I0762918

Rightful Liberty

MERCER UNIVERSITY PRESS

Endowed by

TOM WATSON BROWN

and

THE WATSON-BROWN FOUNDATION, INC.

Rightful Liberty

SLAVERY, MORALITY, AND THOMAS JEFFERSON'S WORLD

Arthur Scherr

MERCER UNIVERSITY PRESS
Macon, Georgia

MUP/H1010

Published by Mercer University Press
1501 Mercer University Drive
Macon, Georgia 31207

25 24 23 22 21 5 4 3 2 1

Books published by Mercer University Press are printed on acid-free paper that meets the requirements of the American National Standard for Information Sciences—Permanence of Paper for Printed Library Materials.

Printed and bound in the United States.

This book is set in Adobe Caslon Pro.

Cover/jacket design by Burt&Burt.

ISBN 978-0-88146-805-2
Cataloging-in-Publication Data is available from the Library of Congress

In memory of Nina

"I am not fond of reading what is merely abstract, and unapplied immediately to some useful science."

— Thomas Jefferson to John Adams, October 14, 1816,
in Lester J. Cappon, ed., *Adams-Jefferson Letters*, 491.

I shall say nothing of your country, because I do not understand either its past or present state, nor foresee its future destiny. Those on the spot possess alone the facts on which a sound judgment can be formed. Believing that forms of government have been attempted to which the national character is not adapted, I expect something will finally be settled as free as their habits of thinking & acting will admit. My only prayer is that it may cost no more human suffering.

— Jefferson to Constantin de Volney, April 20, 1802,
in Barbara B. Oberg, ed., *Jefferson Papers*, 37:295.

Rightful liberty is unobstructed action according to our will, within the limits drawn around us by the equal rights of others. I do not add 'within the limits of the law': because law is often but the tyrant's will, and always so when it violates the right of an individual."

— Jefferson to Isaac H. Tiffany, April 4, 1819,
Jefferson Papers, Library of Congress.

Every people have their own particular habits, ways of thinking, manners, etc., which have grown up with them from their infancy and become a part of their nature, and to which the regulations which are to make them happy must be accommodated.... The institutions of Lycurgus, for example, would not have suited Athens, nor those of Solon, Lacedaemon. The organizations of Locke were impracticable for Carolina, and those of Rousseau and Mably for Poland.

— Jefferson to William Lee, January 16, 1817,
in Lipscomb and Bergh, eds.,
Writings of Thomas Jefferson, 15:101.

That every man shall be made virtuous, by any process whatever, is, indeed, no more to be expected, than that every tree shall be made to bear fruit, and every plant nourishment.

— Jefferson to Cornelius Camden Blatchly, October 21, 1822,
in Lipscomb and Bergh, eds.,
Writings of Jefferson, 15:399–400.

Contents

Preface

When historians think about Thomas Jefferson's political ideas, they usually view him as an eloquent and insistent proponent of "natural rights" who, like most men of the eighteenth-century Enlightenment, that harbinger of modern times, upheld universal rules of politics and morality that individuals and societies should follow to become fully human. Thus, he asserted that political democracy (primarily for White males); direct popular participation in local administration and representative government (republicanism); freedom of speech, thought, and religion; free public education for all; and a distribution of wealth sufficiently equitable that all people had enough to live on comfortably should be the rules by which all societies subsisted. This is part of the story that *Rightful Liberty: Slavery, Morality, and Thomas Jefferson's World* relates. But it is only part of the story.

In *Rightful Liberty*, I concentrate, more than have previous writers, on the ways that Jefferson's thought and action combined the concept of an inborn, universal morality, which all people were theoretically capable of perceiving and obeying—the "moral sense"—with his ideals of democracy and self-government and his attack on the institution of slavery. In an existential leap, Jefferson resolved his inner turmoil over Southern slavery's expansion, which he foresaw would ultimately break up the Union: He proposed that the US government abolish bondage and send the emancipated slaves to Haiti, the Black Caribbean nation that many contemporaries (and historians today) perceived as the greatest worldwide threat to human enslavement.[1]

The moral sense was an instinctive capacity to decide between right and wrong. It did not require an advanced education. According to Jefferson, direct democracy (individual voting) for electing government officials and in deciding local issues, and republican (representative) government over larger land areas

---

[1] Alfred N. Hunt, *Haiti's Influence on Antebellum America: Slumbering Volcano in the Caribbean* (Baton Rouge: Louisiana State University Press, 1988); Adam Rothman, *Slave Country* (Cambridge: Harvard University Press, 2005), 22; Julia Gaffield, *Haitian Connections in the Atlantic World: Recognition After Revolution* (Chapel Hill: University of North Carolina Press, 2015); Janet Polasky, *Revolutions without Borders: The Call to Liberty in the Atlantic World* (New Haven: Yale University Press, 2015); James A. Dun, *Dangerous Neighbors: Making the Haitian Revolution in Early America* (Philadelphia: University of Pennsylvania Press, 2016); Carl L. Paulus, *The Slaveholding Crisis: Fear of Insurrection and the Coming of the Civil War* (Baton Rouge: Louisiana State University Press, 2017).

afforded the greatest opportunity for the average person to exercise their "moral sense." Although theoretically preferring direct democracy (voters' immediate control of all aspects of governmental appointments, law-making, and administration), Jefferson agreed with James Madison and other American republicans that, while it might serve well in towns and small cities, it was impracticable over large populations and landmasses. Representative democracy alone could work over sizeable states.

Jefferson did not exclude women or free Blacks from his moral discourses or ethical calculi. He believed their moral capacities equal to those of White males, that they had equal rights to an education, although he concluded that women, slaves, and children, because of their economic dependence on White men, were denied the possibility of autonomous political judgment. Nevertheless, in France as US minister in the 1780s, he applauded female members of the bourgeoisie and aristocracy who supported revolution against monarchy.

Acutely aware that Black enslavement violated "natural law" and affronted the "moral sense," Jefferson theoretically considered human bondage's existence an unethical perversion in the United States, a society where decent, innately derived moral intuitions ought to dictate behavior. Viewing sociability as essential to morality and the proper exercise of the moral sense, during the Revolutionary era Jefferson predicted that slaveholders' social instincts and moral impulses would eventually lead them to reject enslaving other human beings. However, in old age, he became more pessimistic. Jefferson acknowledged the difficulty of teaching refractory individuals to obey the moral sense, but he believed that educators could artificially instill it by pointing out moral exemplars, demonstrating that in society, honesty was generally the best policy.

Especially as he grew older, Jefferson became aware that for most of the world's peoples the goals of representative government and freedom of thought and religion were not readily attainable. They lived, or rather endured, under oppressive monarchies, aristocracies, and enslavement, actual or virtual, and before they could reach for the objectives of human liberty, self-government, intellectual freedom, and economic prosperity, which Jefferson famously called "the pursuit of happiness," they had to overthrow their oppressors, something often easier said than done. Even after accomplishing this goal, more likely than not they would end up with governments as bad as or worse than the ones they deposed.

Jefferson was convinced that institutionalized religion and monarchical governments, especially those of the absolutist type, impaired the moral sense's development along with the growth of individual freedom and democracy. He upheld the right of revolution, including Gabriel's slave conspiracy in 1800. Jefferson admitted the slave's natural right to revolt in Query XVIII of *Notes on the State of Virginia*. He hoped that slaves, once they gained their freedom and formed their own governments, would achieve happiness and prosperity under democratic regimes they created.

As he proceeded through life, Jefferson perceived that most societies, in Europe and the Americas as well as in other continents he knew little about, were ignorant of the traditions of intellectual freedom, constitutionalism, and representative government that only the people of the United States, and to a lesser extent their British progenitors, had experienced since early modern times.[2] Consequently, during his political career Jefferson traversed a winding road, leading from the embrace of natural rights and political universalism, the insistence that no form of government that perpetuated the domination of the few over the many was acceptable or should be permitted to exist, to a tolerance of regimes that, after overthrowing previous oppressors, instituted forms of government far from the democratic or republican ideals he championed. He eventually found himself hoping, sometimes vainly, that the people of those nations that failed to achieve the liberal ideals of freedom of thought and political democracy he savored would eventually succeed in erecting regimes embracing freedom of thought and political self-government. He resigned himself to envisaging this prospect for the distant future, which he would not live to witness.

First in France, whose democratic Revolution terminated in Napoleon's dictatorship and empire, ending in the return of the old Bourbon kings; then in the Black governments of Saint-Domingue/Haiti, whose slaves, after emancipating themselves from White European colonial masters and rulers, were forced to submit to monarchs, emperors, and dictators of their own color; and finally in Latin America, where numberless revolts against Spanish monarchical rule terminated in native-bred monarchies and dictatorships under heavily Roman Catholic influences, Jefferson's expectations that other nations would join the United States' republican community were dashed. Confronted by such blatant refutations of his original hopes, which arose at the outset of the French Revolution in 1789, that other peoples and nations would slide smoothly into paths of self-rule, Jefferson's political thought gradually evolved from a belief in political universals and natural rights—ideals he had once expected all peoples readily to adopt once they had overthrown the "unnatural" monarchies that had nonetheless survived for centuries—to a reluctant and assessment of cultural relativism, a recognition that progress in the individual and collective pursuit of happiness was not as easy or as natural as he expected.

In old age, Jefferson, in accordance with his implicit albeit unformulated doctrine of cultural relativism, resigned himself to the inevitability of Europe's monarchies and the dictatorships emerging under Bólivar, O'Higgins, Iturbide,

---

[2] Bernard Bailyn, "Political Experience and Enlightenment Ideas in Eighteenth-Century America," *American Historical Review* 67/2 (January 1962): 339–51.

and others in the Western Hemisphere. Most significantly, he respected the dictatorial Black regime that emerged in Haiti after its independence from France in 1804. He understood that recently self-liberated slaves, no matter their color, would, if only because they were victims of their blighted, enslaved past, experience difficulty in transitioning to popular, democratic government.

Nevertheless, during his presidency and into his retirement and old age, Jefferson accepted the Black-governed state's legitimacy (though not granting it formal diplomatic recognition, which no other government had done in any case) despite its racial character and its absolutist regime. As president, he promoted the free conduct of US trade with Haiti, except for a two-year period from 1806–1808 when he hoped, by opportunistically appeasing France and accepting, but not enforcing, a congressional embargo on Haiti-US trade, to gain Napoleon's support for the US takeover of the Floridas from Spain. Many historians deny that Jefferson supported the Black government in Haiti under the heroic Toussaint Louverture and his successors. However, at the beginning of his presidency, in 1801, he advised Virginia's governor James Monroe to sponsor legislation permitting the deportation of Blacks convicted of "conspiracy and insurrection" to Haiti instead of sentencing them to death.

Jefferson was convinced that institutionalized religion and monarchical governments, especially those of the absolutist type, impaired the moral sense's development along with individual freedom and democracy. He had always believed in the right of revolution, including Gabriel's slave rebellion in 1800. After leaving the presidency, Jefferson favored state and congressional legislation to emancipate all the US's slaves and transport them to Haiti. Perhaps he expected that former slaves, with a vague knowledge of the White man's democracy might help transform the Black absolutist regime into a more representative polity.

After Haiti gained stability under Louverture's leadership in the late 1790s, Jefferson hoped that its competent administration might eventually prove Blacks' intellectual equality with Whites. Moreover, Haiti's survival was indispensable to Jefferson's formula for ending slavery in the US. Beginning in the 1790s, he consistently proposed that the US government emancipate all newborn slaves and, when they reached young adulthood, deport them to Haiti. There, they could assist in establishing the first national government administered solely by African Americans and perhaps help convert it from a dictatorship to a republic. Perhaps fatuously, Jefferson believed that impoverished White workers from Europe would eagerly replace emancipated slaves as plantation workers. He feared that race war would erupt in the South if ex-slaves remained after the US government declared them free. Although anguished by sectional strife over slavery restriction during the debate over Missouri's admission to statehood in 1819–1821, Jefferson accepted Congress's right to bar slavery from the territories.

Jefferson's position on Haiti was the most remarkable example of his effort to accommodate "natural rights" universalism—the notion that the only legitimate governments were those that promoted freedom, democracy, and equal rights for all—to a form of "cultural relativism." The latter concept acknowledged that some cultures, both White and Black, not boasting a heritage of freedom of thought and self-government, would necessarily endure transitional stages, including dictatorship, on the road to what Jefferson hoped would eventually emerge as a politics of freedom and democracy.

Ultimately, Jefferson could not ignore the major flaw in the US republic that rendered his somewhat condescending judgments on the political errors of other countries supercilious if not hypocritical: the institution of Black slavery, in which he and millions of other Americans, mainly in the Southern states, participated. The existence of slavery, the authoritarian rule of one person over another that regarded that Other as a form of property, vitiated, at least to a degree, one of Jefferson's basic philosophical premises—and a major theme of this book—that all human beings possess an inherent "moral sense," which commands them to treat others as an end, not a means; and to respect others as they would desire to be respected. For most of his life, Jefferson wrestled with this conundrum: trying to reconcile the existence of slavery in the United States, an affront to the moral sense of decent human beings, with his claims that Americans were among the most virtuous of peoples. He could have taken refuge in the excuse that most countries, including Great Britain, practiced slavery in their colonies, but he probably recognized that this would have been hypocritical; on the other hand, in old age, in defending the slaveholding South against British abolitionists, he argued that slaves' living conditions and personal security were superior to those of British factory workers, sailors, and soldiers.[3]

Jefferson (who had a reputation as a relatively kind master to his slaves) recognized that he could not reconcile Black slavery's existence with the prevalence of the moral sense among Americans, especially those who owned slaves. Jefferson most likely exculpated himself from the charge that his moral sense was deficient although he emancipated only a few of his slaves. Jefferson was a heavy debtor for most of his lifetime, arising from his inheritance of his father-in-law's debts along with his land and slaves. Therefore, he was prohibited from freeing his slaves by the 1782 manumission law, which stipulated that if debtors emancipated their slaves, their creditors could immediately confiscate them. During the American Revolution and afterward, from the 1770s to the 1790s, he paid off his

---

[3] Jefferson to Thomas Cooper, September 10, 1814, Thomas Jefferson Papers at the Library of Congress, Series 1: General Correspondence, 1651–1827, microfilm reel 47, Manuscript Division, American Memory, Library of Congress, Washington, DC (hdl.loc.gov/loc.mss/mtj.mtjbib021836); cited hereafter as Jefferson Papers, LC.

father-in-law's debts by selling part of his estate, but the purchasers paid him in paper money and bonds, which his creditors, the Bristol, England, firm of Farell and Jones, rejected. After being in effect defrauded by his own debtors, he was never able to pay the debt in full a second time.[4]

In *Notes on the State of Virginia* (ca. 1785), Jefferson admitted that Black slaves' moral sense might be superior to that of those who held them in bondage. For the next thirty years, he projected that slaveholders' consciences (a synonym for moral sense) would improve to the point that they would agree to manumit all their slaves, or they would acquiesce to legislation liberating them en masse when the slaves reached a certain age. However, stunned by the controversy precipitated from 1819–1821 by the debate over Missouri's admission to the Union as a "slave state" (i.e., a state of the Union that permitted slavery), in the last years of his life Jefferson, skeptical that Southern slaveholders' moral sense had matured, or would ever mature to the point that they voluntarily agreed to abolition, urged his friends to advocate legislation to abolish slavery without slaveholders' consent and send the emancipated slaves to the Black republic of Haiti when they reached young adulthood.[5]

By this means, Jefferson reconciled his philosophy of natural rights and political universalism with his later notion of cultural relativism that accepted Haiti's existence as an independent Black state and paradoxically sought to increase its power by deporting millions of freed Southern slaves there. Ironically, Jefferson thereby sought to secure the United States' future, endangered by the controversy between North and South over slavery, which threatened to break up the Union or shatter it in the bloodshed of civil war. At the same time that he attempted to preserve the US as a democratic, White republic, he promoted the existence of the world's only Black-governed nation-state.

Viewing science and reason combined with the moral sense as essential agents of human progress, Jefferson hoped that moral advance would produce happiness and prosperity for all, scientific and intellectual progress, and enshrinement of universal values epitomizing the Enlightenment. His cautious expectations for progress extended to hope for African Americans' political and intellectual growth at home and abroad, embodied in his support for Haiti; his public promotion of the Black mathematician Benjamin Banneker; and his desire that White planters grant former slaves opportunities as self-sustaining free farmers. He favored experiments in Black emancipation and agricultural self-sufficiency

[4] Dumas Malone, *Jefferson the Virginian*, vol. 1 of *Jefferson and His Time* (Boston: Little, Brown, 1948), 442–46; Herbert Sloan, *Principle and Interest: Thomas Jefferson and the Problem of Debt* (New York: Oxford University Press, 1995), 14–25.

[5] Under the rule of President Jean-Pierre Boyer from 1820 to 1844, Haiti called itself a republic although there were no free elections and only a rubber-stamp legislature.

in the slave states, in the late 1780s hoping eventually to set up a colony of free Black farmers on his plantations. In old age, he supported English abolitionist Frances Wright's attempts to subsidize a settlement of free Blacks in Nashoba, Tennessee, a suburb of Memphis. On the small scale, an elderly Jefferson actualized his hopes for promoting Black self-sufficiency, happiness, and prosperity by granting to a free Black farmer (with the unlikely name Patrick Henry) gratis use of the land adjoining his cherished property, the Natural Bridge.

Rightful Liberty tells the story of Jefferson's merger of his universalist, natural rights ethos and his cultural relativism; the latter similar to the concepts expounded most famously in Montesquieu's *Spirit of Laws* (1748). That in the real world he synthesized the two theories by advocating the emancipation of the South's slaves and their deportation to Haiti is a part of his political life and ideology that students of Jefferson's thought and actions have overlooked. In the course of my examination, I analyze further the origins of Jefferson's thoughts on slavery, his general concept of the moral sense, which he sometimes called "conscience," his application of the moral sense ideal to international relations, and the frustrations he experienced in such endeavors.

The book combines Jefferson's political thought with a discussion of his policies as political leader and president, attempting to show how they complemented and diverged from one another. During his presidency, Jefferson feared being targeted for additional abuse from his political enemies if his antislavery sympathies resurfaced. He thereby implied that not all individuals, especially his political foes, possessed a developed moral sense. Nonetheless, he optimistically argued, society was so constituted that one's duties and interests coincided.

To a greater extent than other writers, I examine Jefferson's comments and activities concerning slavery and emancipation after his retirement from the presidency and permanent exit from politics, a time when, no longer burdened by responsibilities that rendered him answerable to the electorate, he could privately express his views more honestly and seeks solutions that accorded more with his true beliefs.

Although I stress particularly the impacts of the Haitian Revolution and the Missouri controversy on Jefferson's "moral sense" ideas and his meditations on slavery, at various points throughout the volume I examine several little-known aspects of Jefferson's attitudes and actions toward free and enslaved Blacks, the institution of human slavery, and the measures he supported involving slavery and abolition during his political career. These chapters include such varied topics as his draft in 1778 of the first Virginia slave manumission law (a law permitting masters to emancipate their slaves) in nearly a century; his reaction to the works of the racist-abolitionist Thomas Branagan; his sponsorship as president of the first national law prohibiting the importation of slaves from overseas; his punishment of the runaway slave James Hubbard, including a whipping; his attempts as a slaveholder to unite slave families and prevent his overseers' exercise of cruelty; and his unknown old-age friendship with the free Black Patrick Henry, whom he permitted to reside rent-free at the Natural Bridge site. Many such aspects of Jefferson's life and thought concerning African Americans, slavery, and race have been ignored by other biographers and historians. (I do not examine Jefferson's relationship with his attractive slave Sally Hemings at any length, in part because historians Annette Gordon-Reed, Jon Kukla, and others have already done so; moreover, little documentation of the relationship has survived.) It is hoped that the fruit of my somewhat anomalous, intensive, and extensive research and reflection will be readers' greater understanding of Jefferson, his time, and his ideas on slavery and morality.

Quotations: With regard to quotations, I generally adhere to Jefferson's spelling and punctuation, and when I have corrected it, I usually indicate this in the notes. Orthography was not uniform for most of Jefferson's life. It did not become so until after publication of Noah Webster's *Dictionary* in 1828. By our standards, Jefferson had a few spelling eccentricities that were quite common among his contemporaries. For example, he spelled the possessive pronoun "its" as "it's," began sentences in the lower case, did not always capitalize proper nouns (including "god"), and spelled words that we spell with "ei" (such as "receive") with "ie" ("recieve"). It may also be appropriate to mention that I use the terms Republican, Democratic-Republican, and (less often) Democratic to represent the political party Jefferson co-founded with James Madison during the 1790s, and with which he was associated thereafter. Jefferson's party is considered the ancestor of the present-day Democratic Party. Ironically, his political enemies, the Federalists, were the first ones to derisively label his party "democrats." During the twenty years after 1790, "democrat" was generally considered a term of opprobrium, linked with the French Revolution and social disorders perpetrated by "the mob."[6]

---

[6] Robert R. Palmer, "Notes on the Use of the Word 'Democracy,' 1789–1799," *Political Science Quarterly* 68/2 (June 1953): 203–26.

Acknowledgments

In the research and writing of *Rightful Liberty: Slavery, Morality, and Thomas Jefferson's World*, I have relied heavily on the resources of several libraries, including Columbia University's Butler and Diamond libraries, the New York Public Library's Schwartzman Research Libraries, the New-York Historical Society Library, the Massachusetts Historical Society Library, New York University's Bobst Library, and the Brooklyn College Gideonse Library. I would like to thank professors Eric Foner, Peter S. Onuf, and Christopher Iannini for reading earlier versions of portions of the text. All statements of fact and opinion in the book are my responsibility.

In the course of educating myself to become a historian—someone who tries to teach, write about, and understand historical events, processes, and personalities, not always under the best of conditions—I have met and learned from (or attempted to learn from) other historians. Among those whom I found exemplars of good will are the following, most of them now in Historians' Heaven: Harold C. Syrett, behind whose gruff exterior lurked a heart of gold; Arthur M. Schlesinger, Jr.: conscious of his uniqueness, he displayed humor, civility, and humility in front of his students; the young Eric Foner, who relished hanging out with and joking with his students and could never fully comprehend his ascent to rock-star status among historians; Elaine F. Crane, a scholar of exemplary kindness, dedication, and modesty; Ari Hoogenboom, who always had time for a former student; and Hans L. Trefousse, who knew everything about Abraham Lincoln, and was eager to learn more. I also wish to thank Dr. Marc Jolley, director of Mercer University Press, for agreeing to publish this controversial study of Thomas Jefferson, who continues to arouse as much wrath and disputation among scholars as if he currently occupied the White House.

Introduction

Jefferson's concepts of human nature and the "moral sense," which he argued all races and peoples possessed, affected his politics and public policies in ways scholars have generally ignored. After first examining Jefferson's ideas on the "moral sense," this work will show their connection with his views on human nature; the African American's place in American and world society; the injustice of slavery, and the prospect that other societies, in addition to his own, might achieve republican government.

Finally, I will argue that Jefferson's views on the "moral sense" changed over time. Initially conceiving its axioms as universal and equally applicable to all societies and races, taking for granted that everyone comprehended the wickedness of murder, slavery, political and religious oppression, and other enormities, by the end of his life Jefferson adopted a more environmentalist, relativist perception of the moral sense. He argued that the moral sense's *context*—the times, places, and mores of the cultures and communities within which it operated—essentially determined what was "moral" for the individual. Jefferson's skepticism in this matter increased following his disillusionment at France's failure to achieve a stable republic, and its Revolution's debacle in Napoleon's dictatorship and empire, the final overthrow of which brought the old Bourbon monarchy's restoration. He was equally disappointed if not surprised at the Haitian slave uprising's rapid termination in an oppressive Black dictatorship. Ultimately, he accepted the view that human nature was not the same everywhere, and that disparate societies and natural environments determined its formation. Nonetheless, everyone wanted "happiness."[1]

---

[1] "The equal rights of man, and the happiness of every individual, are now acknowledged to be the only legitimate objects of government." (Jefferson to A. Coray, Oct 31, 1823 (Writings of Thomas Jefferson, 15: 482 [20 volumes, Washington, DC, 1903]). Jefferson applied his theory of environmentalism to defend the U.S.'s extensive federal republic against the strictures of critics who pointed to Montesquieu's *Spirit of Laws* (1748) for evidence that republican governments could only succeed in small territories, but large landmasses (empires) required monarchy for competent governance. He praised the pluralist diversity that existed among the states of the Union. Jefferson to François d'Ivernois, February 6, 1795, and Jefferson to François de Marbois, June 14, 1817, in Merrill D. Peterson, ed., *Thomas Jefferson: Writings*, Library of America, vol. 17 (New York: Viking/Library of America, 1984), 1024, 1410–11, and Jefferson to Nathaniel Niles, March 22, 1801, in Paul L. Ford, ed., *Writings of Thomas*

Jefferson's strangely conciliatory attitude toward the Black government of Haiti, both as president and in private life, demonstrates his extension of the doctrine of moral relativism to condone a Black dictatorship composed of rebellious slaves. Indeed, the Haitian rulers set up a government that prohibited its citizens from owning land. They worked as sharecroppers for the government, keeping only one-fourth of their produce. Deprived of freedom of speech, religion (Roman Catholicism was the established church), and the press, Haitian citizens suffered a fate was not much better than under France's colonial slave regime.[2]

Nevertheless, Jefferson, while not formally recognizing Haiti diplomatically during his presidency, did not share the fears of many Northerners and Southerners that the island nation posed a military threat to the United States or to Southern slavery. Several of his letters, both as president in 1801 and after his retirement from the presidency, revealed his desire to help the war-shattered Haitian polity get back on its feet. In November 1801, responding to an inquiry from his friend, Virginia's governor James Monroe, Jefferson suggested that, instead of executing slaves convicted of "conspiracy and insurrection," like those recently involved in Gabriel's conspiracy near Richmond, the government of Virginia should deport them to Haiti. Jefferson did not fret that they would gain their freedom there though Monroe disliked the idea of rewarding rebellious slaves with liberty.[3]

Jefferson, 10 vols. (New York: G.P. Putnam's Sons, 1892–1899), 8:24. Jefferson's ambivalence toward Montesquieu is summarized in David W. Carrithers, "Montesquieu, Jefferson, and the Fundamentals of Eighteenth-Century Republican Theory," *French-American Review* 6/2 (Fall 1982): 160–68.

[2] Several studies conclude that working and living conditions in parts of Cap Français in the north where the slave revolt began in August 1791 were less intolerable than they were on neighboring plantations. Forster and Breathett argued that slavery in Saint-Domingue was less brutal than elsewhere in the West Indies (David Geggus, "Slave Society in the Sugar Plantation Zones of Saint-Domingue and the Revolution of 1791–93," *Slavery and Abolition* 20 [1999]: 31–46; George Breathett, "Catholicism and the *Code Noir* in Haiti," *Journal of Negro History* 73 [1988]: 1–11; Robert Forster, "Slavery in Virginia and Saint-Domingue in the Late 18th Century," in Philip Boucher, ed., *Proceedings of the Thirteenth and Fourteenth Meetings of the French Colonial Historical Society* [Lanham, MD: University Press of America, 1990], 1–13; Stewart R. King, *Blue Coat or Powdered Wig: Free People of Color in Pre-Revolutionary Saint-Domingue* [Athens: University of Georgia Press, 2001]).

[3] Jefferson to James Monroe, November 24, 1801, in Peterson, ed., *Jefferson: Writings*, 1097. Gabriel's rebellion, as it is sometimes called, was a planned massive slave uprising in August 1800 that failed because of a great rainstorm and Gabriel's betrayal by two slaves. See Douglas R. Egerton's detailed, somewhat romanticized *Gabriel's Rebellion* (Chapel Hill: University of North CarolinaPress, 1993), whose inaccuracies and exaggerations historian Michael L. Nicholls points out in several works, especially *Whispers of Rebellion: Narrating Gabriel's Conspiracy* (Charlottesville: University of Virginia Press, 2012).

In the last years of his life, Jefferson again proposed that Virginia undertake a program of compulsory emancipation that would eventually free all the slaves and deport them to Haiti.[4] Thus, Jefferson was ready to use Haiti as a "receptacle" as he called it, for liberated slaves. He downplayed the fact that Haiti's rulers allowed their Black citizens little freedom of any kind and prohibited Whites from settling or owning property. Particularly in old age, he eschewed racial hatreds. His gradually maturing philosophical doctrine of cultural relativism impelled him to favor sending African Americans to their own "republic."

---

[4] Jefferson to Jared Sparks, February 4, 1824, in Paul L. Ford, ed., *Works of Thomas Jefferson*, 12 vols. (New York: G. P. Putnam's Sons, 1904–1905), 12:334–39.

Chapter 1

Jefferson's Idea of "Natural History": Notes on Virginia, Montesquieu, and Slavery

In his time as well as ours, Thomas Jefferson was renowned for his polymath versatility and inventiveness, qualities his peers recognized by continuously re-electing him president of the American Philosophical Society from 1797 to 1815. Jefferson's only full-length book, *Notes on the State of Virginia* (which he originally self-published in Paris for friends and acquaintances in 1785), a daringly radical work for those days, gained notoriety for its numerous controversial speculations on such varied topics as race, climate, democracy, gender, religion, and the size of animals in Europe and America. Many of the chapters (designated "queries") were glossed with an empirical and scientific veneer. More resolutely than most American intellectuals, Jefferson divorced science from religion. He composed such crisp statements in theoretical support of atheism, a less acceptable creed in those days than it is even today, as, "It does me no injury for my neighbor to say there are twenty gods, or no god. It neither picks my pocket nor breaks my leg."[1]

Among Jefferson's multifarious interests was the burgeoning science of "natural history," which merged present-day biology, zoology, and anthropology. Anticipating the twentieth-century academic discipline of physical anthropology, in *Notes* Jefferson proposed to combine the scientific study of physical nature, the origin of human cultures, and their interaction. Of non-White races inhabiting his state, he provocatively observed, "To our reproach it must be said, that though for a century and a half we have had under our eyes the races of black and of red men [Native Americans], they have never yet been viewed by us as subjects of natural history."[2] Among the relevant definitions in the *Oxford English Dictionary*, by "natural history" Jefferson probably meant the second, "the facts relating

[1] For Jefferson's lapidary statement on freedom of religion, see Query XVII, "The Different Religions Received into that State?" in Jefferson, *Notes on the State of Virginia*, ed. William H. Peden (Chapel Hill: University of North Carolina Press, 1955), cited hereafter as Peden, ed., *Notes on the State of Virginia*.

[2] Peden, ed., *Notes on the State of Virginia*, 143.

to the natural objects, plants, or animals of a place, the natural phenomena of a region, as observed or described systematically."[3]

One of Jefferson's primary goals in *Notes* was to disprove the derisive claims of European natural scientists and general savants, especially Georges Louis Leclerc, comte de Buffon, Cornelius G. DePauw, and Abbé Guillaume Raynal, that all living things degenerated or were inferior in the New World. Their list included plants, animals, and human beings, among them those European immigrants who had settled in the thirteen colonies (Raynal's view) as well as the Indigenous peoples (American Indians). Disproving these charges, Jefferson composed several chapters of *Notes* informing readers that his own scientific investigations and archeological digs, as well as those of others, uncovered ample evidence that, dating from prehistoric times, North American plants and animals were at least as large as Europe's were. During the late 1780s, when he served as US minister to France, he provided visible proof. He instructed General John Sullivan and other Americans to amputate New England moose antlers, dig up mammoth skeletons and the bones of the megatherium (giant sloth), which he called *megalonyx*, panther skins, and other evidence of North American mammals' great size, dating back millions of years, for dispatch to Paris. He went to extremes to demonstrate that the flora and fauna of the United States were at least as large as the Old World's. Since one of his objectives in *Notes* was to validate the physical and intellectual equality of the people of the United States with those of Europe, and the equal size and strength of its animals (if not their superiority), he was probably less of an arrogant "American exceptionalist" than some scholars depict him. His mission of defending the United States—its people, climate, geography, and topography—as a worthwhile place where human beings and things did not degenerate and where animals and people were not threatened with mass starvation from its inaccurately described "cold and humid" weather, distanced him and his countrymen from the (largely enslaved) African population. (Virtually all European Enlightenment philosophers had already concluded that Blacks, especially in Africa, which they regarded as literally and figuratively a Dark Continent, were inferior to Whites; indeed, as David Hume said in his famous essay "On National Characters," in his *Political Essays*, they were sure that White Europeans were superior to all other races.[4])

Therefore, it is possible that Jefferson deliberately pointed out the "inferior" nature of Blacks, or at least his "suspicion" of it, in Query XIV of *Notes* in his quest to prove that Americans were as good as Europeans. Indeed, this objective may help explain his lifelong insistence that Native Americans, despite their

---

[3] *Oxford English Dictionary*, online edition, s.v., "natural history."

[4] David Hume, "Essay 12: Of National Characters," in Knud Haakonssen, ed., *David Hume: Political Essays* (Cambridge: Cambridge University Press, 1994), 86n.

ostensible "savagery" and "uncivilized" mode of life, would be the intellectual equals of White European-descended Americans if exposed to the "right" environment and opportunities, while he was less certain of the same results with the African-descended Blacks. Just as his defense of the American environment's hygienic parity with the European environment dictated praise for the American Indian, the authentic child of America, it also roused him to insist in advance, that the Black, especially in his/her condition as debased slave, was not paradigmatic of the American citizen's potential and capacities. Thus, of necessity part of the *Notes*' purpose was to exclude Blacks from the American polity and the American natural environment. In *Notes*, Jefferson felt impelled reluctantly to admit his "suspicion" of Black inferiority. He considered it part of his mission to emphasize that Blacks were neither literally nor figuratively "Americans," thereby precluding the possibility that Buffon and his successors, DePauw and Raynal, would present the African in America as additional (and, Jefferson perhaps thought, irrefutable) evidence of the American's "inferiority" to the European. He had to stress that Blacks were not "really" Americans, and therefore not relevant to Raynal and Buffon's charges of "degeneration": they were already "degenerated" when they arrived, generally as slaves, on Virginia's shores. Thus, Jefferson had to consider Blacks (West Africans) alien to America, in diametric contrast to the American Indian, whose talents and creativity he often praised as the authentic representation of the American Man, albeit "uncivilized."

In pursuing his goal of disproving Raynal and Buffon, Jefferson wanted to guard against European critics embarrassing him and his literary creation, *Notes*, which he admired and defended throughout his life, despite frequent "modest" disclaimers.[5] Most of all, he sought to uphold the reputation of his country and its inhabitants. Jefferson at least implied, in advance, that since Africans had already degenerated in Africa, Europeans could not assert that living in the New World had caused Black slaves to *become* degenerated ("inferior").

On the other hand, Jefferson never doubted Blacks' right to liberty as fellow human beings. Unfortunately, a few historians, distorting a sentence in Query XIV of *Notes* in which the would-be "natural historian" Jefferson wrote, in general terms, "It is not against experience to suppose, that different species of the same genus, or varieties of the same species, may possess different qualifications [i.e.,

---

[5] See, for instance, Peden, ed., *Notes on the State of Virginia*, xix; Dorothy Medlin, "Thomas Jefferson, André Morellet, and the French Version of *Notes on the State of Virginia*," *William and Mary Quarterly* 35/1 (January 1978): 85–99; Jefferson to G. Clerici, August 15, 1787, in Julian P. Boyd et al., eds., *The Papers of Thomas Jefferson* (Princeton: Princeton University Press, 1950–), 12:39; E. Millicent Sowerby, ed., *Catalogue of the Library of Thomas Jefferson* (Washington, DC: Library of Congress, 1952–1959), 4:301, 310–12.

characteristics]," have argued that he thus excluded Blacks from the human species. Although Jefferson never engaged in a full-scale exegesis of what he meant by "natural rights," he always said that Blacks had a natural right to freedom, and it was only the convenience and selfishness of White society that made them slaves. As he put it in a letter to Abbé Henri Grégoire in 1809, after denouncing the immorality of slavery, he said that, even if Blacks were found to be intellectually unimpressive, "Whatever be their degree of talent it is no measure of their rights."[6]

Although scholars have exploited his words about "different species of the same genus" to berate him as a parochial-minded bigot, a slaveholding racist, Jefferson's speculations on African Americans in Query XIV as possibly a different "variety" or "race of animals" from Whites, and, along with American Indians, suitable "subjects of natural history" primarily expressed his interest in natural science. Although he "advance[d] it therefore as a suspicion only, that the blacks, whether originally a distinct race, or made distinct by time and circumstances, are inferior to the whites in the endowments both of body and mind," he never denied Blacks' humanity. He called them "a whole race of men," whom he was reluctant to label inferior to Whites in the "rank in the scale of beings which their Creator may perhaps have given them." Somewhat hypocritically, among Jefferson's justifications for his drastic proposal to expel the Black slave population after the state emancipated them was to hinder interbreeding between the races. He knew that miscegenation that produced fertile offspring occurred between White workers and Black slaves on his estates, proving that they were members of the same species. Moreover, he reputedly fathered six children with Sally Hemings many years after writing this book. Nonetheless, at this time he asserted, "Will not a lover of natural history, then, one who views the gradations in all the races of animals with the eye of philosophy, excuse an effort to keep those in the department of man as distinct as nature has formed them? This unfortunate difference of colour, and perhaps of faculty, is a powerful obstacle to the emancipation of these people."[7] On the other

[6] Jefferson, *Notes on Virginia*, in Peterson, ed., *Jefferson: Writings*, 270; Jefferson to Abbé Grégoire, February 25, 1809, in Peterson, ed., *Jefferson: Writings*, 1202. For one historian's attack on Jefferson as a polygenist (believer that Blacks were a separate species), see Robert Pierce Forbes, "'The Cause of this Blackness': The Early American Republic and the Construction of Race," *American Nineteenth Century History* 13/1 (March 2012): 65–94.

[7] Jefferson, *Notes on Virginia*, in Peterson, ed., *Jefferson: Writings*, 270. For the sexual relations between White artisans that Jefferson occasionally hired in building Monticello, and the enslaved women, see Lucia Stanton, *"Those Who Labor for My Happiness": Slavery at Thomas Jefferson's Monticello* (Charlottesville: University of Virginia Press, 2012), and Jack McLaughlin, *Jefferson and Monticello: The Biography of a Builder* (New York: H. Holt, 1988), 122, and ch. 4, "To Possess Living Souls."

hand, he may have thought that under conditions of Black freedom, such miscegenation would recur more frequently as free Blacks left their isolated plantation for farms, towns and cities.

However, Blacks' hypothetical inferiority did not impair their right to liberty and an equal chance at happiness that others enjoyed. In referring to "the gradations in all the races of animals," he was not asserting that African Americans were subhuman creatures, but like the "natural historian" he aspired to be, that Blacks and Whites alike, as naked, thinking apes and mammals, were members of the "human" race or family.[8]

In wistful letters to his friends, Jefferson playfully applied similar naturalistic criteria to himself. Depicting himself as an object for scientific investigation, in 1785 he drolly called himself an "animal" in a letter to the Marquis de Chastellux, who had visited Monticello four years earlier. The marquis sent Jefferson, in Paris as United States minister, galley proofs of his famous *Travels in North-America in the Years 1780-81-82* (Paris, 1786), including glowing descriptions of Jefferson's graciousness, intellect, and scientific achievements. Jefferson politely replied that he "read [it] with a continued blush from beginning to end, as it presented me a lively picture of what I wish to be, but am not. No, my dear Sir, the thousand millionth part of what you there say, is more than I deserve." Facetiously advising Chastellux to delete the laudatory section, he spoke of himself (in the third person) as a beast like the American mammoth whose skeleton he had sent to Buffon, the famous French naturalist: "It might perhaps have passed in Europe at the time you wrote it, and the exaggeration might not have been detected. But consider that the animal is now brought there, and that every one will take his dimensions for himself." He humorously continued, "The friendly complexion of your mind has betrayed you into a partiality of which the European spectator will be divested."[9] In a famous letter written in 1823, he reiterated his conclusion that man, far from being in a separate zoological category from other mammals, was "a rational animal."[10]

Similarly, Jefferson labeled himself a "savage" in a letter to his close friend Charles Bellini, an Italian scholar who had arrived in Virginia in the 1770s. As the state's governor, Jefferson served from 1779 to 1781 on the board of visitors of William and Mary College and was instrumental in Bellini's appointment as professor of modern languages. "Behold me at length on the vaunted scene of

---

[8] Desmond Morris, *The Naked Ape* (New York: McGraw-Hill, 1967).

[9] Jefferson to Marquis de Chastellux, September 2, 1785, in Peterson, ed., *Jefferson: Writings*, 826. An extract of Chastellux's panegyric to Jefferson may be found in Adrienne Koch, ed., *Jefferson*, Great Lives Observed (Englewood Cliffs: Prentice Hall, 1971), 87–88.

[10] Jefferson to Judge William Johnson, June 22, 1823, in Peterson, ed., *Jefferson: Writings*, 1470.

Europe!" he wrote him four years later, describing his impressions of Paris after several months; "You are, perhaps, curious to know how this new scene has struck a savage of the mountains of America."[11]

When Jefferson wrote in the Declaration of Independence, "All men are created equal," he was urging society to adopt ideals that human beings' moral sense knew were right, but which, amid the historical predominance of the more selfish and evil human qualities, had been cast aside. Jefferson said that Blacks, and everyone else, had a natural right to liberty. For Jefferson, natural rights were, at least theoretically, a moral imperative based on Nature, not necessarily scientific but rooted in "common sense" and reason, not in the Bible or the laws and decrees of past, usually monarchical and despotic regimes. As Locke and Rousseau put it, natural rights were "prior" to political society.[12]

On the other hand, Jefferson's scientific renown, such as it was, rested on *Notes on Virginia*, which, whatever its defects, was the first lengthy interpretive description of an American state's politics, geography, and culture available to Europeans. The liberal pro-American Europeans who bought it generally ignored its negative opinions of Blacks and praised Jefferson as the first political figure publicly to demand the abolition of slavery, freedom of thought and religion, political democracy, and other humanitarian causes. Conservatives, especially members of the Federalist Party, continually derided *Notes*' liberal views in politics and religion. Politically motivated to embarrass Jefferson, Federalists sometimes denounced what they depicted as *Notes*' unduly favorable statements about Blacks and stigmatized him as an abolitionist. Indeed, in Jefferson's time, attitudes toward *Notes* were determined mainly by one's party identification as a Federalist or a Republican. Jefferson's "towering" reputation as a scientist or "natural philosopher" was mocked by leading Federalists, especially South Carolina congressional representatives William L. Smith and Robert G. Harper.[13]

---

[11] Jefferson to Charles Bellini, September 30, 1785, in ibid., 833. On Jefferson's friendship with Bellini, see Malone, *Jefferson the Virginian*, 285, and Malone, *Jefferson and the Rights of Man*, vol. 2 of *Jefferson and His Time* (Boston: Little, Brown, 1951), 18, 82–83.

[12] Jefferson to Francis W. Gilmer, 7 June 1816, in Ford, ed., *Writings of Thomas Jefferson*, 10:32–33, makes this clear. As late as 1857, for example, Frederick A. Ross, in *Slavery Ordained of God* (Philadelphia: J. B. Lippincott & Co., 1857), 98–102, warned that, although abolitionists quoted Jefferson against slavery, the Bible defended slavery as compatible with God's law.

[13] See William L. Smith, *The Pretensions of Thomas Jefferson to the Presidency Examined; and the Charges against John Adams Refuted* (Philadelphia, n.p., 1796), 9–12, for Federalist charges that Jefferson was a covert abolitionist. Clement C. Moore (composer of the poem "'Twas the Night before Christmas"), *Observations upon Certain Passages in Mr. Jefferson's Notes on Virginia: Which Appear to Have a Tendency to Subvert Religion, and Establish a False Philosophy* (New York: Furman and Loudon, 1804), attacked Jefferson as an atheist, whose hypothesis

In *Notes*, in addition to discoursing on "natural history," Jefferson boldly propounded novel theories about a complementary discipline in social science, the study of what Enlightenment philosophers had begun to call "human nature."[14] He attempted to justify his opinion that Virginia's Black slaves should be emancipated and compelled to immigrate to their own independent state, among other reasons because of his "suspicion" that Blacks were racially inferior to Whites. (However, for Jefferson the most important consideration was his expectation that the freed Black masses would interminably struggle with Southern Whites for domination, ending in race war.[15]) Invoking popular scientific concepts of the Great Chain of Being, Jefferson challenged his readers with the idea that "natural history" validated his desire to separate Blacks and Whites, in order to maintain the purity of the (probably) superior Whites and thus maintain "an effort to keep those in the department of man as distinct as nature has formed them."[16] He muted this statement, with its implication that Blacks were an inferior "race of [human] animals" to Whites, by including it as one in a long list of reasons for his belief that after its mass emancipation, it was unwise for the Black community to remain with its former White masters.[17]

Despite his support for the deportation of African Americans after emancipation, for the time being Jefferson sought to assess Blacks and other races' similarities to and differences from Whites. He favored investigating the physical and cultural characteristic of Blacks and Native Americans. He regarded American Indians as physically and mentally equal to Whites, as was earlier suggested, possibly because they were indigenous to the New World; among his objectives in *Notes* was to prove that America's physical environment was at least as healthy as that of Europe. With specific reference to African Americans' intelligence, he ambivalently wrote,

> The opinion, that they are inferior in the faculties of Reason & Imagination must be hazarded with great diffidence. To justify a general

that Blacks were a separate or inferior species rejected the biblical idea that all peoples were derived as a single creation from Adam and Eve. For Federalist derision of Jefferson's expertise as a naturalist, see Linda K. Kerber, *Federalists in Dissent: Imagery and Ideology in Jeffersonian America* (Ithaca: Cornell University Press, 1966).

[14] On the development of the idea of "human nature" as an outgrowth of the Scottish and French enlightenments, see Arthur O. Lovejoy, *Essays in the History of Ideas* (Baltimore: Johns Hopkins Press, 1948), and Henry Vyverberg, *Human Nature, Cultural Diversity, and the French Enlightenment* (New York: Oxford University Press, 1989). See also Daniel J. Boorstin, *The Lost World of Thomas Jefferson* (New York: Henry Holt, 1948).

[15] Peden, ed., *Notes on the State of Virginia*, 138.

[16] Ibid., 143.

[17] Query XIV, Peden, ed., *Notes on the State of Virginia*, 138.

> conclusion, requires many observations, even where the subject may be submitted to the Anatomical knife, to Optical glasses, to analysis by fire, or by solvents. How much more then where it is a faculty, not a substance, we are examining; where it eludes the research of all the senses; where the conditions of its existence are various and variously combined; where the effects of those which are present or absent bid defiance to calculation; let me add too, as a circumstance of great tenderness, where our conclusion would degrade a whole race of men from the rank in the scale of beings which their Creator may perhaps have given them.[18]

In considering Blacks and Native Americans proper subjects for "natural history," what we would call ethnology or physical anthropology, Jefferson merely proposed to study them in the same manner that Whites studied their own societies and "civilizations." He was not alone in this proclivity. For example, Thomas L. McKenney, appointed superintendent of Indian Affairs in 1816, was intent on proving to doubters the physical and intellectual equality of American Indians and Whites and their existence as members of the same human species (monogenesis). An ardent pro-Native American government official, he inelegantly recommended forcing skeptical Whites to dissect Native American corpses to verify their physical kinship. A Quaker, McKenney was alarmed by rumors that Lewis Cass, governor of Michigan Territory, detested American Indians and viewed them as a separate, inferior species (polygenesis). "I hope he has considered them as Human Beings," McKenney wrote, "because, if he has not, I shall believe the good book is profane to him, which says, 'of *one blood*, God made all the nations to dwell upon the face of the earth.' And were this not satisfactory an Anatomical examination would prove it—And it might be an affair of Mercy to let *skeptics* have a few Indians for dissection."[19]

"Natural history," including Linnaean classification and the "Great Chain of Being," comprised a curious blend of biology and anthropology wherein humans and animals were congruent subjects of investigation. It is difficult for us to comprehend such a mentality in our anti-historical, present-minded age. Many scholars ignore Jefferson's consciousness that his "suspicion" of Black intellectual inferiority was almost universally upheld by his era's White "natural historians." They generally agree with Winthrop D. Jordan's observation in *White over Black*, that Jefferson's "derogation of the Negro...constituted, for all its qualifications, the

---

[18] Ibid.

[19] Thomas L. McKenney to Christopher Vandeventer, June 21, 1818, Christopher Vandeventer Collection, Clements Library, University of Michigan, quoted in Francis Paul Prucha, "Scientific Racism and Indian Policy," in Prucha, *Indian Policy in the United States* (Lincoln: University of Nebraska Press, 1981), 180–97, 185 (quotation).

most intense, extensive, and extreme formulation of anti-Negro 'thought' offered by any American in the thirty years after the Revolution."[20] Nevertheless, Jordan's monumental work amply demonstrates that writers often expressed even more "extreme" views for over a century *before* the Revolution and would do so after the Revolution as well.[21]

Irascible, brilliant John Adams, Jefferson's antislavery contemporary and quondam friend, more favorably evaluated his intent. Jefferson sent Adams a privately printed first edition of *Notes* from Paris in 1785. After reading Query XIV, Adams wrote him, epitomizing the response of antislavery readers to Jefferson's ambivalent text, "I think it will do its Author and his Country great Honour. The Passages upon slavery are worth Diamonds. They will have more effect than Volumes written by mere Philosophers."[22]

Ironically, Jefferson believed that Blacks, despite their brutal enslavement, were more moral and benevolent than their White masters. In this same section of *Notes*, Query XIV, he asserted that although Blacks might be less intelligent than Whites, they were more virtuous. "Whether further observation will or will not verify the conjecture, that nature has been less bountiful to them in the endowments of the head, I believe that in those of the heart she will be found to have done them justice," he insisted. He denied that "depravity of the moral sense" existed among Blacks, slave or free. Indeed, Jefferson argued, even though one might expect an enslaved individual of any race, White or Black, to behave immorally and commit theft almost instinctually, because he was deprived of all property, even the most

---

[20] Winthrop D. Jordan, *White over Black: American Attitudes toward the Negro, 1550–1812* (Chapel Hill: University of North Carolina Press, 1968), 481.

[21] For the widespread "scientific" opinion of Black inferiority before *Notes on the State of Virginia* appeared, see Mark M. Smith, *How Race Is Made: Slavery, Segregation, and the Senses* (Chapel Hill: University of North Carolina Press, 2006), 13–14; Jordan, *White over Black*, 245–65 and passim. See also John Immerwahr, "Hume's Revised Racism," *Journal of the History of Ideas* 53/3 (July–September 1992): 481–86; Larry R. Morrison, "'Nearer to the Brute Creation': The Scientific Defense of American Slavery before 1830," *Southern Studies* 19/3 (1980): 228–42; Morrison, "The Proslavery Argument in the Early Republic, 1790–1830" (Ph.D. diss., University of Virginia, 1975). Unlike Jordan's *White over Black*, Bruce Dain's more recent *Hideous Monster of the Mind: American Race Theory and the Early Republic* (Cambridge: Harvard University Press, 2002) does not view *Notes on Virginia* as a unique, groundbreaking racist polemic but appreciates that its racial doctrines emerged in part out of Jefferson's self-styled role as a "natural historian." "Rather than being a founding document of a new American 'scientific racism,' *Notes* was a home-grown interpretation of an increasingly obsolescent natural philosophy," Dain argues (37–38).

[22] John Adams to Jefferson, May 22, 1785, Cappon, ed., *Adams-Jefferson Letters* (1959; repr., Chapel Hill: University of North Carolina Press, 1988), 21; also quoted in Joseph J. Ellis, *American Sphinx: The Character of Thomas Jefferson* (New York: Knopf, 1997), 86.

basic property in his own body, Black slaves were invariably honest and self-controlled. "Notwithstanding these considerations which must weaken their [Black slaves'] respect for the laws of property," he claimed, "we find among them numerous instances of the most rigid integrity, and as many as among their better instructed masters, of benevolence, gratitude and unshaken fidelity." In light of their enslaved condition, they were perhaps morally superior to Whites. Purveying only a tentative judgment of their intellectual abilities, Jefferson cautiously concluded, "The opinion that they are inferior in the faculties of reason and imagination, must be hazarded with great diffidence."[23] Such relatively favorable views of Black character were hardly typical in the young United States, even in New England, where many writers continued to depict African Americans as "savage" and ignorant during and after the Revolution, despite the Massachusetts Supreme Court decision in 1783 that slavery in the state was illegal.[24]

If we consider "racism" to mean George Fredrickson's definition in his book of the same name, an ideology that posits Blacks' innate inferiority to Whites, an inferiority that cannot be mitigated by any means, an inherent and irremediable intellectual and mental defect which cannot disappear over time or across generations, then Jefferson was not a racist. Even in *Notes on Virginia*, which scholars cite to justify their charges of racism, he implied that he was searching for evidence to demonstrate Blacks' mental equality with Whites.[25]

Indeed, in *Notes*, Jefferson voiced a higher opinion of the moral, and even the intellectual potential of Blacks than did most of his contemporaries in the public, political sphere. As if directly responding to modern historians' accusations of racial bias, seldom made against him in his lifetime, Jefferson wrote to Marquis de Chastellux in 1785, "I believe the [American] Indian, then, to be, in body and mind, equal to the white man. I have supposed the black man, in his present state, might not be so; but it would be hazardous to affirm, that, equally cultivated for a few generations, he would not become so."[26]

Historians George Fredrickson, David Waldstreicher, and other scholars

---

[23] Peterson, ed., *Jefferson: Writings*, 269–70 (Query XIV of *Notes on Virginia*).

[24] Patricia R. Bradley, *Slavery, Propaganda, and the American Revolution* (Jackson: University Press of Mississippi, 1989); Elise Lemire, *Miscegenation* (Philadelphia: University of Pennsylvania Press, 2002); Joanne Pope Melish, *Disowning Slavery: Gradual Emancipation and Race in New England, 1780–1860* (Ithaca: Cornell University Press, 1998); Arthur Scherr, *John Adams, Slavery, and Race: Ideas, Politics, and Diplomacy in an Age of Crisis* (Santa Barbara: Praeger/ABC-CLIO, 2018).

[25] George Fredrickson, *Racism: A Short History* (Princeton: Princeton University Press, 2002), 59.

[26] Jefferson to Marquis de Chastellux, June 7, 1785, in Peterson, ed., *Jefferson: Writings*, 801.

who analyze Jefferson's racial views from a cultural perspective conclude that he was not a thoroughgoing racist (i.e., one who believed Blacks innately, ineradicably, mentally, and physically inferior to Whites). They argue that he kept an essentially open mind on the issue of whether Blacks, like the Native Americans he admired in many ways, could potentially become "equal" to Whites in intelligence if exposed to a less oppressive environment.[27]

There may be one exception to this conclusion, the ostensibly repulsive commentary by Jefferson in the lengthy Query XIV of *Notes on Virginia*, the source of most of his allegedly racist comments and of historians' attacks upon him. However, if one reads carefully, his only racist comment in that book, which could be construed to label African Americans as ineradicably (physically) inferior in some respect is his assertion, "They secrete less by the kidnies, and more by the glands of the skin, which gives them a very strong and disagreeable odour." Unlike his predecessors and contemporaries, Jefferson attempted, in accordance with his desire to advance the pursuit of "natural history," to provide a scientific basis for this alleged inherent Black odor. Referring to the findings of the scientist Adair Crawford, a British physician and chemist who wrote *Experiments and Observations on Animal Heat* (1779), Jefferson continued, "This greater degree of transpiration renders them more tolerant of heat, and less so of cold, than the whites. Perhaps too a difference of structure in the pulmonary apparatus, which a late ingenious experimentalist [Crawford] has discovered to be the principal regulator of animal heat, may have disabled them from extricating, in the act of inspiration, so much of that fluid [water vapor] from the outer air, or obliged them in expiration, to part with more of it."[28]

The concept of Black "odour" did not originate with Jefferson. It is likely that he imbibed the idea from his intellectual mentor, the Scottish philosopher Henry Home, Lord Kames, one of the most prestigious scientists and "common sense" philosophers of the era. Like David Hume, Immanuel Kant, and many others, Kames was convinced of Black inferiority, believing that the economic and intellectual condition of Africans on the African continent indisputably proved it. In a multivolume work considered the apogee of scientific acuity, Kames tersely wrote in the 1770s, a few years before *Notes on Virginia*, "The black

[27] David Waldstreicher, *Slavery's Constitution: From Revolution to Ratification* (New York: Hill and Wang, 2009), 58–59; John C. Greene, *American Science in the Age of Jefferson* (Ames: Iowa State University Press, 1984), 321–22; Fredrickson, *Racism*, 59.

[28] Query XIV, "Laws," in Peden, ed., *Notes on the State of Virginia*, 139, 288n. Following the nearly universal tendency among historians to discredit Jefferson, even the outstanding scholar Gordon S. Wood castigates Jefferson's *Notes on Virginia* as an "abhorrent" and "repugnant" "racist" document ("The Radicalism of Thomas Paine and Thomas Jefferson Considered," in *The Idea of America* [New York: Penguin, 2011], 213–28).

colour of Negroes, thick lips, flat nose, crisped woolly hair, and rank smell, distinguish them from every other race of men."[29] Nonetheless, with the fickleness of a philosopher, Lord Kames upheld cultural diversity in the matter of racial color. "The various colours, though they affect us differently, are all of them agreeable in their purity," he asserted. "But custom has regulated this matter in another manner; a black skin upon a human being is to us disagreeable, and a white skin is probably not less so to a negro."[30]

During the Revolutionary era, one did not have to be a great philosopher or even a litterateur to be conversant with the concept of Black odor. Adam Stephen, a Virginia general in the Continental Army, jokingly derided the actions of his state's departed governor, Lord Dunmore, who before fleeing the colony in November 1775 decreed from his warship *The William* that he would emancipate all slaves joining him in fighting the rebels. In 1777, Stephen anticipated that Dunmore would recommend a British invasion of Virginia, "in order to add some more odoriferous beauties to his Ethiopian seraglios." Apparently, Stephen was not au courant with the latest "scientific" findings, as epitomized by the scientist and philosopher Lord Kames. Kames deliberately distinguished between "Negroes" and "Abyssinians," another name for Ethiopians, who, he said, despite living in the same climates as those in "Negroland," were much more aesthetically pleasing, with "their complexion a brown olive, features well proportioned," and apparently odorless.[31] Borrowing wording from the admired "moral sense" theorist Kames, Jefferson likewise decried Blacks' "very strong and disagreeable odour," a dictum of "natural history" that, as a novice natural philosopher, he was unwilling to challenge when such venerable scholars as Immanuel Kant, Henry Home (Lord Kames), and David Hume expounded it.[32]

---

[29] Henry Home, Lord Kames, *Sketches of the History of Man*, 2d ed., 4 vols. (Edinburgh, 1778), 1:25, quoted in Smith, *How Race Is Made*, 14.

[30] Henry Home, Lord Kames, *Elements of Criticism*, 2d ed. (Edinburgh, 1763), 2:113. See also Wylie Sypher, *Guinea's Captive Kings: British Anti-Slavery Literature of the Eighteenth Century* (Chapel Hill: University of North Carolina Press, 1942), 51.

[31] Adam Stephen to Richard Henry Lee, April 22, 1777, quoted in Woody Holton, "Rebel against Rebel: Enslaved Virginians and the Coming of the American Revolution," *Virginia Magazine of History and Biography* 105 (Spring 1997): 157–92, at 178n, Kames, *Sketches of the History of Man*, 1:25, quoted in Smith, *How Race Is Made*, 14.

[32] On Blacks' alleged odor, see Jefferson, *Notes on Virginia*, Query XIV, in Peterson, ed., *Jefferson: Writings*, 265. For Lord Kames's influence on Jefferson's moral sense and thought, see Bernard W. Sheehan, *Seeds of Extinction: Jeffersonian Philanthropy and the American Indian* (New York: W.W. Norton & Company, 1973), 22–32. On major European philosophers' nearly universal depiction of Blacks, whether free or enslaved, as having an extremely offensive odor, see Smith, *How Race Is Made*, 14; and the other sources cited in note 24 above. Claims about an oppressed ethnic group's offensive odor are almost always made by an hegemonic race

Another egregious statement Jefferson made against African Americans in Query XIV of *Notes* was his assertion that Black men preferred White women sexually because they were more beautiful than Black women. He sought support for this canard in the "scientific" analogy that male orangutans preferred Black women to females of their own species. He did not invent this fantasy by himself. As scholars involved with eighteenth-century thought are well aware, he could have garnered this scenario from diverse sources. Among them were travel accounts, "scientific" treatises like the works of such prototypical anthropologists as Lord Monboddo and Jean-Jacques Rousseau that posited that monkeys were primitive humans who lacked language, and Voltaire's great conte, *Candide*, in which Paraguayan native women take monkeys (who, Candide's valet Cacambo explains, are "one-quarter human") as their lovers. Apparently, Jefferson did not think that such unflattering comparisons were offensive to Blacks. He called himself an orangutan, perhaps indicating his unconscious sexual preference for Black women; indeed, over the past twenty years, most historians have concluded that he eventually fathered six children with his mixed-race slave Sally Hemings who was three-quarters White. Complaining to his White former paramour Maria Cosway about the cold, rainy weather in France when he was US minister there in 1789, and possibly commencing a sexual relationship with his teenage quadroon slave, he said, "I am an animal of a warm climate, a mere Oran-ootan [*sic*]."[33]

---

or nationality about subaltern groups, as they were made in the late-nineteenth and early twentieth centuries against Jews (even by other renowned Jews, such as Ludwig Wittgenstein, Sigmund Freud, and Otto Weininger) (Sander Gilman, *Freud, Race, and Gender* [Princeton: Princeton University Press, 1993]).

[33] Jefferson to Maria Cosway, January 14, 1789, in Douglas L. Wilson and Lucia Stanton, eds., *Jefferson Abroad* (New York: Modern Library, 1999), 275; Voltaire, *Candide: Or Optimism* (1759), chapter 16. For the universally accepted [pseudo]-"scientific" belief that monkeys and orangutans were primitive versions of humans, see Mary L. Bellhouse, "Candide Shoots the Monkey Lovers: Representing Black Men in Eighteenth-Century French Visual Culture," *Political Theory* 34 (December 2006): 741–84; Brett Mizelle, "'Man Cannot Behold it without Contemplating Himself': Monkeys, Apes and Human Identity in the Early American Republic," *Pennsylvania History* 66 (Special Supplemental Issue) (1999): 144–73; Robert Wokler, "Perfectible Apes in Decadent Cultures: Rousseau's Anthropology Revisited," *Daedalus* 107/3 (Summer 1978): 107–34; Wokler, "The Ape Debates in Enlightenment Anthropology," *Studies on Voltaire and the Eighteenth Century* 192, Section 12 (1980): 1164–75; Christopher Fox, Roy Porter, and Robert Wokler, *Inventing Human Science: Eighteenth-Century Domains* (Berkeley: University of California Press, 1995), 43–45. Robert Wokler, "Tyson and Buffon on the Orang-utan," *Studies on Voltaire and the Eighteenth Century* 155 (1976): 2301–19, notes that Buffon and his contemporaries often failed to distinguish between chimpanzees, orangutans, and monkeys although the first two are great apes and lack tails. See also Arthur Lovejoy, "Monboddo and Rousseau," in his *Essays in the History of Ideas*, 38–61.

Unfortunately, historians' present-mindedness often impels them to pigeonhole Jefferson as a more thoroughgoing racist than he was for his time and place.

Even abolitionists like the Pennsylvania Quaker Charles Thomson agreed with *Notes on Virginia*'s conclusions as to Blacks' possible intellectual inferiority. However, Thomson warned Jefferson that his depiction of Blacks' mental shortcomings in Query XIV might inadvertently provide ammunition for proslavery writers who insisted that Blacks were suited only for slavery, not freedom. Thomson also had misgivings about Jefferson's favorable comparison of contemporary Southern slaveholders' allegedly benign treatment of their slaves as opposed to the ancient Romans, who exercised absolute power over their chattel in a cruel, arbitrary manner, according to ancient texts like the writings of Cato the Elder. They ostensibly murdered their slaves for such trivial reasons as accidentally breaking a glass, tortured them to procure legal evidence, and segregated male and female slaves on their plantations (*latifundia*). (Horrifying to relate, Jefferson's drunken nephew, Lilburne Lewis, inflicted similar sadistic brutality, murdering a young slave.[34])

Thomson advised Jefferson to delete the parts of Query XIV that disparaged Black abilities, notwithstanding their possible intellectual inferiority, because those sections would potentially justify their enslavement, which both he and Jefferson opposed. "And though I am much pleased with the dissertation on the differences between the Whites and blacks & am inclined to think the latter a race lower in the scale of being yet for that very reason & because such an opinion might seem to justify slavery I should be inclined to leave it out," he advised. Jefferson followed some, but not all of Thomson's recommendations.[35]

Most of Jefferson's negative "racial" observations emerged from his personal aesthetic preferences. Since most racial groups claim to prefer the physical characteristics of their ethnic group to any other and consider their race the most intelligent, the frequent accusation that his "suspicion" that Blacks were less intelligent and attractive than Whites was "racist" is true in a broad sense. However, such reasoning would probably fit most people, even Jefferson's detractors, under the same category. Ironically, Jefferson was not embarrassed to compare himself with a simian creature who was supposedly part-human, even in a letter to his

---

[34] Horrifically, in 1811, Lilburne Lewis, Jefferson's mentally unbalanced nephew, in a drunken rage beheaded one of his slaves for breaking a pitcher and instructed another slave to dismember and hide his body. Before he could be tried for murder, he killed himself. His brother Isham, an accomplice, escaped from jail and fled to New Orleans (Boynton Merrill, Jr., *Jefferson's Nephews: A Frontier Tragedy* [New York: Avon Books, 1978] 257).

[35] Charles Thomson to Jefferson, [March–April 1784], Jefferson Papers, Coolidge Collection, Massachusetts Historical Society, Boston, MA, quoted in Douglas L. Wilson, "The Evolution of Jefferson's *Notes on the State of Virginia*," *Virginia Magazine of History and Biography* 112/2 (2004): 98–133, n62.

paramour. Although such sentiments horrify us today as politically incorrect, they were less grating to Jefferson's ears. He did not intend to ridicule Blacks, although we perhaps assume that he wanted to, when he mentioned the orangutan's sexual attraction to African American women. He did not mean such ostensibly "scientific" ideas in any way to justify human bondage.

Beginning in his youth, Jefferson had developed an aversion to slavery. This attitude can be garnered from the notes in his *Legal Commonplace Book*, which Jefferson literary scholar Douglas L. Wilson estimates he compiled from 1769 to 1778. Of those authors who were not attorneys or indispensable legal authorities, he spent most time abstracting the Charles de Secondat Baron de Montesquieu's renowned work, *The Spirit of Laws* (Paris, 1748). It is probable that Jefferson copied the extracts from the volume shortly after he purchased Montesquieu's collected works in 1769. The book ostensibly inspired, or confirmed, many of Jefferson's lifelong beliefs. For instance, for the first time he wrote here, what he was to reiterate more poetically in *Notes on Virginia* around ten years later, "The culture of the earth is the greatest work of man."[36]

Jefferson wrote three pages abstracting Montesquieu's antislavery arguments, with special emphasis on the Bordeaux judge and political philosopher's conviction that human enslavement violated natural law, and his suggestions on how to gradually abolish bondage. In one of his summary sentences, Jefferson wrote,

> 789. Civil Slavery. (1) In a democracy where everyone is equal, and in aristocracy where the laws must make efforts so that everyone is as equal as the nature of government can permit, slaves are against the spirit of the constitution. They only serve to give to citizens a power & a luxury that

[36] Gilbert Chinard, ed., *The Commonplace Book of Thomas Jefferson: A Repertory of His Ideas on Government* (Baltimore: Johns Hopkins University Press, 1926), 277 (quotation); pp. 257–96 contain Jefferson's notes on *The Spirit of Laws.* His notes on Montesquieu's ideas about slavery extend from 277–80. Jefferson's notes on Montesquieu are in French. The translations are mine; Chinard did not supply any. For conjectural estimates of the dates when Jefferson compiled his various commonplace books, see Douglas L. Wilson, "Thomas Jefferson's Early Notebooks," *William and Mary Quarterly* 42/4 (October 1985): 433–52. For Jefferson's purchase of Montesquieu's collected works in 1769, see Perkins, Buchanan and Brown (a merchant firm) to Jefferson, October 2, 1769, in Boyd et al., eds., *Papers of Thomas Jefferson* 1:34; Kevin J. Hayes, *The Road to Monticello: The Life and Mind of Thomas Jefferson* (New York: Oxford University Press, 2008), 113; Sowerby, ed., *Catalogue*, 3:2 (entry number 2325). After I wrote this chapter, a definitive edition of Jefferson's Legal Commonplace Book appeared; see David T. Konig and Michael P. Zuckert, eds., *Jefferson's Legal Commonplace Book*, (Princeton University Press, 2019), part of the Papers of Thomas Jefferson, Second Series. I have retained the citations to Chinard's earlier edition.

> they should not have. No matter what kind of slavery there is, it is necessary that civil laws try to remove from it abuse [of the slave by the master] on the one hand and danger [to the slave-holder from rebellious slaves] on the other.[37]

According to Jefferson's notes and abstracts of Montesquieu, the law of reason denied the master power to require of the slave anything beyond personal labor services. Borrowing from Montesquieu, he insisted that the slaves' sexual morality and personal virtue were behaviors beyond the master's power to control. "The laws of modesty are a natural right & must be preserved," he wrote. Montesquieu recommended the universal application of a feature of medieval Lombardy's law concerning slaves (who were usually White): "If a master rapes the wife of a slave, both are free."[38]

Summarizing the ideas in Montesquieu's Book XV, chapter 12, Jefferson argued that a "reasonable state" should not permit an excessive number of slaves. Slaves were the natural enemies of social peace, and in large numbers, they would be dangerous. Attempting to explain the sources of slave revolt, Jefferson wrote that nothing brought a man closer to feeling like a beast than to constantly observe free men and not be free. Where all men were downtrodden serfs, as in the feudal governments of Europe, less likelihood of slave uprising existed. Paraphrasing Montesquieu, Jefferson summarized, "It is not surprising that in moderate governments, the state has been so troubled by slave revolts and that this happens so rarely in despotisms."[39]

If a government's policies toward slaves were moderate and humane, it might surmount the inherent dangers of containing an excess of bondsmen. The

---

[37] Chinard, ed., *Commonplace Book*, 278.

[38] Ibid.

[39] Ibid., 279. I have translated Jefferson's notes from the original French. A comparison of their contents with Book XV of Volume One of *Spirit of Laws*, in which Montesquieu gives his ideas about slavery, reveals that Jefferson copied them nearly verbatim. In the above instance, chapter 12, a two-paged chapter titled, "Danger from the multitude of slaves," Montesquieu wrote, "It is not therefore to be wondered at, that moderate governments have been so frequently disturbed by revolts of slaves; and that this so seldom happens in despotic states" (Montesquieu, *The Spirit of the Laws*, 4th ed., 2 vols. [Edinburgh: A. Donaldson, 1768], 1:319, Book XV ["Slavery"], chapter 12 ["Danger from the multitude of slaves" 318–19]). After Jefferson had served in Europe as US minister to France for a few years, he disputed Montesquieu's assertions. "In Turkey," he wrote, "which Montesquieu supposes more despotic, insurrections are the events of every day." His inquiries revealed that abortive uprisings took place more often in "despotisms," like the Ottoman Empire, where all were theoretically slaves, than in constitutional monarchies like Britain and republics like the United States (Jefferson to James Madison, December 20, 1787, microfilm reel 8, Jefferson Papers, LC [hdl.loc.gov/loc.mss/mtj. mtjbib003193]).

citizens of simple republics, generally small farmers who were not ashamed to labor, were ordinarily kinder to their slaves than in governments whose peoples considered physical labor degrading. Initially, the ancient Romans lived, worked, and ate meals beside their slaves. They were benevolent and fair-minded to them, avoided legislation regulating their private lives, and thereby earned the slaves' loyalty. However, as they became rulers of an empire, the Romans' moeurs changed for the worse. Their morals declined; slave-owners became violent, sadistic, and cruel; and the government passed brutal laws to establish their security against their irate bondsmen, who now viewed them as enemies.[40]

Jefferson's notes emphasized placing legal limits on both the slave-owner and the government and safeguarding the slave's minimal legal rights. In all cases, the magistrate was responsible for ensuring that slaves received adequate food and clothing, enforcing these provisions by law. The law must also require that masters continue to take care of their slaves in sickness and in old age. Jefferson jotted down Montesquieu's observation that ancient Greek law specified that slaves whose masters treated them brutally could request sale to other owners. In addition, Montesquieu advised that if a master and a slave strongly disliked each other, they should be separated at least temporarily. If a slave suffered abuse by someone other than his owner, the owner was entitled to prosecute the reprobate in court. Although the laws frequently denied slaves the "natural right" to physically defend themselves against an owner, they must receive the substitute right to resort to the civil courts for justice. In ancient Athens, the law severely punished those who beat slaves owned by others, sometimes imposing the death penalty. With good reason, the Athenians feared to compound their injustice to the slave by adding the deprivation of all physical safety to his loss of liberty.[41]

In a republic containing many slaves, Montesquieu advised, public safety required a substantial number's periodic emancipation. When too many slaves inhabited a polity, it was difficult to keep them under control. If an excessive number were manumitted, however, it was probable that many would be unable to find jobs (*ils ne peuvent pas vivre)*, and the nation would be threatened by hordes of starving freedmen. There was also a danger that if the government freed large numbers of slaves and granted them civil rights and the suffrage, they would take revenge on the state for past injustices by voting for barbaric laws that would expropriate or humiliate the free classes. Montesquieu mentioned the case of the Volsinienses, an ancient Etruscan (Italian) community, who when the Etruscans freed and granted them the suffrage, passed prurient laws that gave them the right of the first night, to sleep with virgins the night before their wedding. Montesquieu concluded by warning of the dangers in freeing a large number of slaves all

[40] Chinard, ed., *Commonplace Book*, 279.

[41] Ibid., 279.

at once. To employ a later generation's language, he preferred "gradual" to "immediate" emancipation. In writing down his comments on this topic at length, so it seems did Jefferson, who expressed support for gradual emancipation in most of his future writings.[42]

At this time, Jefferson also indicated an interest in how slaves might nonviolently achieve self-sufficiency and eventual freedom by their own efforts. Jotting down methods he would later use as a slaveholder, he wrote, "There are diverse ways to introduce new citizens without disruption into a republic. The laws can favor the *pecule* [peculium, or savings], and give the slaves a way to purchase their liberty," generally by temporarily hiring themselves out to someone for wages, with their master's approval. "They can follow the Law of Moses with the Hebrews, set time limits to enslavement, limiting it to six years," essentially what the colonists had called indentured servitude. Montesquieu analyzed means by which the number of slaves could gradually be reduced. "It is easy to liberate a certain number of slaves every year, especially those whose age, health, and industry, would have the greatest ability to survive" in the outside world. "One can even cure the evil at its roots," Montesquieu pointed out, by replacing slaves with free workers. They could perform some of the tasks involving "commerce and navigation" performed by bondsmen, who were often forced to be jacks-of-all-trades. This strategy, Montesquieu predicted, ultimately "will diminish the number of slaves."[43]

In *Notes on Virginia* and other writings throughout his career, Jefferson expounded his ideas about emancipating slaves and reducing the enslaved population by replacing slaves with free European immigrants. He did not acknowledge the evident influence of Montesquieu's *Spirit of Laws* in this context, but it was undoubtedly there. And Montesquieu was generally considered an antislavery Enlightenment *philosophe*, unlike Voltaire, who was often unfairly labeled proslavery.[44]

---

[42] Ibid.

[43] Ibid., 279–80.

[44] Arthur Scherr, "Thomas Jefferson, White Immigration, and Black Emancipation: Part II," *Southern Studies* 23/1 (Spring/Summer 2016): 1–26; Pierre Pluchon, *Négres et Juifs au XVIIIe siècle: Le racisme au siècle des lumières* (Paris: FeniXX, 1984), 156–57; F. T. H. Fletcher, "Montesquieu's Influence on Anti-Slavery Opinion in England," *Journal of Negro History* 18/4 (October 1933): 414–25.

Chapter 2

The Emergence and Growth of Jefferson's Moral and Political Relativism

Acknowledging that diverse ways existed of evaluating his fellow citizens' political competency, Jefferson voiced confidence that Americans were capable of self-government. They possessed the prerequisite education and moral sense, as well as the practical experience in political participation. Nevertheless, with slight condescension, as one "natural aristocrat" to another, he wrote Du Pont concerning to the latter's plan for the South American Colombians, "We both consider the people as our children, and love them with parental affection. But you love them as infants whom you are afraid to trust without nurses; and I as adults whom I freely leave to self-government." Alluding to Du Pont's constitution, he said,

> Liberty, truth, probity, honor, are declared to be the four cardinal principles of your society. I believe with you that morality, compassion, generosity, are innate elements of the human constitution; that there exists a right independent of force; that a right to property is founded in our natural wants, in the means with which we are endowed to satisfy these wants, and the right to what we acquire by those means without violating the similar rights of other sensible beings.[1]

In other words, Jefferson thought that "all conditions of society" were best served by a government administered on "moral principles" similar to those of his own nation.

While thus declaring that it was natural to desire property for oneself, Jefferson believed that the equal rights of others to property, especially in land, limited the "natural right" to property. The right to property thereby became linked to a "right to subsistence," as Rousseau termed it in *The Social Contract*, rather than an unlimited right to material acquisition, as Locke conceived it in *The Second Treatise of Government*'s "labor theory of property." In Locke's schema, governmental restrictions on an individual's assets could be circumvented by profits' conversion into money, stock certificates, etc. Jefferson seemed closer to Rousseau than to Locke in his determination to ensure that no one suffered from poverty

[1] Jefferson to Du Pont, April 24, 1816, in Ford, ed., *Works of Thomas Jefferson*, 11:523.

and potentially starvation, rather than guaranteeing the rich the right to monopolize capital and impede the lower classes' survival. "No one has a right to obstruct another, exercising his faculties innocently for the relief of sensibilities made a part of his nature," Jefferson wrote, by which he meant everyone had gotten into the habit of eating and would prefer to own property in furtherance of that objective, necessary to the "pursuit of happiness." Moreover, curtailment of the unlimited individual right to acquire property followed from what Jefferson called man's "innate sense of justice" and the natural protection of minority rights. "Justice is the fundamental law of society," he asserted, presumably referring to those societies where the moral sense exercised hegemony:

> That the majority, oppressing an individual, is guilty of a crime, abuses it strength, and by acting on the law of the strongest breaks up the foundations of society; that action by the citizens in person, in affairs within their reach and competence, and in all others by representatives, chosen immediately, and removable by themselves, constitutes the essence of a republic; that all governments are more or less republican in proportion as this principle enters more or less into their composition.[2]

The moral sense and representative democracy, its agent, displayed their excellence by facilitating continental expansion and Manifest Destiny, being "capable of extension over a greater surface of country than one of any other form."[3]

Political democracy, and the majority's respect for the minority's rights and freedoms, constituted the "sacred principle," the keystone of the moral sense that invariably characterized the best form of government. This was the democratically oriented republic. As Jefferson expressed it in his first inaugural address in 1801: "All, too, will bear in mind this sacred principle, that though the will of the majority is in all cases to prevail, that will to be rightful must be reasonable; that the minority possess their equal rights, which equal law must protect, and to violate would be oppression."[4]

Jefferson denied that for all peoples and nations to immediately achieve this goal was the summum bonum, the object of desire for all legitimate governments. To his regret, he knew that some peoples would achieve it sooner, others later, and some perhaps not at all. The last two categories made his occasional recourse to inchoate ideas of cultural relativism necessary. The last letter he wrote, in

---

[2] Ibid.

[3] Ibid. For man's "innate sense of justice," see Jefferson to Justice William Johnson, June 12, 1823, in Peterson, ed., *Jefferson: Writings*, 1470.

[4] Jefferson's First Inaugural Address, March 4, 1801, in Peterson, ed., *Jefferson: Writings*, 492–93.

celebration of the upcoming July 4 semi-centennial, expressed his cautious hope that what he perceived as the United States' glowing example of liberty and democracy would be successfully imitated around the world, by "some parts sooner, to other parts later, but finally to all…to assume the blessings and security of self-government."[5]

To his ultimate dismay, Jefferson admitted that even the classes offered at his budding University of Virginia might fall to the vagaries of his community's and the state legislature's ideas of cultural relativism. In 1814, discussing his intentions with the religious radical and scientific polymath Thomas Cooper, Jefferson agreed that theology was not a practical topic of instruction at a secular school, even one of higher education. "I agree with yours of the 22d that a professorship of Theology should have no place in our institution," he wrote. "But we cannot always do what is absolutely best. Those with whom we act, entertaining different views, have the power and the right of carrying them into practice." Prepared to compromise on religious instruction with his evangelical foes John Hartwell Cocke and Reverend John Holt Rice, who wielded influence with legislators (Cocke was also a member of the University's Board of Visitors, or directors), Jefferson continued, "Truth advances, & error recedes step by step only; and to do our fellow men the most good in our power, we must lead where we can, follow where we cannot, and still go with them, watching always the favorable moment for helping them to another step."[6]

The anticlerical Thomas Cooper sardonically riposted that teaching religion at a university might be appropriate where there was an established national church, but even in that case such classes would properly be conducted within a department of politics rather than theology. He bluntly stated, "If you are to teach theology in your university on the ground of its truth, who is to judge which System is true?"[7] If anything, Jefferson exceeded Cooper in his disdain for theological rigmarole. Equating theology with "charlatanerie," he relegated medical theories to the same lowly category. "Perhaps I should concur with you also in excluding the *Theory* (not the *Practice*) of medecine [*sic*]," he wrote Cooper. "This is the charlatanerie of the body, as the other [theology] is of the mind."[8]

---

[5] Jefferson to Roger C. Weightman, Washington, DC, July 4 Committee on the Fiftieth Anniversary of American Independence, June 24, 1826, ibid., 1517.

[6] Jefferson to Thomas Cooper, October 7, 1814, microfilm reel 47, Jefferson Papers, LC (hdl.loc.gov/loc.mss/mtj.mtjbib021861), also printed in J. Jefferson Looney, ed., *The Papers of Thomas Jefferson: Retirement Series* (Princeton: Princeton University Press, 2004–), 8:12–13, hereafter cited as Looney, ed., *Jefferson Papers: Retirement Series.*

[7] Thomas Cooper to Jefferson, September 22, 1814, microfilm reel 47, Jefferson Papers, LC (hdl.loc.gov/loc.mss/mtj.mtjbib021836).

[8] Jefferson to Thomas Cooper, October 7, 1814, Jefferson Papers, LC, and printed in Looney, ed., *Jefferson Papers: Retirement Series*, 8:12–13.

Applying his pragmatic, empirical and physical attitude to the medical field, Jefferson had no patience with those who sought to adopt centuries-old antiquated theories to the attack on disease. He had much more respect for those, like Drs. Edward Jenner and Benjamin Waterhouse, who used their common sense and experimented on animals before trying their discoveries (in their case the all-important smallpox vaccine) on human beings.[9]

Jefferson balanced his adherence to cultural relativism with his staunch, perhaps quixotic adherence to the universalist belief that a society in which all received an education would implement "progressive amendments with the progressive advances of the human mind" in justice and fair play. Praising a clause in a recently proposed constitution for Spain allowing only literate individuals to vote (this had also been part of the defunct French Constitution of 1795, which Jefferson may have forgotten), Jefferson enthusiastically wrote Du Pont, "Enlighten the people generally, and tyranny and oppressions of body and mind will vanish like evil spirits at the dawn of day." For the South Americans—and perhaps also for the Haitians—Jefferson considered a system of educational literacy as potential salvation. A competent system of public education was the indispensable vehicle for social and intellectual progress. "Although I do not, with some enthusiasts, believe that the human condition will ever advance to such a state of perfection as that there shall no longer be pain or vice in the world," he confided to Du Pont, "yet I believe it susceptible of much improvement, and most of all, in matters of government and religion; and that the diffusion of knowledge among the people is to be the instrument by which it is to be effected."[10]

Jefferson's tenuous hopes for improving the "human condition," which he acknowledged was "susceptible of much improvement," while he was uncertain that such potential "advances" would become reality, reveal that Jefferson was no Pollyanna. As others have pointed out, Jefferson naively placed too much importance on education in securing progress, although he more broadly defined it as "the diffusion of knowledge," not merely formal schooling. By this phrase, Jefferson implied that he would not accept the teaching of lies, "false facts," and propaganda as an authentic "diffusion of knowledge," even if those who "learned" it were literate, like the Germans in the time of Nazi terror.[11]

---

[9] See Rebecca Fields Green, "'Simple, Easy, and Intelligible': Republican Political Ideology and the Implementation of Vaccination in the Early Republic," *Early American Studies* 12/2 (Spring 2014): 301–37.

[10] Jefferson to Du Pont, April 24, 1816, in Ford, ed., *Works of Thomas Jefferson*, 11:523–24.

[11] Jefferson said that those who wrote or printed slander, which he called "false facts," should be prosecuted in the courts by private individuals (Jefferson to Madison, July 31,1788, in Boyd et al., eds., *Papers of Thomas Jefferson*, 13:442–43).

Nonetheless, upholding the concept of cultural relativism that he had recently adopted, Jefferson concluded by concurring with Du Pont's decision that the South Americans were best suited to an indirect system of election by a propertied electorate, rather than a more democratic suffrage. Perhaps with Haiti also in mind, Jefferson pithily observed, "You are right in the case referred to you; my criticism being built on a state of society not under your contemplation [the United States]. It is, in fact, like a critic on Homer by the laws of the Drama."[12]

He feared that, lacking a substantive system of public, secularized education, the Colombians, whose masses had been infected with "ignorance and bigotry" by their previous Spanish monarchical rulers, lacked the "capacity to understand and to support a free government." If they rejected Du Pont's moderate constitution, they would, he predicted, ultimately turn to a military dictator for security. Now, praising Du Pont's document, which he had criticized when comparing it by the standards of the US Constitution's representative republicanism, Jefferson assured him, "For such a condition of society, the constitution you have devised is probably the best imaginable." The indirect system of election would recruit the natural aristocracy, but, Jefferson feared, not restrain it from future corruption and oppression. As he said, "It is certainly calculated to elicit the best talents; although perhaps not well guarded against the egoism of its functionaries. But that egoism will be light in comparison with the pressure of a military despot, and his army of Janissaries." Regarding military dictatorship, such as that imposed by Toussaint, Dessalines and Christophe in Haiti, and Tsar Alexander I in Russia, as the most abhorrent form of government, Jefferson viewed with relief the prospect that the Latinos would adopt Du Pont's constitutional structure. He concluded his letter with an eloquent testimony to cultural relativism in government, despite its imperfections, and the limits of moral sense philosophy: "Like Solon to the Athenians, you have given to your Columbians, not the best possible government, but the best they can bear."[13] But the issue of slavery was not subject to compromise.

By vitiating the moral sense's precepts of natural justice, White slaveholders—including Jefferson—became outlaws no longer entitled to the protection of natural law themselves. Loosely complementing his antislavery rhetoric, Jefferson observed that morality as well as immorality might be taught by example, "for

---

[12] Jefferson to Du Pont, April 24, 1816, in Ford, ed., *Works of Thomas Jefferson*, 11:522.

[13] Ibid., 524. For a similar point of view, see Jefferson's support of Rousseau's proposal of a constitutional monarchy rather than a republican constitution for Poland (Jefferson to William Lee, January 16, 1817, in Andrew A. Lipscomb and Albert Ellery Bergh, eds., *The Writings of Thomas Jefferson*, 20 vols. [Washington, DC: Thomas Jefferson Memorial Association, 1903–1904], 15:101, discussed further below).

man is an imitative animal" (Query XVIII). Broadening this perspective, he implied that individuals who did not respect the freedom or rights of others did not deserve freedom. As Jefferson wrote Francis Gilmer in June 1816, "natural law" protects only those who obeyed it in their dealings with others.[14]

During his brief retirement from politics, in a letter from Monticello in 1795 to Francis D'Ivernois, a Genevan philosopher and educator, Jefferson defined the nominal restraints he would impose on individual freedom. He explained that the limits of "liberty…[though] in the insulated man, bounded only by his natural powers, must, in society, be so far restricted as to protect himself against the evil passions of his associates, & consequently, them against him." In another letter the same year, in which he boasted of setting up a nail factory at Monticello, profitably operated by slave children's labor, Jefferson proclaimed himself "a warm zealot for the attainment & enjoiment [*sic*] by all mankind of as much liberty, as each may exercise without injury to the equal liberty of his fellow citizens." He also praised the United States' temptations as an "asylum" for European political refugees, though it "offer[ed] nothing…but an entire freedom to use their own means & faculties as they please."[15]

During this 1790s period of retirement, Jefferson for the first time since *Notes on Virginia* expressed pessimism about human nature and his country's political future. Disconcerted by Senate passage of the pro-British Jay Treaty, Jefferson concluded that even in the United States, politics had become a dirty game whereby the rich and their demagogic underlings ran the government, exploiting the poor and obtaining advantages for themselves. Apparently, he considered Jay's Treaty an instance of this kind of oppression and injustice. In summer 1795, writing to Mann Page, an old Virginian friend who requested that Jefferson visit a new academy at Fredericksburg he had set up, Jefferson expressed growing concern about the republic's political future. Although he did not accept Page's invitation, he agreed that a good education was essential to the success of a democratic society. At the same time, he maintained an elitist perspective on the matter, which he expressed as early as *Notes on Virginia*, arguing that some individuals were better fitted for advanced learning than others: "I do most anxiously wish to see the highest degrees of education given to the higher degrees of genius,

---

[14] Jefferson to Francis W. Gilmer, June 7, 1816, in Ford, ed., *Writings of Thomas Jefferson*, 10:32–33. For an argument that implies that Jefferson did *not* advocate such a concept of freedom, see François Furstenberg, *In the Name of the Father: Washington's Legacy, Slavery, and the Making of a Nation* (New York: Penguin, 2006), 207.

[15] Jefferson to François D'Ivernois, February 6, 1795, and Jefferson to Démeunier, April 29, 1795, in Peterson, ed., *Jefferson: Writings*, 1024, 1027–28. The nail factory ended up a financial loss, and he eventually abandoned it (McLaughlin, *Jefferson and Monticello*, 111).

and to all degrees of it so much as may enable them to read and understand what is going on in the world, and to keep their part of it going on right; for nothing can keep it right but their own vigilant distrustful superintendance." Thus, Jefferson believed that, although only select members of society were suitable rulers, in a democratic republic all citizens must be responsible for supervising and vigilantly controlling the conduct of their leaders. As a matter of course, the people should be well educated to enable them to perform this function competently.[16]

After briefly discussing education, Jefferson digressed, denouncing the recently ratified Jay Treaty. In an unusually cynical and pessimistic discourse, he deplored the ubiquitous triumph of malevolent "rogues" over the virtuous in American society and politics. According to classical republican theory and the cyclical concept of history, this foreboded the republic's imminent doom. As Jefferson angrily, sardonically put it, "I do not believe, with the Rochefoucaults and Montaignes, that fourteen out of fifteen men are rogues: I believe a great abatement from that proportion may be made in favor of general honesty." Jefferson thought that manipulative and deceitful "rogues" were generally more successful in society and politics than honest and virtuous men were. Pairing the "higher classes" (the wealthy) with the corrupt "rogues," he convolutedly observed, "I have always found that rogues would be uppermost [in society], and I do not know that the proportion is too strong for the higher orders, and for those who, rising above the swinish multitude, always contrive to nestle themselves into the places of power and profit." Regarding demagogues as one type of "rogue," he warned, "These rogues set out with stealing the people's good opinion, and then steal from them the right of withdrawing it, by contriving laws and associations against the power of the people themselves."[17]

---

[16] Jefferson to Mann Page, August 30, 1795, in Boyd et al., eds., *Papers of Thomas Jefferson*, 28:440.

[17] Jefferson to Page, August 30, 1795, ibid., 440–41. Jefferson was using the term "swinish multitude," made famous by the conservative Anglo-Irish Whig leader Edmund Burke in his denunciation of popular movements in *Reflections on the Revolution in France* (1789), in an ironic sense. For the cyclical theory of history that was respected by the Founding Fathers, a legacy of Plato, Aristotle, Polybius, and ancient Greek and Roman political thought, predicting that all governments evolved toward inevitable anarchy followed by tyranny, see Stow Persons, "The Cyclical Theory of History in Eighteenth Century America," *American Quarterly* 6/2 (Summer 1954): 147–63; John R. Howe, Jr., "Republican Thought and the Political Violence of the 1790s," *American Quarterly* 19/2, Part 1 (Summer 1967): 147–65; Lance Banning, "Jeffersonian Ideology and the French Revolution: A Question of Liberticide at Home," *Studies in Burke and His Time* 17 (1976): 5–26; Banning, "Republican Ideology and the Triumph of the Constitution, 1789 to 1793," *William and Mary Quarterly* 31/2 (April 1974): 167–88; and John E. Crowley, "Classical and Other Traditions for the Understanding of Change in Post-Revolutionary America: The Idea of Decline," in John W. Eadie, ed., *Classical Traditions in Early*

Perceiving those who vacillated between the Federalist and Republican parties as quasi-rogues, Jefferson now asserted that in politics there was only one legitimate or moral path, that of his Republican Party. He castigated former secretary of state Edmund Randolph, who claimed to be "a man of no party" in the *Vindication* (1795), a pamphlet he wrote defending his conduct after Washington dismissed him for ostensibly treasonous collusion with the French minister to the United States, Joseph Fauchet. Jefferson derided Randolph's claims that his political career was marked by impartiality—"his opinions not containing any systematic adherence to party, fall sometimes on one side and sometimes on the other." After reading Randolph's tract, he concluded, "The fact is that he has generally given his principles to the one party and his practice to the other; the oyster to one, the shell to the other."[18]

Randolph's nominal adherence to Jeffersonian Republicanism while his actual policies as Cabinet officer dovetailed with Federalism provoked Jefferson's wrath at what seemed to him hypocrisy. Of Randolph he disdainfully observed, "Whether his conduct is to be ascribed to a superior view of things, an adherence to right without regard to party, as he pretends, or an anxiety to trim between both, those who know his character and capacity will decide." He believed that vacillation between parties at this critical period in the republic's political life was immoral. To Jefferson, the Federalists represented the threatened restoration of a monarchical-type government similar to Great Britain's, which deprived the average person of dignity and natural rights. On the other hand, a victory for his Democratic-Republicans signified the survival and progression of free government and majority rule embodied in the American Revolution. Believing that Whigs and Tories alike were unduly subservient to the centralizing policies of Prime Minister William Pitt and King George III, Jefferson scorned Britain's current parliamentary regime as merely a struggle for power and patronage between the Ins and the Outs, divorced from moral or ideological principles or substantive issues. As Jefferson bluntly put it in his letter to Virginia congressman William Branch Giles:

> Were parties here divided merely by a greediness for office, as in England, to take a part with either would be unworthy of a reasonable or moral man. But where the principle of difference is as substantial and as strongly pronounced as between the republicans and the Monocrats [i.e., monarchists] of our country I hold it as honorable to take a firm and decided part, and

America (Ann Arbor: Center for the Coordination of Ancient and Modern Studies, University of Michigan, 1976), 213–53.

[18] Jefferson to William Branch Giles, December 31, 1795, in Boyd et al., eds., *Papers of Thomas Jefferson*, 28:565–66.

as immoral to pursue a middle line, as between the parties of Honest men, and Rogues, into which every country is divided.[19]

In many ways, Jefferson's comments on Jay's Treaty and the growth of political parties in 1795 mark the commencement in his Weltanschauung of a consciousness of the moral and political relativism that existed in Western culture. He argued that parties in England were formed merely on the basis of "greed for office," but that in the United States, where the majority ruled, partisan conflict pitted advocates of monarchy against friends of republicanism (which in Jefferson's opinion was synonymous with Democratic-Republicanism); in other words, "evil" versus "good." Jefferson continued to uphold this stance as late as 1813. He denied English writer John Melish's assertions, similar to Jefferson's earlier observations to Giles on British politics, that the party controversy between Republicans and Federalists was merely a contest for office and patronage between Ins and Outs. Writing to Melish, who had sent him his recent book about the American scene, Jefferson continued to insist, "The question of preference between monarchy and republicanism, which has so long divided mankind elsewhere, threatens a permanent division here."[20]

Despite the culturally relativistic view Jefferson applied to other peoples, races, and countries, he continued to perceive the conflict between parties in the United States in absolute terms of right and wrong, primarily because of his nation's more egalitarian political and economic evolution. He applied different criteria and expectations to other peoples, less blessed than America with a British colonial heritage of comparative liberty and relative freedom from external control, with large spaces of open land and a temperate climate. These latter factors, more than any inherent superiority of character, enabled American settlers to merge "the freest principles of the English constitution, with others derived from natural right and natural reason," and to enjoy the happiest lives on the planet. He boasted that the American people, despite some setbacks and harassment of their foreign trade by Britain and France, went on, "puzzled and prospering beyond example in the history of man. And I do believe we shall continue to growl [grow], to multiply and prosper until we exhibit an association, powerful, wise, and happy, beyond what has yet been seen by men."[21]

As is well known, Jefferson considered farmers the most "virtuous" citizens, and best qualified to administer a democratic republic. Most Americans were small farmers, and, Jefferson argued, they "are the chosen people of God, if ever he had a chosen people" (Jefferson did not believe He did), because, ideally, they

[19] Ibid., 566.

[20] Jefferson to John Melish, January 13, 1813, in Peterson, ed., *Jefferson: Writings*, 1268.

[21] Query VIII, "Population," Peden, ed., *Notes on the State of Virginia*, 84; Jefferson to John Adams, January 21, 1812, in Cappon, ed., *Adams-Jefferson Letters* (1959), 2:291.

resisted "corruption of morals," especially by moneyed wealth and bribery. They were "independent," self-sufficient people, utilizing "their own soil and industry," producing their own food and clothing for "subsistence," unlike merchants, artisans, and laborers of the cities, who depended "on the casualties and caprice of customers."[22]

These yeomen generally elected to office the most competent "natural aristocrats," Jefferson was sure, men of the greatest knowledge and integrity. American agrarian voters were most suited to conduct public affairs directly, in person, at the local level (in districts that he called "wards") and elect the right individuals to administer the laws in state and national governments, not because they were somehow exceptional, or divinely inspired, but because of their vocation as farmers. On the other hand, because of the high ratio of population to land, most Europeans had ended up oppressed by nobles, clergy, and monarchs. They were primarily serfs or city workers, in neither case able to choose the economic independence indispensable to political and intellectual independence. Indirectly answering Crévecoeur's famous question, "What is the American, this new man?" Jefferson began, in a famous letter to John Adams in 1813, by describing what he *was not*. Jefferson concluded that the economic and social conditions of the United States, with its great abundance of arable land, unlike the comparatively scant landmass of most European monarchies, forever made an institutionalized aristocracy impossible. Consequently, he wrote, "we should further consider that, before the establishment of the American states, nothing was known to History but the Man of the old world, crouded [*sic*] within limits either small or over-charged, and steeped in the vices which that situation generates. A government adapted to such men would be one thing; but a very different one that for the Man of these states." "The Man of these [United] States" was not inherently more virtuous than the European canaille, Jefferson contended; rather, the abundance of available land and the prosperous expanding economy enabled Americans to avert class warfare, bypass the need for an institutionalized aristocracy, and sustain representative democracy. Jefferson's utopian picture ignored the plight of the laboring poor and the unemployed, comprising nearly twenty percent of the nation's population, and the enslaved, another ten percent, but it was valid for the remainder, whose condition was more pleasant than that of European peasants. He continued, "Here every one may have land to labor for himself if he chuses [*sic*]; or, preferring the exercise of any other industry,

[22] Query XIX, Peden, ed., *Notes on the State of Virginia*, 164–65. The two-page chapter, titled "Manufactures," is mostly about the harmful effects of cities and urban "mobs," and their incapacity for self-government because they were dependent on wages and "customers." Nevertheless, Jefferson quietly contradicted himself, admitting that commercial farmers depended on selling their commodities to customers. He wrote, "It is better to carry provisions and materials to workmen there [in Europe]," than to encourage European artisans and city workers to immigrate to the United States, "and with them their manners and principles" (165).

may exact for it such compensation as not only to afford a comfortable subsistence, but wherewith to provide for a cessation from labor in old age." As he observed to Adams (who had never thought the French Revolution would succeed), in the United States, unlike revolutionary France, "every one, by his property, or by his satisfactory situation, is interested in the support of law and order. And such men may safely and advantageously reserve to themselves a wholesome controul [*sic*] over their public affairs, and a degree of freedom, which in the hands of the Canaille of the cities of Europe, would be instantly perverted to the demolition and destruction of every thing public and private." Jefferson claimed that the French Revolution, at its outset a movement for greater human freedom and equal rights, failed because its most active supporters, the "mobs of the cites, the instrument used for its accomplishment, debased by ignorance, poverty, and vice, could not be restrained to rational action." Unflatteringly implying that the urban "mobs" were irrational tools, manipulated by their intellectual and social superiors, he predicted that farmers would be more active in promoting the next, less violent but more enduring revolution.[23]

Thus, Jefferson assumed relative cultural differences and political capacities existed between the city resident and the farmer, claiming that the latter had greater aptitude for self-government because he was more self-controlled and more economically independent. In essence, Jefferson maintained that two subcultures existed in the United States: the virtuous, independent yeoman, who, because he was self-sufficient, raising his crops and fabricating most of his clothing, did not depend on customers' patronage, and in sharp contrast, denizens of the cities, merchants, lawyers, artisans, and laborers, reliant on employers and clients for their income. By Jefferson's criteria, in terms of cultural relativism, the farmer was more suited than the urbanites to vote and hold office because of his alleged spirit of independence.[24]

In Query XIX of *Notes*, as in various letters he wrote during the 1780s, Jefferson eloquently asserted the moral superiority of farmers. However, on his part, this was more theoretical posturing than a basis for government policy. Jefferson himself would have admitted that most farmers engaged in commercial activities, and that those who raised crops above subsistence level relied on exporting them

---

[23] Jefferson to John Adams, October 28, 1813, Cappon, ed., *Adams-Jefferson Letters*, 391.

[24] Ibid. In many ways, Jefferson's theory anticipated Frederick Jackson Turner's "Significance of the Frontier in American History" (1893), whose emphasis on the frontier farmer's independence, individualism, and integrity as epitomizing the national character influenced academic disciplines for many years. Richard Hofstadter, *The Age of Reform: From Bryan to F.D.R.* (New York: Alfred A. Knopf, 1955), chapter 1, remains one of the best refutations of Jefferson's "agrarian myth," pointing out that farmers have always depended on buying and selling.

abroad to secure an income and a better life. He knew that this was true of himself, his planter friends, and of most farmers. During the War of 1812, he even advocated allowing farmers to ship wheat and other provisions to the British armies in Spain and Portugal, which offered high prices, despite the recent US declaration of war on Great Britain. He rationalized that, if the British troops were fighting on the Iberian Peninsula, they would *not* be fighting in the United States, thereby reducing the number of men they could send across the Atlantic and indirectly assisting the American war effort.[25] Indeed, in Query XXII of *Notes on Virginia*, he upheld American farmers' right to transport their farm surpluses all over the world.[26]

Proud that the US had succeeded to a greater extent than other nations in achieving political liberty (although it was confined primarily to White adult males), freedom of thought, and progress in disseminating knowledge, the elderly Jefferson was cautiously confident that his nation's liberating "light" would transcend the Holy Alliance's efforts to crush republican revolutions in Spain, Italy, and Portugal. Labeling Austria, Russia, and Prussia, monarchies that repressed reform abroad, the "Northern triumvirate," he predicted their ultimate failure. "I shall not die without a hope that light and liberty are on steady advance," he said, and that they would eventually triumph as the uplifting Renaissance had overcome medieval "conquering ruffians," the Goths, Tartars, and Visigoths. "And even should the cloud of barbarism and despotism again obscure the science and liberties of Europe," he exhorted, sounding much like Winston Churchill over a hundred years later, when he praised the United States as the civilized world's salvation against the Nazi hordes, "this country remains to restore light and liberty to them. In short, the flames kindled on the 4th. of July 1776 have spread over too much of the globe to be extinguished by the feeble engines of despotism. On the contrary they will consume those engines, and all who work them."[27]

Although he never ceased proclaiming democracy, popular rule, and freedom of thought in all spheres as the ideal absolute that all peoples and governments should attain, Jefferson's observations of history and his own time led to the realization that such a utopian outcome was unlikely in his lifetime. This practical perspective caused him to admit the utility of the idea of cultural relativism. Perhaps Jefferson's most forthright espousal of cultural relativism was in

---

[25] Jefferson to Madison, June 29, 1812, microfilm reel 46, Jefferson Papers, LC (hdl.loc.gov/loc.mss/mtj.mtjbib021152). In general, see Donald R. Hickey, "American Trade Restrictions during the War of 1812," *Journal of American History* 68/3 (December 1981): 517–38.

[26] Scherr, *Thomas Jefferson's Haitian Policy* (Lanham, MD: Lexington Books, 2011), 315–16.

[27] Jefferson to John Adams, September 12, 1821, in Cappon, ed., *Adams-Jefferson Letters* (1959), 2:575.

analyzing religious dogmas and the adherence to diverse absurd rituals and liturgies by different faiths, especially Christian ones, which led to innumerable senseless wars, murders, and persecutions. He insisted that the moral doctrines summarized in Jesus' Sermon on the Mount constituted the prototype of a universal creed acceptable to all religions, archetypes of the "moral sense" he contended was innate in almost every sane person.

Shortly after his retirement from the presidency, Jefferson wrote James Fishback, a radical Lexington, Kentucky, Presbyterian who later became a Baptist minister, his ideas about the prevalence of the "moral sense" among all cultures. He eloquently expounded his view that the universal, pervasive "moral sense," which should operate when every society formulates its laws, might be harmoniously combined with the diverse customs and mores of each culture, allowing it to preserve its uniqueness. Although Jefferson did not believe in the divine quality of revelation, and Fishback, author of a pamphlet titled, *Is Revelation True?* (1809) did, the former president appreciated Fishback's apparent tolerance of diversity on such issues of Christian dogma as the Mass. "I thank you for the pamphlet you were so kind as to send me," he began his letter.

> At an earlier period of life I pursued enquiries of that kind with industry & care. Reading, reflection & time have convinced me that the interests of society require the observation of those moral precepts only in which all religions agree (for all forbid us to murder, steal, plunder, or bear false witness) and that we should not intermeddle with the particular dogmas in which all religions differ, and which are totally unconnected with morality.

Surveying the disparate rituals and liturgies of Protestantism and Catholicism, for example, Jefferson concluded, "In all of them we see good men, & as many in one as another."[28]

After thus expounding his adherence to cultural diversity in matters of religious faith, Jefferson posited a physiological basis for different individuals' attraction to different religions. In many ways, Jefferson believed, one's religious faith resembled individual adherence to different political parties. But, perhaps to accommodate the devout Fishback, who believed in divine revelation, Jefferson paid lip service to the Creator's role in molding human thought. (Jefferson did think that the "moral sense" was God-given, as he had explained as early as 1787 to Peter Carr and would explain again to Thomas Law in 1814.) To Fishback, he wrote, "The varieties in the structure & action of the human mind as in those of the body, are the work of our creator, against which it cannot be a religious duty,

---

[28] Jefferson to James Fishback, September 27, 1809, microfilm reel 44, Jefferson Papers, LC (hdl.loc.gov/loc.mss/mtj.mtjbib020083), and Looney, ed., *Jefferson Papers: Retirement Series*, 1:563–66.

to erect the standard of uniformity." Thus, as far as the deist Jefferson was concerned, God upheld diversity in religions when they obeyed universal moral rules; he did not favor one religion over another. This was one more reason to permit freedom of thought in matters of religion, just as in matters of politics, science and other aspects of life. Although it was among God's rules that societies and governments permit people to think and act differently from one another, God also supposedly imposed identical, instinctive moral ideas on all races, colors, and creeds in order to sustain social existence. "The practice of morality being necessary for the well-being of society, he [God] has taken care to impress it's [*sic*] precepts so indelibly on our hearts that they shall not be effaced by the subtleties of our brain," Jefferson argued. Conveniently overlooking most religions' blatant disobedience of the Ten Commandments, Jefferson thought in terms of the ideal rather than reality at this point: "We all agree in the obligation of the moral precepts of Jesus, & no where will they be found in greater purity than in his discourses." Concealing his general hostility to the Protestant clergy, whose orthodox evangelicals he considered primitive and obscurantist and resented for their opposition to the Democratic-Republican Party and their campaign libels against him as an atheist, he ended on a conciliatory note. At this halcyon time of his life, Jefferson merely stated, "It is then a matter of principle with me to avoid disturbing the tranquility of others by the expression of any opinion on the innocent questions on which we schizmatise." As a deist, Jefferson adopted no liturgical or ritualistic beliefs or practices, which, taking a placatory stance, he now labeled "innocent questions." He probably believed it prudent to avoid a new statement of his religious views to someone like Fishback whom he did not know. He ended by asserting his admiration for Fishback's "candor, moderation & ingenuity with which you appear to have sought truth. If all the writers & preachers on religious questions had been of the same temper, the history of the world would have been of much more pleasing aspect."[29]

Expounding similar views to John Adams, Jefferson agreed with him that "the four words, 'be just and good,'" properly summed up the only dogma all religions should teach. Upholding his concept of the moral sense, which in at least rudimentary form was innate in all individuals and cultures, Jefferson said, "What all [religions] agree in is probably right, what no two agree in most probably wrong." Elaborating the pith of his "religion," he told Adams that a would-be biographer had recently inquired of him what his religious views were. His response, he said, was, "'say nothing of my religion. It is known to my god and myself alone. It's [*sic*] evidence before the world is to be sought in my life. If that

[29] Ibid.

has been *honest and dutiful to society*, the religion which has regulated it cannot be a bad one.'"[30]

By the late 1790s, confronted with the unpleasant fact of the interminable, unprecedentedly bloody wars of the French Revolution followed by Napoleon's attempt to achieve Continental supremacy, Jefferson had adopted the view that the murder and destruction of his own species were natural to man. This viewpoint undoubtedly contradicted his belief in the universal "moral sense," but he did not dwell on his inconsistency. He probably would have explained that citizens and subjects were forced to serve in the military and kill strangers because of their evil, power-hungry rulers. In this, he was similar to late eighteenth-century radicals like "Gracchus" Babeuf, Thomas Paine, and James T. Callender, all of whom said that if all governments were republicanized, wars would diminish in number or disappear.[31]

Although a few years later Jefferson despised Callender for exposing his ostensible sexual relationship with his slave Sally Hemings, he was initially impressed by the Scottish radical's political thought. Callender's two-volume attack on the British government, *The Political Progress of Britain* (1792–1795), upheld the virtues of democracy and denounced corrupt, predatory monarchies that forced their people to go to war to increase rulers' power, prestige, and wealth. One of Callender's themes was proto-psychoanalytic: monarchs exacerbated the latent evil and violent tendencies in their subjects and turned them against foreign "enemies." Jefferson stressed this idea in a letter to Madison that praised Callender's two-volume set. "The Political progress is a work of value and of a singular complexion," he wrote. "The eye of the author seems to be a natural achromatic, which divests every object of the glare of colour.... One is disgusted indeed with the ulcerated state which it presents of the human mind: but to cure an ulcer we must go to it's [*sic*] bottom: and no writer has ever done this more radically than this one." After admitting the impression that Callender's stark account had made on him, Jefferson expressed an often-suppressed cynical and pessimistic side of himself. "The reflections into which he leads one are not flattering to our species," he observed. "In truth I do not recollect in all the Animal kingdom a single species but man which is eternally and systematically engaged in the destruction of it's [*sic*] own species." Alluding to Thomas Hobbes's classic account of the so-called

---

[30] Jefferson to John Adams, January 11, 1817, in Cappon, ed., *Adams-Jefferson Letters* (1959), 2:506. Jefferson's italics.

[31] On this topic, see Sir Michael Howard, *War and the Liberal Conscience* (Cambridge: Cambridge University Press, 1986); Reginald Stuart, *War and American Thought from the Revolution to the Monroe Doctrine* (Kent: Kent State University Press, 1982); and, from a different perspective, J. L. Talmon, *Origins of Totalitarian Democracy* (London: Secker & Warburg, 1952).

"state of nature" in *Leviathan* (1651), Jefferson, like Jean-Jacques Rousseau, felt that the Hobbesian view of the state of nature as violent and lawless pervaded the contemporary relations between nations. He bitterly continued, "What is called civilization seems to have no other effect on him [humankind] than to teach him to pursue the principle of bellum omnium in omni [an imitation of Hobbes's slogan, "war of all against all"] on a larger scale, and in place of the little contests of tribe against tribe, to engage all the quarters of the earth in the same work of destruction." In this manner, Jefferson anticipated Freud's *Civilization and Its Discontents* (1931), which argued that the "civilized" countries of Europe exercised their collective "death instinct" by mass murder during World War I, the unprecedented violence of which killed about eleven million people, compared to which the violence of the "savage" tribes of the underdeveloped world was picayune.[32]

Jefferson noted that man, rather than the proverbial wild beasts of the jungle, was the true brute. As he bluntly put it, "When we add to this that as to the other species of animals, the lions and tygers are mere lambs compared with man as a destroyer, we must conclude that it is in man alone that Nature has been able to find a sufficient barrier against the too great multiplication of other animals and of man himself."[33]

Thus, Jefferson, with tongue in cheek, like Voltaire's Candide; his contemporary, Wilhelm Woolff; and the medieval Christian church fathers, claimed to perceive that good might come out of evil: world overpopulation and consequent ecological disaster might be prevented by cataclysmic, interminable warfare, for which mankind had an ostensibly innate proclivity. For Parson Thomas Robert Malthus, the ensuing, inevitable mass starvation when lustful English laborers produced too many children for the food supply to handle prevented world overpopulation. If the people failed to practice "moral restraint" (sexual abstinence), sporadic wars, disasters, and famines would invariably help reduce population. For Jefferson, whose American clime purveyed ample amber fields of grain to fill hungry bellies, international warfare was "an equilibrating power against the fecundity of generation."[34]

Ending his philippic against the culture and society of his time on a lighter note, Jefferson observed that metaphorical warfare could also occur on the battlefields of politics and cabinets, as he had experienced in his conflict with Hamilton

---

[32] Jefferson to James Madison, January 1, 1797, in Barbara Oberg, ed., *Papers of Thomas Jefferson* (Princeton: Princeton University Press, 2003–), 29:248. Hereafter cited as Oberg, ed., *Jefferson Papers*.

[33] Ibid.

[34] Ibid. I am referring to Thomas Robert Malthus's famous *Essay on Population* (1798).

in Washington's cabinet. "My situation points my views chiefly to his wars in the physical world," Jefferson, retired for the time being to his Monticello plantation, wrote his friend Madison, engaged in battling the Federalists from his seat in Congress. "Yours perhaps exhibit[s] him as equally warring in the Moral one. We both, I believe, join in wishing to see him softened."[35]

Jefferson continued to deplore the violence and bloodshed of the wars between France and Great Britain for world domination. He lamented that the United States, mistreated by both powers, especially the British, was forced to enter the fray. During the War of 1812, Napoleon's incessant warfare so appalled Jefferson that he was initially relieved at his overthrow and replacement by the Bourbons. At least temporarily, he adopted the view that old-fashioned kings were less dangerous to peace and therefore to the lives of their subjects than were dictatorial emperors like Bonaparte. Shortly before Napoleon returned for his more enlightened Hundred Days interval, Jefferson wrote William Short that he favored the "restoration of the Bourbons" rather than "continual civil wars" in France. At the same time, since this was during the War of 1812, he feared that Britain would have greater military resources available to use against the US following Napoleon's defeat. He favored peace as soon as possible between the United States and the British, believing this would promote their "mutual affections and mutual interest & happiness." He reluctantly concluded, as he had to Madison as early as 1797, that war and self-destruction seemed to be natural to the human mind. "The destructive passions seem to have been implanted in man, as one of the obstacles to his too great multiplication."[36]

On the international scale, Jefferson applied concepts of cultural relativism to the question of slavery as early as 1786. At that time, in Paris as US minister, advising Jean Nicholas Démeunier, a French scholar immersed in writing an encyclopedia article about the United States, he theoretically condoned slave uprisings. He informed Démeunier that, in 1776, he and George Wythe had proposed in the Virginia legislature a bill for the gradual abolition of slavery (the rough text of which apparently appeared in Query XIV of *Notes*), but they and their followers were stymied for lack of support. In phraseology similar to Query XVIII of *Notes*, Jefferson, rising to rhetorical heights, expressed his disappointment at the outcome, and suggested that Démeunier insert these words (without attribution) into the text of the encyclopedia article:

> What a stupendous, what an incomprehensible machine is man! Who can endure toil, famine, stripes, imprisonment & death itself in vindication of

---

[35] Jefferson to James Madison, January 1, 1797, in Oberg, ed., *Jefferson Papers*, 29:248.

[36] Jefferson to William Short, August 20, 1814, in Jefferson Papers, Massachusetts Historical Society Collections, series 7, vol. 1 (1900): 205; Jefferson to James Madison, January 1, 1797, in Oberg, ed., *Jefferson Papers*, 29:248.

> his own liberty, and the next moment be deaf to all those motives whose power supported him thro' his trial, and inflict on his fellow men a bondage, one hour of which is fraught with more misery than ages of that which he rose in rebellion to oppose. But we must await with patience the workings of an overruling providence, & hope that that is preparing the deliverance of these, our suffering brethren [the slaves]. When the measure of their tears shall be full, when their groans shall have involved heaven itself in darkness, doubtless a god of justice will awaken to their distress, and by diffusing light & liberality among their oppressors, or at length by his exterminating thunder, manifest his attention to the things of this world, and that they are not left to the guidance of a blind fatality.[37]

In this letter, Jefferson reiterated his earlier view that (1) slavery violated natural and divine laws and was a travesty of human relationships of reciprocity and equality; and (2) slaves were morally justified in killing their masters because their action accorded with both human and "godly" justice. It is surprising that his inflammatory views, which, if taken seriously by slaves, would lead them to murder their masters, did not arouse more shock and outrage among Jefferson's planter neighbors. Perhaps equally surprising, Jefferson sought publication of these provocative and potentially suicidal thoughts.

During this period, while he served as US minister to France, Jefferson was preoccupied with the question of justice between nations and was convinced that it was analogous to justice and moral conduct between individuals. For him, as for many Americans during the Revolutionary era, the issue of "gratitude" held a prominent place in their thoughts about sociable and decent conduct. The Americans' Whig leaders, convinced that the British had been ungrateful for colonial loyalty and military assistance over nearly two centuries of Continental competition for North America, found in their injured feelings additional justification for rebelling and declaring independence. In the Declaration of Independence, Jefferson aptly alluded to their resentment as an "agonizing affection." On both the personal level and the level of international relations, Jefferson joined other liberal thinkers in arguing that, with individuals and nations alike, "gratitude" should be an incumbent response to good deeds and consideration from others, a reciprocal policy of "sincerity" and "affection."[38]

---

[37] Jefferson to Jean Nicholas Démeunier, June 26, 1786, in Peterson, ed., *Jefferson: Writings*, 592.

[38] On gratitude's significance among the "affections" civic-minded republicans felt during the colonial and Revolutionary eras, see Jay Fliegelman, *Prodigals and Pilgrims: The American Revolution Against Patriarchal Authority, 1750–1800* (Cambridge: Cambridge University Press, 1982), 93–106, 177, 214–19, 233, 250–54; Barry P. Schwartz, *George Washington: The Making of an American Symbol* (New York: Free Press, 1987), 54, 98–101; Gordon S. Wood,

Jefferson emphasized the importance of "gratitude" in French-American relations in a letter to James Madison in August 1789, one of his last missives as US minister to France.[39] Disappointed that the new Congress had failed to reciprocate France's trade concessions to the United States, foremost among them permitting New England whale and fish oils to enter the country, for which he had striven as minister, Jefferson made some general comments about the importance of gratitude as a component of human nature. Alarmed by Madison's failure to persuade Congress to legislate special privileges for America's ally France on tariff and tonnage duties instead of charging all foreign nations the same rates, Jefferson nonetheless tried to see the brighter side of human character. Rejecting cynics who said that men might behave well as individuals, but not in a group, Jefferson silently disputed his friend's harsh analysis of human nature in *The Federalist*, nos. 10, 49, and 55. Jefferson observed, "He who says that I will be a rogue when I act in company with a hundred others, but an honest man when I act alone, will be believed in the former assertion, but not in the latter." Disdaining such misanthropes, Jefferson wrote in Latin, "I would say with the poet hic niger est, hunc tu Romane cavetto," a line from the Roman poet Horace, which translated, means, "That man is a knave, Roman, beware of him."[40]

The Radicalism of the American Revolution (New York: Vintage Books, 1992), 225; and Melvin Yazawa, *From Colonies to Commonwealth: Familial Ideology and the Beginnings of the American Republic* (Baltimore: Johns Hopkins University Press, 1985). For the concept of gratitude's role in international diplomacy, see Gerald Stourzh, *Benjamin Franklin and American Foreign Policy* (Chicago: University of Chicago Press, 1954), 149–50, 159, 164. For the controversy over gratitude and loyalty to the Mother Country within the Empire, see, e.g., Richard Koebner, *Empire* (Cambridge: Cambridge University Press, 1961); Eliga H. Gould, *The Persistence of Empire: British Political Culture in the Age of the American Revolution* (Chapel Hill: University of North Carolina Press, 2000); Kathleen Wilson, *Island Race: Englishness, Empire, and Gender in the Eighteenth Century* (London: Routledge, 2003); Eliga H. Gould and Peter S. Onuf, eds., *Empire and Nation: The American Revolution in the Atlantic World* (Baltimore: Johns Hopkins University Press, 2005).

[39] Jefferson to James Madison, August 28, 1789, in Boyd et al., eds., *Papers of Thomas Jefferson*, 15:364–69.

[40] Jefferson to Madison, August 28, 1789, in James Morton Smith, ed., *The Republic of Letters: The Correspondence between Thomas Jefferson and James Madison, 1776–1826*, 3 vols. (New York: Norton, 1995), 1:629. See also William T. Hutchinson and William M. E. Rachal, eds., *Papers of James Madison* (Chicago: University of Chicago Press, 1961–1991), 12:363–65. The Latin phrase has been variously translated. The one above is from Hugh Percy Jones, *Dictionary of Foreign Phrases and Classical Quotations* (Edinburgh: John Grant, 1963), 51. The source of the quotation is Horace, *Satires*, Book I, Satire IV, line 85, in his *Satires, Epistles, and Ars Poetica* (1970 reprint), 54–55. Hutchinson and Rachal, eds., *Papers of James Madison*, and Smith, ed., *Republic of Letters*, 12:365n, use, "That man is Black of heart; of him beware, good Roman."

At the same time, Jefferson sought reassurance that Madison shared his benevolent view of human nature, and was, like him, a decent, moral man: "If the morality of one man produces a just line of conduct in him, acting individually, why should not the morality of 100 men produce a just line of conduct in them acting together? But I indulge myself in these reflections because my own feelings run me into them: with you they were always acknowledged." He evidently sought solace from Madison, a prominent congressman from Virginia who dominated the nation's First Congress. Hoping that the people's representatives would prove their republican virtue by future legislation and correct the injustice to the French, he continued, "Let us hope that our new government will take some other occasion to shew [*sic*] that they mean to proscribe no virtue from the canons of their conduct with other nations."[41]

Perhaps Jefferson was unduly optimistic about Madison's confidence in man's all-pervasive moral sense. Both in *Federalist* no. 10 and later, Madison asserted that mass man, man in the crowd, was more dangerous to his fellows than as an isolated individual. Jefferson believed that individuals and governments—which, as Plato said in *The Republic*, despite Jefferson's frequent disparagement of it, were merely the individual writ large—should act morally and righteously toward one another. During the 1780s, Madison expressed contempt for the "mob," the assembled masses. As he wrote in *Federalist* no. 10, "If the impulse and the opportunity be suffered to coincide, we well know that neither moral nor religious motives can be relied on as an adequate control [to thwart an organized political majority's appetites]. They are not such on the injustice and violence of individuals, and lose their efficacy in proportion to the number combined together; that is, in proportion as their efficacy becomes needful."[42]

After Jefferson returned home from France, exhilarated by the beginning of its revolution in favor of popular rule and the "rights of man," his faith in the virtue, fair-mindedness, and "gratitude" of fellow members of the political elite was strong. In 1790, upon assuming the office of secretary of state in charge of US foreign relations, he was confident that Congress would reciprocate for special privileges the French monarchy had already granted to American tobacco and whale oil exports. Although Madison backed him in Congress in fighting for increased commercial privileges for France, they were defeated. Nevertheless,

---

[41] Jefferson to Madison, August 28, 1789, in Hutchinson and Rachal, eds., *Papers of James Madison*, 12:363.

[42] [James Madison] *Federalist*, no. 10, in Jacob E. Cooke, ed., *The Federalist* (Middletown, CT: Wesleyan University Press, 1961), 61. See also Thomas Lindsay, "James Madison on Religion and Politics: Rhetoric and Reality," *American Political Science Review* 85/4 (December 1991): 1336n16. Jefferson derided Plato's *Republic* as nonsensical and irrelevant to the real world, in Jefferson to John Adams, July 5, 1814, Cappon, ed., *Adams-Jefferson Letters*, 432–33.

Jefferson informed one of his friends among the liberal French nobility that he would strive to promote better relations between the two allies. "Be assured that to do this is the first wish of my heart," he wrote. "I have but one system of ethics for men and for nations—to be grateful, to be faithful to all engagements and under all circumstances, to be open & generous, promotes in the long run even the interests of both; and I am sure it promotes their happiness." At this time, he felt particularly friendly toward the French. They were advancing on the road to republican self-government through the reforms made by the National (Constituent) Assembly, their country's first representative body, which was composing the nation's first constitution.[43]

Although the rulers of Spain, a country that Jefferson often attempted to intimidate during his presidency might disagree, he believed that he applied this theory of what Alexis de Tocqueville later called "enlightened self-interest" to his administration's diplomacy with foreign nations. In his second inaugural address on March 4, 1805, he claimed that by impartiality to all nations, he had gained respect for the republic and preserved peace. "We have done them justice on all occasions, favored where favor was lawful and cherished mutual interests and intercourse on fair and equal terms," he proclaimed. "We are firmly convinced, and we act on that conviction, that with nations as with individuals, our interests soundly calculated, will ever be found inseparable from our moral duties; and history bears witness to the fact, that a just nation is taken on its word, when recourse is had to armaments and wars to bridle others."[44]

Believing that human society was constructed so that one's duties and interests were usually in harmony, Jefferson considered most people naturally virtuous. Like a Benthamite Utilitarian, he thought that good deeds, more than good intentions, would be rewarded. In 1807, he expounded his idea of the affinity between "duties and interests" in a letter to leading Philadelphia Quaker merchant, abolitionist, and philanthropist James Pemberton, who sought to protect Native Americans' rights to their lands while "civilizing" them and acclimating them to White men's modern technology. President Jefferson explained and defended his administration's policy of trading manufactured goods with the Indians at exorbitant prices in exchange for their land. With less grazing land available, the

---

[43] Jefferson to Madame d'Enville, April 2, 1790, in Peterson, ed., *Jefferson: Writings*, 965–66. See Merrill D. Peterson, "Thomas Jefferson and Commercial Policy, 1783–1793," *William and Mary Quarterly*, 3d ser., 22/4 (October 1965): 584–610; Albert Hall Bowman, *The Struggle for Neutrality: Franco-American Diplomacy during the Federalist Era* (Knoxville: University of Tennessee Press, 1974), 31–34.

[44] Jefferson's Second Inaugural Address, March 4, 1805, in Adrienne Koch and William Peden, eds., *Life and Selected Writings of Thomas Jefferson* (New York: Modern Library, 1944), 339.

Indians would have to adjust to smaller holdings, which they could cultivate with advanced tools and the scientific agricultural methods White agents taught them. Pleased that the "Five Civilized Tribes" of the Southeast, as they were called (Creeks, Cherokees, Choctaws, Chickasaws, and Seminoles) cooperated with his policy, although the Northern Shawnees resisted, Jefferson asserted, "It is a proof the more of the indissoluble alliance between our duties and interests, which if ever they appear to lead in opposite directions, we may be assured it is from our own defective views."[45] Since moral conduct benefited even one's selfish interests in the long run, once individuals and nations became aware of this "moral fact," peace, prosperity, and happiness were inevitable. Jefferson must have had such thoughts, if only in his most optimistic moments.[46]

[45] Jefferson to James Pemberton, November 16, 1807, in Lipscomb and Bergh, eds., *Writings of Jefferson*, 11:394–95.

[46] On "moral facts," see Jefferson to Richard Rush, October 20, 1820, ibid., 15:283–84.

Chapter 3

The Moral Sense, Jefferson's Cultural Relativism, Christianity, and Race

Jefferson rejected categorical condemnation of Black culture in either Africa or America. Such disapproval would have impugned his hopes that Black slaves would eventually be emancipated and live responsibly in freedom. During his presidency and after his retirement, arguing in favor of the deportation of emancipated Blacks to Sierra Leone or other parts of Africa, he observed that they might help educate and "civilize" the natives. By means of this strategy, he was trying to placate his correspondents rather than satisfy any conviction of his own that the Africans needed to convert to Christianity or learn Western ways. He never proposed making an effort to convert Blacks to Christianity, either in Africa or America.[1]

Jefferson eventually adopted ideas of cultural relativism. Although he believed that the Western concepts of democracy, representative government, and freedom of thought and religion ideally were best for society and the individual, he was aware that, largely because of their rulers' evil natures, most cultures and societies throughout the world had historical experiences antipathetic to realizing this paradigm. On matters of religious belief, Jefferson assumed that all religious dogmas and rituals were equally valid or invalid, and that those beliefs were all good that denounced murder, theft, and other crimes; preached the Judeo-Christian doctrine, "love thy neighbor"; and advocated justice and fairness toward all the world's peoples.[2]

He made this clear in several letters on religion after he retired from the presidency. He explained to a Quaker leader, Michael Megear, that he agreed with his objections to Protestant "missionary and Bible societies" journeying abroad to convert Asians and Africans even though they had their own religions,

---

[1] Jefferson to Monroe, June 2, 1802, in Ford, ed., *Works of Thomas Jefferson*, 10:375; Jefferson to Rufus King, July 13, 1802, microfilm reel 26, Jefferson Papers, LC (hdl.loc.gov/loc.mss/mtj.mtjbib011539). Jefferson to John Lynch, 21 January 1811, in Peterson, ed., *Jefferson: Writings*, 1239–41.

[2] Arthur Scherr, "Thomas Jefferson versus the Historians: Christianity, Atheistic Morality, and the Afterlife," *Church History* 83/1 (March 2014): 60–109.

which they were not trying to foist on American Protestants. He preferred "instruction and assistance" in reading, writing, and perhaps morals to the children of the United States' laboring poor "within the same social pale," if they desired it. However, he opposed sending religious "agents...to persons whom we know not, and in countries from which we get no account, when we can do it at short hand, to objects under our eye, through agents we know, and to supply wants we see."

Jefferson was painfully aware of the atrocities committed in the name of religious faith. These included the murders of Jews during the Crusades, Spanish Inquisition, and other pogroms; the fanatical Wars of the Protestant Reformation in Germany (1520s–1550s); the Wars of Religion in France (1550s–1590s); and the Thirty Years War between Protestants and Catholics in Germany and Bohemia (1618–1648), in which millions were killed over picayune differences of dogma and liturgy. He also knew about the executions of Baptists, witches, and Quakers in both Europe and Puritan Massachusetts in the seventeenth century. Ridiculing the obsession of Jedidiah Morse, Lyman Beecher, and other Congregationalist and Presbyterian revivalists with converting the world to Protestantism, he charged that they would howl with anger if the Pope sent Jesuit missionaries to New England to convert its Puritans to Roman Catholicism:

> I do not know that it is a duty to disturb by missionaries the religion and peace of other countries, who may think themselves bound to extinguish by fire and fagot the heresies to which we give the name of conversions, and quote our own example for it. Were the Pope, or his holy allies, to send in mission to us some thousands of Jesuit priests to convert us to their orthodoxy, I suspect that we should deem and treat it as a national aggression on our peace and faith.[3]

Integral to Jefferson's cultural relativism was his opposition to the preaching of Christian dogma to non-Christians. He argued that insistence on the infallibility of Biblical Revelation, a concept rejected by most peoples, strengthened the atheist's position that God did not exist, and that the universe had existed throughout time. Himself a deist, Jefferson wrote, "I think that every Christian sect gives a great handle to Atheism by their general dogma that, without a revelation, there would not be sufficient proof of the being of a god." Obviously, those non-Western cultures that did not espouse Christianity, but practiced Islam, Hinduism, Judaism, or Buddhism, and believed in God without believing in the Trinity or other aspects of Christian Revelation, were damned according to Christian dogma. "Now one sixth of mankind only are supposed to be

---

[3] Jefferson to Michael Megear, May 29, 1823, in Lipscomb and Bergh, eds., *Writings of Jefferson*, 15:434.

Christians," Jefferson continued. According to these Christian acolytes, "the other five sixths then, who do not believe in the Jewish and Christian revelation, are without a knolege [*sic*] of the existence of a god!" At the same time, Jefferson pointed out that most peoples, "in the proportion of a million at least to Unit [i.e., one]," believed in the existence of some kind of God, though not the Christian one. Such "unanimous sentiment," under the rule of the majority that, in this letter, Jefferson apparently chose to follow in religion as well as politics, rendered the deistic concept of God more credible than the atheistic credo that God never existed.[4]

However, for Jefferson, who sympathized with atheists and insisted that they should enjoy religious freedom, the important point was to allow each society and ethno-cultural group to worship God in its own way and not coerce them into adopting the dogmas purveyed by a more powerful religious or governmental faction.[5] This tenet was one aspect of his cultural relativism.

Jefferson never exhibited any enthusiasm about converting either Africans or Native Americans (American Indians) in the United States to the Christian faith. He insisted that whether or not one believed in God, or what kind of god they believed in, was their personal choice and no business of other people or of the government.[6] Modifying his cultural relativism, Jefferson sought to validate his hope that all enslaved Blacks would be eventually emancipated and immigrate to a territory where they could live in freedom under a government of their own choice, rather than continue in relative subjection to their former White masters. Assimilating Blacks to Anglo-American party systems, Jefferson, as in Query XIV of *Notes on Virginia*, occasionally acknowledged African Americans' potential political acumen.[7]

Jefferson's most pejorative comment about Blacks' capacity for self-government occurs in a seldom-noted sentence of his famous letter to Benjamin Rush on September 23, 1800. Although his words defending religious freedom, "I have sworn upon the altar of God, eternal hostility against every form of tyranny over

---

[4] Jefferson to John Adams, April 11, 1823, in Dickinson W. Adams, ed., *Jefferson's Extracts from the Gospels* (Princeton: Princeton University Press, 1983), 410–11.

[5] For Jefferson's view that atheists were not necessarily immoral—indeed it was possible for them to be more virtuous than Christians—see Jefferson to Thomas Law, June 13, 1814, ibid., 355–56.

[6] For Jefferson's opposition to Reverend Jedidiah Morse's plan to create an organization, sponsored by the national government, to convert American Indians to Christianity, see Jefferson to Jedidiah Morse, March 6, 1822, in Ford, ed., *Works of Thomas Jefferson*, 12:222–27; Jefferson to James Madison, February 25, 1822, and Jefferson to James Monroe, March 19, 1822, ibid., 227–28; and Monroe to Jefferson, March 14, 1822, in Stanislaus M. Hamilton, ed., *Writings of James Monroe*, 8 vols. (New York: G. P. Putnam's Sons, 1898–1903), 6:213.

[7] Peden, ed., *Notes on the State of Virginia*, 138.

the mind of man," are inscribed atop the Jefferson Memorial, the same letter also reported the occurrence of Gabriel's "attempt at insurrection in this state." Rush had been corresponding with Jefferson about recent travelers' accounts of expeditions to West Africa, which the doctor apparently thought provided evidence of Africans' ability to learn Western habits. Jefferson, who kept up with the proto-anthropology of his time, had recently read Scottish explorer Mungo Park's report on his attempt to discover the mouth of the Niger River, *Travels in the Interior of Africa* (1799). Park, the first White man to travel to Nigeria and write a book about his experiences, had discovered that most Nigerians served other Nigerians as slaves. This African slavery predated Mohammed's conquest. Having witnessed several instances of wars between African tribes merely for revenge or to obtain domestic chattel for their own use, Park discovered that parents often even sold their children into slavery, especially in times of famine precipitated by tribal wars for slaves. African slavery was an inherited condition; most slaves were descendants of those originally seized in war. In light of the ancient, indigenous nature of African slavery and endemic tribal violence, Park doubted that the end of the European slave trade to the Americas would affect West Africans' enslavement of one another. "If my sentiments should be required concerning the effect which a discontinuance of that commerce would produce on the manners of the natives," he warned naïve philanthropists, "I should have no hesitation in observing, that, in the present unenlightened state of their minds, my opinion is, the effect would neither be so extensive or beneficial, as many wise and worthy persons fondly expect."[8] Influenced by Park's account, Jefferson wrote Rush: "I have not seen the work of Sonnoni which you mention, but I have seen another work on Africa, (Parke's,) which I fear will throw cold water on the hopes of the friends of freedom."[9]

Jefferson thus implied that Park's depiction of the "uncivilized" behavior of the Africans, including wars, endemic slavery, cannibalism, mutilation, and other

---

[8] Mungo Park, *Travels in the Interior Districts of Africa Performed in the Years 1795, 1796, and 1797* (1816 London ed.), excerpted in David Northrup, ed., *The Atlantic Slave Trade*, 2d ed. (Boston: Houghton Mifflin Co, 2002), 32–38. For West African chieftains' involvement in the international slave trade, see Winston McGowan, "African Resistance to the Atlantic Slave Trade in West Africa," *Slavery and Abolition* 11/1 (1990): 5–29.

[9] Jefferson to Benjamin Rush, September 23, 1800, in Peterson, ed., *Jefferson: Writings*, 1082. Jefferson was responding to a letter from Rush that mentioned "a translation of Sonnoni's travels into Egypt," which "will be memorable from the information they gave to Buonaparte in that country" (Rush to Jefferson, August 22, 1800, microfilm reel 22, Jefferson Papers, LC [hdl.loc.gov/loc.mss/mtj.mtjbib009413] and in Oberg, ed., *Jefferson Papers*, 32:112). Jefferson and Rush, who misspelled the surname, were referring to C. S. Sonnini's *Travels in Upper and Lower Egypt*, 3 vols. (London: John Stockdale, 1799).

atrocities, indicated that their descendants in Virginia might not be capable of handling their liberty in a Western, democratic fashion. Jefferson regrettably overlooked the existence of ritual mutilation, burning alive, scalping, decapitations, and other unpalatable conduct as part of the aggressive behavior of many cultures, White "Europeans" (especially when punishing slaves who murdered or conspired to murder their masters) and American Indians among them.[10]

Forty years after writing *Notes*, Jefferson interpreted Blacks more favorably as figures within "natural history." He wrote English abolitionist Frances Wright, who visited him with the Marquis de Lafayette at Monticello, that he was confident that the slaves, if emancipated, would work diligently to ensure their survival. Rather than labeling Africans "savages," he viewed them, like himself, as actors in the natural world successfully struggling with their environment: "It would be a solecism to suppose a race of animals created, without sufficient foresight and energy to preserve their existence. It is disproved, too, by the fact that they [Blacks] exist, and have existed through all the ages of history."[11]

Jefferson argued that Blacks' endurance under conditions of adversity and slavery in both Africa and America proved their intelligence and personhood. He rejected the "opinion" that "moral urgencies are not sufficient to induce him to labor; that nothing can do this but physical coercion." With ostensibly scientific objectivity, he insisted on giving the "man of color" an opportunity to succeed as an autonomous small property owner. Ignoring Black African tribal chiefs' participation in domestic slavery and their role in the international slave traffic, Jefferson urged further investigation and exploration of independent West African "nations" to ascertain the extent of their skill in commercial farming, a desideratum of civilization. (It is difficult to believe that he was unaware that West African peoples had initiated the most advanced practices of rice cultivation, which increased their enslaved value to South Carolina planters.) "We are not sufficiently acquainted with all the nations of Africa," he observed, "to say that there

---

[10] See David J. Silverman, "Racial Walls: Race and the Emergence of American White Nationalism," in Ignacio Gallup-Diaz et al., eds., *Anglicizing America: Essays in Honor of John M. Murrin* (Philadelphia: University of Pennsylvania Press, 2015), 181–204.

[11] Jefferson to Miss Frances Wright, August 7, 1825, in Lipscomb and Bergh, eds., *Writings of Jefferson*, 16:120. See also Boorstin, *Lost World of Thomas Jefferson*, 96–98, for a brief analysis of his correspondence with Wright. For insightful accounts of Jeffersonian "natural history," including Jefferson's argument that Blacks' adaptability defined them as members of the human species along with Whites, despite their ostensible intellectual inferiority, see Boorstin, *Lost World of Thomas Jefferson*, 88–98, 197–98, and Charles A. Miller, *Jefferson and Nature: An Interpretation* (Baltimore: Johns Hopkins University Press, 1988). See also John C. Greene, "The American Debate on the Negro's Place in Nature, 1780–1815," *Journal of the History of Ideas* 15/3 (June 1954): 384–96, and Greene, *American Science in the Age of Jefferson*.

may not be some in which habits of industry are established, and the arts practised which are necessary to render life comfortable."[12]

In Query 18 of *Notes on Virginia* (1782), Jefferson defended slaves' moral right to revolt against their White masters and erect an independent commonwealth. "The whole commerce between master and slave is a perpetual exercise of the most boisterous passions, the most unremitting despotism on the one part, and degrading submissions on the other," he asserted. He ominously warned that God, by reversing slaves' and masters' roles, would eventually punish Whites who withheld emancipation. Brutality toward slaves perverted the moral fiber and industriousness of slave-owners and the children who emulated their conduct, "for man is an imitative animal." Jefferson contended that the enslaved were neither captives, prisoners of war, nor aliens, but fellow "citizens" whose rights the Whites had violated because they and the politicians who represented them held a monopoly on power. "And with what execration should the statesman be loaded, who permitting one half the citizens thus to trample on the rights of the other," he rebuked his Southern contemporaries, "transforms those into despots, and these into enemies, destroys the morals of the one part, and the amor patriae of the other." Thus anticipating (and justifying) future slave revolts, Jefferson condemned apathetic "statesmen" for tolerating an invidious situation for both types of "citizens," masters and slaves (although it required a stretch of the imagination to accept Jefferson's view that slaves were citizens), which "destroys the morals of the one part [masters], and the amor patriae of the other [slaves]." Employing the oxymoron that ostensible Southern republican political leaders were simultaneously "despots," Jefferson cast doubt upon the whole concept of the United States' virtuous republicanism.[13]

As Jefferson pointed out, it was impossible for a slave to feel loyalty to a country that forced him to labor for others without pay, cheated him of the free use of his "faculties" for his own benefit and self-actualization, and took away his pride in raising children, destined to inherit his own "miserable condition." By depriving other human beings of their liberty, White Virginians had flouted the credo of natural, God-given rights expounded by Jefferson in the Declaration of Independence. Whites thereby forfeited the right to their own freedom,

---

[12] Jefferson to Frances Wright, August 7, 1825, in Lipscomb and Bergh, eds., *Writings of Jefferson*, 16:120. See also Peter S. Onuf, "'To Declare Them a Free and Independent People': Race, Slavery, and National Identity in Jefferson's Thought," *Journal of the Early Republic* 18/1 (Spring 1998): 1–46; and Onuf, *Jefferson's Empire: The Language of American Nationhood* (Charlottesville: University of Virginia Press, 2000), 147–88. Peter H. Wood, *Black Majority* (New York: Norton, 1974), is a classic account of the significance of West Africans' origination of scientific methods of rice cultivation.

[13] Peden, ed., *Notes on the State of Virginia*, Query XVIII, 162–63.

inadvertently justifying a future slave revolt in which, if defeated, masters might reasonably expect to be enslaved if not exterminated. They had abandoned God, who would condone African American vengeance, since Whites had violated his axiom that all people have the right to liberty. As Jefferson put it, revealing his national feeling and painfully aware of the tenuous slaveholding ground it rested on, "Can the liberties of a nation be thought secure when we have removed their only firm basis, a conviction in the minds of the people that these liberties are of the gift of God? That they are not to be violated but with his wrath?"[14]

Jefferson rashly permitted his name to appear on *Notes*' title page, in an era when pseudonyms were considered safer and more respectable. Moreover, he melodramatically warned, atypically affecting religious zeal (perhaps to attract evangelical Virginia readers), "I tremble for my country when I reflect that God is just; that his justice cannot sleep forever; that considering numbers, nature and natural means only, a revolution of the wheel of fortune, an exchange of situation is among possible events; that it may become probable by supernatural interference!"[15]

Reflecting the emphases of Scottish common sense philosophers Adam Smith and David Hume, Jefferson's profound observation that "man is an imitative animal" covered the underlying motives for both slaves' resistance and masters' brutality. Just as the children of masters learned the techniques of disciplining and degrading bondsmen by observing their parents, slaves discerned the "*loveliness* of freedom" by viewing the self-assurance and prosperity of their owners.[16]

Convinced from an early age that slavery caused a slave's moral degeneration no matter what his race or ethnicity, Jefferson insisted in *Notes* that Blacks

---

[14] Ibid., 163. The noun "nation" was hardly in use at this time, and Jefferson's *Notes* was perhaps the first significant work by a North American writer to employ it in reference to the United States.

[15] Dumas Malone, *Jefferson and the Ordeal of Liberty*, vol. 3 of *Jefferson and His Time* (Boston: Little, Brown, 1962), 480; Query XVIII of *Notes on Virginia*, in Peterson, ed., *Jefferson: Writings*, 288–89; Thomas Jefferson, *Notes on the State of Virginia*, ed. Thomas Perkins Abernethy (New York: Harper & Row, 1964), 156. Miller, *Jefferson and Nature*, 69–70, argues that Jefferson's invoking divine intervention to abolish slavery reveals a feeling of urgency on the matter since he generally did not trust the supernatural or mention Divine Providence. Peden, ed., *Notes on the State of Virginia*, 292n., likewise observes, "This is one of the very rare examples of Jefferson's speaking of miracles with anything less than extreme skepticism." For the use of pseudonyms, see Douglass G. Adair, "A Note on Certain of Hamilton's Pseudonyms," in H. Trevor Colbourn, ed., *Fame and the Founding Fathers: Essays by Douglass Adair* (New York: Norton, 1974); and Eran Shalev, "Ancient Masks, American Fathers: Classical Pseudonyms during the American Revolution and Early Republic," *Journal of the Early Republic* 23/2 (Summer 2003): 151–72.

[16] Jefferson to Thaddeus Kosciusko, February 21, 1799, in Oberg, ed., *Jefferson Papers*, 30:52–53.

innately had the same moral sense as Whites. Although he was dubious that Black slaves deserved their reputation for stealing, he argued that if they did often steal, it was because of their awareness that their masters deprived them of their bodies and the fruits of their labor, as well as the right to personal property. "That disposition to theft with which they have been branded," he said, "must be ascribed to their situation, and not to any depravity of the moral sense. The man, in whose favour no laws of property exist, probably feels himself less bound to respect those made in favour of others."[17]

Because some Blacks were free and at least nominally, already members of the "patriae," Jefferson, unlike most of his Virginia contemporaries, would not deny Blacks who owned themselves at the time of the Revolution the rights of citizens. Less humanely, legislation of which Jefferson was among the sponsors in the Virginia assembly from 1776 to 1779 during the Revisal of the Laws, envisaged the reduction of the African American presence, slave or free, in the state. It is possible that his colleagues initiated this legislation, which would have barred free Blacks from other states from immigrating to Virginia and forced future manumitted slaves to leave the state within a year, or else find themselves "outside the protection of the laws."[18] Such provisions were not in the draft constitutions he wrote for Virginia in 1776 and 1783. The latter, one of the most radical antislavery documents to emanate from the South during the Revolution, not only barred the entry of new slaves into the state but also prohibited the "continuance of slavery" after December 31, 1800, "all persons born after that date being hereby declared free."[19] That Jefferson attached his name to this document and published it as an Appendix to *Notes* reveals that it expressed his true opinions on the matter. Probably expecting to exit public life after his service as US minister to France ended (he had the book published in 1787 in London by John Stockdale during his residence in Paris), he did not fear public recrimination over his stance.

In June 1776, when Jefferson, a member of the Second Continental Congress in Philadelphia, was compiling a new constitution for the state of Virginia simultaneously with writing the Declaration of Independence, he did not exclude free Blacks from the polity. Perhaps infused with the idealism of the Revolution and the memorable document he was writing, and his obiter dictum doctrine "that all men are created equal," his constitution avoided the issue of color. Immediately after prohibiting the future entry of slaves into Virginia ("No person hereafter coming into this country shall be held in slavery under any pretext whatever"), paving the way for slavery's diminution and eventual disappearance from

---

[17] *Notes on Virginia*, Query XIV, in Peterson, ed., *Jefferson: Writings*, 269.

[18] See the discussion of this legislation below.

[19] "Appendix No. 2: Draught of a Fundamental Constitution," in Peden, ed., *Notes on the State of Virginia*, 214.

the state, his draft of the constitution defined citizenship. "All persons who by their own oath or affirmation or by other testimony shall give satisfactory proof to any court of record that they propose to reside" in Virginia, for an unspecified number of years in two drafts, although one draft stipulated seven years (his hypothetical date, mimicking Britain's colonial naturalization laws of 1740), he wrote, "and who shall subscribe to the fundamental laws shall be considered as residents & entitled to all the rights of persons natural born." There was no mention of color, race, ethnicity, or national origin. The next clause of Jefferson's constitution, which guaranteed the right to bear arms, also failed to specify Whiteness as a criterion: "No freeman shall be debarred the use of arms (within his own lands or tenements)."[20]

Seemingly uninspired by the egalitarian revolutionary fervor of 1776, Jefferson's colleagues in the House of Delegates in 1779 were less solicitous of the rights of free Blacks as citizens. Although Jefferson was the main draftsman of the revision of the laws, he left the assembly for Monticello on June 1, 1779. The revisal committee did not present the final version of the citizenship bill to the assembly until two weeks later. Their version restricted citizenship to Whites. Unlike Jefferson's one-man draft of a state constitution in 1776, the bill enacted in 1779 specified, "that all white persons born within the territory of this commonwealth," those who had been residents for two years before the act's passage, and future White immigrants, were citizens. Expanding its racial definition of citizenship to other states, the law continued, "The free white inhabitants of every of the states [*sic*], parties to the confederation," would be entitled to the "rights & privileges" of Virginia's citizens.[21]

The first naturalization law passed by Congress in 1790 likewise confined national citizenship, at least in terms of immigrants, to Whites. It stipulated that, after two years residence in the United States and one year in a specific state, "any alien, being a free white person...may be admitted to become a citizen."[22] Thus, even after the United States was united under the Constitution, Jefferson's fellow politicians were less advanced in matters of racial justice for free Blacks than he was in 1776.

---

[20] Jefferson's draft of Virginia constitution, 1776, in Boyd et al., eds., *Papers of Thomas Jefferson*, 1:353 (second draft). There were three nearly identical drafts. For the first and third drafts of Jefferson's citizenship provisions, see ibid., 1:344, 363. Virginia's laws had long permitted free Blacks and even slaves to own guns (Arthur Scherr, "Research Note: A Note on Slaves and Guns in Revolutionary Virginia," *Southern Studies* 25/2 [Fall/Winter 2018]: 79–92).

[21] "A Bill Declaring Who Shall Be Deemed Citizens of This Commonwealth," in Boyd et al., eds., *Papers of Thomas Jefferson*, 2:476.

[22] For the text of "An Act to Establish a Uniform Rule of Naturalization," passed March 26, 1790, see U.S. Congress, *Annals of Congress*, 1st Congress: 2205–206.

Notes also defended the American Indian against claims European travelers and scientists made about his inferiority. Jefferson pointed out that the denigrators of the North American Indian—Cornelius de Pauw, Buffon, William Robertson, and Abbé Raynal—had never seen one, and relied on the memoirs of explorers. As for the South American Indian, Spanish travelers had observed him in a degraded state, "after he had passed through ten generations of slavery. It is very unfair, from this sample, to judge of the natural genius of this race of men."[23] Thus, Jefferson believed that enslavement was at least partly responsible for the alleged lassitude and ostensible "inferiority" of non-White races, both Blacks and Native Americans.

After visiting the European countryside as US minister to France, Jefferson further defended the natural intellectual equality of North American Indians, comparing them favorably with "primitive," rural White European farm laborers. "The proofs of genius given by the Indians of North America, place them on a level with whites in the same uncultivated state," he informed Chastellux. He found scant intellectual difference between Indians and French peasants. Having spent much time in his childhood among the Cherokee Indians, he wrote, "The North of Europe furnishes subjects enough for comparison with them, and for a proof of their equality. I have seen some thousands [of Indians] myself, and conversed much with them, and have found in them a masculine, sound understanding." It is possible that Jefferson gained this insight by his reading of Voltaire. The great French thinker's famous sociological study, *Essai sur les Moeurs*, a work Jefferson admired, praised North American Indians for practicing de facto political democracy and refuted charges that they lacked facial hair (*poil)*, and were less virile, energetic, and intelligent than White Europeans. Trustworthy European and American informants had attested to "the genius of this people," Jefferson said.[24]

In *Essai Sur Les Moeurs*, one of Jefferson's favorite books, Voltaire, who had never left Europe, argued that Europeans "were content to call North Americans *Savages*, though the latter were less 'savage' in most respects than the peasants living near our European coasts." Jefferson often endorsed Voltaire's books during the 1780s. He recommended Voltaire's *Essai* (he called it his "histoire universelle") in his famous letter to Peter Carr in 1787. He often referred to Voltaire in *Notes on Virginia*. Alluding to an aphorism in Voltaire's *Philosophical Dictionary*, Jefferson wrote to Charles Bellini (in the letter we have already cited) that from what he had seen of France, "The truth of Voltaire's observation, offers itself perpetually, that every man here must be either the hammer or the anvil." Not

---

[23] Jefferson to Marquis de Chastellux, June 7, 1785, in Peterson, ed., *Jefferson: Writings*, 800–801.

[24] Ibid., 801.

long before he died, he recommended Voltaire's *Histories* of Louis XIV and XV to a college student. Jefferson owned several editions of Voltaire's writings, including his *Philosophy of History* (1763), which consisted of extracts from *Essai sur les Moeurs*. He sold this to the Library of Congress in 1815, along with Voltaire's *Philosophical Dictionary* (1765), two editions of Voltaire's collected works, totaling 58 volumes, and others. Nonetheless, Jefferson was so fond of Voltaire's *Essai sur les Moeurs et l'ésprit des nations* that he retained a six-volume French-language edition (Paris, 1792) until he died.[25]

On the other hand, Jefferson criticized Native American culture for forcing women to perform most of the physical labor and farming, while men devoted themselves primarily to hunting and war, allegedly wasting most of their time in idleness. "As to their bodily strength, their manners rendering it disgraceful to labor, those muscles employed in labor will be weaker with them, than with the European laborer; but those which are exerted in the chase, and those faculties which are employed in the tracing an enemy or a wild beast, in contriving ambuscades for him, and in carrying them through their execution, are much stronger than with us, because they are more exercised," he graphically explained. Although he deplored the Indians' mistreatment of their women, it was, ironically, to Virginia's early Powhatan tribe that he first ascribed the quality that he (and the Scottish commonsense philosophers) called the "moral sense." Admiring the Indians' comparatively anarchical society, he praised their resistance to "any laws, any coercive power, any shadow of government. Their only controuls are their manners, and that moral sense of right and wrong, which, like the sense of tasting and feeling, in every man makes a part of his nature." For Jefferson to ascribe a full quota of the moral sense to the illiterate Native American at this comparatively early period in his philosophical career is not surprising, since he

---

[25] *Essai sur les Moeurs* (1754; Paris, 1963), ch. 151, "The Possessions of France in America," 2:371, quoted in Claudine Hunting, "The *Philosophes* and Black Slavery, 1748–1765," *Journal of the History of Ideas* 39/3 (July–September 1978): 405–18, 413n (quotation); Jefferson to Peter Carr, August 10, 1787, in Boyd et al., eds., *Papers of Thomas Jefferson*, 12:18–19. For Jefferson's references to Voltaire in *Notes on Virginia*, see Peterson, ed., *Jefferson: Writings*, 155–56, 190–91; Jefferson to Charles Bellini, September 30, 1785, ibid., 833. For Jefferson's admiration for Voltaire's writings in old age, see Jefferson to George Washington Lewis, October 25, 1825, in Koch and Peden, eds., *Life and Selected Writings of Thomas Jefferson*, 723. For Jefferson's sale of Voltaire's works to the Library of Congress, see Sowerby, ed., *Catalogue*, 2:21–22, 5:170–71. For Jefferson's ownership of *Essai sur les Moeurs* until he died, see Volume 7: Jefferson's Second Library, Offered for Sale at Public Auction, February 27, 1829, item #73 on image 6, Series 7: Miscellaneous Bound Volumes, Jefferson Papers, LC (hdl.loc.gov/loc.mss/mtj.mtjbib026579).

always regarded the moral sense as a faculty essentially apart from abstract intellect or reasoning power.[26]

Indeed, he implied that the two faculties were nearly antithetical. As he wrote in his famous letter to his nephew Peter Carr in 1787, "This [moral] sense is submitted, indeed, in some degree, to the guidance of reason; but it is a small stock which is required for this; even a less one than what we call common sense. State a moral case to a plowman and a professor. The former will decide it as well and often better than the latter because he has not been led astray by artificial rules" that would cloud an objective appraisal of the situation's moral purport.[27]

In addition to admiring Indians' minimal government and their intuitive response to moral issues, Jefferson respected their skill as hunters and primitive artists. He concluded that if their environment was changed, they could become more intellectual and domesticated. As he put it in his letter to Chastellux, "I believe the Indian, then, to be, in body and mind, equal to the white man."[28]

In addition to Indians and Blacks, Jefferson argued that such other intellectually underdeveloped groups as Virginia's children possessed a potential quantum of "moral sense." This accorded with his assumption that the moral sense was something intuitive and innate, which children, such as his daughter Martha (who was also a woman, a gender that Jefferson, in common with Aristotle's concept of *akuron*, believed was emotionally and physically "weaker" than man, although not intellectually so) might possess without going to school to learn about it.[29]

In a letter in 1783 to his daughter Martha, Jefferson propounded an early, rudimentary elucidation of the moral sense. This was shortly after he explained in *Notes on Virginia* that Black slaves and North American Indians, as well as Whites, were born with this moral "instinct." Here he associated the moral sense with death and the afterlife more than in any later commentaries, probably because he had not yet recovered from his wife's death over a year before. Perhaps he thought his ten-year-old daughter unprepared for sophisticated philosophical discourses. Martha had written him about her fears of the world coming to an end, and Jefferson sought to reassure her that these rumors, spread by fanatical

---

26 For Jefferson's critique of male Indians' "barbarous" treatment of women in "submitting [them] to unjust drudgery, see *Notes*, Query VI, in Peterson, ed., *Jefferson: Writings*, 185–86. For Jefferson's assertion of the Indians' moral sense, see *Notes*, Query XI, ibid., 220 (quotation); Jefferson to Chastellux, June 7, 1785, ibid., 801. In old age, Jefferson happily reminisced about his intimate childhood acquaintance with Virginia's Cherokees (Jefferson to John Adams, June 11, 1812, ibid., 1263).

27 Jefferson to Peter Carr, August 10, 1787, in Peterson, ed., *Jefferson: Writings*, 902.

28 Jefferson to Chastellux, June 7, 1785, ibid., 801.

29 Jefferson to Martha Jefferson, December 11, 1783, ibid., 784. For Jefferson's reference to women as the "weaker sex," see Jefferson to John Hampden Pleasants, April 19, 1824, microfilm reel 54, Jefferson Papers, LC (hdl.loc.gov/loc.mss/ mtj.mtjbib024992).

religious sects, should not be taken seriously. Writing more childishly about religious matters than was his custom, he explained, "The almighty has never made known to any body at what time he created it, nor will he tell any body when he means to put an end to it, if ever he means to do it." Turning to the more general question of the inevitability of death, which he equated with his daughter's fear of the end of the world, he wrote, "As to preparations for that event, the best way is for you to be always prepared for it. The only way to be so is never to do nor say a bad thing." He called the moral sense the "conscience" in this letter and characterized it as more a conscious consideration of the effect of one's actions on others (somewhat in the manner of Helvétius, whom he later criticized) than as an instinctive reflex commanding one to do the right thing. "If ever you are about to say anything amiss or to do any thing wrong, consider before hand," he advised. "You will feel something within you which will tell you it is wrong and ought not to be said or done: this is your conscience, and be sure to obey it."[30]

Although Jefferson was only forty years old at this time and his daughter only ten, death was constantly on his mind, perhaps because of the recent death of his wife, and he conveyed his view of the moral sense to her in that light. Not long afterwards, he became ill when he attended Congress at Annapolis, and suffered various ailments when he first arrived in Paris as US minister-at-large in 1784 to negotiate free trade treaties, before his appointment as US minister to France to succeed Benjamin Franklin in 1785. As a man of simple tastes in clothes, although he preferred expensive fabrics, he told Abigail Adams that he was exasperated by the elaborate style of dress with which he had to adorn himself during his presentation at King Louis XVI's court. He was angered by the cost of mourning dress that he was required to wear when attending a royal funeral. He was also tired of the requirement that he powder his hair and contemplated cutting it off. Abigail Adams observed his exasperation and wrote her uncle about it:

> Mr. Jefferson who is really a man who abhors this shew and parade fully as much as Mr. Adams [her husband, US minister to the Netherlands and Great Britain, John Adams], yet he has not been long enough enured [*sic*] to it, to Submit with patience or bear without fretting. Back they had to go [Adams and Jefferson] to Paris to lay by their mourning until the next death. His hair too is an other affliction which he is tempted to cut off. He

[30] Jefferson to Martha Jefferson, December 11, 1783, in Peterson, ed., *Jefferson: Writings*, 784.

expects not to live above a Dozen years; and he shall lose one of those in hair dressing.[31]

Jefferson probably thought of death with less humor than he conveyed to Abigail Adams in connection with the burdens of powdering hair and dressing up to attend royal funerals. As he pointed out to his daughter with regard to the universality of the moral sense: "Our maker has given us all, this faithful internal Monitor, and if you always obey it, you will always be prepared for the end of the world: or for a much more certain event which is death. This must happen to all: it puts an end to the world as to us, and the way to be ready for it is never to do a wrong act."[32]

Although Jefferson implied that one should exercise the moral instinct in order to prepare properly for death, he did not mention the prospect of an afterlife, telling his daughter that death "puts an end to the world as to us." Not long before his death, he gained a renewed appreciation of the inauthenticity of religious devotion, perceiving that many fanatical believers used it as a crutch to ward off their fear of death. Of women in Richmond who attended evangelical "Presbyterian" churches and seemed enraptured by their "priests," he wrote to the notorious freethinker Dr. Thomas Cooper, "They pour forth the effusions of their love to Jesus in terms as amatory and carnal as their modesty would [not?] permit them to use to a more earthly lover."[33] In less derisive moments, Jefferson's religious ideology upheld the view that one should exert one's "conscience" in order to treat one's fellow human beings fairly in this lifetime, not to secure a happy afterlife in some mythical paradise. It was a hard and sad lesson for a child to learn.

Regarding the physical manifestations of a defective moral sense, Jefferson's perceptions were inadvertently harsh. As US minister to Paris in 1785, he entered into a discussion of the significance of blushing that irritated Abigail Adams ("Nabby") Smith, the daughter of John and Abigail Adams. Probably having begun to formulate the idea of the "moral sense" that he expounded in completed

---

[31] Abigail Adams to Cotton Tufts, September 8, 1784, in Lyman H. Butterfield, ed., *Adams Family Correspondence*, 14 vols. (Cambridge: Belknap Press of Harvard University Press, 1963–2019) 5:458–59. See also David McCullough, *John Adams* (New York: Simon & Schuster, 2001), 319.

[32] Jefferson to Martha Jefferson, December 11, 1783, in Peterson, ed., *Jefferson: Writings*, 784. See also Johann N. Neem, "Beyond the Wall: Reinterpreting Jefferson's Danbury Address," *Journal of the Early Republic* 27/1 (Spring 2007): 139–54. Neem extensively quotes the letter to Martha, perhaps ascribing undue importance to it as a definitive exposition of Jefferson's ideas of the moral sense.

[33] For his derisive comment on women's religious enthusiasm at revival meetings, see Jefferson to Thomas Cooper, November 2, 1822, microfilm reel 53, Jefferson Papers, LC (hdl.loc.gov/loc.mss/mtj.mtjbib024489).

form in a letter to Peter Carr in 1787, Jefferson implied that when one blushed, one felt that one had done something wrong, or violated one's conscience. "Mr. J. decided not agreeably to my opinion or belief," Nabby wrote in her journal, "that we never blushed but for the consciousness of something wrong in what was said or done, that caused the blush." "I do not believe it," she innocently continued. "A person so subject to blush as myself, should be interested in removing every idea of evil from it."[34] Jefferson should have understood that blushing was more often caused by embarrassing thoughts than by bad acts.

As one might expect, Jefferson believed that living under a democratic regime increased the strength of one's moral sense. He thought that his daughter, though only a child, would understand the principles of the moral sense because she had grown up under a democratic form of government. Over thirty years later, he seemed less confident that *adult* South American revolutionaries, who had lived under a Roman Catholic autocracy, were sufficiently well-versed in the principles of morality and fair play to succeed in instituting representative government. In this, he reluctantly expressed agreement with French *économiste* Pierre Samuel Du Pont de Nemours, in a famous letter of April 24, 1816, reacting to a constitution his friend had written for the South American Colombians that instituted indirect, relatively undemocratic forms of election for the legislature. Simultaneously, rumors that a new constitutional convention, demanded by west Virginians meeting at Staunton, would soon occur in Virginia placed issues of democracy and self-government at the forefront of Jefferson's thoughts.[35]

Jefferson's letter to Du Pont applied to specific circumstances the opinions he had stated as a general principle to Thomas Law two years earlier. Jefferson assumed that the "moral sense," like any mental or physical skill, was improved and strengthened by exercise. He argued that the South Americans, novices in self-government, were deficient in the degree of "moral sense" necessary to install a representative democracy, acquired only by actual experience in self-government such as Virginians had had for over two centuries. Commenting on Du Pont's constitution for the South American states, Jefferson expounded his emerging concept of cultural relativism. He observed, "I suppose it well formed for those for whom it was intended, and the excellence of every government is its adaptation to the state of those to be governed by it."[36] Since the people of the United

---

[34] Journal entry, May 9, 1785, in Caroline De Windt, ed., *Journal and Correspondence of Miss Adams, Daughter of John Adams* (New York: Wiley and Putnam, 1841), 73.

[35] Jefferson to Du Pont de Nemours, April 24, 1816, in Ford, ed., *Works of Thomas Jefferson*, 11:519–25.

[36] Ibid., 519 (quotation); Jefferson to Thomas Law, June 13, 1814, in Lipscomb and Bergh, eds., *Writings of Jefferson*, 14:143.

States had long subsisted in comparative political and economic equality, thereby strengthening their "sense of justice" and consequent ability to practice moral self-government, "For us it would not do."[37]

Like Montesquieu, Jefferson emphasized that certain "moral principles" characterized each form of government. In *The Spirit of Laws* (1748), Montesquieu had asserted,

> Law in general is human reason, inasmuch as it governs all the inhabitants of the earth: the political and civil laws of each nation ought to be only the particular cases in which human reason is applied. They should be adopted in such a manner to the people for whom they are framed that it should be a great chance if those of one nation suit another.... They should be in relation to the nature and principle of each government.

Montesquieu seemingly contradicted himself, first positing the universality of human reason and then proclaiming that it differed for each country, so that each country's laws must differ. Montesquieu continued, "They [the laws] should be in relation to the climate of each country, to the quality of its soil, to its situation and extent, to the principal occupation of the natives, whether husbandmen, huntsmen, or shepherds; they should have relation to the degree of liberty which the constitution will bear; to the religion of the inhabitants, to their inclinations, riches, numbers, commerce, manners, and customs."[38] Ironically, for Montesquieu human reason varied with climate and territory. Jefferson upheld this aspect of his political sociology.

Contrasting his countrymen with the South Americans, who had no experience with self-rule but who had suffered interminable oppression by a union of Roman Catholic Church and Spanish State, Jefferson boasted, "We of the United States...are constitutionally and conscientiously democrats." He stressed the natural sociability of humankind, enhanced by self-government's contributions to community social and economic betterment. "We consider society as one of the natural wants with which man has been created; that he has been endowed with faculties and qualities to effect its satisfaction by concurrence of others having the same want," he asserted. "When, by the exercise of these faculties, he has procured a state of society," he continued, he and his fellow citizens, "whom he cannot exclude from its use or direction more than they him," must "jointly" and reciprocally "regulate and control" it.[39]

---

[37] Jefferson to Du Pont de Nemours, April 24, 1816, in Ford, ed., *Works of Thomas Jefferson*, 11:519.

[38] Charles de Secondat, Baron de Montesquieu, *The Spirit of Laws* (1748; Amherst, NY: Prometheus Books, 2002), 6 (Book I, "Of Laws in General," Part 3, "Of Positive Laws").

[39] Jefferson to Du Pont de Nemours, April 24, 1816, in Ford, ed., *Works of Thomas Jefferson*, 11:519–20.

Thus, what Jefferson called men's "moral faculties" were necessary for them to fulfill their inborn need for society and socialization. He was perhaps alluding to the "faculty psychology," represented by Lord Kames, Thomas Reid, and Adam Smith, that was popular at the time, and brought society and voluntary social controls together. This was a schema that Alexis de Tocqueville would later label "enlightened self-interest," and which Daniel Walker Howe, a major historian of ideas, has applied to *The Federalist Papers*. Howe explains that faculty psychology "treated self-interest as an intermediate motive, sometimes partial, short-term, and passionate (in the derogatory sense of 'selfish passions'), but capable of being collective, long-range, and rational."[40]

Influenced by faculty psychology, Jefferson extended its scope. He insisted that representative democracy, starting from town meetings (he called them "wards") and local government, working up to the state and national levels, was a natural outgrowth of the United States' egalitarian and reciprocal society, based on the faculty psychology its rulers and ruled unconsciously practiced. As Jefferson put it, in words similar to those he used during this period with many other correspondents, among them John Taylor and Samuel Kercheval, "We think experience has proved it safer, for the mass of individuals composing the society, to reserve to themselves personally the exercise of all rightful powers to which they are competent, and to delegate those to which they are not competent to deputies named, and removable for unfaithful conduct, by themselves immediately."[41]

Despite his assurance that Americans nearly universally possessed the moral faculty, Jefferson, adhering to his belief in a "natural aristocracy," expressed most famously in a letter to John Adams of October 28, 1813, implied that well-educated politicians and political philosophers ideally possessed a greater degree of virtue, knowledge, and "moral sense" than their constituents. On the other hand, demonstrating greater faith in the American people than most of his contemporaries, he granted their capability of serving as jurors, electing their legislatures, congressmen, and president directly, and their senators by indirect methods. He explained that this was because, even though they were "unqualified for the management of affairs requiring intelligence above the common level," their moral capacity rendered them "competent judges of human character," enabling them to choose "representatives, some by themselves immediately, others by electors chosen by themselves."[42]

---

[40] Daniel Walker Howe, "The Political Psychology of *The Federalist*," *William and Mary Quarterly* 44/3 (July 1987), 485–509, 491 (quotation).

[41] Jefferson to Du Pont de Nemours, April 24, 1816, in Ford, ed., *Works of Thomas Jefferson*, 11:520.

[42] Ibid., 520.

Perhaps inadvertently, Jefferson's letter to Du Pont raised the important question whether the people's leaders possessed more virtue, intelligence, and "moral sense" than the people themselves, and the implications this posed for conflict between Jefferson's related doctrines of "natural aristocracy" and "moral sense." Although Jefferson did not answer this question directly, he concluded, "We believe that this proximate choice and power of removal is the best security which experience has sanctioned for ensuring an honest conduct in the functionaries of society."[43] Although agreeing with Du Pont that the South Americans might not be ready for democratic self-government, Jefferson thought that, ideally, rulers should be directly elected by the ruled, in order to feel most strongly connected to the people's interests and well-being. In Jefferson's opinion, if election by tiers of electors was carried too far, "they are also farther and farther removed from the control of the society; and the human character, we believe, requires in general constant and immediate control, to prevent its being biased from right by the seductions of self-love."[44]

Jefferson apparently believed that elected officials, including "natural aristocrats," were as susceptible to corruption and ambition—to "becoming wolves," as he wrote Edward Carrington in January 1787—as their constituents. "Cherish therefore the spirit of our people, and keep alive their attention," he advised Carrington.

> Do not be too severe upon their errors, but reclaim them by enlightening them. If once they become inattentive to the public affairs, you & I, & Congress & Assemblies, judges & governors shall all become wolves. It seems to be the law of our general nature, in spite of individual exceptions; and experience declares that man is the only animal which devours his own kind for I can apply no milder term to the governments of Europe, and to the general prey of the rich on the poor.[45]

At least when pondering the repressive governments of Europe and the threat that the Massachusetts government would handle Shays' Rebellion too harshly, Jefferson did not think the "moral sense" strong. Indeed, in some ways this letter to Carrington seems to belie Jefferson's later claims for the essential goodness of human nature and the possession by all a moral sense that inclined them to help others. On the other hand, seven months later he strongly expressed to his nephew Peter Carr his certainty of the ubiquity of the "moral sense,"

---

[43] Ibid., 521.

[44] Ibid.

[45] Jefferson to Edward Carrington, January 16, 1787, in Peterson, ed., *Jefferson: Writings*, 880–81.

perhaps hoping that his younger model of "the American, this new man" would be more benign than some of his contemporaries were.[46]

Jefferson rendered a similarly pessimistic verdict in 1795 when he wrote Mann Page that "rogues would be uppermost" in political life. Ironically, their possession of intelligence and education, the mead of "natural aristocrats," made "rogues" more dangerous. The voters needed to watch and restrain them.[47] In light of his awareness that "rogues" might be successful in politics, Jefferson's confidence in a "natural aristocracy," or even his certainty that one would arise was far from unlimited. To make matters worse, as his antislavery pronouncements often admitted, the prevalence of slavery and slaveholders in the South sullied his and his fellow agrarian Virginia "natural aristocrats" and "philosophers in politics" pretensions to unquestioned public virtue. Apparently it was only when he meditated on abstract philosophical principles rather than social and political realities that Jefferson could confidently invoke the moral sense that everyone possessed, and could learn to strengthen, like a muscle, through "exercise."[48]

---

[46] Jefferson to Peter Carr, August 10, 1787, ibid., 901–902.

[47] Jefferson to Mann Page, August 30, 1795, in Boyd et al., eds., *Papers of Thomas Jefferson*, 28:440.

[48] Jefferson to Peter Carr, August 10, 1787, in Peterson, ed., *Jefferson: Writings*, 901–902. See also Jefferson to Thomas Law, June 13, 1814, discussed further below.

Chapter 4

Gabriel's Rebellion (1800) Impels Jefferson's Search for a Haitian/African Sanctuary

Even in his youth, as a member of Virginia's House of Delegates early in the Revolution, Jefferson had favored deporting refractory slaves rather than executing them. Among the rejected acts in his revisal of Virginia's laws between 1778 and 1779, submitted to the state assembly as a series of 126 bills on June 18, 1779, was Bill No. 64. This was a proposal that "slaves guilty of any offence (Manslaughter, counterfeiting, Arson, Asportation of vessels, robbery, burglary, housebreaking, horsestealing, larceny) punishable in others [free persons] by labor in the public works, shall be transported to such parts in the West Indies, S. America or Africa, as the Governor shall direct, there to be continued in slavery." This was one of the sections of "A Bill for Proportioning Crimes and Punishments in Cases Heretofore Capital," for which Jefferson was largely responsible. An opponent of capital punishment for both free individuals and slaves, he wished to severely restrict its incidence.[1]

To his colleague and lifetime friend Edmund Pendleton, Jefferson explained at this time his sympathy for Blacks and his acute awareness that their enslavement was an inexcusable crime. Wishing to ameliorate "the sanguinary hue of our penal law" for Whites and Blacks alike, he favored imposition of the death penalty only for the crimes of murder and perhaps treason, rather than the vast array of felonies to which it then applied. He continued, "Rape, buggery &c. punish by castration," and all other crimes (committed by free persons) with hard labor. "But as this would be no punishment or change of condition to slaves (*me miserum!*) let them be sent to other countries. By these means we should be freed from the wickedness of the latter," he noted, justifying the humane change by its benefits for the public as well as mercy to the slaves. "Laws thus proportionate and mild should never be dispensed with." He desired that law be impartial to the

[1] The bill was defeated. Jefferson originally transmitted this bill, part of the series of laws on crimes and punishments prepared by a committee consisting of himself, George Wythe, and Edmund Pendleton, in a letter to Wythe, November 1, 1778 (Boyd et al., eds., *Papers of Thomas Jefferson*, 2:504n, 504–506).

greatest practicable degree: "Let mercy be the character of the lawgiver, but let the judge be a mere machine. The mercies of the law will be dispensed equally & impartially to every description of men; those of the judge, or of the executive power, will be the eccentric impulses of whimsical, capricious designing man."[2]

Jefferson's proposals toward Blacks were comparatively benevolent. During the colonial period and extending into the antebellum era, many slaves who committed the crimes he enumerated were sentenced to death by county courts. In Virginia under British rule, a slave usually suffered execution if he broke into a house and stole items worth more than five shillings. Manslaughter carried the death penalty for slaves who killed free persons. However, by a law passed in 1765 they could plead "benefit of clergy" the first time they killed another slave, and thereby avoid capital punishment. Although the House of Delegates apparently never voted on Jefferson's 1778 bill, between 1785 and 1831 judicial punishments inflicted upon slaves were mitigated slightly.[3]

Jefferson respected the rationality of would-be Black rebels. He sympathized with their desire for freedom even though he could not support it, certainly not if they remained within the United States. Although he seldom mentioned his personal slaves, and even haughtily claimed to regard his slave property as an insignificant "bagatelle," he feared that immediate, full-scale, compulsory emancipation might result in race war and probably ruin his shaky economic fortunes, especially should he morally regress and decide to sell slaves to help pay his debts. (Ironically, by the 1782 manumission act, renewed in 1792 and thereafter, it was illegal for Jefferson, as an indebted planter, to free any slaves, whom his creditors could then confiscate.) Thus, Jefferson often stipulated Black banishment as an indispensable precondition for mass emancipation.[4]

---

[2] Jefferson to Edmund Pendleton, August 26, 1776, in Boyd et al., eds., *Papers of Thomas Jefferson*, 1:505, and Peterson, ed., *Jefferson: Writings*, 756–57.

[3] For the data on slave crime and punishment, see Philip Schwarz, *Twice Condemned: Slaves and the Criminal Laws of Virginia, 1705–1865* (Baton Rouge: Louisiana State University Press, 1988), 21, 76–77, 218–21. In 1848, the legislature abolished "benefit of clergy" for slaves, resulting in an increased number of executions (289–91).

[4] For Jefferson calling his slave ownership a "bagatelle," see Jefferson to John Holmes, April 22, 1820, in Lipscomb and Bergh, eds., *Writings of Jefferson*, 15:249. Jefferson occasionally made exceptions to this rule of exile, voicing support for experimental, isolated colonies of free Blacks working side by side with Whites. See Jefferson to Edward Bancroft, January 26, 1789, in Boyd et al., eds., *Papers of Thomas Jefferson*, 14:492; Jefferson to Frances Wright, August 7, 1825, in Lipscomb and Bergh, eds., *Writings of Jefferson*, 16:120; and Jefferson to William Short, January 18, 1826, microfilm reel 55, Jefferson Papers, LC (hdl.loc.gov/loc.mss/mtj.mtjbib025635), all discussed elsewhere in this volume. For the 1792 law prohibiting indebted slaveholders from manumitting their slaves, which prevented Jefferson from freeing his slaves, either by deed during his lifetime or by last will and testament, see "An Act to reduce

As early as the mid-1790s, when it seemed that the Haitian slave revolt would succeed, Jefferson favorably considered the possibility that "St. Domingo" (as Americans called it) would serve as a haven for Virginia's slaves once the state adopted a full-scale program of general emancipation. Although Jefferson favored liberal reforms during what historians have come to regard as an "Atlantic Revolution" or "the Age of the Democratic Revolution," at times he approached the issue of a Southern slave insurrection with fear and trembling, on the assumption that the slaves would obtain assistance from foreign powers. He occasionally speculated that British invading forces, French revolutionaries, or even, in his most pessimistic moments, Northern state militias inspired by abolitionists might offer significant military assistance to Black rebels. Believing emancipation was inevitable, he considered it prudent for Virginia slaveholders to liberate their slaves before a full-scale insurrection (probably something similar to Nat Turner's later Rebellion or worse), perhaps with the assistance of British or French armies, took place. He expressed concern about slave uprisings only on a few occasions, including the undeclared war between the US and France, 1798–1800, when he seemingly feared that the French Directory or Haiti's ruler Louverture might instigate slave revolts; during the War of 1812, when he thought the British might incite them, as they did in Virginia in 1775; and, if only hypothetically, during the Missouri crisis in 1820, predicting that Southern slaves, if emancipated by a Northern-controlled Congress, would indiscriminately attack Southern Whites.[5] In the last case, he melodramatically assumed that Congress would proclaim immediate emancipation (something he knew would not happen in his lifetime) without stipulating that the freed slaves must leave the United States.

Occasionally, seeking to frighten his fellow slaveholders into passing laws to abolish the evil institution, action he had always favored provided the freed slaves were compelled to leave the republic, he stressed the inevitability of a successful Southern slave upheaval. During the late 1790s, Jefferson argued that the spread

---

into one, the several acts concerning slaves, free negroes, and mulattoes," December 17, 1792, Samuel Shepherd, ed., *Statutes at Large of Virginia from October Session 1792 to December Session 1806, Inclusive*, 3 vols. (1835; repr., New York: AMS Press, 1970), 1:127–28.

[5] For Jefferson's ostensible fear that the Northern states would assist slave revolts at the time of the undeclared war with France, see Jefferson to Madison, February 12, 1799, in Smith, ed., *Republic of Letters*, 2:1095. (The context indicates that Jefferson was being sarcastic, which he often was with friends.) For his opinion during the War of 1812, see Jefferson to Edward Coles, August 25, 1814, microfilm reel 47, Jefferson Papers, LC (hdl.loc.gov/loc.mss/mtj.mtjbib021817). For his alarm during the Missouri debates, see Jefferson to John Adams, January 22, 1821, in Lipscomb and Bergh, eds., *Writings of Jefferson*, 15:308–309, discussed elsewhere in this volume. Most of Jefferson's correspondence that I mention in this volume is found at Founders Online (a standard scholarly resource) at the National archives.

of revolutionary violence from the Caribbean to Virginia was only a matter of time, making it imperative that the state emancipate its slaves before they seized their freedom through bloody revolt. He was acutely aware of "the passions the prejudices and the real difficulties" involved, and the controversy over "the mode of emancipation," as he wrote legal expert St. George Tucker. The state assembly rejected, as too radical, Tucker's 1796 plan for emancipating Virginia's slaves, but rendering their lives so miserable by racist laws similar to the later "Black Codes" that he expected them to emigrate voluntarily. Paradoxically, in 1797 Jefferson welcomed the successful slave revolt on "St. Domingo," as Americans called Haiti. He began to consider Haiti or other rebellious West Indian islands (which he expected would eventually win their independence), as the proper home for emancipated Southern slaves.[6]

Seemingly undaunted by the knowledge that Haitian slaves had murdered their French overlords, a fate every Virginia slaveholder dreaded, Jefferson sounded a Nestorian note. "Perhaps the first chapter of this history, which has begun in St. Domingo, and the next succeeding ones which will recount how all the whites were driven from all the other islands," he advised Tucker, "may prepare our minds for a peaceable accomodation [*sic*] between justice, policy and necessity, and furnish/facilitate an answer to the difficult question Whither shall the coloured emigrants go?"[7]

Foreseeing future sectional political conflict between Northern and Southern Whites, Jefferson doubted that the Northern states would help the South subdue a slave uprising, although the Constitution required them to do so. Consequently, Jefferson hoped the slaves would be freed by peaceful means, before they erupted in a violent rebellion. Speedy implementation of a "plan" of emancipation was essential to forestall a slave uprising. Advising that gradual emancipation *might* obviate future slave revolts, Jefferson admonished, "If something is not done, and soon done, we shall be the murderers of our own children." During the late 1790s more than later, Jefferson seemed alarmed by the violence of the French Revolution, which he had enthusiastically supported initially. Perhaps deliberately, to frighten his correspondents into embracing emancipation, he stressed the likelihood of a slave uprising in Virginia, abetted by White French "Jacobin" agents provocateurs. "The revolutionary storm now sweeping the globe will be upon us; and happy if we make timely provision to give it an easy passage

---

[6] Jefferson to St. George Tucker, August 28, 1797, in Oberg, ed., *Jefferson Papers*, 29:519. According to one historian, in many ways, such as slaves' ability to own small plots of land, sell produce in town, and the frequency of manumission and legal protection from excessive cruelty by their owners, bondage under the *Code Noir* was less harsh in eighteenth-century Haiti than in Virginia (Forster, "Slavery in Virginia and Saint-Domingue in the Late 18th Century," 1–13).

[7] Jefferson to St. George Tucker, August 28, 1797, in Oberg, ed., *Jefferson Papers*, 29:519.

over our land," he warned. Somewhat trepidatiously for a man who had once said, "The tree of liberty must be refreshed from time to time with the blood of patriots and tyrants," Jefferson speculated that the French government, currently involved in altercations with the U.S. in the Caribbean, might attempt to incite southern slaves to violent revolt. This possibility increased the urgency of granting the slaves peaceful emancipation in the near future, he reasoned. Indeed, he considered a Southern slave revolt for liberty a legitimate part of the worldwide democratic revolution: "From the present state of things in Europe and America the day which begins our combustion must be near at hand, and only a single spark is wanting to make that day tomorrow," he advised Tucker. Jefferson regretted that the legislature had not yet implemented a plan of liberation, for "every day's delay lessens the time we may take for emancipation."[8]

Jefferson's expressed doubt that the Northern states, most of which had abolished slavery, would help suppress a slave revolt increased his letter's tone of urgency. "Some people derive hope from the aid of the confederated states," he warned. "But this is a delusion. There is but one state in the Union which will aid us sincerely if an insurrection begins;" he said, probably alluding to South Carolina, whose population was over fifty percent enslaved, "and that one may perhaps have it's [*sic*] own fire to quench at the same time."[9] Emphasizing Southerners' isolation may have been Jefferson's means of increasing support for gradual emancipation among slaveholding legislators.

Somewhat paradoxically for one who professed the angst about the Haitian Revolution that Jefferson had voiced in writing to Tucker, Jefferson's letter to James Monroe of November 24, 1801, amply expressed his conviction that Haiti was the optimal destination for both conspiratorial slaves and freedmen. He was impelled by the belief that, no matter what atrocities or injustices Toussaint Louverture's regime perpetrated (and Louverture was less brutal than his successors, Dessalines and Henry Christophe), since the government was run by Blacks it was the proper haven for Black rebels, present and future. Monroe had bombarded the president with letters—on June 15 and November 17, 1801—conveying the Virginia legislature's requests for assistance.[10] For a Southern state government to ask special attention from the national government in any sphere, let alone the emancipation of slaves, was itself an unprecedented event.

---

[8] Ibid.

[9] Ibid.

[10] Monroe to Jefferson, June 15 and November 17, 1801, in Hamilton, ed., *Writings of James Monroe*, 3:292–95, 302. He wrote Jefferson again on February 13, 1802 (ibid., 3:336–38), informing him that the Virginia assembly now preferred a distant African destination for slave insurrectionists to one closer to home in Haiti or the western territories (perhaps it felt safer that way).

Undoubtedly aware of the epochal nature of Monroe's letters, Jefferson replied cautiously. He did not consider ordinary criminal slaves, whom he called "common malefactors," proper candidates for deportation; they ought to remain in Virginia. While understanding that "conspiracy, insurgence, treason, rebellion" of the type involved in the "tragedy of 1800" formed the first object of the House of Delegates' resolution, Jefferson sensed that it might foreshadow "a much larger scope" of operation, such as the deportation of manumitted or state-emancipated slaves. Responding one by one to the assembly's proposals, Jefferson opposed Virginia's purchasing public lands in the Midwest for a Black state. Less optimistically than in *Notes on Virginia*, nearly twenty years before, Jefferson now rejected the possibility that a Black republic within the nation's public heartland might grow from a Virginian "colony within our limits…to become a part of our union." Such a government, run by Black slave rebels might be dangerous both for Virginia and "the other States—especially those who would be in the vicinity."[11]

The Spanish Southwest and Mexico were occupied mainly by "Indian natives." Jefferson believed they would not willingly alienate the ownership of land to a Black rebel state. He maintained his opposition to the presence of a colony of Black rebels within US borders, which might pose a military danger to neighboring members of the Union and, more importantly, occupy territory that White farmers desired. Jefferson's republican racial imperialism anticipated that the growing White population would eventually, in "distant times…cover the whole northern, if not the southern continent, with a people speaking the same language, governed in similar forms, & by similar laws; nor can we contemplate with satisfaction either blot or mixture on that surface." Despite his skepticism, he promised to sound out the European governments which "hold possessions on the southern continent," including Spain, France, and Portugal, as well as the British in Canada, about their receptivity to setting up a Black state.[12]

Jefferson was much more enthusiastic about deporting the Black revolutionaries to the West Indies and especially to Haiti, the realm of successful slave rebellion. Jefferson's initial reaction to news of Black massacres of Whites in Saint-Domingue (the French word for present-day Haiti) in July 1793 is notable for its sang-froid. As secretary of state, from Philadelphia, on July 14, 1793 (ironically, the anniversary of Bastille Day), he wrote about this event to his son-in-law, Virginia state senator Thomas Mann Randolph, Jr. At the end of a letter primarily concerned with Jefferson's request for a carriage horse from his home, Monticello, he commented on the slaves' recent murders of the White population at Port-au-Prince in Haiti's West Province. Led by the White Girondin French

[11] Jefferson to Monroe, November 24, 1801, in Ford, ed., *Works of Thomas Jefferson*, 9:316.

[12] Ibid., 316–17.

commissioners Léger Félicité Sonthonax and Étienne Polverel, the rebels erupted with great violence. "You will have heard, before you recieve [*sic*] this, of the massacre of about one half of the inhabitants of Port au Prince, & the flight of the other half, who are arrived or about to arrive in the Chesapeake," he reported. "A similar massacre has taken place in Martinique, and I think it cannot be doubted but sooner or later all the whites will be expelled from all the West India islands." Rather than urging Randolph to rouse the Virginia assembly to equip the militia with weapons, increase slave patrols, and strengthen laws suppressing slave insubordination and gatherings, Jefferson pointed to the massacres of Whites in the West Indies as a wake-up call to Virginians to free their slaves—and transport them to the crucible of Saint-Domingue itself. He calmly recommended to his son-in-law, "What is to take place in our Southern states will depend on the timely wisdom & liberality of their legislatures. Perhaps the measures they ought to begin to think of may be facilitated by having so near an asylum [St. Domingo] established."[13] Thus, far from regarding Haiti as a dagger pointed at the South, Jefferson considered it a potential "asylum" for bondspersons whose liberation he thought would benefit everyone concerned. And, he was strangely grateful that Saint-Domingue was so close to American shores, probably, as his later writings indicate, because that would reduce the cost of transporting the Blacks.

Eight years later, with his predictions of Black victory and French expulsion seemingly fulfilled, Jefferson, now president of the United States, revived his recommendation to deport Virginia's Black insurrectionists to Haiti. As Jefferson pragmatically observed, in the company of Toussaint, Dessalines, and Christophe, these conspirators would be praised as heroes rather than dreaded as monsters. Using a language of nature similar to that he had employed twenty years earlier in *Notes on Virginia*, Jefferson certified the Blacks' aptitude for the Caribbean climate, "a more probable & practicable retreat for them" than frigid Canada: "Inhabited already by a people of their own race & color; climates congenial with their natural constitution; insulated from the other descriptions of men; nature seems to have formed these islands [the West Indies] to become the receptacle of the blacks transplanted into this hemisphere."[14]

By contrast, Jefferson doubted that Great Britain, Spain, or even the American Indians would welcome a colony composed of insurrectionary slaves. Voicing a proclivity for the republic's territorial expansion, he reiterated an oft-expressed hope that, eventually, huge chunks of both North and even South America, populated by White immigrants from the United States, would join the Union as its

[13] Jefferson to Thomas Mann Randolph, Jr., July 14, 1793, microfilm reel 18, Jefferson Papers, LC (hdl.loc.gov/loc.mss/mtj.mtjbib007733).

[14] Jefferson to Monroe, November 24, 1801, in Ford, ed., *Works of Thomas Jefferson*, 9:317.

political and commercial allies: a White man's country. Always hoping to profit from "Europe's distresses," he anticipated the United States taking over Spain's North American empire when its enervated monarchy inevitably got involved in a European war. This was his meaning when he wrote Monroe that, "our present interests may restrain us within our own limits, [but] it is impossible not to look forward to distant times, when our rapid multiplication will expand itself beyond those limits, & cover the whole northern, if not southern continent."[15]

During this period Jefferson, repelled by Europe's endless wars, Napoleon's recent transformation of France's Revolutionary republic into a dictatorship, and his own country's hairbreadth escape from such repressive Federalist measures as the Alien and Sedition Acts and an increased Army, stressed the United States' unique representative democracy. Pondering why American cities seemed more susceptible to yellow fever epidemics than those of Europe, where "men [were]...piled on one another...with impunity," and unaware that mosquitoes arriving with the Haitian immigrants brought the yellow fever virus. Jefferson wondered whether "our cloudless skies and the solar heat consequently accumulated" generated contagions from which Europe's depressing cloud cover protected its population. He abruptly turned this inquiry to political applications. "I strongly suspect that our geographical peculiarities may call for a different code of natural law to govern our relations with other nations from that which the conditions of Europe have given rise to there," he wrote in June 1800 to Samuel Latham Mitchill, a New York Democratic-Republican chemistry professor at Columbia College elected to Congress the following year. Relieved that Republicans and moderate Federalists had recently gained control of Congress, terminating the Sedition Act and disbanding the Additional Army, Jefferson likened these encouraging events to awakening from a drug-induced sleep. "I sincerely join in your congratulations on the revival of those principles on which our republic has been founded," he wrote. "Perhaps future ages may never know the real soporific which, in gentle slumbers, was carrying them [the American people] to their grave."[16]

---

[15] Jefferson to Monroe, November 24, 1801, in Peterson, ed., *Jefferson: Writings*, 1097–98. For Jefferson's proclivity for imperial expansionism, his belief that United States citizens should occupy the Floridas, Canada, Texas ("Techas"), and Cuba, see Jefferson to Archibald Stuart, January 25, 1786, in Boyd et al., eds., *Papers of Thomas Jefferson*, 9:218; Jefferson to Madison, April 27, 1809, in Lipscomb and Bergh, eds., *Writings of Jefferson*, 12:276–77; and Jefferson to Monroe, May 14, 1820, in Ford, ed., *Writings of Thomas Jefferson*, 10:158–59.

[16] Jefferson to Samuel Latham Mitchill, June 13, 1800, in Oberg, ed., *Jefferson Papers*, 32:18. Ascribing inordinate importance to this letter, early Jefferson scholar Gilbert Chinard regards it as an early manifestation of the onset of Jefferson's "naïve and almost unconscious imperialism" (*Thomas Jefferson: Apostle of Americanism* [Boston: Little, Brown, 1929], 398). More

More painfully aware than ever of republicanism's tenuous uniqueness, Jefferson thereafter stressed the American people's significance in preserving that form of government and pointing the way for the rest of the world, whose peoples, he hoped, would ultimately likewise enjoy life, liberty, and the pursuit of happiness. Apparently, he envisioned the Black, self-liberated people of Haiti eventually sharing the blessings of liberty with White Europeans and Americans. At least, he considered Haiti the most appropriate sanctuary for the Southern states' slave population, which he expected, and seemingly hoped, would gain their freedom in the near future and find the erstwhile "Pearl of the Antilles" a welcoming home.

During the election campaign of 1800, Jefferson admitted that some southern Whites, dreading Black retaliation, might want to slaughter any Blacks even remotely connected with Gabriel's conspiracy, an abortive scheme by Henrico County slaves to burn Richmond, kill most of the town's Whites, kidnap Governor Monroe, and demand a separate enclave where Blacks could live in freedom. "Those who have escaped from the immediate danger, must have feelings which would dispose them to extend the executions," he surmised. "Even here [Albemarle County], where every thing has been perfectly tranquil," despite the general revulsion against further executions, "a familiarity with slavery and a possibility of danger from that quarter prepare the general mind for some severities." Painfully aware of the suspiciousness endemic to human nature that vitiated the moral sense, Jefferson discovered that many Virginians believed that the Adams Administration helped foment the rebellion. At least this was what he had heard during a visit to his alternate plantation, Poplar Forest in Bedford County in the west, a few months after the conspiracy was crushed. "I am sincerely sorry I was absent when you were in the [Albemarle County] neighborhood," he wrote Monroe in November 1800, whom he believed knew more about the details of the insurrection than anyone else. "I wished to learn something of the excitements, the expectations & the extent of this negro conspiracy, not being satisfied with the popular reports." Some of his Bedford neighbors thought that the US Army, which was under Federalist control, had deliberately made it easy for rebellious slaves to procure weapons to facilitate a successful revolt. As he wrote Monroe, "I learnt with concern in Bedford that the important deposit of arms near New London is without even a centinel to guard it. There is said to be much powder in it. We cannot suppose the federal [Adams] administration takes this method of offering arms to insurgent negroes: yet some

---

accurately, one may view it as one of many observations Jefferson made in the aftermath of Bonaparte's *coup d'état* of *Brumaire* that the United States would only preserve its republican government by isolating itself from the influence of other countries, including the former French ally, which had itself prematurely abandoned republicanism.

[Whites] in the neighborhood...suspect it." While seemingly discrediting the view that Federalists covertly supported slave revolt so that they could criticize Republican mismanagement in the state, Jefferson advised Monroe, as Virginia's governor, to alert the Army to its negligence: "Would it not be justifiable in you to suggest to them the importance of a guard there? In truth the deposit should be removed to the [James] river."[17] Jefferson apparently gave some credence to the idea that the Adams Administration, from either ignorance or malice, would encourage the unthinkable—an armed slave uprising.

Appalled by reports of Whites' thirst for vengeance after Gabriel's unsuccessful uprising in August 1800, Vice President Jefferson advised Governor Monroe to propose a law allowing him to sell the surviving rebels outside the boundaries of the United States rather than kill them. Rather self-contradictorily, he surmised that his home county, Albemarle, where "there is a strong sentiment that there has been hanging enough," would endorse mercy. Jefferson believed that public opinion at home and abroad would denounce perpetuation of Virginia's brutal policy of suppression. He argued, "The other states & the world at large will forever condemn us if we indulge a principle of revenge, or go one step beyond absolute necessity." This was especially true, since the "rebellion," as some historians erroneously label it, had been an utter failure, both because two slaves (whom the assembly later freed as their reward) betrayed its intent to authorities, and because a bitter rainstorm prevented the enslaved persons from meeting at the assigned location. Indeed, no Whites died during this conspiracy.[18]

A few months later, on December 31, 1800, the Virginia House of Delegates, responding to petitions from angry constituents who vented their racial

---

[17] Jefferson to Monroe, September 20, 1800 (first quotation) (hdl.loc.gov/loc.mss/mtj.mtjbib009432), and Jefferson to Monroe, November 8, 1800 (second quotation) (hdl.loc.gov/loc.mss/mtj.mtjbib009471), both microfilm reel 22, Jefferson Papers, LC. Historians have noted, and even supported, farfetched Federalist charges that the Republicans, and perhaps French *agents provocateurs* in Richmond, encouraged Gabriel's cohorts. They have likewise ignored Jefferson's mention of Republican suspicions that Federalists were behind the conspiracy. For one prominent example of such scholars, see Douglas R. Egerton, "Gabriel's Conspiracy and the Election of 1800," *Journal of Southern History* 56/2 (May 1990): 191–214. Michael L. Nicholls's careful studies, his article, "'Holy Insurrection': Spinning the News of Gabriel's Conspiracy," *Journal of Southern History* 78/1 (February 2012): 37–68, and his book *Whispers of Rebellion*, discredit most of the information in the Federalist press about the "Rebellion" as partisan exaggeration. This was true of "news" printed in the Philadelphia and New York newspapers, which only received second-hand information. Nicholls questions or refutes many of Egerton's assumptions, which Egerton elaborated at length in his frequently cited book, *Gabriel's Rebellion*.

[18] Jefferson to Monroe, September 20, 1800, in Ford, ed., *Writings of Thomas Jefferson*, 7:457–58.

hatred by demanding repeal of the 1782 manumission act, sought an alternative to passing a law that denied the possibility of slave emancipation and limited slaveholders' rights. It requested Monroe "to correspond with the President of the United States on the subject of purchasing lands without [i.e., outside] the limits of this State, whither persons obnoxious to the laws, or dangerous to the peace of Society, may be removed." Ostensibly, free Blacks, whom some Virginians considered prima facie "dangerous," might potentially fall under the resolution's terms as well as rebellious slaves. It is possible that a House of Delegates committee received a copy of Jefferson's letter of September 20, 1800, to Governor Monroe, since it followed the presidential candidate's recommendations. The assembly proposed, "that a law ought to pass, authorising [*sic*] the executive to transport certain slaves, now under sentence of death, for conspiracy, to be sold for the benefit of the commonwealth." The lower house passed both resolutions, and on January 2, 1801, the state senate concurred, "requesting the Governor to correspond with the President of the United States, on the subject of purchasing lands, &C."[19]

Aware from his youth of Blacks' right to claim their natural rights, Jefferson hesitated to criticize slave revolts; indeed, he never did so. Yet, numerous historians, often basing their conclusions solely on conjecture, insist that he opposed the slave revolt on Haiti virtually from its inception in 1791 and forced Congress to pass legislation to suppress it after winning the presidency in 1801.[20]

---

[19] *Journals of the Virginia House of Delegates, 1801* (Shaw and Shoemaker, comps., *American Bibliography: A Preliminary Checklist for 1801, Items 1–1702* [New York: Scarecrow, 1958], item #1585) 47, 48; *Journal of the Senate of the Commonwealth of Virginia* (Richmond, 1800; Shaw-Shoemaker #1586), 49, 51; *Calendar of Virginia State Papers from January 1, 1799 to December 31, 1807* (Richmond: Flournoy, 1890), 9:195.

[20] I undertook an examination of these scholars' citations to Jefferson's letters and other expressions of his views and concluded that their readings of Jefferson's statements on the Haitian slave uprising often distort what Jefferson actually said (Scherr, *Jefferson's Haitian Policy*; and Scherr, "Jefferson's 'Cannibals' Revisited: A Closer Look at his Notorious Phrase," *Journal of Southern History* 77/2 [May 2011]: 251–82). Among numerous pro-Federalist historiographical interpretations of the debate on United States assistance to Haitian independence, see, for instance, Donald R. Hickey, "America's Response to the Slave Revolt in Haiti, 1791–1806," *Journal of the Early Republic* 2/4 (Winter 1982): 361–79; Michael Zuckerman, "The Power of Blackness: Thomas Jefferson and the Revolution in St. Domingue," in Zuckerman, *Almost Chosen People: Biographies in the American Grain* (Berkeley: University of California Press, 1993), 175–218; and Garry Wills, *"Negro President": Jefferson and the Slave Power* (New York: Houghton Mifflin, 2003). Timothy M. Matthewson, "George Washington's Policy toward the Haitian Slave Revolution," *Diplomatic History* 3 (Summer 1979): 321–36; Matthewson, "Jefferson and Haiti," *Journal of Southern History* 61 (May 1995): 209–48; and Clifford Egan, *Neither Peace nor War: Franco-American Relations, 1803–1812* (Baton Rouge: Louisiana State

Jefferson acknowledged Blacks' political potential, as he did in the letter to Frances Wright designating the African tribes as "nations." Earlier, in *Notes on Virginia*, he had warned that, if granted their freedom, African Americans might organize into "parties, and produce convulsions which will probably never end but in the extermination of the one or the other race." He had long been painfully aware of Blacks' capacity for group unity and political organization.[21]

Jefferson recognized Haiti's possibilities for demonstrating Black political versatility. At the beginning of his presidency, responding to inquiries from the Virginia assembly and his friend Governor James Monroe, Jefferson suggested Haiti as an outlet for "exporting," instead of executing, Virginia slaves convicted of "conspiracy and insurrection." He respected Blacks' justifiable rebelliousness as a violent reaction to the deprivation of freedom—a natural human response to slavery.[22]

Attempting to justify slave revolts following Gabriel's abortive Richmond plot, Jefferson seemingly expected Virginia's public opinion to condone bondspersons' recourse to violence to achieve liberty. "They [the public] cannot lose sight of the rights of the two parties, & the object of the unsuccessful one," he believed. He thought the future deportation of would-be rebels would resolve a dilemma that might otherwise end in great carnage. As he explained to Monroe, "Our situation is indeed a difficult one: for I doubt whether these people [Blacks] can ever be permitted to go at large among us with safety." Nonetheless, he advised Monroe against issuing a preliminary deportation proclamation, which might spur fugitive insurrectionists to attempt to liberate their imprisoned comrades before departure. He thought Monroe ought to confine all insurrectionary slaves in a fortified garrison until the Virginia assembly, which possessed most of the political power, decided whether to deport them. "Surely the legislature would pass a law for their exportation [*sic*], the proper measure on this & all such occasions?" he argued.[23] "Exportation," i.e., transportation or deportation, would serve Jefferson's purpose of removing Blacks from Virginia, either as emancipated freepersons or conspiring slaves. As he would later habitually do in matters connected with slavery and race, as well as with regard to his religious views, he requested Monroe to respect his confidentiality.

University Press, 1983), 56–62, disclose that President Washington staunchly opposed the Haitian insurrection. With Secretary of the Treasury Alexander Hamilton's support, he lent France funds and munitions to suppress the uprising. Involved in its own "undeclared war" with France in the West Indies from 1798 to 1800, the Adams Administration found it expedient to assist Black general Toussaint Louverture against a likely common enemy.

21 Jefferson to Miss Frances Wright, August 7, 1825, in Lipscomb and Bergh, eds., *Writings of Jefferson*, 16:120; Peden, ed., *Notes on the State of Virginia*, 138.

22 Jefferson to Monroe, November 24, 1801, in Peterson, ed., *Jefferson: Writings*, 1097.

23 Jefferson to Monroe, September 20, 1800, in Ford, ed., *Writings of Thomas Jefferson*, 7:457–58.

Jefferson may have viewed Gabriel's abortive August 1800 conspiracy as signifying the coming of the race wars he fearfully predicted in Queries XIV and XVIII of *Notes on Virginia*. However, he did not fear that Blacks would revive the rebellion; on the contrary, he thought that White racists might exploit the recent disturbances to justify massacring Blacks, presaging racial war. As was often the case, Jefferson feared the negative impact that glaring reminders of Southern slavery and racial exploitation would have on public opinion in the other states and abroad, which would denounce Virginia's brutal policy of suppression. He argued, "The other states & the world at large will forever condemn us if we indulge a principle of revenge, or go one step beyond absolute necessity."[24]

In the atmosphere of shock following the discovery and suppression of Gabriel's conspiracy, the Virginia legislature took action toward the rebels that earlier might have seemed unconventional or unduly liberal. In January 1801, the assembly passed a law based on Jefferson's 1778 proposal (although his list did not include conspiracy and insurrection) and his recent letter to Monroe. It allowed the governor, "with the advice of council," to sell "slaves under sentence of death for conspiracy, insurrection, or other crimes" to purchasers (usually slave traders) who promised to transport them out of the United States.[25] The law existed until 1858, when condemned slaves were sentenced to remain in Virginia as state-owned laborers on the public works.[26]

Governor Monroe and the assembly were inclined to expand Jefferson's notions concerning the "exportation" of rebellious Blacks like those involved in Gabriel's Conspiracy to include free Blacks. Several months after Jefferson's election as president, Monroe, following the Virginia assembly's instructions, informed him of the state's request that Virginia or the United States purchase public lands "in the vacant western territory of the United States" as a prison settlement for individuals "obnoxious to the laws or dangerous to the peace of society." Monroe astutely proposed that Jefferson consider foreign territory held by countries outside the United States and contact "friendly powers" that owned land "either on this Continent or a neighboring [Caribbean] Island to which we might send such persons." Surmising that the Virginia Assembly would appreciate a choice of "alternatives," he thought that "mature" consideration might lead it to "prefer" deporting them overseas to settling them on land dangerously close to the state's borders. Monroe favored sending slaves to land held by a cooperative European power in the Western Hemisphere. More charitable than public execution or individual sales abroad, mass deportation followed "motives of humanity." "Under

---

[24] Ibid.

[25] "An Act to empower the Governor to Transport Slaves Condemned, when it shall be deemed expedient," passed January 15, 1801 (Shaw-Shoemaker #1584), 24.

[26] Schwarz, *Twice Condemned*, 27–29.

the existing law [they] might be doomed to suffer death," Monroe emphasized, alluding to the recently passed law's provision that convicted slaves would be eligible for sale abroad rather than hanging only if the Governor's Council unanimously voted for it in each case. Monroe recommended extending the law to permit the perhaps forcible deportation—Monroe called it "transportation"—of *all* Blacks, not merely convicted rebels, to the public lands; foreign colonies in North or South America; or some "neighboring Island," although he did not specifically mention Saint-Domingue (Haiti). Noting the "condition of those people" and "the embarrassment they have already occasioned us"—meaning all African Americans, free as well as enslaved—he advocated a "more enlarged construction of the resolution" extending "the field of practicable expedients...on the widest possible scale." If free Blacks, in addition to condemned rebels, became candidates for deportation, Monroe advised, a greater selection of "an alternative of places" was advisable.[27]

As Monroe admitted, the Virginia assembly's resolution initially "was produced by the conspiracy of the slaves which took place in this city and neighborhood last year [Gabriel's Rebellion] and is applicable to that description of persons only"—convicted rebels and conspirators. Monroe pointed out that its more sweeping possibilities could authorize the state to "transport" abroad, or to some Midwestern colony carved from the public lands, *all* Blacks, including freedmen. He asked Jefferson's advice and assistance in obtaining territory, either in the United States or abroad, for a Black colony.[28]

In responding to Monroe, Jefferson, despite emphasizing that he considered mutinous slaves as the "persons" primarily intended by the Virginia assembly, and probably considering the forced deportation of free Blacks unfair, grasped the legislature's desire to deport free African Americans. Alluding to Gabriel's thwarted slave revolt of the year before, Jefferson said, "Conspiracy, insurgency, treason, rebellion, among that description of persons who brought on us the alarm, and on themselves the tragedy of 1800, were doubtless within the view of every one" of the legislators who proposed a colony for seditious Blacks. He understood, without endorsing, Monroe's point that the assembly resolution conveyed "a much larger scope" of interpretation. Nonetheless, Jefferson rejected the idea that Virginia ought to purchase Western lands for a colony of Black rebels

---

[27] Monroe to Jefferson, June 15, 1801, in Hamilton, ed., *Writings of James Monroe*, 3:292–95; also in *James Monroe Papers in Virginia Repositories* (12 microfilm reels; University of Virginia, 1969), reel 2. Arthur Scherr, "Governor James Monroe and the Southampton Slave Resistance of 1799," *The Historian* 61/3 (Spring 1999): 557–78, provides a different perspective on Monroe's actions at this time.

[28] Monroe to Jefferson, June 15, 1801, in Hamilton, ed., *Writings of James Monroe*, 3:293.

"within our limits, and to become a part of our union," although the assembly had never suggested creating a state of slave conspirators and would probably have been terrified at the thought that those it wished "removed" would govern an autonomous domain.[29]

Jefferson believed that such a disgruntled, outcast group residing within American borders on arable soil would endanger both Virginia and the United States, whether as convicted co-conspirators sentenced to hard labor or free self-governing individuals. Favoring the settlement of both North and South America exclusively by Whites and assimilated American Indians, he thought the mainland should be off-limits to a projected colony of Black revolutionaries. Nor did he expect that the British or Spanish authorities or the American Indians who controlled the "foreign" territories under consideration would consent to a Black enclave. Empathizing with the slaves, at least theoretically, Jefferson, envisaging their arrival in frigid areas of Canada or the Northwest public lands, doubted "whether that race of men could long exist in so rigorous a climate."[30] Furthermore, neither British Canada nor Native American territory on the continent would be a likely "receptacle" for the Black rebels because their current inhabitants would not be sufficiently "disinterested" to help Virginia solve its slave problem by accepting potentially violent residents.[31]

In his letter to Monroe, Jefferson implied that the governor would be better equipped than the legislature to find an appropriate haven for the slaves. Jefferson may have had Saint-Domingue's volatile situation in mind. In July 1801, its governor-general, the great Black leader and former slave, Toussaint Louverture, defying Napoleon Bonaparte, wrote and promulgated a constitution making himself governor of the colony for life, with power to choose his successor. Jefferson looked favorably upon Louverture's assumption of power. He evidently alluded to this epochal event when he observed the selection of an appropriate slave locale might be frustrated by "the vast revolutions & changes of circumstances which are now in a course of progression," and the ensuing "possibilities that...a change

[29] Jefferson to Monroe, November 24, 1801, in Peterson, ed., *Jefferson: Writings*, 1097.

[30] Ibid.

[31] Jefferson to Monroe, November 24, 1801, in Ford, ed., *Works of Thomas Jefferson*, 9:316. In this instance, Jefferson's sensitivity on the matter of climate in relation to governmental structures may show the influence of Montesquieu, one of the favorite authors of his youth, although by the time he became president he was less enthusiastic. See Montesquieu's *Spirit of Laws*, Book XIV, "Of Laws in Relation to the Nature of the Climate." For Jefferson's evolving attitude toward Montesquieu's work, see Sowerby, ed., *Catalogue*, 3:3–11 (entry #2327); Carrithers, "Montesquieu, Jefferson, and the Fundamentals of Eighteenth-Century Republican Theory," 160–68; and Joyce Appleby, "What is Still American in the Political Philosophy of Thomas Jefferson?" *William and Mary Quarterly* 39/2 (April 1982): 287–309.

of sovereignty, of government, or of other circumstances," might "totally derange" the feasibility of "any particular plan." Ostensibly agreeing, Monroe argued that the federal executive should participate with him in selecting territory on which banished slave conspirators could settle, although he thought that at the state's end final preparations might more suitably be undertaken by the legislature than the constitutionally shackled governor.[32] In addition, Jefferson probably preferred to deal personally with his old friend Monroe in such delicate matters than negotiate with the Virginia legislature, which had already annoyed him by demanding the allocation of public lands for a slave colony.

A few years later, the Virginia legislature assumed that the Louisiana Purchase's vast territory, encompassing the south-central states and the Great Plains, would provide enough land for the state to dispose of its free Blacks and future subversive slaves and freed persons, and that its western extremities would be safely distant from Virginia. Indeed, in February 1805, the state legislature requested that its congressional representatives exert "their best efforts" to obtain from the "General Government a competent portion of territory, in the country of Louisiana [not Orleans Territory, which became the state of Louisiana], to be appropriated to the residence of such people of color as have been or shall be emancipated in Virginia, or may hereafter become dangerous to the public safety."[33]

The proposal probably shocked Jefferson. His moral sense must have told him that there was no justification for Blacks who had lived peacefully in quasi-freedom in Virginia, despite the legal and social discrimination against them, to suffer exile from their home state; he had earlier expressed to Monroe his objections to using the public lands for this purpose. He intended the public lands for settlement by White farmers and (after the Louisiana Purchase was secured in 1803) American Indians, who would eventually be forced to surrender their hunting grounds east of the Mississippi to the United States. He was likely aware that, in his home county, Albemarle, free Blacks (most of whom were mixed race) were relatively prosperous, enjoyed sexual freedom including miscegenation, were

---

[32] Jefferson to Monroe, November 24, 1801, in Peterson, ed., *Jefferson: Writings*, 1098–99; Monroe to Jefferson, December 21, 1801, in Hamilton, ed., *Writings of James Monroe*, 3:322–24.

[33] For the text of the Virginia assembly's resolutions in 1805, see *American State Papers: Senate, 9th Congress, 2nd Session, Miscellaneous* (Washington, DC: Gales and Seaton, 1834) 1:466–67, and Rev. Philip Slaughter, *Virginian History of African Colonization* (Richmond: MacFarlane and Fergusson, 1855), 1–6. It is likely that Virginia expected slaves convicted of conspiracy to continue in slavery there, although, more humanely than in the past, they would not be executed.

respected by their White neighbors, and received the equal protection of the laws.[34] President Jefferson never replied to his state's final request.

[34] See Kirt Von Daacke's excellent case study of Albemarle County in the early nineteenth century, *Freedom Has a Face: Race, Identity, and Community in Jefferson's Virginia* (Charlottesville: University of Virginia Press, 2012). On the significance of the Louisiana Purchase in Jefferson's relations with the Indians, see Sheehan, *Seeds of Extinction*, 245–46. In general, see also Anthony F. C. Wallace, *Jefferson and the Indians* (Cambridge: Harvard University Press, 1999).

Chapter 5

Jefferson, Slavery, and the Branagan Affair

During his presidency, Jefferson remained sympathetic to supporters of emancipating and deporting slaves. Attempting to avoid additional abuse from his political enemies, he also wanted his views kept secret. When Thomas Branagan (1774–1843), an Irish abolitionist who advocated Blacks' emancipation and compulsory deportation to their own colony in Louisiana, asked Jefferson to subscribe to his book, *Serious Remonstrances, addressed to the citizens of the Northern States, and their representatives*, an antislavery work he published in Philadelphia in 1805, Jefferson refused to contact him directly.[1]

Branagan was a fascinating figure. According to his autobiographical statements, he was born into a well-to-do Roman Catholic family in Ireland on December 28, 1774. His mother died when he was five. Because his father was overly strict, he ran away from home at the age of sixteen to work on a slave ship bound for West Africa. Although he wrote that the Africans treated him with kindness, he was undeterred from working in the slave trade and eventually became a slave-dealer himself. Calling himself "Thomas Branagan, late slave-trader" in his books, he sold the enslaved in Grenada in the British West Indies and in Savannah, Georgia. Later, enrolling aboard an English privateer, he plundered the ships of French aristocrats fleeing the Haitian slave revolt during the 1790s. Eventually regretting his evil ways, he claimed he later returned the prize money, about which he seemingly had more guilt than about selling human beings. Following such diverse, risky, roguish maritime occupations, Branagan turned to the hardly more respectable role of overseer on a plantation in Antigua in the British

---

[1] Thomas Branagan, *Serious Remonstrances, addressed to the citizens of the Northern states, and their representatives...* (Philadelphia: Thomas T. Stiles, 1805). About the same time, Branagan wrote *A Preliminary Essay on the Oppression of the Exiled Sons of Africa* (Philadelphia: J. W. Scott, 1804), as well as *Avenia; or, a Tragical Poem on the Oppression of the Human Species* (Philadelphia: J. Cline, 1810).

West Indies, but ultimately, he said, "preferred virtue in rags, to vice arrayed in costly clothing."[2]

Having initially converted from Roman Catholicism to the Methodist faith, Branagan adopted the antislavery views held by many members of that denomination. Quitting his job as a West Indian overseer, he arrived in Philadelphia in 1798 and emerged as an antislavery Methodist preacher and writer. With a neophyte's zeal, between 1804 and 1805 he wrote four antislavery pieces, two of prose and two of verse. Calling himself "an illiterate child of nature," divinely inspired to compose abolitionist poems and tracts, he admitted that his poem *Avenia* borrowed from Homer and other pagan poets. Traumatized by witnessing (and perhaps inflicting) torture on captured African slaves in the past, he hoped to expiate his sins by denouncing slavery. He named the African hero in his poem by the cognomen of a late, great Haitian leader: "Louverture."[3]

Branagan's writings made up in energy for what they lacked in logic. He hoped to recruit the president's assistance for his abolitionist publications. Praising Jefferson's "exalted character" in a letter to him in May 1805, Branagan enclosed his "*Preliminary Essay on Slavery*, being well convinced that the subject matter of it will attract your attention, and perhaps prove a stimulus to your encouraging the 'Tragical Poem' which the enclosed Essay is merely intended as an introduction to."[4] He promised to send him the poem upon publication "whether you patronize me by your respectable signature or not." He presciently considered abolition the most critical issue confronting the American people:

> Of all the publications which may be productive of public utility, there is none more deserving of general attention, none more intrinsically momentous to the citizens of American! [*sic*] than the subject matter of my *Tragical Poem*. To every nation, savage, or civilized, it must be deemed Important, but to the *Body Politic*, whose Very existence exclusively depends

[2] Most of the biographical information in this and the following paragraphs is from Lewis Leary, "Thomas Branagan: Republican Rhetoric and Romanticism in America," *Pennsylvania Magazine of History and Biography* 77/3 (July 1953): 332–52. Branagan's quotations are from p. 334.

[3] Ibid., 341–42.

[4] Thomas Branagan to Jefferson, May 7, 1805, microfilm reel 33, Jefferson Papers, LC (hdl.loc.gov/loc.mss/mtj.mtjbib014673). Branagan's book was titled *A Preliminary Essay on the Oppression of the Exiled Sons of Africa: consisting of animadversions on the impolicy and barbarity of the deleterious commerce and subsequent slavery of the human species; to which is added, a desultory letter written to Napoleon Bonaparte, anno domini 1801* (Philadelphia: Printed for the author by John W. Scott, 1806). Branagan referred to himself as "Thomas Branagan, late slave-trader" on the title page.

upon the purity of their political principles, it must be doubly important.[5]

Commencing his career as a writer of sentimental literature about slavery and African Americans, Branagan's *Preliminary Essay on the Oppression of the Exiled Sons of Africa* bemoaned the isolation of the Black subjected to the horrors of the slave trade. Historian Winthrop D. Jordan observed, "Branagan's writings offered a tear on every page." Authors who, like Branagan, expressed *sensibilité* for slaves' sufferings became popular among abolitionists in the first decades of the nineteenth century. They gained notoriety by compiling exaggerated descriptions of the atrocities perpetrated by both races in the lost French colony of Saint-Domingue.[6]

Claiming to have again converted, now to Quakerism under the influence of Anthony Benezet's writings, Branagan's views on slavery seemed close to those of Friends like John Parrish of Maryland. Parrish hoped to facilitate gradual emancipation by encouraging slaves to purchase their freedom, emulating what he thought was a frequent emancipation mode in the Spanish American colonies. Unlike Branagan, who found interracial sex in Philadelphia disgustingly frequent Parrish argued that miscegenation was unlikely in the cities because of the "natural aversion and disgust," exacerbated by slavery, which Blacks and Whites felt for each other. The racist-abolitionist Parrish hoped that, after numerous manumissions occurred, Blacks would depart voluntarily and organize a colony in the western public lands.[7]

For Branagan, slavery's continued existence betrayed American liberty. He ostentatiously observed, "The lassitude of the Citizens of both modern, as well as antient republics, in not guarding with indefatigable assiduity, the palladiums of their respective governments, was the logical cause of their premature annihilation." Slavery's presence would inevitably lead to the downfall of American republicanism, as in ancient Greece and Rome.[8]

While hinting that he would accept a gratuity (perhaps he had heard about Jefferson's reputation for generosity), Branagan preferred the more lasting

---

[5] Thomas Branagan to Jefferson, May 7, 1805, microfilm reel 33, Jefferson Papers, LC (hdl.loc.gov/loc.mss/mtj.mtjbib014673).

[6] Jordan, *White over Black*, 369; Matt Clavin, "Race, Revolution and the Sublime: The Gothicization of the Haitian Revolution in the New Republic and the Atlantic World," *Early American Studies* 5/1 (Spring 2007): 1–29; Bruce Dain, "Haiti and Egypt in Early Black Racial Discourse in the United States," *Slavery and Abolition* 14/3 (December 1993): 139–61.

[7] John Parrish, *Remarks on the Slavery of the Black People* (Philadelphia: Kimber, Conrad & Co., 1806), 41–44, quoted in Jordan, *White over Black*, 549.

[8] Thomas Branagan to Jefferson, May 7, 1805, microfilm reel 33, Jefferson Papers, LC (hdl.loc.gov/loc.mss/mtj.mtjbib014673).

assistance of a presidential blurb. "Though a poor man in a pecuniary point of view, I do not by any means solicit the least assistance in that respect," he assured him. "If you will be so kind as to give your signature, in order to facilitate the publication, it will be considered as a special favour & will be received with unfeigned gratitude." Again appealing to Jefferson's vanity and revealing his own egotism, he extravagantly praised his "work of destiny" as facilitating world revolution, something he thought Jefferson supported:

> May heaven bless & prosper you and as you have been may ever continues [*sic*] to be a patron to a work of destiny and the means of keeping the glowing taper of republicanism from being extinguished; but fanning it to a flame which will illuminate the benighted minds of the enslaved, the wretched, the degraded Sons of europe [*sic*], Asia and Africa.

He advised Jefferson to grasp posterity's gratitude by assisting him, a recent convert to abolitionism. As comrades and "friends to the liberties of the people, he assured him, "the greatest favour I can wish you is that, you may have an equal share in the affections of every individual in America & the world as you have in mine & that the Supreme being must Crown you with never fading laurels in paradise where I hope to have the ineffable pleasure of congratulating you after we drop the burthen of mortality." Concluding by pledging Jefferson his "respect & veneration," he added, "P.S. If you should feel disinclined to give your signature your order for a few copies will be thankfully received & punctually attended to."[9]

Jefferson considered it unwise for him as president to endorse an antislavery diatribe publicly. Sympathizing with Branagan's views, he employed antislavery senator George Logan of Pennsylvania as an intermediary. He wrote Senator Logan at length on this seemingly insignificant matter. "I received last night a letter from Mr. Thomas Brannagan [*sic*] 163 S. Water St., Philadelphia, asking my subscription to the work announced in the enclosed paper," he explained. "The cause in which he embarks is so holy, the sentiments he expresses in his letter so friendly that it is highly painful to me to hesitate on a compliance which appears so small." Thus, Jefferson evinced his antislavery opinions. "But that is not it's [*sic*] true character," he continued, "and it would be injurious even to his views, for me to commit myself on paper by answering his letter." As he often did with others, he argued that even to bring up the question of abolition would

[9] Ibid., received by Jefferson, May 10, 1805. For additional information on Branagan, see Beverly Tomek, "From Motives of Generosity as Well as Self-Preservation': Thomas Branagan, Colonization, and the Gradual Emancipation Movement," *American Nineteenth Century History* 6/2 (2005): 121–47.

counterproductively arouse a legion of defenders of slavery.[10] As president, he thought he should not speak on such a divisive issue, which would compromise his political authority as leader of the whole nation, especially in the slaveholding South. "I have most carefully avoided every public act or manifestation on that subject," he confessed. "Should an occasion ever occur in which I can interpose with decisive effect, I shall certainly know & do my duty with promptitude & zeal. But in the meantime it would only be disarming myself of influence to be taking small means."[11]

Unlike his actions during the years encompassing the Declaration of Independence and *Notes on Virginia*, roughly 1776–1787, which historian Gordon S. Wood calls those of the "creation of the American Republic," as president Jefferson hesitated to write publicly as an antislavery man. He accurately told critics that his *Notes*, with its medley of radical antislavery, racist, and abolitionist sentiments expressed far more articulately than any other major political figure had dared, was widely available in numerous editions (and reprinted throughout the eighteenth and nineteenth centuries, both during his lifetime and after his death).[12] By contrast, Hamilton, the Adamses, Washington, and Pickering published nothing against slavery in their lifetimes.

Describing Jefferson's brief attack on slavery in the *Summary View of the Rights of British-America* (1774), historian David Waldstreicher notes, "Jefferson was unusual in his direct condemnation of slavery."[13] This observation was even more apposite to Jefferson's wide-ranging denunciation of slavery in *Notes on Virginia*, a book whose publication he authorized, carrying him as author on the title page. It is well known that in 1787, Jefferson, claiming to be mortified by André Morellet's French translation of the book, which appeared in Paris, used that as an excuse to publish the book under his own name, in a widely available English version. Before that, he had purportedly sent two hundred copies of his original English printing, made in Paris, to people in the United States and France, including his friends John Adams and James Madison. Eager to make his work public but restrained by false modesty and perhaps fearing that his harsh attacks

---

[10] Jefferson to Jean Nicholas Déméunier, June 26, 1786, in Boyd et al., eds., *Papers of Thomas Jefferson*, 10:63.

[11] Jefferson to George Logan, May 11, 1805, in Ford, ed., *Works of Thomas Jefferson*, 9:141–42.

[12] The interested reader may check OCLC's WorldCat.org or Charles Evans, *Early American Imprints*, for easy verification that Jefferson's *Notes* were printed and reprinted in numerous editions in Boston, Philadelphia, Newark, London, and Paris throughout the late eighteenth and early nineteenth centuries. See also Ford, ed., *Works of Thomas Jefferson*, 3:313–45, for a detailed examination of *Notes*' provenance.

[13] Waldstreicher, *Slavery's Constitution*, 38.

on slavery and Virginia's undemocratic constitution might arouse Southern backlash, he waited until, encouraged by his friends Madison, Monroe, and Adams, he took steps to oversee its publication in the United States. He probably had little anxiety that his antislavery comments would arouse outrage in his home state because during the 1780s he was optimistic that Virginia and Maryland would soon abolish slavery.[14] John C. Miller ignored the evidence when he observed, "Had Jefferson had his way, the only book he ever wrote would not have been published and his opinions on slavery would not have become public knowledge during his lifetime."[15]

In fact, Jefferson was so enthusiastic about *Notes on Virginia* that he sent the Stockdale English-language edition to virtual strangers, excusing his conduct with the warning that the French translation was very poor. (However, modern scholars say that the translation was well done.) For instance, worried that the inferior French translation "might make it's [*sic*] way to your country," he sent an Italian acquaintance, who did not even know of the book's existence, the English edition, "which has been lately printed in London."[16]

In later years, Jefferson showed great pride in the book, often referring people to its pages when they asked for specific information on his views. He claimed that, except for a few areas like his previous opposition to domestic manufactures, his opinions remained the same.[17] When Jefferson originally published a limited English-language edition of *Notes* in Paris, it appeared without his name as author, but those who received it were his friends and knew his identity. After a French translation bearing his name, which he considered flawed, appeared, he did not hesitate to reprint it in English in London, with the help of publisher John Stockdale, whose work he approved.[18] His interest in publishing the controversial book is explicable by his decision during the 1780s not to return to politics, after his humiliating experience as governor of Virginia from 1779 to 1781. The rise of the Hamiltonian fiscal system, the French Revolution, and the advent of political parties, one of which he founded, precipitated his return to the political arena.

---

[14] Jefferson to Richard Price, August 7, 1785, in Boyd et al., eds., *Papers of Thomas Jefferson*, 8:356; Peden, ed., *Notes on the State of Virginia*, xix; Medlin, "Thomas Jefferson, André Morellet, and the French Version of *Notes on the State of Virginia*," 85–99.

[15] *Wolf by the Ears: Thomas Jefferson and Slavery* (New York: Free Press, 1977), 39.

[16] Jefferson to G. Clerici, August 15, 1787, in Boyd et al., eds., *Papers of Thomas Jefferson*, 12:39.

[17] Jefferson to Mr. Lithgow, January 4, 1805, microfilm reel 32, Jefferson Papers, LC (hdl.loc.gov/loc.mss/mtj.mtjbib014212).

[18] Sowerby, ed., *Catalogue*, 4:310–12, 301.

Jefferson's later public silence contrasted with his antislavery sentiments in Queries XIV and XVIII of *Notes* and the projected 1783 constitution he added as an appendix to the book's 1787 London edition. He invariably referred those who asked about his views on slavery to the comments he had made in *Notes*.[19] Jefferson's proposed constitution, which he published as an addendum to *Notes* in 1787, imposed the gradual abolition of slavery. Prohibiting the introduction of additional slaves into the state, it barred the "continuance of slavery beyond the generation which shall be living on December 31, 1800: all persons born after that day being hereby declared free." By inserting a specific, operational provision abolishing slavery in the constitution—the "fundamental law"—while most Northern states abolished slavery by means of "ordinary" legislation, Jefferson demonstrated the significance he attached to emancipation.[20]

Arguing that his support for Branagan's antislavery work would probably backfire, Jefferson defended his quiescence. Emphasizing his political pragmatism, he explained, "The subscription to a book on this subject is one of those little irritating measures, which, without advancing its end at all, would, by lessening the confidence & good will of a description of friends composing a large body [Southern Republican slaveholders], only lessen my powers of doing them good in the other great relations in which I stand to the publick." Jefferson probably had in mind such acts of his administration as the repeal of internal taxes and the Louisiana Purchase, which had been in the interest of all farmers, not only slaveholders. As president, he did nothing special to benefit slaveholders.[21]

---

[19] For example, see Jefferson to Jared Sparks, February 4, 1824, and Jefferson to James Heaton, May 20, 1826, both in Peterson, ed., *Jefferson: Writings*, 1484–87, 1516.

[20] Peden, ed., *Notes on the State of Virginia*, 214. Historians who tend to depict Jefferson as indifferent to, or supportive of slavery include David B. Davis, *The Problem of Slavery in the Age of Revolution, 1770–1823* (Ithaca: Cornell University Press, 1975), 164–84; William Cohen, "Jefferson and the Problem of Slavery," *Journal of American History* 56 (December 1969): 503–26; John P. Diggins, "Slavery, Race, and Equality: Jefferson and the Pathos of the Enlightenment," *American Quarterly* 28/2 (Summer 1976): 206–28; Conor Cruise O'Brien, "Thomas Jefferson: Radical and Racist," *Atlantic Monthly* 278/4 (October 1996): 53–74. William W. Freehling, *The Road to Disunion* (New York: Oxford University Press, 1990), 121–31, has an ambivalent view of Jefferson as a "conditional emancipator" who favored emancipation and colonization but never risked his reputation on behalf of Black liberty, always complaining that the time was not yet right to take a stand. For comparative analyses of emancipation in the North and the South, see Arthur Zilversmit, *The First Emancipation: The Abolition of Slavery in the North* (Chicago: University of Chicago Press, 1967); Freehling, *Road to Disunion*, 131–34; and Gary B. Nash, *Race and Revolution* (Lanham, MD: Madison House Books, 1990), 3–55.

[21] Jefferson to George Logan, May 11, 1805, in Ford, ed., *Works of Thomas Jefferson*, 9:141–42. As president, Jefferson preferred secrecy and confidentiality regarding statements of

Jefferson was unduly worried about the feelings of this obscure, eccentric abolitionist. Perhaps this was because Branagan shared his view that Blacks and Whites could not peacefully live together. Like Jefferson, Branagan claimed to be repulsed by Blacks' physical characteristics and favored their emancipation followed by forced deportation. As Winthrop D. Jordan, the foremost scholar on White racial attitudes in the early republic, wrote, Branagan thought that Whites would benefit from expelling the "twin evils of Negroes and slavery." Although Branagan was "the most prolific of antislavery writers," Jordan says, "[he] was appalled at the thought of permitting revengeful, oversexed, emancipated Negroes to remain in the country." Branagan hoped to resolve the hostility between Blacks and Whites by giving Blacks their own country in the Louisiana Territory, two thousand miles from White-occupied areas, ruled by Black officials chosen by the president. On the other hand, Branagan would not prohibit those degraded Whites who wanted to live with Blacks, or "who wish to be manufactured to black," as he put it, from residing in these African American sanctuaries. Branagan opposed African Americans remaining in the settled United States under any circumstances. He believed their presence endangered the success of the American democratic experiment, which, like Frances Wright and many other British expatriates, he cherished at the expense of Black equality.[22]

Although Branagan lacked any political influence, which might intimidate Jefferson, the President showed him surprising respect. He earnestly wrote Logan, "I cannot be easy in not answering Mr. Brannagan's letter, unless he can be made sensible that it is better I should not answer it; & I do not know how to effect this, unless you would have the goodness, the first time you go to Philadelphia, to see him and to enter into an explanation with him."[23] Sensing (perhaps too generously) Branagan's essential decency, Jefferson was reluctant to hurt his feelings or dissuade him from his goal. Still, now that he had achieved the pinnacle of power and popularity as president, he refused to reiterate publicly his support for so controversial an issue as the abolition of slavery, with its divergent effects on slave-holding and non-slaveholding parts of the country.

Despite its justice, exhorting the nation's representatives to adopt abolitionism would have impugned Jefferson's credibility as a national leader. Since both sections were nearly equal in power at this time, slavery was an issue that

---

his religious opinions as well as his views on the controversial topic of slavery. During his retirement, he asked his correspondents to keep his words out of the newspapers when he made controversial observations about current political events. See, e.g., Jefferson to P. H. Wendover, March 13, 1815, in Lipscomb and Bergh, eds., *Writings of Jefferson*, 14:280.

[22] Branagan, *Serious Remonstrances*, 22n., 36–37, quoted in Jordan, *White over Black*, 549; Gail Bederman, "Revisiting Nashoba: Slavery, Utopia, and Frances Wright in America, 1818–1826," *American Literary History* 17/3 (Fall 2005): 438–59.

[23] Jefferson to Logan, May 11, 1805, in Ford, ed., *Works of Thomas Jefferson*, 9:142.

endangered the Union, precisely because of its sensitivity and moral weight. North and South had always been aware of their differences, the primary one being the prevalence of slavery in the latter. To the extent that it existed, slavery was gradually being eliminated and replaced by free labor in the North. Moreover, the North was becoming increasingly commercial and industrialized while the South, at least in part because of slavery, remained dependent on agriculture. Fearing it might result in Southern secession, politicians from both sections hesitated to demand the abolition of slavery in the Southern states. Moreover, Northern merchants and factories flourished by manufacturing and exporting tobacco, cotton, sugar, and other staples produced by Southern slaves.[24]

Despite his desire to end slavery, Branagan was offensively, perhaps pathologically anti-Southern and anti-Black. In some ways he was a prototype of the North Carolina racist abolitionist Hinton Rowan Helper, whose famous *Impending Crisis of the South* (1857) expounded many of the same views.[25] Branagan's *Serious Remonstrances* charged that the freed slaves immigrating from the South to the North, especially to nearby Pennsylvania, were lazy and immoral. He insisted that Southern slaveholders had deliberately "exported" them to Philadelphia and other Northern cities, "where we have to provide for, and support them, with all their vices." The presence of these "contaminated negroes," whose departure energized the South, enervated Northern society. "They [Southerners] get the benefit, we get the trouble," Branagan argued. Branagan poetically described free Blacks' pernicious influence on the North. Slavery, he wrote, was "a large tree planted in the South, whose spreading branches extend to the North; the poisonous fruit of that tree when ripe fall[s] upon these states." In harsher words than Jefferson had used in *Notes* while expressing similar views, Branagan warned that Blacks were "the inveterate enemies of Americans." Like John Taylor of Caroline, he feared that Northern free Blacks would assist slave uprisings in neighboring states. He mistakenly cited Delaware, a border state where slavery was moribund, as a case in point.[26] In light of their immorality, which may have been the fault of

---

[24] John Richard Alden, *The First South* (Baton Rouge: Louisiana State University Press, 1961); Matthew Mason, *Slavery and Politics in the Early American Republic* (Chapel Hill: University of North Carolina Press, 2006).

[25] David Brown, "Attacking Slavery from Within: The Making of *The Impending Crisis of the South*," *Journal of Southern History* 70/3 (August 2004): 541–76.

[26] Branagan, *Serious Remonstrances,* 33–34, 92, 36. See the discussion in Melish, *Disowning Slavery in Massachusetts,* 226–27. In 1862, Delaware had only two thousand slaves (Eric Burin, *Slavery and the Peculiar Solution: A History of the American Colonization Society* [Gainesville: University Press of Florida, 2005], 162). For Taylor's ideas, see his book, *Arator: Being A Series of Agricultural Essays, Practical & Political: in Sixty-four Numbers,* 4th ed. (Petersburg: Whitworth & Yancey, 1818), and Keith M. Bailor, "John Taylor of Caroline: Continuity,

slavery, Branagan argued freed slaves should be required to settle in a part of the Louisiana Territory specially reserved for them.

Discussing Black atrocities against Whites in Saint-Domingue (which were, however, usually perpetrated by military expeditions rather than individuals' actions), Branagan predicted that freedmen in the US would soon emulate them, since they "are jealous of their liberties and would wade through seas of blood, when an opportunity would offer, to vindicate their rights." He confessed that he had been "naive" and "specious" in earlier assuring readers that free Blacks would become useful citizens once they were educated. He lamented that his home state, Pennsylvania, bordered on slave states whose slaveholders found it convenient to send their manumitted slaves there. Branagan reluctantly concluded that southern Blacks would never voluntarily leave the United States because they could easily go north to Pennsylvania and receive public assistance.[27]

Although Jefferson refused to endorse Branagan's work publicly, he possessed copies of some of his books though it is not clear whether he purchased them or received them as gifts from Branagan. The catalog of Jefferson's final library, auctioned off in 1829, listed one of Branagan's philosophical works, which was sold in a combined volume with a socialist's writings: *The Pleasures of Contemplation, being a desultory investigation of the harmonies, beauties, and benefits of nature; to which is appended Some Causes of Popular Poverty...By Dr. Cornelius C. Blatchley* (Philadelphia, 1817). Jefferson also owned Branagan's book on slavery, not only in the original gift from Branagan, but as part of a two-volumes-in-one set of Branagan's works published in 1808. He listed this in his library catalog as *Branagan on the oppression of the exiled sons of Africa* [originally published in 1804] *& Branagan's Beauties of Philanthropy*.[28]

Jefferson's reluctance to denounce Branagan's hard-core racist views indicates his acute awareness of the dark, Hobbesian side of human nature that thwarted unadulterated benevolence, even for professed abolitionists. Jefferson, like Branagan, combined a desire to abolish slavery with an insistence on deporting the freed slaves from the land where most of them were born. This schema hardly recognized their "equal rights" with their fellow citizens. Rather, it revealed that Jefferson, like Branagan, advocated it as the lesser of two evils; in other

---

Change, and Discontinuity in Virginia's Sentiments toward Slavery, 1790–1820," *Virginia Magazine of History and Biography* 75 (1967): 290–304.

[27] Branagan, *Serious Considerations*, 47–54.

[28] Branagan's *Pleasures of Contemplation* is listed in Volume 7: Jefferson's Second Library, Offered for Sale at Public Auction, February 27, 1829, Series 7: Miscellaneous Bound Volumes, Jefferson Papers, LC (hdl.loc.gov/loc.mss/mtj.mtjbib026579). *The Beauties of Philanthropy* (1808) was a theological excursion into the cyclical theory of the rise and fall of empires (James Gilreath and Douglas L. Wilson, eds., *Thomas Jefferson's Library: A Catalog with the Entries in his own Order* [Washington: Library of Congress, 1989], 56).

words, he considered it preferable to retaining the Blacks in slavery, for both Blacks and Whites.

On the other hand, Jefferson, as he implied in his letter to Logan, was ready to use presidential power to attack slavery when it was feasible. In December 1806, in his sixth annual message to Congress, Jefferson, even before the Constitution allowed, recommended that the national legislature consider prohibiting the importation of slaves as soon as possible, so that it would take effect in January 1808, the earliest date the Constitution permitted. Many Southern states had already prohibited slaves from entering their borders, even those arriving from neighboring states, because the natural reproduction of slave mothers furnished ample numbers for their exploitation. Only South Carolina continued to import slaves from Africa. Indeed, Jefferson was misleading (although the members of Congress probably knew he was exaggerating) in implying that his request was momentous, and hinting that African tribal chieftains did not eagerly participate in selling their people into bondage. He proclaimed,

> I congratulate you, fellow citizens, on the approach of the period at which you may interpose your authority, constitutionally, to withdraw the citizens of the United States from all further participation in those violations of human rights which have been so long continued on the unoffending inhabitants of Africa, and which the morality, the reputation, and the best interests of our country, have long been eager to proscribe.[29]

Probably to Jefferson's dismay, his seemingly innocuous proposal provoked a storm of controversy in Congress between the "free" and "slave" states when Congress debated the specifics of a bill prohibiting the importation of slaves from abroad. One of its provisions, introduced into the Senate by antislavery Democratic-Republican Stephen R. Bradley of Vermont, prohibited slave ships from traversing the Southern states' coasts even in the course of the domestic slave trade, on the pretext that they might be carrying slaves smuggled in from Africa or the West Indies. This section provoked members from the slave-holding states in the House of Representatives, especially Peter Early of Georgia and John Randolph of Roanoke, Virginia, into bitter opposition. They charged that the bill's covert purpose was to abolish the slave trade entirely, which Randolph denounced as unconstitutional. He suspected the measure presaged a Northern attempt to enact "universal emancipation" in the near future that would lead to the breakup of the Union. Randolph warned that the Southern people would "set the law at

---

[29] Jefferson's Sixth Annual Message to Congress, December 2, 1806, in Peterson, ed., *Jefferson: Writings*, 528; Stephen J. Goldfarb, "An Inquiry into the Politics of the Prohibition of the International Slave Trade," *Agricultural History* 68/2 (Spring 1994): 20–34; David L. Lightner, *Slavery and the Commerce Power: How the Struggle against the Interstate Slave Trade Led to the Civil War* (New Haven: Yale University Press, 2006).

defiance." In response to this barrage of unexpected opposition from Southern proslavery states' righters like Randolph (who later, as an act of "Christian charity," emancipated his slaves in his will), a House and Senate conference committee revised the provision to prohibit only small coastal slave trading ships of less than forty tons burden, which were more likely to smuggle slaves illegally. Led by Randolph and Early, the Southern members of the House of Representatives rejected this compromise as well, but they lost by a vote of 63 to 49. More than four-fifths of the Northern members supported this further curtailment of the slave trade within US borders, which went beyond the prohibiting the importation of foreign slaves; and over seventy-five percent of the Southern members opposed it.[30]

Sympathizing with Randolph's point of view, Henry Adams in his classic *History of the United States* agreed that the "coastwise prohibition cut far more deeply into the constitutional rights of slave-owners" than any of the bill's other clauses and was, in effect, an unconstitutional encroachment on the states' domestic police. Adams criticized Jefferson for letting his opposition to slavery supersede his respect for the Constitution. "[On] March 2, 1807, President Jefferson approved this alarming measure," he wrote, in a seldom-noted denunciation of Jefferson's opposition to slavery. "He at least had no constitutional scruples, and paid no attention to the scruples of others." Jefferson probably did not expect that he would have to oppose his fellow slaveholders and reject his class interests in proposing to abolish the foreign slave trade. His original message did not propose to restrict the coastal domestic slave trade. Nevertheless, he signed the bill, enacting a law that, Adams observed, "shocked the pride and threatened the property of every slave-owner in the South."[31]

Henry Adams's ostensible sympathy with slavery, a facet of his scholarship that most historians ignore, may have had something to do with his grandfather John Quincy Adams's readiness to acquiesce to the slaveholders' point of view during his active political career before losing the presidency in 1828. Although a US Senator, Adams did not participate in the debate on the slave-trade bill in 1807. While noting that it was discussed at length in Congress, he hardly mentioned it in his famous *Diary*. "I took, and intend to take, no part in the debates

---

[30] See the accounts of the congressional debate over the slave trade during Jefferson's administration in Don E. Fehrenbacher, *The Slaveholding Republic* (New York: Oxford University Press, 2001), 144–54; and Henry Adams, *History of the United States of America during the Administrations of Thomas Jefferson* (1903; repr., New York: Cambridge University Press, 1986) 842–57.

[31] Adams, *History of the United States*, 842–57, 854 (quotation).

on this subject," he wrote in his entry for January 15, 1807. His entry for January 27, 1807, merely said, "The Slave Prohibition Bill passed without a division."[32]

Jefferson's modestly antislavery measure was the only major action against human bondage initiated by a president before Lincoln's presidency.[33] It would perhaps be too much to claim that Jefferson's brief correspondence over a year before with an eccentric, not entirely respectable young Irish author influenced his action. Nevertheless, if we recall Jefferson's pledge to Logan about Branagan, that, "should an occasion ever occur in which I can interpose with decisive effect [against slavery], I shall certainly know & do my duty with promptitude & zeal," the possibility exists.[34]

---

[32] Charles Francis Adams, ed., *Memoirs of John Quincy Adams, Comprising Portions of his Diary from 1795 to 1848*, 12 vols. (Philadelphia, 1874–1877), quoted in Fehrenbacher, *Slaveholding Republic*, 384n52. As Monroe's secretary of state, John Quincy Adams's opposition to the Slave Trade Act of 1819, a major piece of antislavery legislation, was apparently motivated by political expediency. This law repealed a proslavery feature of the 1807 act that stipulated that slaves illegally imported into the United States would be confiscated and turned over to state authorities, which in most cases (in the Southern states) meant that they would be resold into slavery. The Slave Trade Act of 1819 transferred the power over the illegally imported slaves into the hands of a federal marshal, and the president was empowered to return them to Africa. For this purpose, Congress appropriated $100,000. When the American Colonization Society promptly offered to set up a West African colony for illegally imported African slaves and add to their number US free Blacks and future manumitted slaves willing to reside in Africa, Monroe favored the idea. He believed the colony would provide the Africans a sanctuary and eliminate the possibility that they might end up re-enslaved in the South, if no other means were found to return them to Africa. Adams opposed the idea, not because he believed that free Blacks should remain in the United States and struggle against slavery, but because he considered it unconstitutional for the national government to assist a private enterprise (Fehrenbacher, *Slaveholding Republic*, 153–54). (In this instance, Adams's strict constructionist view sharply contrasted with the ideas he expounded in his Inaugural Address as president in 1825, with its startling proposals for government assistance to the arts and sciences, promotion of roads and canals, a national university, and other nationalistic initiatives.)

[33] William W. Freehling, "The Founding Fathers and Slavery," *American Historical Review* 77/1 (February 1972): 81–93.

[34] Jefferson to George Logan, May 11, 1805, in Ford, ed., *Works of Thomas Jefferson*, 9:141–42.

Chapter 6

Thomas Jefferson, Thomas Law, and the "Moral Sense"

Jefferson's conception of the moral sense and the role of the social substructure in forming "virtuous" behavior changed over time. Jefferson conceived of conscience as merging innate benign feelings towards one's *semblables* with a proto-Freudian internalization of social norms and rules (the Superego). When his eleven-year-old daughter Patsy wrote him about rumors that the world was coming to an end, he told her not to worry about it, but to prepare for her personal demise by never saying or doing a "bad thing." He claimed that she would instinctively know, by the voice of "conscience," if she was about to commit a wrong act, and this would restrain her. Writing to his little girl, who was too young to feel the need to submit to the pressures of socialization, he stressed the inborn aspects more than the social derivation of conscience/moral sense. "Our maker has given us all, this faithful internal Monitor," he said, "and if you always obey it, you will always be prepared for the end of the world: or for a much more certain event which is death."[1]

During the 1780s, although he emphasized moral behavior as a byproduct of the individual's search for social approval, he thought each person should form his own opinions without fear of social rejection. As he explained to his nephew Peter Carr in 1787, discussing the existence of God, "Do not be frightened from this inquiry by any fear of its consequences. If it ends in a belief that there is no god, you will find incitements to virtue in the comfort and pleasantness you feel in its exercise, and the love of others which it will procure you." At this stage, Jefferson apparently had adopted the French philosophe Helvétius's opinion that benevolent acts sprang from the individual's self-congratulating "pleasure" in performing them, and the social approval ("love of others") he received, not from the guidance of the inborn moral sense. The demand for religious freedom that obsessed Jefferson throughout the 1770s, in his Bill for Religious Freedom and *Notes on the State of Virginia*, was rooted in his idea that reason was a vital component

---

[1] Jefferson to Martha Jefferson, December 11, 1783, in Boyd et al., eds., *Papers of Thomas Jefferson*, 6:380–81; and Peterson, ed., *Jefferson: Writings*, 784.

of morality and religion. In theological matters, Jefferson advised Peter to reject prevailing prejudices and enthusiasms, and rely on his own reason: "Your own reason is the only oracle given you by heaven, and you are answerable, not for the rightness, but uprightness of the decision," he advised.[2] Therefore, at this time, Jefferson derived the moral sense, at least in part, from individual self-gratification at social approval and the operations of reason. It was essentially an egotistical faculty.

On the other hand, Jefferson traced another aspect of the moral sense. Though present at birth, the moral sense was not essentially an innate faculty, like a later century's psychoanalytic id or ego. It was more a social construct, like the Freudian superego—a tabula rasa, waiting for its contents to be filled, molded by the individual's contacts and contracts with society. The moral sense embodied social conditioning more than the "innate sense of justice" (a complement of the call to individual[ist], self-centered rights he issued in the Declaration of Independence) he wrote about to Justice William Johnson in 1823, although the latter was among its preconditions.[3]

As early as August 1787, Jefferson hinted at this concept in his letter to Peter Carr: "Man was destined for society," he wrote. "His morality therefore was to be formed to this object. He was endowed with a sense of right and wrong merely relative to this." The moral sense, which Jefferson called "conscience," is inborn, but its content is formed and developed, like parts of the body, by the demands and norms of society as the individual gets older. "The moral sense, or conscience, is as much a part of man as his leg or arm," he wrote. "It is given to all human beings in a stronger or weaker degree," and "may be strengthened by exercise." Jefferson believed that a proper regimen of reading, such as Laurence Sterne's novels, to "encourage as well as direct your feelings," and the conscious practice of moral habits and actions would strengthen the "moral sense."[4]

---

[2] Jefferson to Peter Carr, August 10, 1787, in Koch and Peden, eds., *Life and Selected Writings*, 432–33.

[3] Jefferson to William Johnson, June 12, 1823, in Peterson, ed., *Jefferson: Writings*, 1470; Jean M. Yarbrough, "Race and the Moral Foundations of the American Republic: Another Look at the Declaration and the *Notes on Virginia*," *Journal of Politics* 53/1 (February 1991): 90–105. For an argument that emphasizes the individualist ethos within Jefferson's Declaration, see Michael Zuckert, "Founder of the Natural Rights Republic," in Thomas S. Engeman, ed., *Thomas Jefferson and the Politics of Nature* (Notre Dame: Notre Dame Press, 2000), 11–58.

[4] Jefferson to Peter Carr, August 10, 1787, in Boyd et al., eds., *Papers of Thomas Jefferson*, 12:15. He particularly recommended Sterne, a favorite author of him and his wife: "The writings of Sterne particularly form the best course of morality that ever was written" (15). On this topic, see Andrew Burstein and Catherine Mowbray, "Jefferson and Sterne," *Early American Literature* 29/1 (January 1994): 19–34.

In this same letter, Jefferson contradicted himself. He argued that morality, which even the illiterate possessed, could *not* be learned in college. "He who made us would have been a pitiful bungler if he had made the rules of our moral conduct a matter of science," Jefferson insisted. "For one man of science, there are thousands who are not." Making the extreme claim that "this sense is the true foundation of morality," he estimated that it was "given to all human beings in a stronger or weaker degree," but "may be strengthened by exercise, as may any particular limb of the body." Neither reasoning power nor an advanced education was required for exerting the moral sense in the right direction, Jefferson concluded: "This sense is submitted indeed in some degree to the guidance of reason; but it is a small stock which is required for this: even a less one than what we call Common sense. State a moral case to a ploughman and a professor. The former will decide it as well, and often better than the latter, because he has not been led astray by artificial rules." Jefferson was not only expounding the virtues of "cultivators of the earth," as was his wont but also implying a moral equivalence between the Southern slaveholder and the successful rebellious Saint Dominguan slave, who was also a *cultivateur* of the soil ("ploughman"). The "moral sense" was possessed by Haitian rebels as well as others, at least after they defeated the French, and, no longer enslaved, they achieved moral autonomy and responsibility for their actions and made their will law.[5]

Jefferson considered as "moral facts" his opposition to slavery and his simultaneous belief that it was dangerous to the slaveholder for his slaves to be immediately emancipated without providing for their departure from the country. In contrast to informational facts describing actual events, "moral facts" were opinions with universal or almost universal moral value. "I do not know that, in your situation, the opinions of your countrymen may not be as desirable to be known to you as facts," he explained to an overseas friend during the Missouri

---

[5] Jefferson to Peter Carr, August 10, 1787, in Boyd et al., eds., *Papers of Thomas Jefferson*, 12:15. Among Jefferson's most famous statements about the moral superiority of farmers to other citizens, see *Notes on Virginia*, Query XIX; Jefferson to John Jay, August 23, 1785, and Jefferson to James Madison, October 28, 1785, and December 20, 1787, all in Peterson, ed., *Jefferson: Writings*, 290–91, 818–19, 842, 918. Morton G. White, *Philosophy of the American Revolution* (New York: Oxford University Press, 1978), argues that Jefferson based his "natural rights" philosophy in the Declaration of Independence on the concept that all people possessed the "moral sense," which enabled them to determine right from wrong, and hence was a barometer of their natural equality. White asserts that Jefferson was greatly influenced by the intuitionalist ideas of Jean-Jacques Burlamaqui, which he merged with those of John Locke. By this means, according to White, Jefferson's epistemology asserted that one should employ one's reason to confirm the judgments of the moral sense.

crisis in 1820. "They constitute, indeed, moral facts, as important as physical ones to the attention of the public functionary."[6]

Jefferson's concept of "moral facts" reveals the divergence between his "moral sense" sensibility and the "perspectivism" of Friedrich Nietzsche a hundred years later. Diametrically opposed to Jefferson's notion of the "moral fact," Nietzsche (who was probably unaware of Jefferson's views) wrote, "There are no moral facts whatever. Moral judgment has this in common with religious judgment, that it believes in realities which do not exist." Nietzsche asserted, "Morality is only an interpretation of certain phenomena, more precisely a misinterpretation."[7] It is hardly likely that Jefferson would have agreed with these nihilistic statements despite his own cultural relativism: he believed in certain absolute ideas of right and wrong, such as the criminalization of murder. (It is likely that Nietzsche did also.)

The moral sense's proper "exercise" consisted of faithful obedience to society's laws and norms. As he declared to a group of friends that called to welcome him after he returned from Europe in 1790, Jefferson generally assumed that "the will of the majority" and "the Natural law of every society" were identical; they were "the only sure guardian of the rights of man" and the "holy cause of freedom." He conceded that the majority's will was fallible, that "it may sometimes err. But its errors are honest, solitary and short-lived." "Let us then, my dear friends, for ever bow down to the general reason of the society," he advised. "We are safe with that, even in its deviations, for it soon returns again to the right way."[8]

Although Jefferson might want to keep slaves and women out of political life, he did not deny them a "moral sense," as human beings who participated in society. Sociability was as natural to humans as sight, hearing, or the possession of limbs—or a heart, perhaps, since he considered that the seat of feeling. As he instructed his young nephew, "An honest heart being the first blessing, a knowing head is the second."[9]

Jefferson needed friendship. A few years after his wife's death, striving to recover from the tragedy, Jefferson, writing from Paris, begged his closest friend, James Madison, to join James Monroe as his future Virginia neighbor. "Agreeable

---

[6] Jefferson to Richard Rush, October 20, 1820, in Lipscomb and Bergh, eds., *Writings of Jefferson*, 15:283–84.

[7] Friedrich Nietzsche, *Twilight of the Idols* (Harmondsworth: Penguin, 1969), 55.

[8] Jefferson's Response to the Address of Welcome by the Citizens of Albemarle County, February 12, 1790, in Boyd et al., eds., *Papers of Thomas Jefferson*, 16:179.

[9] Jefferson to Peter Carr, August 19, 1785, in Peterson, ed., *Jefferson: Writings*, 815. See also Jefferson to James Fishback, September 27, 1809, microfilm reel 44, in Jefferson Papers, LC (hdl.loc.gov/loc.mss/mtj.mtjbib020083).

society is the first essential in constituting the happiness & of course the value of our existence," he said. If he could convince them to move closer to his Monticello estate, "I should beleive [*sic*] that life had still some happiness in store for me."[10]

In 1814, continuing to emphasize the importance of friendship and human contact in his famous letter to Thomas Law, the elderly Jefferson decided that one could teach sociability, a precondition for the "moral sense," to those who lacked it, "by [means of] education, by appeals to reason and calculation."[11] Having encountered unsociable individuals, he was ready to put the fear of God into them, in the form of the rewards and punishments of the afterlife.

Jefferson's correspondent, Thomas Law (1759–1834), was a fascinating character. An English native, Law was son of an Anglican bishop, the bishop of Carlisle, and was related to other members of the High Church aristocracy. As a fiscal official in India, he developed an impartial land tax system. Enthusiastic about George Washington and republicanism, Law decided to immigrate to the United States in 1793. He became closely acquainted with Washington and married the president's step-granddaughter in 1796. As an official of the East India Company, he had fathered three illegitimate sons with an Indian mistress. When he moved to Washington, he took two mixed-race sons with him, hoping they would meet with less discrimination than they had in England. Southern plantation owners accepted them, and they eventually attended Harvard and Yale. President Washington accepted the children into his household as well. After his marriage, Law inherited several slaves from Washington's stepson, Jackie Custis, including a few that Jackie had fathered. An opponent of slavery, Law emancipated these persons. Law lost a great deal of money in Washington, DC, real estate speculations (whose later appreciation in value made his descendants wealthy). Although a failure in business, he gained fame by his proposals for a national currency.[12]

Bankruptcy did not deter Law from writing to Jefferson, whom he addressed as an equal from his first letter in April 1801 requesting that the new president intervene to restore the capital's real estate values.[13] His May 1814 letter was

---

[10] Jefferson to James Madison, December 8, 1784, in Boyd et al., eds., *Papers of Thomas Jefferson*, 7:559. For a full-scale study of Jefferson's reliance on friendship, see Andrew Burstein, *The Inner Jefferson: Portrait of a Grieving Optimist* (Charlottesville: University Press of Virginia, 1995).

[11] Jefferson to Thomas Law, June 13, 1814, Peterson, ed., *Jefferson: Writings*, 1338.

[12] For a sketch of Law, see "Law, Thomas" in the *Dictionary of National Biography*. On his relationship with the Washingtons, see Henry Wiencek, *An Imperfect God: George Washington, His Slaves, and the Creation of America* (New York: Farrar, Straus and Giroux, 2003), 289–90.

[13] Thomas Law to Jefferson, April 12, 1801, microfilm reel 23, Jefferson Papers, LC (hdl.loc.gov/loc.mss/mtj.mtjbib009965).

enclosed with his latest book, *Second Thoughts on Instinctive Impulses* (Philadelphia, 1813), which impressed the Monticello philosopher. Hinting that he valued women's role as moral custodians, Law told Jefferson that he intended his book "to be perused by the female sex which has so much influence on man from the cradle to the grave." He cited a recent magazine article that validated his theory that a "boy of sensibility" should be treated with "encouragement and benevolence" rather than "oppression & contempt," if parents wished him to improve his school performance. Blending psychology, phrenology, and rudimentary physiology, Law noted, "The phenomena of mind are influenced by a peculiar conformation of the Brain, & also by its chemical composition, directly by the blood & indirectly by air, exercise & food." He wished to add to this "physiological" knowledge his opinion that "education" vitally stimulated the brain. "As printing disseminates moral sensations arising from moral circumstances, the human race is more & more spiritualised or operated upon by divine moral laws," he argued, causing "violations of right" to be "more execrated" by society. Confident that Jefferson was an avid student of ethics and morals, Law concluded, "[Forgive] me for claiming your attention to a subject which many persons deem unimportant, but which I am convinced is deemed by you worthy of attention."[14]

In another letter, Law recurred to ethical discourse, ostensibly inspired by the empiricist ideas expressed in a fictional preacher's "short sermon on Truth" in *Memoirs of Bryan Perdue* (1805), Englishman Thomas Holcroft's obscure novel. "Matters of fact alone meaning thereby those things which are common & subject to the examination of the senses are the only things that can be called truths, as known to man," Law believed. Human beings could not have certain knowledge of "higher truths," especially of a religious nature. To demand universal conformity to religious dogma was not only to "speaketh that which is wickedly false," the sermon continued, but to espouse "the root & wickedness of hell, for it hath at all times & among all nations, engendered the worst passions, hatred, revenge," the carnage of religious war, "fire, sword & universal destruction." Like Jefferson, Law favored religious freedom.[15]

Although Jefferson respected freedom of religion in theory, his manipulation of the concept of immortality as a fillip for potentially antisocial individuals suggests that he considered the afterlife, the fount of Christian belief, primarily as an anodyne for the masses rather than believing in its reality.[16] Although willing to employ immortality to persuade potential criminals to obey the law, a subtle

---

[14] Thomas Law to Jefferson, May 3, 1814, microfilm reel 47, Jefferson Papers, LC (hdl.loc.gov/loc.mss/mtj.mtjbib021712).

[15] Ibid.

[16] Arthur Scherr, "Thomas Jefferson, Immortality, and the Fear of Death: A Reconsideration," *Cithara* 56/1 (November 2016): 43–74.

form of disrespect for religion as "superstition," Jefferson did not view such legerdemain as violating his sacred principle of the separation of church and state. On the other hand, implying that Jefferson melded religious and secular outcomes, political scientist Jeremy D. Bailey argues that in Query XVIII of *Notes*, Jefferson based his threat that God would intervene to emancipate Southern slaves, if their masters refused to do so, on the assumption of all people's equality as "children of God."[17] However, Jefferson's threat of divine retribution in Query XVIII was unique in his corpus of writings and intended more for public consumption than as testimony to his authentic expectation of divine intervention against slavery.

On a more secular level, Bailey deplores as sacrilegious Jefferson's "suspicion" that Blacks might not be intellectually equal to Whites. If Jefferson were not convinced that all peoples had equal abilities, Bailey boldly asserts, he should not have insisted that all races should be equal before the law. Bailey overlooks Jefferson's basic assumption that equality before the law was all persons' natural right, including African Americans. For example, as Jefferson famously wrote to Henri Grégoire in 1809 defending slaves' right to freedom, "whatever be their degree of talent it is no measure of their rights. Because Sir Isaac Newton was superior to others in understanding, he was not therefore lord of the person or property of others."[18] Jefferson's tendency to manipulate the idea of immortality in order to obtain a peaceful, law-abiding society implied that he considered the desire for an afterlife characteristic of all racial groups irrespective of color, an aspect of the moral and legal equality of human beings, and of their potential intellectual equality as well.

Like Voltaire, Jefferson considered the idea of immortality helpful in keeping the masses from committing violent acts and breaking the laws. In this endeavor, Jefferson contended, religion and a prospective afterlife were shallow substitutes for an authentic moral sense, possessed by most Blacks and Whites alike, irrespective of race, vocation, or condition of servitude, as he emphasized in Query XIV of *Notes*. In later life, Jefferson conceded that the "moral sense" was not entirely innate, but also in part a matter of learning or conditioning. In addition to the idea of rewards and punishments in the afterlife for one's conduct in this one, Jefferson listed for Thomas Law several other substitutes or supplements for an absent or defective moral sense. These included fear of criminal punishment; a moral system of education that emphasized appeals to reason; the desire

---

[17] Jeremy D. Bailey, "Nature and Nature's God in *Notes on the State of Virginia*," in Christopher Nadon, ed., *Enlightenment and Secularism* (Lanham, MD: Lexington Books, 2013), 231–40, at 236–37.

[18] Ibid., 236; Jefferson to Henri Gregoire, February 25, 1809, in Peterson, ed., *Jefferson: Writings*, 1202.

for the love and approval of others and acceptance by one's society; and the cultivation of a Franklinesque, pragmatic, "Poor Richard's" outlook, with "demonstrations by sound calculation that honesty promotes interest in the long run." At the end of this somewhat seamy list, Jefferson placed belief in the afterlife as an ersatz spur to morality, implying that it was the least reliable means of installing even a superficial form of the moral sense: "ultimately the prospects of a future state of retribution for the evil as well as the good done while here."[19]

In Jefferson's most developed statement of his doctrine of the "moral sense," his letter to Thomas Law in 1814, he acclaimed Law's book, *Second Thoughts on Instinctive Impulses* (1813), as best reflecting his current opinions. It "contained exactly my own creed on the foundation of morality in man," he asserted. Law sent Jefferson the book, which Jefferson read en route to Poplar Forest from Monticello. Jefferson professed surprise at the "variety of opinions" on morality Law discussed. But he was comforted by the thought that "the Creator" made the "moral principle so much a part of our constitution as that no errors of oeconomy or of speculation might lead us astray from its observance in practice." Insisting on his belief in God, Jefferson was relieved that atheists, who rejected God, could be moral individuals. Therefore, contrary to some arguments, the love of God was not the true root of morality, nor was the aesthetic concept of "the beautiful."[20]

Complaining that Cardinal Wollaston was too "whimsical" in defining love of "*truth* as the foundation of morality," Jefferson viewed him as, in a sense, putting the cart before the horse; truth could not be considered "the foundation of morality." Moreover, that morality and kindness emanated solely from one's "*love of God*," he observed, was refuted by the presence of moral atheists. He specifically mentioned French atheists, such philosophes as Diderot, d'Holbach, and Condorcet, "known to have been among the most virtuous of men." He denied that "taste"— artistic, poetic, or aesthetic values—was synonymous with morality or the "moral faculty." In Jefferson's reasoning, no moral relationship could exist with oneself; that was mere "egoism," antisocial and amoral. A critic might ask: How could a "moral sense" exist at birth, if human consciousness did not really exist until a baby was eight months old? On the other hand, if morality was inborn, shouldn't one have a moral relationship with oneself first of all?[21]

Since Jefferson asserted that God was the source of the moral sense, and that "the Creator" made the "moral principle...a part of our constitution," some critics

---

[19] Jefferson to Thomas Law, June 13, 1814, in Peterson, ed., *Jefferson: Writings*, 1338.

[20] Thomas Law to Jefferson, May 3, 1814; Jefferson to Thomas Law, June 13, 1814, in Peterson, ed., *Jefferson: Writings*, 1337.

[21] Jefferson to Thomas Law, June 13, 1814, in Lipscomb and Bergh, eds., *Writings of Jefferson*, 14:141.

might have thought it contradictory for him to assert that atheists could have a fully developed moral sense. Contrary to some arguments, he said, the love of God was not the root of morality, nor was the aesthetic concept of "the beautiful." The innate, "natural" love of one's fellow beings (similar to what Adam Smith called "sympathy" and Rousseau called "compassion") inspired "these good acts" toward others "because nature hath implanted in our breasts a love of others, a sense of duty to them, a moral instinct, in short, which prompts us irresistibly to feel and to succor their distresses." Contrary to the renowned philosophe Helvétius, he said, instinct, rather than "self-interest," "egoism," or "self-love," inspired kindly acts.[22]

Jefferson argued that "egoism" or "self-love" was not the root of morality, but its enemy. "Take from man his selfish propensities, and he can have nothing to reduce him from the practice of virtue," concluded Jefferson, who was himself egotistical though he would not admit it. Although substantial, Jefferson's approval of the empiricist philosophe Helvétius's book *De l'ésprit* was qualified: he agreed with him to the limited extent that one's pleasure at being kind to others is a source of morality. "These good acts give us pleasure, but how happens it that they give us pleasure?" he queried Law. It was because nature "hath implanted in our breasts a love of others, a sense of duty to them, a moral instinct, in short." Thus, the impulsions of "instinct" (similar to what would later be called "human nature") rather than "self-interest," as Helvétius had argued, inspired kindly acts.[23]

Hence, Jefferson claimed that "nature" planted morality in people from birth; he simultaneously attributed this activity to God. The simplest explanation for this discrepancy is that Jefferson, like Bolingbroke, pantheistically regarded the "laws of nature and nature's God" as virtually identical.[24]

According to Jefferson, selfishness could be "subdued" by "education, instruction or restraint," to grant virtue supremacy. Although praising Helvétius (whom he never met) as "one of the best men on earth," Jefferson deplored his idea that virtuous acts were founded on self-interest because they made us feel

---

[22] Thomas Law to Jefferson, May 3, 1814; Jefferson to Thomas Law, June 13, 1814, in Peterson, ed., *Jefferson: Writings*, 1337.

[23] Ibid.

[24] Jefferson's original rough draft of the preamble to the Declaration of Independence, which refers to Americans' right to "assume among the powers of the earth the equal & independant [*sic*] station to which the laws of nature & of nature's god entitle them" indicates Bolingbroke's influence. See also Douglas L. Wilson, "Jefferson and Bolingbroke: Some Notes on the Question of Influence," in Garrett Ward Sheldon and Daniel L. Dreisbach, eds., *Religion and Political Culture in Jefferson's Virginia* (Lanham, MD: Rowman and Littlefield, 2000), 112–13; and Harold Hellenbrand, *The Unfinished Revolution: Education and Politics in the Thought of Thomas Jefferson* (Newark: University of Delaware Press, 1990).

better about ourselves. He quoted Helvétius's masterpiece, *De l'ésprit,* which argued that the virtuous man, nauseated by the sight of misery, consequently acting to eliminate the "spectacle," "is forced to succor the unfortunate object." Perhaps considering Helvétius's explanation too immediatist, too much based on the sensations of the moment, Jefferson corrected concepts he may have considered insufficiently profound. Rather than being rooted in "self-interest," benevolent action was the product of an intrinsic discrimination between good and evil. In words similar to those he wrote his nephew Peter Carr twenty-seven years earlier, he reiterated, "The Creator would indeed have been a bungling artist had he intended man for a social animal, without planting in him social dispositions."[25] Assisted by the growth of the rational faculty, these innate "social dispositions" further matured and evolved through human interaction with other members of society.

Although Jefferson criticized the banality of Helvétius's view that "egoism & self-interest" were the "basis of morality," his own concept of morality, primarily a social one, was shallow at its core: "I consider our relations with others as constituting the boundaries of morality."[26]

On the other hand, Jefferson was aware that many individuals had criminal—what we might call today "psychopathic" or "sociopathic"—propensities. He merely considered them exceptions to his general rule of human sociability and benevolence. Those born without moral (i.e., social) feelings, analogous to the sensory deficiencies of the deaf or blind, may sometimes be taught the moral sense that others innately possess, or they can be shown its practical advantages in terms of getting ahead in daily life. (Unfortunately, we cannot identify these psychopaths as easily as we do the innately deaf and blind.) By acting decently, one obtained love, popularity, social acceptance: this was the idea that "honesty promotes interest in the long run." Other social deterrents to evildoing were an awareness of legal penalties and the belief in a future state of rewards and punishments. The agents of these edifying functions, which for some individuals artificially replaced a weak inborn moral sense, are "the moralist, the preacher, and legislator," Jefferson said, realistically if rather cynically.[27]

---

[25] Jefferson to Law, June 13, 1814, in Lipscomb and Bergh, eds., *Writings of Jefferson,* 14:142. See also Jefferson to Peter Carr, August 10, 1787, in Boyd et al., eds., *Papers of Thomas Jefferson,* 12:14–15.

[26] Jefferson to Thomas Law, June 13, 1814, in Lipscomb and Bergh, eds., *Writings of Jefferson,* 14:138–44, 139–40, 140 (quotation). See also the definitive compilation of Jefferson's writings (available in fewer libraries because of its high price), Looney, ed., *Jefferson Papers: Retirement Series,* 7:412–16.

[27] Jefferson to Law, June 13, 1814, in Lipscomb and Bergh, eds., *Writings of Jefferson,* 14:143.

Further grounding the moral sense in traits of socialization and social conformity, Jefferson observed, "The same actions are deemed virtuous in one country and vicious in another," because "nature has constituted *utility* to man the standard and test of virtue." Unfortunately, Jefferson did not explain or provide any examples of what he meant by this dictum. Perhaps he had Montaigne's cannibals in mind. Cannibalism was a social trait seldom found in western European societies but considered acceptable under certain wartime conditions by Montaigne's Brazilian Indians (and, as Voltaire wrote in *Candide* and elsewhere, Europeans might also resort to *anthropophage* in times of siege). Seemingly, for Jefferson it all boiled down to our modern-day aphorism, "when in Rome do as the Romans do": "Men living in different countries, under different circumstances, different habits and regimens, may have different utilities; the same act, therefore, may be useful, and consequently virtuous in one country, which is injurious and vicious in another differently circumstanced," he wrote.[28]

Did such "useful acts" include the horrors of genocide, slavery, and female genital mutilation, which rulers and people in "different countries" had approved at various times and places for centuries after Jefferson's death? Such actions seemed to violate the moral sense and the natural rights of every individual.[29] Jefferson would have rejected such ideas in theory and practice, especially since he seldom rendered obeisance to social conformity in the real world. He would have considered governments that pursued such activities, and their citizens, as perverting the moral sense and abandoning human decency for the amoral advancement of their own short-term interests.

Jefferson would have considered murder and genocide as opposed to the moral sense and natural law and therefore impermissible because they violate his definition of liberty as doing anything not harmful to others.[30] He would also have noticed that such amoral acts, even if certain perverse societies and religions extolled them, were objectionable because they ultimately threatened the well-being of society as a whole. Pondering such matters after retiring from the presidency, he continued to dismiss the mumbo-jumbo of various theological dogmas. He satisfied himself with the conclusion that, "Reading, reflection & time have

[28] Ibid., 1338 (italics in original). See also Lipscomb and Bergh, eds., *Writings of Jefferson*, 14:143.

[29] For a recent defense of female genital mutilation that argues that women in the West African and Muslim societies that practiced it endorsed it as making them feel more "womanly" and more assimilated into their culture, see Richard A. Shweder, "What about 'Female Genital Mutilation'? And Why Understanding Culture Matters in the First Place," *Daedalus* 129/4 (Fall 2000): 209–33.

[30] Jefferson to François D'Ivernois, February 6, 1795, and Jefferson to Démeunier, April 29, 1795, in Peterson, ed., *Jefferson: Writings*, 1024, 1027–28.

convinced me that the interests of society require the observation of those moral precepts only in which all religions agree (for all forbid us to murder, steal, plunder, or bear false witness). These are the articles necessary for the preservation of order, justice, & happiness in society." This was a rather short list; if Jefferson thought more seriously about it, he would have probably included a greater number of crimes.[31]

Unfortunately, Jefferson's rhetoric in such statements as his letters to Law and Fishback was susceptible to another, disconcerting interpretation: that in his mind, in certain public, social matters that involved implementing the "moral sense," natural rights potentially took a backseat to a social conformity he considered odious in his personal life. In theory, even the horrendous institution of human slavery, which was widely practiced in Jefferson's plantation society, and by Jefferson himself, might fall under the broad umbrella of "*utility* to man."[32]

Strangely, Jefferson's words quoted above, if taken out of context without reference to Jefferson's life and thought, recommended a kind of totalitarian democracy. This seeming aberration in his thought seems to flow from his regard for the "will of the majority" as a moral absolute; as he said in his inaugural address, "have we found angels in the form of kings to govern him [the voter]?" Of course, as he said in that same great address, he always believed, "that will to be rightful must be reasonable; that the minority possess their equal rights, which equal law must protect, and to violate would be oppression." Nevertheless, Jefferson did not always appreciate how his "universalist" belief in the sanctity of the majority's will potentially conflicted with his other, more basic, inventory of universal rights. These included the right of all minorities, political, religious, gender, ethnic, etc., to think and express their ideas, religious and/or secular, in complete freedom and equality without intimidation from government or majorities, which sometimes, as in various pogroms, lynchings, and genocides throughout history, became virtual "mobs." On several occasions, as in his famous letter to Adams on "natural aristocracy," he based the (White male) voter's political competence on the United States' agrarian ambience, where, in his opinion, ample farmland existed for all, and "every one, by his property, or by his satisfactory situation," had a stake in society and in obeying the laws. Contented with their economic plenitude and equality of opportunity, Americans could be trusted with a "wholesome controul over their public affairs, and a degree of freedom, which in the hands of the Canaille of the cities of Europe, would be instantly perverted to the

[31] Jefferson to James Fishback, (draft), September—1809, in Looney, ed., *Jefferson Papers: Retirement Series*, 1:564. Not knowing who Fishback was, Jefferson did not mail this letter but sent a much shorter, more innocuous message.

[32] See, e.g., Cohen, "Jefferson and the Problem of Slavery," 503–26.

demolition and destruction of every thing public and private."[33] Ensconced in their agricultural cornucopia, Jefferson implied, Americans' English constitutional heritage of limited government and good luck in having a large land supply, rather than any innate political genius explained their success in self-rule when compared with other peoples.

Among Jefferson's other fundamental natural rights (for free persons) was the right to the fruits of their labor, without "obstruction" from other members of society and minimal taxes and financial harassment by government institutions, whose corruption and alienation from the people were measurable by the amount of their extortions.[34] He expressed this idea most succinctly in his first inaugural address, defining "a wise and frugal Government, which shall restrain men from injuring one another, shall leave them otherwise free to regulate their own pursuits of industry and improvement, and shall not take from the mouth of labor the bread it has earned," as "the sum of good government."[35]

---

[33] First inaugural address, March 4, 1801, in Peterson, ed., *Jefferson: Writings*, 492–93; Jefferson to John Adams, October 28, 1813, ibid., 1309.

[34] Jefferson to Du Pont, April 24, 1816, in Ford, ed., *Works of Thomas Jefferson*, 11:523.

[35] Jefferson's First Inaugural Address, March 4, 1801, in Peterson, ed., *Jefferson: Writings*, 494. See also Johann N. Neem, "Developing Freedom: Jefferson, the State, and Human Capability," *Studies in American Political Development* 27/1 (April 2013): 36–50. Neem's basic thesis is simple: Jefferson's lifetime goal was to remove artificial, government-imposed barriers to equal opportunity and level life's playing field. Less convincingly, Neem claimed that Jefferson hoped that the State "would provide citizens opportunities to enjoy their freedom" and "realize their potential" (49–50). This latter phrase evokes Aristotle's concept of the Good Life or psychologist Abraham Maslow's ideology of "self-actualization" more than anything that Jefferson advocated. To the extent that Jefferson voiced a concept of the ideal life, it was in his embarrassingly simple view that small farmers were the happiest individuals, God's "chosen people," and "the most precious part of a state" (*Notes*, Query XIX, and Jefferson to Madison, October 28, 1785, in Peterson, ed., *Jefferson: Writings*, 290, 842). Neem argues that Jefferson's rejected proposal for public land redistribution among the landless, his bills for religious freedom and grammar school education for all, and his support for "internal improvements" (federal building of interstate roads and canals) were measures by which Jefferson believed government would enable people to realize their potential. They were, respectively, means to achieve widespread suffrage (by satisfying Virginia's property requirement of twenty-five acres of cultivated land for voters), a modicum of literacy, economic independence, and the right to freedom of thought for all. They might embody preconditions for "happiness," the minimum that individuals had the right to expect from government, but they hardly comprised the State's active attempt to "develop each individual's faculties—his or her potential as a citizen and human being," that Neem claims (50). Neem again demonstrates his tendency to expound interpretations *a priori* without basing them on Jefferson's views when he asserts that, "in the case of African Americans he justified inequality by citing African Americans' lack of opportunity as proof of inferiority" (46). Jefferson never said anything so illogical; as we have seen (e.g., Jefferson to Short, September 8, 1823, in Lipscomb and Bergh, eds., *Writings of Jefferson*, 15:469–70 [also

Jefferson's belief in the theoretical omnipotence of the people hardened with age. He denounced the unelected federal judiciary's undemocratic "usurpation" of the powers of the states and over competing branches of the national government in determining which laws and actions were constitutional. He insisted that the people themselves, preferably in representative national conventions, possessed virtually unlimited authority. It was "an axiom of eternal truth in politics," he explained in to Judge Spencer Roane in 1819, "that whatever power in any government is independent, is absolute also.... Independence can be trusted nowhere but with the people in mass. They are inherently independent of all but moral law."[36] And morality, according to Jefferson, was an integral "part of our [physical] constitution."[37]

microfilm reel 53, Jefferson Papers, LC [hdl.loc.gov/loc.mss/mtj.mtjbib024751], and Jefferson to Frances Wright, August 7, 1825, in Lipscomb and Bergh, eds., *Writings of Jefferson*, 16:120), he argued exactly the opposite: that slavery and (what he considered) the primitive conditions of Africa hindered Blacks from realizing their potential, even as freedpersons. More convincing is Boorstin's argument in *Lost World of Thomas Jefferson* that Jefferson did not consider it government's role to define "ends" for society or individuals, but rather to allow each person to decide what they wanted to do with their life, as the laws of nature directed.

[36] Jefferson to Judge Spencer Roane, September 6, 1819, in Ford, ed., *Writings of Thomas Jefferson*, 10:141. In 1801, during the crisis precipitated by the electoral tie between Jefferson and Aaron Burr and the ensuing decision in the House of Representatives, Jefferson several times asserted his confidence that a popularly elected convention, as the highest sovereign authority, was best equipped to settle the disputed contest. See, e.g., Jefferson to Joseph Priestley, March 21, 1801, in Koch and Peden, eds., *Life and Selected Writings*, 563.

[37] Jefferson to Thomas Law, June 13, 1814, in Peterson, ed., *Jefferson: Writings*, 1337.

Chapter 7

Thomas Jefferson, Thomas Law, and Moral Sense Applications in Politics and Society: "The Earth Belongs to the Living"

As a slave-owner, Jefferson generally combined pragmatic matters of profit with kindness and humanity, in accordance with his "moral sense" views. This application of what Alexis de Tocqueville later called "enlightened self-interest" may have been the result of his general philosophy of ethics and metaphysics, as he developed it throughout his life.

Replying to arguments that Nature had not specifically labeled virtuous and vicious acts and that there was no consensus between different countries about what behavior was good or evil, Jefferson offered a nebulous answer. Although he assumed that all cultures regarded murder and robbery as wicked, he admitted, "We find, in fact, that the same actions are deemed virtuous in one country and vicious in another." Without citing an example (although he may have had the institution of slavery in mind, which was not useful in the "country" of the northern United States), he explained to the budding moral philosopher Thomas Law that men in different countries, with diverse habits and circumstances, had "different utilities": varying criteria for what was useful to their society's members.[1]

After expounding this precocious view of cultural (and moral) relativism, Jefferson backtracked to a more rationalist, universalist, Enlightenment schema. He joined Law in expounding one of his own favorite concepts, "the general existence of a moral instinct," "the brightest gem with which the human character is studded." The lack of it was "degrading" to an individual. Recurring to the teachings of Lord Kames, he noted that he and many other philosophers upheld the existence of an innate moral sense. However, Jefferson criticized Kames's

---

[1] Jefferson to Thomas Law, June 13, 1814, in Lipscomb and Bergh, eds., *Writings of Jefferson*, 14:143. See also John H. Schaar, "...And the Pursuit of Happiness," *Virginia Quarterly Review* 46/1 (Winter 1970): 1–26. For Jefferson's excoriation of murder, see Jefferson to James Fishback, September 27, 1809, microfilm reel 44, in Jefferson Papers, LC (hdl.loc.gov/loc.mss/mtj.mtjbib020083), and Looney, ed., *Jefferson Papers: Retirement Series*, 1:563–66. This letter has been discussed above.

Principles of Natural Religion for being too optimistic in claiming that an "impulsive feeling" spurred individuals to perform their duties. Considering himself less idealistic, Jefferson asserted that such a generalization about public and personal obligations might apply more readily to an entire society than to a single person: "This is correct, if referred to the standard of general feeling in the given case, and not to the feeling of a single individual," he commented. "Perhaps I may misquote him, it being fifty years since I read his book."[2] Anticipating David Reisman's "other-directed individual" of *The Lonely Crowd*, Jefferson apparently thought that Kames inadequately appreciated the role social conformity played in many aspects of individual behavior.

By the time he died, Jefferson had concluded that no infallible means existed to define good or bad human actions in all times and places, what Immanuel Kant would call a "universal law." In his most careful analysis of morality, his letter to Thomas Law in 1814, he said, in a statement already quoted, "The same actions are deemed virtuous in one country and vicious in another," because "nature has constituted *utility* to man the standard and test of virtue. Men living in different countries, under different circumstances, different habits and regimens, may have different utilities. The same act, therefore, may be useful, and consequently virtuous, in one country, which is injurious and vicious in another differently circumstanced." On this basis, Jefferson criticized Lord Kames, charging that he had assumed that "moral sense" was properly definable by reference to the views of a single individual. Jefferson, indirectly mimicking Jean-Jacques Rousseau's General Will, now argued that "the standard of general feeling" within the community was the best determinant of right and wrong.[3]

---

[2] Jefferson to Thomas Law, June 13, 1814, in Lipscomb and Bergh, eds., *Writings of Jefferson*, 14:144. On Jefferson's reading of Lord Kames, see Adrienne Koch, *The Philosophy of Thomas Jefferson* (New York: Columbia University Press, 1943), and Sheehan, *Seeds of Extinction*, 22–32. Jefferson was referring to Kames's *Essays on the Principles of Morality and Natural Religion; with other Essays concerning the proof of a Deity* (Edinburgh: R. Fleming, for A. Kincaid and A. Donaldson, 1751).

[3] Jefferson to Thomas Law, June 13, 1814, in Peterson, ed., *Jefferson: Writings*, 1338–39. Ari Helo and Peter Onuf, "Jefferson, Morality, and the Problem of Slavery," *William and Mary Quarterly* 60/3 (July 2003), 571–98, has much stimulated my thought on the moral sense. It contains a useful explanation of Lord Kames's ideas, which intrigued Jefferson in his youth. Several scholars have emphasized Jefferson's admiration for Lord Kames's version of moral sense theory and faculty psychology. Despite his belief in the moral sense, Lord Kames was a polygenist and argued for inherent Black inferiority and a separate creation of the races. For Kames's influence on Jefferson, albeit not specifically in racial matters, see Jay Fliegelman, *Declaring Independence: Jefferson, Natural Language, and the Culture of Performance* (Redwood City: Stanford University Press, 1993); Koch, *Philosophy of Jefferson*, 17–19, 29, 45, 52; Jean Yarbrough, "Jefferson and Property Rights," in Ellen Frankel Paul, ed., *Liberty, Property, and the*

Writing to Thomas Law, expounding his most developed views on the "moral sense" or "moral instinct," he called "Lord Kaims" "one of the ablest advocates" of the moral sense concept. However, he went on to criticize Kames for ostensibly propounding the view that each individual, rather than the "community," ought to determine what was right and wrong. Jefferson may have misinterpreted Kames's views in *Essays on Morality and Natural Religion* since in his classic, *Elements of Criticism*, a book Jefferson owned for many years, Lord Kames said that a single standard of literary "taste" or excellence existed, valid for humanity as a whole. It was derived from a universal "sense or conviction of a common nature, not only in our own species but every species." This viewpoint seems at variance with Jefferson's ascription to Kames of an individualist doctrine wherein each person's morality was equally valid, although Kames's universalist assumption of one "correct" standard of excellence contradicted the cultural relativism Jefferson expounded in his letter to Thomas Law and elsewhere later in life.[4]

By contrast, some of Lord Kames's colleagues in the Scottish "common sense" or moral sense school, among them Adam Ferguson, expounded ideas of cultural relativism long before Jefferson, and may have influenced the Virginian. In his *Principles of Moral and Political Science*, published in 1792, for instance, Ferguson developed the idea that proper, "polite" customs varied depending on one's country, degree of social exposure, or ethnographic group. "Where societies differ in point of manners, on whichever side the advantage of superior intelligence may lie, persons of the best disposition may appear defective in politeness, where the manner of shewing [*sic*] it is not familiar to them," he was certain, "but this no more incapacitates the peasant for politeness in the city, than the citizen for politeness in the country." They merely had to learn the customs of the country by living in it. Consequently, a well-bred gentleman was tolerant of those unfamiliar with his milieu's mores and customs. "If the peasant appears rustic in the town," Ferguson asserted, "the citizen [i.e., townsman] may appear frivolous, ignorant or affected in the country; and of the two that person is most deficient in breeding, who is furthest gone in the mistake, that the local habits of a society

---

Foundations of the American Constitution (Albany: State University of New York Press, 1989), 65–83; Helo and Onuf, "Jefferson, Morality, and the Problem of Slavery"; Sheehan, *Seeds of Extinction*, 24, 27–30.

[4] Jefferson to Thomas Law, June 13, 1814, in Peterson, ed., *Jefferson: Writings*, 1338–39; Kames, *Elements of Criticism* (1762), quoted in Fliegelman, *Declaring Independence*, 74.

to which he himself is accustomed, are the standards of good manners to mankind."[5]

Ferguson continued his panegyric to cultural diversity by upholding the Kantian dictum that one's intentions are what count, and that if they are pure, one is virtuous (in Ferguson's phrase, "polite"). "The real standard of manners, as far as it can be collected from external expressions, is the ingenuity, candour, and disposition to oblige, from which these manners proceed," he asserted.[6] Deploring the burgeoning culture of capitalist competition as invidious to his vaunted, rather aristocratic ethos of genteel "politeness," Ferguson denounced those who were only "conscientious" in matters when they stood to profit at others' expense. He argued that this was not good manners, but hypocrisy: "In societies where men are taught to consider themselves as competitors, and every advantage they gain as comparative to that of some other person, the conscientious may be faithful and true to his engagements, in what he is pleased to think matters of real concern; but the emulation in which he has been nursed is a fretful passion, and politeness, under its influence, cannot be any other than the effect of disguise." Despising those capitalistic businessmen of "ordinary society" who put a dollar sign on everything and demurred at helping their fellow man, Ferguson said, "The interested and sordid make no allowance for good or ill offices that neither fill nor empty the pocket. With such persons as these, even virtue itself is illiberal, and kindness unmannerly."[7]

Deploring the selfish habits of "ordinary society," Ferguson preferred the company of the genteel, who did not exhibit "an affected indifference, or real insensibility" to the needs of others. Understating his admiration for "the offices of mere good breeding," he admitted that politeness was most often found among the rich ("the higher ranks of life"), who cultivated it as part of their social code.

[5] Adam Ferguson, *Principles of Moral and Political Science*, 2 vols. (Edinburgh: W. Creech, 1792), 2:375–76. For some observations on Jefferson's opinion of the Scottish "moral sense" philosophers, his failure to adequately acknowledge their influence upon his thought, and his reluctance to consider the Scottish philosophers separately from the generality of European Enlightenment *philosophes*, see Gilman M. Ostrander, "Jefferson and Scottish Culture," *Historical Reflections* 5/2 (Winter 1978): 233–48.

[6] Ferguson, *Principles of Moral and Political Science*, 2:376. There is no evidence that Kant influenced Ferguson, however.

[7] Ibid. For an incisive depiction of the importance of politeness and good manners in eighteenth-century American society's transition from aristocracy to republicanism, followed by democracy and individualism, see Wood, *Radicalism of the American Revolution*, and Richard L. Bushman, *The Refinement of America* (New York: Alfred A. Knopf, 1992). For a European emphasis, see Peter Gay, *The Enlightenment: An Interpretation: Vol. 2: The Science of Freedom* (New York: Knopf, 1969).

On the other hand, Ferguson argued, even a "savage" could be polite, if imbued with a "passion for the real and superior distinctions of courage and fortitude."[8] An avid reader of Ferguson, Adam Smith, and other "common sense" philosophers, Jefferson admired Ferguson's work. A copy of the second edition of his great *Essay on the History of Civil Society* (1768) was in the library he sold to Congress in 1815.[9] Ferguson's work may have further stimulated Jefferson's moral relativism.

Law shared Jefferson's admiration for Lord Kames and was conversant with his writings. He cited Kames in an earlier book, *Thoughts on Instinctive Impulses*, published in 1810. In this work, as in *Second Thoughts*, he claimed to be writing "a composition for a lady," viewing women as the appropriate purveyors of morality and the moral sense. In the 1810 volume, more arcane than its successor, Law hoped to construct rational laws of ethical behavior.[10]

Adopting views akin to those of Rousseau's *Discourse on the Origin of Inequality*, which Jefferson himself reiterated in different form in several letters, Law argued that man feels spurred to increase his knowledge only when stimulated by the emotion of "social feeling." He admitted that some men behaved unethically and xenophobically (e.g., Englishmen tended to be anti-French). Nevertheless, he insisted, "God is love," while (perhaps inadvertently) quoting the atheistic communist, Abbé de Mably's words that one finds the rules of morality in his own heart.[11] Jefferson complemented Mably's stance with his view that the innate germ of moral sense is nourished most by one's moral social actions.

Law sent Jefferson the earlier treatise in November 1810. In a letter included with the book, Law flatteringly wrote, "The accompanying may perhaps afford amusement during a leisure hour at Monticello, I should be happy if I could contribute a moment of pleasure to one who has rendered millions happy & promoted principles which have averted calamities." A few weeks later, Law reminded Jefferson, "I did myself the pleasure of forwarding to you my Pamphlet on Instinctive impulses." Jefferson took his time reading the book. On January 15, 1811, he replied from Monticello, "An absence from home of some length [probably at his Bedford County estate, Poplar Forest, ninety miles west of

---

[8] Ferguson, *Principles of Moral and Political Science*, 2:376–77. Allan Silver, "Friendship in Commercial Society: Eighteenth-Century Social Theory and Modern Sociology," *American Journal of Sociology* 95/6 (May 1990): 1474–504, esp. 1484–87, misreads Ferguson's statements as an attack on pre-commercial, Old Regime social mores, when it was more the opposite.

[9] Sowerby, ed., *Catalogue*, 3:20–21.

[10] Thomas Law, *Thoughts on Instinctive Impulses* (Philadelphia: Jane Aitken, 1810), iii–iv.

[11] Ibid., 5. For Jefferson's espousal of a Rousseauist socioeconomic creed, see his letter to Madison, October 28, 1785, in Peterson, ed., *Jefferson: Writings*, 841–42.

Monticello] has prevented my sooner acknoleging [*sic*] the receipt of your letter covering the printed pamphlet which the same absence has as yet prevented me from taking up, but which I know I shall read with great pleasure."[12]

Indulging in theological speculation despite his later volume's warnings against religious dogma, Law argued that people should not blame God for human intemperance and suffering. To make God responsible is to incriminate God and deny individuals freedom of will. Divine Providence was essentially kind; God's "despotism" should not be stressed at "the expense of his benevolence." "Our sufferings natural and moral" are the "consequences of freedom of the will," Law insisted.

Even more than Jefferson did, Law relied on Lord Kames, whom he often quoted, as in the following: "Wisely is it ordered and agreeably to the system of Providence, that we should have nature for our instructor." With Kames, he believed that "color, figure, & motion" constituted "external signs of passion" that help us understand others. Indulging in semiotic analysis, Law pointed out that while the "arbitrary signs" conveyed by words were not universally the same, the expressions on an individual's face when experiencing certain emotions, which one communicated to others, were universal. Quoting Lord Kames, he cited such other major secular thinkers as Locke, the poet Sir William Jones, Alexander Pope, and the Philadelphia epidemiologist Dr. Thomas Beddoes, to help prove his point that infants are able to "read" the emotions of others "intuitively" in their facial expressions.[13]

On the other hand, Law was unconvinced by Locke's argument that we can know the rules of morality by means of our reason and the Idea of a Supreme Being. Law believed that most people acted out of passion and pursued evil even when reason warned against it. Echoing Adam Smith, Law mentioned the empathic power of "sympathy" in inspiring human benevolence; the moral sense: "Men may by reason conceive the pangs of childbirth, but woman more sensibly owns a sympathetic emotion."[14] Physical desires and sensations had priority over reasoning: "Pleasures and pains must be felt before we can deliberate about them,"

---

[12] Thomas Law to Jefferson, letter received November 14, 1810, Law to Jefferson, December 22, 1810, and Jefferson to Law, January 15, 1811, in Sowerby, ed., *Catalogue*, 3:323. Surprisingly, Law's *Second Thoughts*, which Jefferson read and which occasioned his famous letter of June 13, 1814, is not listed in Sowerby. Perhaps Jefferson did not sell the book to Congress, or he may have lost it or given it to someone. It is not listed in Nathaniel Poor's *Catalogue* of Jefferson's final library, auctioned off in 1829 after his death (*Catalogue of President Jefferson's Library. A Catalogue of the extensive and valuable library of the late President Jefferson* [Washington, DC: Gales and Seaton, 1829]).

[13] Law, *Thoughts on Instinctive Impulses*, 13.

[14] Ibid., 17.

Lord Kames said. Espousing a strict Lockean sensationalism, Kames argued that the economy of nature dictated that our "first impressions" of others were most powerful. If "objects continue to affect us as deeply as at first," he observed, "the mind would be totally engrossed with them and have no room left either for action or reflection."[15]

Law stressed that without the prior existence of the senses and passions, reason would lack raw materials for deriving ideas of right and wrong. Our "instincts" tell us what moral information we need to know: "Without pleasures and pains and instinctive emotions and impulses, what could operate upon us but force?" Law rhetorically queried. This contrasted with Locke's claim that "morality [was] among the sciences capable of demonstration" by reason, as much as was mathematics. Nevertheless, Law himself hoped that "ultimately ethical propositions will be as clearly ascertained as any in Euclid."[16]

Less optimistic than Jefferson about the moral sense's guiding power, Law endorsed Helvétius's hedonism and fear of public disapproval as spurs to virtuous conduct. He asserted, "Without the emotions which produce aversion to wrong, and without a fear of forfeiting the esteem and of incurring the displeasure of others, and the apprehension of future punishment [by God], &c., a man would not be restrained from violating another's right, and would only calculate the risque of legal punishment, and encounter it as a sailor hazards the dangers of the ocean." While admitting a role for reason in setting up individual moral boundaries, Law, like the neo-Lockean, Burlamaqui, argued that reason acted only in conjunction with emotions, "instinctive feelings," that existed prior to it. These were creations of sensory, sentimental experiences and responses. As he poetically described it, "Was not the scene in existence, were not the emotions antecedent to reason? What were they but materials for reason to operate upon?"[17]

According to Law and his authorities, society existed only because most people, exercising "the original constitution of human nature," possessed social sentiments, causing us to rejoice instinctively "with the glad of heart, weep with the mourner, and shun those who threaten danger, this is a contrivance no less illustrious for its wisdom than its benevolence." The distinguished essayist Joseph Addison agreed that the Creator supplied us with innate emotional instincts.[18] Assembling this diverse array of authorities, Law, while giving an incrasing role to the moral senses controverted Locke, who argued that morality might be

---

[15] Ibid., 18.

[16] Ibid., 18 (first quote), 16 (second quote), iv (third quote).

[17] Ibid., 18–20.

[18] Ibid., 13–14 (quotes from Kames), 16 (Addison).

included "among the sciences capable of demonstration" by fulfilling our duties to God and man as rational beings, not as social and benevolent individuals.[19]

Further delineating this "moral instinct," Jefferson, in the manner of Sterne, Lord Shaftesbury, and Adam Smith, ultimately defined it as mere sociability. With a hint of irreverence for the Deity and an inflated appreciation of humankind's social talents, Jefferson lectured Law, a willing pupil: "The Creator would indeed have been a bungling artist, had he intended man for a social animal, without planting in him social dispositions. It is true they are not planted in every man, because there is no rule without exceptions."[20]

Notwithstanding his acknowledgment of social conformity's influence in enforcing the norms imposed by laws and customs, Jefferson eschewed defending the "legal," socially acceptable institution of Black slavery. Far from justifying slavery, Jefferson's "moral sense" implicitly rejected it by emphasizing our duty to others. Even lawmakers' powers extended only so far as "to declare and enforce only our natural rights and duties, and to take none of them from us," Jefferson wrote in 1816, reiterating ideas he expressed as early as Query XVII (on religion) of *Notes on Virginia*. Persisting in an elementary Lockean view he had held for many years, Jefferson argued,

> No man has a natural right to commit aggression on the equal rights of another; and this is all from which the laws ought to restrain him. Every man is under the natural duty of contributing to the necessities of the society; and this is all the laws should enforce on him; and, no man having a natural right to be the judge between himself and another, it is his natural duty to submit to the umpirage of an impartial third.[21]

In Jefferson's opinion, the moral sense was intrinsically linked with the enforcement of natural law: both were "natural" and inborn. And slavery, as Jefferson had been saying since the Declaration of Independence, violated "the rights of human nature."[22]

The "sense of justice and injustice" was "derived from our natural organization," Jefferson asserted. He vehemently rejected the Hobbesian view (to which, to his regret, the admired philosopher Destutt de Tracy subscribed) that,

---

[19] Ibid., 16.

[20] Jefferson to Thomas Law, June 13, 1814, in Peterson, ed., *Jefferson: Writings*, 1337 (quotation); see also Jefferson to Carr, August 10, 1787, ibid., 901, for the consistency of his social philosophy over time.

[21] Jefferson to Francis W. Gilmer, June 7, 1816, in Ford, ed., *Writings of Thomas Jefferson*, 10:32–33.

[22] On the Declaration of Independence, see Allen Jayne, *Jefferson's Declaration of Independence: Origins, Philosophy and Theology* (Lexington: University Press of Kentucky, 1998), 124.

humankind being selfish and evil, morality was "founded on convention only." By respecting each other's rights, the American Indians, whom Jefferson considered the prototype of natural man, disproved this ad hoc notion of morality. Jefferson insisted that Native Americans verified his "syllogism" for social relationships: "Man was created for social intercourse; but social intercourse cannot be maintained without a sense of justice; then man must have been created with a sense of justice." Rather than create an organized police force, Native Americans employed "public opinion" to chastise those who "violate the rights of another," by shaming them. In the most "serious" cases, wrongdoers were "tomahawked as a dangerous enemy."[23]

Thus, Jefferson pointed to Native Americans to confirm his idea that the moral sense was natural. As an outgrowth of this, he claimed, the only natural and moral form of government was direct democracy, which the American Indians practiced, and the only natural form of government by "regular" or "positive laws" was representative democracy, not monarchy as Hobbesian theorists argued. Rather than "the patriarchal or monarchical form," the Cherokees, the first Indian tribe in Jefferson's experience to set up a polity establishing "regular laws, magistrates, and government," chose a legislature consisting of representatives elected from each town. They rejected monarchy, a polity that Jefferson had long ago discarded as being based on the premise that humankind was incapable of self-government: "Of all things, they least think of subjecting themselves to the will of one man. This, the only instance of actual fact within our knowledge, will be then a beginning by republican, and not by patriarchal or monarchical government, as speculative writers have generally conjectured."[24] Denying the historical priority of monarchy and patriarchy, Jefferson's political deductive reasoning implicitly questioned the legitimacy of slavery, an institution derived in part from patriarchal oppression.

Jefferson consistently upheld the "syllogism" that natural "justice" and the moral sense confirmed that republicanism and political equality were self-evident social instincts. However, in old age, he embraced the view that natural law justified a degree of economic *inequality*. He became less friendly in his view of the ancient direct democracies of Athens and Rome as well. Acutely conscious that they held large numbers of slaves and that ancient citizens were often swayed by

---

[23] Jefferson to Francis W. Gilmer, June 7, 1816, in Ford, ed., *Writings of Thomas Jefferson*, 10:32–33. Jefferson also mentioned to John Adams his regret that Tracy denied the idea of an innate moral sense, but "adopts the principle of Hobbes, that justice is founded in contract solely, and does not result from the construction of man" (Jefferson to Adams, October 14, 1816, in Cappon, ed., *Adams-Jefferson Letters* [1988], 492).

[24] Jefferson to Francis W. Gilmer, June 7, 1816, in Ford, ed., *Writings of Thomas Jefferson*, 10:32–33, and Lipscomb and Bergh, eds., *Writings of Jefferson*, 15:24–25.

demagogues, he deplored the ancient republics as imperialistic and militarist states, inhabited by ignorant hedonists incapable of self-government. In his old age, New England town meetings and the more "extended" republican polity created by the United States Constitution were the main sources of his political enthusiasm. "So different was the state of society then, and with those people, from what it is now, and with us," he wrote regarding the ancient Greeks in 1816, "that I think little edification can be obtained from their writings on the subject of government....They knew no median between a democracy (the only pure republic, but impracticable beyond the limits of a town) and an abandonment of themselves to an aristocracy, or a tyranny independent of the people." Jefferson was confident that government by popularly elected representatives, republicanism or "representative democracy," as practiced in the United States was superior. "The introduction of this new principle of representative democracy has rendered useless almost everything written before on the structure of government," he boldly commented, "and in a great measure, relieves our regret, if the political writings of Aristotle, or of any other ancient, have been lost, or are unfaithfully rendered or explained to us."[25] Jefferson overlooked the fact that the ancient Athenians and Spartans also utilized elected magistrates. (The Spartans elected ephors and the Athenians chose archons who executed the laws while the Romans had their senators and tribunes.)

Jefferson continued to emphasize that the American republic's political and economic progress superseded the practices of the ancient democratic city-states and made them irrelevant. In a letter to a Greek political philosopher in 1823, he insisted that, "the circumstances of the world are too much changed" for the United States to emulate the brutal, militarist ancient Greek polities. "The government of Athens, for example," he pointed out, "was that of the people of one city making laws for the whole country subjected to them. That of Lacedaemon [Sparta] was the rule of military monks over the labouring class of the people, reduced to abject slavery. These are not the doctrines of the present age. The equal rights of man, and the happiness of every individual, are now acknowledged to be the only legitimate objects of government."[26]

---

[25] Jefferson to Isaac H. Tiffany, August 26, 1816, in Lipscomb and Bergh, eds., *Writings of Jefferson*, 15:65–66.

[26] Jefferson to A. Coray, October 31, 1823, ibid., 15:482. See also Koch, *Philosophy of Jefferson*, 149–61. For Jefferson's familiarity with ancient Greek and Roman constitutions, see Carl J. Richard, "A Dialogue with the Ancients: Thomas Jefferson and Classical Philosophy and History," *Journal of the Early Republic* 9/4 (Winter 1989): 431–55, and his book, *The Founders and the Classics: Greece, Rome, and the American Enlightenment* (Cambridge: Harvard University Press, 1994).

When people were educated and the majority of them were small landholders, the situation in many parts of the United States, Jefferson unqualifiedly endorsed the idea that they should directly govern and directly elect their local and state officials to the greatest practicable extent. He remained devoted to the concept of "town-meeting democracy" and the "ward system," which permitted voters within localities to participate in devising the education, civil and criminal laws and regulations, and poor relief administration in their communities.[27]

At the same time, Jefferson appreciated representative government as more likely than direct democracy to safeguard an extensive land area against dictatorship and demagoguery. "It seems that the smaller the society the bitterer the dissensions into which it breaks," he said, alluding to the Italian Renaissance city-states. "Perhaps this answers all the objections drawn by Mr. Adams from the small republics of Italy. I believe ours is to owe its permanence to its great extent, and the smaller portion comparatively, which can ever be convulsed at one time by local passions."[28] Thus, Jefferson reiterated his friend Madison's immortal conclusions in *Federalist* no. 10.

There were times, however, as during the most desperate stages of the American Revolution, when the thirteen colonies were near defeat, that Jefferson would have condoned demagoguery though not dictatorship. In 1785, agreeing with British radical Richard Price, one of the Mother Country's few advocates of American independence, that the "federal head" (Congress) required more power in order to gain respect from European countries and access to their trade, he said that the American people were gradually adopting this point of view. He hoped they would soon abandon their localist predilections. As he put it, in an early statement of his democratic faith, "The happiness of governments like ours wherein the people are truly the mainspring, is that they are never to be despaired of. When an evil becomes so glaring as to strike them generally, they arouse themselves, and it is redressed." At the point that they became aware that extreme measures were necessary, they would grant greater power to their leaders, who might even assume demagogic characteristics: "He only is then the popular man and can get into office who shews [*sic*] the best dispositions to reform the evil," Jefferson said flatly.[29]

---

[27] For Jefferson's admiration for New England's local democratic institutions despite the section's opposition to his party and his policies, see Arthur Scherr, "Thomas Jefferson's Nationalist Vision of New England and the War of 1812," *Historian* 69/1 (Spring 2007): 1–35.

[28] Jefferson to Robert Williams, November 1, 1807, in Lipscomb and Bergh, eds., *Writings of Jefferson*, 11:389, quoted in Koch, *Philosophy of Jefferson*, 151.

[29] Jefferson to Richard Price, February 1, 1785, in Boyd et al., eds., *Papers of Thomas Jefferson*, 7:630.

Despite its ostensibly demagogic aspect, Jefferson believed that the tendency of capable leaders to arise at the right time epitomized the best "character in our governments." He thought that the people's flexibility and willingness to obey the best men had saved the Revolution after such disasters as the British capture of Charleston in September 1780. "Calamity was our best physician," he assured Price. He said that, likewise, popular anger at the advantage that European countries were taking of American disunity and Congress's lack of the power to levy retaliatory tariffs would soon precipitate their demand that Congress obtain such powers. Despite his hortatory rhetoric, during the 1780s when he resided in France, Jefferson remained doubtful of popular readiness to give Congress greater powers. He predicted that a "calamity" such as war between two states of the Union would be necessary to obtain public consent. "At that moment the hand of the union will be lifted up and interposed, and the people will themselves demand a general concession to Congress of means to prevent similar mischiefs," he concluded.[30]

Jefferson further expressed his emerging political relativism following his election as president, mildly praising his enemies, the Hamiltonian Federalists. He pledged that as president his main goal was to interfere with the people's daily lives as little as possible, tax them as little as possible, and run the country's affairs with the utmost frugality. He implied that Hamilton and his colleagues, despite what he now considered their wise fiscal policies, had failed to follow similar guidelines. "If we can prevent the government from wasting the labours of the people, under the pretence of taking care of them," he said, echoing his first inaugural address,

> they must become happy. Their finances are now under such a course of application as nothing could derange but war or federalism. The grip of the latter [Federalism] has shewn itself as deadly as the jaws of the former. Our adversaries say we are indebted to their providence for the means of paying the public debt. We never charged them with the want of foresight in providing money; but with the misapplication of it after they had levied it. We say they raised not only enough, but too much: and that after giving back the surplus we do more with a part than they did with the whole.[31]

Jefferson was crowing too loudly over his repeal of the internal taxes, made possible only because of greatly increased revenue from import duties following

---

[30] Ibid., 631. Jefferson used the verb "interpose" to describe congressional intervention to prevent wars between the states. This was the same term that Madison used in the Virginia Resolutions to defend the necessity for individual states to prevent the enforcement of unconstitutional laws like the Alien and Sedition Acts by the national government.

[31] Jefferson to Thomas Cooper, November 29, 1802, in Oberg, ed., *Jefferson Papers*, 39:84.

the temporary cessation of European hostilities and reduced military expenses after the end of the US's undeclared war with France. During the 1790s, the Republican Party in Congress usually favored increased, direct taxation of land in order to keep up payments on the interest and principal of the public debt, which they wanted to pay off more quickly than did the Federalists. Jefferson had always been acutely aware that taxpayers grumbled about taxes, and that land taxes, whose burdens they felt directly, in contrast to "invisible" indirect taxes on imports and excises on commodities, were particularly unpopular. During the undeclared war with France (1798–1800), Jefferson expected that the Federalists would fall from power because of the high taxes they imposed, among them direct taxes on lands, houses, and slaves. Early on, he predicted that the "disease of the imagination," the public hysteria for war with France stimulated by Adams, the Federalists, and the notorious "XYZ Affair," French agents' demand in October 1797 for a bribe before negotiations could proceed, would soon end. "Indeed, the doctor is now on his way to cure it, in the guise of a tax gatherer."[32]

By no means was Jefferson a carte-blanche advocate of demagoguery. Perhaps thinking of the Gracchi brothers' schemes of "agrarian law," designed to divide the land holdings of the rich among the poor, or Julius Caesar's successful efforts to bribe the people to support his dictatorship, Jefferson criticized the illiterate, "demoralised and depraved" ancient Romans. Unlike many thinkers, he considered the Roman Republic an immoral polity and its people invariably ignorant and corrupt, "from the rape of the Sabines to the ravages of the Caesars." He disapproved of the imperialistic aims of ancient Greece and Rome, both the Republic and the Empire. Despite his admiration for Cicero's rhetoric and patriotism, Jefferson thought that the Roman people were so corrupt and ignorant that not even Cicero could have rendered them competent for a self-governing republic, which required morality and literacy of its citizens. Writing to John Adams in 1819, he argued, "steeped in corruption vice and venality as the whole nation was...what could even Cicero, Cato, Brutus have done, had it been referred to them to establish a good government for their country? They had no ideas of government themselves but of their degenerate Senate, nor the people of liberty, but of the factious opposition of their tribunes."[33]

Reiterating Montesquieu's idea that a people's national character shaped their laws, with "virtue" as the necessary principle of republics just as honor was essential to monarchy and moderation to aristocracy, in old age Jefferson considered the citizens of the Roman Empire so debased that they were ripe candidates

---

[32] Jefferson to John Taylor, November 26, 1798, microfilm reel 21, Jefferson Papers, LC (hdl.loc.gov/loc.mss/mtj.mtjbib009149).

[33] Jefferson to John Adams, December 10, 1819, in Cappon, ed., *Adams-Jefferson Letters* (1959), 2:549–50.

for despotic rule. He observed, "No government can continue good but under the controul of the people; and their people were so demoralised and depraved as to be incapable of exercising a wholsome [*sic*] controul." As far as Jefferson was concerned, the ancient Romans would have had to start learning virtuous principles from scratch: "Their minds were to be informed, by education, what is right and what wrong, to be encoraged [*sic*] in habits of virtue, and deterred from those of vice by the dread of punishments, proportioned indeed, but irremissible; in all cases, to follow the truth as the only safe guide."

Only the "inculcations" of morality and education could prepare the Romans, or any other people whose innate "moral sense" had atrophied, for self-government, but this would have taken more than a generation to achieve, by which time dictators or emperors would likely have "quashed" the effort. Unlike many of his contemporaries, who glorified the Roman Republic, Jefferson lamented that its "unenlightened and vitiated" people had never had "one single day of free and rational government."[34] Because of what Jefferson, perhaps inordinately, considered their indispensability in generating the public and private virtue and reasonableness essential to representative democracy, public education and large-scale projects of higher learning like his University of Virginia were crucially important to him, especially in his later years.

Disputing the views of ancient Roman radicals like the Gracchi and modern French communists and Babeuvists, Jefferson argued that the inheritance of unequal sums of wealth was natural and inevitable, if testators freely chose to bequeath different amounts to their offspring. Adhering to this view, in old age Jefferson opposed most forms of progressive taxation. "Whether property alone, and the whole of what each citizen possesses, shall be subject to contribution, or only it's [*sic*] surplus after satisfying his first wants, or whether the faculties of body and mind shall contribute also from their annual earnings, is a question to be decided," Jefferson wrote concerning American tax policy. He believed that society was undecided about whether income or property should bear the heaviest burden:

> But, when decided, and the principle settled, it is to be equally and fairly applied to all. To take from one, because it is thought that his own industry and that of his father has acquired too much, in order to spare to others, who, or whose fathers have not exercised equal industry and skill, is to

[34] Ibid. See also Meyer Reinhold, *Classica Americana: The Greek and Roman Heritage in the United States* (Detroit: Wayne State University Press, 1984), 108–109, and Richard, *Founders and the Classics*, ch. 4.

> violate arbitrarily the first principle of association, the *guarantee* to every one of a free exercise of his industry, & the fruits acquired by it.[35]

More philosophically, he was not surprised that the French physiocrats (also called *Economistes*) Quesnay and Turgot, originators of the discipline of political economy in the mid-eighteenth century, had elicited little support. Their proposal that the sole form of taxation should be a land tax (*l'impôt unique*) because, they argued, land and its products were the sole source of real wealth, was predictably, not very popular with most landholders, apart from the few who were also political philosophers, like John Taylor of Caroline. In Taylor's view (and Jefferson probably agreed with him somewhat although he never specifically said so), farmers paid most of the taxes in the form of excises and tariffs, but they were unaware they were doing so since these taxes were paid initially by merchants and manufacturers. Therefore, if farmers paid a direct tax on their land, they would be more aware of their contribution and more attentive to how the government was spending their money. Expounding his appreciation for political relativism in the matter of taxation, Jefferson took for granted that there was no absolutely "right" or "wrong" tax; that all depended primarily on what the people were most willing to pay. As he put it, assessing the physiocrats' unpopularity:

> Their opinions on production, and on the proper subjects of taxation, have been particularly controverted; and whatever may be the merit of their principles of taxation, it is not wonderful they have not prevailed; not on the questioned score of correctness, but because not acceptable to the people, whose will must be the supreme law. Taxation is in fact the most difficult function of government—and that against which their citizens are most apt to be refractory. The general aim is therefore to adopt the mode most consonant with the circumstances and sentiments of the country.[36]

Throughout his career, most famously in his first inaugural address, Jefferson had argued that, like political democracy and freedom of thought and religion, each person's guarantee to the fruits of their labor was a natural social axiom. One would consider a presidential inaugural address a strange occasion to make such a declaration of faith today, but the "Jacobinism" of the French Revolution cast a long shadow, and Jefferson and the Democratic-Republicans were constantly tarred with its brush during the election campaigns of 1796 and 1800. In 1801, Jefferson thought it necessary to convince the people that he was not a wild-eyed Babeufist or Maratist radical. He had pushed for the abolition of primogeniture and entail in the Virginia legislature in the late 1770s, liberating private

[35] Jefferson to Joseph Milligan, April 6, 1816, microfilm reel 48, Jefferson Papers, LC (hdl.loc.gov/loc.mss/mtj.mtjbib022403).

[36] Ibid.

property from perpetual hereditary restraints and providing for equal inheritance of intestate estates by all children, male and female. In his second inaugural address, Jefferson again sought to reassure Americans that he favored private property, free enterprise, and the inheritance of wealth by one's heirs. He sought to distance himself from the socialism and communism that some European extremists advocated during the French Revolution, and which his political opponents imputed to him and his party during election campaigns. In his second inaugural in 1805, he told the nation that he favored maintaining "that state of property, equal or unequal, which results to every man from his own industry, or that of his fathers."[37]

In this connection, philosopher Maurizio Valsania's discussion of what he considered Jefferson's hostile appraisal of Native American cultures seems relevant. In an essay based on slender evidence, Valsania criticized Jefferson's progressivism as arising from Jefferson's racial preference for "whites." In Valsania's hypothesis, Jefferson considered Whites a superior race because their economic system of private (landed) property better enabled them to conquer the chaotic natural wilderness of the New World, while Blacks and Native Americans, who lacked a concept of private property, could not compete with them. This thesis suffers from several logical and empirical flaws: It overemphasizes Jefferson's conviction of the importance of private property; bizarrely assumes that he inscribed possession of private property as a hereditary trait unique to the "white race"; and ignores the fact that American Indians had been engaged in conquering nature in America for thousands of years before White men arrived. He also overlooked the fact that Blacks, both free and enslaved, had always desired to accumulate private property to the extent allowed them.[38]

Valsania's assumptions are factually untenable. Not all American Indian tribes practiced a communal system of land ownership. For instance, the Iroquois practiced individual land-ownership although land was heritable by the clan or the tribe rather than individuals. On the Iroquois, Daniel Richter, a leading authority explains, "Food, clothing, tools, houses, land, and other forms of property belonged to those individuals and kin groups who needed and made use of them. Conversely, excess or abandoned property was largely free for the taking, and in times of shortages all shared in the meager fare."[39] In *Death and Rebirth of the*

[37] Jefferson's Second Inaugural Address, March 4, 1805, in Peterson, ed., *Jefferson: Writings*, 522.

[38] Maurizio Valsania, "'Our Original Barbarism': Man vs. Nature in Thomas Jefferson's Moral Experience," *Journal of the History of Ideas* 65/4 (October 2004): 627–45, at 640–42.

[39] Daniel K. Richter, *The Ordeal of the Longhouse: Peoples of the Iroquois League in the Era of European Colonization* (Chapel Hill: University of North Carolina Press, 1992), 21–22. This

Seneca, anthropologist Anthony F. C. Wallace similarly wrote about the Senecas, one of the Six Nations of Iroquois. "All land was national land; an individual could occupy and use a portion of it and maintain as much privacy in the tenure as he wished, but this usufruct title reverted to the nation when the land was abandoned," he explained. "There was little reason to bother about individual ownership of real estate anyway: there was plenty of land."[40] Private property was respected, at least during the lifetime of the individual who held it.

Jefferson was well aware that the most modern ("progressive") Christian Indians, especially in Georgia, engaged in private landholding similar to their White persecutors, and that numerous tribes had at least partially privatized systems of land ownership. Indeed, in *Notes on Virginia* and throughout his career, Jefferson maintained that American Indians were as intelligent as White men.[41] Adopting a program that he considered beneficial to both American Indians and land-hungry White settlers, whom he could not deter from invading Indian lands, he sought to convince Native Americans to become small farmers rather than retain hunting cultures requiring vast acreages for stalking game.[42] Likewise, during his lifetime of experience as a slaveholder, Jefferson often rewarded slaves for good service with cash bonuses and small plots of land to raise crops for their own consumption and sell at market in small quantities. He was aware that free Blacks

---

depiction of Native Americans' property arrangements was nearly identical to that which Jefferson, in his famous "earth belongs in usufruct to the living generation" letter to Madison, September 6, 1789, considered all societies' property arrangements according to "natural law." He argued that it was only the "municipal" or "positive laws" enacted by different states and nations that made individual property hereditable by kin or others in a decedent's last will and testament (Jefferson to Madison, September 6, 1789, in Peterson, ed., *Jefferson: Writings*, 959–64). Indeed, Jefferson praised Native Americans' communal systems (Jefferson to James Madison, January 30, 1787, in Peterson, ed., *Jefferson: Writings*, 882, and Jefferson to John Adams, June 11, 1812, ibid., 1263).

[40] Anthony F. C. Wallace, *Death and Rebirth of the Seneca* (New York: Knopf, 1970), 24.

[41] Jefferson to Marquis de Chastellux, June 7, 1785, in Peterson, ed., *Jefferson: Writings*, 801.

[42] Sheehan, *Seeds of Extinction*, 167–74. See also M. Andrew Holowchak, ed., *Thomas Jefferson and Philosophy: Essays on the Philosophical Cast of Jefferson's Writing* (Lanham, MD: Lexington Books, 2013), 57. Unaware that Jefferson sarcastically manipulated public opinion's stereotype of American Indians as ignorant and primitive as metaphors for his New England Federalist political enemies, whom he dismissed as religious fanatics, Holowchak stressed occasions when Jefferson complained that the American Indians' "government" was defective because they were too reverential of the past.

and the slaves on his plantations showed an affinity for cultivating private plots of land and eagerly desired private property.[43]

In his later years, Jefferson continued to advocate the principle of individuals' control of the disposition of their private property. In old age, he preferred the equal division of inherited estates among all children when the testator's will did not favor a specific child, over more drastic measures like progressive taxation of the wealth, income, or inheritances of the rich. "If the overgrown wealth of an individual be deemed dangerous to the state the best corrective is the law of equal inheritance to all in equal degrees and the better as this enforces a law of nature, while extra taxation violates one," he explained to a publisher.[44] He considered such a policy naturally just, because in accord with parental "affections," as he put it in his famous letter of October 1785 to James Madison.[45]

Apart from the natural "affections" that people generally felt for their spouses and children, no "natural law" required society to convey parents' properties at their death to children or even to those specified in their last will and testament. This all took place by what Jefferson called "municipal," rather than natural law. As Jefferson had originally explained in his "earth belongs to the living" letter to Madison in September 1789, there were no "natural laws" by which a family member, creditor, or other legatee could inherit the land (and probably other personal property) of a decedent. In his view, "the portion occupied by an individual ceases to be his when himself ceases to be, and reverts to the society," which invariably passes laws for disposing of it. "But the child, the legatee or creditor takes it, not by any natural right, but by a law of the society of which they are members," he argued. As a corollary to this insight, Jefferson said that, "no man can by *natural right* oblige the lands he occupied, or the persons who succeeded him in that occupation, to the paiment [*sic*] of debts contracted by him." He concluded that the existing government had the sole right, by "municipal law," to regulate "individual inheritance of property." He specifically applied his theory to the question of public responsibility for paying the national debt, an issue

---

[43] Philip J. Schwarz, *Slave Laws in Virginia* (Athens: University of Georgia Press, 1996), 35–62.

[44] Jefferson to Joseph Milligan, April 6, 1816, microfilm reel 48, Jefferson Papers, LC (hdl.loc.gov/loc.mss/mtj.mtjbib022403). The French Revolution had emulated Jefferson's Virginia policy of abolishing laws of primogeniture and entail. In April 1791, France's Legislative Assembly had decreed the division of intestate estates equally among all children, regardless of sex or birth order. In 1794, the National Convention of the Reign of Terror went further, in declaring that illegitimate children recognized by their parents were entitled to an equal share of estates where there was no will (Suzanne Desan, *Family on Trial in Revolutionary France* [Berkeley: University of California Press, 2004], 141–42).

[45] Jefferson to James Madison, October 28, 1785, in Boyd et al., eds., *Papers of Thomas Jefferson*, 8:682.

vigorously discussed in both France and the United States in 1789. Insisting that regulations involving debts, property and inheritance depended on each society's legislation, rather than being subject to a universal, "natural law," Jefferson argued that individual inheritances and the payment of individual and government debts rested on each legislature's "municipal" laws. Society had not made them subject to a higher, absolute "natural law" of right and wrong. On the other hand, permanent public debts inherited by succeeding generations, unlike private property inherited by individual beneficiaries who became responsible for the legator's debts, were invalid by the "natural law" which, he said, was "self evident, '*that the earth belongs in usufruct to the living*; that the dead have neither powers nor rights over it." Jefferson implied that, on the collective, national level, the natural law that "the earth belongs to the living" stood on a par with the immortal "self-evident truths" he listed in the Declaration of Independence: "that all men are created equal; that they are endowed by their creator with inherent and inalienable rights; that among these are life, liberty, & the pursuit of happiness."[46]

Presenting his emerging theory of moral and political relativism, Jefferson explained to Madison that each living majority of citizens should have the power to pass new laws involving public debts (and, he concluded later, in his July 1816 letter to Samuel Kercheval, private debts) every generation, which he estimated at nineteen or twenty years. He wrote Madison,

> I suppose that the received opinion, that the public debts of one generation devolve on the next, has been suggested by our seeing habitually in private life that he who succeeds to lands is required to pay the debts of his ancestor or testator, without considering that this requisition is municipal only, not moral, flowing from the will of the society which has found it convenient to appropriate the lands become vacant by the death of their occupant on the condition of a paiment [*sic*] of his debts; *but that between society and society, or generation and generation there is no municipal obligation, no umpire but the law of nature.*[47]

---

[46] Jefferson to James Madison, September 6, 1789, in Peterson, ed., *Jefferson: Writings*, 959–64, esp. 959–60 (first and second quotations; Jefferson's italics) Jefferson's original version of the Declaration of Independence, in his *Autobiography*, in Peterson, ed., *Jefferson: Writings*, 19.

[47] Jefferson to James Madison, September 6, 1789, in Peterson, ed., *Jefferson: Writings*, 959–64, at 962 (my italics). In later life, Jefferson argued that all laws and constitutions should automatically be subject to reconsideration, revision, or repeal every twenty years. See Jefferson to Samuel Kercheval, July 12, 1816, microfilm reel 49, Jefferson Papers, LC (hdl.loc.gov/loc.mss/mtj.mtjbib022494) and in Peterson, ed., *Jefferson: Writings*, 1401. The government already limited inheritance of estates in such laws as the manumission acts, which prohibited debtors from emancipating slaves in their wills.

In this case, the "law of nature" simply referred to the brutal, inevitable fact of the death of individuals and generations, and their replacement in society and governmental administration by successor generations. With stark objectivity, Jefferson stated this factor of inevitable death, which in his opinion invalidated the equity of any permanent laws relating to public debts, in his letter of 1789 to Madison: "We seem not to have perceived that, by the law of nature, one generation is to another as one independant [*sic*] nation to another."[48]

In stronger terms, Jefferson continued, "No society can make a perpetual constitution, or even a perpetual law. The earth belongs always to the living generation. They may manage it then, and what proceeds from it, as they please, during their usufruct. They are masters too of their own persons, and consequently may govern them as they please. But persons and property make the sum of the object of government." Calculating, based on the French naturalist George Buffon's mortality statistics that the majority of those currently alive would be dead within nineteen years, Jefferson concluded that the laws made during their lifetimes should die with them, unless renewed by the current voting population. As he put it, "Every constitution, then, and every law, naturally expires at the end of 19 years. If it be enforced longer, it is an act of force and not of right."[49]

Such a doctrine was potentially anarchical; but Jefferson provided the safety valve of "municipal law" to maintain the realistic need for upholding the necessity to pay public and private debts, even if idealistic "natural law" might disavow their validity after twenty years. In any case, in the matter of public debts, annual legislative appropriations would be required to pay them promptly. So, if Congress ever repudiated public debts, reduced the interest payments on them, or by other means applied a "sponge" to them, in that period's phrase, as Britain's House of Commons occasionally did in reducing public debt interest payments after 1694,

---

[48] Jefferson to Madison, September 6, 1789, in Peterson, ed., *Jefferson: Writings*, 962. This letter probably contained his most careful distinction between "municipal law," the positive laws enacted by a state, and the more fundamental "natural law" that denied the natural justice of the inheritance of personal property, or national or personal debts from one generation to another. This is a feature of Jefferson's widely examined political principle that "the earth belongs to the living generation" that scholars, such as Herbert Sloan in his article, "'The Earth Belongs in Usufruct to the Living,'" in Peter S. Onuf, ed., *Jeffersonian Legacies* (Charlottesville: University Press of Virginia, 1993), 284, tend to overlook. The letter is conveniently printed in Peterson, ed., *Jefferson: Writings*, 959–64. The best study of Jefferson's lifelong doctrine that the "earth belongs to the living generation" remains Adrienne Koch, *Jefferson and Madison: The Great Collaboration* (1950; repr., New York: Oxford University Press, 1964), 62–96.

[49] Jefferson to James Madison, September 6, 1789, in Peterson, ed., *Jefferson: Writings*, 963.

Jefferson's dictum might be applied in practice.[50] Thus, laws, like the governments and societies that wrote them, far from being absolute and unchangeable, constantly evolved with cultural transitions from one generation to the next, in an eternal state of social, political and moral relativism.

Although by "municipal law," Jefferson was responsible for paying his father-in-law's debts in exchange for accepting his lands and slaves, American and French taxpayers might seek legislation to escape the collective burden of paying preceding regimes' taxes, for which "natural law" did not hold them permanently responsible. They could do this by putting a time limit of one generation (about twenty years, according to Jefferson) as the period for which public debts could be legally contracted.

In his revolutionary letter to Madison of September 6, 1789, Jefferson also advocated stronger patent protections for inventors. Perhaps envisioning himself as one who would need such protection in the future, he thought that the profits to inventors should be guaranteed to them for nineteen years, the span of his "generation," rather than the fourteen years that British (and later American) law provided.[51] Twenty years later, Jefferson found himself forced to pay a fee to Oliver Evans, the brilliant inventor of steam engines, grain elevators, and numerous other devices, for constructing a sophisticated, steam-operated grain mill and grain elevator based on his models. He paid the required fee but protested that a man's ideas should be available gratis to the rest of the community. Embellishing this concept, seemingly inspired by his economic self-interest, with an ideological rationale, he expounded a Rousseauist, communistic thesis on the origins of private property that came straight out of Rousseau's *Discourse on the Origin of Inequality Among Men* (1755). Writing during the War of 1812, he may have felt more justified in denouncing the British precedent, which he had formerly approved. Reiterating views expressed in his letters to Madison from Revolutionary-era France in 1785 and 1789, he now argued that there was no natural right to private property, which was merely a convenient social convention. If the proprietor had no natural right to his own tangible, private property, he had even less right to the exclusive possession of his ideas and inventions, Jefferson now reasoned.[52]

---

[50] On Britain's public debt, see Peter G. M. Dickson, *The Financial Revolution in England: A Study in the Development of Public Opinion, 1688–1756* (London: Macmillan, 1967). For the debate on funding (annually paying interest on) the US Revolutionary War debt during the period from 1775 to 1790, see E. James Ferguson, *The Power of the Purse: A History of American Public Finance, 1776–1790* (Chapel Hill: University of North Carolina Press, 1961).

[51] Jefferson to Madison, September 6, 1789, in Peterson, ed., *Jefferson: Writings*, 964.

[52] Jefferson to Isaac McPherson, August 13, 1813, in Koch and Peden, eds., *Life and Selected Writings*, 629–30. For Jefferson's earlier letters, see Jefferson to Madison, October 28, 1785, and Jefferson to Madison, September 6, 1789, both excerpted in ibid., 388–90, 488–93.

Deploring the notion that inventors and their heirs should hold a permanent monopoly on their inventions, Jefferson tried to demonstrate the absurdity of such reasoning. "It has been pretended by some, (and in England especially) that inventors have a natural and exclusive right to their inventions, and not merely for their own lives, but inheritable to their heirs," he began. Casting doubt on the justice of any inherited property ownership, he said, "While it is a moot question whether the origin of any kind of property is derived from nature at all, it would be singular to admit a natural and even an hereditary right to inventors." Perhaps alluding to Rousseau, or Thomas Paine's *Agrarian Justice* (1797), Jefferson said, "It is agreed by those who have seriously considered the subject, that no individual has, of natural right, a separate property in an acre of land, for instance." Like Rousseau in the *Second Discourse*, Jefferson contended that in the state of nature (he seemed to think that this really existed) the ownership of land was temporary and really amounted only to possession for the duration of the individual's occupancy. Land was naturally the property of the whole community, Jefferson argued, seemingly adopting Native American customs in this matter. "By an universal law, indeed, whatever, whether fixed or movable, belongs to all men equally and in common, is the property for the moment of him who occupies it, but when he relinquishes the occupation, the property goes with it." Reiterating Rousseau's arguments, but omitting Rousseau's realistic (and Hobbesian) emphasis that even temporary ownership was often determined by who had greater physical force at his disposal, he hinted that private property was not invented by the Neanderthal man: "Stable ownership is the gift of social law, and is given late in the progress of society."[53]

Insisting that the ownership of real and personal property, especially after the original possessor had died, was a product of "social law," and not a natural right, Jefferson now applied the same criteria to intellectual property. He argued that intangible possessions, such as one's ideas and inventions, were not the profitable, hereditary assets of those who thought them up: "It would be curious then, if an idea, the fugitive fermentation of an individual brain, could, of natural right, be claimed in exclusive and stable property." An idea belongs to its creator as long as he keeps it to himself; once he divulges it to others, it belongs to society, as a "fugitive fermentation" spreading to other fermenting minds, who will put it to

[53] Jefferson to Isaac McPherson, August 13, 1813, in Koch and Peden, eds., *Life and Selected Writings*, 630. For the law passed during Jefferson's administration, and which he did not veto, see "An Act for the relief of Oliver Evans," which gave Evans patent privileges for fourteen years, in emulation of British laws (William Waller Hening, ed., *Statutes at Large of Virginia*, 13 vols. [Richmond: Bartow, 1823], 6:70–71; available at catalog.hathitrust.org/Record/009714930).

diverse uses. In one of his most famous dictums, Jefferson continued, "If nature has made any one thing less susceptible than all others of exclusive property, it is the action of the thinking power called an idea, which an individual may exclusively possess as long as he keeps it to himself; but the moment it is divulged, it forces itself into the possession of every one and the receiver cannot dispossess himself of it."[54]

An essential characteristic of the mental construct, or idea, is that it is in many cases involuntary; once one has got it into their head, so to speak, one cannot get rid of it. Jefferson made this point effectively in his Statute of Virginia on Religious Freedom. In that great document, he emphasized that the state could not force an individual to adopt a religion he did not believe even though the idea of God might involuntarily have presented itself to him as a child in a certain guise, perhaps taught by his parents, and he preferred to retain that concept rather than a new one.

Presenting ideas as liberating forces, Jefferson's letter to McGregor stressed that, unlike a loan of money or goods, the giver did not lose anything when others discovered his immaterial idea (the exception being, he should have added, if the idea was an invention which the inventor might expect to earn him money; or a book he wrote etc.). "Its [an idea's] peculiar character, too, is that no one possesses the less, because every other possesses the whole of it," he said, self-servingly in Evans's case. (Indeed, Jefferson demanded repeal of the tariff on imported books although he never said that copyright laws for written works like his *Notes on Virginia*, whose pirating he suffered under the Articles of Confederation, should be overthrown.[55]) Borrowing, without attribution, a metaphor from Voltaire's *Philosophical Dictionary*, he observed, "He who receives an idea from me, receives instruction himself without lessening mine; as he who lights his taper at mine, receives light without darkening me." He argued that "nature" exempted ideas from being caught and caged; they could spread without obstruction by the physical environment. Only human societies could impede their progress by repressive laws and decrees:

> That ideas should freely spread from one to another over the globe, for the moral and mutual instruction of man, and improvement of his condition, seems to have been peculiarly and benevolently designed by nature, when she made them, like fire, expansible over all space, without lessening their

---

[54] Koch and Peden, eds., *Life and Selected Writings*, 630. The complete text of Jefferson to Isaac McPherson, August 13, 1813, is available in Peterson, ed., *Jefferson: Writings*, 1286–94, and Looney, ed., *Jefferson Papers: Retirement Series*, 6:379–86.

[55] See Jefferson to Jared Sparks, February 4, 1824, in Peterson, ed., *Jefferson: Writings*, 1487.

density in any point, and like the air in which we breathe, move, and have our physical being, incapable of confinement or exclusive appropriation.[56]

Carrying his reasoning to its logical extreme, Jefferson concluded that patents for inventions were against natural law, and in a sense illegal. "Inventions then cannot, in nature, be a subject of property," he asserted. "Society may give an exclusive right to the profits arising from them, as an encouragement to men to pursue ideas which may produce utility, but this may or may not be done, according to the will and convenience of the society, without claim or complaint from any body."[57]

Societies and governments pronounced inventions the personal property of the inventors, giving them exclusive access to the profits derived therefrom for a fixed period. By natural law, once someone else had figured out how to make the invention, he should have obtained equal rights to it. He claimed that only Britain and the United States possessed patent legislation ("a legal right to an exclusive use of an idea," as he put it), ostensibly to encourage inventors. However, according to Jefferson, those countries that had no laws providing patent rewards for inventors were just as "fruitful" of "new and useful devices" as the Anglo-Americans were. He thought that the well-being of society, rather than the profit of the inventor, should be the main factor involved. "Generally speaking, other nations have thought that these monopolies produce more embarrassment than advantage to society," he pointed out.[58]

By denying inventors the "natural right" to get rich through the profits of their inventions, Jefferson perhaps thought he was blocking a modern road to economic inequality between citizens. This may not have been his primary motive, however. Indeed, he seems to have been inspired to curtail patent rights by the stark fact that he had to pay to use Evans's invention, even though he claimed that one of his workers had set up the grain elevator at Monticello during his presidency without his knowledge, and "no judicial decision" was on the books validating the pertinent law.[59] Apparently, Jefferson thought his "natural right" to

---

[56] Jefferson to Isaac McPherson, August 13, 1813, in ibid., 1291. See Voltaire's *Philosophical Dictionary*: "It is with books as with the fires in our grates; everybody borrows a light from his neighbor to kindle his own, which is in turn communicated to others, and each partakes of all" (from "Miscellany," in Ben Ray Redman, ed., *Portable Voltaire* [New York: Penguin, 1977], 227).

[57] Ibid., 1291–92.

[58] Jefferson to Isaac McPherson, August 13, 1813, in Peterson, ed., *Jefferson: Writings*, 1292.

[59] Ibid., 1293–94. Selfish motives likewise guided Jefferson's rage at the tariff on imported books. A compulsive bibliophile, he considered "the duty on imported books" an

keep his money in his pocket had been violated, or that he was, as in the days before the Revolution, a victim of "taxation with[out] representation."

More appropriately, monopolies of land in the hands of the rich and powerful, as he perceived was the case among the French nobles when he lived in France in the years before the French Revolution, aroused Jefferson's disgust and recommendations for reform. To limit the prerogatives of wealth, he urged progressive taxation and the exemption of the poorer classes from taxation. As a last resort, a portion of the sprawling, unutilized plantations of the wealthy should be confiscated and distributed among the landless. He eloquently wrote, "Whenever there are in any country uncultivated lands and unemployed poor, it is clear that the laws of property have been so far extended as to violent natural right." Anticipating his doctrine that "the earth belongs to the living," and that those with excessive land and other wealth retained it, not by "natural right" but because the laws protected them, he continued, "The earth is given as a common stock for man to labor and live on. If for the encouragement of industry we allow it to be appropriated, we must take care that other employment be provided for those excluded from the appropriation. If we do not, the fundamental right to labor the earth returns to the unemployed." Turning from Ancien Régime France to the US, where the same logic denied his "natural right" to own several plantations and hundreds of slaves, he continued, "It is too soon yet in our country to say that every man who cannot find employment, but who can find uncultivated land, shall be at liberty to cultivate it, paying a moderate rent. But it is not too soon to provide by every possible means that as few as possible shall be without a little portion of land. The small landholders are the most precious part of a state."[60]

When Jefferson utilized the concept of natural law and "natural right" to denounce or limit economic inequality, the same reasoning invariably invalidated slavery. In this respect, he disagreed with other Jeffersonian Republicans, including correspondents in the leading Republican newspaper, the *Washington National Intelligencer*, edited by Republican activist Samuel Harrison Smith.

Despite its Republican editorial position, the *National Intelligencer* reflected a diametrically opposed concept of the moral sense during this period. Defending

---

atrocity. "I hope a crusade will be kept up against it, until those in power shall become sensible of this stain on our legislation, and shall wipe it from their code, and from the remembrance of man, if possible," Jefferson wrote Jared Sparks, February 4, 1824, ibid., 1487. The historian/littérateur Henry Adams concluded at the end of the century that inventors like Oliver Evans, John Fitch, Eli Whitney, and Robert Fulton often came from the poorer classes; their innate genius speeded economic mobility. For Adams's point of view, see his *History of the United States*, 123–25.

[60] Jefferson to James Madison, October 28, 1785, in Peterson, ed., *Jefferson: Writings*, 841–42.

slavery with a perverse version of moral sense theory, it asserted that slaves "perform their daily labor not as a task enforced by fear...but rather under the influence of an instinct which impels them to the voluntary performance of what they are conscious is their duty."[61] To this claim Jefferson would have replied, adhering to the opinions he had expressed in *Notes on Virginia* in the 1780s, that no human being, especially a slave, can ever instinctively regard as their duty acts commanded by a society that denies them their right to property, and enforces its dictates under the threat of the lash.

ꝏ

Jefferson wrote one of his last letters about the moral sense at the close of 1816, to his old friend and former political rival, John Adams. Here again Jefferson described the moral sense as God-given, "natural," and social, and so designed that human beings would want to help each other. Opposing what he called the "Hobbesian" premise that "justice is founded in contract solely, and does not result from the construction of man," Jefferson argued that the conception of justice is "instinct, and innate." He thought that the moral sense was intrinsic to the human personality, "as much a part of our constitution as that of feeling, seeing, or hearing; as a wise creator must have seen to be necessary in an animal destined to live in society." Accepting a priori that "every human mind feels pleasure in doing good to another," Jefferson reiterated the relativistic views earlier stated in his letter to Thomas Law. Now he urged, "that the non-existence of justice is not to be inferred from the fact that the same act is deemed virtuous and right in one society, which is held vicious and wrong in another; because as the circumstances and opinions of different societies vary, so the acts which may do them right or wrong must vary also." Although Jefferson's moral sense would not justify deliberate murder or oppression of minorities, others could distort his viewpoint as a means to justify such unintended consequences. Therefore, one society or culture might consider vicious what another considered virtuous. He qualified the potentially dangerous implications of such cultural/moral relativism by asserting, as a Benthamite Utilitarian might, "Virtue does not consist in the act we do, but in the end it is to effect."[62]

Jefferson always bounded his ideas of personal and political morality by stating that one's "liberty" consisted in doing anything not harmful to others. Hence, Jefferson eschewed following the rule of "the greatest good for the greatest

[61] *National Intelligencer*, April 30, 1813, quoted in Frank A. Cassell, "Slaves of the Chesapeake Bay Area and the War of 1812," *Journal of Negro History* 57/2 (April 1972): 155.

[62] Jefferson to John Adams, October 14, 1816, in Cappon, ed., *Adams-Jefferson Letters* (1959), 2:492.

number," since he would never, under any circumstances, permit the violation of the rights of minorities or individuals merely because they were weaker than the majority. As he wrote Adams, "If it [the act] is to effect the happiness of him to whom it is directed, it is virtuous, while in a society under different circumstances and opinions the same act might produce pain, and would be vicious. The essence of virtue is in doing good to others, while what is good may be one thing in one society, and its contrary in another."[63]

He ended by asserting that, though many writers differed on "the foundation of morals," they reached the same conclusions. Their similar inferences proved that they "were guided, unconsciously, by the unerring hand of instinct."[64] As Adrienne Koch notes, this letter to Adams exhibited Jefferson's belief "that the social nature of man is in every respect as natural as his physical equipment or mental make-up."[65]

To a certain extent, Jefferson had metamorphosed from an Enlightenment man to a political Romantic. In an earlier letter to Adams, he more closely connected morality with the emotions, or "passions," than he usually did. For himself, he denied that the passion of "grief" had value in the human emotional economy or in the quest for the right moral action. Indeed, he connected morality with his own joie de vivre. "How much pain have cost us the evils which have never happened?" he wondered, as he often did in letters to friends.[66] "My temperament is sanguine. I steer my bark with Hope in the head, leaving Fear astern. My hopes indeed sometimes fail; but not oftener than the forebodings of the gloomy." He admitted that even the "happiest life" experienced times of anguish, pain, and tragedy. Still, he did not think grieving about them decreased their painfulness. Thus, he concluded, "I have often wondered for what good end the sensation of Grief could be intended. All our other passions, within proper bounds, have an useful object." He regarded grief as a useless passion, one that did not guide the grieving to moral conduct or anything useful. According to Jefferson, "The perfection of the moral character is, not in a Stoical apathy, so hypocritically vaunted, and so untruly too, because impossible, but in a just equilibrium of all the passions." He did not consider grief a legitimate passion; perhaps it was rather the

---

[63] Ibid.

[64] Ibid.

[65] Koch, *Philosophy of Jefferson*, 20.

[66] Jefferson to John Adams, April 8, 1816, Cappon, ed., *Adams-Jefferson Letters* (1988), 467. See also Jefferson to William Short, November 28, 1814, in Lipscomb and Bergh, eds., *Writings of Jefferson*, 14:217, and Jefferson to Thomas Jefferson Smith, February 21, 1825, microfilm reel 54, Jefferson Papers, LC (hdl.loc.gov/loc.mss/mtj.mtjbib024892), for similar remarks.

negation of passion: "I wish the pathologists then would tell us what is the use of grief in the economy [of passions], and of what good it is the cause, proximate or remote."[67]

In his own way, Jefferson was a Byronic type, striving for the *élan vitale*, even in old age. He believed that one should seize the day and strive for as much physical and intellectual pleasure as possible, casting aside past tragedies as events that could not be undone. His intense mourning after his wife's death may have belied these sentiments; his grief, though, was short-lived, and within a few years in Paris, he was indulging in romantic flings with the much younger (and married) Maria Cosway and (possibly) a teenager named Sally Hemings. He accepted human frailty, including his own, although he tried to hurt others as little as possible in achieving his own pleasure.

---

[67] Jefferson to John Adams, April 8, 1816, Cappon, ed., *Adams-Jefferson Letters* (1988), 467.

Chapter 8

War and International Morality: Examining Another Form of Evil

After retiring from the presidency, Jefferson had more leisure to develop his doctrine of moral and cultural relativism. Partly because of the unprecedented loss of life and violence of the Napoleonic Wars, he increasingly tended to agree with pessimists who felt that an individual lost his moral sense when he submerged himself in a crowd, a mob, or even "civilized" groups like legislative bodies. He believed that the unprecedented violence and loss of life during the Napoleonic Wars and the unrelenting struggle of the British and the French powers for victory indicated that human nature had regressed to virtual barbarism from the rational and humane heights achieved by the Enlightenment only a few decades earlier. Jefferson contended that the US government was the only polity that pursued fairness, virtue, and decency in its foreign policy (apparently, he did not count the dispossession of the American Indians as "foreign policy").

From the tranquility of retirement, Jefferson viewed his and his successor James Madison's attempts to prevent war by the Embargo and Non-Intercourse Acts as epitomizing reason, which the savage warring powers failed to appreciate. "At any other period," he wrote, "the even-handed justice we have observed towards all nations, the efforts we have made to merit their esteem by every act which candor or liberality could exercise, would have preserved our peace, and secured the unqualified confidence of all other nations in our faith and probity." But the "hurricane" of war had obliterated all "physical and moral" considerations, "reason as well as right." In ordinary times, governments would have striven to obey the dictates of the "moral sense" in international and individual arenas alike. Now that only the US sought to apply "moral sense" dicta—the "laws of nature" that posited the identity of duties and interests in international relations—other nations considered its government naïve and gullible. "All those calculations which, at any other period, would have been deemed honorable, of the existence of a moral sense in man, individually or associated, of the connections which the laws of nature have established between his duties and his interests, of a regard for honest fame and the esteem of our fellow men, have been a matter of reproach to us, as evidences of imbecility," he charged. Benjamin Franklin's old apothegm that honesty was the best policy was seemingly no longer valid: "As if it could be a folly for an honest man to suppose that others could be honest also, when it is their interest to be so." He conjectured that, even if Bonaparte were assassinated, though it "would, to be sure, remove the first and chiefest apostle of the desolation of men and morals, and might withdraw the scourge of the land," the British, with their control of the sea lanes, posed an even greater and more permanent danger. "What is to restore order and safety on the ocean?" he rhetorically asked. Theoretically, he blamed all the British people for that country's demand for tribute from all nations that plied the oceans. Unlike the case of Napoleon in France, "stupid" King George III's death would have little effect on British foreign policy's demoniac character, "and his ministers, however weak and profligate in morals, are ephemeral. But his nation is permanent, and it is that which is the tyrant of the ocean. The principle that force is right, is become the principle of the nation itself. They would not permit an honest minister, were accident to bring such an one into power, to relax their system of lawless piracy." Thus, the British people (or "nation") themselves, ruled by greedy merchants, bankers, landed aristocrats, and textile corporations and their obsessive desire to monopolize the world's markets, who fed the populace the chauvinistic pap of super-patriotism, ate away at any moral fiber they possessed, making them virtually immoral monsters.[1]

Still, at least in 1810, Jefferson praised the people and government of the United States, to whose president (little James Madison) they all looked for guidance and leadership, as upholding the "reasonable" doctrines of international morality and justice. In Jefferson's opinion, they would continue to support the Democratic-Republican Party, because "they are kept so well informed of the state of things as to judge for themselves, to see the true sources of their difficulties [French and especially British aggression], and to maintain their confidence undiminished in the wisdom and integrity of their functionaries." He asserted that the government must "go straight forward, pursuing always that which is right," seemingly equating this with a policy of "peaceable coercion," although as president he abandoned the Embargo policy after only a year as ineffectual, and deciding that war for freedom of the seas was inevitable. In retirement, he hinted that the government should prepare for war and that President Madison must take the lead in this endeavor. "Let nothing be spared of either reason or passion," he wrote exuberantly, "to preserve the public confidence entire, as the only rock of our safety. In times of peace the people look most to their representatives; but in war, to the executive solely. It is visible that their confidence is even now

[1] Jefferson to Caesar Rodney, February 10, 1810, in Peterson, ed., *Jefferson: Writings*, 1217.

veering in that direction; that they are looking to the executive to give the proper direction to their affairs, with a confidence as auspicious as it is well founded."[2]

Thus, Jefferson, who generally believed the legislature was the most important branch of government, thought that in emergencies connected with war and foreign affairs, the president must take the lead. He followed his advice, both during the Louisiana crisis of 1802–1803 and in preparing in 1808–1809 for the possibility of war, proposing increasing the army to ten thousand men and expanding the navy, while he instituted the Embargo Act in a last-ditch search for peace.[3]

Jefferson's alacrity in accepting the necessity of war and urging his successors to organize for victory, the high-minded suggests he had abandoned dictums of international morality, peace, and virtue, which he claimed he and the American people who revered him embodied. It was this "exceptionalism," so to speak, that inspired him to propose the Embargo instead of entry into the worldwide war, which he feared would lead Americans into a cult of militarism, governmental dictatorship, and violence like the European nations. He denounced the immorality of the rulers of Britain and France, who used their power to intimidate the rest of the world. Because they violated the "law of nature," which enjoined universal peace and morality, Jefferson claimed during the War of 1812 (at other times he said that the law of nature exhibited ubiquitous violence), they would ultimately meet their downfall. "Throwing off all restraints of morality, all pride of national character, forgetting the mutability of fortune, and the inevitable doom which the laws of nature pronounce against departure form justice, individual or national," he asserted, "[they] have dared...to set up force instead of reason, as the umpire of nations, degrading themselves from the character of lawful societies."[4]

However, Jefferson too, eventually became inclined to condone the sadistic acts of governments and nations during the previous decade: their pursuit of war and the aggrandizement of the executive power for conducting war. During his presidency, comparing the British and the French, he wrote to James Monroe, U.S. minister to Great Britain, "We consider each as a necessary instrument to hold in check the disposition of the other to tyrannize over other nations." During

---

[2] Ibid., 1217–18.

[3] See Theodore Crackel, *Mr. Jefferson's Army* (New York: New York University Press, 1987); Adams, *History of the United States*, 1061–82.

[4] Jefferson to John Wayles Eppes, September 11, 1813, in Looney, ed., *Jefferson Papers: Retirement Series*, 6:491. For an example of one of Jefferson's pessimistic estimates of human nature as violent and unjust, see Jefferson to Edward Carrington, January 16, 1787, in Peterson, ed., *Jefferson: Writings*, 880–81.

the War of 1812, he hoped the United States would soundly defeat the British enemy, but not so severely that the British would be unable to maintain the European balance of power against France in the future.[5]

In a long letter to William Short during the War of 1812, Jefferson revealsed an increasing moral relativism. He even supported the Hamiltonian funding plan, which he had so zealously opposed during the 1790s, now preferring it to Congressional imposition of heavy taxes on land, slaves, and houses to pay for the war. Indeed, Jefferson seemed sympathetic to the Eastern states' reluctance to pay war taxes. He was in arrears on his federal and state taxes throughout the War of 1812 and believed that the Democrats were misguided in levying high land taxes to pay for the conflict's costs in a pay-as-you go policy, rather than restricting current disbursements to normal government expenses and interest on war loans. In his letter to Short of November 28, 1814, after Congress passed a $6 million tax on houses, lands, and slaves to finance the War of 1812, he recommended adopting for the war's duration the old Hamiltonian principle of "funding" the debt—merely paying the interest—rather than a "sinking fund" that paid installments of both interest and principal. In view of the conflict's heavy expenses, the latter would be too burdensome during wartime. He frankly wrote Short, a political nonentity who blamed Madison for the war and thought it had ruined the economy, that he considered Congress's fiscal policies unwise. (It did not restrain him that his son-in-law, John Wayles Eppes of Virginia, chaired the House Committee on Ways and Means). "I wish I could see them [Congress] get into a better train of finance," he lamented. "If anything could revolt our citizens against the war, it would be the extravagance with which they are about to be taxed. It is strange indeed, that at this day, and in a country where English proceedings are so familiar, the principles and advantages of funding should be neglected, and [tax] expedients resorted to." With the zeal of a New England Federalist, he mercilessly criticized the Democratic Congress's fiscal policies. "Their new bank, if not abortive at its birth, will not last through one campaign; and the taxes proposed cannot be paid," he argued. In his opinion, the patriotic Southern states suffered most from wartime embargoes and British blockades, while the Easterners unconscionably smuggled goods across borders and overseas. "How can a people who cannot get fifty cents a bushel for their wheat, while they pay twelve dollars a bushel for their salt, pay five times the amount of taxes they ever paid before?" he protested, perhaps thinking of his own predicament. "Yet that will be the case in all the States south of the Potomac. Our resources are competent to

---

[5] Jefferson to James Monroe, January 8, 1804, Jefferson Papers, LC, quoted in Joseph I. Shulim, "Thomas Jefferson Views Napoleon," *Virginia Magazine of History and Biography* 60/2 (April 1952): 293.

the maintenance of the war if duly economized and skillfully employed in the way of anticipation. However, we must suffer, I suppose, from our ignorance in funding, as we did from that of fighting, until necessity teaches us both."[6]

Jefferson was less interested in a balanced budget—and more concerned about the high taxes Congress was forcing him and other farmers to pay—than he had been in times past. The paragon of republican virtue and frugality in government had given way to the hard-bitten businessman having difficulty paying his debts, primarily because wartime Congressional and British embargoes and blockades kept his goods, especially wheat, bottled up in port without overseas outlets.[7] Along with the dreadful loss of life and economic and natural resources of a country, usually to no purpose, war for Jefferson had the further odious effect of increasing his taxes and making them harder to pay because of government blockades of his produce for export.[8]

When Napoleon's Army was defeated by the European coalition at the end of 1814, Jefferson feared that unemployed French veterans, like powerful armies in ancient history without a war to fight, might turn to oppressing their fellow citizens. At the same time, he agreed with his former ward, William Short, who had made a fortune from various speculations and investments but had never forgotten a love affair he consummated in France at the beginning of its revolution with the young wife of a French duke, that France was an idyllic spot. Although professing relief at the "monster" Napoleon's downfall, Jefferson presciently expected that Bonaparte might eventually return or be replaced by another general-turned-dictator. He wrote Short,

> You intimate a possibility of your return to France, now that Bonaparte is put down. I do not wonder at it. France, freed from that monster, must again become the most agreeable country on earth. It would be the 2d choice of all whose ties of family & fortune give a preference to some other one, and the 1st of all not under those ties. Yet I doubt if the tranquility of France is entirely settled. If her Pr[a]etorian bands are not furnished with

---

[6] Jefferson to William Short, November 28, 1814, in Lipscomb and Bergh, eds., *Writings of Jefferson*, 14:217, and Peterson, ed., *Jefferson: Writings*, 1357–58. For an examination of Short's attitude, see George Green Shackelford, *Jefferson's Adoptive Son* (Lexington: University Press of Kentucky, 1993).

[7] See Steven Harold Hochman, "Thomas Jefferson: A Personal Financial Biography" (PhD diss., University of Virginia, 1987), 264–68.

[8] One of Jefferson's many denunciations of war as wasteful and as providing excuse for governments to assume arbitrary power over their citizens is his letter to Samuel Kercheval, July 12, 1816, often cited in this study and found on microfilm reel 49, Jefferson Papers, LC (hdl.loc.gov/loc.mss/mtj.mtjbib022494) and in Peterson, ed., *Jefferson: Writings*, 1401.

employment on her external enemies, I fear they will recall the old, or set up some new Caesar.[9]

Stating in such matter-of-fact terms the decline of French republican virtue, which would have greatly pained him had he been forced to admit it as secretary of state in 1793, in old age Jefferson embraced a realist position on world politics. Emblematic of Jefferson's increasingly cynical perspective was his support of Napoleon's overthrow of the restored Bourbon monarchy in January 1815, when he escaped from exile on the Italian island of Elba and returned to Paris during the thunderous Hundred Days. Resuming his rule from March through May 1815 following a popular referendum, and hoping to appease the British so that they would leave him alone, Bonaparte instituted such reforms as the abolition of the slave trade in France and its colonies.[10] In retrospect, after reading the prison-keeper Barry O'Meara's memoir of Napoleon's final years on St. Helena, where O'Meara witnessed his gradual poisoning, tortures, and other humiliations, Jefferson admitted that the book revealed Bonaparte's great intelligence, but his inability to apply it to constructive purposes. He concluded that Napoleon's great shortcoming was that he lacked a moral sense, an ability to empathize with the sufferings of others. This moral defect enabled him to engage in endless wars that cost the lives of "tens of millions." Revealing his increasing moral relativism, Jefferson nonetheless concluded that the great European powers that defeated and imprisoned him were even more devoid of a moral sense than Napoleon was, attested by the degradations and deprivations they inflicted upon him.[11]

☙

By 1815, Jefferson considered naïve his earlier expectations of humanity's inevitable and irreversible progress although they had never been a mainspring of his philosophy.[12] By 1815, abandoning his previous confidence in human improvement, expressed so eloquently in a letter to William Greene Munford in

---

[9] Jefferson to William Short, November 28, 1814, in Peterson, ed., *Jefferson: Writings*, 1359.

[10] R. S. Alexander, *Napoleon* (London: Arnold, 2001), 75; Jerome Reich, "The Slave Trade at the Congress of Vienna: A Study in English Public Opinion," *Journal of Negro History* 53/2 (April 1968): 140.

[11] Jefferson to John Adams, February 25, 1823, in Cappon, ed., *Adams-Jefferson Letters* (1988), 589.

[12] Jefferson seldom proclaimed his belief in the inevitability of human progress, and even then, it was often tentative. For that reason, Ari Helo's thesis in *Thomas Jefferson's Ethics and the Politics of Human Progress: The Morality of a Slaveholder* (Cambridge: Cambridge University Press, 2014), is slightly misleading.

1799, Jefferson cautiously welcomed Napoleon's escape from exile in the island of Elba and his resumption of rule in France for the unique Hundred Days. Despite Bonaparte's aggressiveness and ambition, Jefferson recommended that the European Allies accept him as France's ruler because the people had received him enthusiastically after his return, and he believed in respecting the people's voice. When Jefferson learned that the British and the Prussians intended to invade France and topple Napoleon, he regretted that the oppressed subjects of royal governments were again forced to blindly undertake meaningless carnage. Drawing parallels to the Roman Empire, he wrote, "I look on this new conflict of the European gladiators, as from the higher forms of the amphitheatre, wondering that man, like the wild beasts of the forest, should permit himself to be led by his keeper into the arena, the spectacle and sport of the lookers on." He admitted that he did not "see the issue with the sanguine hopes of our friend M. Dupont. I fear, from the experience of the last twenty-five years, that morals of necessity do not advance hand in hand with the sciences."[13] Thus, the bloody, seemingly endless Napoleonic Wars impelled Jefferson's increasing cynicism about human nature's perfectibility.

After Napoleon's final defeat at the Battle of Waterloo, Jefferson, perhaps tailoring his opinions to his audience, resumed his castigation of the enigmatic liberal despot. When his protégé George Ticknor, a political conservative who had just toured Europe, informed him that Bonaparte had emphasized military training in the schools and universities, Jefferson (who himself favored military training and engineering, creating the US Military Academy at West Point in 1802) feigned horror. He said that Napoleon was a monster who deserved the greatest suffering because of his unparalleled "atrocities" against humanity. "What sufferings can atone for his crimes against the liberties and happiness of the

---

[13] Jefferson to Monsieur Correa de Serra, June 28, 1815, in Lipscomb and Bergh, eds., *Writings of Jefferson*, 14:330–31. Jefferson to William Green Munford [or Mumford], June 18, 1799, discussed further below, is in Koch, ed., *Jefferson*, 61–63. In his last letters to Jefferson, Pierre Samuel Du Pont de Nemours, a French physiocrat leader, *idéologue* and pacifist, expressed hope that the South American colonies would adopt republicanism. In this letter to Correa, Jefferson was probably referring to Du Pont's acceptance of the restored Louis XVIII's constitutional monarchy in France as long as it guaranteed civil liberties. Du Pont early turned against Napoleon, at least in part because Napoleon disparaged his abilities and never offered him a major political office after he returned to France from the United States in 1802; Du Pont had expected a prestigious appointment. Having maintained a friendly relationship with Talleyrand throughout his life, after Napoleon's downfall Du Pont continued requesting political appointments from the resilient foreign minister (Raymond F. Betts, "Du Pont de Nemours in Napoleonic France, 1802–1815," *French Historical Studies* 5/2 (Fall 1967): 188–203).

human race?" he protested.[14] The man whose genius and seeming mission to safeguard the French Revolution Jefferson had admired when he was a triumphant general fighting for the Republic during the late 1790s, he now ostensibly considered a downtrodden maniac.[15]

In the political sphere, despite exercising a benevolent despotism over hundreds of slaves, Jefferson had contempt for monarchs and those, like Napoleon, who aspired to a kingly domination over their fellow citizens. Shortly after retiring from the presidency, he derided the hereditary rulers of Europe as lazy, stupid "animals." He reflected, "These animals had become without mind and powerless; and so will every hereditary monarch be after a few generations."[16] In 1815, Jefferson called Napoleon, a self-proclaimed monarch who rose from the middle classes, a carnivorous "kite" who threatened to "eat" his own people. Even more vehemently disparaging the recently restored Louis XVIII whom Bonaparte had briefly deposed, Jefferson now demanded that the Allies respect the rights of the French people and return Bonaparte to power:

> I trust that the allied powers will be sensible that they have neither the right nor the power to impose on France a ruler which she rejects, or to displace one [Napoleon] who, from being originally an Usurper, seems now to have become a legitimate despot, by the will of the great body of the nation. They have rejected their king dog, and preferred a kite [an individual who preys on others, a metaphor derived from a predatory, carnivorous bird similar to a hawk]. They have a right to be eaten, if they chuse it.[17]

At least in theory, Jefferson seemed unruffled by the prospect of cannibalism.[18]

Before the Battle of Waterloo, Jefferson was prepared to endorse the legitimacy of Bonaparte's new government, recently ratified by a plebiscite. He opposed Tsar Alexander I's occupation of Paris: "As far as we can judge from appearances Bonaparte, from being a mere military Usurper, seems to have become

---

[14] Jefferson to George Ticknor, November 25, 1817, microfilm reel 50, in Jefferson Papers, LC (hdl.loc.gov/loc.mss/mtj.mtjbib023002); printed in George T. Curtis, *Life, Letters and Journals of George Ticknor*, 1:301.

[15] For Jefferson's changing views on Bonaparte, see Shulim, "Thomas Jefferson Views Napoleon," 288–304.

[16] Jefferson to Governor John Langdon, March 5, 1810, in Peterson, ed., *Jefferson: Writings*, 1221–22.

[17] Jefferson to George Ticknor, July 4, 1815, in Sigmund Diamond, ed., "Some Jefferson Letters," *Mississippi Valley Historical Review* 28/2 (September 1941): 236.

[18] On Jefferson's use of the term, "cannibals," see Scherr, "Jefferson's 'Cannibals' Revisited."

the choice of his nation; and the allies, in their turn, the usurpers & spoliators of the European world." Jefferson further expounded his persisting devotion to each nation's right to self-determination. "The right of nations to self government being my polar star," he said, "my partialities are steered by it, without asking whether it is a bonaparte or an alexander [*sic*] toward whom the helm is directed."[19] He was aware that Tsar Alexander had not been chosen by the people although Napoleon was. Therefore, he was disappointed when Alexander entered France and installed Louis XVIII, and the Quadruple Alliance sent Napoleon to die on the island of St. Helena.

Employing this pessimistic, culturally relativist perspective he viewed the British Parliament's members, whose corruption and gratification of selfish interests mocked the ideal of "balanced government." In 1810, he wrote to New Hampshire's Democratic-Republican Governor John Langdon, that in Great Britain, where the party battle was merely between Ins and Outs for the plums of office—unlike his depiction of the United States to John Melish three years later—men in groups revealed their evil nature. Britain's undemocratic regimes forced the voiceless masses to go along with them: "This is the true character of the English government in practice; however different its theory; and it presents the singular phenomenon of a nation, the individuals of which are as faithful to their private engagements and duties, as honorable, as worthy, as those of any nation on earth, and whose government is yet the most unprincipled at this day known."[20]

After the French Revolution terminated in Napoleon's dictatorship and interminable warfare, ending in a restored Bourbon monarchy, Jefferson expressed less confidence that other ethnic groups, including the "enlightened" French, could adopt republican government. He depicted the American people and their Anglo-Saxon British forebears, despite the latter's "corrupt" polity, alone as capable of instituting popularly elected legislatures.

Extremely pleased by his election as the nation's third president in 1801, Jefferson later exuberantly referred to his victory as the "revolution of 1800."[21] But he knew that his "revolution," such as it was, was doomed to be incomplete because of laws passed during the administrations of his predecessors and the general habits and customs of the American people, who were becoming increasingly involved in commerce, finance, and manufacturing. At the end of his first year as president, he wrote a French friend, "What is practicable must often control what is pure theory; and the habits of the governed determine in a great degree what is

---

[19] Jefferson to José Corrêa de Serra, June 28, 1815, in Looney, ed., *Jefferson Papers: Retirement Series*, 8:569.

[20] Jefferson to John Langdon, March 5, 1810, in Peterson, ed., *Jefferson: Writings*, 1220.

[21] Jefferson to Judge Spencer Roane, September 6, 1819, in ibid., 1425.

practicable. Hence the same original principles, modified in practice according to the different habits of different nations, present governments of very different aspects." He was aware that the divergences in history, culture, and traditions between the United States and France played a great role in the contrasting outcomes of their revolutions. "The same principles reduced to forms of practice accommodated to our habits, and put into forms accomodated [*sic*] to the habits of the French nation, would present governments very unlike each other." Hypothetically allowing that a great political philosopher well acquainted with French habits would perhaps be able to devise them a "free government," Jefferson doubted the advent of such a prodigy. Instead, he predicted, "many unsuccessful experiments I fear are yet to be tried before they will settle down in freedom & tranquility."[22]

In 1817, after the Bourbon restoration, he wrote Lafayette, indirectly reminding him that in 1789 he had doubted the intellectual ability of the French to go beyond constitutional monarchy, because regal rule was the only government they had historically experienced. Indeed, he wittily wrote Lafayette early in the French Revolution that one must not expect people accustomed to autocracy "to be transferred from despotism to liberty, in a feather-bed." Pointing out that the foreign troops of the Quadruple Alliance would eventually leave France, he tried to be optimistic, predicting that the French people were sufficiently well educated to adopt liberalizing reforms. "What government she [France] can bear, depends not on the state of science, however exalted, in a select band of enlightened men," he soberly pointed out, "but on the condition of the general mind. That, I am sure, is advanced and will advance.... For I consider your foreign military oppressions as an ephemeral obstacle only."[23]

Jefferson felt greater misgivings about the potential of the South American revolutions for achieving liberty, civil equality, and representative government. Even though Simón Bolívar and other revolutionaries were expelling the benighted Spanish monarchy, they possessed the same feudal, authoritarian mindset as the governments they overturned. As Jefferson wrote incisively, "I wish I could give better hopes of our southern brethren," whose future after their inevitable independence from Spain was moot. "What will then become of them? Ignorance and bigotry, like other insanities, are incapable of self-government." They would end up miserable under the heel of dictators, he feared: "They will fall under military despotism, and become the murderous tools of the ambition of their

---

[22] Jefferson to Pierre Samuel Du Pont de Nemours, January 18, 1802, in Oberg, ed., *Jefferson Papers*, 36:391. I have retained Jefferson's spelling but modernized his punctuation.

[23] Jefferson to Lafayette, May 14, 1817, in Peterson, ed., *Jefferson: Writings*, 1407; Jefferson to Marquis de Lafayette, April 2, 1790, in Boyd et al., eds., *Papers of Thomas Jefferson*, 16:292–93.

respective Bonapartes." Of course, he assured Lafayette of his sincere "wish to see them and all mankind exercising self-government, and capable of exercising it. But the question is not what we wish, but what is practicable?" "As their sincere friend and brother then," Jefferson recommended their return to Spain as self-governing dominions under the protection ("guarantee") of France, Russia, Holland, and the United States, who would prevent the motley array of new states in South America from fighting among themselves like the ancient Greek city-states. He relied on the South Americans' increasing experience in representative government to accelerate "their emancipation from their priests, and advancement in information," to "prepare them for complete independence."[24] Although England lagged behind only the United States in advancement in constitutional government, Jefferson excluded it from the "confederacy" of guarantors of Latin-American independence. He considered England's government excessively "selfish" and obsessed with material gain, "incapable of honorable patronage or disinterested co-operation; unless, indeed, what seems now probable, a revolution should restore to her an honest government, one which will permit the world to live in peace."[25]

Contrary to many historians' assumptions, despite his frequent criticisms of the British government and society for oppressing the poor and barring most White adult male citizens from the vote, Jefferson respected the British. He was of British descent, and he appreciated the British as forerunners of republicanism and constitutional government. He was ready to forgive the recent unpleasantness between the two countries, culminating in the War of 1812, and demonstrated his own refreshing aptitude for civilized behavior and international comity in dealing with British citizens. When a member of the English gentry, George Flower, arrived at Poplar Forest in 1817 with a letter of introduction from Lafayette, hoping to begin an English colony on the prairies of Illinois, Missouri, or Iowa, he responded enthusiastically. (Jefferson must have also enjoyed Flower's comment that Jefferson treated his slaves better than English factory workers and city laborers were treated, which he said almost tempted him, despite his original antislavery fervor, to become a Virginia planter himself.) Jefferson informed Flower that the Public Land Office usually restricted the number of acres a group of settlers could receive, unless they promised some particular benefit to the national economy, as had a recent Swiss settlement for wine production, and the French for olive oil and wines. However, Jefferson thought that an English colony, composed of people who spoke the same language and favored the same republican principles as the United States, should receive some "favoritism" for

---

[24] Jefferson to Lafayette, May 14, 1817, in Peterson, ed., *Jefferson: Writings*, 1408–409.

[25] Ibid., 1409.

displaying a "special national advantage," even though Flower could only offer for tangible consideration "an improved system of farming, interesting to so great a proportion of our citizens."[26]

In supporting Flower's petition on the individual level, Jefferson demonstrated—as his friend President Monroe was doing on an international level by negotiating the Rush-Bagot Treaty, creating an unfortified border between Canada and the United States, the first such agreement in modern times—that for citizens and governments, "duties and interests" could be reciprocal. Such outcomes fulfilled Jefferson's own optimistic philosophy of international relations, results disappointingly rare in the world of his time.

---

[26] Jefferson to George Flower, September 12, 1817, in Lipscomb and Bergh, eds., *Writings of Jefferson*, 15:139–40. On Flower's search for a republican form of government to reside in, and his strangely favorable impression of slavery on Jefferson's Poplar Forest plantation, see Mary Ann Salter, "George Flower Comes to the Illinois Country: A New Look at Motivations," *Journal of the Illinois State Historical Society* 69/3 (August 1976): 213–23.

Chapter 9

"A Capitulation between Conflicting Interests and Opinions": Jefferson's Political Roles for Women, Slaves, and "Infants"[1]

In debating moral issues with Thomas Law, George Washington's relative by marriage, Jefferson was not excluding women from his ethical calculi. He was certainly aware that Law directed his book specifically to the "fair sex." In his writing, Jefferson was not excluding women from consideration in employing the generic term "mankind," a habitual term of communication that was the norm for Western society from antiquity until the 1970s and the advent of the "second wave" of feminism, the women's rights movement. For example, in his letter to Peter Carr in 1787, Jefferson wrote, "The moral sense, or conscience, is as much a part of man as his leg or arm. It is given to all human beings in a stronger or weaker degree, as force of members is given them in a greater or less degree."[2] Women were "human beings"; so were Blacks and slaves. Until relatively recently, people in modern societies condescendingly (and patriarchally, influenced by the story of Adam and Eve) considered women (an often subordinate) part of "mankind."

Jefferson was not a proto-feminist, unlike his correspondent William Godwin, Mary Wollstonecraft's husband.[3] Like virtually all his male contemporaries, he never demanded that women have the right to vote and participate equally with men in politics. On the other hand, he did believe that girls, particularly his own daughters Martha ("Patsy") and Mary ("Polly"), should have an education in the liberal arts equal to that of their young male counterparts, so that they could teach their children if public schools or male tutors were unavailable. Bill 79 of his Revisal of Virginia's Laws, proposed in 1778, was uniquely democratic in

---

[1] Jefferson to Samuel Kercheval, September 5, 1816, microfilm reel 49, Jefferson Papers, LC (hdl.loc.gov/loc.mss/mtj.mtjbib022568). See the discussion below.

[2] Jefferson to Peter Carr, August 10, 1787, in Peterson, ed., *Jefferson: Writings*, 901.

[3] William Godwin to Jefferson, September 6, 1808, microfilm reel 42, Jefferson Papers, LC (hdl.loc.gov/loc.mss/mtj.mtjbib019027).

providing a free primary school education for all free persons, apparently including Blacks. His bill, defeated by the state legislature, provided that Virginia's counties should be divided into "hundreds," or townships (which he later called "wards"), with a free, tax-supported school in each:

> At every of [*sic*] these schools shall be taught reading, writing, and common arithmetick, and the books which shall be used therein for instructing the children to read shall be such as will at the same time make them acquainted with Graecian, Roman, English, and American history. At these schools all the free children, male and female, resident within the respective hundred, shall be intitled to receive tuition gratis, for the term of three years, and as much longer, at their private expence, as their parents, guardians or friends shall think proper.[4]

Thus, girls and free Blacks would have the same opportunity for higher education as White boys, if their parents or patrons had the money and were willing to pay for it. If knowledge was the road to happiness, each free child in Virginia's wards or "hundreds" would receive an opportunity to embark to some length on that course.[5] As philosopher Mark Holowchak suggests, "Wards are to be structured such as to provide for the happiness and independence of the citizens in them." Citizens would be inclined to participate in government because, through such institutions as education, the government attempted to secure their happiness and fulfill their "social nature."[6]

By promoting each citizen's participation in local government through their performance of various administrative functions and the election of local officers,

[4] Virginia Revisal of the Laws, Bill 79, in Boyd et al., eds., *Papers of Thomas Jefferson*, 2:528. Jon Kukla's statement, in *Mr. Jefferson's Women* (New York: Vintage, 2007), 173, that Jefferson refused to include girls within this educational plan is incorrect. Unfortunately, the system of scholarships, by which one extremely intelligent *boy* from every ten schools whose parents could not afford to pay for his further education would receive annually renewable subsidies from the state, was so meager that it was hardly significant, as Daniel J. Boorstin pointed out in *Lost World of Thomas Jefferson*, 223–24.

[5] The idea that free public education was the panacea for economic and social inequality reached fruition in the years after Jefferson's death, but he foreshadowed it in many of his writings although some scholars claim that his idea that a "natural aristocracy" should guide the nation was unduly elitist. See, for example, Rush Welter, *Popular Education and Democratic Thought in America* (New York: Columbia University Press, 1962).

[6] Mark Andrew Holowchak, "Individual Liberty and Political Unity in an Expanding Nation," ch. 3 of Holowchak, ed., *Jefferson and Philosophy*, 52–55, 52 (first quotation), 55 (second quotation). Holowchak writes, "Jefferson's ward system was his way of ensuring that democratic ideals and political stability could survive in a country that was expanding territorially and progressing at a rapid technological and scientific pace" (56).

the wards increased the people's feeling of community and their understanding and appreciation of working democracy. Jefferson believed such local entities as schools, and local officials like boundary arbitrators, overseers of the poor, road and bridge administrators, were vital to the success of republican government. Notwithstanding New England's dismaying adherence to his Federalist opponents for much of his political life, he most admired its town meetings, which he considered the closest approximation to his ward idea. "My partiality for that [ward] division is not founded in views of education solely, but infinitely more as the means of a better administration of our government and the eternal preservation of it's [*sic*] republican principles," he wrote Virginia governor Wilson Cary Nicholas in 1816. "The example of this most admirable of all human contrivances in government is to be seen in our Eastern states; and it's [*sic*] powerful effect in the order and economy of their internal affairs, and the momentum it gives them as a nation, is the single circumstance which distinguishes them so remarkably from every other national association."[7] In Jefferson's opinion, the town meeting or "ward" (perhaps even more than the absence of slavery) made New Englanders so unique as to constitute them a separate "nation."

Jefferson was willing to support women's limited participation in politics, particularly if they favored republicanism rather than monarchy or Hamiltonian Federalism. When the son of Robert Gamble, a Richmond Federalist merchant whom Jefferson hoped to convert to the Democratic-Republican Party, visited England "on commercial concerns," Jefferson advised James Monroe, US minister to Great Britain, to befriend him. He noted, "His [Gamble, Sr.'s] two daughters have remained two good republicans." He hoped the son might soon join them.[8]

Of course, Jefferson's assessment of female political acumen at the outset of the French Revolution depended on which side of the political fence the women in question were on. If he perceived them as friends of liberal reform, he applauded their involvement in politics. If he viewed them as indolent aristocrats who indulged in luxury and corruption, he opposed them, just as he would if they were male. When Jefferson was in Paris as US minister observing the early stages of the French Revolution in 1788 and 1789, he criticized the aristocratic women of the Court whom he suspected used their influence and their wiles to manipulate the king's ministers into doing favors for their friends. Suspecting that Queen Marie Antoinette and her entourage of power-hungry representatives of the sovereigns of Europe were infiltrating Louis XVI's ministry, Jefferson felt alarmed

---

[7] Jefferson to Wilson Cary Nicholas, April 2, 1816, microfilm reel 48, Jefferson Papers, LC (hdl.loc.gov/loc.mss/mtj.mtjbib022402).

[8] Jefferson to James Monroe, June 15, 1805, microfilm reel 33, Jefferson Papers, LC (hdl.loc.gov/loc.mss/mtj.mtjbib014811).

but powerless. In December 1788, writing George Washington about the contest for power between the king, the Parlement of Paris, and the Estates General, Jefferson doubted that a "thorough reformation of abuse" would occur. As a supposedly "naïve" American, Jefferson purveyed a unique outlook on events. He advised that the current state of political disorganization, even desperation, among Europe's male politicians furnished an opportunity for women to exert decisive influence on the political struggle, which they might employ either to increase the power of the people (the Third Estate) or the nobles and the Court. As far as Jefferson could tell, the Frenchmen in power were not even aware of the weight that women wielded on events. "In my opinion a kind of influence, which none of their [French officials'] plans of reform take into account, will elude them all," he observed. "I mean the influence of women in the government." He then elaborated on what he considered aristocratic women's conspiratorial role in exerting political authority over powerful men, a state of affairs that he thought inconceivable in the United States. (This was before such women as Abigail Adams, Maria Reynolds, and Dolly Madison arrived on the political scene.[9]) Informing Washington, the most influential man in the United States, about events in Paris, he painted a picture of persistent, most likely beautiful women, twisting important men around their fingers—or at least trying to:

> The manners of the nation [France] allow them [women] to visit, alone, all persons in office, to sollicit [*sic*] the affairs of the husband, family, or friends, and their sollicitations [*sic*] bid defiance to laws and regulations. This obstacle may seem less to those who, like our countrymen, are in the precious habit of considering Right, as a barrier against all sollicitation [*sic*]. Nor can such an one, without the evidence of his own eyes, believe in the desperate state to which things are reduced in this country from the omnipotence of an influence which, fortunately for the happiness of the [female] sex itself, does not endeavor to extend itself in our country beyond the domestic line.[10]

Jefferson decried this kind of female involvement in politics, which the tenets of republican political conduct rendered illegitimate, mainly because he interpreted Frenchwomen as aiding aristocratic special interests rather than the entire

---

[9] See Catherine Allgor, *Parlor Politics: In Which the Ladies of Washington Helped Build a City and a Government* (Charlottesville: University Press of Virginia, 2000); Allgor, *Perfect Union: Dolley Madison and the Creation of the American Nation* (New York: Henry Holt & Co., 2006); and Allgor, *Dolley Madison: The Problem of National Unity* (Boulder: Westview Press, 2013).

[10] Jefferson to George Washington, December 4, 1788 (misdated by Jefferson as November 4, perhaps betraying his concern), in Boyd et al., eds., *Papers of Thomas Jefferson*, 14:330.

community, represented by the rising bourgeoisie. By contrast, he praised French women's support for increasing the Third Estate's power at the impending meeting of the Estates General, convened by Louis XVI to handle the government's bankruptcy crisis. "All the handsome young women, for example, are for the *tiers état*, and this is an army more powerful in France than the 200,000 men of the king," he reported enthusiastically in spring 1789 to David Humphreys, US minister to Portugal.[11]

Desiring additional recruits to the middle-class reform campaign in France, Jefferson sought young female allies. He was confident that women could abandon their alleged obsessions with fashions and material things for more important issues. "The change in this country, since you left it, is such as you can form no idea of," he explained to Humphreys. "The frivolities of conversation have given way entirely to politicks—men, women and children talk nothing else; and all you know talk a great deal."[12] Somewhat anomalously, Jefferson exuberantly included women and children along with men as members of the political nation.

Years later, Jefferson retained a more vivid impression of the luxury-loving queen, Marie Antoinette, than of the great Girondist thinker Madame Roland, or the French washer-women, *enragées*, and "fish-wives" whose raucous acts spurred the early French Revolutionary *journées*. He viewed women's participation in the Revolution as a fad rather than a product of sincere political convictions. In his autobiography, written at age seventy-seven, he concluded that, despite their salons and reading, French bourgeois women's support for liberal causes or institutional reforms was somewhat flippant. He ascribed much of the credit for the French Revolution to the American Revolution's example, especially in inspiring French veterans of the American Revolution with ideals of liberty and equality. Along with French and English political theorists, the American Revolution had "awakened the thinking part of the French nation in general, from the sleep of despotism." He observed that "young" French officers who had fought in the American Revolution "came back with new ideas and impressions," which the press "disseminated." It soon became stylish to favor liberal ideas, and bourgeois and aristocratic women alike wanted to be à la mode. "Politics became the theme of all societies, male and female," Jefferson recalled, "and a very extensive and zealous party was formed, which acquired the appellation of the Patriotic

---

[11] Jefferson to David Humphreys, March 18, 1789, in Boyd et al., eds., *Papers of Thomas Jefferson*, 14:677. Kukla misrepresents Jefferson's meaning in this letter, claiming that it reveals his "censoriousness" of French women's political activity when it shows the opposite (*Mr. Jefferson's Women*, 156).

[12] Jefferson to David Humphreys, March 18, 1789, in Boyd et al., eds., *Papers of Thomas Jefferson*, 14:676.

party." With a mixture of praise and contempt, Jefferson described most supporters of reform as political dilettantes rather than people who took seriously the epochal events they were witnessing: "This [Patriot] party comprehended all the honesty of the kingdom, sufficiently at leisure to think, the men of letters, the easy Bourgeois, the young nobility, partly from reflection, partly from mode; for these sentiments became [a] matter of mode, and as such, united most of the young women to the party."[13]

For most of his life, Jefferson ethnocentrically maintained, especially after the French Revolution's collapse in the Reign of Terror in 1794, that Americans' relatively wide distribution of property and diffusion of education who compared to Europe's oppressed feudal classes enabled them uniquely to succeed as a self-governing republic. He concluded that most revolutions were bound to fail because those involved did not, could not, know what they were doing. Indeed, later, voicing doubts about the ability of freed slaves and new South American nations to institute popular government, Jefferson pointed out that even the comparatively literate and "enlightened" French masses were too poorly educated and politically inexperienced to maintain republicanism. Despite his admiration for French bourgeois culture and politesse, he was aware, somewhat like his antithesis Edmund Burke, that French historical experience exhibited few examples of representative institutions replacing an overthrown monarchy. As he wrote Humphreys, when preparations were underway to convene the Estates-General for the first time in nearly two hundred years, "In fine I beleive [*sic*] this nation will in the course of the present year have as full a portion of liberty dealt out to them as the nation can bear at present, considering how uninformed the mass of their people is. This circumstance will prevent their immediate establishment of the trial by jury." Jefferson considered trial by jury essential in providing equality before the law.[14]

---

[13] Dumas Malone, ed., *Autobiography of Thomas Jefferson* (New York: Capricorn Books, 1959), 81. See also Hellenbrand, *Unfinished Revolution*, 121–22. Jefferson's observation that French war veterans played a major role in spreading anti-aristocratic ideas was confirmed by French historians, such as the Marxist scholar Albert Soboul. See Forrest McDonald, "The Relation of French Peasant Veterans of the American Revolution to the Fall of Feudalism in France," *Agricultural History* 25 (1951): 151–61, which relies on Soboul.

[14] Jefferson to David Humphreys, March 18, 1789, in Boyd et al., eds., *Papers of Thomas Jefferson*, 14:677. On the relatively high literacy rate among adult men and women in France before the French Revolution, see Simon Schama, *Citizens: A Chronicle of the French Revolution* (New York: Knopf, 1989), 180; and John Markoff, "Literacy and Revolt: Some Empirical Notes on 1789 in France," *American Journal of Sociology* 92/2 (September 1986): 323–49. For an example of Jefferson's insistence on the importance of trial by jury, see Jefferson to Du Pont de Nemours, April 24, 1816, in Peterson, ed., *Jefferson: Writings*, 1385–86.

Although Jefferson as president once briefly commented to Albert Gallatin, who apparently suggested a woman for a minor government post, "The appointment of a woman to office is an innovation for which the public is not prepared, nor am I," he did not have a low opinion of women's political acumen compared with men, all things being equal.[15] He was merely unwilling to attract negative attention to his administration, furnish ammunition for Federalist ridicule, or defy public opinion by appointing a woman to office, something neither of his predecessors had done. Indeed, he was willing to give a female ruler, Catherine II (later dubbed The Great), tsarina of Russia, high marks despite her absolutist regime. In 1810, analyzing the rulers of Europe, for whom he had great contempt, he disparaged its kings as lazy, drunken dullards. He believed that their incompetence was at least partly the result of long-time inbreeding among the ruling families, and consequently ascribed Catherine's superior performance to her descent from a more junior branch of royalty, one less subjected to inbreeding. He considered her less mentally impaired than her male counterparts. Recalling his service as US minister to France, he reminisced,

> While in Europe, I often amused myself with contemplating the characters of the then-reigning sovereigns of Europe. Louis XVI was a fool, of my own knowledge. The king of Spain was a fool.... [He then listed several other monarchs, all fools]. All these were Bourbons. The Queen of Portugal, a Braganza, was an idiot by nature. And so was the king of Denmark.... There remained, then, none but old Catherine, who had been too lately picked up to have lost her common sense. In this state Bonaparte found Europe, and it was this state of its rulers which lost it with scarce a struggle.[16]

Jefferson generally respected women's intelligence. He urged his daughters to acquire an education in history and foreign languages far in advance of that available to most men of the time. Nevertheless, as Jefferson explained in his letter of September 5, 1816, to Virginia's democratic reformer Samuel Kercheval, he thought that women were too economically dependent on men to participate in politics. At this time, professing little confidence in *male* rationality and political acumen, he feared that women would distract male voters at polling places with their feminine charms, to which he regretted that men, himself probably included, were susceptible.[17]

---

[15] Jefferson to Albert Gallatin, January 13, 1807, in Henry Adams, ed., *Writings of Albert Gallatin*, 3 vols. (1879; repr., New York: Antiquarian Press, 1960), 3:328.

[16] Jefferson to John Langdon, March 5, 1810, in Peterson, ed., *Jefferson: Writings*, 1221.

[17] Jefferson to Samuel Kercheval, September 5, 1816, microfilm reel 49, Jefferson Papers, LC (hdl.loc.gov/loc.mss/mtj.mtjbib022568); see Joyce Appleby, "Introduction: Jefferson and

A closer examination of Jefferson's letter to Kercheval reveals he sincerely adhered to a doctrine of erratic political progress and tolerant cultural relativism. He merged political expediency, rules of political ethics and morality, and acquiescence in the state's prevailing political practices. The letter's main topic was whether Virginia's slaveholders should gain additional representation for their counties in the state legislature, based on number of slaves, under the terms of a projected new state constitution. (Under the existing constitution, passed in 1776, the number of slaves did not overtly affect representation in the state legislature; each county elected two representatives, but areas in the west that did not have slaves had not recently been divided into separate counties.) Jefferson opposed counting each county's number of slaves in determining representation in the state legislature, even though each slave embodied "three-fifths" of a free person under the 1787 Philadelphia Convention's compromise apportioning seats in the federal lower house, enforced until after the Civil War. "I have been told that, on the question of equal representation [for counties in the legislature], our fellow-citizens in some sections of the state claim peremptorily a right of representation for their slaves," Jefferson objected. He believed that only the free population should be the basis for the number of votes each county held in the state assembly. Applying classical Whig republican principles to determining suffrage qualifications, he assumed that political justice dictated that slaveholders (himself included) should gain no political advantages from the unethical practice of holding persons in bondage. "Principle will, in this, as in most other cases, open the way for us to correct conclusion," he began. He continued,

> Were our state a pure democracy, in which all its inhabitants should meet together to transact all their business, there would yet be excluded from their deliberations 1. infants, until arrived at years of discretion. 2. women, who, to prevent depravation of morals and ambiguity of issue, could not mix *promiscuously* in the meetings of men. 3. slaves, from whom the unfortunate state of things with us takes away the rights of will and of property.[18]

Jefferson extended his analysis from direct democracy, wherein every citizen voted on every issue, to representative democracy, the creation of Americans' "new science of politics," as Alexander Hamilton called it. Contending that women and slaves, as economic dependents of their White male overlords, were constrained from formulating authentic, autonomous opinions of their own,

---

his Complex Legacy," in Onuf, ed., *Jeffersonian Legacies*, 10, for the view that Jefferson's ideal republic excluded Blacks, women, and Native Americans.

[18] Jefferson to Kercheval, September 5, 1816. Italics mine. Spelling and punctuation modernized.

Jefferson bluntly continued, "Those then who have no will could be permitted to exercise none in the popular assembly; and of course could delegate none to an agent in a representative assembly. The business in the first case [direct democracy], would be done by qualified citizens only; and in the second by the representatives of qualified citizens only."[19]

Therefore, Jefferson was ready to exclude women, children, and slaves from political deliberations: children, because they lacked the requisite knowledge and maturity; women, primarily because they might use their wits and wiles to impair their menfolk's decisions although Jefferson apparently considered them competent in political understanding; and slaves, male and female, who legally lacked property. As human property, slaves had no political "wills" of their own, no autonomous existence. They were essentially (and dangerously, if allowed into the political sphere) extensions of their owners' views and objectives.

Adhering to "classical republican" canons, Jefferson considered it fair to deprive "unqualified" women, slaves, and youngsters of the right to vote. He also objected to including the number of slaves in determining counties' representation in the state legislature, which would only increase the power of aristocratic, large slaveholders, whose wealth did not mirror the average citizen's interests. Indeed, to deny slaveholders additional representation was a logical corollary to the political axiom by which "willless" slaves were denied a political identity.[20]

Jefferson was not naïve. He understood that Virginians, like other Southerners, would not want to lose the *national* advantage that slave-holding states already possessed, in Congress and the Electoral College, within the United States Constitution's "three-fifths" ratio of representation for a state's slave population. Jefferson agreed with their stance, albeit unenthusiastically, based on individual and state self-interest, political pragmatism and expediency, and obedience to existing political contracts between the states. Thereby he resorted to his doctrine of political relativism, entailing compromise solutions to conflicts between parties and sections. Seeking slaveholders' acquiescence to apportionment of the state legislature based on the number of free citizens alone, Jefferson matter-of-factly accepted the "representation" of slaves under the national Constitution while rejecting it for that of Virginia: "It is true that, in the General [United States] constitution our state is allowed a larger representation on account of its slaves," he said. "But every one knows that that constitution was a matter of compromise, a capitulation between conflicting interests and opinions."[21]

---

[19] Ibid. Italics mine. Spelling and punctuation modernized.

[20] Ibid.

[21] Ibid.

This phrase, "a capitulation between conflicting interests and opinions," is a good summation of Jefferson's political relativism. Reiterating his quest for political "truth," he said, "In truth, the condition of different descriptions of inhabitants in every country is a matter of *municipal arrangement*, of which no foreign country has a right to take notice. All its inhabitants are men as to them."[22] In this instance, by "foreign country," he anomalously meant the US government and its Congress; and considered the noun "men" as encompassing women, as in the term "mankind," which was universally acceptable in those times.

Employing the concept of incompatible, "foreign" entities in his letter to Kercheval, Jefferson applied the metaphor, "foreign country," to the United States government and Congress, because the government's national responsibilities were "foreign" to the states' domestic political arrangements and largely involved the Union's conduct toward "foreign" nations. Jefferson pointed out that each state was entitled to institute regulations for electing and apportioning its legislature independent of every other state and of the rules prevailing in Congress. Thus, Virginia could rightly refuse to give slaveholders extra votes for their slaves in county representation, even though the national Census counted each slave as three-fifths of a free person. Jefferson's handwriting became increasingly microscopic as he filled the page. He continued, "Thus, in the New England states, none have the powers of citisens [*sic*] but those, whom they call *freemen*; and none are *freemen* until admitted by a vote of the freemen of the town. Yet in the general government [i.e., the United States Congress] these non-freemen are counted in their quantum of representation and of taxation" as full individuals, although they were not allowed to vote in their home states. "So slaves, with us, have no powers as citisens [*sic*]; yet in representation in the General government they count in the proportion of 3 to 5 and so also in taxation."[23]

Jefferson's September 1816 letter to Kercheval concluded with a powerful statement of his doctrine of political relativism: "Whether this [the additional representation the slave states received in Congress] is equal is not here the question. It is a capitulation of discordant sentiments and circumstances, and is

---

[22] Ibid. Italics mine.

[23] Ibid. Jefferson's emphasis. Jefferson's comments applied to Connecticut rather than Massachusetts, where male citizens who possessed sixty pounds worth of personal property or a freehold with an annual income of £3 had the right to vote. In the US Constitution, of course, each slave was counted as three-fifths of a free person in apportioning both state representation in the lower house and assessing the amount of "direct taxes" (e.g., land, poll, or house taxes) that Congress might choose to levy on each state in the future. The income tax was considered unconstitutional because it could not be fairly or sensibly levied on each state in proportion to its population.

obligatory on that ground. But this view shows there is no inconsistency in claiming representation for them from the other states, & refusing it within our own."[24]

A virtuoso politician even in his politically powerless old age—moreover, his friends presidents Madison and Monroe did not often take his advice—Jefferson manifested political acumen and pragmatism. He employed "classical republican" rhetoric, appealing to conservatives, in order to advance his more modern, liberal democratic agenda for Virginia (universal White manhood suffrage and equal electoral districts, with no extra seats for slave-holding counties).[25]

Thus, Jefferson insisted on recognizing principles of political justice and (White) majority rule within his own state although he did not specifically exclude free Blacks from the vote. By the same token, political expediency dictated that the existing representation of three-fifths of the slave population (for both Northern and Southern states) in Congress remain, so as not to alienate Virginians who might agree to omit that provision from their state constitution.

Many other political leaders, Republican and Federalist, held views similar to Jefferson's on refusing to grant slaves, women and "infants" suffrage and political responsibility.[26] Indeed, one of the most conservative Massachusetts Federalists, Judge Theophilus Parsons of Newburyport, labeled by John Hancock as organizer of the conservative "Essex Junto" political machine, voiced kindred ideas in *The Essex Result*, a pamphlet written in 1778 during the debate over Massachusetts's constitution and a major influence on John Adams. Parsons warned that women were naturally too "delicate" and "tender" for political activity, a tendency fortified by their sheltered domestic lives. Although advocating a bicameral

---

[24] Ibid.

[25] For Jefferson's negligible impact on the presidencies of his friends James Madison and James Monroe, see Roy J. Honeywell, "President Jefferson and his Successor," *American Historical Review* 46/1 (October 1940): 64–75; J. C. A. Stagg, *Mr. Madison's War: Politics, Diplomacy, and Warfare in the Early American Republic, 1783–1830* (Princeton: Princeton University Press, 1983), 438–39; George Dangerfield, *The Era of Good Feelings* (New York: Harcourt, Brace, 1952), 293–301; Harry Ammon, *James Monroe: The Quest for National Identity* (New York: McGraw-Hill, 1971), 476–88.

[26] For useful summaries of "classical republican," Whig ideology's role in determining voting eligibility, and the general political deference of the poor and middling classes to the rich, see Jack P. Greene, *All Men Are Created Equal* (Oxford: Clarendon Press, 1976); Charles Sydnor, *Gentlemen Freeholders: Political Practices in Washington's Virginia* (Chapel Hill: University of North Carolina Press, 1952); Richard R. Beeman, "Deference, Republicanism, and the Emergence of Popular Politics in Eighteenth-Century America," *William and Mary* Quarterly, 3d ser., 49/3 (July 1992): 401–30; Jack R. Pole, "Historians and the Problem of Early American Democracy," *American Historical Review* 67/3 (April 1962): 626–46; Ronald P. Formisano, "Deferential-Participant Politics: The Early Republic's Political Culture, 1789–1840," *American Political Science Review* 68/2 (June 1974): 473–87.

legislature with proportional representation in both houses, a liberal concept, he considered government primarily a tool to protect property. "Every freeman, who hath sufficient discretion, should have a voice in the election of his legislators," he said. By this, he implied a property requirement for voters, since "the legislative body should be so constructed, that every law affecting property, should have the consent of those who hold a majority of the property."[27]

Though rhetorically insisting on legislative representation for every "person" in the state, Parsons, adopting Burke's concept of virtual representation, would bar mentally and physically "dependent" women, children, slaves, and poor Whites from voting. As he put it, "All the members of the state are qualified to make the election, unless they have not sufficient discretion, or are so situated as to have no wills of their own." Epitomizing the classical Whig theory of suffrage, Parsons continued, "Persons not twenty-one years old are deemed of the former class, from their want of years and experience. The municipal law of this country will not trust them with the disposition of their lands, and consigns them to the care of their parents or guardians." Women, no matter what their age, lacked the mental acuity to vote, primarily because, in consideration of their natural "delicacy," a male-dominated society prevented them from gaining appropriate life experience. Otherwise, they were ostensibly as intelligent as men: "Women what age soever they are of, are also considered as not having a sufficient acquired discretion, not from a deficiency in their mental powers, but from the natural tenderness and delicacy of their minds, their retired mode of life, and various domestic duties. These concurring, prevent that *promiscuous* intercourse with the world, which is necessary to qualify them for electors," he said.[28]

Ironically, in justifying the exclusion of women from the suffrage, Parsons used the same erotically suggestive term Jefferson employed nearly forty years later, although contrary to Jefferson, he argued that women's isolation from the "promiscuous" affairs of the world incapacitated them for public participation. (By contrast, Jefferson thought women's presence in politics would distract *men* from acting responsibly, because women represented social activities and pleasures more mundanely "promiscuous" than the serious business of political decision-making.) Parsons apparently ascribed women's alleged political ineptitude to both nature and environment. Their minds were naturally too "tender" for the political rough-and-tumble, partly because the "retired mode of life" that a male-dominant society imposed on them impeded an acquaintance with current political affairs. While women's judgmental "discretion" was innately inadequate for

---

[27] [Theophilus Parsons], *The Essex Result* (1778), in Charles S. Hyneman and Donald S. Lutz, eds., *American Political Writing During the Founding Era, 1760–1805*, 2 vols. (Indianapolis: Liberty Press, 1983), 1:497–98.

[28] Ibid. Italics mine. Jefferson used the same adjective in his letter to Kercheval.

their participation in politics, Parsons pointed out, slaves' "situation," depriving them of freedom of will, rendered them far more incapable. "Slaves are of the latter case and have no wills," he admitted, pointing out that slavery deprived Blacks of a social identity. "But are slaves members of a free government? We feel the absurdity, and would to God, the situation of America and the tempers of its inhabitants were such, that the slave-holder would not be found in the land." He raged against an institution that had no place in a land whose people supposedly stood for liberty.[29]

Like many Massachusetts political conservatives, Parsons championed a strong executive, high property requirements for voters, and an established church. Many of his ideas were implemented in the Massachusetts Constitution of 1780, which he helped John Adams to draft. Among the most extreme Massachusetts conservatives, Parsons's opposition to slavery, an insignificant institution in his home state, did not mean that he advocated the rights of the poor and downtrodden. By contrast, many Southern politicians, such as John Taylor of Caroline (Virginia) and Charles Pinckney of South Carolina, who favored universal suffrage for White males supported Black enslavement.

When discussing questions of political theory with legalistic individuals like the Schoharie, New York, attorney Isaac Hall Tiffany (1777–1859), Jefferson was more likely to resort to old-fashioned Enlightenment ideals and universally valid principles than in writing the political activist Kercheval. In 1819, after sending Jefferson a model of the three branches of the US government and their powers, Tiffany hinted that he wanted Jefferson to translate Aristotle's *Politics*. As a prelude to this task, he requested from the elderly Monticello squire definitions of such terms as "liberty" and "republic." In reply, Jefferson offered a definition of liberty similar to Hobbes's *Leviathan*, which maintained that liberty was essentially nothing more than the physical ability to move where you had the power to go in the absence of physical impediments. Revealing the influence of Locke's *Second Treatise of Government* and Montesquieu's *Spirit of the Laws*, he merged Hobbes's idea of absolute physical freedom of movement with respect for the equal rights of others and his old-age concept of political relativism.

Perhaps Jefferson was also thinking of Adams's observations, in *Defence of the Constitutions* (1787) and elsewhere, that the term "republic" was so widely used and abused by political thinkers that it could mean anything or nothing.[30]

---

[29] *The Essex Result* (1778), ibid. See also Rosemarie Zagarri, *The Politics of Size: Representation in the United States, 1776–1850* (Ithaca: Cornell University Press, 1987), 39–40.

[30] John Adams, *Defence of the Constitutions of Government of the United States*, vol. 3, ch. 9, "Padua," in Charles F. Adams, ed., *Works of John Adams*, 10 vols. (Boston: Little, Brown & Co., 1851), 5:453. See also Gerald Stourzh, *Alexander Hamilton and the Idea of Republican Government* (Stanford: Stanford University Press, 1970), 44, 55.

Whatever his inspiration, Jefferson observed that definitions of the "terms liberty & Republicanism…have been so multifariously applied as to convey no precise idea to the mind of Liberty than I would say that, in the whole plenitude of its extent, it is unobstructed action according to our will. But rightful liberty is unobstructed action according to our will, within the limits drawn around us by the equal rights of others." This became the traditional liberal definition of liberty expounded by John Stuart Mill in *On Liberty*. Giving his definition a more radical emphasis than Locke, Jefferson continued, "I do not add 'within the limits of the law': because law is often but the tyrant's will, and always so when it violates the right of an individual." Implying that each citizen, including women and free Blacks, ought to participate in governance by his definition of "republic," Jefferson went on, "I will add 2dly that a pure republic is a state of society in which every member, of mature and sound mind, has an equal right of participation, personally, in the direction of the affairs of the society."[31] Thus, Jefferson modified the cultural relativism of his letter to Thomas Law by denying that a tyrant's rule could be legitimate, and by insisting that no political culture or form of government could violate, rightfully or legally, the equal rights and desires of others for happiness and the good life. In a sense, he presaged the succinct formula of his letter to Coray in 1823, "The equal rights of man, and the happiness of every individual, are now acknowledged to be the only legitimate objects of government."

As he often did, Jefferson reiterated Madison's views in *Federalist* no. 10. He confessed that only a small town or city-state could efficiently enact direct individual participation in law-making and governance. In larger areas, the voters would have to be satisfied with electing representatives, expecting them to behave as honest surrogates, and to follow their constituents' desires and directions as much as possible. Emphasizing that a "pure republic" could only operate over a small land area, Jefferson revealed that his idea of a "pure republic" was what others meant by Athenian-style "direct democracy" in the town hall, or the Boston town meeting. He said, "Such a regimen is obviously impracticable beyond the limits of an encampment, or of a very small village." As the republic grew in territory and population, the election of "deputies" (delegates and representatives, such as state legislators and congressmen) became increasingly urgent. But the government was less "republican" (what we would call democratic), the more the voters were required to resort to representation, instead of making personal political decisions in their own town-meeting–type scenarios. "When numbers, distance, or force, oblige them to act by deputy," he explained, "then their

---

[31] Jefferson to Isaac H. Tiffany, April 4, 1819, microfilm reel 51, Jefferson Papers, LC (hdl.loc.gov/loc.mss/mtj.mtjbib023463).

government continues republican in proportion only as the functions they still exercise in person are more or fewer and as in those exercised by deputy the right of appointing their deputy is *pro hac vice* [for specific occasions] only, or for more or fewer purposes or for shorter or longer terms."[32]

In the recent past, Jefferson had discussed republicanism in this way; especially in 1816, when rumors flew of a new Virginia constitutional convention, and his friend Du Pont de Nemours struggled to help South America's Colombians create a government. In Jefferson's old-age radical mindset, he might logically have denoted the representative stage of a "republic" as an "elective aristocracy," as did Jean-Jacques Rousseau (whom he seldom mentioned) in *The Social Contract*.[33]

Indeed, Jefferson's idea of the "pure republic" had become nearly identical to Rousseau's definition of "democracy" in his *Social Contract* (1762). Rousseau asserted that the people were free only when they made political decisions in person, and that the English people were therefore free only when they (or at least the small percentage who could vote) chose members of the House of Commons. However, Jefferson did not mention the Genevan's masterpiece. Instead, he renewed his fervent recommendation of Destutt de Tracy's volume lauding America's extended republic and representative democracy, the *Review of Montesquieu* (1818), which, partially translated by Jefferson and published by Philadelphia Democrat William Duane a "few years ago," Jefferson considered one of the best books on government ever written. He called it "the ablest political work which the last century of years has given us."[34] Jefferson's enthusiasm for Tracy's work was ephemeral, however. None of his books was among those he recommended as outstanding political treatises for the University of Virginia the year before his death.[35]

Perhaps one reason for his seeming loss of enthusiasm for Tracy was the French philosopher's failure to examine at length the topic of human enslavement. If only because Jefferson was a slaveholder in a slaveholding society, that offense to "human nature" was constantly on his mind, lending it a critical importance it could not have for a European.

---

[32] Ibid.

[33] The letters I am alluding to are Jefferson to Pierre Samuel Du Pont de Nemours, April 24, 1816; Jefferson to John Taylor of Caroline, May 28, 1816; and Jefferson to Samuel Kercheval, July 4, 1816, all in Peterson, ed., *Jefferson: Writings*, 1384–88, 1391–95, 1395–403.

[34] Jefferson to Isaac H. Tiffany, April 4, 1819, microfilm reel 51, Jefferson Papers, LC (hdl.loc.gov/loc.mss/mtj.mtjbib023463).

[35] University of Virginia, "Regulations, Political Science," March 4, 1825, in *The Complete Jefferson*, ed. Saul K. Padover (New York: Tudor Publishing, 1943), 1046.

Chapter 10

Jefferson on the Abolition of Slavery: From Richard Price to Edward Coles

When his father died in 1808, young Edward Coles inherited a dozen slaves and a small, debt-ridden plantation in Albemarle County. He owed a small sum from his father's estate, $500, but did not find any takers for his landholdings at the high price he wanted. Sickened from observing enslaved Blacks, a disgrace to the republic's ideals of human freedom, he postponed his departure for the "free" Midwestern states and the emancipation of his slaves until he could get wealthy from selling his inheritance at a high price. In spring 1819, after eleven years as a slaveholder, with money in his pocket arising from his brother's purchase of his farm and his success with Illinois real estate investments and bank stock purchases, he left for Illinois, intending to free his slaves there. He directed his slaves, who had grown in number from twelve to nineteen, to precede him on flatboats. He had promised his family that he would not inform his slaves of their impending freedom in advance because of his relatives' fear that they might spread the news, encouraging slave rebellions on their plantations. He kept his bondspersons unaware of his intention to free them before they reached Illinois; perhaps he was not certain himself what he would do.[1]

Seventeen of his slaves departed for Illinois ahead of him. Two elderly women stayed behind because they chose not to separate from their husbands or children, whom Coles's mother owned. When the flatboat expedition reached western Pennsylvania, Coles, having caught up with the slave contingent, told them of his decision to free them and provide land for the heads of three families.[2]

Several years before taking the leap of moving with his slaves from Virginia to Illinois, Coles engaged in a momentous correspondence with his Albemarle County neighbor, Thomas Jefferson, a family friend. Advocating the "general

---

[1] According to his biographers, Coles was "naturally indecisive" (Kurt E. Leichtle and Bruce G. Carveth, *Crusade against Slavery: Edward Coles, Pioneer of Freedom* [Carbondale: Southern Illinois University Press, 2011], 20, 39, 40 [quotation], 60; see also Marie Jenkins Schwartz, *Ties That Bound: Founding First Families and Slavery* [Chicago: University of Chicago Press, 2017], 306–307).

[2] Leichtle and Carveth, *Crusade against Slavery*, 59–60.

emancipation" of Virginia's slaves, Coles wrote Jefferson in July 1814, at the height of the War of 1812, several years after inheriting slaves from his father. Urging Jefferson to compose a "plan" and "invaluable Testament" for abolishing slavery in Virginia, he was certain that the "immortal author of the Declaration of Independence" was best suited to influence the public on this matter. Linking the Declaration's antislavery exhortations with attacks on the "ignominious bondage" foisted upon Virginia by "British Colonial policy," he predicted that the elderly Jefferson's prestige would increase in the "course of nature" after he died. From Coles's perspective, even if Jefferson's hoped-for antislavery proclamation achieved nothing during his lifetime, after his death his "disciples" would pursue his goal until they achieved victory. For his part, Coles confided to Jefferson that he had detested slavery from childhood, and early decided that he would never be a slaveholder. Therefore, he wrote Jefferson this farewell letter because he had made up his mind "not to hold them; which decision has forced me to leave my native state, and with it all my relatives and friends."[3]

Jefferson's reply, written during a critical point in the War of 1812, dodged the issue. He made clear that he considered slavery antithetical to the moral sense, an amoral and immoral institution. He asserted that during his long political career, he had never been in a position to force through emancipation. Probably with *Notes* in mind, Jefferson said that the public had long been aware of his hostility to slavery. As the years progressed, he grew increasingly convinced that, "the love of justice and the love of country plead equally the cause of those [Black] people, and it is a moral reproach to us that they should have pleaded it so long in vain." Focusing his attention on his home state, he self-righteously deplored Virginia political leaders' refusal to enact antislavery measures to terminate "our present condition of moral and political reprobation." He admired Coles's desire to manumit his slaves as honorable "to both the head and heart," epitomizing a pure moral sense.[4]

Like Coles, as a young man Jefferson decided that slavery and forced labor violated his "moral sense" of right and wrong. Jefferson's lengthy youthful commentary (probably composed before 1775) on a passage from Lord Kames's *Essays on the Principles of Morality and Natural Religion*, written into his copy of the book, baldly rejected the justifications for enslavement advanced by the ancient

---

[3] Edward Coles to Jefferson, July 31, 1814, in Looney, ed., *Jefferson Papers: Retirement Series*, 7:503–504; and in "Letters of Edward Coles: Second Installment," *William and Mary Quarterly* 7/2 (April 1927): 97–113, at 97–98. Much of the correspondence is printed in Ralph L. Ketcham, "The Dictates of Conscience: Edward Coles and Slavery," *Virginia Quarterly Review* 36 (Winter 1960). The letter is also available online (founders.archives.gov/documents/Jefferson/03-07-02-0374).

[4] Jefferson to Edward Coles, August 25, 1814, microfilm reel 47, Jefferson Papers, LC (hdl.loc.gov/loc.mss/mtj.mtjbib021817).

Romans, seventeenth-century Puritans, and the great English jurist Lord Edward Coke in the 1650s. According to Jefferson's marginal comments, the eighteenth-century liberal thinkers Burlamaqui and Montesquieu who accepted the idea that ransom was a legitimate demand to make for the return of a prisoner of war, like philosophers in ancient cultures, accepted the rationale that slavery was proper commutation for the death penalty that a conqueror could allegedly impose upon enemies in a "just war." Even Locke's renowned *Second Treatise of Government* assumed that enslavement was proper substitution for the death penalty in war, while it also indirectly continued the "state of war." Pious writers argued that non-Christian "infidels" deserved enslavement. Jefferson accepted neither justification for slavery, either that of wartime booty or the slave's punishment for "paganism."[5] He regarded slavery strictly as an unjust economic institution that violated the human and natural rights of those subjected to it. He also acknowledged that it was an inherited, convenient institution for him and his fellow Southerners.[6]

Jefferson admired Lord Kames, an early "moral sense" theorist who opposed slavery because it denied the enslaved individual's autonomous right to exercise

---

[5] Koch, *Philosophy of Jefferson*, 18. For Locke's endorsement of the idea that enslavement could be justified by the winner of a "just war" as commutation for killing his vanquished foe, see Helo and Onuf, "Jefferson, Morality, and the Problem of Slavery," 583–614, at 589. On British attempts to justify slavery by citing Ham's derision of his father Noah's nakedness and the dehumanized status of captives taken in wars, concepts the prestigious Sir Edward Coke affirmed, see Jordan, *White over Black*, 54–56. Another popular justification for slavery was that "infidels," especially Muslim Turks, centuries-long enemies of Europe's Christian powers, deserved enslavement; moreover, Turks and North African Barbary pirates enslaved captured Christians (Jordan, *White over Black*, 55–56).

[6] Ultimately, slavery proved unprofitable to Jefferson, precipitating his economic ruin because he had more slaves than he could use and, in old age, moral principles prohibited him from separating families by selling slaves to strangers although the money would have come in handy to reduce his debts. Such factors resulted in his being what one might call "slave-poor." For the adverse economic effects a slave "surplus" had on Jefferson's plantation profits, see Stanton, "Thomas Jefferson: Planter and Farmer," in Francis D. Cogliano, ed., *Wiley-Blackwell Companion to Thomas Jefferson* (Malden, MA: Wiley-Blackwell, 2012), 253–70. Washington's and Madison's plantations also operated at a loss, the result of owning too many slaves and of declining wheat and tobacco prices (Furstenberg, *In the Name of the Father*, 72–74). Washington owned over three hundred slaves when he died. On a visit to Mt. Vernon after Washington's death, Abigail Adams noted, "Mrs. [Martha] Washington with all her fortune finds it difficult to support her family, which consists of three hundred slaves" (Furstenberg, *In the Name of the Father*, 73). Unlike Jefferson, in old age James Madison, in reduced financial circumstances because of poor wheat and tobacco crops and low prices, decided to sell slaves to reduce his debts (David B. Mattern, "James Madison and Montpelier: The Rhythms of Rural Life," in Stuart Leibiger, ed., *Wiley-Blackwell Companion to James Madison and James Monroe* [Malden, MA: Wiley-Blackwell, 2013], 304).

his moral sense, an innate quality in everyone, which required use to establish itself firmly. Among the writers whom Jefferson selected who were not professional attorneys, the extracts from Kames's moral treatises included in his *Legal Commonplace Books* were exceeded only by his excerpts from Montesquieu's *Spirit of the Laws*.[7]

Jefferson appreciated the role that time and the evolution of the moral sense played in a people's ability to adopt representative government. Even in his youth, he thought that the collective moral sense of communities and nations would eventually target the abolition of slavery as a goal. He viewed the replacement of the "savage" custom of killing prisoners of war with lifetime bondage, followed by its comparatively more benevolent evolution into holding prisoners for ransom, as presaging slavery's ultimate demise. He predicted that wartime combatants' demands for ransom would finally give way to allowing freedom to prisoners of war, and eventually to slaves, whose bondage theoretically evolved from the prisoner of war status. Jefferson logically observed, "If we have no right to the life of a captive, we have no right to his labor; if none to his labor we have none to his absent property [ransom] which is but the fruit of that labor. In fact, ransom is but commutation [for enslavement] in another form."[8]

Jefferson denied that enslavement, or even the less odious ransom, was a moral replacement for the supposed customary, "barbaric" right to kill captured enemies in wartime. He considered enslavement automatically void since, according to natural law, no individual could be a slave. Therefore, the institution of slavery itself was an illegal violation of natural law and natural rights.[9] Beginning with *Notes on Virginia*, he proposed that the state emancipate enslaved children and send them to new territories free from bondage once they reached young adulthood; separating families was the price of freedom.

[7] On Lord Kames's moral sense philosophy, see Koch, *Philosophy of Jefferson*, 17–19. Wilson, "Thomas Jefferson's Early Notebooks," 433–52, dates the compiling of Jefferson's commonplace books from 1769 until the late 1770s. The most recent scholarly edition of Jefferson's commonplace books is David T. Konig and Michael P. Zuckert, eds., *Jefferson's Legal Commonplace Book* (Princeton: Princeton University Press, 2019).

[8] Jefferson's commentary, written into his copy of Lord Kames, *Essays on the Principles of Morality and Religion*, 147–49, quoted in Koch, *Philosophy of Jefferson*, 18. Jefferson was aware that John Locke, Montesquieu, and Burlamaqui, three of his favorite thinkers, condoned the immoral policy of holding prisoners of war for ransom. For John Locke's view that slaves, and even convicts condemned to lifetime imprisonment, had the right to seek freedom violently, see Milton Mayer, *If Men Were Angels* (New York: Atheneum, 1972), 116–17.

[9] This was his argument in one of his first legal cases, in which he bluntly asserted, "Under the law of nature, all men are born free" (Jefferson's "Argument in the Case of Howell vs. Netherland," in Ford, ed., *Works of Thomas Jefferson*, 1:470–81).

Jefferson qualified his support for Black freedom in one critical respect: In addition to theoretically opposing procreation between Blacks and Whites, he feared that, once emancipated, Blacks would battle the Whites for a share of political and economic power, precipitating great bloodshed. Therefore, his emancipation proposals stipulated that the Black masses depart Virginia after emancipation. His stance differed somewhat from Locke's position that slavery constituted a continuation of the "state of war" between master and slave; from Jefferson's perspective, emancipation without exportation of the freed slaves would be the state of war. Jefferson justified deporting freed slaves to their own independent colony not as punishment but as liberation, even if he expected some slaves to fear the unknown, as anyone would. He considered deportation a cruel necessity. As Jefferson made clear in the draft of the Declaration of Independence and in various parts of *Notes on Virginia*, he considered slavery a violation of natural rights (the "rights of human nature"): illicit by moral and natural, though unfortunately, not by positive (that is, statute) law.[10]

In an obscure chapter of *Notes on Virginia*, titled "Population," Jefferson early voiced his disgust with slavery. After briefly describing the House of Burgesses' passage of laws imposing prohibitive tariffs on the importation of slaves, which the royal Privy Council in Great Britain invariably disallowed (vetoed) with "a joyful sanction from the then sovereign" (who supported the slave-trading interest), Jefferson called slavery a "blot in our country." He praised the Virginia Assembly for passing a law in 1778 (which he drafted) that "perpetually prohibited" the importation of slaves, commenting, "This will in some measure stop the increase of this great political and moral evil, while the minds of our citizens may be ripening for a complete emancipation of human nature."[11] Observing that Virginia's slave population increased faster than did the free White population, Jefferson, unlike "fire-eaters" who later argued that such facts proved that slavery was a "positive good" for all, grimly noted, "Under the mild treatment our slaves

---

[10] Koch, *Philosophy of Jefferson*, 18; Locke, *Second Treatise of Government*, Chapter 4, "Of Slavery" (New York: Macmillan, 1997). See also Onuf, *Jefferson's Empire*, 175; Helo and Onuf, "Jefferson, Morality, and the Problem of Slavery," 590–91; and Jayne, *Jefferson's Declaration of Independence*, 123–25.

[11] Query VIII, *Notes on Virginia*, "Population," in Peterson, ed., *Jefferson: Writings*, 214. Jefferson claimed authorship of the 1778 "act prohibiting the importation of slaves," one of numerous laws he drafted as leading member of the Committee of Revisors, in "A Memorandum of Services to My Country," which emphasized his services in providing Virginia with new crops from abroad and listed none of his public offices (Peterson, ed., *Jefferson: Writings*, 702). Jefferson composed this memorandum, unpublished during his lifetime, in 1800, for his amusement, after reports of his death circulated in Federalist newspapers.

experience, and their wholesome, though coarse, food, this blot in our country increases as fast, or faster, than the whites."[12]

Jefferson had expressed qualified optimism about planters' amenability to abolitionism in *Notes*, particularly in his indignant Query XVIII. In that famous chapter, he said he detected an increasing tendency for slaveholders to improve their slaves' living conditions and eventually acquiesce in "a total emancipation," inviting their own "extirpation" by God if they refused.[13] He restated this conviction in more secular, temperate language in an August 1785 letter to the English abolitionist and deist philosopher Richard Price. After receiving Price's recent book on the American Revolution, Jefferson sent him a copy of *Notes on Virginia* via US minister to Great Britain John Adams. With his usual feigned modesty concerning the book, which he prized and on which he worked diligently for several years, Jefferson explained that it was a revised and expanded version of a report he had written for the secretary of the French legation at Philadelphia, François de Barbé-Marbois, at the request of Joseph Jones, a Virginia delegate to Congress. "The vices however of their original composition were such as forbid material amendment," he confided. He sent Price one of the numerous English-language copies he anonymously printed in France (he supposedly ordered two hundred) to send to important people, "as a testimony of the respect which the writer bears him." He was undecided about whether to allow *Notes*, with its controversial antislavery opinions that would antagonize fellow Southerners, to appear in the United States. For the time being, he said, "unwilling to expose them [*Notes*] to the public eye, he asks the favor of Doctor Price to put them into the hands of no person on whose care and fidelity he cannot rely to guard them against publication."[14]

Price lauded *Notes* as a brilliant antislavery manifesto. "This has been, indeed, a most acceptable present to me," he wrote. "I have read it with Singular pleasure and a warm admiration of your Sentiments and character." He exclaimed, "How happy would the united States be were all of them under the direction of Such wisdom and liberality as yours!" "But this is not the case," he believed. Price was an antislavery, radical Welsh Presbyterian clergyman with

---

[12] Query VIII, "*Population*," in Peden, ed., *Notes on the State of Virginia*, 87.

[13] *Notes on Virginia,* Query XVIII.

[14] Jefferson to Richard Price, June 1785, in D. O. Thomas, ed., *Correspondence of Richard Price*, 3 vols. (Durham: Duke University Press, 1991–1994), 2:288. For Jefferson's intensive work on *Notes on Virginia*, to which he referred correspondents for his opinions on most issues (especially slavery) until the end of his life, see Wilson, "The Evolution of Jefferson's *Notes*," 98–133. In one of his last letters, he advised a Quaker correspondent who wished for a statement from him against slavery to read his *Notes* because his opinions had not changed (Jefferson to James Heaton, May 20, 1826, microfilm reel 55, Jefferson Papers, LC [hdl.loc.gov/loc.mss/mtj.mtjbib025735]).

Unitarian tendencies. He lived in London and preached to wealthy congregations of Dissenters still subjected to civil disabilities by the Anglican government. He had learned from South Carolina Whig leader and abolitionist Henry Laurens that that state's leading politicians, Speaker of the House of Representative John F. Grimké and wealthy planter and Charleston merchant Ralph Izard, denounced Price's "measures for preventing too great an inequality of property and for gradually abolishing the Negro trade and Slavery." Although he welcomed Jefferson's antislavery stance, Price regretted having prematurely praised the American Revolution as a harbinger of liberal reform. He felt "ridiculous" because slavery and class distinctions still pervaded the Lower South. He bitterly remarked, "It will appear that the people who have been Struggling so earnestly to save *themselves* from Slavery are very ready to enslave *others*; the friends of liberty and humanity in Europe will be mortify'd, and an event which had raised their hopes will prove only an introduction to a new Scene of aristocratic tyranny and human debasement."[15]

Only a few months earlier, Price praised the United States as a land of liberty. His pamphlet, titled *Observations on the Importance of the American Revolution and the Means of Making It a Benefit to the World* (1785), extolled the Revolution as a battle for republican virtue and democratic rule that would culminate in the abolition of slavery in the states. He sent Jefferson a copy of the book and was probably encouraged by Jefferson's exaggerated report that, "I have read it with very great pleasure, as have done many others to whom I have communicated it."[16]

For Price as for Jefferson, the growth of slavery was a major symptom of a republic's decline into luxury and perversion. Neither man gave the issue of abolition the priority it deserved, pretending that slavery would somehow gradually disappear without their active intervention to secure legislation to eliminate it. In this respect, Price was more derelict than Jefferson, who had composed a constitution that would abolish slavery in Virginia as an appendix to his *Notes*, published in England in 1787 and reprinted in America while he was in France. Price's ideology was essentially more conservative than Jefferson's was. He had less democratic fervor than the Virginian, wished to preserve social distinctions between rich and poor, and he supported sumptuary laws to curb the lower classes' drunkenness. He considered Blacks as probably intellectually inferior to Whites. Influenced by the writings of French *economiste* Jacques Turgot, he agreed with

---

[15] Richard Price to Jefferson, July 2, 1785, in Boyd et al., eds., *Papers of Thomas Jefferson*, 8:258–59. On Richard Price, see Anthony Page, "'A Species of Slavery': Richard Price's Rational Dissent and Antislavery," *Slavery and Abolition* 32 (March 2011): 53–73.

[16] Jefferson to Richard Price, February 1, 1785, in Boyd et al., eds., *Papers of Thomas Jefferson*, 7:630.

Jefferson that the Black population must be transported from the United States once slavery was abolished in order to preserve cultural homogeneity and civil peace. Price considered the political "slavery" that White Americans endured at the hands of the British monarchy and Parliament before the American Revolution, and the deprivation of full civil liberties that Presbyterian "rational dissenters" like him continued to experience in England, as odious as the far more oppressive hereditary personal enslavement Blacks suffered. Price agreed with John Taylor of Caroline and other slaveholders (including Jefferson at times, as in his 1814 letter to Thomas Cooper) that members of the class of White "labouring poor," especially in England, were treated as badly as slaves. Despite being a theoretical abolitionist and a member of the British Abolition Society, which favored prohibition of the slave trade and (eventually) slavery, Price eschewed delivering antislavery sermons. He was unwilling to antagonize those of his wealthy London parishioners who were merchants engaged in the slave trade or who were connected with British West Indian planters. Essentially a classical liberal republican, he condoned social inequality and was snobbish and patronizing toward the poor. He was far more enthusiastic about the early stages of the French Revolution (he died in 1791) than about ending Black slavery in the US or the West Indies. Price welcomed the possibility that the French Revolution would lead to an alliance between a British republic, whose people he expected would overthrow the monarchy, and the American and French republics; the abolition of feudalism; and the establishment of civil equality for all Europeans. He was generally more conservative in matters of race and slavery than Jefferson was.[17]

Price was reassured when reliable sources like Jefferson and Benjamin Franklin informed him that British reports of disorder, riots, and mass bankruptcies in the new republic were English fabrications. Nonetheless, he hoped the states would grant Congress more power, within limits. He feared that the American people were growing too devoted to luxuries, especially "along the Sea coast...and in some of the principal towns," symptoms of national decline that might eventually result in exchanging republicanism for monarchy. Expounding the classical republican ethos, Price warned, "The character of popular governments depending on the character of the people, if the people deviate from Simplicity of manners into luxury, the love of Shew, and extravagance, the governments must become corrupt and tyrannical."[18]

In replying to Price's critique, Jefferson indicated his adherence to what David Hume called the "constant and universal principles of human nature." Urging Price to continue to compose antislavery pamphlets, he assured him that they would favorably affect the new breed of potentially antislavery, younger Virginia

[17] Page, "'Species of Slavery,'" 53–73, passim.

[18] Richard Price to Jefferson, March 21, 1785, ibid., 8:53.

office-holders. He dismissively explained the greater willingness of Northerners to abolish slavery as flowing from the institution's relatively minor role in their society and economy, rather than as a manifestation of greater republican virtue or morality than their Southern neighbors possessed. Desiring to acquaint Price with the sectional peculiarities of the South and the diverse receptions his antislavery pamphlet might receive there, Jefferson, who resided in Paris and experienced firsthand few responses to Price's work, surmised,

> Southward of the Chesapeak [*sic*] it will find but few readers concurring with it in sentiment on the subject of slavery. From the mouth to the head of the Chesapeak, the bulk of the people will approve it in theory, and it will find a respectable minority ready to adopt it in practice, a minority which for weight and worth of character preponderates against the greater number, who have not the courage to divest their families of a property which however keeps their consciences inquiet.[19]

Thus, Jefferson believed that in theory, the majority of those who lived in the Chesapeake region—Virginia, North Carolina, and Maryland—were repulsed by slavery. However, only a noble minority would willingly part with their slaves; for the majority, economic dependence on human bondage took priority over "republican" or liberal notions of freedom for all. More starkly, he expected that planters in South Carolina and Georgia, obsessed by the wealth they gained from slave-plowed fields of rice, cotton, and indigo, would hardly consider abolitionist recommendations. Essentially, he viewed men as motivated by their economic self-interest. When it came to non-slaveholding Northerners, Jefferson acknowledged their opposition to slavery, albeit with a tinge of sarcasm. In the North, he wrote Price, "you may find here and there an opponent to your doctrine as you may find here and there a robber and a murderer, but in no greater number. In that part of America, there being but few slaves, they can easily disencumber themselves of them, and emancipation is put into such a train that in a few years there will be no slaves Northward of Maryland." He found little heroism or superior morality in Northerners' rejection of slavery. Indeed, he implied that those Virginians who deplored slavery were of superior probity. They were also more determined than Maryland's slaveholders, he said, to abandon an execrable labor system. Predicting that Virginians were about to undertake a great debate over abolishing the "enormity" of slavery, he was confident that ultimately its antislavery forces would achieve a "sacred" triumph. He depicted the imagined scene of conflict for Price in heroic terms:

---

[19] Jefferson to Richard Price, August 7, 1785, in Boyd et al., eds., *Papers of Thomas Jefferson*, 8:356.

> This [Virginia] is the next state to which we may turn our eyes for the interesting spectacle of justice in conflict with avarice and oppression: a conflict wherein the sacred side is gaining daily recruits from the influx into office of young men grown and growing up. They have sucked in the principles of liberty as it were with their mother's milk, and it is to them I look with anxiety to turn the fate of this question.[20]

Jefferson specifically mentioned his friend and mentor George Wythe, veteran law professor at the College of William and Mary, as a fervent enemy of slavery who indoctrinated his students in his republican principles.[21]

Although Jefferson's letter sought to convince Price that slavery would soon be abolished in every state but South Carolina and Georgia, Price's reply skeptically noted that Henry Laurens had likewise reassured him. Although "honored" by Jefferson's suggestion that he continue to edify the "young persons under preparation for public life at the College of William and Mary at Williamsburgh [*sic*]" by writing about slavery and republicanism, he refused, insisting that his vocation was religion not politics. "It is a very happy circumstance for *Virginia* that its young men are under the tuition of so wise and virtuous a man as you say Mr. Wythe is," he remarked congenially. "Young men are the hope of every state; and nothing can be of so much consequence to a state as the principles they imbibe and the direction they are under."[22] Although Jefferson also relied on America's youth at this time, his confidence in the republican virtue of the younger generation shrank over the years.

Even when the Federalists attempted to crush his Democratic-Republican Party during the "American Reign of Terror" of 1798–1800, when, stressing the likelihood of a French invasion, government prosecutions of opposition newspapers and imprisonment of Jeffersonian writers and editors proliferated, Jefferson, at least on paper, remained cheerful. However, shocked by the enthusiasm that various young men's organizations demonstrated for fighting France and praising President Adams in "patriotic addresses" during the undeclared quasi-war with France, he was less confident of youths' republican virtue than in the past. In June 1799, writing to William G. Munford, a would-be disciple, trying to encourage this young man who had dropped out to return to the College of William and Mary, Jefferson composed one of his most eloquently optimistic letters. "I am among those who think well of the human character generally," he asserted. Reiterating the "moral sense" teachings he had conveyed to Peter Carr at length in 1787, he continued, "I consider man as formed for society, and endowed by nature with those dispositions which fit him for society." He admiringly alluded to

---

[20] Ibid., 356–57.

[21] Ibid.

[22] Richard Price to Jefferson, October 24, 1785, ibid., 8:668.

Condorcet's famous *Sketch of the Progress of the Human Mind* (1793), in which, shortly before committing suicide in a French prison, the French mathematician and philosopher outlined various stages of human improvement through the ages and claimed that humanity was capable of perfectibility. "I believe also, with Condorcet, as mentioned in your letter," Jefferson assured Munford, "that his ["man's"] mind is perfectible to a degree of which we cannot as yet form any conception." Insisting that there was much knowledge still to be gained by extended study in mathematics, astronomy, chemistry, natural history, medicine, pharmacology, and other sciences, he exulted, "great fields are yet to be explored to which our faculties are equal, & that to an extent of which we cannot fix the limits."[23] He did not list the discipline of politics, perhaps sensing that that was a field dependent on *fortuna* (chance) more than on mathematical reasoning.

At this point in his letter, Jefferson felt compelled to stress the significance of the American experiment in civil liberty, religious freedom, and popular government. It was an achievement unique in a world universally (with the tottering exception of France) under the domination of monarchies. The US record for freedom of thought (perpetuated in the Bill of Rights) exceeded what the ancient republics in Greece and Rome had achieved before their fall. Perhaps attempting to overcome his anxiety about current political conditions in the United States, where the Republican press and foreigners hostile to the Adams Administration (even the great English scientist Joseph Priestley) faced fines, imprisonment, or exile, he wrote Munford, "I join with you in branding as cowardly the idea that the human mind is incapable of further advances. This is precisely the doctrine which the present despots of the earth are inculcating; & their friends here re-echoing; & applying especially to religion and politics; 'that it is not probable that any thing better will be discovered than what was known to our fathers.'" After thus mockingly paraphrasing President Adams's speech of over a year before (which still shocked him) responding to a "patriotic address" from young Philadelphia Federalists acclaiming his resistance to France's diplomatic insults and maritime depredations, Jefferson mockingly continued, "We are to look

---

[23] Jefferson to William G. Munford, June 18, 1799, in Oberg, ed., *Jefferson Papers*, 31:127–28. Before Condorcet completed his sketch, he committed suicide, expecting that Robespierre would have him guillotined for his moderate Girondin political views. For Jefferson's later, more restrained acceptance of Condorcet's view of progress, see Jefferson to Du Pont de Nemours, April 24, 1816: "I do not, with some enthusiasts, believe that the human condition will ever advance to such a state of perfection as that there shall no longer be pain or vice in the world" (Peterson, ed., *Jefferson: Writings*, 1387).

backwards then & not forwards for the improvement of science, & to find it amidst feudal barbarisms."[24]

Castigating his atavistic political and intellectual enemies, among whom during the late 1790s he included even his scholarly fellow Revolutionary Adams, Jefferson's mood rose from the depths to a rhetorical crescendo of confidence and fervor for the triumph of Americans' open, free society and "mind" over governmental efforts to stifle them. "Thank heaven the American mind is already too much opened, to listen to these impostures," he proclaimed. "And while the art of printing is left to us science can never be retrograde. What is once acquired of real knowledge can never be lost."[25]

Sounding a more desperately heroic note, Jefferson concluded, "To preserve the freedom of the human mind then & freedom of the press, every spirit should be ready to devote itself to martyrdom; for as long as we may think as we will, & speak as we think, the condition of man will proceed in improvement."[26] Thus, Jefferson believed that the natural goodness and intelligence of man (his "moral sense" and "genius") would supersede government efforts to oppress him and brainwash him into an automaton at the whim of the authorities. Perhaps he thought it necessary to convince young Mumford of this by this zealous harangue.

Nonetheless, Jefferson became confused at this critical point in US history. He was less confident than he pretended to be, and his concluding words to Mumford were illogical. Jefferson was acutely aware of the culpability of Adams, whom he derisively paraphrased in this letter; Secretary of State Timothy Pickering; the great ex-president Washington and other Grand Old Men of the Federalist Party, as well as the comparatively younger Hamilton, who in 1799 was forty-four years of age. Still, he instructed Mumford that the older generation was not responsible for the threat to freedom of thought. Somehow, the younger generation had ushered in the current Federalist hegemony. "The generation which is going off the stage has deserved well of mankind for the struggles it has made," he observed although his ambitions for the presidency excluded him from the departing cohort, "& for having arrested that course of despotism which had overwhelmed the world for thousands & thousands of years. If there seems to be danger that the ground they have gained will be lost again, that danger comes from the generation your contemporary." Upholding his doctrine, "the earth belongs to the living generation," devised ten years earlier in revolutionary Paris,

---

[24] Oberg, ed., *Jefferson Papers*, 31:128. Mumford's letter to him has been lost, but it must have been inspiring to evoke Jefferson's lapidary words. Adams's May 7, 1798, address to "the Young Men of the City of Philadelphia" is quoted in Oberg's note to this letter (129).

[25] Jefferson to William G. Munford, June 18, 1799, in ibid., 128.

[26] Ibid.

Jefferson may have needed to remove doubts that his generation adequately preserved the libertarian heritage for posterity. He was reluctant to consider the possibility that faint-hearted heroes like him had not fought vigorously enough against villains like Hamilton, Adams, and the venerated Washington, whom Jefferson denounced for supporting repressive Federalist legislation.[27]

Suppressing thoughts of violent death (perhaps desiring Washington and Adams as victims), he admonished, "that the enthusiasm which characterises [*sic*] youth should lift it's [*sic*] parricide hands against freedom & science, would be such a monstrous phaenomenon as I cannot place among possible things in this age & this country." Calling up fond recollections of his alma mater, the College of William and Mary, he soothingly ended, "Your college at least has shewn itself incapable of it; and if the youth of any other place have seemed to rally under other banners it has been from delusions which they will soon dissipate."[28]

The passage of time further dimmed Jefferson's memory and the long-distance hopes he entertained from Paris in 1785. Nearly thirty years after his letter to Price, he wrote his young antislavery friend Edward Coles that he had long been aware that, before 1776, Virginia's revolutionary leaders were too much accustomed to the habit and profits of slavery to abolish it. He "soon saw that nothing was to be hoped" from them on that issue, he admitted. He echoed the language of his letter to Price and in Query 18 of *Notes*. As he recalled of the older generation, "Nursed and educated in the daily habit of seeing the degraded condition, both bodily & mental, of these unfortunate beings, not reflecting that that degradation was very much the work of themselves & their fathers, few minds had yet doubted but that they were as legitimate subjects of property as their horses or cattle." Although colonial Virginians indignantly defended their liberties to the point of Revolution when they became "alarmed" at British endeavors to restrict them, he charged, "it was not easy to carry them the whole length of

---

[27] Arthur Scherr, "'Monuments of Mortal Decay': Thomas Jefferson's Changing Perspective on George Washington," *Southern Studies* 27/1 (Spring/Summer 2020): 1–64, discusses Jefferson's ambivalent feelings toward Washington at length. Marshall Smelser, "George Washington and the Alien and Sedition Acts," *American Historical Review* 59/2 (February 1954): 322–34, briefly discusses Washington's support for the repressive laws.

[28] Jefferson to Mumford, June 18, 1799, in Oberg, ed., *Jefferson Papers*, 31:128. On Jefferson's death wish for Washington, see R. W. G. Vail, ed., "A Dinner at Mt. Vernon: From the Unpublished Journal of Joshua Brookes (1773–1859)," *New-York Historical Society Quarterly* 31/4 (April 1947): 72–85; Benjamin Rush to Jefferson, March 12, 1801, microfilm reel 23, Jefferson Papers, LC (hdl.loc.gov/loc.mss/mtj.mtjbib009789). The best study of college students' reaction to the Federalist/Jeffersonian party warfare is Steven J. Novak, *The Rights of Youth: American Colleges and Student Revolt, 1798–1815* (Cambridge: Harvard University Press, 1977).

the principles which they invoked for themselves," to endorse freedom for their slaves. As in his later *Autobiography* (where he claimed to have proposed a manumission law when he first entered the colonial assembly in 1769), he told Coles that, in the House of Burgesses he had joined senior delegate Richard Bland in a vague antislavery measure to safeguard slaves' legal rights. (This was perhaps a forerunner of his 1776–1778 emancipation proposal detailed in *Notes*, or his bill to abolish the death penalty for slaves in numerous cases). But the assembly "denounced" Bland "as an enemy to his country" for his efforts.[29]

Excusing his failure to fight slavery in his home state after the Revolution, Jefferson pointed out that his duties during the Revolution were primarily on the national congressional stage. He surprisingly omitted his unsuccessful efforts to gain passage of the antislavery Ordinance of 1784, which prohibited slavery after 1800 in all the nation's territories, North and South, and the proposed constitution he published as an appendix to *Notes*, which barred slavery in Virginia after 1800. He was a diplomat overseas for most of the postwar pre-Constitutional period, "so that from that time till my return from Europe in 1789," and until retiring from the presidency in 1809, he had "little opportunity of knowing the progress of public sentiment here [in Virginia] on this subject."[30] Nor was there much chance of gaining passage of antislavery measures in Congress had he attempted it during his presidency, when he often faced serious immediate crises, such as the Louisiana controversy with France, New England secessionist plots,

---

[29] Jefferson to Edward Coles, August 25, 1814, microfilm reel 47, Jefferson Papers, LC (hdl.loc.gov/loc.mss/mtj.mtjbib021817); Jefferson to Richard Price, August 7, 1785, in Boyd et al., eds., *Papers of Thomas Jefferson*, 8:356–57. Although the *Journals* of the House of Burgesses do not mention Bland and Jefferson's motion, it is known that Virginia Quakers, headed by Robert Pleasants, approached Richard Bland in 1769 or 1770 requesting him to propose a manumission law. See A. Glenn Crothers, *Quakers Living in the Lion's Mouth: The Society of Friends in Northern Virginia, 1730–1865* (Gainesville: University Press of Florida, 2012), 45; John B. Boles, *Jefferson: Architect of American Liberty* (New York: Basic Books, 2017), 28–29; Jay Worrall, Jr., *The Friendly Virginians: America's First Quakers* (Athens: Iberian, 1994), 225; and Stephen B. Weeks, *Southern Quakers and Slavery* (1896; Baltimore: Johns Hopkins Press, 1968), 205; Jefferson to Richard Price, August 7, 1785, in Boyd et al., eds., *Papers of Thomas Jefferson*, 8:356–57. For Query XVIII of *Notes on* Virginia, castigating slaveholders' cruelty, see Peterson, ed., *Jefferson: Writings*, 288–89; for Jefferson's comments in his *Autobiography*, ibid., 5. For Jefferson's 1776 proposal to substitute deportation for the death penalty for slaves convicted of diverse crimes, see Jefferson to Edmund Pendleton, August 26, 1776, in Boyd et al., eds., *Papers of Thomas Jefferson*, 1:505; Peterson, ed., *Jefferson: Writings*, 756–57; and Boyd et al., eds., *Papers of Thomas Jefferson*, 2:504.

[30] Jefferson to Edward Coles, August 25, 1814, microfilm reel 47, Jefferson Papers, LC (hdl.loc.gov/loc.mss/mtj.mtjbib021817).

the threat of war with France and Great Britain, the Embargo Act, and Aaron Burr's alleged treasonable conspiracy.

The rest of Jefferson's letter to Coles was imbued with moral sense rhetoric. Ominously referring to "St. Domingo" (Haiti), he discussed Virginia's failure to emancipate its slaves and his confidence in the slaves' ultimate liberation. Attempting to justify his inaction on slavery during his two prominent decades in public life after returning from France in 1789, he impugned apathetic "public sentiment on this subject." Plainly, he had found Americans, including the youth of Coles's ilk, deficient in the qualities of moral sense requisite to achieve Black emancipation. He wrote,

> I had always hoped that the younger generation, recieving [*sic*] their early impressions after the flame of liberty had been kindled in every breast, & had become as it were the vital spirit of every American, that the generous temperament of youth, analogous to the motion of their blood, and above the suggestions of avarice, would have sympathized with oppression wherever found, and proved their love of liberty.... But my intercourse with them, since my return has not been sufficient to ascertain that they had made towards this point the progress I had hoped.[31]

Despite applauding Coles's "welcome" though "solitary voice" in favor of emancipation, Jefferson concluded that the "general [public] silence" displayed "an apathy unfavorable to every hope." However, Jefferson warned, "the hour of emancipation is advancing, in the march of time." At the nadir of American fortunes in the War of 1812, Jefferson ominously suggested that invading British troops, impelled by military necessity more than ideological conviction, would violently correct Virginians' moral shortcomings, liberating slaves who fought on the British side and, emulating Haitian revolutionaries, killed their masters. Black freedom, Jefferson admonished, would take place, "whether brought on by the generous energy of our own [Virginian] minds," driven by a revived moral sense, "or by the bloody process of St. Domingo, excited and conducted by the power of our present enemy, if once stationed permanently within our Country, and offering asylum & arms to the oppressed." In light of British support for slave troops during the American Revolution and the runaway slaves who, wearing the uniforms of the British Colonial Marine Company, were currently burning down Washington, he was euphemistic in concluding that a British-subsidized slave revolt was "a leaf of our history not yet turned over."[32]

Obviously, the Haitian Revolution was in Jefferson's thoughts in summer 1814 when invading British troops armed runaway Virginia slaves to resist their

---

[31] Ibid.

[32] Ibid.

masters: the high point of British success during the War of 1812. The day that British troops invaded and set fire to the capital, employing runaway slaves they had earlier formed into a Colonial Marine Company, Jefferson was coincidentally writing Coles and thinking about Haiti. Jefferson expected the British to use Black troops to win the war (although he could not yet know about the burning of the President's House). Surely, he remembered that Lord Dunmore, royal governor of Virginia in the first year of the American Revolution, had twice during 1775 issued proclamations offering freedom to runaway slaves who joined his troops against their former masters. Now, ostensibly alarmed, Jefferson warned Edward Coles that "the hour of emancipation" might arrive "by the bloody process of St. Domingo," with the powerful assistance of British troops, especially if, as the result of a peace treaty, they gained a beachhead "permanently within our Country."[33]

Apparently fearing that the British might create a permanent buffer zone for runaway slaves near Washington or elsewhere in the South, if they seized territory on the US mainland, Jefferson utilized his political creativity. He invented a solution to his state's racial problem, vindicated Black political equality, and demonstrated flexibility in accepting the moral sense's application to diverse political regimes, encapsulated in the graphic metonym, "the bloody process of St. Domingo."[34]

Recurring to his proposal in Query 14 of *Notes*, Jefferson's letter to Coles recommended for Virginia a policy of gradual emancipation, without compensation to masters, freeing newborn Blacks, educating and deporting them at state expense, and replacing them with White labor, including immigrants. "I have

---

[33] Jefferson to Edward Coles, August 25, 1814, in Ford, ed., *Works of Thomas Jefferson*, 11:417–18. It is possible that Jefferson knew that British troops and naval forces were engaged in a *Blitzkreig* attack (as historian Robert A. Rutland calls it) on Washington, DC, when he wrote this letter (Rutland, *Presidency of James Madison* [Lawrence: University Press of Kansas, 1990], 160–65). He may have just learned that runaway slave troops under British command were burning Washington and sending his friend President Madison to flight (Malone, *Sage of Monticello*, vol. 6 of *Jefferson and His Time* [Boston: Little, Brown, 1981], 120). For slaves' military participation with the British in the War of 1812, see Gene A. Smith, *The Slaves' Gamble: Choosing Sides in the War of 1812* (New York: St. Martin's Publishing Group, 2013), esp. chapter 5; Alan Taylor, *Internal Enemy: Slavery and War in Virginia, 1772–1832* (New York: W. W. Norton, 2013), 301–305; Cassell, "Slaves of the Chesapeake Bay Area," 144–55, and Christopher T. George, "Mirage of Freedom: African Americans in the War of 1812," *Maryland Historical Magazine* 91/4 (Winter 1996): 426–50. On Lord Dunmore's efforts to recruit slaves to fight for the British in 1775–1776, see Holton, "Rebel against Rebel," 157–92.

[34] Indeed, the British agitated for a Native American "border state" in the American Midwest from the American Revolution until the War of 1812 (William T. Hagan, *American Indians*, 3rd ed. [Chicago: University of Chicago Press, 1993], 72–73).

seen no proposition so expedient on the whole, as that of emancipation of those born after a given day, and of their *education* and expatriation at a proper age," he wrote.

> This would give time for a gradual extinction of that species of labor and substitution of another, and lessen the severity of the shock which an operation so fundamental cannot fail to produce. For men probably of any colour, but of this color we know, brought [up] from their infancy without necessity for thought or forecast, are by their habits rendered as incapable as children of taking care of themselves, and are extinguished promptly wherever industry is necessary for raising the young. In the mean time they are pests in society by their idleness [he warned,] and the depredations to which this leads them.[35]

Such statements revealed Jefferson's guilt, his projection and denial of *his* dependence on slaves, who in large part raised food for themselves on their garden plots and took care of themselves in most other ways as well. Indeed, their labors provided Jefferson's sustenance, and enslaved women may occasionally have been wet-nurses for members of his family. Although he failed to explain the manner in which, if Blacks were so helpless, they would be able to fend for themselves after being emancipated and sent to an unfamiliar locale, he must have expected their "education," which would render them literate and worldly-wise, to facilitate their success in this respect.

Another seeming contradiction in Jefferson's letter was that he now apparently thought that slaveholders' moral sense, suddenly infused with a "generous energy" by worrisome, sporadic slave revolts during the War of 1812, would acquiesce in a plan causing them severe economic loss. He imputed any deficiency in Blacks' morality and intelligence to the regimen of slavery the Whites inflicted upon them. He was now ostensibly more aware of the disadvantages slaves suffered than in *Notes*, which strongly implied that racial inferiority prevented Blacks from reaching the literary and philosophic heights achieved by slaves in ancient Greece. Now he asserted that "*men probably of any colour*" when oppressed by the conditions slavery imposed, would find themselves so emotionally and mentally handicapped that they would likely be unable to survive and raise children as freedpersons.[36]

To some extent, Jefferson applied similar infantilizing assumptions to Whites unaccustomed to civil freedom. During the debates over a form of

---

[35] Jefferson to Edward Coles, August 25, 1814, microfilm reel 47, Jefferson Papers, LC (hdl.loc.gov/loc.mss/mtj.mtjbib021817). My italics.

[36] Ibid. My italics. By contrast, in the highly praised abolition of slavery in the British West Indies in 1833, the monarchy paid masters to free their slaves.

government for the French and Spanish inhabitants of Louisiana (Orleans Territory) during his presidency, he doubted that they would easily adjust to a popularly elected assembly and provisions for trial by jury, freedom of religion, and freedom of the press. "Our new fellow citizens are as yet as incapable of self-government as children," he observed at the time.[37] Unlike Spanish and French Whites in Louisiana, however, Black slaves had never controlled their economies or possessed legal rights.

Extending his reasoning about slavery's status of infantilization, Jefferson's letter to Coles anticipated that Black freedpersons, if allowed to remain in Virginia, would wallow in poverty and indolence, neglect their children, and turn to crime. However, he now more powerfully recognized that Whites had not given slaves an opportunity to retain the fruits of their labor, a prerequisite for authentic human exertion.[38] Implying his continued belief in Blacks' innate inferiority, nonetheless he concluded with his customary warning that miscegenation would "degrade" Whites' eugenic superiority: "Their [Blacks'] amalgamation with the other color produces a degradation to which no lover of his country, no lover of excellence in the human character can innocently consent."[39]

Although subtly retaining *Notes*' "suspicion" of Blacks' mental inferiority, Jefferson's letter to Coles reasserted his view that slavery, especially in a society as politically and educationally progressive as the United States, perverted slaveholders' "moral sense" and stigmatized republicanism. He expressed a negative opinion of his fellow slaveholders perhaps more strongly than he had in the past. On the other hand, his racial prejudices against Blacks, no matter how reluctantly expressed; his assumption that Whites would discriminate against free Blacks in both North and South, rendering their existence intolerable; and his conviction that emancipation would be feasible only if Blacks were deported afterwards, remained little changed from what they were thirty years earlier.[40]

---

[37] Jefferson to DeWitt Clinton, December 2, 1803, microfilm reel 29, Jefferson Papers, LC (hdl.loc.gov/loc.mss/mtj.mtjbib012968).

[38] Jefferson to Edward Coles, August 25, 1814, microfilm reel 47, Jefferson Papers, LC (hdl.loc.gov/loc.mss/mtj.mtjbib021817) (quotation); see also Jefferson to William Short, September 8, 1823, in Lipscomb and Bergh, eds., *Writings of Jefferson*, 15:469–70.

[39] Jefferson to Edward Coles, August 25, 1814, Jefferson Papers, LC. In *Notes on Virginia*, he wrote, referring to the mixed-race population, "The improvement of the blacks, in body and mind, in the first instance of their mixture with the whites, has been observed by every one, and proves that their inferiority is not the effect merely of their condition of life" (Query XIV, in Peden, ed., *Notes on the State of Virginia*, 141).

[40] M. Andrew Holowchak, "'The spirit of the master is abating': The Myth of Jefferson's Racism," in *The Elusive Thomas Jefferson: Essays on the Man behind the Myth* (Jefferson, NC: McFarland, 2017), 95, 101, 106–108.

Implying that, as an old man, his moral sense was too jaded to lead the fight for Black liberation, Jefferson urged young Coles to remain in Virginia, "buckle the armour of Hector" and replace him in the public sphere and in the legislature, agitating for Black emancipation. His letter was imbued with sentimental, "moral sense" rhetoric. Excusing his failure to take a more prominent antislavery stance, he appealed to Coles's sympathy for the elderly, lamenting that, like King Priam, Hector's father in the *Iliad*, "I have overlived the generation with which mutual labors & perils begat mutual confidence and influence." The "enterprise" was more appropriate "for the young; for those who can follow it up, and bear it through to its consummation." Simultaneously urging Coles to remain in Virginia and fight for emancipation and doubting the project's success, he implied that the practical path of a kindly, paternalistic slaveholder possessed a modicum of virtue. He explained, "My opinion has ever been that, until more can be done for them, we should endeavor, with those whom fortune has thrown on our hands, to feed and clothe them well, protect them from all ill usage, require such reasonable labor only as is performed voluntarily by freemen, & to be led by no repugnancies to abdicate them, and our duties to them."

Downplaying his responsibility for slaveholding, Jefferson pointed out that the laws prohibited him from freeing his slaves. (He probably meant that his status as a debtor whose slaves remained collateral for his creditors under various Virginia statutes, including those of 1782, 1792, 1794, 1803, 1814, and 1819, made it illegal for him to free his slaves, who would consequently be seized by his creditors). As he put it, "The laws do not permit us to turn them loose, if that were for their good." He considered it more immoral to sell one's slaves to unfamiliar individuals—for "to commute them for other property is to commit them to those whose usage of them we cannot control"—than to retain them. Nevertheless, Jefferson concluded by recommending that Coles defy the Establishment rather than abandon his state. The best course was to seek to alleviate his "country's unfortunate condition" by becoming a member of the legislature and fighting for the "truly christian doctrine" of emancipation until he succeeded. "It is an encouraging observation that no good measure was ever proposed, which, if duly pursued, failed to prevail in the end," Jefferson naively wrote, pointing to British legislation suppressing the international slave trade for inspiration. Adapting one of his favorite Gospel aphorisms, he advised Coles, "Be not weary in well-doing," shifting responsibility for emancipation onto him. He assured Coles that "honorable & immortal consolation" would be his reward if he pushed emancipation through the Virginia assembly.[41]

---

[41] Jefferson to Edward Coles, August 25, 1814, microfilm reel 47, Jefferson Papers, LC (hdl.loc.gov/loc.mss/mtj.mtjbib021817). Several historians misread the letter, claiming

Positing that moral sense propositions applied to Whites at least as much as to Blacks, Jefferson ended the letter on the opposite note from where it began, optimistically asserting that White *American* politicians' virtue would evolve sufficiently to pass African American liberation and deportation through the Virginia assembly, if idealists like Coles stuck around to lead the way. Thus, he reasserted his doctrine of human benevolence and progress, even amid war and foreign invasion, despite White legislators' failure to advance Black emancipation in his state or elsewhere in the South.

In his effort to exonerate himself from charges of harboring proslavery sympathies, perhaps Jefferson protested too much. In any case, he was an old man with little influence or political power. Even in the powerful position of president, he could have done little to abolish slavery, other than to recommend prohibiting the importation of slaves, an act that he performed in 1806. Out of office, there was no way he could abolish slavery by an effort of will. Despite his strong friendship with Madison and Monroe, his successors in office paid little attention to his suggestions, rejecting even his few requests to appoint close friends to minor offices. His recommendations on conducting the War of 1812 were ignored by his closest friend, President James Madison, and even by his son-in-law, John Wayles Eppes, chairman of the House Ways and Means Committee. Burdened by his dead father-in-law's debts as well as his own, Jefferson could not free his own slaves even if he wanted to; Virginia law prohibited debtors from manumitting their slaves. Therefore, he might justifiably complain, as he did to Coles, that for him to publicly condemn slavery and agitate for its abolition, a "salutary but

---

Jefferson urged Coles to take no action against slavery, and merely remain a passive Virginia slaveholder; see, for example, Davis, *Problem of Slavery in the Age of Revolution*, 182. For laws prohibiting debtors from freeing their slaves, see, for example, the 1819 law, "An Act Reducing to One, the Several Acts concerning Slaves, Free Negroes and Mulattoes," passed March 2, 1819, in *Revised Code of the Laws of Virginia*, 2 vols. (Richmond: Thomas Ritchie, 1819), 1:433–34; Jefferson to Edward Coles, August 25, 1814, in Ford, ed., *Works of Thomas Jefferson*, 11:419–20. The basis for this aphorism, "Let us not grow weary in well-doing, for in due season we will reap a harvest," is from Galatians 6:9. Coles never attempted to abolish slavery in Virginia. As governor of Illinois, he kept slavery from flourishing legally in a state where Jefferson's Ordinance of 1784 would have abolished it after 1800. There are several biographies of Coles, a fascinating personality, among them Suzanne Cooper-Guasco, *Confronting Slavery: Edward Coles and the Rise of Antislavery Politics in Nineteenth-Century America* (Dekalb: Northern Illinois University Press, 2013), and Leichtle and Carveth, *Crusade against Slavery*. Cooper-Guasco, "'To Put into Complete Practice Those Hallowed Principles': Edward Coles and Antislavery Nationalism in Early Nineteenth-Century America," *American Nineteenth Century History* 11 (March 2010): 17–45, shows that by 1830, Coles, conscious of the racism prevalent in White male society, supported the transportation projects of the American Colonization Society.

arduous work" which no major public figure had ever undertaken, would be "like bidding old Priam to buckle the armour of Hector." Demanding immediate abolition would make him look like a hypocrite, since as a debtor, his hold on his slaves was tenuous at best. "This enterprise is for the young; for those who can follow it up, and bear it through to it's [*sic*] consummation," he finally advised. "It shall have all my prayers, and these are the only weapons of an old man."[42]

Rejecting Jefferson's excuses, Coles insisted that, as a retired president in good repute with the people of his state, Jefferson would be a decisive force if he publicly demanded the "gradual emancipation" of the slaves. As "the first of our aged worthies," he would surely serve as a "rallying point for its [emancipation's] friends." Seeking to rebut Jefferson's assertions that age inhibited his effectiveness as an antislavery crusader, Coles, with an imperfect knowledge of US history, argued that Benjamin Franklin was even older than Jefferson was when he forced through the abolition of slavery in Pennsylvania in 1780. "Your time of life I had not considered an obstacle to the undertaking," he asserted. "Doctor Franklin, to whom, by the way, Pennsylvania owes her early riddance of the evils of Slavery, was as actively and usefully employed on arduous duties after he had past your age as he had ever been at any period of his life."[43] In fact, Franklin was overseas as US minister to France when Pennsylvania abolished slavery under the radical Constitutionalist Party in 1780. Forgotten figures like Timothy Matlack and George Bryan accomplished abolition, not Franklin, who only espoused the abolitionist cause a few months before his death in 1790.[44]

In any case, history has shown that few if any ex-presidents exert much influence on major events during their retirements. Even George Washington, who had little interest in abolishing slavery, treated his slaves harshly, and owned more slaves than Jefferson did, never contemplated action against slavery. Despite his great prestige and popularity, which led President John Adams to drag him out of retirement to serve as nominal commanding general of the US Army during the undeclared war with France from 1798 to 1800, Washington remained at

---

[42] Jefferson to Edward Coles, August 25, 1814, in Looney, ed., *Jefferson Papers: Retirement Series*, 7:604. On Jefferson's lack of influence on Madison, his closest friend and erstwhile political ally, see for example, Honeywell, "President Jefferson and his Successor," 64–75. President James Monroe's rejection of Jefferson's advice in 1823 to join England in an alliance on behalf of the new South American governments, instead adopting Secretary of State John Quincy Adams's position and unilaterally proclaiming the Monroe Doctrine, most starkly reveals his insignificant influence.

[43] Edward Coles to Jefferson, September 26, 1814, in Looney, ed., *Jefferson Papers: Retirement Series*, 7:704.

[44] David Waldstreicher, *Runaway America: Benjamin Franklin, Slavery, and the American Revolution* (New York: Hill and Wang, 2004), depicts Franklin as a supporter of slavery.

Mount Vernon and was content to let his protégé Alexander Hamilton, as second-in-command, do all the work.[45]

Nor did James Madison, who lived for ten years after Jefferson's death, attempt to foster state emancipation legislation. Coles incessantly urged him to emancipate his slaves, but he kept putting him off because of his poor financial circumstances in old age, which necessitated that he sell land and slaves to make ends meet. Ironically, in 1834, two years before he died, Madison, in reduced financial circumstances because of poor wheat and tobacco crops and low prices, was forced to sell sixteen slaves, who had become more of a burden to him than an economic advantage, to a relative in Louisiana. He sent the proceeds to Edward Coles to pay off a debt he owed him. His will directed that his wife Dolley, Coles's cousin, free his slaves after his death if it were financially feasible. However, because Madison's estate remained insolvent until her death, she never did.[46]

Despite (or perhaps because of) following the dictates of humanitarianism and emancipating his slaves, Edward Coles died financially secure, unlike his more famous slaveholding friends, Jefferson and Madison, who, in part because of the expenses incurred by holding large numbers of human property, some of them elderly and unproductive, for whose subsistence they had to provide, died mired in debt.[47]

Even more ironically, the antislavery Jefferson had the last word on prohibiting bondage in Illinois, the state to which Coles moved in 1819, where he emancipated his slaves. It was an apt epilogue to Jefferson's abolitionist Ordinance of 1784. During Coles's statewide campaign against slavery as Illinois's governor, he reprinted Jefferson's letter of August 25, 1814, in local newspapers, to prove that the Sage of Monticello detested slavery. On the eve of a statewide referendum over holding a constitutional convention to legalize slavery, Coles's friends quoted Jefferson's famous condemnation in Query XVIII of *Notes* as evidence that some slaveholders did not consider human bondage a panacea for the White man's economic woes. Thus, despite his earlier protests to Coles that old age rendered him physically and politically impotent, Jefferson inadvertently, with "one foot in the grave," assisted by his young friend Coles, spoke out decisively against slavery.[48]

---

[45] Smelser, "George Washington and the Alien and Sedition Acts," 322–34.

[46] Mattern, "James Madison and Montpelier," in Leibiger, ed., *Wiley-Blackwell Companion to James Madison and James Monroe*, 304.

[47] Susan Dunn, *Dominion of Memories: Jefferson, Madison, and the Decline of Virginia* (New York: Basic Books, 2007).

[48] "Hear Both Sides" ("The immortal Jefferson"), *Edwardsville Spectator*, July 20, 1824, p. 1 (quotation); *Illinois Intelligencer*, June 4, 1822; *Edwardsville Spectator*, July 6, 1822; James Simeone, *Democracy and Slavery in Frontier Illinois: The Bottomland Republic* (DeKalb: Northern Illinois University Press, 2000), 28. In a letter Jefferson wrote at age eighty-two, he said he

Later, Coles and Jefferson's grandson, Thomas Jefferson Randolph, utilized Jefferson's 1814 letter to Coles in Virginia's abortive debates over ending slavery. When Coles visited Richmond to observe the constitutional convention in October 1829, he hoped by republishing Jefferson's letter to him to encourage movements for abolition. However, his efforts failed abysmally. Proslavery Tidewater and Northern Neck conservatives maintained control of the debates. Coles unwisely published Jefferson's letter in the October 23, 1829, edition of the antislavery *Genius of Universal Emancipation*, a Philadelphia newspaper neither popular nor widely available in Virginia. Demanding abolition as a member of the Virginia legislature six months after Nat Turner's rebellion in 1831, Thomas Jefferson Randolph likewise quoted Jefferson's pro-abolition 1814 letter to Coles, who had recently visited Randolph in Albemarle County and urged him to fight for emancipation. However, Randolph's attempts to abolish slavery also failed.[49] Ironically, these disappointing results suggest that Jefferson, who had only modest success in his old age even in obtaining funds for his brainchild, the University of Virginia, and was unpopular with Virginia's burgeoning evangelical interest groups, accurately forecast that his antislavery proclamations would fail to convince the state legislature to abolish bondage.

---

had "one foot in the grave, and the other uplifted to follow it" (Jefferson to Frances Wright, August 7, 1825, microfilm reel 55, Jefferson Papers, LC [hdl.loc.gov/loc.mss/mtj.mtjbib 025495]).

[49] Cooper-Guasco, "'To Put into Complete Practice Those Hallowed Principles,'" 31–37.

Chapter 11

Jefferson's Road Not Taken: Edward Coles and Slavery

As was seen in the preceding chapter, about the same time that Jefferson corresponded with Thomas Law, he wrote Edward Coles (1786–1868), a young antislavery Virginian who, lacking the material attachments and financial impediments that Jefferson confronted as owner of Monticello and Poplar Forest, had for many years intended to leave Virginia out of "repugnance" for slavery. Coles appeals to the romantic imagination: a young, idealistic individual who gave up his material comforts as a son (albeit the youngest) of one of the First Families of Virginia, to free his slaves and accompany them to Illinois. In 1808, when his father, John, died, Coles was twenty-two years old. John Coles was a slaveholding merchant and planter, close friend of Jefferson, and owner of the Albemarle County estate Enniscorthy, where Jefferson and his family took refuge when Tarleton's troops invaded Monticello in June 1781. Edward Coles had early decided that slavery was wrong, at least in theory. He promised himself that he would emancipate the twelve slaves he inherited and sell Rockfish, the small 782-acre plantation he inherited at the western edge of Jefferson's own Albemarle County. His father's plantations had produced tobacco, wheat, and corn and consisted of hills and rich bottomland.[1]

Hindered by low commodity prices, congressional trade embargoes, and British blockades, young Coles's Rockfish was productive but not profitable. Lacking a personal attachment to his slaves, Coles's father often rented them out. Despite young Coles's theoretical abhorrence of slavery, perhaps imbibed at Bishop James Madison's lectures at the College of William and Mary, his alma mater, he had whipped a slave on at least one occasion, despite his youth and his

---

[1] Leichtle and Carveth, *Crusade against Slavery*, 20; "John Coles, II," in Thomas Jefferson Encyclopedia, Thomas Jefferson Foundation, Monticello, Charlottesville, VA (monticello.org/site/research-and-collections/john-coles-ii).

short period of slaveholding.[2] Apparently, he did not differ much from Jefferson in his conduct as a master.

Attracted to neither slavery nor farming, Coles sought to sell the Rockfish farm as soon as he inherited it, but he was determined to make money on the deal. As he told his family, whom he did not immediately inform that he intended to free his slaves, he was "disposed to sell," but "not so much bent on it as to make a sacrifice." He insisted that Rockfish was worth at least $15,000, but he refused to part with it at a price under $17,000. His desire to immediately free his slaves and pay his small, inherited debt did not exceed his determination to make a profit on the land.[3] Consequently, Coles took his time emancipating his bondspersons, who increased in number from twelve to nineteen between 1808 and 1819, when he finally pulled up stakes and left for Illinois. The young intellectual, more at home in urbanizing Washington than on the farm, found it hard to make a profit as a business-minded planter at Rockfish, where he spent little time. Although the debt he inherited along with his father's land and slaves was only $500, he postponed any attempt to pay it until he got a good price for his father's estate, hoping it would enable him to marry well, leave Virginia, and start a family in free territory.[4]

Despite his youth, as a slaveholding planter from 1808 to 1819, Coles felt the landed aristocrat's urge to clear his debt and make a profit. In pursuing this objective, he hired additional slaves from his sister to work his lands. At the same time, he sought a high price for his plantation before selling it, which was difficult to achieve at the time. His brother Walter offered to buy the land from him as early as 1813, but Edward was holding out for a higher price. He ended up selling the property to Walter, who paid him a good price (exactly how much is uncertain) in 1817.[5]

Coles probably could have easily paid the debt on Rockfish, and he had no wife or children to support. By Virginia law, he could not manumit his slaves unless he paid his debts; but of course, he could always leave the state with them and free them somewhere else. Apparently, young Coles liked being a member of

---

[2] Cooper-Guasco, *Confronting Slavery*, ch. 1. In Coles's manuscript autobiography, held by the Historical Society of Pennsylvania (HSP), his biographers note, he "reflected (with some pride, it appears) that he had treated his slaves with all the kindness and attention in his power and forbid whipping in every case but one." Coles's autobiographical notes in Edward Coles Papers, HSP, paraphrased in Leichtle and Carveth, *Crusade against Slavery*, 39 (quotation); on John Coles's slaves, see *Crusade against Slavery*, 20.

[3] Cooper-Guasco, *Confronting Slavery*, 35, 17, 234.

[4] Bruce G. Carveth, "Edward Coles," in Library of Virginia, *Encyclopedia Virginia* (encyclopediavirginia.org/Coles_Edward_1786–1868).

[5] Leichtle and Carveth, *Crusade against Slavery*, 39.

the Virginia aristocracy. He was the cousin of Dolley Madison, wife of President James Madison. He became the president's personal secretary at the end of 1809, replacing his older brother Isaac, who got into trouble after beating up a congressman and resigned. Edward enjoyed city life and high society. He was Madison's secretary until 1816, after which he toured Europe for a year. He insisted that he wanted to sell his land, leave the state, and free his slaves, but he desired top dollar for his property; and it was difficult to sell land at a high price during the War of 1812, when money was scarce, agricultural prices were low, and British blockades ruled the seas. Coles's wheat harvests at Rockfish were poor, but his slaves also raised tobacco and hemp. An absentee landlord, he resided in Washington, DC, relying on an overseer to supervise and discipline his slaves.[6]

Residing in Washington and receiving a salary as President Madison's personal secretary, Coles enjoyed himself and was something of a spendthrift. In 1812, alluding to the debt left him by his father, he complained, "I commenced my operations as a farmer more than four years ago, with a debt of $500." Partly because of his inexperience as a farmer and his absence in Washington, albeit with a salary "sufficient to support me," Coles ostensibly failed to save enough money to pay off the slight debt, preferring to use his funds to buy land in Illinois. (Perhaps he had already decided to eventually move there and free his slaves.)[7] He preferred the politics and high society of the nation's capital to working on a farm together with his slaves. He never lived on his plantation. Instead, he rented out the lands as early as 1809 and hired his father's trusted overseer, a Mr. Weatherd, to manage the estate.[8]

By contrast, Jefferson's debt was over $100,000 in 1826 money. Aside from money he spent on wine and books in Paris and on extravagant hospitality during his presidency and in retirement, Jefferson was rather frugal; the debt was mainly the legacy of his father-in-law, John Wayles, whose estate he inherited in the 1770s. He paid his debt to his father-in-law's creditors with bonds from his own debtors that he deposited in the state treasury, but they refused to accept them, requiring him to pay the debt twice. (The notes from Jefferson's debtors, in state paper money, proved worthless, leaving him deeper in the hole.) In addition, Jefferson lost tens of thousands of dollars to tenants and debtors who did not pay him, including vast sums he lent to shirking friends as recently as 1818, most disastrously his grandson's father-in-law, Wilson Cary Nicholas. In that year, in a gesture of noblesse-oblige, Jefferson guaranteed a $20,000 bank loan to

---

[6] David Ress, *Edward Coles and the Vote to Forbid Slavery in Illinois, 1823–1824* (Jefferson, NC: McFarland, 2006), 40.

[7] Cooper-Guasco, *Confronting Slavery*, 60, 66; Edward Coles to brother [John] Coles, March 26, 1812, and June 2, 1813, Coles Papers, HSP.

[8] Ibid., 62, 254n43.

Nicholas, who had formerly assisted him as president of the Richmond branch of the Bank of the United States. A year later, Nicholas went bankrupt and soon died. Jefferson was left responsible for paying $1200 annual interest on the loan, plus eventually the principal. Squashing whatever possibility he had of getting out of debt, emancipating his slaves, or even retaining his Monticello estate, "our friend WCN gave me the *coup de grace*," Jefferson lamented to Madison a few months before he died.[9] The untoward consequences of his loans to Nicholas and others not only prevented him from freeing his slaves but, by the incessant anxiety they caused him, probably helped precipitate his own death.

In his younger days, when there was a greater likelihood that he would succeed in paying his debt to his and his father-in-law's British creditors, Jefferson took on national responsibilities as a congressman and US minister to France, which probably hindered his quest for solvency. As minister, he was out of the country for over five years and was required to pay for diplomatic outfits and entertainments, much of it out of his own pocket since the Confederation Congress was virtually bankrupt. (He accepted the French mission, seeking to overcome his depression over his wife's death.) For most of his life, until retiring from the presidency, he did not personally reside on his plantations and left their management to friends and overseers.[10]

At least for a while, Jefferson expected his slaves' labor to pay his debts. In 1786 and 1787, from Paris, he informed his estate manager Nicholas Lewis that he would do almost anything to become solvent but wished to avoid selling more slaves. Pondering their fate, in December 1786, he wrote Lewis, "I am miserable till I shall owe not a shilling: the moment that shall be the case I shall feel myself at liberty to do something for the comfort of my slaves."[11] He lamented seven

[9] Jefferson to James Madison, February 17, 1826, quoted in Boles, *Jefferson: Architect of American Liberty*, 489–91. After Jefferson's death, his grandson Thomas Jefferson Randolph advertised Monticello for sale, claiming that the debts of the estate were over $107,000. On Jefferson's debts, see Hochman, "Thomas Jefferson: A Personal Financial Biography," 264–68, and passim; "Debt," Thomas Jefferson Foundation, Thomas Jefferson Encyclopedia (monticello.org/site/research-and-collections/debt). See also Sloan, *Principle and Interest*, ch. 1.

[10] Hochman, "Thomas Jefferson: A Personal Financial Biography." For Jefferson's quest to overcome his depression, see Jefferson to Chastellux, November 26, 1782, in Peterson, ed., *Jefferson: Writings*, 780–81.

[11] Jefferson to Nicholas Lewis, December 19, 1786, in Boyd et al., eds., *Papers of Thomas Jefferson*, 10:615. Virginia law prohibited debtors from manumitting their slaves, either in deeds or in their wills. "An act to authorize the manumission of slaves," passed at May 1782 session of legislature, in Hening, ed., *Statutes at Large*, 11:39–40.

months later, "The torment of mind I endure till the moment shall arrive when I shall owe not a shilling on earth is such really as to render life of little value."[12]

More ominously, Jefferson warned that his slaves could only avoid being sold away from his Bedford and Albemarle County plantations if they worked arduously enough to enable him to make a profit sufficient to pay his debt to his father-in-law's creditors. Specifically linking the slaves and his debts, unconsciously *blaming* the slaves for his fiscal predicament, he said that he wanted to free the slaves he had inherited from Wayles but that only they could make that possible by working harder so that he could pay his debts. Wishing his daughters to possess the security derived from inheriting his estates, he ruled out selling his land. Regarding the alternative of selling the slaves, he defensively wrote Lewis,

> Nor would I willingly sell the slaves as long as there remains any prospect of my paying my debts with their labour. In this I am governed solely by views to their happiness which will render it worth their while to use extraordinary exertions for some time to enable me to put them on an easier footing, which I will do the moment they have paid the debts due from the estate, two-thirds of which have been contracted by [Wayles] purchasing them.[13]

Initially, Jefferson leased out his land and slaves as a halfway measure in the 1780s and early 1790s. Because the Wayles' estate debt was so heavy and the interest payments continued to mount, he found it necessary to betray his promise to his slaves. Lucia Stanton, the leading authority on Jefferson and slavery at Monticello, writes, "In the end, he sold over 50 slaves in the early 1790s, but made only a dent in his British debts."[14]

---

[12] Jefferson to Nicholas Lewis, July 29, 1787, in Boyd et al., eds., *Papers of Thomas Jefferson*, 11:640.

[13] Ibid. Although the transcription in the *Jefferson Papers* uses the words "extraordinary cautions" (see founders.archives.gov/documents/Jefferson/01-11-02-0564), an examination of image 3 of the manuscript, available online (in the American Memory Database of Jefferson's Papers; see hdl.loc.gov/loc.mss/mtj.mtjbib002845), reveals that the correct word is more likely "exertions" than "cautions." The word is transcribed as "exertions" in Ford, ed., *Works of Thomas Jefferson*, 5:311. The letter does not appear in H. A. Washington, ed., *Writings of Thomas Jefferson*, 9 vols. (New York: Riker, 1853–1854), or in Lipscomb and Bergh, eds., *Writings of Jefferson.*

[14] "[Jefferson's] Negroes alienated from 1784 to 1794, inclusive," Sol Feinstone Collection, David Library of the American Revolution, on deposit at American Philosophical Society (also available at classroom.monticello.org/media-item/jeffersons-farm-book-page-25-negroes-alienated-from-1784–1794-inclusive/), cited by Stanton, "Thomas Jefferson: Planter and Farmer," ch. 16 of Cogliano, ed., *Wiley-Blackwell Companion to Thomas Jefferson*, 253–70, 257 (quotation). See also Malone, *Jefferson and the Ordeal of Liberty*, 178–79, 529–30.

In familial and personal relationships involving inherited estates, the young aristocrat Edward Coles was perhaps more fortunate than Jefferson. Purchasing Rockfish in fall 1817, Edward Coles's oldest brother Walter provided him with a substantial amount of money. Edward had been trying to sell the estate since 1810, but Virginia's economy was in decline and he had few takers. During this entire period, young Coles was out-of-state and did not promote the sale. As Coles's biographers Leichtle and Carveth observe, "Walter's offer to purchase Edward's legacy must be viewed as a remarkable brotherly gesture—a testament to the bonds of family. Walter understood that he was empowering Edward to fulfill his pledge to free his slaves" although Walter and the rest of the family opposed the idea. Judging from Coles's possession of ample amounts of capital the following year, the sale price must have been at least $17,000.[15]

After Coles reached Illinois, a slaveholding family friend, Jefferson's confidant President James Monroe, appointed him register of federal lands at Edwardsville, Illinois (named after Governor Ninian Edwards, not Edward Coles). This job, a position he held from 1819 to 1821, provided him with additional funds to emancipate his slaves, buy 160 acres of cheap prairie lands for the heads of three slave families, and set up as a farmer on his own homestead.[16]

Coles finally agreed to his brother's offer to purchase the property and used a portion of the cash he received, which must have approximated the $17,000 he sought, to buy additional land out west. Walter and his sister Rebecca joined him in his land speculations, each splitting one-third of a six-thousand-acre tract of fertile land in Lincoln County, Missouri, called El Prado. He was not deterred by the fact that Missouri was inhabited by slaveholders, since his objective at this time was to increase his income.[17] Apparently, he had paid in cash the substantial amount of $10,000 for his share of the land, twenty times the value of the debt that impeded him in freeing his slaves, and this before Walter bought his estate. In 1815, he optimistically observed, "I do not think that I am extravagant in my calculations, when I say that $10,000 in the hands of only a tolerably judicious man will in five years be worth $100,000."[18]

---

[15] Leichtle and Carveth, *Crusade against Slavery*, 56 (quotation).

[16] Carveth, "Edward Coles," encyclopediavirginia.org/Coles_Edward_1786–1868; Robert M. Sutton, "Coles, Edward," in John A. Garraty, ed., *American National Biography* (hereafter *ANB*), 24 vols. (New York: Oxford University Press, 1999), 5:226–28. On Edward Coles, see also Schwartz, *Ties That Bound*, 306–307; Ress, *Coles and the Vote to Forbid Slavery*, 40, 75–77; Leichtle and Carveth, *Crusade against Slavery*, 20–60. Nicholas Gordon, *The Man Who Freed his Slaves: A Narrative of the Life of Edward Coles*, is a useful online biography.

[17] Leichtle and Carveth, *Crusade against Slavery*, 60–67; Leichtle and Carveth, *Crusade against Slavery*; Coles Collection, HSP, cited ibid., 60.

[18] Edward Coles [1815], quoted in Cooper-Guasco, *Confronting Slavery*, 67.

That year, Coles acquired six thousand acres of land in Madison and St. Clair counties near Edwardsville, Illinois Territory, buying them at cheap prices. He purchased land cheaply on visits to Illinois in 1815 and 1818.[19] Ironically, by 1818, the year that Jefferson went irretrievably bankrupt, Coles had become wealthy. His land speculations were fruitful, and he gained $13,000 in profits from his stock in the Farmers Bank of Virginia and the Second Bank of the United States, acquired perhaps on the advice of his friend, Nicholas Biddle, president of the BUS and one of the richest men in America.[20]

For the time being, Coles refrained from moving to the frontier of Missouri, Illinois, or anywhere else, preferring the genteel society of Washington and Philadelphia, and even traveling to Tsarist Russia as Madison's personal representative. After this mission, he vacationed in Europe and the British Isles for a year.[21] Reluctant to commit himself to a rugged life in the West and complaining of a leg injury contracted at the College of William and Mary and generally poor health, he delayed freeing his slaves for over ten years after acquiring them.[22]

In 1816, President Madison sent Coles on a delicate diplomatic mission to Russia to explain the case of Nicholas Kosloff, Russian consul general in Philadelphia. Before a federal court released him, Kosloff was imprisoned by a state court for eighteen hours for raping a twelve-year-old servant girl; rape was a common-law crime for which he had diplomatic immunity. André de Daschkoff, the Russian minister, himself reportedly an abuser of young girls, heatedly denied that Kosloff had committed rape and threatened the US with retaliation. The Madison Administration, fearing a deterioration of relations, decided to send Coles to explain Kosloff's imprisonment to the Russian monarch. Coles admired the wealth and luxury of the tsar and nobility of St. Petersburg.[23]

After returning from Europe in 1817, Coles visited Illinois. His European experiences followed him to Edwardsville, which he visited in 1818, anticipating settling there with his freed slaves. He mocked the people's backwoods ways, touting his membership in the FFVs (First Families of Virginia) and his acquaintance with Tsar Alexander I and the "Ladies of the Courts." He alienated the

---

[19] Sutton, "Coles, Edward," *ANB*, 5:227. See also Simeone, *Democracy and Slavery*, 26; Robert M. Sutton, "Edward Coles and the Constitutional Crisis in Illinois, 1822–1824," *Illinois Historical Journal* 82/1 (Spring 1989): 3–46, at 36, discusses Coles's land purchases.

[20] Gordon, *Man Who Freed the Slaves*, chapter 14, citing Edward Coles's Account Books, HSP.

[21] Ibid.

[22] Ibid.; Leichtle and Carveth, *Crusade against Slavery*, passim.

[23] Irving Brant, *James Madison, Commander in Chief, 1812–1836* (Indianapolis: Bobbs-Merrill, 1961), 397–98, 409, 411; Leichtle and Carveth, *Crusade against Slavery*, 50–55.

editor of the local newspaper, who depicted him as an arrogant aristocrat. Contrary to accepted knowledge, Coles did not emancipate all his slaves on a flatboat on the Ohio River en route to Illinois in June 1819. At least seven remained in his service until 1825, as indentured servants although he retained them in his household at least in part because they were elderly or their health was too poor for him to emancipate them.[24]

On July 4, 1819, after President James Monroe appointed Coles registrar of the Edwardsville land office, Coles, promulgating his decision from his new post, publicly emancipated half the slaves he inherited from his father. Coles did not know much about farming. After settling in Illinois in 1819, he bought a great deal of poor farmland on the prairie, mainly because it was cheap. Surmising that prairie land was situated in a healthier climate than the marshy bottomland, initially he did not seem aware of its inferior fertility. Between 1819 and 1821, he relied primarily on his income as registrar of the US Land Office at Edwardsville and from real estate speculations and bank stock investments.[25]

Although Coles's aristocratic snobbishness alienated him from some voters, in 1822 he ran as an antislavery candidate for governor of Illinois, spending thousands of dollars of his own money for publicity. Elected by a narrow margin, it was his first, and last, election victory. In December 1822, in his first message to the state legislature, he recommended a law explicitly abolishing slavery.[26]

Although Coles won the governorship by a close vote in 1822, the poor Whites of his neighborhood resented his haughty demeanor. Hoping to eventually purchase slaves themselves, they were unimpressed by his passionate desire to abolish the institution in the state permanently. His political opponents used these factors against him. "He was an easy target on the wealth and status issue," an historian observes. "Besides the Edwardsville farm worked by hired men and servants, he owned over 6,000 acres of land [in Madison and St. Clair counties], much of it granted as a consequence of his appointed positions."[27]

Elected governor with 33 percent of the vote, Coles won a plurality because the two proslavery candidates divided the rest of the votes between them. The residents of the state were largely proslavery, as was the state legislature. When

---

[24] Simeone, *Democracy and Slavery*, 17–18, 222n5; Coles to editor of the *Illinois Intelligencer*, June 4, 1822, reprinted in the *Edwardsville Spectator*, July 6, 1822, in Clarence W. Alvord, ed., *Governor Edward Coles*, in *Collections of the Illinois State Historical Library* (Springfield: Illinois State Historical Library, 1920), 15:261–63. More generally, see ibid., 40–47, 312, 330, 349, 353–54, 363.

[25] Ress, *Coles and the Vote to Forbid Slavery* 75–77.

[26] Simeone, *Democracy and Slavery*, 18.

[27] Simeone, *Democracy and Slavery*, 26 (quotation).

Coles asked the legislature to pass an abolition law, proslavery politicians insisted that only a constitutional convention could do that; they expected such a convention would legalize slavery. When the legislature passed a vote for a popular referendum to decide on holding a constitutional convention, Coles and his abolitionist allies conducted a large-scale campaign against it. Coles employed his own money to purchase newspapers and distribute antislavery handbills, warning that a convention would benefit large slaveholders. The referendum was resoundingly defeated in a large turnout of voters in 1824, mainly because of Coles's efforts.[28]

The defeat of the referendum was Coles's greatest achievement as governor. His demand for legislation abolishing slavery and most of his proposals for increased internal improvements, government investment in canal enterprises, and a modernized state penitentiary system that substituted solitary confinement for corporal punishment suffered defeat. His recommendation for state-supported universal public education had more success. However, in 1830, when he ran for a Senate seat, the legislature rejected him. He was also defeated for Congress. On the personal side, he made great profits from his St. Louis-area investments in real estate. In fall 1831, he moved to Philadelphia and never returned to Illinois. At age forty-seven, he married Sally Logan Roberts, of a prominent Philadelphia Quaker family. They had three children, one of whom died fighting for the Confederacy in the Civil War. As a Philadelphia businessman, Coles's primary interest was in accumulating wealth. During the 1830s, he became rich from real estate investments, both his own and those he inherited from his father-in-law, Hugh Roberts. He owned land in Virginia, Missouri, Illinois, Ohio, Wisconsin, and Philadelphia, but the source of most of his wealth was real estate investments in downtown St. Louis, Missouri, a slave state. He spent only thirteen of his eighty-two years in Illinois, but they were the most important of his life.[29]

Coles often visited Philadelphia and formed friendships with its wealthiest inhabitants, among them the wealthy and powerful Biddle, president of the Second Bank of the United States, an institution that radical Democrats depicted as the stronghold of rich oligarchs who fleeced the poor. Philadelphia's urban aristocracy proved congenial to Coles, who had no objection to the maldistribution of personal income not directly derived from slaveholding. "Despite his

[28] Ress, *Coles and the Vote to Forbid Slavery*, passim. Despite Coles's apparent success, various forms of quasi-slavery persisted in Illinois until several state supreme court decisions during the 1840s declared it illegal and the constitution of 1848 permanently abolished it (Newton N. Newborn, "Judicial Decision Making and the End of Slavery in Illinois," *Journal of the Illinois State Historical Society* 98/1 & 2 [2005]: 7–33.0

[29] Edward Coles Account Books, Historical Society of Pennsylvania, cited in Leichtle and Carveth, *Crusade against Slavery*, 170, 241n9; Sutton, "Coles, Edward," *ANB*, 5:227–28.

republican protests," Coles's biographers write, "Coles had cultivated a taste for high society. Philadelphia, with its salons and clubs and the whirl of a lively society crowd, fulfilled him in ways that Illinois never did."[30]

Coles was optimistic about Black prospects. Writing the Philadelphia Quaker merchant and antislavery philanthropist Roberts Vaux, whom he wanted to contribute to his antislavery political campaign, he said that his experiment in freeing his slaves and granting them land fulfilled his hopes that they would prove Black competence under the right conditions. "They have all behaved uniformly well, and are honest, industrious and prosperous," he reported.[31]

However, despite his antipathy to slavery and his satisfaction with his former slaves' success in creating new lives in Illinois, especially the father and son Ralph and Robert Crawford, by 1830 Coles's encounter with White Illinoisans' racial prejudices, along with his slaveholding Virginia background, convinced him that Jefferson was right: the two races could not live happily together. Coles ultimately agreed that after emancipation, the freedpersons must be exiled. During the debate in 1831–1832 over abolition in Virginia, perhaps seeking to appease Thomas Jefferson Randolph and other Virginia abolitionists whose opinion of Blacks was low, he labeled slaves an "ignorant, immoral and degraded race" although he considered these negative qualities effects of slavery, rather than innate. Like most antislavery Southerners, Coles had decided that Blacks' "degraded" condition and their likely obsession with vengeance (or at least political equality, if not hegemony, which for White slaveholders amounted to much the same thing) after centuries of slavery, made it necessary for the Whites to exile them after emancipation for the mutual survival of both races. (Indeed, he had not emancipated his slaves when he was in Virginia—though he had plenty of money after lucrative real estate investments in Missouri and his brother's purchase of Rockfish—and he could have petitioned the legislature to allow them to remain; instead he had moved with them to Illinois.) He agreed that the government should compel young Blacks to leave for Africa after emancipation. Hoping that James Madison would manumit his slaves in his will, he expected that an awareness that they would be deported to Africa would allay his fears of ensuing social disorder.[32]

---

[30] Leichtle and Carveth, *Crusade against Slavery*, 150 (quotation).

[31] Edward Coles to Roberts Vaux, 1824, quoted in Nicholas Guyatt, *Bind Us Apart: How Enlightened Americans Invented Racial Segregation* (New York: Oxford University Press, 2016), 309.

[32] Cooper-Guasco, *Confronting Slavery*, 158–62; Leichtle and Carveth, *Crusade against Slavery*, 127; Schwartz, *Ties That Bound*, 309. Neither Madison nor his widow, Dolley, ever freed his slaves (*Ties That Bound*, 309).

In December 1831, following Nat Turner's bloody, unsuccessful slave revolt, Coles, after moving permanently to Philadelphia that November, offered advice to Jefferson's grandson Thomas Jefferson Randolph, a freshman member of Virginia's assembly. Coles advised Randolph to press for passage of a gradual emancipation and deportation law, which he considered essential to Virginia's survival. Like Governor Thomas Mann Randolph eleven years earlier, he recommended banishing all Blacks from the state, including those already free, paying for their transportation to Africa by means of a poll tax on slaves and free Blacks; it was a harsher proposal than any Jefferson had ever supported. He advised that all slaves be freed at the age of twenty-one, but he was not clear whether they would be forced to labor for their masters until that date or treated as wards of the state. At the age of twenty-one, the ex-slaves would be forced to work for a few years to reimburse the government for their one-way trip to Africa. He thought that the state legislature should submit this idea to the voters in a referendum for their decision.[33]

Coles argued that White planters retained slavery, an "unnatural" institution contravening "the spirit of the age," primarily because they enjoyed dominating an ostensibly inferior race. He insisted that Virginia slavery was unprofitable both because of the soil's exhaustion over the years and the slaves' crude agricultural practices, which inspired planters to sell them or replace them increasingly with superior free White labor. Other reasons for Virginia Whites to abolish slavery were the "innumerable evils & perilous consequences" of retaining "a race of beings so dissimilar, & between whom [*sic*] there are such adverse interests & strong prejudices, and who neither as bond or free can amalgamate & become domiciliated [*sic*] with the Whites." If Blacks remained enslaved, he warned, they would increasingly endanger the Whites' peace and prosperity. As he put it, they "must continue to become more & more injurious to society, valueless as labourers, & dangerous as enemies." Coles predicted that soon the Deep South states, which bought slaves from Virginia, would pass laws prohibiting such purchases, further impoverishing and endangering Virginia planters who lacked other use for their excess slaves. He warned that eventually the Blacks would increase in numbers and power and become more resistant to serving as slaves, forcing the increasingly impoverished and outnumbered Whites to emancipate them.[34]

---

[33] Edward Coles to Thomas Jefferson Randolph, December 29, 1831, in "Letters of Edward Coles: Second Installment," 97–113, at 105–107; Leichtle and Carveth, *Crusade against Slavery*, 150–54.

[34] Edward Coles to Thomas Jefferson Randolph, December 29, 1831, in "Letters of Edward Coles: Second Installment," 105–106.

Ultimately, even if the slaves failed to rise up in massive revolts, provoking "efforts at mutual extermination," Coles predicted, the masters would emancipate "their Slaves as no longer of any value, & be forced to turn loose upon Society this ignorant, immoral & degraded race." Like Jefferson before him, Coles emphasized the danger of allowing Blacks to remain in the state, as either slaves or free persons. He expected endless violent confrontations between the races for power and possession of the land—what he called "a contest between the two casts [*sic*] for the occupancy of the State"— if the government liberated the slaves and permitted them to remain.[35]

Emulating Jefferson's words from 1814, Coles urged Whites to remain in Virginia and restore its racial "consistency" by emancipating and deporting all slaves and free Blacks, granting them their "rights" and then displacing them from the country. He recommended financing the compulsory "transportation" of free Blacks to Africa, both those already free and those manumitted in the future, by a small poll tax on free Blacks and slaves. The specifics of the law he proposed were virtually identical to Jefferson's recommendations in Query XIV of *Notes*, except for the provisions specifying a poll tax and deporting free Blacks to Africa as the compulsory destination of those emancipated by the government once they reached adulthood.[36]

Coles's efforts were unavailing, just as his struggle to convince the Illinois legislature to pass a law specifically abolishing slavery when he was governor had been. In 1832, the Virginia legislature rejected Randolph's suggestion for a statewide referendum to abolish slavery, which included many features of Coles's harsh emancipation plan. It decided to retain slavery unaltered. Like their famous forebear, the efforts of Jefferson's biological heir Thomas Jefferson Randolph and his intellectual heir Edward Coles against the Slave Power had failed.[37]

---

[35] Ibid., 106.

[36] Ibid., 106–107 (quotation).

[37] Cooper-Guasco, *Confronting Slavery*, 159–62; Leichtle and Carveth, *Crusade against Slavery*, 150–55. Leonard L. Richards, *The Slave Power: The Free North and Southern Domination, 1780–1860* (Baton Rouge: Louisiana State University Press, 2001).

Chapter 12

Jefferson "at Home" with His Slaves: The James Hubbard Incident

By the time he composed his fragmentary autobiography in 1821 at the age of seventy-seven, having reached a disillusioned old age, Jefferson relinquished much of his optimism about the American people's benevolence. His *Autobiography*, marred by superficiality, eccentric emphases in terms of events, and often-lackluster writing style compared to his other works, conveyed his jadedness. Written in 1821, it revealed his doubts that human nature, even in Virginia, was sufficiently benign to convince the legislature to enact slaves' emancipation. He acknowledged that at some point between 1776 and 1778 he, Edmund Pendleton, George Wythe, George Mason, and Thomas Ludwell Lee, a committee for revising the state's laws, had discussed a gradual emancipation act. Jefferson, Wythe, Pendleton, and Mason were among the greatest men in Virginia, but they seemingly lacked sufficient moral sense or confidence in its passage to produce such a bill. Jefferson started out matter-of-factly to explain, "The bill on the subject of slaves was a mere digest of the existing laws respecting them, without any intimation of a plan for a future & general emancipation. It was thought better that this should be kept back, and attempted only by way of amendment whenever the bill should be brought on." After implying the committee felt exceedingly cautious about broaching abolition, Jefferson claimed that it agreed in principle with the plan he would publish a few years later in *Notes*' Query XIV. "The principles of the amendment however were agreed on, that is to say, the freedom of all born after a certain day [the post-nati principle], and deportation at a proper age," he wrote.[1] The committee seemed ready to take the decisive step of introducing the revolutionary proposal for slave emancipation.

However, the committee's confidence in human nature and the moral sense quickly eroded, and they finally rejected the idea of proposing a gradual emancipation bill to their colleagues. Perhaps after conversing with their fellow legislators or sending up some kind of trial balloon, they became discouraged. As Jefferson vaguely put it in his old age, recognizing that his earlier, sporadic

[1] Jefferson's *Autobiography*, in Ford, ed., *Works of Thomas Jefferson*, 1:76.

predictions of popular support for abolition were over-optimistic, "It was found that the public mind would not yet bear the proposition, nor will it bear it even at this day." As he had been doing for forty years, Jefferson, now in his autobiography, renewed his warning that race war was inevitable if the assembly failed to pass, or the people did not accept, an emancipation bill: "Yet the day is not distant when it [public opinion] must bear and adopt it, or worse will follow." Suddenly rising to his wonted eloquence, Jefferson disclosed his persisting, lifelong opinion that the two races could never live together in peace and freedom. "Nothing is more certainly written in the book of fate than that these people are to be free," he asserted. "Nor is it less certain that the two races, equally free, cannot live in the same government. Nature, habit, opinion has drawn indelible lines of distinction between them." In contrast to his discussion in Query XIV of *Notes*, his autobiography said nothing about his opinion of Blacks' mental and physical qualities. Perhaps he regarded the two races as potential equals, but for all that still lethal to each other. He believed there was still time to undertake emancipation, before the slaves took up the "dagger" to accomplish it by force. He advised, "It is still in our power to direct the process of emancipation and deportation peacefully and in such slow degree as that the evil will wear off insensibly, and their [the slaves'] place be *pari passu* filled up by free white laborers."[2]

Although Jefferson certainly preferred that the emancipated enslaved masses leave the United States, unlike some Southern leaders, including Thomas Mann Randolph, Jr., and the political philosopher John Taylor of Caroline, he never proposed to force the existing free Black population into exile.

Jefferson was consistent in recommending that White laborers replace the Blacks; apparently, he thought that Whites, perhaps immigrants from Germany or Ireland, would be willing to perform, at low wages, the same work that slaves had involuntarily done for room and board. This had been his stance since writing *Notes on Virginia* in the 1780s, an idea that he expressed at greater length to Edward Bancroft from Paris in 1789 although, in contrast to his later opinions, he then envisioned Blacks and Whites working side by side in his fields, as free individuals.[3]

---

[2] Ibid., 77. "Shall we present them [the slaves] with freedom and a dagger?" Jefferson wrote to John Adams around this time, during the great controversy over slavery in Missouri and its abolition there and in the entire Louisiana Purchase, which northern Federalists and many Republicans advocated. Jefferson opposed Congress's arrogating power to abolish slavery in the states where it had long existed, which he feared might happen if it prohibited slavery in the new state of Missouri (Jefferson to John Adams, January 22, 1821, in Cappon, ed., *Adams-Jefferson Letters* [1959], 2:570).

[3] Jefferson to Edward Bancroft, January 26, 1789, in Boyd et al., eds., *Papers of Thomas Jefferson*, 14:492.

Jefferson ended his autobiography's ruminations on a pessimistic note, employing the unusual analogy between nineteenth-century Southern masters and slaves and Spanish Christians and Moors in 1492. The short-lived Spanish constitutional monarchy recently (in 1820) abolished the Inquisition, perhaps bringing it to Jefferson's mind. He alluded to that evil institution's atrocities against Jews and to Ferdinand and Isabella's expulsion of the North African Muslims ("Moors") from Spain, in their quest for ethnic and religious cleansing and a homogeneous nation-state. He euphemistically called the Spaniards' deportation and sporadic executions of the Moors a "deletion." "If on the contrary it [emancipation] is left to force itself on, human nature must shudder at the prospect held up," he admonished. "We should in vain look for an example in the Spanish deportation or deletion of the Moors. This precedent would fall far short of our case."[4]

In comparing the Moors' tragic fate in Spain with his expectation that White militias and armies would massacre Southern slaves seeking liberty through revolution or liquidate them if government emancipated them without banishing them, Jefferson did not feel his life endangered by their *continuance* in slavery. If the slaves were emancipated en masse and permitted to remain in Virginia, however, he envisaged a race war that the Whites would inevitably win—just as the Spaniards defeated the Moors—at the price of needless bloodshed and atrocity.

Predicting sickening carnage if adult Blacks were emancipated but not deported, Jefferson inadvertently exposed his flawed moral sense, in failing to concede the possibility that the two races could live together. However, he had some justification for this dread, in light of the internal warfare and annihilation of the Whites in Haiti, the first country where Black slaves had overthrown White rule. Jefferson unflatteringly compared Southern masters to fanatical Roman Catholic Spaniards, obsessed with achieving national unity and religious uniformity; slaves were surrogates for the helpless Moors, whose Turkish protectors were permanently expelled from southern Spain in 1492. In this manner, Jefferson revealed his disillusionment with the Southern gentry, who had made no efforts toward abolition. He implied that his opinion of Americans' moral sense had declined to the point that he considered them akin to the religious bigots and rabid nationalists of Europe, whom he despised. He held a higher opinion of the moral integrity, and therefore of the social justice, of the ostensibly primitive Native American tribes, and even of the stateless Black slave.

---

[4] *Autobiography*, in Ford, ed., *Works of Thomas Jefferson*, 1:77. After 1492, the Moors were permitted to stay in Spain under close surveillance. Philip II persecuted them, and they revolted in 1568, after which they were nearly exterminated. In 1609, the remaining Moriscos (Moorish converts to Christianity) were expelled from Spain.

As early as *Notes on Virginia*, in discussing the American Indians, whose Virginian Cherokee and Mingo tribal leaders he knew personally, Jefferson depicted the moral sense as a social as well as an innate function, an inborn seedling that reached fruition under proper social conditions and constraints. Explaining how Native Americans, who lived without an organized government or a written language, maintained law and order, Jefferson observed, "Their only controuls are their manners, and that moral sense of right and wrong, which, like the sense of tasting and feeling, in every man makes a part of his nature. An offence against these is punished by contempt, by exclusion from society, or, where the case is serious, as that of murder, by the individuals whom it concerns."[5]

Jefferson understood the system of retributive justice characteristic of many coastal Indian tribes, in which the kin (clan) of the aggrieved party sought revenge on wrongdoers.[6] In a letter discussing the Indians' form of government written many years later, Jefferson once more noted that they had no "monarchical" or executive functionary. Headmen ruled by persuasion rather than by coercing the disobedient. Nonetheless, despite their virtually anarchical condition he believed they had a strong moral sense. From their customs, he derived his late-life axiom, "Man was created for social intercourse; but social intercourse cannot be maintained without a sense of justice; then man must have been created with a sense of justice."[7]

Apart from the "innate sense of justice," the details of the "moral sense" were filled in by society rather than inborn, varying with different cultures and social norms. It was an outgrowth of environmentalism, a new ethnographic term.[8] Like the American Indians, Jefferson's concept of the "moral sense" understood the role of shame and public opinion in forming a socialized personality.[9]

He applied this shaming approach to the disciplining of his slaves. After his men apprehended James (or "Jame") Hubbard, a recidivist runaway slave who

---

[5] *Notes on Virginia*, Query XI, in Peden, ed., *Notes on the State of Virginia*, 93. See also Sheehan, *Seeds of Extinction*, 31.

[6] Wilcomb E. Washburn, *The Indian in America* (New York: Harper & Row, 1975), 17–20.

[7] Jefferson to Francis W. Gilmer, June 7, 1816, in Ford, ed., *Works of Thomas Jefferson*, 11:535.

[8] On Jefferson's concept of the moral sense as an outgrowth of an environmentalist ethic, see Sheehan, *Seeds of Extinction*, 32–39, 85–87, 98, 115, 189–90.

[9] Jefferson to Judge William Johnson, June 22, 1823, in Peterson, ed., *Jefferson: Writings*, 1470 ("innate sense of justice"). For Jefferson's favorable assessment of Native Americans' near-anarchical society and their free-spirited personalities, see Jefferson to Edward Carrington, January 16, 1787; Jefferson to James Madison, January 30, 1787, in Peterson, ed., *Jefferson: Writings*, 880–81, 881–82; *and Notes on Virginia*, Queries 6 and 11.

foraged for provisions from other plantations, surviving on their stolen resources for a whole year (thereby humiliating Jefferson in the eyes of his planter neighbors and friends), Jefferson had him brought back to Monticello "in irons. I had him severely flogged, in the presence of his old companions, and committed to jail." He had not punished Hubbard the first time he ran away, which was a sign of weakness in the eyes of his slaves. Despite his attempt to employ the slaves' opinion to intimidate the disobedient bondsman, Jefferson concluded that Hubbard was incorrigible. By necessity a student of slave psychology, Jefferson advised Reuben Perry, the artisan to whom he had sold Hubbard in absentia, "The course he has been in, and all circumstances convince me he will never again serve any man as a slave. The moment he is out of jail and his irons off he will be off himself."[10]

After retiring from the presidency, therefore, Jefferson ostensibly revealed a sadistic aspect of his personality in his abuse of the young Monticello nail-maker Jame Hubbard. Apparently, he had formerly favored this slave but felt Hubbard had flouted his earlier benevolent treatment by pilfering and selling nails and by making several runaway attempts, the last of which lasted a year. Bitter toward Hubbard for these betrayals despite Jefferson's earlier forgiveness of the nail "theft" and other instances of kind treatment toward him (and his parents, who lived at Poplar Forest, Jefferson's Bedford County plantation), Jefferson wanted revenge.

Although superficially methodical in his account keeping, a product of his obsessive interest in detail, Jefferson was a poor fiscal manager, generally unaware that he was deeply in debt.[11] Maintaining a veneer of efficiency, he resented all the more the economically unproductive expenses he had incurred in paying slave catchers and placing newspaper advertisements to recapture Jame. He was forced to hire two acquaintances, Reuben Perry and Isham Chisolm, to track down Hubbard. After Jame was brought back to Monticello, Jefferson detailed his punishment to Perry, who with his brother John were construction workers on his

---

[10] Jefferson to Reuben Perry, April 16, 1812, in Edwin W. Betts, ed., *Thomas Jefferson's Farm Book...* (Princeton: [Published for the American Philosophical Society by] Princeton University Press, 1953), 34–35. The first time James Hubbard ran away, in 1805, he used forged passes provided by the son of Jefferson's Monticello overseer Gabriel Lilly. See Jefferson to David Bradley and David Bradley to Jefferson, both October 6, 1805, ibid., 20–21. See also McLaughlin, *Jefferson and Monticello*, 115–16.

[11] On Jefferson's ineptitude in managing the finances of his plantations, partly because he was preoccupied with public affairs as president, see McLaughlin, *Jefferson and Monticello*, 377–79; introduction to James A. Bear and Lucia C. Stanton, eds., *Jefferson's Memorandum Books*, 2 vols. (Princeton: Princeton University Press, 1997), 1:xvii–xxi.

home. He intended to "pay" Perry, at least in part, by transferring to him the refractory slave. In April 1812, he wrote Perry,

> Having recieved [*sic*] information in March that Jame Hubbard had been living in Lexington [a town in the Shenandoah Valley in western Virginia, near Jefferson's Natural Bridge] upwards of a twelvemonth, I engaged a man (Isham Chisolm) to go after him. He got there five days after Hubbard had run off from there, having committed a theft. He [Chisolm] returned of course without him. I engaged him [Chisolm] to start a second time, offering a premium of 25. D [dollars] in addition to yours [Perry's], besides his expences. He got upon his tract [i.e, trail], & persued [*sic*] him into Pendleton county, where he took him and brought him here [Monticello] in irons.[12]

Irritated by reports that Hubbard had "committed a theft" from neighboring planters during his flight, as well as by memories that he stole boxes of nails a few years earlier when employed with a dozen other young male slaves at Monticello's nail factory, Jefferson considered Hubbard an incorrigible miscreant whose brazen acts further discredited Jefferson's shaky reputation for efficiency. Seemingly forgetting the sentiments he had earlier emblazoned in the Declaration of Independence and in writing *Notes on Virginia*, documents which stressed that all people rightfully desired freedom to pursue life, liberty, and happiness, Jefferson ostensibly condoned his actions in having Hubbard whipped.[13]

Although in *Notes* he argued that the slave, in effect deprived of life by the master, was justified in stealing in retaliation for society's injustice, Jefferson was obviously unwilling to apply his own maxim to this slave, for whom he had perhaps developed a personal hostility. In Hubbard's case, Jefferson granted the persona of a cruel, business-oriented slave-owner priority over that of the libertarian philosopher and benign master. Irked by Hubbard's ostensibly incorrigible desire for freedom—something Jefferson had always considered "natural"—he wanted him out of his sight and transported out of the state. That he may have unconsciously felt guilt over denying Hubbard's right to freedom provided additional incentive for him to remove this unpleasant jab to his conscience. Hubbard had

---

[12] Jefferson to Reuben Perry, April 16, 1812, in Betts, ed., *Jefferson's Farm Book*, 34–35. Pendleton County is in present-day West Virginia, suggesting that Hubbard got rather far in his flight. For the deed of sale of James Hubbard, who was on the run, to Reuben Perry of Bedford County, in exchange for Perry's doing "Carpentry or House-joinery" at Poplar Forest (the venue was later changed to Monticello), see Conveyance of James Hubbard to Reuben Perry, February 1811 and September 3, 1812, in Looney, ed., *Jefferson Papers: Retirement Series*, 3:411–12.

[13] Jefferson to Reuben Perry, April 16, 1812, in Betts, ed., *Jefferson's Farm Book*, 34–35.

been an unprofitable business expense, and as a plantation owner and manager Jefferson could not tolerate such losses. Writing as if Hubbard were an obdurate horse to be gotten rid of, he advised his new "owner," Perry, that Hubbard would unceasingly persist in his escape attempts. "It will therefore unquestionably be best for you to sell him. I have paid for his recovery 70D. all I ask for it is that he may be sent out of the state."[14] Jefferson perceived the Hubbard incident as personally humiliating.

Despite his exasperation with Hubbard's rebelliousness, Jefferson's moral sense, as in earlier justifying slave revolt in *Notes* and elsewhere, prohibited disparaging a slave's desire for freedom as improper or a sign of criminality.[15] Although he willingly enacted the harsh master's role and ordered Hubbard whipped the second time he ran away, a decision repulsive to our values, those times were more brutal in some ways than our own. Historian Kenneth M. Stampp wrote regarding whipping, "Nearly every slaveholder used it, and few grown slaves escaped it entirely." As the historian Edward E. Baptist has most recently emphasized, the threat of whipping and other, even harsher physical punishment characterized the institution of Black slavery. Unfortunately, flagellation was a common feature of numerous other absolute or arbitrary forms of subjugation, among them homeless people's subjection to bondage in England under the Statute of Vagabonds in 1553. In armies, navies, and prisons, where the discipline and obedience of masses of potentially rebellious, violent men were essential to the effectiveness and even survival of those who supervised them, whipping was a common practice in the Anglo-American world.[16]

Flogging was often utilized in the armed forces, including the US Continental Army during the American Revolution. General George Washington

---

[14] Jefferson to Perry, April 16, 1812, in Betts, ed., *Jefferson's Farm Book*, 34–35. On this incident, see also Cohen, "Jefferson and the Problem of Slavery," 516.

[15] For instance, in Query 14, Jefferson, argued that all slaves, whatever their color, were brutally deprived of personal property and their right to their own labor. This perennial abuse justified slaves' alleged tendency to steal from their masters. For a different view, see Helo and Onuf, "Jefferson, Morality, and the Problem of Slavery," 610–14.

[16] Edward E. Baptist, *The Half Has Never Been Told: Slavery and the Making of American Capitalism* (New York: Basic Books, 2014), 120–21, 122, 134, 141–42, 261–65, 305; Kenneth M. Stampp, *The Peculiar Institution: Slavery in the Antebellum South* (New York: Knopf, 1956), 174–78, 209–210, 174, quote; and Eugene D. Genovese, *Roll, Jordan, Roll: The World the Slaves Made* (New York: Pantheon Books, 1974), 63–67, 124–25, 379–80, 502–11, 619–20. For the enslavement and whipping of homeless vagabonds in England during the 1500s, see Louis Ruchames, "The Sources of Racial Thought in Colonial America," *Journal of Negro History* 52/4 (October 1967): 251–72, at 259. On the whipping of White convicts, see also John J. Navin, "Intimidation, Violence, and Race in British America," *The Historian: A Journal of History* 77/3 (Fall 2015): 464–97; and Edmund S. Morgan, *American Slavery, American Freedom: The Ordeal of Colonial Virginia* (New York: Norton, 1975), passim.

favored subjecting disobedient soldiers to a lethal two hundred lashes. As commander of the Continental Army, Washington condoned brutality toward the lowly, impoverished enlisted men, while treating his officers, who generally came from the "better sort," respectfully. Washington and his officers were glad when Congress in 1776 amended the Articles of War to increase the limit on the number of lashes inflicted on disobedient soldiers, deserters, looters, and bounty jumpers from thirty-nine to one hundred and increased the number of crimes imposing the death penalty, while exempting commissioned officers from corporal punishment. As the war went on and conditions for the troops grew unendurable, Washington became more intolerant. During the notoriously bitter winter at Morristown, New Jersey (1780–1781), he issued General Orders to his officers permitting them to inflict over one hundred lashes, up to five hundred, on soldiers who looted, even though these instructions violated the Articles of War. In February 1781, seeking to legalize his arbitrary conduct, Washington recommended that Congress increase the whipping limit to five hundred lashes. When Congress finally voted on the measure in June 1781, his proposal was defeated, six states to three, although the individual delegates favored it, 14 to 13. Naval officers also frequently employed flogging, and its use in the armed services did not end until the Civil War. Black sailors as well as White were whipped. According to one historian, "Humanitarians pointed out that the sailor was worse treated than the slave."[17]

Annette Gordon-Reed, a leading Jefferson historian, argues that Jefferson was more humane than most planters in trying to avoid physically punishing his slaves. Emphasizing that he preferred appeasing them with incentives to work hard, she favorably compared him with his more efficient, albeit less compassionate grandson, Thomas Jefferson Randolph, who flogged them in front of his sister Ellen Randolph Coolidge, and her young son, Thomas Jefferson Coolidge, who

---

[17] Harold D. Langley, "The Negro in the Navy and the Merchant Service, 1798–1860," *Journal of Negro History* 52/4 (October 1967): 273–86, quotation at 282. James Kirby Martin and Mark Edward Lender, *"A Respectable Army": The Military Origins of the Republic, 1763–1789*, 3rd ed. (Malden, MA: Wiley, 2015), 76, 134–35; Caroline Cox, *A Proper Sense of Honor: Service and Sacrifice in George Washington's Army* (Chapel Hill: University of North Carolina Press, 2004), 99–101, 268–69, n65. In the Navy, slaves often gained exemption from flogging if they were the personal property of naval officers. Flogging was abolished in the US Army and the Navy around the time of the Civil War.

was only six at the time.[18] Even Edward Coles, who famously took his bondspersons to Illinois in 1819 and freed them there, admitted he whipped his slaves.[19]

☙

The altercation with Hubbard suggests that Jefferson was all too human in the matter of being made a fool of, especially by a Black slave, whom he had pardoned the first time he ran away, and whom he undoubtedly regarded as intellectually his inferior. Despite his repeated denials that he did not consider slaves chattel, he may have viscerally felt cheated of his "property" when a slave ran away, especially if, like Hubbard, they took nails or other supplies that Jefferson considered part of his "capital."

The nailery ended up a financial loss for Jefferson. His neighbors failed to pay him for the nails, and he could not compete with the big nail factories springing up. These factors perhaps unconsciously increased his anger at Hubbard, who worked there. In addition, Jefferson may have found Hubbard repulsive because the young slave was "very stout," a physique the svelte Jefferson perhaps considered the result of self-indulgence, indolence, and malingering. In writing to Daniel Bradley, the jailer of Fairfax County where Hubbard was caught after his first escape in October 1805, Jefferson wrote,

> I was yesterday informed that you had in custody in the jail at Fairfax a negro man of mine who ran away from my estate in Albemarle county 3 or 4 weeks ago. He is about 20 years of age, very stout, is a nailer by trade & called James Hubbard. My informant says he [Hubbard] confessed at once the truth of his case, that he had three passes which he said had been given him by the son of mr. [Gabriel] Lilly my manager. Mr. George Swink who gives me this information, & goes about the middle of this month on a visit to Albemarle, agrees to take this man with him to whom therefore I will ask the favor of you to deliver him when called for & in the meantime to keep him in jail.[20]

---

[18] Annette Gordon-Reed, *The Hemingses of Monticello: An American Family* (New York: Norton, 2008), 602; Thomas Jefferson Coolidge, *The Autobiography of T. Jefferson Coolidge, 1831–1920* (Boston: Houghton Mifflin, 1923), 2–3.

[19] Cooper-Guasco, *Confronting Slavery*, ch. 1; Coles's autobiographical notes in Edward Coles Papers, HSP, paraphrased in Leichtle and Carveth, *Crusade against Slavery*, 39.

[20] Jefferson to Daniel Bradley, Washington, October 6, 1805, in Betts, ed., *Jefferson's Farm Book*, 20–21. On Jefferson's eventual failure to profit from the nailery, largely because of his lax bookkeeping; inability to practice a bourgeois, entrepreneurial ethos; and persistently maintaining the worldview of an aristocratic "gentleman," see Oriol Pi-Sunyer, "Thomas

Jefferson probably wanted to ensure that Hubbard did not escape and make him look foolish again. He apparently perceived the forged passes used by Hubbard in 1805 to effect his escape as adding insult to injury, a sign of the slave's "ingratitude" for kindly treatment as one of his slave "family." He was especially interested in getting his hands on the forged passes, which were ostensibly the instruments of his (Jefferson's) humiliation. "It would be important to me to recieve [*sic*] the passes immediately because mr. [Gabriel] Lilly sets out on Thursday for Kentucky [for which he was departing permanently because Jefferson would not give him a sufficient raise as an overseer]," he wrote, "& if he can get the passes into his hands before he goes I am sure he will probe the forgery to the bottom."[21]

Jefferson's seeming obsession with retrieving the passes and his rage at discovering that his overseer's son fabricated them, suggest that he considered Hubbard's exploitation of this sign of legality, legitimacy, and the White man's superior "civilization" in betraying his confidence to be an immoral aberration from "moral sense" imperatives. Had Jefferson consistently looked at things more objectively, from the stance he adopted in Query XIV of *Notes* twenty-five years before, he would have seen the moral imbecility of that perspective. Indeed, the Hubbard incident is probably the only affair relating to slavery in which Jefferson showed inhumanity and perhaps exploited his prerogatives as a slaveholder for sadistic psychological gratification more than for purely economic objectives.[22]

Despite Jefferson's aberration from his own "moral sense" standards in Hubbard's case, he usually applied to the treatment of his slaves the maxim that if one behaved morally toward one's fellow beings, one would benefit in the end—biblically speaking, "Do unto others as you would have others do unto you." Internalizing Southern law's ambiguity, he considered slaves valuable property as well as persons. In surmising that the increasing death rate of infant slaves was caused by overseers' failure to treat pregnant women benignly, he warned his employees

---

Jefferson: Reluctant Manufacturer," *Janus: Revue Internationale de l'histoire des Sciences* 51 (1964): 226–34. Jack McLaughlin, a leading scholar on Jefferson's activities at Monticello, agrees. "The nail business never lived up to Jefferson's expectations," he writes, "because of his frequent absences, inefficient management, undependable slave labor, and the difficulty of getting paid for nails that had been purchased on credit" (*Jefferson and Monticello*, 111).

[21] Jefferson to Daniel Bradley, Oct 6, 1805, in Betts, ed., *Farm Book*, 20–21.

[22] For Jefferson's naive view of his slaves as part of his "family," see, e.g., Lucia C. Stanton, "'Those Who Labor for My Happiness': Thomas Jefferson and His Slaves," in Onuf, ed., *Jeffersonian Legacies*, esp. 148–53. The phrase quoted in Stanton's title is from a letter Jefferson wrote explaining the reasons for his retirement from public life (Jefferson to Angelica Schuyler Church, November 27, 1793, in John Catanzariti, ed., *Papers of Thomas Jefferson* [Princeton: Princeton University Press, 1950–2017], 27:449–50).

that he considered harshness toward expectant mothers wasteful as well as immoral. He wrote Joel Yancey, his plantation manager at Poplar Forest, that "the loss of 5. little ones in 4 years induces me to fear that the overseers do not permit the women to devote as much time as is necessary to the care of their children. that they view their labor as the 1st object, and the raising of their child but as secondary."[23]

Jefferson already had more slaves than he could profitably use. However, he did not want his White employees or his slaves to consider him an unduly softhearted, effeminate master. Therefore, he could not bluntly say that a human life, even that of an infant slave, deserved respect. Instead, he resorted to the market psychology of Adam Smith. He instructed Yancey, "I consider the labor of a breeding woman as no object, and that a child raised every 2 years is of more profit than the crop of the best laboring man. In this, as in all other cases, providence has made our interests and our duties coincide perfectly." Thus, assuring Yancey that he was following the "providential" rules of "Nature and Nature's God," as he wrote in the Declaration of Independence, he concluded, "I must pray you to inculcate upon the overseers that it is not their [the females'] labor, but their increase which is the first consideration with us."[24]

A year later, his identical advice to his former son-in-law, John Wayles Eppes, reiterated the self-evident importance of female slaves in reproducing plantation life. "I know of no error more consuming to an estate than that of stocking farms with men almost exclusively," he explained. "I consider a woman who brings a child every two years as more profitable than the best man of the farm. What she produces is an addition to capital, while his labors disappear in mere consumption."[25] On the surface, Jefferson's business acumen viewed slaves as little better than breeding animals. He inadvertently added a corollary to Marx's later surplus labor theory of value that one might call "the pregnant slave's reproductive theory of value." Nevertheless, if what he said, that kindness to the pregnant slave also helped increase one's profits, was coldly capitalistic, its results were humane. Especially in old age, after he retired from the presidency, refrained from purchasing additional slaves, and refused to sell any, Jefferson wanted his overseers to encourage his slaves to marry other slaves who resided on his plantations. Otherwise, they might become intimate with slaves from distant estates

---

[23] Jefferson to Joel Yancey, January 17, 1819, Founders Online, National Archives (founders.archives.gov/documents/Jefferson/03-13-02-0522). Spelling and punctuation in original.

[24] Jefferson to Joel Yancey, January 17, 1819, quoted from Betts, ed., *Jefferson's Farm Book*, 43, in Cohen, "Jefferson and the Problem of Slavery," 518.

[25] Jefferson to John Wayles Eppes, June 30, 1820, in Betts, ed., *Jefferson's Farm Book*, 45–46, quoted in Cohen, "Jefferson and the Problem of Slavery," 518n.

whom they met casually and marry them. Then such a male slave would request to visit his wife elsewhere, his labor would be lost, and if his "wife" (slave marriages had no legal standing) became pregnant and belonged to a different owner, the other planter, not Jefferson, would reap such physical benefits as the additional slave children provided.

Jefferson espoused this shockingly mercenary—though paradoxically humane—policy in an 1815 letter to Jeremiah A. Goodman, his reputedly callous overseer at Poplar Forest in Bedford County. After hearing from one of his Tomahawk Plantation (Bedford County) slaves, Phill Hubbard (brother of the ill-fated Jame), who journeyed to Monticello to complain that Goodman punished his wife because Phill visited her at her father's home, Jefferson reproached the overseer. Jefferson not only defended Phill against Goodman's alleged disrespect for his marital state but also showed surprising familiarity with and respect for the slave. "Phill Hubbard arrived here the 2d day after Christmas," he notified the overseer. "His subject of complaint is exactly what you supposed. He says that he and Dick's [the bride's father] Hanah [*sic*] had become husband & wife, but that you drove him repeatedly from her father's house and would not let him go there, punishing her, as he supposes, for receiving him." (It is surprising that Jefferson, in light of his supposed long-term relationship with Sally Hemings, did not suspect Goodman of jealousy of Phill's intimate relationship with Hannah, and that Goodman may have sexually abused her before Phill abruptly arrived on the scene.) Jefferson instructed Goodman to send Phill and Hannah from the Tomahawk estate to the other Poplar Forest plantation, Bear Creek, where Phill said they would be happier away from the brutish overseer. Goodman admitted to Jefferson, without remorse, that on Christmas Day, unaware that she and Phill were about to be married, he had slapped Hannah "three or foure times for some words she had bin makeing use of." Perhaps she had spoken disrespectfully to the overseer. Goodman suspected that after getting a beating, she broke off the "engagement" with Phill, perhaps thinking he had not sufficiently protected her. According to Goodman, this may have been the reason that Phill, his best worker, "went off in drunking [*sic*] madness." He became "Like a mad man and Said he would not stay here." Goodman assured Jefferson that if Phill wanted Hannah for a wife, he would try to reconcile them, but from Phill's testimony, it is likely that Goodman was lying.[26]

---

[26] Jeremiah A. Goodman to Jefferson, December 30, 1814, and Jefferson to Jeremiah Goodman, January 6, 1815, in Looney, ed., *Jefferson Papers: Retirement Series*, 8:173–74, 185–86; Edwin Betts, ed., *Thomas Jefferson's Garden Book, 1766–1824* (Philadelphia: American Philosophical Society, 1944), 540. See also McLaughlin, *Jefferson and Monticello*, 128.

Jefferson took the slaves' side. He instructed Goodman to supply the newlyweds Hannah (a rather common name on Jefferson's plantations) and Phill with a wedding present of sorts: a new cooking pot and bed, "which I always promise them when they take husbands at home, and I shall be very glad to hear that others of the young people follow their example."[27]

Although dependent on overseers, Jefferson considered them generally servile, worthless philistines. He despised them, perhaps unjustly, believing they fawned on the plantation owners, who hired and humiliated them. In 1815, describing Virginia society for the Virginia lawyer, judge, and historian William Wirt, he wrote that overseers were "the most abject, degraded and unprincipled race, always cap in hand to the Dons who employed them, and furnishing materials for the exercise of their pride, insolence and spirit of domination." This depiction of overseers contrasts with the reality that many overseers, among them his favorite, Edmund Bacon, left Jefferson when he rejected their demands for higher pay. Jefferson indirectly acknowledged their hard work and diligence when he asked his friends for help in finding cheap but competent replacements. Perhaps his negative assessment was partly sour grapes.[28]

Despite the overseer's wickedness and immorality in violently keeping a husband from his wife (and Goodman admitted he had slapped Hannah), Jefferson ostensibly considered Goodman's primary fault not his brutal disregard of human affections but his needlessly disrupting the slave quarters' harmony. As Jefferson put it, "Certainly there is nothing I desire so much as that all the young people in the estate should intermarry with one another and stay at home. They are worth a great deal more in that case than when they have husbands and wives abroad." The aging Jefferson could not be everywhere at once, and he visited Poplar Forest never more than once or twice a year (and that was after 1817). This pragmatic metaphysician had to rely on Goodman whether he liked it or not, and as a student of man's nature he was aware he had to treat him gently. He was trying to restrain Goodman from afar while not affronting his vulgar macho sensibilities,

---

[27] Jefferson to Jeremiah Goodman, January 6, 1815, in Looney, ed., *Jefferson Papers: Retirement Series*, 8:174.

[28] Jefferson to William Wirt, August 5, 1815, in Lipscomb and Bergh, eds., *Writings of Jefferson*, 14:337. For Jefferson's request for assistance in finding a new overseer to replace Gabriel Lilly, who left because Jefferson would not give him a sufficient raise, see Jefferson to John Strode, June 5, 1805, microfilm reel 33, Jefferson Papers, LC (hdl.loc.gov/loc.mss/mtj.mtjbib 014782). On the difficulty of finding good overseers, see also Charles Clay to Jefferson, July 30, 1801, microfilm reel 49, Jefferson Papers, LC (hdl.loc.gov/loc.mss/mtj.mtjbib022490). For a recent generally favorable depiction of overseers as respectable citizens, see Laura Sandy, "Divided Loyalties in a 'Predatory War': Plantation Slavery and Overseers during the American Revolution," *Journal of American Studies* 48/2 (May 2014): 357–92.

which automatically led him to beat slaves rather than empathize with them. Goodman likely viewed brutality as the most effective way to keep the Poplar Forest estates productive. His more enlightened employer disagreed.[29]

In accordance with his pragmatic support for the slave, Jefferson directed that Phill and his wife live together happily, for their well-being and his own. His letter revealed that he respected the slaves' wishes and tried to follow their desires for enhancing their pursuit of happiness, to the extent a slave could conceive of such a thing. "Phill has been long petitioning me to let him go to Bearcreek [Bear Creek, Jefferson's Poplar Forest farm near Tomahawk] to live with his family, and Nanny [another slave, living at Monticello] has been as long at me to let her come to the Poplar forest. We may therefore now gratify both, by sending Phill & his wife to Bearcreek, and bringing Nanny and any one of the single men from there, that is to say Reuben, Daniel, or Stephen."[30]

Jefferson wanted to distance the newlyweds from Goodman. He also demonstrated knowledge of the slaves' living conditions, even at faraway Poplar Forest, which he had only recently begun visiting for extended periods during the summer. "No new house will be wanting," he wrote Goodman, who should have known all these details since he was the Poplar Forest overseer, "because Phill can take the house Nanny leaves, and Nanny may take the house which Cate's [this was probably Phillip Hubbard's mother-in-law] Hanah leaves." He insisted that Goodman not retaliate on Phill for running away to Monticello to inform against him, although it is hard to see how Jefferson could protect Phill in Bedford County from the distance of Monticello: "I would by no means have Phill punished for what he has done; for although I had let them [the slaves] all know that their runnings [*sic*] away should be punished, yet Phill's character is not that of a runaway. I have known him from a boy and that he has not come off to sculk from his work."[31] Unlike many other slaveholders, Jefferson was familiar with his slaves' personalities and defended them when necessary.[32]

---

[29] Jefferson to Goodman, January 6, 1815, in Betts, ed., *Jefferson's Garden Book*, 540. For the commencement of Jefferson's regular visits to Poplar Forest late in life, see Jefferson to José Corrêa da Serra, June 14, 1817, in Looney, ed., *Jefferson Papers: Retirement Series*, 11:439.

[30] Jefferson to Goodman, January 6, 1815, in Betts, ed., *Jefferson's Garden Book*, 540.

[31] Ibid.

[32] Lucia C. Stanton, *Free Some Day: The African American Families of Monticello* (Charlottesville: Thomas Jefferson Foundation, 2000), 78–79; Philip J. Schwarz, "Thomas Jefferson and the Law of Slavery," in Schwarz, *Slave Laws in Virginia*, 35–62; McLaughlin, *Jefferson and Monticello*, 94–145. Jefferson often collectively referred to his plantations in Bedford County, near present-day Lynchburg in western Virginia, as "Poplar Forest." They included the plantations of Poplar Forest, Bear Creek, and Tomahawk. Jefferson's Albemarle County plantations included Shadwell and Lego north of the Rivanna River, and Monticello and Tufton south of the Rivanna. See Malone, *Jefferson and the Ordeal of Liberty*, 198–99.

Jefferson preferred that Goodman exercise moderation in disciplining slaves, even those who had allegedly committed crimes. In the case of the runaway slave Hercules, whom other slaves accused of poisoning them as a bogus doctor, Jefferson instructed Goodman to be lenient. In July 1813, he wrote him from Monticello

> Hercules arrived here on the 22d. having been discharged from Buckingham jail on the 20th where he had been confined as a runaway: the folly he has committed certainly justifies further punishment, and he goes in expectation of receiving it, for I have assured him that I leave it to yourself altogether and made him sensible that he deserves &ought to recieve [*sic*] it. I believe however it is his first folly in this way, and considering his imprisonment as a punishment in part, I refer it to yourself whether it may not be passed over for this time, only letting him receive the pardon as from yourself alone, and not by my interference, for this is what I would have none of them [the slaves] to suppose.

At this time, Jefferson wanted to disguise his kindness to a slave, fearing to gain a reputation with bondsmen as an unduly lenient master who would condone wrong-doing.[33]

In the case of Sally (not the older, more famous Sally Hemings), Jefferson conditionally sold Goodman one of his slaves, a five-year-old girl. He soon changed his mind, pretended that the overseer had not received fair value, and paid handsomely for her return to Monticello. Jefferson apparently proposed to pay his overseer more than he expected for the return of a poorly performing infant slave. Indeed, it is possible that Goodman was the infant's father since Jefferson refers to her as "Sally Goodman" in the bill of sale to Jeremiah Goodman. Perhaps the callous Goodman was contemplating raising his own child at Poplar Forest but had second thoughts and let Jefferson keep her, especially when Jefferson offered him a lot of money to retain the child. Jefferson may have felt guilty about separating such a small child from her mother (who probably resided at Monticello), and even more for subjecting her to Goodman's tender mercies. The postscript to the bill of sale for Sally by which Jefferson deeded her to his overseer, dated November 30, 1815, indicates that she had never left Monticello. It states, "The said girl Sally remains in my possession by agreement in the care of her mother until either the sd. Jeremiah Goodman or myself chuses that she shall be taken into his possession."[34]

---

[33] Jefferson to Jeremiah Goodman, July 26, 1813, in Betts, ed., *Jefferson's Farm Book*, 36.

[34] Jefferson to Jeremiah Goodman, November 30, 1815, microfilm reel 48, Jefferson Papers, LC (hdl.loc.gov/loc.mss/mtj.mtjbib022216).

With surprising philanthropy, Jefferson was eager to compensate Goodman for what he pretended was his employee's loss. Sally was a young child, and apparently a poor worker (perhaps in the nailery or a spinning facility). Nonetheless, Jefferson decided to reimburse Goodman amply, writing somewhat incoherently, "With respect to the girl Sally, the fair thing is to consider the bargain as annulled, and for me to repay you the sum allowed for her, 150D. with interest till repaid: but I cannot undertake the repayment but in all May 1819. I had as live [*sic*] pay in May [18]18 as in Aug. [18]18 but I could not do this conveniently. This with the repayment of her clothing comes to something more than you propose." Taking substantial time to determine the precise amount he owed his overseer, Jefferson held back the letter for ten days and added a postscript: "P.S. July 30, 1817. The only contribution you have given to the clothing or subsistence of the child being the sum of 15.D. allowed me for corn in a subsequent account, I mean that that shall also be repaid with interest."[35] Jefferson retained Sally in his "family." She never left Monticello.[36]

Despite Goodman's harshness toward slaves, Jefferson respected his competence as a manager. Nonetheless, by treating him generously in the case of little Sally, he perhaps hoped to instill Goodman with a greater degree of the "moral sense." He also instructed him in fairness toward others. For instance, when S. J. Harrison, a tobacco merchant, agreed to purchase Jefferson's tobacco crop, Jefferson told Goodman to be careful in storing the tobacco and to make sure that it was of good quality. Once more employing a variant of the Golden Rule, he said, "We ought to do not only what is just, but liberal, in the case of Mr. Harrison, to merit his future confidence."[37]

Jefferson made only a token effort to discipline his slaves. He attempted to keep secret his refusal to punish Phill for fleeing to Monticello to complain about an unjust overseer when he should have been working at Tomahawk plantation, and he advocated leniency for Hercules. Jefferson was naturally an ineffectual disciplinarian, shying away from direct physical confrontation with anyone, even his slaves. Theoretically, he believed in freedom for all, and the use of compulsion repelled him. Moreover, he felt a natural disgust with the institution of slavery, considering it a "moral and political depravity." As he explained to a friend, whose help he requested in finding a new manager for his Monticello plantation during

[35] Jefferson to Jeremiah Goodman, July 20, 1817, in Betts, ed., *Jefferson's Farm Book*, 41.

[36] See "Conveyance of Sally Goodman to Jeremiah A. Goodman, November 30, 1815," in Looney, ed., *Jefferson Papers: Retirement Series*, 9:215–16, and notes. Sally never left Monticello. She remained in Albemarle County until her death in 1870.

[37] Jefferson to Jeremiah Goodman, February 5, 1813, in Betts, ed., *Jefferson's Farm Book*, 303.

his presidency, he preferred to encourage his slaves to work by offering incentives rather than punishment: "I love industry & abhor severity."[38]

With regard to free labor, comparing the British and American qualities of life, Jefferson argued that the American people were far "happier" than the English were. "In England, happiness is the lot of the aristocracy only," he insisted, who, he said, composed fewer than four percent of the population. In the United States, virtually everyone was happy because "most of the laboring class," "the great mass of our population...possess property, cultivate their own lands, have families, and from the demand for their labor are enabled to exact from the rich and the competent such prices as enable them to be fed abundantly, clothed above mere decency, to labor moderately and raise their families."[39]

More questionably, Jefferson insisted that even lowly slaves had better living conditions than most British laborers, soldiers, and sailors. This observation was part of Jefferson's nationalism and his brand of American "exceptionalism," in which he argued that, because the vast majority of Americans were more prosperous than most Europeans were and had more freedom, they were "happier." Anticipating Karl Marx's theory of the surplus value of labor, Jefferson argued that Britain's urban and rural "aristocracy, comprehending the nobility, the wealthy commoners, the high grades of priesthood, and the officers of government," paid the laboring classes the minimum amount needed to keep them alive and working. Indifferent to the fate of the surplus population that was not needed or suited for labor, they abandoned the latter, who became "the eleemosynary class, or paupers, who are about one-fifth of the whole."[40]

Anticipating Marx, Malthus, and Darwin, Jefferson depicted a struggle among the lower classes for survival, controlled and manipulated by the rich, in which only the fittest were able to stay out of pauperism:

---

[38] Jefferson to Thomas Cooper, September 10, 1814 (first quotation), and Jefferson to John Strode, June 5, 1805 (second quotation), Jefferson Papers, LC. On Volney's description of a slaveholder's ludicrous histrionics toward his slaves at the time he visited Virginia and Monticello in summer 1796, which a recent writer mistakenly identified as Jefferson, see Constantin Volney's *"Rélation inedite"* (unpublished manuscript journal), quoted in John Leman *Jefferson's Demons* (New York, 2005), 90, 127. Indeed, one might expect such bumbling, feckless attempts at coercion from Jefferson, a slaveholder who had no stomach for enforcing discipline on his slaves. However, an expert study of Volney, which Leman cites, reveals that Jefferson was *not* the clumsy, whip-toting master. See Jean Gaulmier, *L'Idéologue Volney, 1757–1820: Contribution à l'Histoire de l'Orientalisme en France* (Geneva: Sletkine, 1980), 370–72.

[39] Jefferson to Thomas Cooper, September 10, 1814, in Lipscomb and Bergh, eds., *Writings of Jefferson*, 14:182.

[40] Ibid. See also Claudio J. Katz, "Thomas Jefferson's Liberal Anti-Capitalism," *American Journal of Political Science* 47/1 (January 2003): 1–17.

> The aristocracy, which have the laws and government in their hands, have so managed them as to reduce the third description ["of persons," the paupers and beggars] below the means of supporting life, even by labor; and to force the second ["the laboring class"], whether employed in agriculture or the [mechanic] arts, to the maximum of labor which the construction of the human body can endure, and to the minimum of food, and of the meanest kind, which will preserve it in life, and in strength sufficient to perform its functions.[41]

Depicting the English ruling classes as despicable villains, Jefferson charged that they forced the artisan class, including journeymen, day laborers, and master craftsmen, to work with the utmost diligence and skill merely to survive. Because of this brutal competition, they surpassed the mechanic classes of the other nations in ability. Tragically, most of the people, "less dexterous individuals" without such skills, were forced to become beggars who "furnish[ed] materials for armies and navies to defend their country, exercise piracy on the ocean, and carry conflagration, plunder and devastation, on the shores of all those who endeavor to withstand their aggressions." These plebeians were "tools" of the rich, enabling "the luxury, the riot, the domination and the vicious happiness of the aristocracy." The unskilled, impoverished majority contributed to their own tragic impoverishment and degradation by the aristocracy, in whose "hands, the paupers are used as tools to maintain their own wretchedness, and to keep down the laboring portion by shooting them [in their roles as soldiers] whenever the desperation produced by the cravings of their stomachs drives them into riots. Such is the happiness of scientific England." By Jefferson's accounting, the wealthy aristocracy certainly lacked a moral sense. These immoral great merchants, financiers, and landed nobility had coerced the vast majority of the people into amoral, starving, self-destructive automatons who did their bidding.[42]

Claiming that British laborers, soldiers, and sailors had less secure access to nourishment and guarantees for their health, safety, and family stability than most slaves did, Jefferson pointed out, as his friend Thomas Paine had done earlier in *Agrarian Justice* (1797), that the royal government rejected responsibility for protecting them from nearly certain impoverishment in old age. By contrast, an aged Virginia slave could not be ejected from the plantation when he became too old to labor; if such a slave were manumitted, his former master had to guarantee him an income by law. Jefferson excitedly pointed to the physical abuse and dangers suffered by British sailors, who, when they were not being whipped by their officers, endured malnutrition and perilous naval encounters with Napoleon's

---

[41] Jefferson to Thomas Cooper, September 10, 1814, in Lipscomb and Bergh, eds., *Writings of Jefferson*, 14:181.

[42] Ibid., 181–82.

French and Spanish fleets. Forced like slaves into service by impressment, British seamen, like the British laboring classes, virtually lacked an independent will or identity, surviving at the whim of the rich and powerful. As Jefferson put it,

> Has not the British seaman, as much as the African, been reduced to this bondage by force, in flagrant violation of his own consent, and of his natural right in his own person? and with the laborers of England generally, does not the moral coercion of want subject their will as despotically to that of their employer, as the physical constraint does the soldier, the seaman, or the slave?[43]

In Jefferson's opinion, the British "aristocracy's" mistreatment of the laboring poor and the government's abuse of army and navy personnel were even more outrageous than masters' conduct toward Virginian slaves, whose existence, he argued, was generally more secure. In ending his letter to Cooper, however, Jefferson returned to a basic, inescapable truth: the suffering which England's White proletariat endured in no way justified or mitigated the even more debasing hereditary enslavement of Blacks in the United States. "But do not mistake me," he said,

> I am not justifying the wrongs we have committed on a foreign people [African Blacks], by the example of another nation committing equal wrongs on their own subjects. On the contrary, there is nothing I would not sacrifice to a practicable plan of abolishing every vestige of this moral and political depravity. But I am at present comparing the condition and degree of suffering to which oppression has reduced the man of one color, with the condition and degree of suffering to which oppression has reduced the man of another color; equally condemning both.[44]

---

[43] Jefferson to Thomas Cooper, September 10, 1814, in Lipscomb and Bergh, eds., *Writings of Jefferson*, 14:183. For an informative brief study of the relatively good living conditions of Virginia slaves at this time, and their access to a diverse diet and outside income by selling produce they grew on their own garden plots, see John T. Schlotterbeck, "The Internal Economy of Slavery in Rural Piedmont Virginia," *Slavery and Abolition* 12/1 (May 1991): 170–81.

[44] Jefferson to Thomas Cooper, September 10, 1814, in Lipscomb and Bergh, eds., *Writings of Jefferson*, 14:184. Historian John C. Miller attempts to depict Jefferson in old age as intellectually accommodating himself to slavery (*Wolf by the Ears*, 251). He quotes only those parts of this letter where Jefferson criticized the harsh treatment of British sailors, claiming that this is proof that he condoned slavery. Miller omits the sentences where Jefferson denounced slavery and said he wanted it abolished. More recently, political scientist Thomas Merrill cited Miller's book to confirm his own preconceived notion that Jefferson staunchly defended slavery. Merrill's neglect to read Jefferson's writings to discover his opinions led him to conclude that Jefferson was a proslavery ideologue (Merrill, "The Later Jefferson and the Problem of Natural Rights," *Perspectives on Political Science* 44 [2015]: 122–30).

Perhaps Jefferson's invidious comparison between Britain and the United States insufficiently stressed "moral sense" considerations that potentially facilitated antislavery legislation. After all, the US state and national governments, whose officials, elected by a large electorate of supposedly happy, prosperous White males, might be expected to possess a stronger moral sense than the selfish British urban and rural aristocracy, whom he portrayed as solely devoted to power and monetary gain. The British upper classes controlled the government, exercised virtually hereditary power, and unlike politicians in the United States, were not responsible to a vast, literate electorate who voted for them in elections held at brief intervals. In the United States, a democratic polity, the people's representatives, were ostensibly more susceptible to ethical influences than governments controlled by selfish elites. They should have made greater efforts to achieve the gradual abolition of slavery.

☙

Jefferson owned over ten thousand acres of land. He allowed his slaves to sell him provisions they produced on the small plots of land adjoining their cabins. Chickens, eggs, and vegetables were the items most often sold by slaves to accommodate Jefferson's kitchen needs. Slaves obtained money and credit for their goods, but no records exist of what they did with the money they received. An owner of over 200 slaves for most of his life, derived from natural reproduction, in 1810 Jefferson's slave records listed 126 slaves of all ages at his Albemarle properties and 86 on his Bedford properties. In general, Jefferson's overseers and artisans/foremen were White while the laborers, apprentices, and artisans' assistants were slaves, either owned or rented. The records that Anne Cary Randolph, Jefferson's teenage granddaughter, kept at Monticello, are the most detailed existing for the period of his presidency. He did not keep any, being away in Washington, DC.[45]

In his record as a slaveholder, as well as in most other things, recent historians tend to cast Jefferson as more evil than he perhaps deserves. For instance, William Cohen's groundbreaking brief analysis of Jefferson and slavery, a 1969 article in *The Journal of American History*, distorted Jefferson's letters to increase the cogency of his interpretation of Jefferson as essentially a selfish, capitalistic slaveholder. He mocked Jefferson apologists' traditional argument, that Jefferson had little choice but to remain a slaveholder because he was deeply in debt. Citing a letter Jefferson wrote in 1805, Cohen bitingly observes,

---

[45] Gerard W. Gawalt, "Jefferson's Slaves: Crop Accounts at Monticello, 1805–1808," *Journal of the Afro-American Historical and Genealogical Society* 13/1, 2 (Spring/Fall 1994): 19–38, esp. 20–21 and 38.

> It may be argued that, although Jefferson deplored the institution of slavery and particularly the buying and selling of men, the purchases and sales he made were impossible to avoid, since they were for the purpose of paying off debts or uniting families. But in 1805, he said that he was "endeavoring to purchase young and able negro men" for his plantation. Clearly then, he was not merely engaged in a holding operation designed to protect his slaves from a cruel and inhospitable world.[46]

Like later "Jefferson experts," Cohen exaggerated Jefferson's participation in the slave trade. Jefferson purchased only five slaves for the rest of his life after his wife's death in 1782, and except for two instances, he did it either to pay his brother's debts or to unite a separated husband and wife.[47] In any case, it is doubtful that Jefferson, any more than Washington, who owned many more slaves than Jefferson did, really needed more slaves. In 1783, according to Dumas Malone, Jefferson owned 204 slaves, a small army, inherited mainly from his father-in-law John Wayles's estate. At this time, he apparently sold at least fifty slaves, because in 1794 he owned only 155 slaves. He employed only one-third of his slaves regularly in the fields.[48] Jefferson's slaveholdings arose almost entirely from his inheritance from his father and especially his father-in-law, rather than purchase; many of the enslaved were children or elderly persons unfit for labor.

In any case, it seems unfair for Cohen to chastise Jefferson as an "entrepreneurial," conscienceless slaveholder based on a single letter expressing his need for young slaves to work at Monticello. An examination of the letter reveals that Jefferson was not requesting more slaves; on the contrary, the letter uncovers Jefferson's benevolent deed of uniting a slave husband and wife while attempting to disguise this as a shrewd business deal. Jefferson was in the process of building Monticello and needed young slaves like "Brown," the skilled bricklayer he was about to sell, yet he was willing to transfer him to John Jordan, one of the artisans he had hired to finish Monticello even though it would likely hinder the construction project. Jefferson initially offered to sell Brown for $600, a price he called a bargain, so that Brown could be with his wife. Jefferson ended up selling him for $500 because that was all that Jordan was willing to pay, and Jefferson, who had asked Brown what he wished, decided "to indulge his [Brown's] inclinations" to be with his wife. Jefferson did not buy slaves in either of the letters to

---

[46] Cohen, "Jefferson and the Problem of Slavery," 518 (quotation).

[47] Bear and Stanton, eds., *Jefferson's Memorandum Books*, index and passim. Fawn Brodie, *Thomas Jefferson: An Intimate History* (New York: Norton, 1974), 423.

[48] Malone, *Jefferson the Virginian*, 445; Malone, *Jefferson and the Ordeal of Liberty*, 211; Stanton, "Thomas Jefferson: Planter and Farmer," in Cogliano, ed., *Wiley-Blackwell Companion to Thomas Jefferson*, 257.

Jordan cited by Cohen, printed in the *Farm Book*. On the contrary, he protested how much he valued the ability of skilled slaves like Brown, whom he was purportedly selling at a discount, and as he was "now endeavoring to purchase young & able negro men for my own works, it is exactly counter to these views to sell Brown to you as proposed in your letter." But, moved by the humane instincts of the "moral sense," he did so anyway.[49] The letter said the opposite of what Cohen said it did. By quoting a single phrase, Cohen misread the contents of the letter to depict Jefferson as a mean, mercenary slaveholder.

In this instance, perhaps Jefferson sought to deceive himself about his business acumen, pretending that he was not suffering loss from selling Brown, so that the slave could have a happier life. He lied to Jordan about looking for bondspersons to purchase, since he was not really buying any slaves. Thus, he was in "bad faith" to himself. But, it was in a good cause: uniting a slave with his family.

Thus, Cohen overlooked the purport of Jefferson's letter to Jordan, in which he was actually *selling* a slave at a cheaper price than he considered fair in order to unite a slave family. Instead, Cohen makes it seem as if Jefferson were actively negotiating to buy slaves to stock his plantation. Perhaps Jefferson was trying to be a shrewd businessman hoping to get a better price for a slave he did not want by touting Brown's great worth and his need for young slaves "for his own works," to rebuild Monticello, etc. If this were his motive, his attempt to get a better price failed, and he lost a young slave rather than gaining new ones, since none of his letters to Jordan mentioned purchase of slaves.[50]

Jefferson's policies as a slaveholder were not entirely benevolent. For example, although he increased his plantations' wheat production, his persistence in cultivating tobacco, which required slave labor, evinced a degree of hypocrisy and moral myopia. (There is no evidence that Jefferson himself used tobacco in any form.) As early as the 1780s, in a famous section of *Notes on the State of Virginia*, Jefferson stridently objected to planters' cultivation of tobacco because, unlike wheat, it required slave labor, decreased the plantation's self-sufficiency in food, and ruined the soil. Jefferson hoped that Virginians would abandon their wasteful cultivation of tobacco and use their abundant land resources for the production of wheat. He observed that tobacco cultivation was a "culture productive of infinite wretchedness" for the slaves who handled it. Moreover, in the years after Jefferson composed *Notes*, tobacco growing became increasingly unprofitable in

---

[49] Jefferson to John Jordan, December 21, 1805, and February 9, 1806, in Betts, ed., *Jefferson's Farm Book*, 21–22; Jefferson to Thomas Law, June 13, 1814, microfilm reel 47, Jefferson Papers, LC (hdl.loc.gov/loc.mss/mtj.mtjbib021743).

[50] For a more careful account of the "Brown" incident than Cohen provides, see McLaughlin, *Jefferson and Monticello*, 102–103, 113.

Virginia and Maryland, whose planters could not compete with new, more fertile lands in Georgia and on the Mississippi, in present-day Kentucky, Alabama, and Mississippi. Still, he continued to grow tobacco on his plantations until he died.[51]

Surprisingly, a few respectable historians insist that Jefferson's antislavery writings and congressional activities during the 1770s and 1780s never happened. For example, in "Thomas Jefferson and Slavery," historian Cassandra Pybus wrote that Jefferson never suggested manumission during his years in public life. Jefferson's autobiography, his *Notes on the State of Virginia*, his proposed constitution for Virginia in 1783 (appended to the published version of the *Notes* in 1787), and his famous defeated congressional resolution, the Ordinance of 1784, which abolished slavery in the territories of the United States, amply demonstrate that her statement is erroneous. He favored not only manumission but also government-enforced abolition of slavery. Nevertheless, Pybus insists, citing a scholar whose writing on Jefferson is sometimes inaccurate, "As Paul Finkelman (1996) has observed, Jefferson was never sufficiently troubled by the injustice of slavery to risk proposing, or even supporting, efforts to provide for the emancipation of slaves, even as a voluntary, private matter."[52]

In his autobiography, written a few years before he died, Jefferson claimed credit for the first proposal in the Virginia assembly during the Revolution to legalize the manumission of slaves by their owners.[53] He wrote his autobiography for his personal reference and the information of his family, and he probably did not intend to publish the often boring, slapdash work. He did not diligently revise it or delete passages he thought clumsy, as he did with his personal letters, *Notes on Virginia*, and most of his other writing. There was no reason for him to mention the manumission proposal if it were not true. If his goal were posthumous

---

[51] Query XX ("Subjects of Commerce"), in Peden, ed., *Notes on the State of Virginia*, 166.

[52] Cassandra Pybus, "Jefferson and Slavery," in Cogliano, ed., *Wiley-Blackwell Companion to Thomas Jefferson*, 271–83, 273 (quotation). As will be mentioned below, in one case Finkelman invented nonexistent documents and events, involving Jefferson's famous "fire bell in the night" letter to Massachusetts Congressman John Holmes in 1820 (Paul Finkelman, "The Problem of Slavery in the Age of Federalism," in Doron Ben-Atar and Barbara B. Oberg, eds., *Federalists Reconsidered* [Charlottesville: University Press of Virginia, 1998], 142; Jefferson to John Holmes, April 22, 1820, in Peterson, ed., *Jefferson: Writings*, 1433–35. Contrary to Finkelman, Holmes, one of the few New Englanders to support slavery in Missouri during the congressional debates of 1819–1820, never proposed an emancipation plan to Jefferson, and Jefferson never "rebuffed" him. For a detailed study of Holmes's activities defending slavery in Missouri, see Matthew Mason, "The Maine and Missouri Crisis: Competing Priorities and Northern Slavery Politics in the Early Republic," *Journal of the Early Republic* 33 (Winter 2013): 675–700.

[53] Jefferson's *Autobiography* is online at libertyonline.hypermall.com/Jefferson/Autobiography.html and printed in Peterson, ed., *Jefferson: Writings*, 5.

celebrity, he must have known that manumission grew increasingly unpopular in Virginia during his old age. He boldly proposed plans to abolish slavery entirely in *Notes on the State of Virginia* and in his constitution for Virginia in 1783, both of which he published under his own name in 1787. Although, as James Monroe said later, opposition to "domestic slavery…was a generous instinct which grew out of the revolutionary struggle," few of the republic's leaders ever publicized their antislavery views as forthrightly as Jefferson did.[54]

[54] James Monroe to George Hay, December 27, 1819, James Monroe Papers, James Monroe Library and Museum, Fredericksburg, VA; for a similar view to Monroe's, see Nash, *Race and Revolution*; Jordan, *White over Black*; Sean Wilentz, *No Property in Man* (Cambridge, MA: Harvard University Press, 2018).

Chapter 13

Morality versus "Self-Preservation": Jefferson on Slave Revolt, the Missouri Controversy, and the Haitian Panacea

Echoing Jefferson's skeptical political opponents, many scholars reject as hypocritical his conviction that slavery's "diffusion" into Missouri by Virginia slaveholders and others taking slaves purchased in Virginia to the territory would somehow expedite abolition in the Old Dominion. Although this "diffusionist" argument did not originate with him, it fortuitously complemented his recommendation that Virginia gradually abolish slavery and exile the freed slaves to Haiti.[1] Jefferson indirectly validated Haiti's existence by supporting such emancipation legislation. He seemed undeterred by Haiti's identity as a nation-state founded by slave rebels, whose ruler, General Jean-Jacques Dessalines, in 1804 ordered most of its remaining White population annihilated.[2]

Perhaps Jefferson's persisting, albeit limited expectation of humanity's political, social, and moral progress accounts for his approval of material assistance to the Haitian dictatorship by US merchants during his presidency in the early nineteenth century. He had some reason to believe the Haitian government might evolve in a republican direction, among them the rulers' occasional convening of assemblies representing competitors for power, and, most importantly, the

---

[1] New York Republican congressman John W. Taylor, a foremost advocate of the abolition of slavery in Missouri, derided the "diffusionist" argument as a "counterfeit" strategy to "palliate disease by the applications of nostrums…which saves a finger today, but amputates the arm tomorrow" (John W. Taylor, speech in Congress, in *Annals of Congress*, 15th Cong., 2d sess., 1175, quoted in Fehrenbacher, *Slaveholding Republic*, 264). See also William H. Gaines, Jr., *Thomas Mann Randolph, Jr.: Jefferson's Son-in-Law* (Baton Rouge: Louisiana State University Press, 1966), 124–26.

[2] On Dessalines's defeat of the French and war against the remaining Whites, whom he distrusted as traitors, see Philippe R. Girard, *The Slaves Who Defeated Napoleon: Toussaint Louverture and the Haitian War of Independence, 1801–1804* (Tuscaloosa: University of Alabama Press, 2011), 319–25.

republican example of the nearby United States and their close trade relations.[3] In his own way, he admired the steadfast determination of the Haitians to achieve and maintain their freedom from White enslavement. When he learned in June 1802 that Louverture had been stealthily kidnapped by French troops and deported to prison in the Jura Mountains, he was angry at General Victoire Emmanuel Leclerc's trickery. "The account of Toussaint's arrest seems authentic," he wrote. "It will need good evidence to clear Le Clerc of perfidiousness in the eyes of the blacks. Should he fail to establish some new crime on Toussaint, some other black leader will arise, and a war of extermination ensue; for no second capitulation will ever be trusted by the blacks."[4] Throughout his life, he unreservedly considered slave rebellion and Black nationhood as morally legitimate political endeavors.

In Haiti's case as well as others, Jefferson never doubted the justice of slave revolts or the validity of slaves' demands for freedom. In January 1805, shortly after his reelection to the presidency, Jefferson wrote a letter to his private secretary, Virginia state assembly member William A. Burwell, affirming the morality of slave revolt. He went so far as to bestow tacit approval upon the recent massacre of Haiti's White population. When Burwell reported the possibility that the Virginia assembly would repeal the manumission law, probably squelching future abolition legislation, Jefferson expressed contempt for fellow slaveholders' avarice. He considered the news confirmation of his suspicion of their increasing selfishness and amorality. "I have long since given up the expectation of any early provision for the extinguishment of slavery among us," he admitted. "There are many virtuous men who would make any sacrifice to effect it, many equally virtuous who persuade themselves either that the thing [slavery] is not wrong, or that it cannot be remedied, and very many with whom interest is morality." Questioning the moral fiber and philanthropy of his fellow slaveholders, Jefferson added, "The older we grow, the larger we are disposed to believe the last [most selfish] party to be."[5] At this point, he had a low opinion of slaveholders' defective moral sense.

---

[3] For Haitian leader, Toussaint Louverture's cordiality toward the Adams and Jefferson Administrations, see Charles C. Tansill, *United States and Santo Domingo, 1798–1873* (1938; reprinted, Gloucester, MA: Peter Smith, 1967), 16–17, 45, 58–59, 83–84. Jefferson refused in 1801–1802 to embargo supplies and munitions to Haiti despite Napoleon's insistence that he comply with earlier alleged promises to do so (Miller, *Wolf by the Ears*, 135–38; Egan, *Neither Peace nor War*; Brant, *James Madison: Secretary of State, 1800–1809* ((Indianapolis: Bobbs-Merrill, 1941); Malone, *Jefferson the President: First Term*, vol. 4 of *Jefferson and His Time* [Boston: Little, Brown, 1970], 252–53).

[4] Jefferson to John F. Mercer, June 23, 1802, in Oberg, ed., *Jefferson Papers*, 37:659.

[5] Jefferson to William Burwell, January 28, 1805, microfilm reel 32, Jefferson Papers, LC (hdl.loc.gov/loc.mss/mtj.mtjbib014284).

Years earlier, shortly after the American Revolution, Jefferson, eloquently attacking slavery in *Notes*' Query XVIII, seemed more optimistic that slaveholders' humanitarianism would overcome their avarice. Discussing whether his state would abolish slavery, he declared, "I think a change already perceptible, since the origin of the present revolution. The spirit of the master is abating, that of the slave rising from the dust, his condition mollifying, the way I hope preparing, under the auspices of heaven, for a total emancipation, and that this is disposed, in the order of events, to be with the consent of the masters, rather than by their extirpation."[6] Approving the intensification of the slaves' "spirit, rising from the dust," feeling that their aggressiveness and willingness to seize their freedom by force were justified, he likewise applauded the "abatement," or deceleration of the master class's determination to brutally enforce its domination ("spirit"). Thus, Jefferson rashly indicated, in public, that his sympathies lay with the slaves rather than with his own people. It is an indication of slaveholders' guilt during the post-Revolutionary period that his belligerent rhetoric did not cost him much if anything politically at the time. Ironically, it was not until Jefferson's friend John Taylor condemned his antislavery views in his famous work, *Arator*, many years later, that a powerful slaveholding voice arose specifically rebuffing his abolitionism.[7]

Amid an armed White population that substantially outnumbered the slaves, Jefferson's melodramatic assumption in Query XVIII that the enslaved could potentially exterminate the masters and seize their liberty by force was an extremely improbable scenario. More likely, Jefferson did not really believe Query 18's dire predictions, including his uncharacteristic claim, as one who denied divine intervention in human affairs, that "supernatural interference" would emancipate the slaves if their masters refused. Indeed, in Query XIV of *Notes*, he frankly doubted that those who "wish to vindicate the liberty of human nature" would ever defeat the forces of "sordid avarice" and, without invoking God's wrath, more humbly proposed that the state legislature emancipate and "colonize" the slaves in their own independent country.[8] In light of Jefferson's thwarted attempts to propose emancipation and deportation of the slaves as a legislator in 1776–1778, as he alleged in *Notes* and in old age in his autobiography, his motive for Query XVIII's rhetorical alarmism might have been to frighten his Southern readers into passing abolition legislation. As Holowchak observes, Jefferson's doctrine of the moral sense preferred (other things being equal) to regard "humans qua social creatures" as "rational, progressive, and morally sensitive beings." However,

[6] *Notes*, Query 18, in Peden, ed., *Notes on the State of Virginia*, 163.

[7] Taylor, *Arator*.

[8] *Notes*, Query XIV.

Jefferson knew enough about human psychology to comprehend that when fiscal and physical security were at risk, as was the case with emancipation, slaveholders would leave their moral "sensitivity" behind.[9]

Jefferson's political prowess in winning two terms as president and heading the nation's most popular political party had not dulled his awareness of human greed in political and social life. Nor had age increased Jefferson's faith in the diffusion of White beneficence toward Blacks. Even though he thought, probably mistakenly, that slavery was becoming less and less profitable, he warned Burwell that several bloody slave uprisings might be necessary to prod slaveholders into passing emancipation laws. Probably because the prices of wheat and tobacco were falling and that of food for the slaves increasing, Jefferson suggested that abolition would help the slaveholders financially. "Interest is really going over to the side of morality," he wrote. "The value of the slave is every day lessening; his burthen on his master dayly [*sic*] increasing. Interest is therefore preparing the disposition to be just; and this will be goaded from time to time by the insurrectionary spirit of the slaves."[10]

When writing to Burwell in 1805, Jefferson stressed the prospect of sporadic, bloody slave rebellions. However, these anticipated "dreadful scenes & sufferings" seemed not to frighten him, but rather to evoke a sneering "I told you so." About slave discontent, he wrote, "[It] is easily quieted in it's [*sic*] first efforts; but from being local it will become general, and whenever it does it will rise more formidable after every defeat, until we shall be forced, after dreadful scenes & sufferings to release them [slaves] in their own way, which, without such sufferings we might now model after our own convenience."[11]

A few years earlier, Jefferson had not expressed fear over Gabriel's suppressed conspiracy, in which no White casualties occurred. As president, he generally supported the much more serious, successful slave revolution in Haiti, failing to dispatch a diplomatic protest even when its Blacks annihilated most of its remaining White population in March 1804.[12] Though he probably viewed a similar large-scale uprising in Virginia as impossible, he ostensibly wanted to frighten

---

[9] Holowchak, "Individual Liberty and Political Unity," 57 (quotation).

[10] Jefferson to William Burwell, January 28, 1805, microfilm reel 32, Jefferson Papers, LC (hdl.loc.gov/loc.mss/mtj.mtjbib014284). Jefferson's analysis was prescient. The only sustained debate in the Virginia legislature over emancipation occurred in 1831–1832, after Nat Turner's bloody revolt. His grandson, Thomas Jefferson Randolph, led the unsuccessful antislavery faction (Alison G. Freehling, *Drift toward Dissolution* [Baton Rouge: Louisiana State University Press, 1982]).

[11] Jefferson to William Burwell, January 28, 1805, Jefferson Papers, LC. Burwell reported the proceedings in the Virginia legislature in Burwell to Jefferson, January 18, 1805, microfilm reel 32, Jefferson Papers, LC (hdl.loc.gov/loc.mss/mtj.mtjbib014255).

[12] See Scherr, *Jefferson's Haitian Policy*, 388–89.

his protégé Burwell into supporting abolition. He knew that, unlike Haiti, where the slaves outnumbered the White population by ten to one, in Virginia Whites slightly outnumbered Blacks, and their militia and, to a greater extent, individual slaveholders were armed. Whites exercised a monopoly of law and force, so that the outcome of a Black uprising in the state, contrary to the Haitian revolution's Black triumph, might be the annihilation of the slaves. Jefferson preferred not to point out the latter denouement, which, at least for those of sadistic temperaments, might make emancipation legislation seem less urgent. On the other hand, his emphasis on the ubiquitous threat of slave revolts was a means by which he might encourage legislative action for emancipating the allegedly murderous slaves. Burwell, an opponent of manumission in the House of Delegates, needed convincing at a time when pressure on the legislature to repeal even private manumissions was increasing.[13] With Haiti's recent upheaval in the minds of many, Jefferson painted a horrifying picture of future race relations under slavery. If he sufficiently impressed Burwell with the gravity of the situation, his young former secretary might take action against slavery in the state.

As years went by, however, Jefferson reluctantly concluded that the White "master" population continued to suffer from a defective "moral sense" and would never emancipate its slaves. In 1815, writing David Barrow, a Kentucky Baptist minister and abolitionist, he maintained that the solution of gradual emancipation and deportation that he had publicly recommended in Query XIV of *Notes on Virginia* was "still the one most sound in my judgment." However, "unhappily...both parties [masters and slaves] require long and difficult preparation" before its implementation. Regarding the maturation of the masters' moral sense as a vital prerequisite to their consent to abolition, Jefferson's expectations of success were modest:

> The mind of the master is to be apprised by reflection, and strengthened by the energies of conscience, against the obstacles of self interest to an acquiescence in the rights of others; that of the slave is to be prepared by instruction and habit for self government, and for the honest pursuits of industry and social duty. Both of these courses...require time, and the former must precede the latter. Some progress is sensibly made in it; yet not so much as I had hoped and expected.[14]

---

[13] For a brief account of the debate over the 1806 manumission act in the Virginia assembly, a topic that deserves more attention, see Jordan, *White over Black*, 575–80.

[14] Jefferson to David Barrow, May 1, 1815, microfilm reel 48, Jefferson Papers, LC (hdl.loc.gov/loc.mss/mtj.mtjbib022031). For Barrow's antislavery activities in Virginia and Kentucky, see Davis, *Problem of Slavery in the Age of Revolution*, 201, 202, 203, 552–55; James David Essig, "'A Very Wintry Season': Virginia Baptists and Slavery, 1785–1797," *Virginia*

In this, one of his most dispassionate commentaries on the conditions hindering emancipation, Jefferson admitted that the masters' greed and inadequate moral "reformation" disappointed the unwarranted optimism in Query XVIII of *Notes*, more seriously impeding the slaves' liberation than the alleged inferiority Query XIV imputed to Blacks.[15] Nonetheless, Jefferson cautiously continued to apply his conception of the consensual, social, "superego" facets of the moral sense to the question of abolishing slavery. He relied on the masters' moral regeneration, or failing that, governmental action on the state or, more likely, national level to secure justice.

ꝏ

The debate from 1819 to 1821 on Missouri's admission to the Union as a "slave state" gave birth to the question of the legitimacy of Congress's prohibition of slavery in a territory that was on the verge of statehood and whose state constitution legalized human bondage. This became the most crucial issue that ever confronted that body, leading ultimately to the Civil War. When first presented with this matter, the retired Jefferson, who wanted to keep out of public affairs and the newspapers, was reluctant to give his opinion. He eventually accepted the optimistic premise that the reduced number of slaves in Virginia following their departure with their masters for Missouri and other new slave-holding states would enable the Virginia assembly (and others among the "older" slave states) to finance the compensated emancipation of the smaller number who remained and pay for their transportation to foreign territory. (He preferred Haiti.) In April 1820, after the initial crisis ended, Jefferson wrote encouragingly to John Holmes, a Massachusetts/Maine Republican congressman and one of the few Northerners voting for the Missouri Compromise. He accepted the idea, expounded in Holmes's circular letter to his constituents, that slavery's "diffusion" to the Western territories would disperse, rather than augment, the enslaved population. Slaves' movement to new areas, Holmes convinced him, "would make them individually happier" and "facilitate their eventual emancipation" (as Jefferson's paraphrased Holmes). Holmes expounded his advocacy of "diffusion" in his "Letter

---

Magazine of History and Biography 88/2 (April 1980): 170–85, and Essig, *The Bonds of Wickedness: American Evangelicals Against Slavery, 1770–1808* (Philadelphia: Temple University Press, 1982). Barrow's role in the antislavery movement among Kentucky Baptists is stressed in Monica Najar, "'Meddling with Emancipation': Baptists, Authority, and the Rift over Slavery in the Upper South," *Journal of the Early Republic* 25/2 (Summer 2005): 157–86.

[15] *Notes on Virginia*, Queries 14 and 18, in Peterson, ed., *Jefferson: Writings*, 264–70, 288–89.

to the People of Maine," written at Washington, DC, April 10, 1820, which he enclosed in a letter to Jefferson of April 12, 1820.[16]

Jefferson considered the issue of slavery expansion the most important that Congress ever confronted—and the most likely to break up the Union. Despite his opposition to slavery, he believed that Missouri's statehood, even if admitted as a "slave state," was essential to the continuation of the United States as an expansive, potentially powerful republic. To that extent, he accepted slavery as a concomitant of republicanism, at least temporarily. He regarded the "Missouri question," which to him embraced whether Congress had the right to exclude slavery from all states derived from the Louisiana Purchase, as linked with the fate of the republic's ability to expand over time. In his opinion, Missouri, ready for admission to the Union, could no longer be considered a mere fledgling, embryonic territory. Unlike the Northern and Southern territories bordering the Ohio River, which in 1784 he proposed to close to slavery, Missouri had over sixty thousand inhabitants and was ready for statehood. As he wrote John Adams in December 1819, while the country was in the midst of an economic depression partly caused by the Bank of the United States' unpredictable behavior and President Monroe was engaged in frustrating negotiations to purchase Florida from Spain, "The banks, bankrupt law, manufactures, Spanish treaty, are nothing. These are occurrences which, like waves in a storm, will pass under the ship. But the Missouri question is a breaker on which we lose the Missouri country by revolt, and what more, God only knows." He feared that Missouri would break away from the Union and become an independent country (in "revolt") if Congress refused to admit it as a slave state. "From the battle of Bunker's hill to the treaty of Paris, we never had so ominous a question," he believed. Although venerable, the elderly Adams lacked political influence even in Massachusetts. Jefferson may nonetheless have hoped to rouse him to action to restrain Senator Rufus King and other Massachusetts congressmen, such as Maine's Joshua Cushman, who wanted to bar slavery from the Louisiana Purchase. Pondering his old

[16] John Holmes to Jefferson, April 12, 1820, microfilm reel 51, Jefferson Papers, LC (hdl.loc.gov/loc.mss/mtj.mtjbib023788); John Holmes, "Letter to the People of Maine," Washington, DC, April 10, 1820, enclosed in John Holmes to Jefferson, April 12, 1820; Jefferson to John Holmes, April 22, 1820, in Lipscomb and Bergh, eds., *Writings of Jefferson*, 15:249–50 (quotation). This was Jefferson's famous "fire bell in the night" letter. The [Maine] *American Advocate and Kennebec Advertiser*, Saturday, April 29, 1820, printed the "Circular Letter from Mark Langdon Hill to the Citizens of Maine, Concerning his Vote on the Missouri Question, dated March 31, 1820, and Mr. Holmes' Letter to the People of Maine, April 10, 1820." Holmes's circular letter is conveniently reprinted in Noble E. Cunningham, Jr., *Circular Letters of Congressmen to their Constituents, 1789–1829*, 3 vols. (Chapel Hill: University of North Carolina Press, 1978), 3:1109–15.

age and nearness to death, as he often did, Jefferson continued, "It [the Missouri crisis] even damps the joy with which I hear of your high health, and welcomes to me the consequences of my want of it. I thank God that I shall not live to witness its issue."[17]

Even more grimly, Jefferson wrote Hugh Nelson, congressional representative from Albemarle County, that slavery would annihilate the Union. The crisis had seemingly ended with the passage of the Thomas Bill, sponsored by an Illinois Republican senator. It permitted slavery in Missouri while prohibiting it in all future states north of the line 36°30′. Jefferson feared that the law was too lopsided a victory in favor of Northern interests since it barred slavery in most of the Louisiana Purchase—public land. Expecting continued violent controversy over slavery, Jefferson predicted that the boundary would divide free and slave republics once the Union's tragic breakup occurred. "An abstract principle [of barring slavery in places where it could not profitably exist] is to become the line of separation of these States, and to render desperate the hope that man can ever enjoy the two blessings of peace and self-government," he pontificated. "The question sleeps for the present, but is not dead."[18]

Although he considered slavery evil, Jefferson viewed the "abstract principle" of barring bondage from a few new states that would probably not want or need it as in an inferior moral category to the far more vital goal of gradually abolishing slavery in all the states where it existed—an idea he supported. He regretted that America's unique republican Union would likely shatter over this issue of slavery in the territories, which the South considered threatening to its honor and equal

---

[17] Jefferson to John Adams, December 10, 1819, in Cappon, ed., *Adams-Jefferson Letters* (1988), 548–49; Lipscomb and Bergh, eds., *Writings of Jefferson*, 15:232–33. In a readable work designed for a general audience, the popular historian Joseph J. Ellis erroneously wrote concerning this letter, "In his correspondence with Adams, Jefferson's initial reaction to what was being called the Missouri question was calm and assured. He expressed the hope that the issue would pass 'like waves in a storm pass under the ship'" (Ellis, *American Sphinx*, 264, citing Cappon, ed., *Adams-Jefferson Letters* [1959], 2:548–49). Rufus King's speeches against slavery in Missouri started out as a pragmatic argument that perpetuating slavery would reduce the Union's ability to defend itself against external aggressors and domestic rebellions, and they ended as a crusade against bondage's evil and immorality (Robert Ernst, *Rufus King: American Federalist* [Chapel Hill: University of North Carolina Press, 1967], 369–75; Robert Ernst, "Rufus King, Slavery, and the Missouri Crisis," *New-York Historical Society Quarterly* 46 (October 1962): 357–82; and Joseph L. Arbena, "Politics or Principle? Rufus King and the Opposition to Slavery, 1785–1825," *Essex Institute Historical Collections* 101/1 (1965): 56–77.

[18] Jefferson to Hugh Nelson, March 12, 1820, in Lipscomb and Bergh, eds., *Writings of Jefferson*, 15:238. Like Jefferson, the Pennsylvania Society for the Abolition of Slavery, which opposed slavery in Missouri, concluded that, by prohibiting bondage in future states carved from the Louisiana Purchase, the law promoted abolition (Glover Moore, *The Missouri Controversy, 1819–1821* [Lexington: University Press of Kentucky, 1953], 131, 202).

rights in the Union and potentially dangerous to slavery's existence in the older states.

Without illusions about the importance of the slavery question, Jefferson was willing to permit Missouri to retain slavery until the institution was abolished nationally, or its citizens amended their constitution to eliminate it. He was aware that the territory's residents had held slaves under French and Spanish rule, which were guaranteed to them by Article Three of the 1803 US purchase treaty with Napoleon. He emphasized that the Missourians were ready for statehood; not merely an incipient territory, Missouri was an established entity. In that sense, it was unlike the Northern and Southern regions bordering the Ohio River, which Jefferson recommended in 1784 be closed to slavery.

Joining his friends Madison and Monroe, Jefferson, unlike Northern abolitionists, during the debate over Missouri's entry into the Union (1819–1821) briefly argued that Virginians' emigration with their slaves into the Louisiana Purchase, by reducing the number of slaves in his state, would promote Virginia's abandonment of human bondage. By reducing the cost of compensating the state's fewer remaining slave owners and deporting the former slaves, Jefferson argued that planters' migration to Missouri "lightens the difficulty" of abolishing slavery "by dividing it and renders it [abolition] more practicable on the whole." Preferring Haiti, not Africa, as the freedpersons' destination, among other reasons because its greater proximity to the United States would enable the US government to pay for their transportation and grant them financial assistance, he concluded, "the neighborhood of a government of their colour [in Haiti] promises a more accessible asylum than that from whence they came."[19]

One of the reasons Jefferson supported slavery in Missouri was his expectation that some of Virginia's large slaveholders would leave the Old Dominion. They would embark for Missouri and other new slave-holding states with fertile

[19] Jefferson to Short, September 8, 1823, in Lipscomb and Bergh, eds., *Writings of Jefferson*, 15:469–70. For Jefferson, Madison, and Monroe's support of the extension of slavery into Missouri and Arkansas, see Fehrenbacher, *Slaveholding Republic*, 263–66; and Moore's summary in *Missouri Controversy*, 252–56. Ignoring the Missouri crisis's role in stimulating Jefferson to immediately develop plans for the gradual abolition of slavery and the immigration of the freedpersons to Haiti, Moore perceives only negative consequences in Jefferson's reaction to the threatened disruption of the Union. He argues that Jefferson, as well as Madison and other Southern "liberals," became more proslavery and sectionally oriented after the Northern attempt to abolish slavery in the Louisiana Purchase; impelling Jefferson to convert his embryonic University of Virginia from a fount of liberalism and Enlightenment to a bastion of proslavery Southernism. Moore greatly exaggerates Jefferson's stance; he remained devoted to Enlightenment ideals of scientific progress and freedom of thought until his death, arousing much opposition to his university from Presbyterian religious revivalists and proslavery conservatives, who never perceived him as an advocate of slavery.

soil, like Louisiana, Alabama, and Mississippi. Virginia's ensuing diminished slave population and reduced number of influential big slaveholders would render votes from the antislavery western part of the state sufficient to push emancipation through the legislature. Jefferson voiced his approval of the idea of "diffusion" in his famous "wolf by the ear" letter to John Holmes, a Massachusetts Republican congressional representative for the district of Maine and supporter of the Missouri Compromise, who had convinced Jefferson of "diffusion's" feasibility.[20]

Seemingly, Jefferson authentically considered the Union's survival in jeopardy because of the slavery question. However, historian Stuart Leibiger argues that his professions of alarm were mere theatrics, employed to gain Missouri's admission as a slave state and to promote the Virginia Assembly's support for his university, which he advertised as an alternative for large numbers of Southern students receiving an "anti-Southern" higher education in the North. Such alarmism, Leibiger argues, would ostensibly motivate the state to increase funding.[21]

Contrary to Leibiger's assumptions, the letters Jefferson wrote before learning that Henry Clay in the House and Jesse B. Thomas in the Senate, with President Monroe's cooperation, had achieved a compromise, conveyed genuine alarm. On March 3, 1820, Jefferson confessed his anxiety to Monroe, whom he had no reason to mislead. "The Missouri question by a geographical line of division is the most portentous one I have ever contemplated," he said. "[Rufus] King is ready to risk the union for any chance of restoring his party to power and wriggling himself to the head of it. Nor is [DeWitt] Clinton without his hopes nor scrupulous as to the means of fulfilling them." He apparently considered the Union threatened by politicians' ineptitude. Unlike his attitude several months later, he expected the Union's breakup. "I hope I shall be spared the pain of witnessing it either by the good sense of the people, or by the more certain reliance, the hand of death," he lamented. He denounced Federalist politicians as opportunists, ready to manipulate the moral issue of slavery to gain political advantage, even if they destroyed the republic in the process.[22]

Historian Don Fehrenbacher has observed that the constitutional validity of the Missouri restrictionists' argument was dubious: the controversy involved new states, over which Congress lacked authority, not new territories. Regarding the

---

[20] John Holmes expounded his support for "diffusion" in his "Letter to the People of Maine," Washington, DC, April 10, 1820, which he enclosed in a letter to Jefferson explaining his reasoning (April 12, 1820, microfilm reel 51, Jefferson Papers, LC [hdl.loc.gov/loc.mss/mtj.mtjbib023788]).

[21] Stuart Leibiger, "Thomas Jefferson and the Missouri Crisis: An Alternative Interpretation," *Journal of the Early Republic* 17/1 (Spring 1997): 121–30.

[22] Jefferson to James Monroe, March 3, 1820, microfilm reel 51, Jefferson Papers, LC (hdl.loc.gov/loc.mss/mtj.mtjbib023743).

legitimacy of Congress's prohibition of slavery in Missouri, a territory on the verge of statehood whose constitution permitted human bondage, Fehrenbacher questioned the validity of the abolitionists' argument. "The crisis was indeed over the expansion of slavery, but it centered primarily on the process of making new states rather than on the process of creating and governing federal territories," Fehrenbacher observed. "This feature of the struggle put antislavery elements at a serious disadvantage because any effort to introduce a prohibition or restriction at the state-making stage was likely to be, in practical terms, too late, and in constitutional terms, highly questionable."[23]

At least one historian has manipulated the dialogue between Jefferson and John Holmes in April 1820 to present Jefferson as ardently proslavery. In the essay, "The Problem of Slavery in the Age of Federalism," a defense of Federalist attitudes toward slavery in a compendium in which historians eulogized America's most antidemocratic political party, Jefferson's critic, legal historian Paul Finkelman, goes to extremes to "prove" his thesis that Jefferson fervently supported slavery in Missouri. Finkelman charges that Jefferson wrote his famous "fire bell in the night/wolf by the ear" letter in April 1820, during the crisis over Missouri's admission to the Union, to "rebuff" Massachusetts (Maine) Congressman John Holmes's request that he "endorse a restriction on slavery." Holmes never made such a request. He had always supported the Missouri Compromise and considered it a state's right to maintain slavery if it so desired. Jefferson's reply praised his stance, specifically the pamphlet, a circular letter to his constituents that Holmes had just sent him, which explained how the "diffusion" of the slaves would improve their living conditions and make the eventual abolition of slavery more likely. To his Maine constituents, he defended his support for slavery in Missouri if that were necessary to preserve the Union and gain Maine statehood. After receiving and reading Holmes' circular letter, Jefferson attested his approval. He wrote Holmes, "I thank you, dear Sir, for the copy you have been so kind as to send me of the letter to your constituents on the Missouri question. It is a perfect justification to them," he said, for Holmes' congressional stance approving Missouri's entry into the Union as a slave state.[24]

Holmes inspired Jefferson with the idea that the "diffusion" of slavery into Missouri and other new states would promote slavery's demise. Less reliant on human bondage after disposing of their surplus slaves to immigrants westward, plantation owners in Virginia and other states would be friendlier to abolition,

---

[23] Fehrenbacher, *Slaveholding Republic*, 264 (quotation).

[24] Jefferson to John Holmes, April 22, 1820, in Peterson, ed., *Jefferson: Writings*, 1433–34; Finkelman, "The Problem of Slavery in the Age of Federalism," in Oberg and Ben-Atar, eds., *Federalists Reconsidered*, 142 (quotation).

according to Holmes and kindred advocates of "diffusion."[25] Indeed, Holmes contributed the idea that "diffusion" of slavery into Missouri was for the well-being of slaves, and that it would advance progress toward the gradual abolition of the shameful institution, rather than the other way around, as Finkelman claims. Jefferson only expounded the virtues of "diffusion" at the time of the Missouri Compromise, influenced by Holmes.[26]

Other scholars, not only Finkelman (although he uniquely invented the story of Jefferson's "rebuff" of Holmes's nonexistent antislavery crusade) have imputed to Jefferson the invention of the hypocritical or "counterfeit" assumption (as congressman John W. Taylor called it) that the "diffusion" of slavery into Missouri, by slaveholders from neighboring Virginia or purchasers of slaves from Virginians, would promote abolition. Even Jefferson's expert biographer, Dumas Malone, assumed that, as early as 1803, "Jefferson...had come to believe that the diffusion of the slaves already in the country would tend to weaken rather than strengthen the institution he detested." Unusual in such a diligent historian, Malone provided no evidence for this statement, and buried it in a footnote.[27]

Jefferson ephemerally adopted this point of view only after reading Holmes' pamphlet; it was not and did not represent his lifetime opinion. Nevertheless, the concept was sensible, in light of his chimerical hope that Virginia would pass measures to gradually abolish slavery and exile the freed slaves to Haiti. During the debates over Missouri's admission to the Union in 1820, his son-in-law, Virginia governor Thomas Mann Randolph, presented a similar plan, also recommending Haiti to the legislature, which overwhelmingly rejected it as too radical.[28] In keeping with his political axiom that human bondage must end, as he aged in retirement at Monticello, Jefferson became increasingly convinced that the solution to the problem of Southern slavery was the gradual emancipation of

[25] John Holmes expounded his advocacy of "diffusion" in his "Letter to the People of Maine," Washington, DC, April 10, 1820, enclosed in John Holmes to Jefferson, April 12, 1820, Jefferson Papers, LC. It is reprinted in Cunningham, ed., *Circular Letters of Congressmen*, 3:1109–15. On "diffusionist" arguments during the debate over expanding slavery in the territories beginning in 1798, see John Craig Hammond, *Slavery, Freedom, and Expansion in the Early American West* (Charlottesville: University of Virginia Press, 2007), who nevertheless, without evidence, implies that Jefferson originated the idea of "diffusion" (36).

[26] Jefferson to John Holmes, April 22, 1820, in Peterson, ed., *Jefferson: Writings*, 1433–35. Mason, "Maine and Missouri Crisis," 675–700, surprisingly ignores Holmes's diffusionist pamphlet and neglects to mention that Holmes wrote Jefferson advocating "diffusion" as the best way to abolish slavery, a concept that several historians, including Mason (691–92), have claimed Jefferson invented.

[27] Malone, *Jefferson the President: First Term*, 354–55n.

[28] See Gaines, *Thomas Mann Randolph, Jr.*, 124–26.

the slaves and their "transportation" to Haiti. Disappointed at the defeat of his son-in law's proposal, which in any case he criticized for providing insufficient state tax revenues to succeed, Jefferson nevertheless praised his "courage."[29]

Jefferson was probably aware that, of all the likely states to evolve from the Louisiana Purchase apart from Louisiana itself, only Missouri and Arkansas could utilize Black slavery. "Of one thing I am certain, that as the passage of slaves from one State to another, would not make a slave of a single human being who would not be so without it," he confessed to Holmes, who inspired him with the idea, "so their diffusion over a greater surface would make them individually happier, and proportionally facilitate the accomplishment of their emancipation, by dividing the burden on a greater number of coadjutors."[30]

Both Holmes in his pamphlet, and Jefferson in various letters at this time, assumed that the slaves would be "happier" in Missouri. Although slaves' experience was something Jefferson could not foresee, it is possible that he had knowledge of slaves' treatment by slaveholders in the burgeoning state. Whatever his source of information, Jefferson seemed aware that Missouri's small slaveholders often had friendly relations with their slaves. Slaves' proximity to their masters, whose households they often lived in, and their owners' awareness that bondspersons constituted a substantial part of their monetary investment, encouraged a relatively benign, reciprocal relationship. Slaves found they could maneuver and manipulate their masters, openly express their opinions, and escape harsh punishments. When in the years before the Civil War masters sought to limit slaves' tenuous freedoms by eliminating slave meetings and restricting their learning to read and write, the enslaved workers sometimes succeeded in opposing such repression, using the flexibility of the system and the owners' need for their labor to achieve compromise solutions through their resistance.[31]

In the final analysis, Jefferson desired "a general emancipation and *expatriation*" of the United States' Black population. Extending the arguments of Holmes and others, he believed that Missouri's entry into the Union with slavery, as its citizens desired, would indirectly expedite Virginia's, and national emancipation.[32] A diminution of great slaveholders who relied on human enslavement would presumably occur if emigrants were willing to buy their slaves at a good

---

[29] Jefferson to David Bailie Warden, December 26, 1820, in Ford, ed., *Works of Thomas Jefferson*, 12:181. See also Jefferson to Albert Gallatin, December 26, 1820, in Peterson, ed., *Jefferson: Writings*, 1450.

[30] Jefferson to John Holmes, April 22, 1820, in Lipscomb and Bergh, eds., *Writings of Jefferson*, 15:249–50.

[31] These are the conclusions of Diane M. Burke, *On Slavery's Border: Missouri's Small-Slaveholding Households, 1815–1865* (Athens: University of Georgia Press, 2010).

[32] Jefferson to John Holmes, April 22, 1820, in Lipscomb and Bergh, eds., *Writings of Jefferson*, 15:249–50. Jefferson's italics.

price; and eventually the total number of the state's slaveholders would fall, leading to a decrease in that interest group's power and facilitating antislavery action by the House of Delegates. Criticizing Northern Federalists and Republicans who insisted on slavery's immediate abolition in the remainder of the Louisiana Purchase and its gradual exclusion from Missouri, Jefferson argued that they misunderstood the "diffusion" strategy. They ignored the likelihood that if small slaveholders, who had purchased slaves from planters in the older states, spread into Missouri and other new territories, it would enable slavery gradually to disappear from states like Virginia, where he believed it had become less profitable. In a letter written to his friend from Revolutionary War days, the conservative constitutionalist and abolitionist Marquis de Lafayette, when the Missouri dispute revived in December 1820, Jefferson again explained "diffusion's" objectives:

> All know that permitting the slaves of the South to spread into the West will not add one being to that unfortunate condition, that it will increase the happiness of those existing, and by spreading them over a larger surface, will dilute the evil everywhere, and facilitate the means of getting finally rid of it, an event more anxiously wished by those on whom it presses [Southerners who confronted slavery in their daily lives] than by the noisy pretenders to exclusive humanity [Northern antislavery congressmen].[33]

His version of "diffusion" relied on slavery's gradual disappearance first from the older slave-holding states, where he thought it had become less profitable. This would occur if large slaveholders gained outlets for purchasers of their slaves, who would seek new opportunities in Louisiana, Missouri, and the Deep South. (Jefferson failed to take this reasoning to its logical conclusion, which more convincingly tied abolition to *barring* slavery from new states. If slavery in Virginia remained profitable only as long as planters sold their slaves to immigrants, if new states prohibited purchases of slaves from neighboring states, or abolished slavery itself, Virginia planters would be compelled to manumit their superfluous slaves, or enforce an unprecedented, tyrannical system of contraception among enslaved women.) Indeed, from the 1820s to the 1850s, most states, including those of the

[33] Jefferson to the Marquis de Lafayette, December 26, 1820, in Lipscomb and Bergh, eds., *Writings of Jefferson*, 15:301. For Lafayette's abolitionism, see Melvin D. Kennedy, ed., *Lafayette and Slavery: From His Letters to Thomas Clarkson and Granville Sharp* (Easton, PA: American Friends of Lafayette, 1950), and Liliane Willens, "Lafayette's Emancipation Experiment in French Guiana, 1786–1792," *Studies on Voltaire and the Eighteenth Century* 242 (1986).

Lower South that were most dependent on slaves, sporadically prohibited the purchase of slaves from other states for diverse reasons.[34]

Jefferson had reason to assume that, if his state lost slaves to emigration, the institution, having become less popular, would eventually be abolished at least in Virginia, though perhaps not in the United States as a whole. After the Revolution, Virginians increasingly sold slaves to one another. By 1810, the majority of White Virginians were slaveholders with a stake in slavery and the laws that protected it. However, it was around this time that they began selling slaves in large numbers to White immigrants to Missouri and the Lower South, thereby "diffusing" slaves and the institution of slavery throughout the South and West. The 220,000 slaves sold to the Lower South by Upper South states, primarily Virginia and Maryland, from 1790 to 1820 (North Carolina was a relatively minor participant) represented nearly 40 percent of their entire 1790 slave population. This development perhaps led Jefferson to expect the number of Virginian slaveholders to decline in the near future. A reduction in the number of great Virginia slaveholders reliant on the institution would presumably occur if emigrants purchased large numbers of their slaves, or if big Virginia slaveholders decided to leave for Missouri or Louisiana themselves.[35]

Jefferson continued his campaign to explain his motives in justifying Missouri's admission as a slave state in other letters to correspondents at home and abroad. He had apparently abandoned his earlier demand, in the Ordinance of 1784, that Congress prohibit slavery in all US territories. However, Missouri, unlike the Old Northwest in 1784, was part of a massive territory, purchased from a foreign power in an act of doubtful constitutionality and on the verge of statehood. These numerous considerations made its case different from that of the Confederation's territories. Missouri already contained a substantial number of

---

[34] Michael Tadman, *Speculators and Slaves: Masters, Traders, and Slaves in the Old South* (Madison: University of Wisconsin Press, 1989), 13–15, 84–89; Winfield H. Collins, *The Domestic Slave Trade of the Southern States* (1904; repr., Port Washington: Kennicat Press, 1969), 109–39; Stampp, *The Peculiar Institution*, 253; Scherr, *John Adams, Slavery, and Race*, 146–48.

[35] On Virginia slaveholdings in 1810, see Gordon S. Wood, *Empire of Liberty: A History of the Early Republic, 1789–1815* (New York: Oxford University Press, 2009), 524–27. For later years, see Lacy K. Ford, *Deliver Us from Evil: The Slavery Question in the Old South* (New York: Oxford University Press, 2009), 35–37, 76–77, 562n115; John R. Van Atta, *Wolf by the Ears: The Missouri Crisis, 1819–1821* (Baltimore: Johns Hopkins University Press, 2015), 36–37; Tadman, *Speculators and Slaves*, 287–90. In South Carolina and Mississippi in 1860, approximately half the families owned slaves; in Virginia, only one-fourth of the families owned slaves. Thus, some long-range basis existed for expecting that "diffusion" might increase the possibility that a legislative majority in Virginia would eventually abolish slavery though this was less likely in South Carolina. For these figures, see Stampp, *The Peculiar Institution*, 30.

slaves (many had arrived there decades earlier during the Spanish and French occupations) although far fewer than other new states like Alabama and Mississippi. In addition, Jefferson occasionally expressed the fear that if Congress succeeded in Missouri, it might next attempt to abolish slavery in the states where it had long existed, thus precipitating race war, and possibly secession and civil war.[36]

Alienated from slavery ever since he was a young practicing attorney in his twenties who took on slaves' freedom suits pro bono, Jefferson at that time defended the rights of the enslaved to freedom, most famously in the case of *Howell vs. Netherland* in 1770.[37] Fifty years later, a lifetime for most people of his generation according to Buffon's tables of mortality, Jefferson contemplated using the Missouri Compromise as a springboard for emancipation. On the eve of death, overwhelmed with debt, he had little personal economic incentive to defend the "Peculiar Institution." He was aware that he had only a short time to live and that after his death his estate and his slaves would be confiscated to pay his creditors, leaving his family impoverished. He hoped that gradual emancipation would eliminate the likelihood of a civil war over slavery, which he considered the greatest future threat to the Union's survival. He supported Missouri's admission as a slave state because its White inhabitants had expected Congress to permit slavery

[36] For Jefferson's ostensible fear that Congress would abolish slavery in the original thirteen states, which he may have affected to believe in order to frighten his correspondents into supporting the Missouri Compromise, see, e.g., Jefferson to Albert Gallatin, December 26, 1820, in Ford, ed., *Writings of Thomas Jefferson*, 10:177. Despite its antislavery stipulations, Jefferson's godchild, the Northwest Ordinance of 1787, had failed from its inception, for lack of enforcement, to prohibit bondage in the Midwest. The Confederation's appointee as territorial governor, Arthur St. Clair, permitted slavery. Although President Washington and Jefferson, his secretary of state, had the opportunity to reverse his decision and remove him in 1790, they "silently acquiesced in this high-handed action," as historian Don Fehrenbacher noted. Jefferson gained belated retribution on St. Clair, a diehard Federalist, when he became president. In 1802, he fired him as governor of the Northwest Territory (Fehrenbacher, *Slaveholding Republic*, 256–57).

[37] Jefferson's "Argument in the Case of Howell vs. Netherland," in Ford, ed., *Works of Thomas Jefferson*, 1:470–81. For accounts of Jefferson's activities in defending slaves' lawsuits for freedom as a young attorney before 1776, the most famous of which was that of the mixed-race, long-term indentured servant Samuel Howell (*Howell v. Netherland*) in 1770, see Boles, *Jefferson: Architect of American Liberty*, 28–29; Malone, *Jefferson the Virginian*, 120–22. For legal aspects of the case of *Howell v. Netherland* and others in which Jefferson was involved, see Edward Dumbauld, *Thomas Jefferson and the Law* (Norman: University of Oklahoma Press, 1978), 83–85; William G. Merkel, "A Founding Father on Trial: Jefferson's Rights Talk and the Problem of Slavery during the Revolutionary Period," *Rutgers University Law Review* 64/3 (2011): 595–664, at 631; Aaron Schwabach, "Thomas Jefferson as an Unsuccessful Advocate for Freedom in *Howell v. Netherland*," *Thomas Jefferson Law Review* 20 (Spring 1998): 129–37.

when they applied for entry into the Union: a rationale that would later be called "popular sovereignty." At the same time, Jefferson favored prohibiting slavery in the rest of the Louisiana Purchase, where slavery was not established, and he praised the handful of New England Republican congressional representatives who voted for compromise. Ironically, he disagreed with the majority of congressmen from his own state. They voted against the Compromise and muttered threats of secession, resentful that the deal outlawed slavery in most of the national territories.[38] Slavery had become an even more divisive issue in 1820 than it was during the Constitutional Convention in 1787, when James Madison defined it as the great dividing line between the states.[39]

For Jefferson, emancipation and emigration of freed Blacks from the United States were two sides of the same coin. First expressed in Query XIV of *Notes*, Jefferson's anxiety on this score persisted. Unlike the leaders of the American Colonization Society (ACS) created in 1816, he did not wish to uproot the small number of freed former slaves residing in the United States, whom the ACS hoped would leave for Africa on ships they provided for them. Nonetheless, ever since *Notes on Virginia*, albeit with a few exceptions, such as his letter to Edward Bancroft in 1789, he had expressed the view that Blacks and Whites were not meant to live together and would be happier if they lived separately in their own communities or (if possible) nation-states. His belief in White superiority in physical features and, possibly, intelligence, a vestigial racism common to most racial groups, did not extend to a desire for Whites' domestic hegemony and domination over Blacks, which could not occur if all slaves, after emancipation, lived far away in their own domain.

At the time of the Missouri Compromise, Jefferson ostensibly became temporarily obsessed by the fear that, if all US slaves were emancipated at once by order of Congress and *not* exiled abroad, they would attempt to kill off their former White masters, in revenge for past servitude, in a dreadful bloodbath. He did not need the Haitian Revolution to inspire him with such uneasiness. He had imbibed it from his cogitations on slavery during the American Revolution, and to a lesser degree from Gabriel's feckless conspiracy. Such events as Lord Dunmore's efforts to provoke a slave uprising in Virginia in 1775 by offering freedom

---

[38] See Scherr, "Thomas Jefferson's Nationalist Vision of New England," 1–35. For the permutations of the idea of popular sovereignty from Jefferson's time to the Civil War, see Christopher Childers, *The Failure of Popular Sovereignty* (Lawrence: University Press of Kansas, 2016).

[39] Staughton Lynd, *Class Conflict, Slavery, and the U.S. Constitution: Ten Essays* (Indianapolis: Bobbs Merrill, 1967), 159–60.

to slaves who joined the British Army perhaps inspired Jefferson's antislavery polemic in the Declaration of Independence, which Congress deleted.[40]

The flight of thirty of Jefferson's slaves to Cornwallis's troops in 1781 and the smallpox epidemic among those who joined the British Army before the Battle of Yorktown lent substance to his intuitions of chaos. In 1821, Jefferson bluntly expressed his feelings to his Massachusetts friend, John Adams. Adams sympathized with his point of view and opposed risking the Union to emancipate the South's slaves. Jefferson stigmatized the anti-Missouri faction as "the Holy Alliance in and out of Congress," likening it to European autocrats such as Russia's Tsar Alexander or the Emperor of Austria. Insisting that congressional Federalists intended to manipulate the Missouri issue to eventually abolish slavery in all the states, starting with newly admitted Missouri, empowering their commercial and manufacturing interests, risking dividing the Union into commercial ("Athenian") and non-commercial ("Lacedemonian," or ancient Spartan) republics, he dramatically argued,

> The real question, as seen in the States afflicted with this unfortunate population [slaves], is, are our slaves to be presented with freedom and a dagger? For if Congress has the power to regulate the conditions of the inhabitants of the States, within the States, it will be but another exercise of the power, to declare that all shall be free. Are we then to see again Athenian and Lacedemonian confederacies?[41]

[40] On Lord Dunmore's efforts to recruit slaves into the British Army with offers of emancipation, to which Congress alluded in blaming George III for "domestic insurrections" in the Declaration of Independence, see Sidney Kaplan, "The 'Domestic Insurrections' of the Declaration of Independence," *Journal of Negro History* 61/3 (July 1976): 243–55. The phrase "domestic insurrections" was not in Jefferson's original Declaration, and it is likely that the Continental Congress meant Loyalist uprisings as well as slave revolts. Although Kaplan refers to Jefferson's "perennial fear of slave rebellion," he quotes other Virginians, especially young James Madison and Edmund Randolph, not Jefferson, to prove Virginians' fear of slave revolt in 1776. Perhaps because Jefferson considered himself a benevolent slaveholder, was naïve, or doubted the likelihood of slave revolt, he seemed less worried about slave uprisings than his contemporaries were. When Jefferson mentioned the threat of slave rebellion and violence, as in Queries XIV and XVIII of *Notes*, and (although seldom) in his personal correspondence, he used it as a rhetorical device, attempting to convince others of the wisdom of gradual emancipation legislation and exile of the freed slaves.

[41] Jefferson to John Adams, January 22, 1821, in Lipscomb and Bergh, eds., *Writings of Jefferson*, 15:308–309; Adams to Jefferson, February 3, 1821, in Cappon, ed., *Adams-Jefferson Letters* (1988), 571. Both Athens and Sparta held slaves; perhaps the existence of human bondage was not the primary inspiration for Jefferson's analogy. For Adams's attitude toward slavery, see John R. Howe, Jr., "John Adams's Views of Slavery," *Journal of Negro History* 49/3 (July 1964): 201–205, and Scherr, *John Adams, Slavery, and Race.*

Exercising his imagination (as it turned out, correctly) in predicting that war between two sectional republics would follow the separation of North and South, Jefferson was painfully aware of the violent, power-seeking propensities of his own countrymen. Alluding to conflicts between Spartans and Athenians in fifth-century B.C. Greece, Jefferson speculated there might be "another Peloponnesian war to settle the ascendancy between" North and South. Or, perhaps only the slaves would rise up and kill the Whites in the seceded South, as had recently happened in Black Haiti. He rhetorically inquired of Adams, "Is this to be the tocsin of merely a servile war?" of slaves against free Southern Whites. "That remains to be seen; but not, I hope, by you or me. Surely, they [North and South] will parley awhile, and give us time to get out of the way." After hoping that he and Adams would die before the Union's ordeal exploded in maniacal violence, he pessimistically concluded, "What a Bedlamite is man!"[42] Adams similarly predicted a war of slaves against Whites, but unlike Jefferson's letter (although similar to words Jefferson's friend Isaac Briggs recorded him speaking at this time), he assumed Blacks' overwhelming defeat and their extermination by the White majority, with Southern slaveholders receiving assistance from Northern militias (something Jefferson did not expect).[43]

This letter to Adams was among Jefferson's most cynical and pessimistic expostulations. His despair arose from the recognition that human nature, even in his own beloved republic, was marred by the same selfishness and imperfections found in despotic governments in Europe and Latin America. Evidently, it did not disturb him to ascribe malicious intentions to the antislavery elements perhaps because he considered their strategy opportunistic, improper, disreputable, and disruptive. In his calmer moments, he acknowledged that civil war was unlikely in the immediate future. Reacting defensively to the brouhaha in Missouri, he believed that each state should decide for itself how to excise the canker of slavery, as Randolph was attempting to abolish it in Virginia despite setbacks. Jefferson welcomed assistance, especially in the form of money, from the federal government, the Northern states, or Europe in order to expedite slavery's demise. Still, for the moment he objected to Congress initiating measures to abolish human bondage in Missouri, where the majority of White settlers, eager to become

---

[42] Jefferson to John Adams, January 22, 1821, in Lipscomb and Bergh, eds., *Writings of Jefferson*, 15:309. A "Bedlamite" is an inmate of a mental institution or lunatic asylum.

[43] See John Adams to Louisa Catherine Adams, January 13, 1820, Adams Family Papers, 1639–1899, Series IV: Letters received and other loose papers, A: Chronological papers, 1639–1889, microfilm reel 449, Massachusetts Historical Society, Boston, MA, and Howe, "John Adams's Views of Slavery," 202. For Jefferson's predictions of Blacks' annihilation in his conversation with Isaac Briggs, discussed further below, see Merrill D. Peterson, ed., *Visitors to Monticello* (Charlottesville: University of Virginia Press, 1989), 81, 90–92.

part of the Union, had just ratified a state constitution that adopted that "hideous evil," as he labeled human bondage.[44]

In terms similar to those he had employed with Adams, he wrote to his friend, former secretary of the treasury Albert Gallatin, now US minister in Paris, that, if congressional fiat abolished slavery in Missouri and ultimately throughout the Union in an act he suspected was unconstitutional, inhabitants of slave states would have to flee for their lives. Otherwise, he cynically predicted, the emancipated bondsmen would massacre the Whites:

> If Congress once goes out of the Constitution to arrogate a right of regulating the condition of the inhabitants of the States, its majority may, and probably will next declare that the condition of all men within the US. shall be that of freedom, in which case all the whites South of the Patomak [*sic*] and Ohio must evacuate their States; and most fortunate those who can do it first.[45]

However, indicating his strong Unionism, Jefferson did not suggest that the Southern states secede or forcibly resist Congress, even if immediate emancipation en masse took place without "expatriation." He did not specify whether he thought Congress would give Southern Whites time to leave the country with their slaves before the hypothetical emancipation legislation took effect. It is likely that Jefferson's statement was hyperbole designed to alarm Gallatin and enlist him in the move for compromise. Averse to congressional usurpation of power by enforcing immediate abolition without deporting the ex-slaves, Jefferson continued to claim that slavery's "diffusion" to other states would dilute the institution's power within an individual state, presumably by reducing its proportion of slaveholders. Expanding slavery into Missouri would, he argued, improve the lot of slaves in general, "because by spreading them over a large surface, their happiness would be increased, & the burthen of their future liberation lightened by bringing a greater number of shoulders under it."[46]

By the latter phrase, Jefferson must have meant that the greater the number of small slaveholders spread across the South, the less drastic the effects of

---

[44] Jefferson to Richard Rush, October 20, 1820, in Lipscomb and Bergh, eds., *Writings of Jefferson*, 15:283. He called slavery a "hideous blot" in a letter to William Short (Jefferson to Short, September 8, 1823, in Lipscomb and Bergh, eds., *Writings of Jefferson*, 15:469–70).

[45] Jefferson to Albert Gallatin, December 26, 1820, in Ford, ed., *Writings of Thomas Jefferson*, 10:177, and Peterson, ed., *Jefferson: Writings*, 1449. See also David N. Mayer, *Constitutional Thought of Thomas Jefferson* (Charlottesville: University Press of Virginia, 1994), 288–89.

[46] Jefferson to Albert Gallatin, December 26, 1820, in Ford, ed., *Writings of Thomas Jefferson*, 10:177, and Peterson, ed., *Jefferson: Writings*, 1449. Probably his home state of Virginia, whose slaveholders wanted to sell their slaves down South, was foremost in his mind when he made this observation.

anticipated liberation would be on individual large planters in the old states. The number of big planters (who, however, often provided better living conditions for slaves and less often separated slave families than small slaveholders) would decrease because they would most likely sell their surplus slaves to eager young planters emigrating west. With fewer slaves, they would find their economic interests less severely injured by emancipation since fewer planters would own dozens of slaves. Thus, the "number of shoulders" he alluded to were, not the straining, sweating shoulders of slaves carrying heavy loads, but the flaccid shoulders of owners of small numbers of slaves, whose proportion of the slave-holding population would be increased by slavery's dispersion. Jefferson assumed that large slave-owners, at least in Virginia where slavery was reportedly becoming unprofitable for them, would sell many of their slaves to settlers leaving for Louisiana, Missouri, Arkansas, and other emerging slave states.[47] He further explained his views to Isaac Briggs, an old friend and former government official.

In November 1820, Briggs, an antislavery Pennsylvania-born Maryland Quaker and Jefferson's surveyor general south of Tennessee during his presidency, visited Monticello. He dined with Jefferson, joined by a stranger who simply barged into the house and left after drinking some wine, and several women in Jefferson's household, including his daughter Martha Jefferson Randolph, "his sister [Anna] Marks, and three or four of his grand daughters, fine looking young women."[48] Jefferson did not fear to speak frankly about public events in front of the women, whose intellectual acumen impressed Briggs. Pleased that Jefferson said that he looked young for his age, Briggs spent a few days with Jefferson, his daughter, and granddaughters.[49]

As Briggs recalled in a letter to his wife, "Among other political questions, that which has been called the Missouri question stood prominent." Although in March 1820 Congress allowed Missouri territory to retain slavery and instructed its leaders to prepare a state constitution for presentation the following year, Jefferson remained uneasy. In private conversation with a private citizen, Jefferson

---

[47] For a brief comparative discussion of small and large planters' treatment of slaves, see Schlotterbeck, "The Internal Economy of Slavery in Rural Piedmont Virginia," 170–81. However, Burke's discussion of slavery in Missouri depicts small slaveholders in a more favorable light than Schlotterbeck does.

[48] Isaac Briggs described his visit with Jefferson in a letter to his wife and children, November 21, 1820, reprinted in Peterson, ed., *Visitors to Monticello*, 81, 90–92.

[49] Isaac Briggs described his visit with Jefferson in a letter to his wife and children, November 21, 1820, reprinted in Peterson, ed., *Visitors to Monticello*, 81, 90–92. Briggs observed that Jefferson went to bed at 8 p.m. Jefferson's daughter Martha and her daughters chatted with Briggs until 10 p.m. Impressed that Jefferson encouraged the women of the household to develop their intellects, Briggs added, "It seems to be a matter of equal facility with them to write or converse, in French, Spanish, Italian, or their mother tongue" (ibid., 92).

reiterated the views he earlier expressed in his letters to politicians: "He said that nothing had happened since the revolution, which gave him so much anxiety and so many disquieting fears for the safety and happiness of his country." Striking a religious note, perhaps in deference to Briggs's devout Quakerism, Jefferson said he feared that, if in the forthcoming December 1820 session of Congress, "they carry matters to extremities…nothing short of Almighty power can save us. The Union will be broken." If Northerners in Congress again demanded abolition, Briggs paraphrased Jefferson, it might provoke "all the horrors of civil war, embittered by local jealousies and mutual recriminations…. Bloodshed, rapine, and cruelty will soon roam at large, will desolate our once happy land and turn the fruitful field into a howling wilderness." As a byproduct of this frustrating, desolating civil war, Whites in both North and South might turn in anger on the Black population (as indeed happened during the Civil War in the New York City draft riots, and more generally, in Confederate atrocities against captured Black Union troops). Consequently, Jefferson dramatically warned, "Out of such a state of things will naturally grow a war of extermination toward the African[s] in our land."[50]

Jefferson apparently expected a civil war, in which angry lower-class White Southerners would massacre any slaves they could get their hands on, retaliating for losses in men and money during the internecine conflict. His grisly, worst-case scenario was less than precise in its details. He speculated that the Southern states would secede from the Union if the Northern states, at the next session of Congress, renewed their demands that Missouri enter without slavery. A civil war would ensue (Jefferson did not specify how it would start), in which Southerners would vent their frustrations by massacring Blacks. Perhaps he only meant free Blacks since there was little reason for slaveholders to kill slaves, their most costly investment, unless, as happened in later years, Jefferson expected poor Whites to murder slaves suspected of various crimes as a way simultaneously to intimidate wealthy slaveholders they resented, in what historian Bertram Wyatt-Brown aptly called a "degradation ceremony."[51] As in the late 1790s, when Jefferson utilized the Haitian Revolution's ominous example as a means to promote slave

---

[50] Peterson, ed., *Visitors to Monticello*, 90. In late February 1821, Henry Clay formulated a Second Missouri Compromise, seeking to smooth over the Missouri constitution's refusal to admit free Blacks into the state. He inserted a meaningless proviso preceding congressional acceptance of the document, stating that Missouri's constitution did not violate the rights of other citizens of the United States. On Clay and the Missouri Constitution, see Robert Pierce Forbes, *The Missouri Compromise and Its Aftermath: Slavery and the Meaning of America* (Chapel Hill: University of North Carolina Press, 2007), 117–18.

[51] Bertram Wyatt-Brown, *Southern Honor: Ethics & Behavior in the Old South* (New York: Oxford University Press, 1982).

emancipation, he predicted slave upheaval, now including the warning that White Southerners would vent their frustrations by massacring Blacks.[52] Whatever his reasoning, Jefferson concluded that Blacks were doomed to annihilation unless they were soon emancipated and exiled.

In contrast to most of his other statements at this time, which doubted that Southern slaveholders had sufficient "moral sense" to emancipate their slaves, in conversing with Briggs Jefferson implied that, unless impeded by provocative Northern abolitionists, they would soon grant the African Americans their liberty, including "equal rights." Jefferson feared pernicious results from Northern agitation. "Instead of improving the condition of this poor, afflicted, degraded race, terminating, in the ordering of wisdom, in equal liberty and the enjoyment of equal rights (in which direction public opinion is advancing with rapid strides)," he complained, "the course pursued, by those who make high professions of humanity and of friendship for them, would involve them as well as us in certain destruction."[53]

At this point, then, Jefferson emphasized Unionism's fragility. He defensively pointed out that Northern abolitionists, shrilly demanding slavery's prohibition in all the territories, increased slaveholders' fears that Congress would abolish bondage throughout the South.[54] In Missouri's case, revising his nationalistic perspective, Jefferson adopted the Southern moderates' viewpoint. Placing the onus for discord on Northern abolitionists, he predicted the "horrors of Civil War" if the slavery "restrictionists" refused compromise. He expected that, if Northern agitation ceased, southern slaveholders would be less fearful that the government would confiscate their human property. They would ultimately agree to free their slaves and grant them "equal rights."[55]

Giving Northern antislavery psychology a more human face than he usually did, Jefferson appreciated that many Northerners were "honest in their humane views," and really wanted to help the Blacks. However, he told Briggs, in their

---

[52] For Jefferson's earlier warnings of slave revolt, already mentioned, which he said should be obviated by a Virginia emancipation statute, see Jefferson to St. George Tucker, August 28, 1797, in Oberg, ed., *Jefferson Papers*, 29:519.

[53] Peterson, ed., *Visitors to Monticello*, 90. Jefferson's young friend, the Illinois abolitionist Edward Coles, also viewed Northern antislavery agitation and threats that Congress would abolish slavery in the states as impeding the emancipationist cause (Edward Coles to Nicholas Biddle, September 18, 1823, in "Letters of Edward Coles: Second Installment," 97–113, at 103).

[54] Peterson, ed., *Visitors to Monticello*, 90–92.

[55] Ibid., 81, 90–92. The term "restrictionists" refers to those who wanted to restrict the entry of slavery into the new states and territories, including Missouri, and preferably any future states admitted to the Union.

"misguided zeal" they followed "master spirits, who raise the whirlwind and direct the storm." These Federalist demagogues' ostensibly humane intentions "masked" a quest for power, which they intended to achieve even at the risk of a bloody civil war.[56]

Reiterating a primary axiom of his political thought, Jefferson hoped the US would serve as a model of republicanism, democracy, morality, liberty, and happiness for the world's oppressed masses, "which, by its mild and steady light, would be far more powerful than the sword in correcting abuses." Especially after the French Revolution's collapse in the Reign of Terror and Napoleon's dictatorship, Jefferson insisted that the US remained the sole resource for assuring Europeans that "mankind can, if they will, govern themselves, and of relieving them from the oppressions of kingcraft and priestcraft." If the Union broke up, Jefferson feared, the United States' "bright example" would be "lost" and monarchists gloat that its disintegration proved the masses incapable of "self government." Thus, the failure of the "fullest and fairest experiment" in human liberty would "rivet the chains of despotism more firmly than ever."[57] Briggs, who shared Jefferson's fears, reflected that he spoke in an "impressive manner" about his concern for the republic's survival after the Missouri crisis.[58]

Jefferson's sympathy with Missouri residents' demands for slavery suggests that he considered Missouri a de facto state; indeed, it contained a population above sixty thousand, as the Northwest Ordinance of 1787 had originally required.[59] Moreover, he distrusted the motives of the restrictionists, whose leaders he perceived as power-hungry resurrected Federalist demagogues, fatal to republics, rather than sincere antislavery idealists. This consideration provided him with an added incentive for accepting slavery in Missouri, at least until his hoped-for nationwide plan for abolition was implemented.

Apart from his distrust of New York and Pennsylvania Federalist politicians, Jefferson had other reasons for ambivalence toward the extreme abolitionists and their "immediatist" philosophy (i.e., advocating the immediate freeing of all slaves). At times, he imagined them a threat to the Union, a role model he considered essential to the progress of (White) liberty even in Europe, where people

---

[56] Ibid.

[57] Ibid., 91. I have slightly changed the word order. Jefferson's words were similar to those in his famous last letter to Roger C. Weightman, June 24, 1826, celebrating the fiftieth anniversary of the Declaration of Independence (Jefferson to Roger C. Weightman, June 24, 1826, in Peterson, ed., *Jefferson: Writings*, 1517).

[58] Peterson, ed., *Visitors to Monticello*, 92.

[59] In 1820, Missouri had 66,000 inhabitants, but about 10,000 were slaves (Moore, *Missouri Controversy*, 32). By means of the "three-fifths clause," the 10,000 slaves would count as 6,000 free persons. This legally gave Missouri 62,000 "free inhabitants," exceeding the number of 60,000 free persons that the Northwest Ordinance of 1787 required for statehood.

had few civil rights and whose laborers and serfs were little better off than slaves. He incessantly expressed such ideas at this time, to Briggs and others. In a letter to Richard Rush, a native Philadelphian and US minister to Great Britain during James Monroe's presidency, after mentioning news of rioting and repression in France and England, he observed, "Nor is our side of the water entirely untroubled. The boisterous sea of liberty is never without a wave." Unfortunately, the question of slavery restriction had created a rip tide of disharmony between North and South. Jefferson considered Northern politicians, who viewed the conflict over slavery as a means to increase their political power with antislavery voters, insensitive to the internal dangers and difficulties slavery posed for southerners. Northerners exploited the Missouri crisis as a vehicle for a holier-than-thou stance toward the slave-holding South, whose inhabitants alone understood the tragedy of slavery from personal experience, he said. Aware that the Missouri controversy had not yet played out, Jefferson continued to describe slavery's "diffusion" euphemistically as a means by which large slaveholders in states like Virginia would sell their surplus slaves, thus "sharing the evil" of human bondage with new slaveholders. Northern slavery restrictionists in Congress thoughtlessly desired to frustrate this process by legislation like the Missouri emancipation bill. Disappointed by Northern hostility, he long-windedly explained to Rush:

> A hideous evil, the magnitude of which is seen, and at a distance only, by the one [Northern] party, and more sorely felt and sincerely deplored by the other [Southern Republicans], from the difficulty of the cure, divides us at this moment too angrily. The attempt by one [Northern] party to prohibit willing States from sharing the evil, is thought by the other [Southern Republican party] to render desperate, by accumulation [of slaves in "old" slave-holding states like Virginia], the hope of its final eradication.[60]

More optimistically, Jefferson insisted that all sections condemned slavery as an "evil, moral and political," only disagreeing on the "practicable process of cure." He recommended that Northern and Southern congressional parties "cool" off, abandon their paranoid, "visionary fears" of each other's intentions, and recognize that "duty and interest" required peaceful settlement of their differences. Anticipating a brief "separation" of the Union into North and South, he expected a peaceful divorce; after "two or three years," the sections would reunite, "like quarreling lovers to renewed embraces, and increased affections." Far from resting his argument on affectionate sentiments, however, Jefferson concluded that the

---

[60] Jefferson to Richard Rush, October 20, 1820, in Lipscomb and Bergh, eds., *Writings of Jefferson*, 15:283.

self-interest of North and South dictated that they remain a single republic. "The experiment of separation would soon prove to both that they had mutually miscalculated their best interests," he asserted.[61] Even if Congress "in a passion" dissolved the Union, Jefferson was confident that a grass-roots upsurge of the people would be more discerning than their representatives were. Trusting the intelligence of the agrarian majority more than the ambition and avarice of their representatives, he thought, "soberer people," perhaps through the mechanism of two-thirds of the state legislatures, "would call a convention and cement again the severance attempted by the insanity of their functionaries."[62]

Belying his seeming confidence that any rupture of the republic would be temporary and corrected by the direct act of the people, Jefferson viewed the current discord with great sadness. Despite envisioning a happy outcome to his secessionist forebodings, Jefferson feared that even a temporary "schism" would have a "fatal effect" on the current revolutionary movements in Europe. A separation of the states, he warned, would assist "evil" forces throughout the "enslaved world," a term whose ludicrous connotations he apparently ignored in condoning at least a temporary perpetuation of Southern domestic *slavery*. "We exist, and are quoted," he sententiously wrote, "as standing proofs that a government, so modelled [*sic*] as to rest continually on the will of the whole society, is a practicable government."[63]

Partisan and sectional antagonisms over slavery and race closer to home disturbed Jefferson's retirement more than Haiti's existence as a country ruled by former slaves ever did. Alarmed by the conflict over slavery's extension into the Louisiana Purchase's western territories, the elderly Jefferson hoped that good will and moral sense ("sincerity") would deter his old Federalist foes from inflammatory, disunionist talk. He urged Northern Federalists and Republicans to compromise with the South amid their vehement congressional debates between 1819 and 1821. At the same time, he hoped that a congressional logrolling compromise, supporting Missouri's admission to the Union as a "slave state" in exchange

[61] Ibid., 283–84.

[62] Ibid.

[63] Ibid.

for prohibiting slavery in most of the Louisiana Purchase, would not eclipse the fundamental question of slavery's evil per se—an institution that he and many other southerners considered immoral.[64]

[64] Moore's *Missouri Controversy* is the most thorough study of the dispute over slavery involved in the Missouri Compromise although it suffers from its failure to stress the issue of abolishing slavery, an acceptable scholarly stance at the time he wrote. Forbes, *Missouri Compromise and its Aftermath*, covers more ground in briefer compass and emphasizes the abolitionist presence, although implausibly trying to convert President James Monroe into an abolitionist and a religious fundamentalist. In general, see Charles G. Sellers's classic article, "The Travail of Slavery," in Sellers, ed., *The Southerner as American* (Chapel Hill: University of North Carolina Press, 1960), 40–78.

Chapter 14

Jefferson's Sectional Missouri Politics Overcomes His Vision of Destruction

In old age, Jefferson continued in some ways to assert the "Classical Republican" credo of such British political philosophers as James Harrington; the Earl of Shaftesbury; Algernon Sidney, the republican martyr; and one of his favorites, Henry St. John, Viscount Bolingbroke.[1] Adhering to classical republicanism's distrust of Establishment politicians as unethical power-mongers, Jefferson suspected that self-interest and ambition motivated the resurrected Federalists' position on slavery in Missouri. Long retired from politics and frequently pondering his nearness to death, he protested that he was now apolitical. He told former colleagues that, in poor health and not expecting to live much longer, he was preoccupied with personal matters like his "farm" and the University of Virginia rather than politics. "I now am unable to write but with pain, and unwilling to think without necessity," he said. "In this state I leave the world and its affairs to the young and energetic, and resign myself to their care, of whom I have endeavored to take care when young." He confided to his friend Charles Pinckney, a Democratic-Republican congressman from Charleston, South Carolina, "I read but one newspaper and that of my own State [Thomas Ritchie's *Richmond Enquirer*], and more for its advertisements than its news. I have not read a speech in Congress for some years."[2] He made clear to his friends that he would not enter

---

[1] For Jefferson's praise of Algernon Sidney, see, for example, Jefferson to Mason Locke Weems, December 13, 1804, in Founders Online, National Archives (founders.archives.gov/documents/Jefferson/99-01-02-0824).

[2] Jefferson to Charles Pinckney, September 30, 1820, in Lipscomb and Bergh, eds., *Writings of Jefferson*, 15:279. Standard studies on "classical republicanism" include Zera S. Fink, *The Classical Republicans* (Evanston: Northwestern University Press, 1945); J. G. A. Pocock, *The Machiavellian Moment: Florentine Political Thought and the Atlantic Republican Tradition* (Princeton: Princeton University Press, 1975); Pocock, *Politics, Language, and Time* (New York: Atheneum, 1971); Pocock, "The Classical Theory of Deference," *American Historical Review* 81/3 (June 1976): 516–23; and Lance Banning, *The Jeffersonian Persuasion: Evolution of a Party Ideology* (Ithaca: Cornell University Press, 1976). See also Isaac Kramnick, *Bolingbroke and His Circle: The Politics of Nostalgia in the Age of Walpole* (Cambridge: Harvard University

the public sphere, either to express moral opposition to slavery, as Edward Coles urged him to do in 1814, or to champion slavery's expansion into new states, embracing Pinckney's position.

Beneath his veneer of indifference, Jefferson was as angry at his old political foes, the Federalists, as at any time in his life, despite sharing the antislavery views and Unitarian beliefs of many of them.[3] Decrying the motives of the North's "leaders of federalism," in September 1820 Jefferson responded to a letter from the proslavery Pinckney asking for his opinion on various topics, including Missouri. Pinckney considered the agitation over slavery a plot by "these gentry at the northward" to make Rufus King the next president. "As I suppose you take both *Niles Register* & the *National Intelligencer* you have seen my opinion at length on the Missouri Question & particularly on the importance of the State Governments & how much their increase would tend to strengthen & give permanency to our Union," he informed Jefferson.[4]

Jefferson did not hesitate to express to Pinckney, who was instrumental in securing his election as president in 1800, his belief that the Federalists were playing a dangerous, amoral, irresponsible game. "The Missouri question is a mere party trick," he declared. Federalists' latest antics, in shifting the basis of partisan division from the comparatively innocuous "personal principle" of "monarchism" (which in the past Jefferson had considered of the greatest importance) to the potentially "fatal" sectional conflicts over slavery, flirted with breaking up the Union. "The leaders of federalism, defeated in their schemes of obtaining power by rallying partisans to the principle of monarchism, a principle of personal not of local division, have changed their tack," he warned. "They are taking advantage of the virtuous feelings of the people to effect a division of parties by a geographical line." Federalists hoped that their new platform, adhering to Northern "local principles" of antislavery while jettisoning their earlier Anglophile policies of centralized national government and "monarchy," would win them a hitherto elusive majority. In the process, he warned, they irresponsibly risked the Union's survival.[5]

Press, 1968); Bernard Bailyn, *Ideological Origins of the American Revolution* (Cambridge: Harvard University Press, 1967); and Gordon S. Wood, *Creation of the American Republic, 1776–1787* (Chapel Hill: University of North Carolina Press, 1969).

[3] Jefferson to Timothy Pickering, February 27, 1821, and Jefferson to George Thacher, January 26, 1824, in Adams, ed., *Jefferson's Extracts from the Gospels*, 402–404, 414–15.

[4] Charles Pinckney to Jefferson, September 6, 1820, microfilm reel 52, Jefferson Papers, LC (hdl.loc.gov/loc.mss/mtj.mtjbib023886). For Pinckney's position as a "proslavery extremist," see Moore, *Missouri Controversy*, 114–15.

[5] Jefferson to Charles Pinckney, September 30, 1820, in Lipscomb and Bergh, eds., *Writings of Jefferson*, 15:280.

Agreeing with Pinckney on Federalist duplicity, Jefferson once more charged that the Federalists were manipulating Americans' revulsion against slavery to gain political power by hypocritically "wasting Jeremiads on the miseries of slavery, as if we [Southerners] were advocates for it." Unlike Jefferson, South Carolina's "Old Republican" Pinckney, still active in politics after thirty years of veering from Federalism to Antifederalism, opposed the Missouri Compromise. In Congress, Pinckney voted against the "Thomas Proviso," which traded Missouri's admission as a slave state for the prohibition of slavery in the rest of the Louisiana Purchase territory north of 36°30′.[6]

Despite his doubts, Jefferson vaguely hoped that Northern Federalists in Congress, instead of continuing their clamor against the South, would more usefully vote funds to finance the abolition of slavery throughout the nation. Jefferson considered this action the measure of his opponents' "sincerity," a word that had become for him synonymous with his prized term, "moral sense." "Sincerity in their [northern Federalists and restrictionist Republicans] declamations should direct their efforts to the true point of difficulty," he argued, "and unite their counsels with ours in devising some reasonable and practicable plan of getting rid of it [slavery]." In a letter to Jared Sparks three years later, Jefferson used similar urgent albeit offensive terms to stress his desire to eliminate slavery and slaves from the United States. He said that, despite the great expense the US government incurred by emancipating, transporting, and initially subsidizing the millions of former slaves, "getting rid of them" should not be considered "forever impossible."[7]

Pinckney shared Jefferson's anger although unlike Jefferson he opposed all the Missouri Compromise's antislavery features. Jefferson favored the compromise because he considered Congress's acceptance of slavery in Missouri, which, having ratified a state constitution was in his opinion a de facto member of the

---

[6] Ibid. On Pinckney's political activities, see Marty D. Matthews, *Forgotten Founder: The Life and Times of Charles Pinckney* (Columbia: University of South Carolina Press, 2004), 131–42; and Moore, *Missouri Controversy*, 114–15, 122, 125–26, 166, 218, 304.

[7] Jefferson to Charles Pinckney, September 30, 1820, in Jefferson Papers, Library of Congress; Ford, ed., *Works of Thomas Jefferson*, 11:165–66, has a few errors of transcription; Jefferson to Jared Sparks, February 4, 1824, microfilm reel 54, Jefferson Papers, LC (hdl.loc.gov/loc.mss/mtj.mtjbib024921). On the *mentalité* of post-Revolutionary "sensibility" and sincerity, epitomized by the overwhelming public response to the simultaneous deaths of Jefferson and John Adams on July 4, 1826, see Andrew Burstein, *Sentimental Democracy: The Evolution of America's Romantic Self-Image* (New York: Hill and Wang, 1999); Burstein, *America's Jubilee* (New York: Knopf, 2001). See also Sarah Knott, *Sensibility and the American Revolution* (Chapel Hill: University of North Carolina Press, 2009).

Union rather than a territory, the basic point. He was opposed to upholding slavery in the entire Louisiana Purchase.[8]

Perhaps Jefferson exaggerated the malignity of his opponents' intentions. Maintaining his suspicion of Federalist leaders' loyalty to republicanism, Jefferson remembered their laws curtailing his party's freedom of speech in 1798, and years later their activities flouting his Embargo Act and plotting New England's secession from the republic in 1804, 1808, and most blatantly, during the War of 1812, culminating in the Hartford Convention in December 1814. Perhaps most unpardonably from Jefferson's point of view, the Federalists had attempted to deprive him of the presidency in 1800–1801 and hand it over to Burr. These memories pervaded his mind. Thus, he perceived even the slavery dispute as one more expedient by which a powerful minority of Federalist leaders, far from seeking to offer meaningful financial assistance or moral support in helping sister states "get rid" of slavery, defied their Unionist constituents. They intended to maneuver the Northern and Western "free' states out of the Union into their own "antislavery" republic, a separate nation over which they would exercise suzerainty. "Some of these leaders, if they could attain the power, their ambition would rather use it to keep the Union together," Jefferson opined, "but others have ever had in view its separation." Nonetheless, Jefferson predicted, the Western states and territories would remain with the South, depriving the Northern states of their internal free-trade market and their duty-free raw materials. The Federalists' schemes would backfire, "and as manufacturing and navigating States, they will have quarrelled with their bread and butter." More optimistically, he predicted that, after a brief separation, the seceded Northern states would humbly reunite with their Southern and Western comrades: "I fear not, that after a little trial, they will think better of it, and return to the embraces of their natural and best friends."[9] As in his letter a month later to Richard Rush, an abolitionist, Jefferson envisioned a relatively harmonious conclusion to the crisis.

Although the strong Unionist Jefferson drew a happy conclusion to the potential internal crisis, his friend Pinckney was less eager to maintain a united republic. Theoretically justifying the South's secession from a Northern-controlled

---

[8] Forbes, *Missouri Compromise and Its Aftermath*, 98, 105, 112–15. Thomas's amendment was added to a bill that allowed Missouri to form a constitution and state government permitting slavery, and permitted Maine's admission as a "free" state (Moore, *Missouri Controversy*, 87–89).

[9] Jefferson to Charles Pinckney, September 30, 1820, in Lipscomb and Bergh, eds., *Writings of Jefferson*, 15:280–81. For a detailed account of Jefferson's attitude toward New England during the Missouri crisis, see Arthur Scherr, *Thomas Jefferson's Image of New England: Nationalism versus Sectionalism in the Young Republic* (Jefferson, NC: McFarland, 2016), chs. 21 and 22.

government, the South Carolinian Pinckney nonetheless differed from some Virginia congressmen, who considered the Missouri Compromise law ample reason for secession. Instead, he depicted the statute to his anxious constituents as a victory for the slave-holding states that would eventually secure them at least six additional Senate seats. He claimed that the land mass allocated for future "free states" was a worthless wasteland, still in the hands of wary Native American tribes. Pinckney pleased his constituents by insisting that slavery was a positive good for the slave, that Blacks were racially inferior to Whites, and that they had never been citizens in any of the states.[10]

Despite upholding the doctrine that "the earth belongs to the living generation," first announced in a letter to James Madison on September 6, 1789, and reiterating it until he died, Jefferson remained anxious that the recurrence of disputes similar to that over Missouri statehood would dissolve the Union and end the hopes of millions at home and abroad for liberty. To Pinckney, he asserted his generalized disgust with Northern Federalist tactics, which he viewed as duplicitous politicking and a personal insult. In his last letter to Pinckney, he barely concealed his resentment. It pained him to be aware that he was dying, in the physical and metaphorical senses. During the Missouri crisis, Northern and Southern extremists had seemingly ignored the patriotic example of accommodation he and his Revolutionary colleagues had set. Instead, he warned Pinckney, politicians played childish political games, endangering the republic's survival and making him feel spiritually dead:

> This scheme of party I leave to those who are to live under its consequences. We who have gone before have performed an honest duty, by putting in the power of our successors a state of happiness which no nation ever before had within their choice. If that choice is to throw it away, the dead will have neither the power nor the right to control them. I must hope, nevertheless, that the mass of our honest and well-meaning brethren of the other States, will discover the use which designing leaders are making of their best feelings, and will see the precipice to which they are led, before they take the fatal leap.[11]

The younger Pinckney preceded Jefferson to the grave. Financially ruined and in poor health, despite his aristocratic origins, Pinckney supported an equitable apportionment of county representation in the state legislature and universal White manhood suffrage. As a young man during the 1780s, Pinckney was a leading nationalist. He reportedly recommended a congressional veto on state

[10] Moore, *Missouri Controversy*, 6, 114–15, 122, 125–26, 186, 218, 304.

[11] Jefferson to Charles Pinckney, September 30, 1820, in Lipscomb and Bergh, eds., *Writings of Jefferson*, 15:281.

laws as a delegate to the Great 1787 Constitutional Convention. He ended his life supporting his beloved state's secession from the Union, if slavery were threatened. He died in 1824, two years before Jefferson. Perhaps on his deathbed he pondered Jefferson's words, "The dead will have neither the power nor the right to control them."[12]

Thus, Jefferson considered the Missouri crisis an instance where the "moral sense" (or lack of it) of the disputants proved decisive. He agreed with the ethics of abolitionism but distrusted the intentions of politically motivated antislavery leaders. Unlike later "immediatists," such as William Lloyd Garrison and Wendell Phillips, who favored immediate emancipation of the slaves, the more moderate Rufus King, De Witt Clinton, and their allies were adept in political warfare. They did not reject partisan activity or denounce the Constitution as a proslavery document, what Garrison later famously labeled "a covenant with death and an agreement with Hell." Nevertheless, before the Civil War, Garrison and his followers rejected the use of violent means to overthrow slavery and opposed slave insurrections. Pacifists and non-resisters on principle, they deplored the Constitution, which in their opinion legalized war, slavery, and capital punishment. Most Southerners were probably unaware that Garrison's *Liberator* instructed slaves to obey their masters, not revolt, because violence flouted Jesus' teachings.[13] Jefferson would probably have trusted the apolitical fanatic Garrison more than he did Rufus King and the Northern Federalists, who insisted on abolishing slavery in Missouri. He castigated these men as political opportunists whose moral sense was weak.

As early as his late twenties, copying Montesquieu's writings into his Commonplace Book, Jefferson perceived slavery's evil. He knew that the enslaved in Missouri, and all over the world, deserved their natural right to liberty. Passionately attached to his own freedom, he was sure that Black slaves felt the same way. Perhaps for this reason, he seemed certain that if all slaves were immediately emancipated and allowed to remain in the United States, they would act violently in retribution for slavery, even perpetrating serial murder and massacre of the White population. He espoused this view as early as the 1780s in *Notes on Virginia*, long before the Haitian Revolution, conscious that thousands of Southern slaves fled to British lines during the American Revolution (including thirty of his own), although they committed few if any recorded atrocities against soldiers or civilians. Years later, Jefferson avoided exploiting Haiti as an example of Black slaves' revenge on their White masters. However, Dessalines' massacres of White

---

[12] See Robert M. Weir, "Pinckney, Charles," in Garraty, ed., *American National Biography*, 17:533–36.

[13] John Demos, "The Antislavery Movement and the Problem of Violent 'Means,'" *New England Quarterly* 37/4 (December 1964): 501–26.

civilians in 1804, performed as the head of government rather than as some anonymous, newly freed slave, perhaps confirmed his belief in the necessity of exiling the freed slave masses. (Yet, in old age, he never denied individual manumitees' right to remain in Virginia.) Although he alluded to "the bloody process of St. Domingo" in writing Edward Coles in August 1814, he was insisting on the urgency of government action to emancipate the slaves, rather than advocating increased repression.[14] "Justice is in one scale, and self-preservation in the other," Jefferson pithily wrote to Maine congressman John Holmes over five years later, supporting the New England legislator's stance in permitting slavery in Missouri. Jefferson believed that the Southern White population's "self-preservation" necessitated avoiding *immediate* congressional emancipation of all slaves even though "justice" dictated the latter.[15]

Thus, like many antislavery advocates, Jefferson was not an "immediatist." Moreover, he opposed Congress's arrogating what he considered an unconstitutional power to invade intrastate affairs by deciding their inhabitants' "condition," e.g., who could vote, who was a citizen, and who a slave. This was the function of the state governments, and Missouri was ready for statehood. As he bluntly put it, "An abstinence, too, [by Congress] from this act of power, would remove the jealousy excited by the undertaking of Congress to regulate the condition of the different descriptions of men composing a State. This certainly is the exclusive right of every State, which nothing in the Constitution has taken from them and given to the General Government." Descending to particular examples, he wrote, "Could Congress, for example, say, that the non-freemen of Connecticut shall be freemen, or that they shall not emigrate into any other State?"[16]

Interpreting the struggle between advocates of slavery and freedom through the kaleidoscope of "moral sense" theory, Jefferson contended that the Federalists and those "fanaticized" into supporting their demands to abolish slavery in Missouri violated moral sense principles. Their goal, he thought, was to regain political power using the pretext of antislavery zeal to deceive Northern Republicans about the (im)purity of their motives. In the aftermath of overwhelming political

[14] On Jefferson's escaped slaves, see, e.g., Jefferson to William Jones, January 5, 1787, microfilm reel 6, Jefferson Papers, LC (hdl.loc.gov/loc.mss/mtj.mtjbib002454). On the British War of 1812 raids on Bladensburg, Alexandria, and the capital, see Jefferson to Edward Coles, August 25, 1814, in Peterson, ed., *Jefferson: Writings*, 1345; Taylor, *Internal Enemy*, 301–305.

[15] Jefferson to John Holmes, April 22, 1820, in Lipscomb and Bergh, eds., *Writings of Jefferson*, 15:250.

[16] Ibid. In this instance, "freeman" meant, not someone who had been freed from slavery [a *freedman*], but a free individual, generally a White male citizen in New England and in colonial New York City, whom the town corporation or the state government granted a license to practice a trade within its borders.

defeats following the War of 1812, Federalists scrambled to find an issue that could replace the failed one of "whig and tory" (advocacy of legislative versus preference for executive power) in winning votes and stumbled on the formula "of slave-holding & non-slave-holding states." Jefferson acknowledged that their antislavery stance "had a semblance of being Moral," and the issue of slavery superficially held moral weight, but their real goal was a "Geographical" division of parties "calculated to give them ascendancy" by convincing Northern Republicans to join "a coalition" in their seemingly just cause.[17]

Perhaps self-servingly, Jefferson categorically denied that Federalists' desire to restrict slavery had moral content. According to his newly espoused rationale, prohibiting slavery in new regions would not decrease the nation's total number of slaves. Rather, it would merely keep them bottled up in states like Virginia, where they already existed in dangerously high numbers, were increasingly unprofitable to their owners, and furnished abundant raw materials for revolt. In words echoing his letter to Holmes, Jefferson informed Gallatin, "Moral the question certainly is not, because the removal of slaves from one state to another, no more than their removal from one country to another, would never make a slave of one human being who would not be so without it." This was especially true of Virginia, which abolished the importation of slaves from abroad and from neighboring states in 1778 and relied wholly on native births for bondspersons. Turning his opponents' moral claims upside down, Jefferson speculated, "if there were any morality in the question it is on the other side." Again, in his "diffusionist" interpretation, inspired by Holmes' circular letter, extending bondage to Missouri and points west would willy-nilly dilute the power of large planters in the older states and their dependence on slavery, by providing them the opportunity to sell slaves to migrating settlers. This process would "diffuse" bondsmen into smaller groups spread among different states of the Union. Indifferent to the effects their demands for slavery restriction would have on slaveholders or slaves, the Federalists merely sought an issue to secure their political domination in the "free states." Thereby, they hoped ultimately to regain political control of the country. According to Jefferson's calculations, the antislavery "North and East" comprised twelve states, enough to outvote the ten states of the "South & West." The threats of some Federalist extremists to liberate all slaves by congressional fiat imperiled the safe "existence" of the White residents within this "geographical minority," Jefferson warned.[18]

Jefferson ignored the fact that, by opposing New York Republican James Tallmadge's resolution prohibiting slavery in Missouri, extended by fellow New Yorker John W. Taylor to include Arkansas, he was supporting, at least

[17] Jefferson to Gallatin, December 26, 1820, in Peterson, ed., *Jefferson: Writings*, 1448–49.

[18] Jefferson to Gallatin, December 26, 1820, in Peterson, ed., *Jefferson: Writings*, 1448–49.

temporarily, the suppression of slaves' natural rights, consigning them to odious bondage and will-lessness in Missouri. Jefferson preferred to vaunt the greatness (what we call "exceptionalism," but he probably would not) of the US White Republic as an example for the world. He reminded Richard Rush, "As members...of the universal society of mankind, and standing in high and responsible relation with them, it is our sacred duty to suppress passion among ourselves, and not to blast the confidence we have inspired of proof that a government of reason is better than one of force."[19]

Believing that the peoples of other nations would eventually succeed in imitating the US example, he warned Gallatin that a breakup of the Union would thwart Europeans' efforts for liberal reform. "Should this scission take place," he predicted, "one of it's [*sic*] most deplorable consequences would be it's [*sic*] discouragement of the efforts of the European nations in the regeneration of their oppressive and Cannibal governments."[20] For the future well-being of the impoverished and oppressed White masses of Europe, Jefferson considered it imperative to avert the Union's breakup, even over such a crucial matter as abolishing Black slavery. From Jefferson's point of view, tearing the Union into a North and South would not expedite the latter's abolition of slavery; indeed, it would retard that laudable goal by enabling the slave states to entrench themselves within their own self-righteous Union.

Nor did Jefferson seem perturbed that Missouri's constitution prohibited free Blacks coming in from elsewhere. He had proposed something similar as a Virginia legislator. Virginia and other Southern states had passed similar laws during the 1790s to deter free Blacks from Haiti and Africa. (In addition to several Southern states, Ohio law enacted severe sanctions on the entry of free Blacks.) He unenthusiastically acquiesced in Congress's demand that Missouri remove this provision. Even if Missouri agreed to excise the objectionable article (it never really did so but merely reworded it to appease Congress), he expected similar disputes to emerge when other territories applied to enter the Union. Jefferson predicted that if Congress reneged on the Compromise, Missouri would choose to become a self-governing republic, which Congress would eventually, "after pouting awhile, recieve [*sic*]...on the footing of the original states [i.e, with slavery]."[21]

In his old age, Jefferson strangely relished inventing hypothetical scenarios of political disaster involving slavery. If the House of Representatives' antislavery majority directed the Army to force Missouri into the Union without slavery, he

---

[19] Jefferson to Richard Rush, October 20, 1820, in Lipscomb and Bergh, eds., *Writings of Jefferson*, 15:284.

[20] Jefferson to Albert Gallatin, December 26, 1820, in Peterson, ed., *Jefferson: Writings*, 1450.

[21] Ibid.

predicted, the proslavery Senate would veto the measure. If by some miscalculation, the Senate agreed to employ force, Jefferson anticipated the secession of the states south of the Potomac and even of "the three North Western states" (Ohio, Indiana, and Illinois). The Northwest Ordinance of 1787, a Jeffersonian legacy, prohibited slavery in these states. However, they depended on Louisiana, Kentucky, and Missouri for access to the Mississippi River, "however inclined to the other [Northern] side" they felt emotionally, and "would scarcely separate from those who would hold the Misisipi [*sic*] from it's [*sic*] mouth to it's [*sic*] source."[22]

Seeking to shock his politically active friends into getting involved during the crisis, Jefferson conjured up the possibility of the Union's break-up. He did not suggest using armed force to keep the Union together. He preferred to imagine a happy conclusion to the drama, with the states of the Union, realizing their mutual need of each other for prosperity and happiness, reuniting after a temporary separation. Jefferson never advocated using armed force to keep the Union together. In outlining this hypothetical scenario to Gallatin, Jefferson complacently concluded, without limning the outcome, "What next? Conjecture itself is at a loss. But whatever it shall be you will hear from others and from the newspapers." In this manner, he alluded to his belief that he would not be alive to see the rupture of the Union if one took place. He considered cooperation between Virginia and Gallatin's home state of Pennsylvania, from which many anti-Missouri "fanaticised" congressional representatives hailed, essential for the Union's preservation. For this reason, unaware of Gallatin's slight political influence, he somewhat implausibly urged him to abandon his post at Paris, return to Philadelphia, and mediate between the sections. "You might turn the scale there, which would turn it for the whole," he advised, eager to preserve the Union despite his seemingly nonchalant scenario about the possibility that the quarrel over Missouri statehood would destroy it.[23]

Jefferson's passive reaction to Congress's temporary rejection of Missouri's constitution revealed his persisting optimism that the republic's political, social, and moral progress would not be permanently impeded by disputes over slavery and sectional relations. It is a good example of his moral relativism and neutrality in matters involving slavery. He assuaged his fears with the thought that each side

---

[22] Ibid.

[23] Ibid.; Ford, ed., *Writings of Thomas Jefferson*, 10:176. Jefferson probably considered Gallatin, a transplanted Swiss citizen and former resident of Pennsylvania, New York, and Washington, DC, as someone who had picked up numerous friends in these places. However, he had certainly made numerous enemies, especially the Smith brothers of Baltimore, who considered him an obstacle to their political advancement.

sympathized with the other's point of view more than it admitted. Eventually they would together find a "practicable cure" for slavery's blight on the republic.[24]

Months after the dispute was resolved and Missouri formally admitted into the Union on August 10, 1821, Jefferson experienced relief that his goal of an expansive republic survived. He probably perceived that even Federalists dared not recommend compelling "slave states" like Alabama and Mississippi, which had recently entered the Union, and the future state of Florida, all of which had far more slaves than Missouri, to enter the Union as "free states." Thus, when such Federalists as Congressman John Sergeant of Pennsylvania, a leader of the restrictionists, argued in February 1821 that Missouri must enter the Union as a "free state" to balance the impending admission of Florida, which actually was twenty-five years in the future, Democrats took note of their opportunism and apparent hypocrisy on the issue of slavery.[25] Content with Missouri's admission as the first state formed from the Louisiana Purchase, Jefferson considered its rise to statehood as helping to preserve the United States by increasing its westward extent, simultaneously reducing the likelihood of the republic's breakup. He thereby validated his action as president in pursuing the ostensibly unconstitutional act of purchasing Louisiana from France. Writing to Henry Dearborn, secretary of war in his Cabinet at the time, he said, "I still believe that the Western extension of our confederacy will ensure its duration, by overruling local factions, which might shake a smaller association. But whatever may be the merit or demerit of that acquisition, I divide it with my colleagues to whose councils I was indebted for a course of administration, which, notwithstanding the late coalition of clay & brass will, I hope, continue to receive the approbation of our country."[26] For Jefferson, the admission of Missouri was essential to ensure the republic's expansion through the Louisiana Purchase and to enhance his self-esteem as the president who had consummated the unprecedented purchase.

---

[24] Jefferson to Richard Rush, October 20, 1820, in Lipscomb and Bergh, eds., *Writings of Jefferson*, 15:283; Holowchak, "The spirit of the master is abating," 107–108.

[25] Moore, *Missouri Controversy*, 160–61; Malone, *Sage of Monticello*, 342.

[26] Jefferson to Henry Dearborn, August 17, 1821, in Founders Online, National Archives (founders.archives.gov/documents/Jefferson/98-01-02-2258). I have modernized Jefferson's spelling and punctuation.

Chapter 15

Jefferson's Solution to the Slavery Issue Relies on the Nation's Moral Sense

While Jefferson pondered the fate of Missouri and the Union, he considered enlisting the existence of an independent Haiti in the Caribbean in destroying the cancer of slavery. His acquiescence to slavery in Missouri demonstrated his consistent desire to preserve the extended union and his respect for the new state's White majority. However, he tempered his ostensible moral neutrality on slavery with a wish, like a deus ex machina, to bring good out of evil. His "machine" was Haiti, or as it was then spelled, "Hayti." (Some people, including Jefferson at times, still called it "St. Domingo.") He imagined that the Missouri crisis and dual Northern and Southern threats of secession, by revealing slavery's threat to the Union, would advance the movement for slaves' emancipation and resettlement, preferably in Haiti. He appreciated that it had this effect in Virginia, where Governor Randolph in December 1820 urged the legislature to enact a program to emancipate and deport to Haiti 10 percent of the slave population annually. After warning Gallatin that the conflict over Missouri's constitution might shatter the Union, Jefferson ended his letter on an encouraging note, despite criticizing his son-in-law's program as too minuscule:

> Amidst this prospect of evil, I am glad to see one good effect. It [the Missouri crisis] has brought the necessity of some plan of general emancipation & deportation more home to the minds of our people than it has ever been before. Inasmuch, that our governor has ventured to propose one to the Legislature. This will probably not be acted on at this time. Nor would it be effectual, for while it proposes to devote to that object one third of the revenue of the State, it would not reach one tenth of the annual increase.[1]

In his letter to Gallatin at this desperate moment, when the Missouri Controversy threatened to dissolve the Union, Jefferson revived an idea he first elaborated in November 1801. At that time, Governor James Monroe asked him to suggest a proper destination for Virginia to deport slaves convicted of rebellion and conspiracy and perhaps eventually the less "obnoxious" free Blacks. President

---

[1] Jefferson to Gallatin, December 26, 1820, in Peterson, ed., *Jefferson: Writings*, 1450.

Jefferson then argued that, compared with Africa, it would be cheaper and more practicable for the state and national governments to transport emancipated Blacks the relatively short distance to Haiti. The revolutionary leader, Governor-General Toussaint Louverture, had promised to welcome Blacks from other countries arriving in Saint Domingue. Twenty years later, Jefferson reminded Gallatin that an established Black government under mixed-race President Jean-Pierre Boyer likewise sought to attract immigrants to bolster its agricultural and military facilities. Jefferson preferred sending freed Blacks to Haiti instead of Africa, where no functioning Black nation-state existed. He recommended that Virginia confiscate young slaves from their masters and become their "guardian" until they were old enough for the trip to Haiti, a voyage he expected the US government's public "land office" to pay for. Other revenue sources for financing the deportations to Haiti were Virginia state taxes and "charitable contributions" from supposedly guilt-ridden European individuals and purportedly antislavery citizens in the "Eastern states." That section's merchants, especially those from Rhode Island and Massachusetts, were principally involved in the slave trade before Congress, at President Jefferson's behest, declared it illegal in 1807. Atypically expressing confidence in slaveholders' moral sense, Jefferson did not expect Virginia planters to receive compensation for their slaves, but to agree to "give [them] up" to the state as infants. Strangely, he thought that non-slaveholders in Europe and New England would be eager to give "charitable" donations to the emancipation of the slaves. He had never expressed such confidence in the strength of the "moral sense" of Whites before. Perhaps desperation inspired his newfound assurance. He wrote Gallatin,

> My proposition would be that the holders should give up all born after a certain day, past, present, or to come, that these should be placed under the guardianship of the State, and sent at a proper age to S. Domingo. There they are willing to recieve [*sic*] them, & the shortness of the passage brings the deportation within the possible means of [national?] taxation aided by charitable contributions. In this I think Europe, which has forced this evil on us [as a British colony in the eighteenth century], and the Eastern states who have been it's [*sic*] chief instruments of importation [actually, British Liverpool merchants did most of the importing of slaves into the U.S.] would be bound to give largely. But the proceeds of the [national] land office, if appropriated, would be quite sufficient.[2]

---

[2] Ibid. A brief account of the revenue the U.S. government derived from selling public lands in 1820 is in Davis R. Dewey, *Financial History of the United States* (New York: Appleton, 1934), 216–17. The public land office was profitable. Between May 1800 and June 1820, more than 13.6 million acres were sold for $22.6 million, with average annual proceeds of about $1.1

Even before the beginning of his presidency in 1801, Jefferson favored Haiti (called Saint-Domingue or St. Domingo until Dessalines, declaring its independence on January 1, 1804, renamed it "Haiti") as the best destination for liberated slaves. He hoped the US government would one day liberate all slaves en masse, albeit gradually.[3] He maintained this Haitian preference into old age. For instance, his letter to Gallatin in December 1820 applauded the efforts of his son-in-law, Virginia governor Thomas Mann Randolph, Jr., to enact a gradual emancipation law, further discussed below. Jefferson regarded Randolph's attempt as a fortunate, unexpected result of the Missouri controversy, which had nearly brought about Virginia's secession from the Union after the US House of Representatives passed the Tallmadge resolution, forcing the citizens of Missouri to emancipate their slaves as a condition for statehood. Regretting that the state revenues Randolph proposed to allocate for manumission fell far short of what was needed, as we have seen, Jefferson nebulously hoped that the Northern states, and even European governments or wealthy individuals, would prove the sincerity of their antislavery ardor by contributing money toward Virginia's gradual abolition of slavery. He relied primarily on congressional funding, advanced through national public lands sales.

In desiring the national government to undertake the legislation and financing required for abolition, Jefferson granted it a role that even the most ardent nationalists would probably consider unconstitutional. His fellow slaveholders, many of them close friends like Judge Spencer Roane, Charles Pinckney, and John Taylor, would probably recoil from it in horror, as antithetical to their obsession with preventing any national interference with slavery. He would begin by forcing masters to part with newborns who would become wards of the state (either Virginia or the federal government; he was not clear on this), which would eventually expel the adults to Haiti as freedmen. In expecting masters to agree to such a self-sacrificing measure, and in apparently believing that Southern slaveholders, most of them states' righters, would support direct intervention by the national government against slavery, Jefferson manifested his desperate perception that the need to abolish slavery was urgent, as the Union's near break-up over Missouri had revealed. Either he believed that Southern slaveholders' devotion to the Union and their moral sense had grown significantly in a short time, or he

---

million. The Homestead Act of 1820 ended a system of easy credit but reduced the minimum price per acre to $1.25 and the minimum purchase per tract to 80 acres, more feasible for the average farmer than the minimum price of $2.00 per acre and minimum tract of 340 acres under the Land Act of 1800. Acreage sold and revenues greatly increased between 1820 and 1862 (Gary M. Anderson and Dolores T. Martin, "The Public Domain and Nineteenth Century Transfer Policy," *Cato Journal* 6/3 [Winter 1987]: 907).

[3] Jefferson to St. George Tucker, August 28, 1797, in Oberg, ed., *Jefferson Papers*, 29:519.

assumed they felt as desperately as he did about slavery's disruptive power. His seeming expectation that "charitable" individuals in Europe and the New England states would eagerly subsidize this project from their own pockets was an equally idealistic projection of society's moral sense. Or, perhaps he had lost touch with reality.[4]

After an interval of silence during his presidency's troubled last years, Jefferson in retirement often recommended Haiti as the optimal destination for emancipated Southern slaves, the expense of which would be financed by the state or national government. Now able to give advice more freely without the inhibitions and burdens of official position, he unqualifiedly preferred Haiti as the ideal "receptacle" for emancipated slaves. His position was reinforced when Randolph, impelled by the crisis over Missouri's admission as a slave state, proposed in his annual message to the legislature in December 1820 a gradual emancipation plan to deport liberated slaves to Haiti. In this, he was his father-in-law's spokesman, emulating Jefferson's confidential proposals to Governor James Monroe during his presidency, nearly twenty years earlier, as well as to Gallatin in 1820.

In effect, Jefferson argued for the rights of the "living generation" of Southern slaves coming into being, who, unlike their predecessors, would find sanctuary in the first Black-controlled government in modern history: Haiti. Expecting the federal government to finance the subsistence of the emancipated slave children through public land sales until they reached a "proper age for deportation," Jefferson's ambitious program of intervention by the national government exceeded anything proposed with regard to emancipation before the Thirteenth Amendment liberated four million Blacks without compensating their owners.[5]

The day after Christmas, Jefferson wrote nearly identical letters to Gallatin and David B Warden, a former US consul in Paris. At the height of renewed congressional debate over Missouri's admission to the Union as a slave state, he again linked slavery in Missouri, emancipation, and deportation of the freed slaves to Haiti. Proudly informing Warden, an abolitionist sympathizer, of his son-in-law's efforts to abolish slavery, he reported, "Mr. Randolph is at present our Governor, & of course at Richmond. He has had the courage to propose to our legislature a plan of general emancipation & deportation of our slaves." "Altho this is

---

[4] Jefferson to Albert Gallatin, December 26, 1820, in Peterson, ed., *Jefferson: Writings*, 1450, and in Ford, ed., *Writings of Thomas Jefferson*, 10:178. See also Gaines, Jr., *Thomas Mann Randolph, Jr.*, 124–26.

[5] Jefferson to Albert Gallatin, December 26, 1820, in Peterson, ed., *Jefferson: Writings*, 1450, and in Ford, ed., *Writings of Thomas Jefferson*, 10:178. I have modernized spelling and punctuation for greater readability. See also Betty Fladeland, "Compensated Emancipation: A Rejected Alternative," *Journal of Southern History* 42/2 (May 1976): 169–86.

not ripe to be immediately acted on," Jefferson continued, "it will, with the Missouri question, force a serious attention to this object by our citizens, which the vicinage of St. Domingo brings within the scope of possibility."[6]

Jefferson preferred Haiti to Africa as the freedpersons' destination, partly because its proximity would enable the United States, like a surrogate mother country, to assist the emigrants and transport them the shorter distance more quickly and cheaply. This was among the stipulations he mentioned as early as Query XIV of *Notes*, twenty years before Haiti existed. Perhaps more important, Haiti had an established government whose rulers offered to assist Black immigrants.[7]

Perhaps inspired by Jefferson's ideas about Haiti, which he probably learned from him firsthand, Randolph's more cautious proposal for gradual emancipation in his annual message to the Virginia assembly in December 1820 sought slaveholders' voluntary participation.[8] It was therefore less far-reaching than the compulsory procedure that Jefferson had in mind, described in greatest detail in an 1824 letter to Jared Sparks.[9]

Unfortunately, Randolph's scheme, like those of many colonizationists, was not motivated by sympathy for African Americans but hostility. Unlike his son-in-law, Jefferson had never suggested deporting already-free Blacks from Virginia although Monroe and the Virginia Assembly sent him recommendations for such projects during his first term as president. Like John Taylor of Caroline in his book of essays, *Arator* (1810), Randolph was exasperated by free Blacks' alleged involvement in fencing goods stolen by slaves. He argued that these practices financially ruined "the Farmers of Virginia." Not only did he wish to deport future freed slaves to Haiti, he proposed to exile already-free Blacks convicted of "traffic with slaves...to St. Domingo, or Africa, with forfeiture of freedom for returning." Strongly desiring to relieve "posterity" from the doubly "evil blemish" of free Blacks and slavery, and blaming slavery on African chiefs who sold their own people, reviving slavery and the slave trade in Christian Europe and America after its disappearance for centuries, Randolph urged the mandatory "transportation oversea[s]" of all future emancipated slaves. According to Randolph, White

---

[6] Jefferson to Warden, December 26, 1820, in Ford, ed., *Works of Thomas Jefferson*, 12:181.

[7] For Jefferson's earliest statement of his preference for Haiti over West Africa, see Jefferson to Monroe, November 24, 1801, in Lipscomb and Bergh, eds., *Writings of Jefferson*, 10:296–98.

[8] Governor Randolph to the Speaker of the House of Delegates, December 4, 1820, in *Richmond Enquirer*, December 5, 1820.

[9] Jefferson to Jared Sparks, February 4, 1824, in Ford, ed., *Works of Thomas Jefferson*, 12:336–39.

Virginians' sturdiness and moral fiber, and their state's "happy," exhilarating climate enabled them to overcome "the deplorable error of our ancestors in copying an evil institution from savage Africa": Black slave labor and its unprofitability, inefficiency, and ignorance. With great exertion, Virginians had been able to "maintain...our lofty station in the Union." The governor regretted that "the free citizens of the state, and that distinct and inferior race so unfortunately intermingled with them" resided together, even as masters and slaves.[10]

Somewhat contradicting his assertions of slaves' stupidity, Randolph now charged that their lazy work habits and waste of resources were motivated by "reason and self interest": a means of rebelling against enslavement. Thus, Randolph reluctantly admitted that slaves were human, not automatons or animals. As rational beings, it was reasonable for them *not* to work diligently if they received no personal reward. Virginia would make greater economic and social progress without them, Randolph said, by relying solely on "the energy her free citizens have displayed, and the advantages nature had bestowed." Unfortunately, Randolph was too racially prejudiced to consider whether freed slaves would make *good* workers, motivated by self-interest and working for themselves.[11]

Ignoring the racial discrimination free Blacks faced, he blamed their allegedly immoral character for their thefts and marauding. The remedy for these crimes was the "transportation" to Haiti or Africa of free Blacks convicted of illegally trading with slaves. He believed that a "general emancipation" of all slaves should include the deportation of these "needy and idle vagabonds," even though they were free.[12] Despite acknowledging that some masters were brutal and occasionally whipped their slaves, Randolph warned that free Black "vagabonds" were

---

[10] Governor Randolph to the Speaker of the House of Delegates, December 4, 1820, in *Richmond Enquirer*, December 5, 1820. West African chiefs vigorously conducted the Atlantic slave trade, seeking manufactures and guns with which to defeat neighboring tribes. Possessing large slave-holdings long before the Whites arrived, they opposed European efforts to end the slave trade in the 1820s (McGowan, "African Resistance to the Atlantic Slave Trade in West Africa," 5–29; and Stephanie E. Smallwood, "African Guardians, European Slave Ships, and the Changing Dynamics of Power in the Early Modern Atlantic," *William and Mary Quarterly* 64/4 [October 2007]: 679–716). On the other hand, during the early nineteenth century, British and American abolitionists exaggerated the African tribes' brutality toward their neighbors. They accepted hearsay evidence that African chieftains, obsessed with profit and the acquisition of the White man's guns and alcohol, engaged in "unjust wars" with other tribes for the purpose of selling slaves, wantonly murdering innocent women and children in the process (Jeffrey Glover, "Witnessing African War: Slavery, the Laws of War, and Anglo-American Abolitionism," *William and Mary Quarterly* 74/3 [July 2017]: 503–32).

[11] Governor Randolph to the Speaker of the House of Delegates, December 4, 1820, in *Richmond Enquirer*, December 5, 1820.

[12] Ibid.

habitually violent. They threatened White people's security, demanding retribution for past and present injustices. White people could not expect "permanent safety, to persons or property, in the midst of needy and idle vagabonds, who had never known from their birth any law but force, ever impending, indeed in too many cases ever acting somewhere in view!" he emphasized. Indirectly corroborating Jefferson's charges in Query XVIII of *Notes*, Randolph agreed that the master's violence mentally and physically scarred the ex-slave exposed to force or the threat of force, creating a monster obsessed by hatred and a desire for revenge. Randolph concluded that a strong militia was essential to protect Whites from the perpetual menace of free Blacks and slaves.[13]

Ironically, years later, Jefferson's great-grandson, Thomas Jefferson Coolidge, visiting Virginia as a six-year-old, witnessed Governor Randolph's son, abolitionist state legislator Thomas Jefferson Randolph, whip a slave accused of stealing goods, possibly to sell to free Blacks. This brutality outraged young Coolidge's nursemaid, a free Black woman who resided with him and his parents in Boston. Speculating that such cruelty might provoke a slave revolt incited by free Blacks, Coolidge reminisced many years later, "I wonder how indifferent the planters were to the presence of free negroes, who must have caused a very great feeling of discontent among the slaves."[14]

Employing arguments similar to those Jefferson used four years later in writing to Jared Sparks, Randolph pointed out that the "free community" of Haiti was "sufficiently near us to admit of emigration at little cost, and yet separated by a sufficient space of sea, to render the interdiction of return an effective measure." Haiti's president, Jean Pierre Boyer, promised land and jobs for free Blacks, possibly solving Virginia's race problem, Randolph observed. Randolph looked less to the past than to the future: a future in which he hoped only free White people would reside in his state. He proposed that, with Boyer's permission, the United States guarantee Haiti's independence against France and other powers, and "be ready hereafter to interpose its influence, & power if at any time requisite to protect the asylum" Haiti delivered for Southern Blacks.[15] Anticipating a fellow Virginian, President Woodrow Wilson's later doctrine of hemispheric hegemony, he recommended that the national government make Haiti a virtual protectorate.

Emulating Jefferson's earlier statements about Africa's potential as a trade hub, Randolph applied this reasoning to the Haitian experiment. He predicted that the masses of emancipated Virginian Black expatriates would stimulate

---

[13] Ibid. For Query XVIII of *Notes on Virginia*, see Peterson, ed., *Jefferson: Writings*, 288–89.

[14] Coolidge, *Autobiography of T. Jefferson Coolidge*, 2–3.

[15] Governor Randolph to the Speaker of the House of Delegates, December 4, 1820, in *Richmond Enquirer*, December 5, 1820.

native Haitians to prefer US goods, precipitating a revival of trade and "an advantageous commerce with the island in the exchange of our corn, meal, and flour, for their coffee and sugar, to a rapidly increasing amount." As Jefferson had done in letters to Monroe and Sparks, Randolph exaggerated Haiti's political stability, noting that Haitians displayed "facilities for self-government, in a tropical climate, and an insular situation." Hoping that transportation oversea[s]" would eventually be made mandatory for all manumitted slaves, he intended to use the state poll tax on bondspersons to fund his "voluntary" deportation program. He proposed that the state purchase slaves "just arrived to the age of puberty," and twice as many females as males (thereby reducing the reproduction rate).[16]

Although Jefferson's biographers have generally ignored Randolph's proposal, it constituted a radical line of attack on slavery.[17] Alone among Southern governors, Jefferson's son-in-law publicly promoted emancipation and specifically recommended Haiti, which historians usually depict as Southerners' bête noire, as the ideal destination for a colony of free Black exiles.[18] Violating Virginia's states' rights doctrine, Randolph requested help from the United States government in implementing this antislavery project, at that time administered by his and Jefferson's friend, the surprisingly nationalistic Democratic-Republican James Monroe.

In contrast to Jefferson's *Notes*, Randolph charged that African Americans' moral sense was defective. Nonetheless, he speculated that some of their thefts, which deprived Virginians "of the immense advantages for enlightened agriculture, manufactures and commerce, in vain offered by our fertile soil," might have resulted from enslavement's warping of the personality. In any case, he said, their multiple crimes caused the South to lag behind the North in productivity. He lamented, "the want of moral motives and defect of intelligence, the too common absence of settled character, that marks the race degraded by slavery, if not by nature, which supplies so large a majority of the labourers of our state." Because of their natural, "contemptible inefficiency," Black slaves were often employed in

[16] Ibid. For Randolph's failure to pass gradual emancipation legislation through the Virginia legislature, see the brief accounts in Gaines, *Thomas Mann Randolph, Jr.*, 124–26, and Charles S. Sydnor, *The Development of Southern Sectionalism, 1819–1848* (Baton Rouge: Louisiana State University Press, 1948), 96. Jefferson to Monroe, November 24, 1801, in Lipscomb and Bergh, eds., *Writings of Jefferson*, 10:296–98.

[17] Even Dumas Malone's monumental work, *Sage of Monticello*, 381, barely mentions Randolph's proposal. Fawn Brodie's popular biography, *Thomas Jefferson: An Intimate History* (New York: Norton, 1974), 457, also has a few words.

[18] For an example of historians' assumption of the Haitian Revolution's "volcanic" impact on Southern fear of Blacks, see Rothman, *Slave Country*, 22. In general, see Hunt, *Haiti's Influence on Antebellum America*.

servile, ceremonial positions and "unproductive, menial offices," as domestic servants rather than in more useful manufacturing, retarding Southern economic development. Because slaves were incapable of skillful artisanship, Randolph complained, Virginia had to import its finer manufactures ("comforts which refined life requires"). However, he must have known that many of Jefferson's slaves, including members of the Hemings family, were outstanding masons, glaziers, and furniture-makers.[19]

Unlike his son-in-law, Jefferson never directly blamed African warlords for slavery's exportation from Africa to America. Like most American revolutionaries, he preferred to discredit England's Royal African Company, which monopolized the slave trade to the thirteen colonies for much of the colonial period. He also blamed King George III and his Privy Council, who had vetoed numerous laws passed by the Virginia House of Burgesses during the 1760s and early 1770s that prohibited the importation of slaves from overseas. Jefferson's stance was immortalized in his draft of the Declaration of Independence, but he made the point earlier in his *Summary View of the Rights of British-America* (1774). In that precursor of the Declaration, Jefferson denounced the Royal Privy Council's recent veto of several laws the Virginia assembly had passed levying prohibitive duties on slave imports. He stigmatized the Privy Council as the pawn of the powerful Royal African Company. Boldly claiming that "the abolition of domestic slavery is the great object of desire in those colonies, where it was unhappily introduced in their infant state," Jefferson asserted, "But previous to the enfranchisement of the slaves we have, it is necessary to exclude all further importations from Africa." Although, like his son-in-law, he knew that African chieftains profited from the heinous trade and supplied the slaves, he did not hold the Blacks completely responsible. Perhaps he reasoned that warlords possessed a less cultivated "moral sense" than White "Anglo-Saxons" and should therefore bear less blame. Directing his wrath at George III, he argued that the King's veto of Virginia's slave trade prohibition certified that he "preferred the immediate advantages of a few British corsairs to the lasting interests of the American states, and to the rights of human nature, deeply wounded by this infamous practice."[20]

---

[19] Governor Randolph to the Speaker of the House of Delegates, December 4, 1820, in *Richmond Enquirer*, December 5, 1820. Gordon-Reed, *Hemingses of Monticello*, Stanton, *"Those Who Labor,"* and McLoughlin, *Jefferson and Monticello*, have much information on Jefferson's skilled slaves, especially Robert and John Hemings, Burwell Colbert, and Joe Fosset.

[20] Jefferson, *Summary View of the Rights of British-America* (1774), in Peterson, ed., *Jefferson: Writings*, 115–16. Jefferson used the phrase, "British corsairs," which the printer, perhaps seeking to conciliate the King, replaced with "African." Boyd, ed., *Jefferson Papers,* 1:130. Jefferson also blamed the British and George III for the slave trade in *Notes on Virginia* and the *Autobiography*. Peterson, ed., *Jefferson: Writings*, 5 (autobiography), 214 (Query VIII of *Notes*).

Whoever was responsible, Jefferson and his son-in-law agreed that slavery was an evil that hindered the United States' economic growth and more dangerously, its moral purity and reputation abroad as a paradigm of liberty.

ɷ

Nearly fifty years after Jefferson's *Summary View*, English feminist and abolitionist Frances Wright met Jefferson for the first time at Monticello in 1824. She was accompanied by her patron, Jefferson's constant friend from Revolutionary War days, the aging "hero of two worlds," Marquis de Lafayette. Captivated by the author of the Declaration of Independence, she observed that his doughty demeanor belied the effects of a recent severe, debilitating illness that impaired his ability to speak. Only a few weeks before, Jefferson had recovered from an abscess in his jaw that required him to drink liquids through a straw. "Tho' this weakness is painfully evident in the low voice, & occasional languor of the countenance," she wrote admiringly, "his tall well-moulded figure remains erect as at the age of 20, & his step is as light and springy as tho' it could bear him without effort up the steepest sides of his favourite mountains." Jefferson converted Miss Wright to his ideas of Black emancipation and immigration to Haiti. She informed a friend in England that Jefferson told her he wanted to see slavery abolished in Virginia before he died: "Mr. Jefferson is very anxious that some steps which he considers as preparatory to the abolition of slavery at least in this state should be adopted this winter. You will find his plan (that which he proposed, in the Va. Legislature at the time of the revolution) sketched in the *Notes* [Jefferson's book, *Notes on the State of Virginia*]."[21]

Wright's disgust at the racism of many Americans intensified her conviction that Virginia should implement Jefferson's 1780s antislavery project as soon as possible, choosing Haiti as the freedpersons' ultimate destination. "God grant it

---

See also Helo, *Jefferson's Ethics and the Politics of Human Progress*, 42; and David Armitage, *The Declaration of Independence: A Global History* (Cambridge: Harvard University Press, 2007), 58. African chieftains constructed boats to bring slaves to the small forts Whites built along the coastline. European traders purchased them and departed with them in their ships. Indeed, White crewmembers were thrown overboard more often than slaves during the overcrowded Middle Passage, because their bodies were considered less valuable. See Stephen D. Behrendt, "Crew Mortality in the Transatlantic Slave Trade in the Eighteenth Century," *Slavery and Abolition* 18/1 (April 1997): 49–71.

[21] Fanny Wright to Julia Garnett, November 12, 1824, in Cecelia Helena Payne-Gaposchkin, ed., "The Nashoba Plan for Removing the Evil of Slavery: Letters of Frances and Camilla Wright, 1820–1829," *Harvard Library Bulletin* 23/3 (July 1975): 230. Jefferson described his illness in Jefferson to Joseph C. Coolidge, October 24, 1824, in Ford, ed., *Writings of Thomas Jefferson*, 10:323.

be acted upon & that shortly," she wrote. "I am not without hopes that the urgency of the case—the great pressure of the evil upon the industry & prosperity of the country will enforce on the public mind the necessity of a remedy." She was impressed by President Boyer's offer to pay the transportation costs of African Americans wishing to settle in Haiti, an announcement in the newspapers that she learned about from Jonathan Granville, Boyer's envoy. She and Lafayette met Granville in Philadelphia before arriving at Monticello. Echoing Jefferson's ideas, Wright observed, "The near vicinity of Hayti affording a safe & convenient haven for the black population of the U.S. & its President [Haiti's president, Boyer, *not* James Monroe] offering to advance money for its transportation affords great facilities for emancipating gradually the slaves of the South." Borrowing Jefferson's phrase from *Notes on Virginia*, Wright somberly concluded that, in view of the "deeply rooted...prejudice" against Blacks in the "American mind, amalgamation" of the races would occur, if at all, only after great "evils" and "suffering," "including probably a servile war" of slaves against Whites. At the same time, she expected that public indignation at the prospect of "amalgamation" (by which she probably meant interbreeding between Blacks and Whites) would ultimately necessitate government measures for Black emancipation and deportation.[22]

Miss Wright considered Black men physically attractive, pleasant individuals. She enjoyed the company of the handsome mixed-race envoy Jonathan Granville (1785–1839), Boyer's agent to recruit free Blacks for settlement at Port-au-Prince. The Blacks were expected to gradually reimburse Boyer's regime for the cost of transportation to Haiti and gifts of small farms. Granville told her that he had already dispatched four shiploads of Black families to Haiti. The enthusiastic Miss Wright set up an interview between Granville and Lafayette, who treated the "amiable" diplomat with great "affection." "The Haytian Govt. advance the

[22] Fanny Wright to Julia Garnett, 12–14 November 1824, in Cecelia Helena Payne-Gaposchkin, ed., "The Nashoba Plan for Removing the Evil of Slavery: Letters of Frances and Camilla Wright, 1820–1829," *Harvard Library Bulletin* 23/3 (July 1975): 229–31, 230 (quotation). On Frances Wright's abolitionism, feminism, and anticlericalism, see also Bederman, "Revisiting Nashoba," and Lauren Elizabeth Nickas, "Conceiving Happiness: Frances Wright and the Nashoba Experiment," *West Tennessee Historical Society Papers* 61 (2008): 109–21. In 1825, Wright defended miscegenation between consenting adults, but not between masters and slaves. A decade later, she changed her mind and denounced all interracial sexual intercourse as evil in an article in the *Cincinnati Daily Gazette*, February 4, 1836, saying it "violated decency, and brutalized character." In public lectures at that time, she argued that, because Americans considered miscegenation "repulsive," it should be outlawed in the United States (Celia Morris Eckhardt, *Fanny Wright: Rebel in America* [Cambridge: Harvard University Press, 1984], 247, 251).

passage money, lands are apportioned to the emigrants immediately on arrival, the necessary tools are supplied, & the debt is afterwards to be gradually cancelled by the [Black] proprietors," she optimistically reported on the Boyer-Granville "plan" to her friend Julia Garnett in England. "This serves as an incentive to industry & enables the Haytian Govt. to afford the means of transportation to any extent."[23]

Counseling Wright after her departure with Lafayette, Jefferson's intellectual bent for natural history revived. Although, as earlier mentioned, he referred to African Americans as "a race of animals," he did not intend this remark as racist or offensive.[24] Mrs. Wright, who, wishing to demonstrate Black competence, had come to the United States to set up a cooperative farm for free Blacks in Nashoba, Tennessee, did not perceive his comments in that light.

Jefferson aptly concluded his letter to Wright with tentative praise for the Haitian government and the Black settlement in Liberia (also known as Mesurado), financed by the US government and the ACS, commenced in 1822. Concerning African American talents for self-government, he gingerly observed, "The experiment now in progress in St. Domingo [Haiti], those of Sierra Leone and Cape Mesurado, are but beginning. Your proposition has its aspects of promise also." Even should the free-Black Nashoba colony, which Wright hoped to set up in Tennessee, be initially unprofitable, Jefferson assured her, "it may yet, in its developments, lead to happy results." Advising Wright to persevere in her project for Black emancipation, he concluded: "You are young, and have powers of mind which may do much in exciting others in this arduous task."[25] Although wishing her well, he said that age, ill health, and preoccupation with the establishment of the University of Virginia had sapped his already "enfeebled energies."[26] Probably reluctance to get involved in so controversial an experiment had much to do with his public silence as well.

Although it survived from 1825 to 1829, Wright's farm project at Nashoba in western Tennessee, near Memphis, ultimately failed. The seventy-six Black

---

[23] Wright to Garnett, November 14, 1824, in Payne-Gaposchkin, ed., "Nashoba Plan," 231. Perhaps Granville and Wright had exaggerated his success in persuading free Northern Blacks to depart for Haiti. Historian Rayford Logan observes of Granville's efforts, "few Negroes left the United States for Haiti…and many of those had returned as early as March, 1825" (Rayford W. Logan, *Diplomatic Relations of the United States with Haiti, 1776–1891* [Chapel Hill: University of North Carolina Press, 1941], 218).

[24] Jefferson to Miss Frances Wright, August 7, 1825, in Lipscomb and Bergh, eds., *Writings of Jefferson*, 16:120.

[25] Ibid., 120–21.

[26] Jefferson to Frances Wright, August 7, 1825, in Lipscomb and Bergh, eds., *Writings of Jefferson*, 16:121.

freedmen she brought there were unable to make the communal farm function without a greater amount of financial assistance and personal supervision than she was able or willing to provide. Nevertheless, in October 1829, Wright traveled with thirty of the Blacks all the way to Haiti to take advantage of President Jean-Pierre Boyer's offer of free land for African Americans to settle there. Wright remained with her Black associates for six months while they acclimated themselves. She returned to the United States the wife of a French educator and abolitionist, remaining an antislavery activist.[27]

During the last years of his life, Jefferson privately continued to endorse colonization projects for the emancipation of Virginia's slaves and their deportation to the Black Caribbean nation of Haiti after reaching adulthood, "a more accessible asylum" for emancipated slaves than Africa would be.[28] His alacrity in offering unofficial support for Wright's radical Nashoba project of Black self-sufficiency and his assurances about Black capacity for self-rule reveal that in old age his opinion of Blacks was more favorable than derogatory. Although Jefferson had been relatively taciturn about recommending Haiti during the violent monarchical regimes of Dessalines and Christophe, he apparently trusted Boyer's "moral sense" and his "common sense." He advocated fulfilling Boyer's goal of recruiting Blacks from abroad to strengthen his burgeoning nation-state, not fearing that Haiti might encourage slave revolts in the United States or invade its neighbors.[29]

---

[27] On Frances Wright's antislavery activities and her trip to Haiti in 1829, after her Nashoba colony failed, see Hunt, *Haiti's Influence on Antebellum America*, 169–70, and J. Treadwell Davis, "Nashoba: Frances Wright's Experiment in Self-Emancipation," *Southern Quarterly* 11 (October 1972): 63–90.

[28] Jefferson to William Short, September 8, 1823, in Lipscomb and Bergh, eds., *Writings of Jefferson*, 15:469–70. See also Jefferson's letter to Jared Sparks, Massachusetts colonizationist and editor of the *North American Review*, February 4, 1824, in Lipscomb and Bergh, eds., *Writings of Jefferson*, 16:8–14.

[29] See Ada Ferrer, "Haiti, Free Soil, and Antislavery in the Revolutionary Atlantic," *American Historical Review* 117/1 (February 2012): 40–66.

Chapter 16

Jefferson's Late-Life Speculations on the Haitian "Receptacle"

In 1802, Jefferson vacillated between recommending Saint Domingue or the British African colony of Sierra Leone as a possible future site to which Virginia would send slaves convicted of conspiracy and insurrection instead of executing them (as it had done following Gabriel's Rebellion of 1800). His enthusiasm for Haiti was dampened by its recurring wars with invading foreign powers, followed by the ongoing civil war between rival factions of Haitians, which did not finally end until Jean-Pierre Boyer united its northern and southern halves in 1820.[1]

For several years after retiring from the presidency, Jefferson favored the national government financing free Blacks' voluntary emigration to Britain's West African Sierra Leone colony, asserting that they would bring the "seeds of civilization" to the natives and that the Black exodus would be good "for themselves as well as for us." More likely, he was temporarily alienated from supporting Haiti as the best destination because of its constant political turmoil, even after it permanently evicted the French in November 1803 and declared independence a few weeks later. From that point on, things seemed to go downhill, with the new governor-general, Jean-Jacques Dessalines, instituting a harsh dictatorship, ordering the massacre of most of the remaining French Whites, and (probably to Jefferson's distaste) proclaiming himself emperor of Haiti in October 1804. As in 1802, when Jefferson first investigated Sierra Leone as a possible venue to deport insurrectionary slaves, in 1811 he proposed that the government pay off the expense of a voyage there by conducting "mercantile operation[s]" in West Africa, which would profit the US government and reimburse the shippers. He doubted that free Blacks would voluntarily leave the United States for Africa or that newly freed Blacks, manumitted on condition that they depart for a homeland that was foreign to them, would have the enthusiasm to make a success of their

---

[1] Scherr, *Jefferson's Haitian Policy*, 107–10; Jefferson to Governor John Page, December 23, 1803, microfilm reel 29, Jefferson Papers, LC (hdl.loc.gov/loc.mss/mtj.mtjbib013020). Thomas O. Ott, *The Haitian Revolution, 1789–1804* (Knoxville: University of Tennessee Press, 1973), is a useful brief overview of the revolution.

expedition.[2] He apparently took for granted that Blacks would want to remain with their families in the land of their birth, no matter how unjustly it treated them. As late as 1824, Jefferson said that he did not expect all slaves to accept the offer of freedom if as its condition they were forced to leave their homeland. Indeed, he feared that the slaves would rise up against their masters if granted freedom and threatened with deportation. If the Southern states, assisted by the national government, attempted to emancipate and deport all the enslaved, he wrote, "A million and a half [slaves] are within their [White governments'] controul, but 6 millions (which a majority of those [Whites] now living will see them attain) and one million of these fighting men, will say 'we will not go.'"[3]

In any case, the plans during the first years of his presidency for sending a colony of manumitted conspirators to Sierra Leone fell through. In 1803, the British company refused to receive any US Blacks, because those runaway slaves who arrived there after the American Revolution had gained a reputation for violence.[4]

For his part, Jefferson did not perceive these broken rebels as mere criminals. Indeed, he recognized their courage and intelligence, and he surmised that their fellow ex-slaves regarded them as natural leaders and heroes. In July 1802, he wrote to Rufus King, US minister to Great Britain. Urging him to expedite British acquiescence in a slave rebel colony at Sierra Leone, he advised him to persuade them with language similar to that he had used when writing Monroe touting the benefits of "exporting" the rebels to Saint Domingue:

> It is material to observe that they are not felons, or common malefactors, but persons guilty of what the safety of society, under actual circumstances, obliges us to treat as a crime, but which their feelings may represent in a far different shape. They are such as will be a valuable acquisition to the

---

[2] Jefferson to John Lynch, January 21, 1811, in Peterson, ed., *Jefferson: Writings*, 1240 (quotation); Jefferson to Monroe, June 2, 1802, in Ford, ed., *Works of Thomas Jefferson*, 10:375; Jefferson to Dr. Thomas Humphries, February 8, 1817, in Lipscomb and Bergh, eds., *Writings of Jefferson*, 15:102–103.

[3] Jefferson to Jared Sparks, February 4, 1824, microfilm reel 54, Jefferson Papers, LC (hdl.loc.gov/loc.mss/mtj.mtjbib024921); Adam Rothman, "Jefferson and Slavery," in John B. Boles and Randal L. Hall, eds., *Seeing Jefferson Anew: In His Time and Ours* (Charlottesville: University of Virginia Press, 2010), especially 115–20, charges that Jefferson erroneously assumed that emancipated slaves would be intent on revenge against Whites, when they merely desired to live in peace in a land they considered their home.

[4] Egerton, *Gabriel's Rebellion*, 155–60.

settlement already existing there, and well calculated to cooperate in the plan of civilization.[5]

Perhaps naively, Jefferson expected no trouble convincing the British to accept these would-be rebels as settlers in a free African state. Applying his evolving doctrine of cultural relativism, he perceived the obvious: that a society of former slaveholders would regard as evil demons what a society composed entirely of victorious, rebellious slaves, like that of Haiti, would consider comrades-in-arms.[6] Although this was among the most powerful considerations tempting Jefferson to persevere in recommending Haiti as the proper destination for freed slaves over the next twenty years, he needed a different rationale to convince Europe's African colonizers to permit rebellious slaves to inhabit their territory. Therefore, the more Jefferson thought about transporting American Blacks to Africa, the more he stressed that they would redeem White people's sin of slaveholding by teaching "civilization" to African "savages." However, this was a perspective that, because of his doctrine that each culture must advance in freedom and "civilization" (a term he seldom used because of its condescending connotations) at its own pace, he did not really consider valid. Among the reasons he avoided the terms "savagery" and "civilization" was his knowledge that they often served as a rallying cry by which oppressive Christian clergy justified using "fire and fagot," as he called it, to convert alien peoples (and even their own countries' "Jews, Turks, and infidels," as Madison memorably phrased it). Not only was such theological violence an attitude opposed to his belief in cultural autonomy and relativism, it violated the doctrines of religious freedom and freedom of thought and reason that he considered among the most important things in life.[7]

In 1811, Jefferson's Bedford County neighbor John Lynch, a Virginia Quaker abolitionist, revived concepts of savagery and civilization in Jefferson's mind when he informed him that Philadelphia Quaker Anne Mifflin proposed to create a colony of free Blacks in Africa protected jointly by the United States, France, and Great Britain. Their project did not advocate the emancipation of all slaves, and it was essentially a colonizationist, not an abolitionist, venture. Believing that Jefferson's *Idéologue* friends exerted great influence in France, Mrs. Mifflin, widow of Warner Mifflin, one of the greatest Quaker abolitionists, hoped

[5] Jefferson to Rufus King, July 13, 1802, Jefferson Papers, LC.

[6] Although the Blacks residing on Sierra Leone were nominally free, even such leaders of the colony as the famed abolitionist William Wilberforce condoned the use of a form of indentured servitude similar to slavery in order to raise revenue for the Sierra Leone Company (Michael J. Turner, "The Limits of Abolition: Government, Saints, and the 'African Question,' c. 1780–1820," *English Historical Review* 112/446 [April 1997]: 319–57).

[7] Madison to Jefferson, October 17, 1788, in Hutchinson and Rachal, eds., *Papers of James Madison*, 10:297.

that the retired president would secure the French government's assistance for her plan. Unknowingly echoing Jefferson's views, Lynch expected Southern slaveholders would more willingly free their slaves if they thought they would find sanctuary outside the state. Of the link between the African colonization scheme and manumission, Lynch wrote,

> As I presume it must be a gradual work the sooner it is sett [*sic*] on foot the better, and believe if such a Measure was adopted that many would be willing to give up their Slaves that now hold them, and there are many at this time in our State that has [*sic*] already been emancipated, so that best pollicy [*sic*] seems to require it either on the coast of Africa or somewhere Else that may be deemed more proper and convenient.[8]

Replying to Lynch's letter a few weeks later, Jefferson emphasized the "civilizing" benefits of a Black colony in Africa. He nonetheless informed him that while Jamaican rebels (Maroons) deported to Sierra Leone had become diligent and cooperative workers, US slaves who had escaped there after the American Revolution were reportedly insubordinate. Now safely retired from public life, Jefferson voiced the radical hope that the United States government would set up a public "establishment on the coast of Africa," instead of merely authorizing the creation of a private philanthropic colony by Philadelphia Quaker Anne Mifflin.[9]

Seemingly enthusiastic about the Lynch-Mifflin plan of colonizing "the people of color of these States" in Africa "under the supervision of different [European] governments," Jefferson claimed he had long "thought it the most desirable measure which could be adopted, for gradually drawing off" the entire Southern Black population, "most advantageously for themselves as well as for us." The emigrating Blacks, in departing from the United States, "a country possessing all the useful arts," would represent Western civilization. By "transplanting" White culture "among the inhabitants of Africa," Jefferson argued, the ex-slaves would contribute to "render their sojournment and sufferings here a blessing in the end to that country [*sic*]."[10] Thus, Jefferson thought that Blacks, in both Africa and the American South, were capable of imbibing European culture and knowledge, and conveying it to other Africans.

Confident that the US government would at least rhetorically defend a projected African state against European aggressors, Jefferson viewed such a settlement by former Southern slaves as beneficial to the entire United States, "an

[8] John Lynch to Jefferson, December 25, 1810, microfilm reel 44, Jefferson Papers, LC (hdl.loc.gov/loc.mss/mtj.mtjbib020466).

[9] Jefferson to John Lynch, January 21, 1811, in Slaughter, *Virginian History of African Colonization*, 7–8.

[10] Jefferson to John Lynch, January 21, 1811, in Ford, ed., *Works of Thomas Jefferson*, 11:178–81, 178 (quotation).

object so benevolent in itself, and so important to a great portion of its constituents." Seeking a new source of trade for his harried republic at a time when warring Britain and France harassed America's North Atlantic commerce, Jefferson anticipated that an African colony run by the US government would ultimately furnish an outlet for American goods. Relegating the importance of "civilization" to the background, he put US commerce first. He wanted the United States to establish its own colony, perhaps a prototype of later Liberia. "Exclusive of motives of humanity, the commercial advantages to be derived from it might repay all its expenses," he pointed out. However, he doubted that public opinion possessed the foresight to support such an initially expensive endeavor. He was also skeptical that the Blacks would willingly immigrate to Africa, and pessimistic that, lacking political experience and recently brutalized by slavery, they could set up an enduring democratic government. As he put it, "It may perhaps be doubted whether many of these people would voluntarily consent to such an exchange of situation, and very certain that few of those advanced to a certain age in habits of slavery, would be capable of self-government."[11]

As in *Notes on Virginia* thirty years earlier, Jefferson ascribed Blacks' alleged moral or political shortcomings (as opposed to their supposed intellectual limitations) to their enslaved condition—environment—rather than innate mental or emotional deficiencies. Although he feared that White "prejudices" might hinder the project of a tax-supported colony of Blacks abroad, Jefferson remained "prudently cautious" about the future.[12] He remained optimistic at least in part because, especially in old age, he grew increasingly tolerant of socio-cultural diversity. His appreciation of the influence of society and government in molding the diverse aspects of human nature and social norms—what he called "utility"—and defining morally optimal political behavior in different cultures and societies, led him to consider such concepts as the "moral sense" and political democracy itself as culturally relative, although ideally the summum bonum for every people. He may even have condoned a free Black dictatorship for West Africa, similar to that existing in Haiti.[13]

A few years later, another of Jefferson's western Virginia Quaker neighbors, Dr. Thomas Humphreys of Lynchburg in Campbell County, also sought his

[11] Ibid., 180.

[12] Jefferson to Lynch, January 21, 1811, ibid., 181 (I have modified the tense of the quotation without changing the meaning).

[13] See Jefferson to Thomas Law, June 13, 1814, and Jefferson to Pierre Samuel Du Pont de Nemours, April 24, 1816, for examples of Jefferson's growing, albeit regretful, resignation to anti-Enlightenment political trends. Perhaps his acceptance was merely a sign of old age and approaching death. He constantly harped on that theme in his letters as early as 1796. See Jefferson to Philip Mazzei, April 24, 1796, in Peterson, ed., *Jefferson: Writings*, 1037.

endorsement for a plan of gradual emancipation. Of Scottish ancestry and an early settler of Lynchburg, Humphreys was a medical doctor and apothecary. He owned one slave.[14] Humphreys sent Jefferson a petition he addressed to the US House of Representatives recommending all slaves' gradual emancipation, followed by their mandatory deportation to West Africa. John Taylor of Caroline's work, *Arator* (published in book form in 1813), may have influenced his proposal, although Taylor confined his plan to already-free Blacks, whom he desired to exile from Virginia, fearing that they inspired slave revolts. Taylor would have arranged for the Southern state governments to purchase public lands from the US government and grant them gratis to the free Blacks, thus combining the carrot and the stick. If free Blacks refused to settle on the public lands, Taylor said, they would be forced to leave the state anyway.[15]

Humphreys voiced "astonishment" at the conundrum the Southern states presented. Their "enlightened" and "polished" White inhabitants stood in the forefront of modernity in politics, agriculture, literature, commerce, and military and naval expertise. Although seemingly attached to "pure and rational republican principles" for themselves, they simultaneously retained in slavery a million of their "African brethren," "tyrannically traded and trafficked for" in the Dark Continent, "like the beasts of the field." Humphreys insisted that slavery violated the Bill of Rights, the constitutions of the United States and of the individual states, and was "in immediate opposition, to the Fundamental principles, of the Government." He expressed contempt for his White Southern fellow citizens, who, "basking themselves, in the full meridian Blaze of Liberty, and Independence," embraced "the horrid scene of Cruelty and Injustice" they inflicted on Black slaves. As a "degraded part of the country," Humphreys charged, the South did not deserve to "boast" of its "republicanism" and "patriotism," its pretensions to "liberty, equality, and the rights of man." His fellow Virginians were "political hypocrites, and greater Tyrants than the Dey of Algiers, Tripoli, or any other eastern Despots." Mimicking Query XVIII of Jefferson's *Notes on Virginia*, he insisted that, "the effects which slavery had, on the Morals, the Manners, the virtue, the Industry, and Economy of the Inhabitants of the country, in which it is tolerated, merits [*sic*] the highest consideration; But to do Justice to this Subject, would require a volume in which to discuss it." In the states that abolished slavery, he said, the White inhabitants were "generally more virtuous, more sober, more industrious & more attentive to their professional pursuits," accumulated more

---

[14] [The Oldest Inhabitant], *Sketches and Recollections of Lynchburg* (Richmond: C. H. Wynne, 1858), 298–301.

[15] Thomas [misidentified as Reuben] Humphreys to Jefferson, January 1, 1817, microfilm reel 49, Jefferson Papers, LC (hdl.loc.gov/loc.mss/mtj.mtjbib022700). For Taylor's proposal to deport all free Blacks to the public lands, see Taylor, *Arator*, 50.

money, had fewer debts, happier marriages, and greater "peace of mind" than in the slave South. If the Southern states abolished slavery, Humphreys predicted, landholders would sell or lease their large plantations, thereby happily spreading land ownership among the "poorer classes" and increasing the number of landowners. By renting or selling his land, or hiring free laborers to work it, the plantation owner would become wealthier than if he remained a slave owner. Though the agricultural practices accompanying slavery wore out the land, Humphreys predicted that cultivation by free tenants and laborers would promote scientific agricultural techniques and restore nutrients to the soil.[16]

Contending that it was Congress's responsibility to undertake full-scale national emancipation, Humphreys proposed that it begin the annual liberation and deportation of one-tenth of the slave population. His plan envisaged delivering the slaves to a US "commissioner" at the seaports, who would pay the owners for their liberty. The United States government would appoint individuals chosen by the states' congressional delegations to assess the slaves' value, including slave children, by "grades." Exposing his plan's harshness, which unlike anything Jefferson ever suggested included the forced deportation of currently-free Blacks, Humphreys's directive contained the proviso that, "All the free people of colour shall also in like manner be sent off, and that in the course of the first, and second years" of the program's operation. He cruelly sought the exile of free Blacks as well as slaves, intending all African Americans, "bond and free," to be "disposed of" through deportation to Africa. The free Blacks "shall be paid, each, the sum of 20 dollars and shall participate in all the Benefits, and emoluments, in transportation, and settlement, as the slaves themselves, also in provisions, Tools &c."[17]

Detecting Humphreys's strident tone, Jefferson's reply forbore praising Black "civilization" and intelligence. This was unlike his earlier letter to Lynch. He professed enthusiasm about Humphreys's "leading principles of gradual emancipation, of establishment on the coast of Africa, and the patronage of our nation until the emigrants shall be able to protect themselves," which in fact mimicked his plan in *Notes*. For the first time, Jefferson implied that he might favor an American military presence in the African settlement, with "the subordinate details" arranged later. As in his letter to Tucker in 1797, which noted Northern hostility to the Southern states, Jefferson was pessimistic about Northerners' willingness to cooperate in a plan of Black emancipation, expecting they would reject

[16] Dr. Thomas Humphreys to Jefferson, January 1, 1817, Jefferson Papers, LC, enclosing a petition to the U.S. House of Representatives for the gradual abolition of slavery, images 759–64.

[17] Ibid.

bearing part of the financial burden of compensating masters. "The bare proposition of purchase by the United States generally, would excite infinite indignation in all the States north of Maryland," he predicted. "The sacrifice must fall on the States alone which hold them; and the difficult question will be how to lessen this so as to reconcile our fellow citizens to it."[18] Expecting emancipation to be solely a Southern project, Jefferson thought Virginians would bear the burden more gracefully if it involved as little additional taxation as possible.

Insisting on his own humanity and moral sense, Jefferson assured the Quaker of his willingness to bear the financial loss involved in freeing his slaves and permitting their deportation. (He failed to mention that, under current Virginia law, as a debtor, he could not free his slaves, who, after confiscation by his creditors, would probably be worse off than they were under his relatively benevolent despotism.) "Personally I am ready and desirous to make any sacrifice which shall insure their [the slaves'] gradual but complete retirement from the State, and effectually, at the same time, establish them elsewhere in freedom and safety," he asserted. However, he doubted that other White Virginians, especially the young, were equally virtuous. "But I have not perceived the growth of this disposition in the rising generation, of which I once had sanguine hopes," he confessed.[19]

His disappointment with the "rising generation's" indifference toward abolition and "transportation" of the entire slave population must have been profound. In 1785, over thirty years earlier, he had published the antislavery text of *Notes on Virginia* in France, in the original English. He ordered two hundred

[18] Jefferson to Dr. Thomas Humphreys, February 8, 1817, in Ford, ed., *Writings of Thomas Jefferson*, 10:76.

[19] Ibid. See "An Act to Reduce into one, the several acts concerning slaves, free negroes, and mulattoes," passed December 17, 1792, in Shepherd, ed., *Statutes at Large of Virginia*, 1:127–28. Like the original 1782 law, the 1792 act permitted owners to emancipate slaves by deeds or wills, but "all slaves so emancipated, shall be liable to be taken by execution, to satisfy any debt contracted by the person emancipating them before such emancipation is made." The legislature first legalized private manumissions, without requiring prior consent of the legislature or the governor, in 1782. The act passed at the May 1782 session authorized a slaveholder, "by his or her last will and testament, or by any other instrument in writing," to emancipate his slaves. It simultaneously authorized "all and every person and persons, bodies politic or corporate, and their heirs and successors, other than the person or persons claiming under those so emancipating their slaves [i.e., the slaveholder and his family], all such right and title as they or any of them could or might claim if this act had never been made." The 1782 and the 1792 acts thereby prohibited debtors from liberating their slaves. "An act to authorize the manumission of slaves" passed at May 1782 session of legislature, in Hening, ed., *Statutes at Large*, 11:39–40. See the excellent general discussion in Benjamin Klebaner, "American Manumission Laws and the Responsibility for Supporting Slaves," *Virginia Magazine of History and Biography* 63/4 (October 1955): 443–53.

copies printed, intending to send them gratis to the students at the College of William and Mary to stimulate their opposition to human bondage. Dissuaded from this bold action by his friends, who thought it might alienate the students' parents and the college administration, he ended up distributing them to friends and acquaintances, and even total strangers, some prominent, some not.[20] He apparently expected the students to support his liberal sentiments. If his friends convinced him that his arguments would not arouse fierce opposition, he confided to the Marquis de Chastellux in June 1785, "I have printed and reserved just copies enough to be able to give one to every young man at the College. It is to them I look, to the *rising generation*, and not to the one now in power for these great reformations."[21] Thirty-two years later, he used the same phrase, "rising generation," regretfully, as if remembering the unwarranted optimism he had felt in the past.

During the 1780s, he professed hesitation to publish *Notes* in the United States, fearing that his controversial statements opposing slavery and urging democratic reform in Virginia's constitution would have a reverse effect, making them (and him) unpopular. "It is possible that in my own country these strictures might produce an irritation which would indispose the people towards the two great objects I have in view, that is the emancipation of their slaves, and the settlement of their constitution on a firmer and more permanent basis," he wrote Chastellux. However, Jefferson must have known that the book's contents would leak and emerge in the US, since he had already published and distributed numerous copies to people in Virginia and Europe. According to the most careful students of *Notes*, Dustin Gish and Daniel Klinghard, he was merely awaiting the right time to publish it at home. Indeed, he contemplated sending free copies to all the students at the College of William and Mary, hardly a way to keep his ideas secret.[22]

At this time, he was conversant with and enthusiastic about the progress of the newly formed American Colonization Society (ACS), founded in 1816 by Charles Fenton Mercer of Virginia, Henry Clay, and other mildly antislavery Southerners. (He was probably unaware that his correspondence with Monroe in 1801 had inspired Mercer, who stumbled upon their letters, to create the organization.) "Perhaps the proposition now on the carpet at Washington to provide

---

[20] See, for instance, Jefferson to Richard Price, August 7, 1785, in Boyd et al., eds., *Papers of Thomas Jefferson*, 8:356, and Jefferson to G. Clerici, August 15, 1787, in ibid., 12:39.

[21] Jefferson to Marquis de Chastellux, June 1, 1785, in Boyd et al., eds., *Papers of Thomas Jefferson*, 8:184. My italics.

[22] Ibid.; Dustin Gish and Daniel Klinghard, *Thomas Jefferson and the Science of Republican Government: A Political Biography of Notes on the State of Virginia* (Cambridge: Cambridge University Press, 2017). See also Noble E. Cunningham, Jr., *In Pursuit of Reason: The Life of Thomas Jefferson* (Baton Rouge: Louisiana State University Press, 1987), 94–96.

an establishment on the coast of Africa for voluntary emigrations of people of color, may be the corner stone of the future edifice," he wrote Humphreys, alluding to the ACS's lobbying for congressional funding for its colony of freedmen, Liberia (called Mesurado at this time). Although he "prayed for its completion as early as may most promote the good of all," he doubted that Black bondage would end "in my day." He believed, though, that eventually "the day will come, equally desirable and welcome to us as to them."[23]

Paradoxically, Jefferson's expressions of good will toward Blacks during his lifetime accelerated after Haiti's bloody, successful war for independence. As early as 1786, five years before the revolt began, Jefferson, now US minister in Paris, regretted that he, George Wythe, and other Virginia burgesses had failed to pass an act abolishing slavery immediately after the American Revolution. Like Washington, Patrick Henry, and other critics of slavery at the time, he excused their inaction on the grounds of anticipated public opposition. He wrote to the anti-slavery tutor of King Louis XVI's son, "They saw that the moment of doing it with success was not yet arrived, and that an unsuccessful effort, as too often happens, would only rivet still closer the chains of bondage, and retard the moment of delivery to this oppressed description of men." Although Jefferson used this excuse for the rest of his life, blaming others' opposition for his inaction, he made clear that he sympathized with the slaves as an "oppressed description of men," rather than implying that they deserved enslavement because of some innate inferiority or cowardice.[24]

During his retirement from the presidency, Jefferson, as in writing Monroe in 1801, continued to render tentative support to the Haitian Revolution. Ignoring Dessalines's massacre of Whites in 1804, he hoped Haiti would establish a government in which the ex-slaves were happy and peaceful. Shortly after leaving office, Jefferson wrote to his old friend, the Connecticut wit and fervid

---

[23] Jefferson to Humphreys, February 8, 1817, in Ford, ed., *Writings of Thomas Jefferson*, 10:76–77. On the beginnings of the American Colonization Society, whose goal was primarily to deport already-freed Blacks to Africa rather than to agitate for gradual emancipation of all slaves, see Douglas R. Egerton, "'Its Origin Is Not a Little Curious': A New Look at the American Colonization Society," *Journal of the Early Republic* 5 (1985): 463–80; Egerton, "Averting a Crisis: The Proslavery Critique of the American Colonization Society," *Civil War History* 43/2 (June 1997): 142–56, and George M. Fredrickson, *The Black Image in the White Mind: The Debate on Afro-American Character and Destiny, 1817–1964* (New York: Harper & Row, 1971).

[24] Jefferson to Jean Nicholas Démeunier, June 26, 1786, in Boyd et al., eds., *Papers of Thomas Jefferson*, 10:63. For a provocative study that argues that Jefferson and other Founding Fathers believed that slaves were unworthy of liberty in failing to exhibit an inherent love for freedom through perpetual acts of revolt, see François Furstenberg, "Beyond Freedom and Slavery: Autonomy, Virtue, and Resistance in Early American Political Discourse," *Journal of American History* 89/4 (March 2003): 1295–318, and his book, *In the Name of the Father*, 207.

revolutionary Joel Barlow, that he considered Haiti's fate the barometer of African American capability for self-government. Perhaps he had in mind President Alexandre Pétion's benevolent dictatorship in southern Haiti (1807–1818), which had set up a system of small subsistence farms for Haitian soldiers, rather than Henry Christophe's militaristic monarchy in the north. He minimized Haiti's cacophony of bloody civil wars, "empires" and dictatorship. While admitting that he did not concur with the abolitionist French bishop Henri Grégoire on Black intellectual equality in "grade of understanding" with Whites, his letter to the bishop, who had praised Pétion's government in southern Haiti as an inchoate republic, expounded doctrines of cultural relativism and appreciation for diversity. As in *Notes on Virginia*, which Grégoire criticized for implying Blacks' intellectual inferiority, Jefferson expressed willingness to be convinced of Black intellectual parity with Whites. Acknowledging the persecution and racial discrimination Blacks suffered, even as free persons, he explained to Grégoire that his "doubts" about Black intelligence were "the result of personal observation on the limited sphere of my own State, where the opportunities for the development of their genius were not favorable, and those of exercising it still less so. I expressed them therefore with great hesitation."[25] Thus, Jefferson suggested that, were African Americans placed in freedom in an environment that encouraged their artistic and scientific learning, their intellectual prowess would manifest itself.

On the other hand, Jefferson informed Barlow at this time that a letter to him in 1791 from Benjamin Banneker, a free Maryland Black with an eminent reputation as a mathematician and almanac-maker, praised in Grégoire's book, "shows him to have had a mind of very common stature indeed." (Banneker's letter to Jefferson was not a mathematical treatise, but a politically oriented document criticizing Jefferson and other politicians for failing to abolish slavery, which may have annoyed Jefferson.) Insisting that his tentative remarks on Black inferiority in Query XIV evinced open-mindedness, not racial prejudice, and overlooking its array of disparaging comments about Blacks, Jefferson asserted, "It was impossible for doubt [about Black intellectual equality with Whites] to have been more tenderly or hesitatingly expressed than that was in the *Notes on*

[25] Jefferson to Abbé Henri Grégoire, February 25, 1809, in Ford, ed., *Works of Thomas Jefferson*, 11:99–100, quoted in Richard K. Matthews, *The Radical Politics of Thomas Jefferson: A Revisionist View* (Lawrence: University of Kansas Press, 1984), 70; Jefferson to Joel Barlow, October 8, 1809, in Ford, ed., *Works of Thomas Jefferson*, 11:121.

Virginia, and nothing was or is farther from my intentions, than to enlist myself as the champion of a fixed opinion, where I have only expressed a doubt."[26]

Writing to Barlow, a friend without political influence, the elderly Jefferson, who certainly lacked political ambitions by this time, voiced what must have been his sincere belief. Even more surprising than his insistence that he had not suggested Black inferiority in *Notes*, he speculated that the new Haitian state might eventually prove Blacks' intellectual equality, concluding, "St. Domingo will, in time, throw light on the question."[27]

Two years before his death, in a remarkably revealing letter about his view of slavery and its connection with Black equality and morality generally, Jefferson attempted to combine his environmentalist-relativist and Enlightenment-universalist perspectives on human nature. In February 1824, writing to Jared Sparks, a Unitarian minister, historian, and president of Harvard College, Jefferson unburdened himself. He elaborated on their mutual concern with Black emancipation and deportation to Africa, which Sparks, an avid colonizationist who dreamed of visiting the continent, strongly supported. Sparks, who advocated the American Colonization Society's efforts in his prestigious magazine, *The North American Review*, had strong racial prejudices. In an article in the January 1824 issue of his magazine titled "The Colonization Society, or the Advantages and Practicability of Colonization in Africa," written after traveling widely through the South and sent to Jefferson, Sparks asserted that it was unwise, even impossible, for Southerners to retain free Blacks with equal civil rights in their society. "No dream can be more wild than that of emancipating slaves who are still to remain among us free," the Boston Brahmin declared. "We unhesitatingly express it as our belief—and we speak from some experience—that the free people of color as a class in the slaveholding States are a great nuisance to society, more comfortless, tempted to more vices, and actually less qualified to enjoy existence, than the slaves themselves."[28]

---

[26] Jefferson to Joel Barlow, October 8, 1809, in Ford, ed., *Works of Thomas Jefferson*, 11:121; Benjamin Banneker to Thomas Jefferson, August 19, 1791, in Boyd et al., eds., *Papers of Thomas Jefferson*, 22:49–54.

[27] Jefferson to Joel Barlow, October 8, 1809, in Ford, ed., *Works of Thomas Jefferson*, 11:121.

[28] Jared Sparks to Jefferson, January 13, 1824, microfilm reel 54, Jefferson Papers, LC (hdl.loc.gov/loc.mss/mtj.mtjbib024847); Sparks, "The Sixth Annual Report of the American Society for Colonizing the Free People of Color of the U. S.; with an Appendix," *North American Review* 18 (1824), 40–91, 41; "The Colonization Society," in Herbert Baxter Adams, *The Life and Writings of Jared Sparks, Comprising Selections from his Journals and Correspondence*, 2 vols. (Boston: Houghton, Mifflin and Company, 1893), 1:247–48 (quotation). For more on Sparks's support for African colonization, see ibid., 248–51, 257–58. See also John Hammond

By contrast, Jefferson held to a residual belief that there potentially existed a uniform human nature accessible to all humankind, which statesmen were responsible for cultivating. Pityingly describing Southern Black slaves as "these unfortunate people," Jefferson lukewarmly supported Whites' efforts to colonize freed slaves in African regions like Sierra Leone and Mesurado (Liberia) as possibly fulfilling the "rational objectives" he had in view. Reiterating what he had told Lynch and others years before, he suggested that, if these White-organized settlements of freed Blacks successfully "introduce[d] among the aborigines [African natives] the arts of cultivated life, and the blessings of civilization and science," their philanthropic undertakings "may make...some retribution for the long course of injuries we have been committing on their population." Because, for Jefferson, posterity embodied the secular equivalent of immortality, he optimistically concluded that, by perpetuating the "blessings" of civilization in Africa, Whites "shall in the long run have rendered them more good than evil." The ACS differed from religious organizations such as the Roman Catholic Jesuits and Lyman Beecher and Jedidiah Morse's Congregationalist/Presbyterian missionary societies, which, he disgustedly observed, imposed Christianity on foreign nations. "The [American] colonization society is to be considered as a missionary society, having in view, however, objects more humane, justifiable, and less aggressive on the peace of other nations, than the others of that appellation," he reasoned.[29]

Indulging in concrete speculations of national self-interest, Jefferson admitted that Black colonization of Africa was "interesting" (i.e., important) to Whites. It would improve "our physical and moral characters, our happiness and safety," by providing "an asylum" for Blacks and gradually eliminating their presence among White Americans. Alluding to recent congressional appropriations for the ACS made at President Monroe's recommendation, he predicted that the

---

Moore's articles on Sparks's Southern travels, which include excerpts from his journals: "Jared Sparks Visits South Carolina," *South Carolina Historical Magazine* 72 (1971): 150–60; "Jared Sparks in North Carolina," *North Carolina Historical Review* 40 (1963): 285–94; "Jared Sparks in Georgia, April 1826," *Georgia Historical Quarterly* 47 (1963): 425–35; and "Jared Sparks Visits Harper's Ferry, 1819," *West Virginia History* 25 (1964): 81–91.

[29] Jefferson to Jared Sparks, February 4, 1824, in Lipscomb and Bergh, eds., *Writings of Jefferson*, 16:8–13. For Jefferson's hostility to evangelical missions, see also Jefferson to John Adams, November 25, 1816, in Cappon, ed., *Adams-Jefferson Letters* (1988), 496, and Jefferson to Michael Megear, May 29, 1823, in Lipscomb and Bergh, eds., *Writings of Jefferson*, 15:433–34. On the Enlightenment idea that one's fame in the eyes of posterity constituted a secular version of the Christian afterlife, see Carl L. Becker, *The Heavenly City of the Eighteenth-Century Philosophers* (Cambridge: Harvard University Press, 1926), and Peter Gay, *Voltaire's Politics: The Poet as Realist* (Princeton: Princeton University Press, 1959).

national government would help "establish them [the free Blacks] under our patronage and protection, as a separate, free and independent people." Despite his insistence on exiling Blacks from the United States, he maintained that the freed slaves deserved to live in a vicinity "friendly to human life and happiness." Implying that his own preferences deserved universal adoption, Jefferson asserted that, unlike Sparks and the ACS, he opposed an African locale for the Black exodus: "That any place on the coast of Africa should answer the latter purpose [for 'human life and happiness'], I have ever deemed entirely impossible."[30] He expected that most African Americans would not want to return to their Mother Continent, probably because of its unpleasant climate, its Black inhabitants' perennial practice of slavery, and their violent tribal warfare.

Nevertheless, Jefferson had not abandoned the idea of Black deportation and colonization abroad. He considered it of secondary importance that the Blacks from what we now call the "diaspora" return to Africa, replenishing the unpopular colonies of Sierra Leone and Mesurado (which had attracted few free Black immigrants). He opposed their likely leading lives of misery there. For him, African American happiness, in the neighborhood of the United States but not *within* the United States, was of some importance. If the freed slaves were happy where they were sent, they would not want to return to an American South that had enslaved and discriminated against them, and possibly create renewed unrest in the United States. Black "happiness," an outcome beneficial for all, would assuage the consciences of would-be ex- slaveholders like Jefferson and his descendants. As he put it, "The second object [after mass emancipation], and most interesting to us, as coming home to our physical and moral characters, to our happiness and safety, is to provide an asylum to which we can, by degrees, send the whole of that [enslaved] population from among us, and establish them under our patronage and protection, as a separate, free and independent people, in some country and climate friendly to human life and happiness."[31] For Jefferson, this African American Garden of Eden was Haiti.

Weighing fiscal and eudemonic considerations, Jefferson explained to Sparks that the transportation of freed slaves to Africa, if attempted by Southern state governments, would be prohibitively expensive, especially after his calculation that the Black slave population would double from 1.5 million to 3 million

[30] Jefferson to Sparks, February 4, 1824, in Lipscomb and Bergh, eds., *Writings of Jefferson*, 16:10. Under the terms of the Slave Trade Act of 1819, introduced by President Monroe's friend Charles Fenton Mercer and supported by his administration, Congress provided annual appropriations for the ACS on the assumption that slaves illegally imported to the United States would be sent to Liberia (Burin, *Slavery and the Peculiar Solution*, 14–15).

[31] Jefferson to Jared Sparks, February 4, 1824, in Ford, ed., *Works of Thomas Jefferson*, 12:334–35.

within twenty-five years. Although at this time he usually labeled the slaves as "*people* of color" (my italics), thereby attesting their humanity, he was acutely aware that they were human *property*, which he held in substantial numbers, whose owners, whatever their circumstances, theoretically deserved compensation if compulsory emancipation was undertaken. As he actuarially pointed out, "Their estimated value, as property, in the first place (for actual property has been lawfully vested in that form, and who can lawfully take it from the possessors?) at an average of two hundred dollars each, young and old, would amount to six hundred millions of dollars, which must be paid or lost by somebody."[32]

However, for Jefferson, in this matter moral considerations took priority over practical financial ones, even though one basis for his republic's existence was property's sanctity, as a precondition for "the pursuit of happiness." He proposed that the state or national government confiscate slave owners' newborn slaves before masters could complain about their lost "investment." The government would then raise them as wards of the state and deport them to Haiti when they reached adolescence or young adulthood.[33]

In one of his last letters, written to his friend William Short in January 1826, Jefferson, with less than six months to live, reaffirmed his adherence to deporting US African Americans to the nearby Black "republic" of Haiti. There they could live, for the first time in modern Western history, under a government ruled by men of their own race. Alluding to a book Short sent him praising Russian serfdom, Jefferson opined that African Americans, as free men under their own government in Haiti, would be happier than Russia's serfs who, apart from being tied to the land (an odious kind of security) and consequently deprived of all social and indeed physical mobility, were slaves. "On the subject of [Black] emancipation I have ceased to think because not to be a work of my day," he wrote, revealing the consistency of his thought over thirty years in giving independent Haiti his imprimatur. "The plan of converting the blacks into Serfs would certainly be better than keeping them in their present condition, but I consider that of expatriation to the governments of the West Indies of their own colour as entirely practicable, and greatly preferable to the mixture of colour here. To this I have great aversion."[34]

---

[32] Jefferson to Sparks, February 4, 1824, in Lipscomb and Bergh, eds., *Writings of Jefferson*, 16:10. In general, see Fladeland, "Compensated Emancipation: A Rejected Alternative," 169–86.

[33] Jefferson to Sparks, February 4, 1824, in Lipscomb and Bergh, eds., *Writings of Jefferson*, 16:10.

[34] Jefferson to William Short, January 18, 1826, Jefferson Papers, LC.

From the outset of the Black revolution, Jefferson, to a greater extent than his political colleagues, accepted Haiti's legitimacy and legality as a fait accompli.[35] His program for the government's deportation to Haiti of slaves emancipated en masse over dozens of years, until bondage no longer existed in the United States, was patently impossible without diplomatic recognition of the Caribbean regime. In old age, he stressed this factor in conversing with Samuel Whitcomb, a radical Boston bookseller, later a founder of the Massachusetts Workingman's Party, who visited him at Monticello in May 1824. He interviewed Jefferson on diverse aspects of his political and religious credo. Whitcomb recorded that Jefferson, despite reiterating stereotypes about African Americans he had held ever since writing *Notes on Virginia*, both favorable and unfavorable, recommended emancipating and deporting the South's slaves to Haiti and recognizing its government:

> [He] says the south agrees with the Negroes best—that the experiment now making at Hayti is very interesting. He hopes well of their minds though [he] has never seen evidence of genius among them, but they are possessed of the best hearts of any people in the world. Great levity of character, etc. On account of the prejudice of our Nation against the black, he would defer treating with haytians [*sic*] so long as possible, but we must certainly acknowledge their independence.[36]

In 1823, the year before Whitcomb's visit, Jefferson expressed approval of President Jean-Pierre Boyer's mixed-race-controlled Haitian regime. At that time, in another letter to Short, who had not returned to Virginia partly because of his disgust with slavery, he again advocated Black emigration from the US to Haiti. He regretted that, for centuries, the "heteromorph peculiarities of that race" (Blacks' physical and mental differences from Whites, and their apparently more primitive West African civilization) encouraged malevolent Whites to inflict upon them the "hideous blot" of New World slavery. Instead of relying on "the moral necessity which constrains the free laborer to work equally hard," Whites abused their monopoly of power, employing brutal, "physical compulsion" to force Blacks to labor as unpaid slaves. Perhaps too optimistically, Jefferson observed that Virginia's "only blot is becoming less offensive by the great improvement in the condition and civilization of that race, who can now more advantageously compare their situation with that of the laborers of Europe." He was sure that, once permitted the freedom to fend for themselves, enslaved Blacks

[35] Jefferson to Lafayette, June 16, 1792, in Peterson, ed., *Jefferson: Writings*, 991.

[36] Samuel Whitcomb, "Notes on an Interview with Thomas Jefferson May 31, 1824" (manuscript and typescript), reel 9, Thomas Jefferson Papers, University of Virginia. Original owned by Frederick W. Wead.

would become diligent free workers. Rejecting Blacks' unjustified reputation for indolence, he expected the "desperate" situation of slavery to eventually be "redeemed" by liberating the slaves to embark on their own quest for the good life. He insisted on behalf of Virginians, that, "we feel & deplore it [slavery] morally and politically, and we look without entire despair to some redeeming means not yet specifically foreseen. I am happy in believing that the conviction of the necessity of removing this evil gains ground with time." Favorably appraising Missouri and Haiti as locales that inadvertently advanced the abolitionist goal, he ended his letter to Short, "Their [slaves'] emigration to the Westward lightens the difficulty of dividing it [the fiscal burden of abolition] and renders it more practicable on the whole. And the neighborhood of a government of their colour promises a more accessible asylum than that from whence they came."[37]

In this letter to his old friend and protégé, Jefferson summarized his vision of human bondage's demise. Abolition would be accomplished by reducing the number of large slaveholders in Virginia once planters left for Missouri, and in greater numbers, for Louisiana, Mississippi, and other "westward" points, conjoined with the indispensable requirement that Haiti would eventually provide a haven for the liberated Blacks. Jefferson looked to Haiti as their sanctuary. This was despite its dictatorship's incompatibility with American republicanism, its Black citizens legal condition of being tied to the land like serfs (although they generally disobeyed that directive, the "Code Rural," proclaimed by President Boyer), the glaring reality that its government was run by non-Whites, and Whites' prohibition from settling on the island. Jefferson's support of diplomatic relations with Haiti was especially paradoxical and contrary to that of the US government. Neither the United States during the presidency of his successors Madison, Monroe, and John Quincy Adams nor any other country had yet sent diplomatic representatives to Haiti or recognized its independence from France.[38] The *real* Jefferson's desire to fortify Haiti's existence by sending millions of freed slaves there, and in the process recognizing its government, in its time an international pariah, likewise deserves recognition.

---

[37] Jefferson to Short, September 8, 1823, in Lipscomb and Bergh, eds., *Writings of Jefferson*, 15:469–70.

[38] Fehrenbacher, *Slaveholding Republic*, 114–17; Robert L. Stein, "From Saint-Domingue to Haiti, 1804–1825," *Journal of Caribbean History* 19/2 (November 1984): 189–226; Jean-François Brière, *Haiti et La France, 1804–1848: Le Rêve Brisé* (Paris: Karthala, 2008), 37–157; Joachim Benoit, "La Reconnaissance d'Haiti par la France (1825); naissance d'un nouveau type de rapports internationaux," *Revue d'histoire moderne et contemporiane* 22/3 (July–September 1978): 369–96; John Edward Baur, "Mulatto Machiavelli, Jean Pierre Boyer, and the Haiti of His Day," *Journal of Negro History* 32/3 (July 1947): 307–53, esp. 321–30; J. N. Leger, *Haiti: Her History and Her Detractors* (1907; repr., Westport, CT: Negro Universities Press, 1970), 173–91; Tansill, *United States and Santo Domingo*, 122.

Chapter 17

Jefferson's Ambivalence toward Immigration: Turn and Return, 1776–1826[1]

The evolution of Jefferson's adherence to a philosophy of cultural relativism also presented itself in his attitude towards immigration. In an article about Jefferson and slavery, historian James Oakes draws attention to his views on immigration, claiming that he considered Europeans too much indoctrinated by ideas of the infallibility of absolute monarchy to become suitable citizens for the libertarian United States, whose people were more rational because of their venerable republican heritage. In Oakes's words, Jefferson "feared the immigration of Europeans because they came from places where the rule of reason was suppressed and were therefore unfit to participate as equals in American public life."[2]

While it contains a grain of truth, Oakes's depiction of Jefferson transforms him into an elitist aristocrat, prepared to deny European immigrants the touted "life, liberty, and the pursuit of happiness" and "equal rights" (despite their being White males, not women or Blacks). Oakes does not present any evidence for this broad assumption. On the other hand, Jefferson occasionally made detailed remarks about immigration, and I will briefly trace his opinions here.

As a young man in 1776, when he wrote the Declaration of Independence and in the state legislature stood in the forefront of the movement to liberalize Virginia's laws, he proposed measures to favor immigrants, especially Jews. A staunch advocate of religious equality, in submitting his revision of state laws in October 1776 he proposed conferring citizenship on Jewish immigrants and granting them and other "foreigners" who came to Virginia twenty dollars to reimburse their ship passage and fifty acres of free land upon arrival. In a statement

---

[1] The topics of this chapter are discussed at greater length in Scherr, "Thomas Jefferson, White Immigration, and Black Emancipation. Part I: Jefferson's Views on Immigration: From *Notes on the State of Virginia* to Retirement from the Presidency," *Southern Studies* 22/2 (Fall/Winter 2015): 1–36, and "Thomas Jefferson, White Immigration, and Black Emancipation. Part II," 1–26.

[2] James Oakes, "Why Slaves Can't Read: The Political Significance of Jefferson's Racism," in James Gilreath, ed., *Thomas Jefferson and the Education of a Citizen* (Washington, DC: Library of Congress, 1999), 177–92, 185 (quotation).

that perhaps helps to explain why he believed that after emancipation, Black slaves should be forced to leave the state, Jefferson, defending his humanitarian proposals toward immigrants, warned that those denied "full rights" would become the country's "*secret enemies.*" The assembly rejected his bill for naturalizing foreigners perhaps because Jefferson had in mind Jews and possibly Roman Catholics as its beneficiaries. In notes he composed justifying his desire to encourage Jewish immigration, he wrote, "Religion—is theirs less moral[?]" He acclaimed the "Honesty-Veracity" and morality of Jews, jotting down in the course of debate, "Jews [are] advantageous" to the state. He also observed, "All who have not *full rights* are *secret enemies*" of the government, thereby validating his generous measures because of state self-interest and security as well as humanitarianism.[3]

It is natural to consult Jefferson's *Notes on Virginia* when seeking his opinions on political topics in early middle age. Jefferson and his reform-minded followers believed that, by separating themselves from European feudalism and monarchy, they could furnish an example of freedom, democracy, and prosperity for all humankind, particularly their European forebears. As Daniel J. Boorstin succinctly put it, "Jeffersonian isolationism expressed an essentially cosmopolitan spirit."[4] Like Jefferson in Query VIII of *Notes*, kindred political theorists might be especially concerned that, habituated to the incubus of monarchy and aristocracy, European immigrants would spread, willy-nilly, those pernicious doctrines on arrival in the US.

Judging from *Notes*' "Population" chapter (Query VIII), Jefferson apparently feared that unrestricted immigration might threaten or corrupt the republican principles unique to the United States and alien to the monarchial world. Paradoxically, he balanced this hostility with a steadfast belief in the "right of expatriation," a conviction that anyone should be allowed to live anywhere he or she desired, a right the founders of the thirteen colonies had exercised. (He maintained this opinion for his generation in his *Summary View of the Rights of British-America* in 1774.) In Query VIII ("The number of its inhabitants?"), Jefferson sketched a hypothetical scenario of a one-year flood of immigration to Virginia, theoretically doubling the state's population in one year. On this basis, he calculated that, nonetheless, it would take only twenty-eight years longer for Virginia to acquire the same number of people by natural increase as it would if this hypothetical demographic deluge occurred. (According to Jefferson, starting from 1781, Virginia would reach 4,540,922 inhabitants in 1835 if its population doubled in 1781 through immigration, as opposed to achieving that number in 1862 solely by natural increase, without *any* immigration. Jefferson's point was that

---

[3] Jefferson's Bill for the Naturalization of Foreigners [October 1776], in Boyd et al., eds., *Papers of Thomas Jefferson*, 1:558–59n. Italics in original.

[4] Boorstin, *Lost World of Thomas Jefferson*, 229.

natural increase of the existing population was sufficiently great to develop the state's resources and prosperity; an excessive influx of immigrants might result in the thinning out of the state's resources and reduce the prosperity of its current inhabitants even though he theoretically appreciated the humaneness of welcoming the oppressed peoples of Europe. According to his estimates, Virginia's population had doubled every twenty-seven years since 1654, with little immigration. In light of its considerable population growth, Jefferson "doubted" the "good policy" of many Americans' desire to replenish the country's population by vast immigration. "Civil government being the sole object of forming societies," Jefferson feared that a "harmonious...civil government" would elude Virginians if immigrants from European monarchies invaded the state. Virginians' goal of "happiness" would be defeated if they were victims of conflicting political cultures and antagonistic political ideals.[5]

In a wayward interpretation of the "American Dream," Jefferson, rather than stressing that all peoples desired freedom, democracy, and equality, warned that America's unique republic might hold values antipathetic to the reactionary creed the European arrivals had learned in the Old World, and they would reject it. He evinced a cultural relativist credo. "Every species of government has its specific principles," he wrote, showing Montesquieu's influence. "Ours perhaps are more peculiar than those of any other in the universe. It is a composition of the freest principles of the English constitution, with others derived from natural right and natural reason. To these, nothing can be more opposed than the maxims of absolute monarchies."[6]

Perhaps only for argument's sake, Jefferson anticipated that the inhabitants of absolute monarchies like France, Austria, Prussia, and Russia, rather than natives of the British Isles, America's mother country, where constitutional monarchy prevailed and from which most of the immigrants came, would immigrate to Virginia. (He may have expected that Britons would fear to reside in the newly independent state, whose citizens might have vengeful feelings toward them.) He darkly and xenophobically implied that these supposedly pro-monarchical immigrants would attempt to transform the United States from a republic to a monarchy. In a provincial vein alien to his later years, ignoring the likelihood that desperate immigrants would prefer democracy and republicanism to absolutism, he warned, "They will bring with them the principles of the governments they leave, imbibed in their early youth; or, if able to throw them off, it will be in exchange for an unbounded licentiousness, passing, as is usual, from one extreme to

[5] Query VIII, "On Population," Peden, ed., *Notes on the State of Virginia*, 84.
[6] Ibid.

another. It would be a miracle were they to stop precisely at the point of temperate liberty."[7]

It is difficult to believe that Jefferson expected a sudden arrival of immigrants from Central and Eastern Europe, who had never arrived in Virginia in large numbers over the preceding two centuries. On a perhaps unconscious level, Jefferson was referring allegorically to immigrants from Great Britain, the former mother country, for which his hatred grew during the Revolution, and expressing the expectation of many American revolutionaries that Britain was about to decline into absolute monarchy. Like many American Whigs, Jefferson predicted that, under the "corrupt," vigorous rule of George III and his prime minister Lord North, the House of Commons would decay into a mere figurehead and Britain, for all practical purposes, would mutate into an "absolute monarchy."[8]

Not only did many American revolutionaries insist that Britain's government was in irreversible decline toward despotism; conversely, they declared that the only hope for the survival of freedom of thought and representative government rested with the success of the thirteen colonies' struggle for independence. Jefferson shared these perceptions, as his *Summary View* and his original draft of the Declaration of Independence made clear. The violent course of the Revolution resulted in the British army's takeover of much of Georgia and South Carolina. Jefferson was angered by British military aggression toward the Southern states, which injured him both personally and financially in the destruction of his buildings and livestock at Elkhill in June 1781 by Cornwallis's troops, along with the escape of thirty slaves. Concerning his runaway slaves' joining Cornwallis's army, he later said, "He carried off also about 30 slaves: had this been to give them freedom he would have done right, but it was to consign them to inevitable death from the small pox and putrid fever then raging in his camp. This I knew afterwards to have been the fate of 27 of them. I never had news of the remaining three, but presume they shared the same fate."[9]

More importantly from Jefferson's homeostasis, humiliated by British invasions of Virginia during his governorship, he suffered lifetime psychological distress. He was forced to flee the capital, Richmond, after Benedict Arnold's attack in January 1781; he then had to evacuate his home, Monticello, when another, larger British invading force headed by General Cornwallis and Colonel Banastre

---

[7] *Notes on Virginia,* Query VIII, in Lipscomb and Bergh, eds., *Writings of Jefferson*, 2:119–20, 120 (quotation).

[8] The best study of American Whigs' perceptions of the decline of Britain's "republican virtue" and their fears that Britain's "free constitution" was degenerating into a monarchical tyranny and a "corrupted" Parliament remains Wood, *Creation of the American Republic*, ch. 1.

[9] Jefferson to William Gordon, July 16, 1788, in Boyd et al., eds., *Papers of Thomas Jefferson*, 13:362–65. Also available at Founders Online, National Archives (founders.archives.gov/documents/Jefferson/01-13-02-0266).

Tarleton attempted to capture him in June 1781. His two years as governor of Virginia, 1779–1781, marked the nadir of his public life. His inept handling of supplying the Continental Army and Virginia militia in 1781 and his failure to impose military obstacles or militia forces against Arnold's raid on Richmond aroused severe criticism from the highly respected General Nathanael Greene and members of the state assembly. Public outrage at his failing to protect Richmond from invasion culminated in a legislative investigation of his administration in June 1781, supported by Patrick Henry, the state's most popular figure. These proceedings probably angered Jefferson more than anything in his political career. He deliberately stood for a seat in the House of Delegates in order to personally act as his advocate in clearing his name at the session of December 1781. During the debates, he convinced the legislature that he was not personally culpable for the debacles of 1781. The House of Delegates unanimously passed a resolution of commendation and "public gratitude" for his conduct, and the Senate voted its "sincere Thanks...for his impartial, upright, and attentive administration." However, he remained resentful of the dishonor he had endured, and his rage at Britain's aggression was enhanced by a personal component.[10]

During this period of invasion and personal humiliation, tormented by his wife's chronic poor health, Jefferson commenced writing *Notes on Virginia.* His uncharacteristically negative comments on immigration perhaps evolved from his rage at British military aggression and reports of various wartime atrocities in the Carolinas. The British Army's harassment of him, the invasion of Virginia, and the destruction of his Elkhill estate exacerbated the hostility toward Britain that Jefferson expressed, sometimes inappropriately, at various points in *Notes* and provoked the most degrading and unhappy time of his life.

Jefferson was not an inveterate Anglophobe. As a political theorist, he had always appreciated the importance of the British constitutional, common law and republican heritage in providing the foundation for the thirteen colonies' legal and representative government. However, like the other revolutionists, he was convinced that the English had violated the unwritten British constitution by taxing and legislating for the colonies during the 1760s and 1770s. He strongly advocated independence. In August 1775, he wrote his friend and relative, Virginia's attorney general, John Randolph, who had taken a Loyalist stance and was leaving for England, that he favored independence, especially after the fighting at Lexington, Concord, and Bunker Hill. "I...would rather be in dependence on Great Britain, properly limited, than on any other nation on earth, or than on no nation," he explained. "But I am one of those, too, who, rather than submit to the

[10] Malone, *Jefferson the Virginian*, 330–69, 444–45; Cunningham, Jr., *In Pursuit of Reason*, 66–75.

rights of legislating for us, assumed by the British Parliament, and which late experience has shown they will so cruelly exercise, would lend my hand to sink the whole Island in the ocean."[11]

During the Revolution, Jefferson further manifested his rejection of British attempts to "enslave" the colonies, as radicals termed the prewar repressive legislation. As a Virginia legislator and afterward as governor, Jefferson supported laws imposing fines and imprisonment on those who publicly advocated submission to the king and claimed that Britain still ruled the colonies. He also acquiesced in Governor Patrick Henry's advocacy of bills of attainder (legislative trials, overriding due process of law) against Loyalists, bandits, and others who committed murder during their crimes.[12]

Jefferson's contemporary political opponents, such as Alexander Hamilton, and later, historians like Oakes, cited Jefferson's observations in *Notes on Virginia* opposing unlimited immigration after the Revolution to discredit him as a hypocrite for favoring repeal of the Naturalization Laws as president. In fact, in Query VIII of *Notes*, Jefferson was apparently denouncing the British, for whom he, like many other Americans, felt great hostility during the destructive war, in which nearly 26,000 American soldiers and sailors lost their lives (second only to the

---

[11] Jefferson to John Randolph, August 25, 1775, in Peterson, ed., *Jefferson: Writings*, 750. See also Malone, *Jefferson the Virginian*, 209–10.

[12] On the abundant metaphors drawing analogies between Britain's taxation of the colonists and "slavery," see, e.g., Peter A. Dorsey, "To 'Corroborate Our Own Claims': Public Positioning and the Slavery Metaphor in Revolutionary America," *American Quarterly* 55/3 (September 2003): 353–86; Dorsey, *Common Bondage: Slavery as Metaphor in Revolutionary America* (Knoxville: University of Tennessee Press, 2009); Bailyn, *Ideological Origins of the American Revolution*, 22–54, 234. Leonard W. Levy, *Jefferson and Civil Liberties: The Darker Side* (Cambridge: Belknap Press of HUP, 1963), 25–41, discusses Jefferson's support for wartime legislation curtailing Loyalists' rights. Levy portrayed Jefferson as an enemy of civil liberties, but his account of Jefferson's actions during the American Revolution merely revealed that he followed the lead of the Virginia legislature and Governor Patrick Henry. As the best literary craftsman in the assembly, he drafted laws curtailing speech against the cause of independence and in favor of George III when legislative committees requested him to do so. As a fervent supporter of independence, he did not oppose legislation imprisoning or restricting the civil liberties of Tories charged with aiding and assisting the British or suspected of awaiting the opportunity to join them. During the invasions of Virginia in 1781, Jefferson as governor was rightly concerned that Loyalists might aid British troops in their mayhem, but (a fact that Levy ignores) he had no militia or Continental forces to arrest or subdue them if they turned to violence. Levy's evidence sometimes disproved his thesis, as when he mentioned that in 1776 Jefferson composed the most lenient treason statute of the period (28). Inserted later as a provision of the US Constitution, the statute, requiring two witnesses to an overt act of treason to prove a defendant guilty, was cited by Chief Justice John Marshall in 1807 in asserting Aaron Burr's innocence of treason.

Civil War in per capita mortality). Except for a small percentage of Germans, Scotch-Irish, and Irish, before 1790 nearly all the immigrants to Virginia were English (around 70 percent).[13] In questioning the desirability of unrestricted immigration, therefore, Jefferson, ironically, was covertly denouncing the British people, who had shown themselves lacking in virtue by supporting the king's war against the colonies.

Infused with wartime Anglophobia, like many Americans during the Revolution, Jefferson's rage against Britain emerged at unexpected points in *Notes*. For example, Query VI, the longest chapter in the book, bearing the innocuous title, "Productions Mineral, Vegetable and Animal," defended the flora and fauna of the United States against French naturalists Buffon and Raynal. These French scientists charged, without evidence, that the New World's noxious cold and humid climate caused the degeneration of its animals (including human beings, even European immigrants to the colonies) and plants into smaller and inferior varieties and species than those found in Europe. After presenting statistical tables showing that many American varieties of plants and mammals were larger than Europe's, Jefferson addressed French charges that the thirteen colonies had produced no distinguished individuals. He listed Benjamin Franklin, George Washington, and the astronomer David Rittenhouse as proof that the United States had produced its "full quota of genius" proportionate to its small population of three million. However, instead of denouncing French scientists for their anti-American aspersions, he launched into an attack on the British. "The present war having so long cut off all communication with Great-Britain," he wrote,

> we are not able to make a fair estimate of the state of science in that country. The spirit in which she [*sic*] wages war is the only sample before our eyes, and that does not seem the legitimate offspring either of science or of civilization. The sun of her glory is fast descending to the horizon. Her philosophy has crossed the Channel, her freedom the Atlantic, and herself seems passing to that awful dissolution, whose issue is not given human foresight to scan.[14]

In this manner, Jefferson reiterated the common feeling among American political thinkers that the fragile features of representative government, freedom

---

[13] It is estimated that 90 percent of Virginia's population in 1790 was from Great Britain (England, Scotland, Wales, Ireland, and Ulster), and 68.5 percent was from England alone. Similar demographics prevailed for most of the original thirteen states, especially those settled before 1682 (Richard B. Morris, ed., *Encyclopedia of American History* [New York: Harper and Brothers, 1953], 445). For casualty figures during the American Revolution, see Martin and Lender, *Respectable Army*, 207.

[14] Peden, ed., *Notes on the State of Virginia*, 65. Query VI extends from page 26 to page 72.

of thought and speech that existed in Great Britain, were about to disappear, as evinced by its government's cavalier treatment of the thirteen colonies and disrespect for their republican legislative branches. When viewing *Notes* as to some extent a wartime polemic against Great Britain, it emerges that Jefferson was not attacking immigration in principle in Query VIII of *Notes*; he was not rejecting the United States' role as an "asylum for mankind," as Thomas Paine phrased it in *Common Sense*. Jefferson was, if rather indirectly, demonstrating his hostility toward the Mother Country.

In *Notes*, Jefferson did not appear optimistic that immigrants would easily assimilate into the American melting pot. Unlike present-day conservatives who advocate forcing immigrants to learn the English language, Jefferson assumed that they would preserve an attachment to their monarchical forms of government as well as their native tongues, hardly a testimony to his confidence in their resiliency. "These [monarchical] principles, with their language, they will transmit to their children," he warned. Perhaps thinking of Pennsylvania's Germans, he nonetheless expected them to participate actively in politics. "In proportion to their numbers," he warned, "they will share with us the legislation. They will infuse into it their spirit, warp and bias its direction, and render it a heterogeneous, incoherent, distracted mass." This was an extremely vivid (if not very logical) depiction of Jefferson's fears that the country's peace and democracy would be overwhelmed by royalist immigrants who, despite never having held the suffrage, would now eagerly vote for anti-republican government. Superficially, Jefferson seemingly feared the disruption of his homogeneous White Anglophone culture. Contrariwise, he may have been thinking of the numerous Tory Loyalist émigrés when he inveighed against immigration, fearing their return, although most of them, even the Scots and Irish, spoke English. He seems to have had Loyalists in mind when he wrote, "I may appeal to experience during the present contest for a verification of these conjectures." Jefferson's muddled exegesis leads one to conclude that he feared European immigrants, not because they were irrational or illiterate, but because their literacy and political sophistication might lead them to participate in politics.[15] Purely from nostalgia for their mother countries, like William Cobbett, who became a shrill royalist after arriving in the republican US, to which he fled when he faced imprisonment for criticizing the corruption of the

---

[15] Peden, ed., *Notes on the State of Virginia*, 85 (Query VIII: "Population"). In his old age, John Adams claimed that the French Revolution failed because nearly all the French people were illiterate. However, recent historians have discovered that France had the highest literacy rate in Europe (Adams to Jefferson, July 13, 1813, in Cappon, ed., *Adams-Jefferson Letters* [1959], 2:355). For the relatively high literacy rates among adult French men and women of all economic classes on the eve of the French Revolution, see Schama, *Citizens*, 180; Markoff, "Literacy and Revolt," 323–49.

British Army in 1792, they would proclaim the superiority of monarchy to the democracy in which they now basked.[16]

Moderating his tone, Jefferson admitted that his dire predictions of immigration's catastrophe for republicanism were "probable" rather than certain. Denying the need for excessive government incentives for immigration, he believed the country could more safely rely on the native-born for demographic growth. "May not our government be more homogeneous, more peaceable, more durable?" by rejecting a deluge of immigrants, he inquired. He employed the analogy of a sudden flood of American immigrants into royal France, contending that their arrival would threaten the happiness and stability of the kingdom. Likewise, a flood of European immigrants would disrupt Virginia's republicanism and free-enterprise society. Recurring to his usual sense of fairness and justice, he denied that he would bar immigrants from entering the country; he merely would not grant them special privileges or subsidies. As he put it, "If they come of themselves, they are entitled to all the rights of citizenship: but I doubt the expediency of inviting them by extraordinary encouragements." In contrast to his support a few years earlier for subsidies for immigrants, specifically persecuted Jews, he considered most foreigners a drain on the state's resources, which should be reserved for the ever-increasing native-born population. Rather undemocratically, however, he condoned special rewards to tempt skilled workers, who could increase the republic's productivity. "I mean not that these doubts [about the desirability of immigrants] should be extended to the importation of useful artificers," he explained. "The policy of that measure depends on very different considerations. Spare no expence in obtaining them. They will after a while go to the plough and hoe; but, in the mean time, they will teach us something we do not know."[17]

Jefferson thought that skilled immigrants (he may have had in mind British textile factory managers like Samuel Slater), with their specialized knowledge of mechanics and technology, including the latest factory and steam engine machinery, were intelligent individuals who could teach Americans about new inventions. Paradoxically, he expected them eventually to melt peacefully into the homogeneous mass of American farmers, an outcome he seemingly did not think would occur with the average European immigrant. Strangely, Jefferson, who often denounced cities as cesspools of vice, hoped to attract urban foreign artisans,

---

[16] On William Cobbett, see David L. Wilson, *Paine and Cobbett: The Atlantic Connection* (Toronto: McGill-Queen's University Press, 1988); and Mary Elizabeth Clark, *Peter Porcupine in America: The Career of William Cobbett* (New York: Beekman, 1974). Robbie Totten's informative article, "National Security and U.S. Immigration Policy, 1776–1790," *Journal of Interdisciplinary History* 39/1 (Summer 2008): 37–64, overlooks this famous anti-immigrant Jefferson quote, which would have helped substantiate his thesis that some Founding Fathers objected to immigration because they feared it might lead to the entry of foreign subversives.

[17] Peden, ed., *Notes on the State of Virginia*, 85 (Query VIII: "Population").

believing that they could help make the United States more technologically advanced and self-sufficient in manufactures. He had little respect or concern for the average European serf, who probably did not have any knowledge of advanced farm machinery, the best systems of crop rotation and manuring, and other things useful to American farmers. Revealing a selfish, nationalist streak rather than one befitting his later reputation as a "world citizen," Jefferson pointed out that there was plenty of land in America (a feature that he later emphasized was responsible for its people's prosperity and success in self-government), but insufficient knowledge of how to use it in an ecologically productive manner. "The indifferent state of [agricultural productivity] among us does not proceed from a want of knowledge merely," he coldly observed. "It is from our having such quantities of land to waste as we please. In Europe the object is to make the most of their land, labour being abundant: here it is to make the most of our labour, land being abundant."[18]

With its conservative sentiments about immigration, Query VIII does not fit well with the rest of *Notes*, or with the entire corpus of Jefferson's writings. It is not clear when Jefferson completed *Notes on Virginia*. It was a work in progress, begun in 1781 after his retirement from politics. Although Douglas L. Wilson, the leading scholar on the topic, surmises that Jefferson had finished most of it by December 1783, when Jefferson was a member of the Continental Congress meeting at Annapolis, it is likely that he did not write the most important parts until he was in France in late 1784.[19]

In his autobiography, written when he was in his seventies, Jefferson himself suggested that he did not finish writing *Notes* until after he arrived in Europe, probably in early 1785. He recalled that Barbé-Marbois requested information from him about Virginia in late 1780, and his resort to "loose papers" about Virginia's history and geography, collected over the years, which he continued to call "our country" rather than a state. When the book was less than half its final length, he sought to publish it but did not do so because of the high printing costs in the United States. "On my arrival at Paris I found it could be done for a fourth of what I had been asked here [in the United States]," he reminisced. "I *therefore corrected and enlarged them*, and had 200 copies printed under the title of Notes

[18] Ibid.

[19] Wilson, "The Evolution of Jefferson's *Notes*," 98–133. Robert A. Ferguson concludes that Jefferson did not complete *Notes* until early 1785 ("'Mysterious Obligation': Jefferson's *Notes on the State of Virginia*," *American Literature* 52/3 [November 1980]: 381–406). A more recent study of *Notes* shows that Jefferson probably continued to write and revise the book into 1785, when he was in Europe. It concludes that he always intended to publish it eventually (Dustin P. Gish and Daniel Klinghard, "Republican Constitutionalism in Thomas Jefferson's *Notes on the State of Virginia*, *Journal of Politics* 74/1 [January 2012]: 35–51).

on Virginia. I gave a very few copies to some particular persons in Europe, and sent the rest to my friends in America."[20]

Thus, according to Jefferson's own testimony, he did not complete *Notes* until 1784 or 1785, in Europe. Jefferson may actually have been in Europe when he wrote Query VIII; he was sufficiently appalled by the economic inequality and political oppression he viewed there to prefer that the impoverished farm tenants and serfs he observed on the feudal manors not migrate to his country's comparative agrarian paradise, whose cultureshock might drive them insane.[21] Indeed, it is possible that Jefferson disparaged the idea of extensive immigration because of his early experiences in Europe and that he finished *Notes* months after he arrived in Paris with his daughter Martha in October 1784.

As US minister to France, Jefferson was obsessed by the differences he perceived between the economic inequality and absence of representative government in France and the freedom and relative equality of property ownership he knew of in the United States. He resented British anti-US propaganda, which aimed to discourage emigration as well as make Europeans hesitate about trading or investing in the United States.[22] He discovered a silver lining in British malice. In 1785, he sarcastically told a young Dutch friend that, by depicting the US as in crisis, British government and newspaper sources helped Americans discourage Britons from going there. Jefferson was relieved that, by discouraging British financiers from advancing US merchants credit, such negative, albeit false news reports would serendipitously encourage the latter's prudence, virtue, industry, and frugality. Lacking abundant funds, American businessmen and citizens would find their "disposition to luxury checked." Forced to travel all over the world in search of new markets and cheap raw materials, they would become especially resourceful and defeat their British rivals. Their increased spirit of enterprise, combined with Europeans' reluctance to migrate to a country that they heard was impoverished, were blessings in disguise, "all of which I consider as advantageous to us." In attempting to monopolize US freight abroad and crush domestic carriers, Jefferson observed, British shippers had aroused US merchants' anger, inspiring their demands that indolent state governments support

[20] *Autobiography*, in Peterson, ed., *Jefferson: Writings*, 55. My italics.

[21] Brian Steele, "Thomas Jefferson's Gender Frontier," *Journal of American History* 95/1 (June 2008): 17–42, provides some suggestive ideas.

[22] See Jefferson's draft of an anonymous letter to the newspapers, in which he said that the American people were happy and prosperous because they were free, and explained that all the negative reports about the poverty, violence, crime, and anarchy in the states were lies concocted by English newspapers and spread to the European continent ("Reply to the Representations of Affairs in America by British Newspapers" [before November 20, 1784], in Peterson, ed., *Jefferson: Writings*, 571–74).

retaliatory congressional tariff laws, tonnage duties, and national commercial regulations. Jefferson's letter to G. K. Van Hogendorp more overtly expressed his hostility to British influence than did Query VIII's anti-immigrant phraseology.[23]

Initially shocked by experiencing European feudal inequality and injustice, Jefferson expressed in extreme terms his desire for US isolation from Europe, what later generations might inaccurately regard as "American exceptionalism." He wanted to isolate his country from Europe the same way as China allegedly had: "We should thus avoid wars, and all our citizens would be husbandmen." However, reluctantly admitting that Americans desired to trade abroad and that his theoretical goal of isolation was unattainable, Jefferson hoped that he and other US foreign ministers could gain freedom of world trade for the US, another pipe dream.[24]

Jefferson favored political isolation from Europe for practical reasons of national survival and expansion, as well as to preserve the United States' moral purity and "republican virtue." He considered Europe a source of interminable dynastic wars (briefly exacerbated by the abrupt emergence of the republican behemoth, democratic revolutionary France) and believed that European powers, especially the former mother country England, would unceasingly attempt to drag the United States into their conflicts. During the Wars of the French Revolution in the late 1790s, he was hysterically fearful that British economic, financial, and political influence had encroached upon American autonomy in every sphere, and he charged that the British controlled most of the American newspapers. In 1797, he wrote to Elbridge Gerry, whom President John Adams had just appointed one of a trio of envoys to Paris to preserve peace with France, that he hoped that the US would "find some means of shielding ourselves in future from foreign influence, political, commercial, or in whatever other form it may be attempted. I can scarcely withhold myself from joining in the wish of Silas Deane, that there were an ocean of fire between us and the old world."[25]

More forthrightly than in Query VIII, where he irrelevantly decried "absolute monarchies," Jefferson now admitted that he especially feared *British* immigration. He worried that many immigrants would be upper-class British

---

[23] Jefferson to Van Hogendorp, October 13, 1785, in Lipscomb and Bergh, eds., *Writings of Jefferson*, 5:183.

[24] Ibid., 183–84. See the discussion of these themes as they evolved over time in Douglass G. Adair, *Intellectual Origins of Jeffersonian Democracy* (1943; Lanham, MD: Lexington Books, 2000); Drew R. McCoy, *The Elusive Republic* (Chapel Hill: University of North Carolina Press, 1980); McCoy, "Jefferson and Madison on Malthus: Population Growth in Jeffersonian Political Economy," *Virginia Magazine of History and Biography* 88/3 (1982): 259–76.

[25] Jefferson to Elbridge Gerry, May 13, 1797, in Lipscomb and Bergh, eds., *Writings of Jefferson*, 9:385. Silas Deane, who negotiated the wartime alliance between the U.S. and France in 1778, ended up deserting the American cause and seeking asylum in England.

merchants and financiers who intended, not to be good citizens, but to manipulate the US government and people into advancing their own selfish goals and the British government's political aims.

For the average impoverished or oppressed European peasant, Jefferson during his lifetime generally held up the United States as a beacon of liberty to which they might emigrate for freedom and prosperity. If European governments brutally prohibited immigration, fearing depletion of their military base, the American republic might still furnish an inspiring example of liberty and reform to which citizen/subjects might strive to steer their governments by agitation for peaceful change. As a last resort, they might even emulate the "spirit of '76" by waging violent revolution to overthrow intractable kings.[26]

In the years immediately following the American Revolution, however, Jefferson was cautious about advocating unlimited immigration from the Old World to the New. He tended to believe that the United States could only serve as a model for the world if it excluded excessive numbers of European immigrants, especially uneducated laborers from big cities like London and Paris, who might have a penchant for monarchy and ingrained city-bred vices. He acknowledged that the US was destined to play a major world role as an asylum while demurring at the likelihood that unlimited access to asylum might ultimately wreck the US potential as the "republican experiment," by providing a habitat for subversive, anti-republican elements. Although he did not name them in Query VIII, in 1796 he came close. At that time, he listed among the "anti-republican" forces, "all timid men who prefer the calm of despotism to the boisterous sea of liberty, British merchants & Americans trading on British capitals, speculators & holders in the banks & public funds, a contrivance invented for the purposes of corruption, & for assimilating us in all things to the rotten as well as the sound parts of the British model." Thus, Query VIII perhaps targeted Scottish merchants and returning American Tories, whom he warned would eventually attempt to overthrow the country's burgeoning representative democracy if they had the power.[27]

As US minister to France during the 1780s, Jefferson was obsessive (especially before he fell in love with Maria Cosway in October 1786) in favorably comparing US republicanism with France's theoretically absolute monarchy and the economic disparities the people suffered under a waning feudalism. He

[26] See, e.g., among numerous relevant examples, Jefferson to George Flower, September 12, 1817, in Lipscomb and Bergh, eds., *Writings of Jefferson*, 15:139–42. See also Cushing Strout, *The American Image of the Old World* (New York: Harper & Row, 1963), 18–48. On Flower's search for a republican form of government to live in, and his paradoxically favorable impression of slavery on Jefferson's Poplar Forest plantation, see Salter, "George Flower Comes to the Illinois Country," 213–23.

[27] Jefferson to Philip Mazzei, April 24, 1796, in Peterson, ed., *Jefferson: Writings*, 1036–37 (quotation). See also Boorstin, *Lost World of Thomas Jefferson*, 229–30, 291.

assured James Monroe that if he visited France, "It will make you adore your own country, its soil, its climate, its equality, liberty, laws, people, and manners." A burgeoning nationalist and citizen of a new country, perhaps Jefferson protested too much in order to convince himself that he was happiest in his native republic. (Even he invariably admitted that the European architecture and gardens were superior to those of the United States.) "My God!" he exclaimed. "How little do my countrymen know what precious blessings they are in possession of, and which no other people on earth enjoy. I confess I had no idea of it myself." Concluding that no sane American would want to reside permanently in the Old World, he expected a dangerous number of Europeans infected with monarchical doctrines and habits to arrive in the United States. "While we shall see multiplied instances of Europeans going to live in America, I will venture to say, no man now living will ever see an instance of an American removing to settle in Europe, and continuing there," he predicted. Although he hoped that Monroe would visit him in France, he was sure that when he returned to the US he would tell his "countrymen how much it is their interest to preserve, uninfected by contagion, those peculiarities in their governments and manners, to which they are indebted for those blessings."[28]

Extending the critique in Query VIII, which he may well have composed in 1785, Jefferson unflatteringly perceived as a "contagion" the immigrants from monarchies, fearing their retention of nostalgias or patriotic biases toward the governments of their birth. He uncharitably and myopically ignored a more likely scenario: if they were immigrating to the republican US, they most likely rejected the hidebound institutions of monarchy for a land of freedom and opportunity. His wartime-aggravated Anglophobia, his assumption that most European immigrants (whether from Britain or France) would prefer monarchy, and his conviction that native-born Americans' birthrate sufficed for the population to grow amply enough precipitated his atypical clarion call against excessive immigration during the 1780s. Although he knew that most Europeans lived under oppressive feudalistic regimes, he was not very sympathetic with their plight at this time, nor, before the Revolutionary upsurge of the 1790s, were many Europeans eager to move to America's freer, more prosperous climate.

The partisan conflicts of the 1790s helped make Jefferson a more enthusiastic public advocate of a liberalized immigration policy. Except for the White and mixed-race émigrés from Saint-Domingue, fleeing the carnage of the slave upheaval (and bringing their slaves), few Francophone people immigrated to the United States. As in the past, most immigrants came from Great Britain and Ireland; many were lower- or middle-class artisans who drifted toward his

---

[28] Jefferson to James Monroe, June 17, 1785, in Lipscomb and Bergh, eds., *Writings of Jefferson*, 5:21.

Democratic-Republican Party, with its ethos of political and social equality and freedom of opportunity for all. The Federalists, especially New Englanders like Boston congressman Harrison Gray Otis, who in 1795 wished to impose a naturalization fee of twenty-five dollars on all immigrants, and lumped them together as "Wild Irishmen," regarded immigrants as a dangerous nuisance. They considered most immigrants incendiary radicals, and sought to increase the difficulty of naturalization. Many of Jefferson's most articulate supporters, such as Thomas Cooper, William Duane, John Daly Burk, Mathew Carey, and (during the 1790s) James Thomson Callender, were immigrants from England, Ireland, and Scotland with impressive credentials as intellectuals or radical journalists.[29]

Aroused by the new immigrants' rejection of monarchy and their preference for democracy and political reform, Jefferson welcomed them into Democratic-Republican ranks. He was outraged by the Federalist Congress's passage in 1798 of the Alien, Sedition, and Naturalization Acts (the last increased the federal naturalization process from five years to fourteen), a deliberate attempt to eliminate his party. He also considered the Alien Friends Act and the Sedition Act unconstitutional. Consequently, after he became president, his first annual message to Congress in December 1801 proposed to repeal the Naturalization Act (the Sedition Act and the Alien Friends Act had already expired) and restore the naturalization process to five years. He insisted that he did not desire to encourage immigration in order to siphon population from America's monarchical foes abroad and increase the pool of potential soldiers to dispatch on imperialistic military expeditions. Restoring the old naturalization law would expedite "the settlement of the extensive country still remaining vacant within our limits, [and] the multiplications of men susceptible of happiness, educated in the love of order, habituated to self-government, and valuing its blessings above all price."[30]

Convinced that most immigrants savored freedom and democracy and would eschew monarchy's servile mentalité, Jefferson pointed out the injustice of

[29] See Michael Durey, *Transatlantic Radicals and the Early American Republic* (Lawrence: University of Kansas Press, 1997); Edward C. Carter, II, "A 'Wild Irishman' under Every Federalist's Bed: Naturalization in Philadelphia, 1789–1806," *Pennsylvania Magazine of History and Biography* 94/3 (July 1970): 332–46; David A. Wilson, *United Irishmen, United States: Immigrant Radicals in the Early Republic* (Ithaca: Cornell University Press, 1998).

[30] Jefferson's First Annual Message to Congress, December 8, 1801, in Peterson, ed., *Jefferson: Writings*, 503. For the Founders' views on immigration, see also Thomas G. West, *Vindicating the Founders: Race, Sex, Class, and Justice in the Origins of America* (Lanham, MD: Rowman & Littlefield Publishers, 1997), ch. 7. In discussing Jefferson, West mistakenly says that in his first annual message to Congress, "Jefferson proposed immediate naturalization of foreigners instead of the fourteen-year residency then required" (154). Jefferson's message did not specify a particular time-period for naturalization, and the Republican-controlled Congress merely changed it to five years.

the Federalist fourteen-year naturalization law. More severe than Parliament's seven-year naturalization requirement for the colonists, imposed in 1740, the Federalists' law intended to bar citizenship to many current foreign residents, who, "considering the ordinary chances of human life" in those times (a lifespan of around fifty years), would not live to see naturalization. He observed that, before Article One of the Constitution gave Congress power over immigration, many states enforced more lenient laws. (Pennsylvania, for example, granted citizenship to foreigners after one or two years' residence). According to the Constitution, Jefferson reminded Congress, the 1798 law "controls a policy pursued from their first settlement of many of these States, and still believed of consequence to their prosperity." With an eloquence he had not devoted to the subject before, he rhetorically asked, "Shall we refuse the unhappy fugitives from distress that hospitality which the savages of the wilderness extended to our fathers arriving in this land? Shall oppressed humanity find no asylum on this globe?" He asserted his agreement with the Constitutional provisions that the highest public offices should be restricted to long-term residents ("a residence shall be required sufficient to develop character and design"). "But might not the general character and capabilities of a citizen be safely communicated to every one manifesting a bona fide purpose of embarking his life and fortunes permanently with us?" he said, implying that they should exercise the vote.[31]

Ignoring Jefferson's previous fear of an influx of potentially subversive Tories, reasonable when he wrote *Notes*, his greatest foe, Alexander Hamilton, mocked his apparent volte-face on immigration. In an editorial in his newspaper, the *New-York Evening Post*, he dredged up the relevant quotations from Query VIII of *Notes* placing them in columns side-by-side with Jefferson's words in his first annual message advocating liberalized naturalization. Hamilton bluntly called Jefferson's message "a flourish of rhetoric" whose purpose was to gain him additional immigrant votes.[32]

Hamilton's sardonic charges were half-accurate. Disgusted by Federalist persecution of immigrant adherents to his party, Jefferson had returned to a stance he adopted during the Revolution, when in the throes of idealistic zeal he wrote the Declaration of Independence. His 1776 draft constitution for Virginia,

---

[31] Peterson, ed., *Jefferson: Writings*, 508. On the parliamentary statute of 1740, see Morris, ed., *Encyclopedia of American History*, 445.

[32] "Lucius Crassus," "The Examination: Number VII," in Harold C. Syrett, ed., *Papers of Alexander Hamilton*, 27 vols. (New York: Columbia University Press, 1961–1987), 25:491–95. For an unconventional psychological analysis of Jefferson's and Hamilton's statements on immigrants and immigration, see Ali Behdad, "Founding Myths of the Nation; or What Jefferson and Hamilton Forgot about Immigration," *Aztlán: A Journal of Chicano Studies* 25/2 (Fall 2000): 143–49.

composed at Philadelphia, granted citizenship to "all persons" who merely promised to reside in the state for seven years. They "shall be considered as residents and entitled to all the rights of persons natural born."[33] His even more liberal 1783 draft granted citizenship and the vote to anyone who promised to obey the laws and reside within the state for a year. This was practically universal suffrage for all "free male citizens" resident in the county for one year, landholders, or enrollees in the militia; even free male Blacks were apparently included.[34]

After retiring from politics, Jefferson supported antislavery British immigrants who wished to settle as farmers on the frontier. Demonstrating an Anglophilia that he had expressed in private letters and at times in his foreign policy (as in threatening to form an alliance with Great Britain to obtain New Orleans and the Floridas in 1803 and 1805), he claimed to prefer British settlers. He informed Flower that the government opposed non-English immigrants "settling together in large masses, wherein, as in our German settlements, they preserve for a long time their own languages, habits, and principles of government." While the government preferred that the Germans "distribute themselves sparsely among the natives for quicker amalgamation, yet English emigrants are without this inconvenience." Thirty-five years after the Revolution, Jefferson expected British immigrants to adopt republicanism eagerly. He said, "They differ from us little but in their principles of government, and most of those (merchants excepted) who come here, are sufficiently disposed to adopt ours."[35]

In old age, Jefferson's advocacy of European immigration was virtually unqualified. He pledged to assist Flower in obtaining a tract of land, because he desired "to consecrate a sanctuary for those whom the misrule of Europe may compel to seek happiness in other climes." He insisted that American democracy's example would spur liberal reform and eventual revolution across the Atlantic without the military participation of the United States, which would provide a "refuge" and role model for Europe's oppressed. Once Europe's rulers became sufficiently alarmed by their subjects' mass immigration to the American Israel, he continued, they would be more attentive to the "happiness" of their remaining inhabitants. These "task-masters" would take notice, "that when the evils of Egyptian oppression become heavier" than the hardships of immigration,

---

[33] Jefferson's Draft Constitution for Virginia [June 1776], in Boyd et al., eds., *Papers of Thomas Jefferson*, 1:344.

[34] Jefferson's 1783 draft of a constitution for Virginia, which he published in 1785 and 1787 as an appendix to *Notes on Virginia*, is in Peden, ed., *Notes on the State of Virginia*, 210–12.

[35] Jefferson to George Flower, September 12, 1817, in Lipscomb and Bergh, eds., *Writings of Jefferson*, 15:141.

"another Canaan is open where their subjects will be received as brothers, and secured against like oppressions by a participation in the right of self-government."[36]

For Jefferson, the right of "expatriation," leaving one's native country, was natural and self-evident, as he emphasized as early as 1774 in the *Summary View.* His conviction in this matter was strengthened by "the animating consideration," or expectation, that the existence of the American republican model would force monarchs to temper their evil, arbitrary rule in a more benign manner if they desired their subjects to remain within the realm. He enthusiastically told Flower, "a single good government becomes thus a blessing to the whole earth, its welcome to the oppressed restraining within certain limits the measure of their oppressions."[37]

After the War of 1812 concluded in a draw honorable to the United States, Jefferson's hostility to the British government faded, and he hoped that their people would attain the benefits of democracy, either by peaceable reform or by violent revolution. If any government, including the British, should prohibit its people from the right to immigrate to the United States (the British government denied artisans and factory owners this right until 1828), Jefferson urged them to resort to "the other branch of our example…for imitation, to rise on their rulers and do as we have done." He applauded Flower, who provided his countrymen a "good example…a peaceable mode of reducing their rulers to the necessity of becoming more wise, more moderate, and more honest."[38] He assured Flower that the American population's native increase was sufficiently ample for it to achieve world power. He had no desire "of increasing our own population at the expense of other nations," which were "but as a drop in a bucket to those by natural procreation."[39] Pondering the need for White immigrants to replace the labor of over a million Black slaves, whom he hoped government action would liberate and send to their own independent country, Jefferson soon had cause to reassess this judgment.

---

[36] Ibid.

[37] Ibid.

[38] Ibid. Jefferson was familiar with Flower's published narrative of his travels in France and the U.S., in which the British antislavery republican, Morris Birkbeck, accompanied him. Jefferson sent his salutations to Birkbeck, "the associate of your late exploratory journeying, [with whom] I have not the happiness of personal acquaintance; but I know him through his narrative of your journeyings together through France." Birkbeck angered William Cobbett with his later pamphlets urging discontented Englishmen to immigrate to the United States (G. D. H. Cole, *Life of William Cobbett* [New York, n.d.], 225–26).

[39] Jefferson to Flower, September 12, 1817, in Lipscomb and Bergh, eds., *Writings of Jefferson*, 15:141.

Chapter 18

"I Have No Doubt but That They Will Be Good Citizens": Linking White Immigration with Slavery's Abolition

Jefferson's lifelong desire to emancipate and send abroad Virginia's entire slave population, replacing it with huge numbers of White immigrant laborers, necessitated his enthusiastic support for unskilled workers' immigration. (He apparently expected the state's abandonment of slave labor to tempt them to come.) Judging from the ambivalence toward unskilled European workers' immigration he expressed in Query VIII, either he had not sufficiently recognized the need for them or expected to fill the need for labor with native White Virginians. He probably composed Query XIV, with its description of his unsuccessful proposed revisal of Virginia's laws to abolish slavery and deport the freed slaves, at roughly the same time he expressed doubts about excessive European immigration in Query VIII. In Query XIV, he recalled that the assembly regarded the emancipation act he and Wythe proposed as an amendment to a comprehensive bill on slaves, which he called Bill 51, with such hostility that it did not even consider the proposal. The rejected amendment would "emancipate all slaves born after passing the act," allow them to remain "with their parents to a certain age," apparently on the plantation, and have the government supervise their education until the girls were eighteen and the boys twenty-one. At that point, when they were adults, Jefferson expected them to settle their own colony in "such place as the circumstances of the times should render most proper." The state government would provide them with weapons, household and handicraft utensils, even with "seeds, pairs of the useful domestic animals, &c. to declare them a free and independant [*sic*] people, and extend to them our alliance and protection, till they shall have acquired strength."[1]

Of course, Jefferson's plan, more revolutionary than anything officially proposed elsewhere during the American Revolution, never came near fruition. If it had, it would have amounted to state subsidization of a free Black nation with citizens who were furnished with everything they needed, even seeds to plant

---

[1] Query XIV, in Peden, ed., *Notes on the State of Virginia*, 138.

crops; it would have been a project more extensive than the storied proposals of Senator Charles Sumner, Congressman Thaddeus Stevens, and other Radical Republicans after the Civil War to give Blacks "forty acres and a mule." Jefferson's willingness to advocate publicly this extraordinary idea in *Notes on Virginia*, a book he desired as many people as possible to read, suggests that during the late 1780s he fancifully sought fame as an extreme abolitionist perhaps because he intended to withdraw from public life after his mission to France ended. (It is even possible that Jefferson's committee never presented such a proposal, about which no firm evidence exists, but that Jefferson wanted to be publicly associated with it to establish himself as an abolitionist, an erstwhile identity he abandoned after President Washington appointed him secretary of state and he entered the maelstrom of partisan conflict).[2]

Taking for granted his emancipation plan's feasibility, he explained that under its provisions Virginia's government would make a thoroughgoing effort to attract White immigrants from all over the world to fill the slaves' places. Concomitant with the Blacks' gradual liberation over time, Jefferson prognosticated, the state would "send vessels…to other parts of the world for an equal number of white inhabitants; to induce whom to migrate hither, proper encouragements were to be proposed. It will probably be asked, Why not retain and incorporate the blacks into the state, and thus save the expence of supplying by importation of white settlers, the vacancies they will leave?" Jefferson then commenced his—for our times notorious—lengthy explanation that Blacks' rage at their previous enslavement ("ten thousand recollections, by the blacks, of the injuries they have sustained"); "deep rooted prejudices entertained by the whites"; "new provocations" by members of both races against one other; palpable physical and racial differences ("the real distinctions which nature has made"), including Blacks' possible natural inferiority, would provoke perpetual discord, and "will divide us into parties." By the latter phrase, Jefferson perhaps meant competing political and military organizations. Providing a worst case scenario of the "political objections" to retaining hundreds of thousands of emancipated slaves in Virginia, Jefferson, apparently seeking to frighten fellow slaveholders, predicted that such antagonistic racial societies will "produce convulsions which will probably never end but in the extermination of the one or the other race."[3] Therefore, White immigration was indispensable to his project's success, and consequently to the republic's

[2] On Jefferson's virtual obsession with publishing *Notes* in the United States and distributing many copies, see Gish and Klinghard, "Republican Constitutionalism," and their full-length study, *Jefferson and the Science of Republican Government*. According to Gish and Klinghard's monograph, the most thorough yet on *Notes*, Jefferson wanted the book to establish him as a high-minded "lawgiver," consequently a Great Emancipator of the slaves (61).

[3] Query XIV, in Peden, ed., *Notes on the State of Virginia*, 138.

survival and its abandonment of slavery. Judging from his words in Query VIII, however, he was not entirely aware of immigration's significance.

During his European sojourn from 1784 to 1789, imbued with Revolutionary fervor derived from the consummated American and incipient French upheavals, Jefferson continued to ponder slavery's abolishment. His consciousness of the importance of White immigration to provide a substitute labor force for the departed ex-slaves increased. In January 1789, he composed a letter about his views on race, slavery, and emancipation to the scientist Dr. Edward Bancroft, a citizen of Massachusetts who resided in England and spied for the British during the American Revolution. Distant from slavery in pre-revolutionary Paris as US minister, his epistle contained some thoughtful statements on Blacks' capabilities. He stressed that his pessimism about manumission arose from slavery's adverse impact on slaves, and argued that bondage, not race, produced Blacks' ostensible inferiority. Alluding to rumors of Quaker Virginian slaveholders' failed attempts at manumission, Jefferson said, "As far as I can judge from the experiments which have been made, to give liberty to, or rather, to abandon persons whose habits have been formed in slavery is like abandoning children." He heard that many Virginia Quaker landlords had freed their slaves and rented them land as tenants; but they continued to find it necessary to direct their actions and plan their crop-raising, as if still their masters. "What is more afflicting," Jefferson reported, one Quaker "was obliged to watch them daily and almost constantly to make them work, and even to whip them."[4]

Jefferson was told that the Blacks refused to work and preferred to steal and that the Quakers finally returned many of them to slavery. Reluctantly disclosing gossip about the Virginia freedmen's dismal fate, he continued, "These slaves chose to steal from their neighbors rather than work. They became public nuisances, and in most instances were reduced to slavery again."[5] Perhaps these rumors increased his reluctance to advocate the immediate, en masse emancipation of Virginia's slaves, who did not know the meaning of real freedom.

Although the freedmen's alleged failure to behave responsibly distressed him, Jefferson argued that their shortcomings were the inevitable outcome of slavery's brutality rather than innate racial defect. Earlier, in *Notes*, despite his offensive remarks about Blacks, he imputed slaves' alleged tendency to theft to their enslavement, rather than to Blacks' alleged vice, and linked it directly to a slave's lack of social opportunities to cultivate the "moral sense" faculty. He

---

[4] Jefferson to Edward Bancroft, January 26, 1789, in Boyd et al., eds., *Papers of Thomas Jefferson*, 14:492. For Bancroft, see Malone, *Jefferson and the Rights of Man*, 209.

[5] Jefferson to Edward Bancroft, January 26, 1789, in Boyd et al., eds., *Papers of Thomas Jefferson*, 14:492.

reiterated this point of view in his letter to Bancroft, stating his certainty that, "A man's moral sense must be unusually strong, if slavery does not make him a thief." White legislators' brutal laws against free and enslaved Blacks thwarted the moral sense's operation. As Jefferson put it, "He who is permitted by law to have no property of his own, can with difficulty conceive that property is founded in any thing but force."[6]

Aware that his knowledge of these Quakers' allegedly incompetent tenants was essentially rumor, Jefferson "begged" Bancroft not to publicize "this imperfect information," which might hinder emancipation legislation. Intending to verify these things himself, Jefferson refused to let rumors of "discouraging...experiments" deter him. Hoping to ascertain the Quaker settlements' actual condition when he visited Virginia in a few months to set his affairs in order before returning to Paris as minister, he intended to investigate Joseph Mayo, who had reportedly freed two hundred slaves in his will four years earlier. When Jefferson returned permanently to Virginia, he intended to import an equal number of German indentured servants as he held of adult slaves, whom he would emancipate, and "intermingle" them together on fifty-acre farms (the same acreage he wished to allocate to "every person" under his ignored 1776 state constitution), like the "*metayers* [sharecroppers] of Europe." On a determined note, he assured Bancroft, "Notwithstanding the discouraging result of these experiments, I am decided on my final return to America to try this one. I shall endeavor to import as many Germans as I have grown slaves. I will settle them and my slaves, on farms of 50 acres each, intermingled, and place all on the footing of the Metayers [sharecroppers] of Europe."[7] This "experiment" never materialized.

---

[6] Ibid. See also Peter Joseph Albert, "The Protean Institution: The Geography, Economy, and Ideology of Slavery in Post-Revolutionary Virginia" (Ph.D. diss., University of Maryland, 1976), 49, 218.

[7] Jefferson to Edward Bancroft, January 26, 1789, in Boyd et al., eds., *Papers of Thomas Jefferson*, 14:492. The law freed Mayo's slaves on the condition that, supervised by trustees, they first labor sufficiently to provide funds to support the emancipated slaves too young, elderly, or disabled to take care of themselves (and thus become potential public burdens), and that their labor pay off the debts of the estate. The law included the customary proviso that creditors of the estate could seize the slaves to pay Mayo's debts; see Hening, ed., *Statutes at Large*, 12:611–13 (act passed December 13, 1787). In 1785, James Currie wrote Jefferson that news that Mayo emancipated over 120 slaves in his will had reached other slaves, who were resisting their masters, and "struggling for the liberty to which they conceive themselves entitled" (James Currie to Jefferson, August 5, 1785, in Boyd et al., eds., *Papers of Thomas Jefferson*, 8:342–43). See also Albert, "The Protean Institution," 149–50, 218. Albert misread Currie's letter, believing that he was describing an uprising by Mayo's slaves. For Jefferson's 1776 constitution, see Peterson, ed., *Jefferson: Writings*, 343.

Perhaps Jefferson's long absence from Virginia had increased his sympathy for his slaves or convinced him that they were as capable as the European peasants he had observed, some wealthy, some impoverished, on his tours of France, the Netherlands, Italy, and Germany. Contemplating this project, Jefferson was more optimistic about Blacks' future—insisting that the children of his prospective Black freedmen/sharecroppers would become "good citizens"—than he had been before or would be again. Apparently envisioning himself as a kind of surrogate father to these erstwhile freedmen's offspring, he wrote,

> Their children shall be brought up, as others are, in habits of property and foresight, and I have no doubt but that they will be good citizens. Some of their fathers will be so: others I suppose will need government. With these, all that can be done is to oblige them to labour as the labouring poor of Europe do, and to apply to their comfortable subsistence the products of their labour, [Jefferson] retaining such a moderate portion of it as may be a just equivalent for the use of the lands they labour and the stocks [of animals and corn] and other necessary advances.[8]

Although he never attempted this "experiment," during his time as US minister to France, he had something like it on his mind. When he toured the Netherlands and Germany in March 1788, he asked Hermen Hend Damen, an Amsterdam "merchant-broker," about the terms on which German immigrants, mostly from the Palatine, booked passage from Amsterdam to the United States. The merchant told him that the Germans were eager to "go to America, and settle lands on half stocks or metairies [sharecroppers' land]." He said they would be willing to work for as long as eight years for an employer in the United States who paid their passage, one year gratis "as an indemnification for the passage." They "would employ more than fifty acres each," but might expect to receive another fifty acres if they came with their wives. Since Jefferson mentioned *metairies* and fifty acres a few months later in his letter to Bancroft, the Amsterdam broker's information must have affected him.[9]

Jefferson also discussed the project with the great radical Thomas Paine when they were together in Paris during the late 1780s. "I recollect when in France," Paine reminded Jefferson many years later, "that you spoke of a plan of making the Negroes tenants of a plantation." Paine wrote this letter in 1805, after President Jefferson negotiated purchase of the vast Louisiana territory from Napoleon. Unlike Jefferson, who hoped to secure the Louisiana Purchase for the use

---

[8] Jefferson to Edward Bancroft, January 26, 1789, in Boyd et al., eds., *Papers of Thomas Jefferson*, 14:493.

[9] Ibid., 492; Jefferson's Memorandum on a Tour from Paris to Amsterdam, Strasburg, and back to Paris, March 3, 1788, in Peterson, ed., *Jefferson: Writings*, 631.

of Whites and Native Americans, Paine proposed that Congress set aside part of the area as a settlement for free Blacks who agreed to work for plantation owners for one or two years and learn the arts of plantation management. Afterwards, Paine suggested, Congress should grant the African Americans "a tract of land." It is difficult to understand what Paine hoped to accomplish by having free Blacks become planters, and probably eventually slaveholders, although Paine opposed granting free Blacks full civil rights. Perhaps he viewed this scheme as a good way of diffusing the reputedly disruptive free Blacks throughout the country instead of their remaining in the Southern states, where they purportedly instigated slave revolts.[10]

Jefferson seemed not to have taken seriously the initial expense of the resettlement project, either in providing for the needs of emancipated slaves or White European immigrants. In any case, he considered it self-evident that the emancipated slaves and their children would be citizens of the state, hopefully responsible and respectable ones. (In 1783, apparently on Jefferson's recommendation, since his proposed 1776 constitution had referred to "free persons," not color, a 1779 Virginia law, restricting citizenship to Whites was changed to grant citizenship to all "free persons," without mentioning color.) Pondering his hypothetical experiment's results, he was confident that the aging manumitees' "children shall be brought up, as others are, in habits of property and foresight, and I have no doubt but that they will be good citizens." Although he seemed to expect the young emancipated Blacks to behave no differently than White children, he contradicted himself by assuming that their "fathers," primarily responsible for their children's socialization, but who had lived most of their lives as slaves, would be intractable as freedmen: "Some of their fathers will be ['good citizens']: others I suppose will need government. With these, all that can be done is to oblige them to labour as the labouring poor of Europe do."[11] Jefferson's ambiguous

---

[10] Thomas Paine to Jefferson, January 25, 1805, in Philip S. Foner, ed., *Complete Writings of Thomas Paine*, 2 vols. (New York: Citadel Press, 1945), 2:1458 (first quotation), 1464 (second quotation). James V. Lynch, "The Limits of Revolutionary Radicalism: Tom Paine and Slavery," *Pennsylvania Magazine of History and Biography* 123/3 (July 1999): 177–99, argues that Paine never enthusiastically supported abolition, was not in the forefront of the antislavery movement, and feared the consequences of the Haitian Revolution. Nevertheless, Lynch asserts, Paine has gained an unmerited reputation among some scholars as an ardent abolitionist. "Indeed," Lynch concludes, "there seems little doubt that of the two revolutionaries it was Jefferson who harbored the most passionate and intense hatred of slavery" (198).

[11] Jefferson to Bancroft, January 26, 1789, in Boyd et al., eds., *Papers of Thomas Jefferson*, 14:492. One historian misreads this letter, claiming it evoked Jefferson's demand for free Blacks' deportation although it was one of the rare instances when he said the opposite (Christa Dierksheide, "'The great improvement and civilization of that race': Jefferson and the

denouement suggests that he was not as optimistic about his fantasized project as he appeared to be.

Nevertheless, Jefferson viewed White European immigrants as potential colleagues and comrades, as well as friendly competitors of freed Blacks. As a matter of course, he would encourage these unskilled imaginary German Redemptioners (indentured servants) to live on his plantations as part of his experiment in Black self-sufficiency. He seemingly believed that they and the Blacks he intended to emancipate (although he never did so), would together learn the fundamentals of "good citizenship" under his benevolent tutelage. Jefferson seemed convinced that Blacks, even if on average less intelligent than Whites, were sufficiently educable to work efficiently, establish functioning communities, and live in Virginia (or, preferably, according to his consistent later views, somewhere else) as law-abiding citizens.[12]

In the letter to Bancroft and earlier in *Notes on Virginia*, Jefferson proposed that Blacks be taught self-sufficiency and, in some cases, where their "geniuses" merited it, excellence in intellectual endeavors. He relied on the children of the freedpersons, if not the freedmen themselves, to be roughly equal to Whites in abilities if properly educated. Historians have surprisingly ignored his insistence, by the terms of his emancipation scheme in Query XIV of *Notes*, that the freed slaves, both male and female, receive education "at the public expence, to tillage, arts or sciences, according to their geniuses, till the females should be eighteen, and the males twenty-one years of age."[13] This plan, which Jefferson boldly published in *Notes* in 1785 and 1787, was perhaps that era's most startling proposal for Black education (theoretically providing the emancipated Blacks with greater access to schooling than most Whites of the time).

This proposal was not a mere transitory whim of Jefferson's, seemingly contradicting his assertion, in the same chapter of *Notes*, "I advance it therefore as a suspicion only, that the blacks, whether originally a distinct race, or made distinct by time and circumstances, are inferior to the whites in the endowments both of

'Amelioration' of Slavery, ca. 1770–1826," *Early American Studies* 6/1 [Spring 2008]: 165–97, at 176). For the text of the 1783 Virginia law, see "An act for the admission of emigrants, and declaring the rights of citizenship," passed at the legislative session beginning October 20, 1783, in Hening, ed., *Statutes at Large*, 11:322–24. For Jefferson's 1776 constitution, bestowing citizenship on all free "persons," see Jefferson's Draft of a Constitution for Virginia [June 1776], in Boyd et al., eds., *Papers of Thomas Jefferson*, 1:344, 353, 363.

12 For other interpretations of Jefferson at this time, see Patrick Griffin, *America's Revolution* (New York: Oxford University Press, 2013), 218–19; Dierksheide, "The great improvement," and her Ph.D. dissertation, "The Amelioration of Slavery in the Anglo-American Imagination, 1770–1840" (Ph.D. diss., University of Virginia, 2009).

13 *Notes*, Query XIV, in Peterson, ed., *Jefferson: Writings*, 264.

body and mind."[14] He expected African Americans' intellectual faculties to improve through better education and training side by side with Whites under his supervision. Moreover, Jefferson took into account his "suspicion" of Black inferiority when he proposed that they receive a better education. He never denied that, even if perhaps less intelligent than some Whites, Blacks should have the same rights, apparently even the right to vote as equal "citizens." He made this clear on the eve of his retirement from political life in 1809, in a letter to French Bishop Henri Grégoire, a vocal proponent of mulatto intelligence who was less than certain that Blacks were intellectual equals of Whites. Toussaint Louverture supposedly distrusted him because of his friendship for his mixed-race foes.[15]

When Grégoire chastised Jefferson for implying Black intellectual inferiority in *Notes*, and sent him a compilation of the *Literature of the Negroes*, Jefferson retorted that he did not think that individuals were required to earn their freedom by proving their intellectual skills. "Be assured that no person living wishes more sincerely than I do, to see a complete refutation of the doubts I have myself entertained and expressed on the grade of understanding allotted to them [African Americans] by nature, and to find that in this respect they are on a par with ourselves," he protested. As he had declared in *Notes* and other places, he was open to conversion on the question of Black intellectual equality. Unlike *Notes*, which unrealistically compared enslaved Blacks' intellectual achievements unfavorably with those of the Stoic philosopher Epictetus and other ancient Greek slaves, some of them reputedly great poets and scholars, he admitted that under conditions of slavery and racial discrimination, all African Americans, free and enslaved, lacked opportunities to realize their potential. "But whatever be their degree of talent it is no measure of their rights," he insisted. "Because Sir Isaac Newton was superior to others in understanding, he was not therefore lord of the person or property of others."[16]

---

[14] Ibid., 270.

[15] Laurent Dubois, *Avengers of the New World* (Cambridge: Belknap Press of HUP, 2004), 237. Abbé Grégoire's attitude toward Haiti was complex, but corresponded to Jefferson's in several ways. He initially opposed the immediate abolition of slavery in Haiti in 1793, considering the Blacks unprepared and fearing to antagonize the White planter aristocracy. He eventually accommodated himself to the idea, and after Napoleon's ascendancy, he envisaged Saint Domingue as a potential haven for the sabotaged French Revolution. His hope that the Haitians would adopt a form of liberal Christianity, abandon "concubinage" and voodoo and adopt white European mores was disappointed, and he became further alienated from the Black revolution when Dessalines and Christophe proclaimed themselves monarchs and expropriated the people's liberties. He placed greater confidence in the Southern mixed-race (mulatto) Republic, led by Pétion and Boyer, and was personally friendly with Boyer. Jean-François Brière, "Abbé Grégoire and Haitian Independence," *Research in African Literatures*, 35/2 (Summer 2004): 34-43.

[16] Jefferson to Henri Gregoire, February 25, 1809, in Peterson, ed., *Jefferson: Writings*, 1202.

Perhaps alluding to the existence of functioning Black governments in Haiti, Jefferson went on to assert vaguely, "On this subject they are gaining daily in the opinions of nations, and hopeful advances are making towards their re-establishment on an equal footing with the other colors of the human family." Thanking Grégoire for his compendium of Black writings, comprising "the many instances you have enabled me to observe of respectable intelligence in that race of men, which cannot fail to have effect in hastening the day of their relief," Jefferson revealed an open mind on the quest for instances of Black intellectual and literary creativity. On the other hand, he was personally unconvinced by Grégoire's book.[17]

One of Jefferson's most significant statements advocating Black emancipation was his letter in 1824 to Jared Sparks, a member of the American Colonization Society and editor of the *North American Review*, already mentioned. In this document, Jefferson reiterated his hope, first expressed in *Notes*, that newborn Blacks receive special public educational advantages at government expense. Such schooling would suit them for freedom and self-government, and once they reached adulthood, for success in Haiti, where they could participate in ruling a Black "republic" that excluded White oppressors. In his last years, Jefferson admitted his guilt as a slaveholder, and his wish to help "these unfortunate people," victims of a "long course of injuries." Alluding to his assertions in *Notes*, he designated Haiti as the best locale for the Black settlement contemplated in that volume, particularly since its government was already established. His goal was for the US government to emancipate the newborn slaves, compensate their masters for permitting them to be raised by their mothers without working, "until their services are worth their maintenance, and then putting them to industrious occupations [perhaps in a governmental factory], until a proper age for deportation."[18]

Although Jefferson noted that his proposal was nearly identical to that in *Notes*, now he had a specific destination in mind to which to send the Black freed persons. He explained that the Revolutionary ferment of the time engendered by the American Revolution itself had produced an unlikely panacea: "In the plan sketched in the Notes on Virginia, no particular place of asylum was specified; because it was thought possible, that in the revolutionary state of America, then

---

[17] Ibid. Jefferson was probably thinking of the success of Haiti in surviving as an independent country and repelling the European attempts to overthrow it, despite its division into two states, the Republic of Haiti under Alexandre Pétion in the South and the Kingdom of Haiti under Henry Christophe in the North (Jefferson to Joel Barlow, October 8, 1809, in Ford, ed., *Works of Thomas Jefferson*, 11:121). In the letter to Barlow, however, Jefferson also told Barlow that the "genius" of the Blacks discussed in Grégoire's book did not impress him.

[18] Jefferson to Jared Sparks, February 4, 1824, in Ford, ed., *Works of Thomas Jefferson*, 12:334–39.

commenced, events might open to us some one within practicable distance."[19] His incongruous choice was the Black cauldron of revolution and White expulsion and death: Haiti. Emancipated Blacks would not have to fear White enslavement or discrimination there since Whites were prohibited from settling in the country.

By 1824, Jefferson, in less detail than his proposal in Query XIV forty years before, merely recommended training the emancipated Blacks to "industrious occupations." He eschewed mentioning the "arts and sciences." Nonetheless, he made clear that young Blacks should get special training to become self-sufficient and self-governing. Thereby he attempted to rectify the previous wrongdoing that White oppression had inflicted on the slaves, infantilized like "children," even by their benign Quaker masters in the 1780s, as he wrote Bancroft, and, according, to Jefferson, rendered incapable of taking care of themselves. Jefferson consistently emphasized the need to properly educate emancipated slaves to suit them for freedom. He probably intended that the government erect boarding schools for the education of the emancipated young slaves.

In one of the most radical antislavery and nationalistic proposals of the period, Jefferson thus recommended that the US government ("general confederacy") pay for the emancipated children's "nurture with the mother a few years." This could be financed by a "very moderate appropriation of the vacant lands," since Haiti's President Boyer offered to pay for Blacks' transportation in what Jefferson labeled a "short run" trip and to provide work for Black emigrants. Jefferson thought that sale of the public lands his administration had procured by the Louisiana Purchase should be utilized to finance the emancipation scheme. He reasoned that Virginia and Georgia had ceded their colonial-era public lands to the national government in 1784 and 1802 respectively, and such slave-holding states were "the very States now needing this relief" from their alleged slave burden. He stressed that the Northern states, whose congressional representatives had threatened slaveholders with the possibility of total emancipation by congressional action during the debates over Missouri, should eagerly grasp this remedy. "The object, though more important to the slave States," he asserted, "is highly so to the others also, if they were serious in their arguments on the Missouri question." Since he proposed forcing slaveholders to surrender their newborn slaves to the government by means of a special tax, he thought that the Northern states could not demur at using national public lands to finance the upkeep of the young emancipated Blacks and their ultimate transportation as adult freed-persons to Haiti. "The slave States, too, if more interested, would contribute more by their gratuitous liberation, thus taking on themselves alone the first and

---

[19] Ibid. The contents of Jefferson's letter to Sparks are also discussed in Peter S. Onuf, "Every Generation is an 'Independant Nation': Colonization, Miscegenation, and the Fate of Jefferson's Children," *William and Mary Quarterly*, 3d ser., 57/1 (January 2000): 163–66.

heaviest item of expense," he reasoned. Jefferson estimated that within about fifty years, slavery by these means would disappear from the Union, and the "blessed effects" of its abolition be enjoyed by posterity, which would experience "a beatitude forbidden to my age. But I leave it with this admonition, to rise and be doing."[20]

Employing a "loose construction" of the Constitution that made Madison and even Hamilton seem conservatives by comparison, Jefferson knew that it was doubtful that the Constitution permitted slaves' confiscation from their masters, or the national government financing the education and subsistence of young emancipated slave children while they lived with their mothers until young adulthood. He advised Sparks, "I am aware that this subject involves some constitutional scruples. But a liberal construction, justified by the object, may go far, and an amendment of the constitution, the whole length necessary."[21]

Not long after writing to Sparks, Jefferson received a communication from William Turpin, a New Yorker and former South Carolina slaveholder, whom Jefferson's *Notes on Virginia* had inspired to emancipate his sixty slaves. Indeed, Turpin provided funding to send thirty to Haiti. He considered Haiti's duration as proof that Blacks "are capable of Self-Government." Unlike Jefferson, he believed that initially only female slaves should be emancipated and educated; they would teach their children useful skills in preparation for liberation. Unaware that Jefferson's debts prohibited him from freeing his slaves, Turpin urged him to insert a provision in his will emancipating and deporting them to Haiti.[22] Severely ill by this time, Jefferson did not reply to the letter, but its contents must have been pleasingly surprising.

Jefferson continued to maintain, as he had in writing to Bancroft thirty-six years earlier, that unless White society rectified its evil errors by properly educating the Blacks for citizenship and replacing them with White laborers, probably from Europe, his fellow slaveholders would remain responsible for Blacks' alleged ineptitude after emancipation. He no longer argued that Blacks were somehow inferior. Instead, he asserted that, by depriving Blacks of education and opportunities for self-sufficiency, Whites had rendered their experience in freedom

[20] Jefferson to Jared Sparks, February 4, 1824, in Ford, ed., *Works of Thomas Jefferson*, 12:337–38. For events in Haiti, see Baur, "Mulatto Machiavelli," 307–53; on Boyer's effort to attract Black immigrants from the United States, see "Mulatto Machiavelli," 324–28.

[21] Baur, "Mulatto Machiavelli," 338–39.

[22] William Turpin to Jefferson, March 29, 1825, Jefferson Papers, Founders Online, National Archives (founders.archives.gov/documents/Jefferson/98-01-02-5090). Turpin declared his admiration for *Notes on Virginia* and noted the impact that Query XVIII had in his decision to free his slaves, in a letter to Jefferson in November 1809 (William Turpin to Jefferson, received November 5, 1809, Jefferson Papers, Founders Online, National Archives [founders.archives.gov/documents/Jefferson/03-01-02-0513]).

especially harsh, in a sadistic, self-fulfilling prophecy. (In other letters, like that to Grégoire, he also noted the racial discrimination they faced.) Moreover, he expected a substantial White immigration to his state by unskilled laborers, or at least those willing to take unskilled positions, to fill the void on the plantations left by the emancipated Blacks. Thus, he appended the hostility to massive White immigration he had voiced in Query VIII of *Notes*.

In the final years of his life, Jefferson continued to insist that extensive White immigration was essential to his project for the abolition of slavery. In his autobiography, he reiterated both his support for slavery's abolition and his fear that, if human bondage continued, civil war and Black extermination would result. Despite the absence of existing evidence that his 1776 state committee had proposed to abolish slavery, this unpublished narrative of events, written for his family, reiterated that it occurred. Jefferson considered the matter important since he wrote his autobiography with great reluctance, and it was among his most tedious works. However, in discussing the urgency of emancipating and deporting the slaves, he rose to his wonted eloquence. As he put it, an influx of White immigrants was necessary to accomplish Black emancipation and fill the labor void. This would permit the slaves' emancipation "peaceably and in such slow degree as that the evil will wear off insensibly, and their [slaves] place be pari passu [under equal conditions] filled up by free white laborers." He warned that a compulsory exile of the Blacks after an upsurge of slave revolts would be a far bloodier solution.[23]

Jefferson did not seem disturbed at hiring a White immigrant labor force under conditions ("pari passu") similar to those of slaves; indeed, as he wrote Thomas Cooper in 1814, he thought the lives of English laborers more unpleasant than those his slaves endured. Explaining that American workers' living conditions were better than those of the British, he asserted, "Nor in the class of laborers do I mean to withhold from the comparison that portion whose color has condemned them, in certain parts of our Union, to a subjection to the will of others. Even those are better fed in those states, warmer clothed, & labor less than the journeymen or day laborers of England." He even believed slaves' family situation was more secure than that of the English laboring poor. "They [Black slaves] have the comfort too of numerous families, in the midst of whom they live, without want, or the fear of it; a solace which few of the laborers of England possess."[24]

Jefferson's conviction that the working and living conditions of slaves were not especially onerous may explain why he unhesitatingly proposed to replace emancipated Black slaves with White European immigrants, who would perform

[23] Peterson, ed., *Jefferson: Writings*, 44.

[24] Jefferson to Thomas Cooper, September 10, 1814, Jefferson Papers, LC.

the same tasks that slaves performed in the past. Whether such European workers would be found was a question he seemingly did not seriously consider.

In contrast to Jefferson's solicitude for the freed slaves, he did not bother too much about future White immigrants' fate. That he had no qualms about substituting White laborers for Black ex-slaves, whose advanced education in mechanical skills and the "arts and sciences" financed at "the public expence" he would entrust to the state, uncovers a side of his thought that students have devalued. That the White laborers would receive no educational fillips (his vagueness about their remuneration and terms of employment are also worth noting) suggests that he did not insist on special privileges for members of his own race.

In one of his last letters, Jefferson responded to William Short's request for his support of a plan for Black emancipation and sharecropper status, similar to what Jefferson had proposed in 1789 to Dr. Bancroft. In that early document, Jefferson seemed eager to allow Blacks an opportunity to exercise their freedom on Virginian soil. Contrary to his usual position, expounded in *Notes on Virginia* and his last letters, in that instance he intended to keep the emancipated Black laborers on their farms. On the eve of death, however, as he had proposed since the early 1780s, Jefferson, now confident that Haiti was a viable Black state available for settlement, reaffirmed his support for deporting government-emancipated Blacks en masse. In his opinion, that was the best means of surmounting the danger of national dissolution foreshadowed by the recent Missouri crisis.[25]

Jefferson's requirement for the freed slaves' exile from the US was callous. But it was balanced by his intention to bestow on African Americans, along with emancipation, educational privileges rare for the times, helping prepare them for economic self-sufficiency and political self-government in new worlds outside US borders. At the same time, he was oblivious to the future of the (presumably lower class, barely literate) White laborers who would replace millions of Black individuals who would finally inhale the bittersweet air of freedom.

Jefferson's mutedly expressed ambivalence toward the desirability of White European immigration in *Notes* reveals him as less dedicated to human freedom of movement, at least under wartime conditions (perhaps exaggerating the threat of incoming spies and subversives), than he is usually depicted. His enduring conviction, at least in theory, that all African American slaves should be freed and obtain the educational and material prerequisites for successful settlement overseas, and his indifference to the economic and educational circumstances of their purported immigrant substitutes, revealed him capable of recommending action

[25] Jefferson to William Short, January 18, 1826, microfilm reel 55, Jefferson Papers, LC (hdl.loc.gov/loc.mss/mtj.mtjbib025635). On Jefferson's early acceptance of an independent, emancipated Haiti, see Jefferson to Lafayette, June 16, 1792, in Peterson, ed., *Jefferson: Writings*, 991.

benefiting the most oppressed race while expecting White laboring poor to fend for themselves. Ironically, in some sense Jefferson's proposals for Black emancipation and emigration, with poor Whites replacing them as lowly workers, foreshadow, in inchoate form, affirmative action for African Americans.

Chapter 19

Jefferson's Political and Educational Theories Merge Moral Universalism and Cultural Relativism

For much of his life, Jefferson had tried to maintain the optimistic viewpoint that eighteenth-century progress, the acme of "sciences and arts, manners and morals" would persist into the nineteenth century. Unlike the Jean-Jacques Rousseau of *Discourse on the Arts and Sciences* (1750), Jefferson believed that with the wider diffusion of increased knowledge, the capacity of "public opinion" to judge rulers' integrity improved. During the eighteenth century, until the French Revolution, international morality had been part of the "political code" of most European governments, with the exception of the partition of Poland between Russia, Austria, and Prussia, which Jefferson blamed on "the atrocity of a barbarous government [Russia] chiefly." During the Wars of the French Revolution, Great Britain and France "acted on the principle that power was right." According to Jefferson, the ensuing regression to the excesses of international depravity even threatened a renewal of the Spanish Inquisition. Concluding that the only hope for a return to international morality was the European peoples' adoption of republican governments, Jefferson believed that, inspired by the example of the United States' "light from the West," the people would fight for "their rights and their power." He rejoiced at rumors that "the idea of representative government has taken root and growth" at the fringes of Europe, in such places as Belgium, Poland, and Prussia. Although at the cost of unbridled civil war, Jefferson expected that "representative government" would emerge in France and elsewhere in Europe: "The idea then is rooted, and will be established, although rivers of blood may yet flow between them and their object."[1]

Despite optimistic reports that Tsar Alexander I would embark on a new era of justice in Russia's domestic and foreign policies, Jefferson was aware of the empire's dark past in foreign relations. The Great Powers respected international honor, law, and morality for most of the eighteenth century, he recalled, until "the partition of Poland, but this was the atrocity of a barbarous government

---

[1] Jefferson to John Adams, January 11, 1816, in Merrill D. Peterson, ed., *The Portable Jefferson* (New York: Viking Press, 1975), 550–52.

[Russia] chiefly, in conjunction with a small one still scrambling to become great [Prussia], while one only of those already great, and having character to lose [Austria], descended to the baseness of an accomplice in the crime."[2] However, that blatant aggression occurred before Alexander ascended the throne.

Alert to protecting America's national interests, during the War of 1812, when Tsar Alexander, who became Britain's ally after Napoleon invaded Russia, offered to mediate between the British and Americans, Jefferson favored accepting the offer. He expected that Russia, a country with a weak navy that in recent years had often joined the northern European Armed Neutrality seeking to curb British naval power and its arbitrary treatment of neutral trade, would sympathize with the United States. Writing to Madame de Staël, Bonaparte's bitter enemy, Jefferson argued that, by accepting mediation by a British ally, the Madison Administration evinced conciliation toward its current foe. "Our accepting at once, and sincerely, the mediation of the virtuous Alexander, their [Britain's] greatest friend," he said with exaggeration, "and the most aggravated enemy of Buonaparte, sufficiently proves whether we have partialities on the side of her enemy [France]." Pretending that Alexander actually deserved the bizarre nickname "Prince of Peace," he continued,

> I sincerely pray that this mediation may produce a just peace. It will prove that the immortal character [Alexander], which has first stopped by war the career of the destroyer of mankind [Napoleon], is the friend of peace, of justice, of human happiness, and the patron of unoffending and injured nations. He is too honest and impartial to countenance propositions of peace derogatory to the freedom of the seas.[3]

Indeed, fearing that Alexander I would sympathize with American demands for neutral rights and the end of impressment, the British rejected his mediation offer, although the Madison Administration favored it.

Despite Jefferson's approval of Alexander's mediation, Russia's oppression of its eastern European neighbors soon disgusted him. "That the sufferings which France had inflicted on other countries justified severe reprisals, cannot be questioned," he noted. Unfortunately, as Jefferson sardonically pointed out, Tsar Alexander appeared no better than Bonaparte. "I have not yet learned what crimes of Poland, Saxony, Belgium, Venice, Lombardy and Genoa had merited for them not merely a temporary punishment but that of permanent subjugation & a

[2] Jefferson to John Adams, January 11, 1816, in Looney, ed., *Jefferson Papers: Retirement Series*, 9:345–47. He must have been aware that Alexander's mother, Catherine the Great, was responsible for this aggression, and that Alexander was just a boy at the time.

[3] Jefferson to Madame de Staël, May 24, 1813, in Peterson, ed., *Jefferson: Writings*, 1276.

destitution of independence and self government," he lamented. He even feared that Russia, seeking to extend its borders (which the tsar in a notorious 1821 ukase later claimed reached San Francisco), might join Great Britain in renewing the war with the United States after France's defeat.[4]

Writing to John Adams in 1821, Jefferson labeled Russia the foremost enemy of freedom and the antithesis of American standards of liberty and democracy. The Russian Empire, together with the benighted Austrian and Prussian monarchies, formed a "Northern triumvirate, arming their nations to dictate despotisms to the rest of the world." Contemptuous of the Tsar's opportunistic encouragement of Greek independence, designed to weaken Turkey, he now stigmatized Alexander I as "the hypocritical Autocrat." He suspected that, beneath "the iron cover of his Ukazes [*sic*]," he was even more dangerous to Greek freedom than the Turks were. Throughout history, he charged, the Russians and Germans (he had the recent Austrian occupation of Italy particularly in mind) acted as "Northern barbarians, conquering and taking possession of the countries and governments of the civilized world." He hoped that these "conquering ruffians" would eventually be enlightened by "the art of printing," once they got into the habit of reading books. Even if the members of the Holy Alliance continued to reject liberalism and republicanism and crushed their weaker neighbors who were fighting for freedom and independence in Italy, Germany, Poland, and Greece, the United States, he maintained, would remain as a bastion of science and freedom of thought.[5] Thus, Jefferson, far from considering Russia a potential ally of the United States, as Logan hoped, regarded Alexander I as its inevitable enemy.

After 1818, when Europe's dominant powers, united in a "Holy Alliance," crushed democratic revolutions, Jefferson's pessimism revived. He tried to maintain his equanimity, admitting that some cultures were insufficiently prepared for self-government because of past oppression. Lacking experience, their citizens could not adequately cultivate reason and the moral sense and acted self-destructively. "The generation which commences a revolution can rarely compleat [*sic*] it," he candidly observed. "Habituated from their infancy to passive submission of body and mind to their kings and priests, they are not qualified when called on, to think and provide for themselves and their inexperience, their ignorance and bigotry make them instruments often, in the hands of the Bonapartes and

---

[4] Jefferson to George Logan, October 15, 1815, in Looney, ed., *Jefferson Papers: Retirement Series*, 9:90–91.

[5] Jefferson to John Adams, September 12, 1821, in Cappon, ed., *Adams-Jefferson Letters* (1988), 574–75.

Iturbides to defeat their own rights and purposes. This is the present situation of Europe and Spanish America."[6]

In 1822, upon learning that Russia and Turkey were on the brink of war over Greece and aware of Russia's perennial desire for Turkish territory, Jefferson in effect hoped the two tyrants would kill each other off (as some liberal American isolationists, including Senator Harry S. Truman, did over a century later when Hitler invaded Stalin's Soviet Union). Employing one of his favorite derogatory terms ("cannibals"), he wrote Adams,

> To turn to the news of the day, it seems that the Cannibals of Europe are going to eating one another again. A war between Russia and Turkey is like the battle of the kite and snake. Whichever destroys the other, leaves a destroyer the less for the world. This pugnacious humor of mankind seems to be the law of his nature, one of the obstacles to too great multiplication provided in the mechanism of the Universe.

Once more, Jefferson contrasted eastern European "despotisms" with the United States, whose citizens, emulating the Quakers, whom he admired for their simplicity and lack of religious dogma, preferred pecuniary gain to war. "I hope we shall prove how much happier for man the Quaker policy is, and that the life of the feeder [i.e., exporters of farm products] is better than that of the fighter: and it is some consolation that the desolation by these Maniacs of one part of the earth is the means of improving it in other parts," he gloated. "And let us milk the cow, while the Russian holds her by the horns, and the Turk by the tail."[7] Indeed, the serfs of Russia had never known even the modicum of liberty that European and Latin American subjects had experienced. It would be difficult for Jefferson, if he thought clearly, to support Alexander I's tyrannical rule under any circumstances.

Nevertheless, during his retirement from the presidency, Jefferson adopted a cultural relativism that in some ways contradicted his rationalist, universalist Enlightenment creed. In matters of taxation, for example, Jefferson fused cultural relativist concepts with his conviction that the most moral or virtuous government was one in which majority rule took place. He had earlier believed that the best system of revenue was a democratic, graduated, progressive tax in which "all public expences, whether of the general treasury, or of a parish or county…[were] supplied by assessments on the citizens, in proportion to their property."[8]

---

[6] Jefferson to John Adams, September 4, 1823, in Peterson, ed., *Jefferson: Writings*, 1477–78. Among many other letters where Jefferson expressed similar sentiments at this time, see also Jefferson to David Bailie Warden, October 31, 1823, in Diamond, ed., "Some Jefferson Letters," 242.

[7] Jefferson to John Adams, June 1, 1822, ibid., 578–79.

[8] Query XIV, *Notes on Virginia*, in Peterson, ed., *Jefferson: Writings*, 263.

Jefferson's Political and Educational Theories Merge Moral Universalism and Cultural Relativism

In later years, Jefferson's tax views became more conservative. In 1816, anonymously composing the introduction (called a "Prospectus") to Destutt de Tracy's *Treatise on Political Economy*, a defense of laissez-faire and a work that he much admired, Jefferson briefly explained his current ideas on taxation. He was unwilling to commit himself on the merits of the physiocrats' doctrine of the *impôt unique*, the single tax on landowners, which, they argued, should provide all government revenues. Jefferson believed that the correctness of the principle was less important than whether the proposals were acceptable to the people, "whose will must be the supreme law." In his "Prospectus" to Tracy's volume, he observed, "taxation is, in fact, the most difficult function of government, and that against which, their citizens are most apt to be refractory. The general aim is, therefore, to adopt the mode most consonant with the circumstances and sentiments of the country." Adrienne Koch observes after quoting this sentence of the Prospectus, "The very first theoretical point that Jefferson has to make is thus a rejection of universal 'principles' in practical economic policy for governments, and a reminder of his belief in the consent of the governed to the measures of their government."[9]

It had been a fundamental principle with Jefferson since the 1780s that only a body directly elected by the people was justified in levying taxes. During the debate over the US Constitution in 1787, Jefferson, then United States minister to France, gave lengthy commentaries on his opinion of the new mode of government in letters to friends. During this period, Jefferson expressed reluctance to trust the people to elect both houses of the legislature. Indeed, in 1776, when devising a new constitution for his state, he proposed the indirect election of the state senate with a lengthy tenure of nine years, one of his most undemocratic ideas. (On the other hand, the Senate invented by the new US Constitution *was* elected indirectly, by the state legislatures.) However, Jefferson clearly believed that the directly elected lower house of Congress should be responsible for initiating revenue bills, as the Constitution provided, because it was closer to the people and more conversant with their needs. "I like the power given the Legislature to levy taxes, and for that reason solely approve of the greater house being chosen by the people directly," he wrote Madison in December 1787. "For tho' I think a house chosen by them will be very illy qualified to legislate for the Union, for foreign nations [*sic*] &c. yet this evil does not weigh against the good of preserving

[9] "Prospectus" to Antoine Louis Claude, comte Destutt de Tracy, *A Treatise on Political Economy* (Georgetown, DC: Joseph Milligan, 1817), iii, quoted in Koch, *Philosophy of Jefferson*, 150.

inviolate the fundamental principle that the people are not to be taxed but by representatives chosen immediately by themselves."[10]

However, by 1816 Jefferson confined this principle of "no taxation without representation" within a culturally relativist framework. He implied that governments should continue to employ the same mode in which they taxed the people in the past to tax them in the future, because it had received the approval, direct or tacit, of the taxpaying voters themselves. Rejecting universal principles of just taxation proportionate to wealth applicable to all times and places throughout history, he said, "The general aim is, therefore, to adopt the mode most consonant with the circumstances and sentiments of the country." He put this new axiom in its pithiest form in a letter to Judge Spencer Roane in 1821. Adopting the Polybian, cyclical view of governmental and cultural degeneration, Jefferson, after restating his fears that the new generation of Americans was too selfish and fractious to maintain the republic, resigned himself to the possibility that because of changes in American society and culture in the near future, slavery or some other issue might destroy the nation. "It is a law of nature that the generations of men should give way, one to another, and I hope that the one now on the stage will preserve for their sons the political blessings delivered into their hands by their fathers," he said, expressing himself in general terms and not specifically discussing taxation. He ended by accepting the unpredictability of cultural change and historical events: "Time indeed changes manners and notions, and so far we must expect institutions to bend to them."[11]

☙

It is probably no coincidence that Jefferson most fervently endorsed the emancipation and deportation of future generations of Virginia's slaves to Haiti after he embraced an ideology of moral relativism. In contrast to the 1780s–1790s, before the French Revolution's democratic reforms crumbled in Napoleon's dictatorship, in old age Jefferson no longer insisted that all nations follow the same moral rules. He became more dubious of his original theory, first expounded to Peter Carr in 1787, that all individuals possessed a moral sense that only needed cultivation for them to treat each other decently. Although he seldom mentioned

---

[10] Jefferson to Madison, December 20, 1787, in Peterson, ed., *Jefferson: Writings*, 915. For Jefferson's conservative proposals favoring the indirect election of the state senate in his projected constitution for Virginia in 1776, see the trenchant analysis of Elisha P. Douglass, *Rebels and Democrats* (Chapel Hill: University of North Carolina Press, 1955).

[11] Jefferson to Joseph Milligan, April 6, 1816, microfilm reel 48, Jefferson Papers, LC (hdl.loc.gov/loc.mss/mtj.mtjbib022403); Jefferson to Spencer Roane, March 9, 1821, in Lipscomb and Bergh, eds., *Writings of Jefferson*, 15:326, and microfilm reel 52, Jefferson Papers, LC (hdl.loc.gov/loc.mss/mtj.mtjbib024025).

Rousseau, Jefferson probably bestowed qualified approval to *The Social Contract*'s observations on human society, particularly Book I, chapter 8, which asserted that the transition from the "state of nature" to "the civil state" imbued human beings' actions with a formerly absent "moral quality" rather than its being wholly innate. Similarly, Jefferson believed that as human reason matured, a greater number of members of society would increase in their capacity to achieve the public good and a more equitable sociopolitical order, although most governments would fail to realize this potential. He described this idea of cumulative, modest social progress most eloquently in his famous letter of July 12, 1816, to Samuel Kercheval, endorsing democratic reforms in Virginia's constitution. "Some men look at constitutions with sanctimonious reverence, and deem them like the arc of the covenant, too sacred to be touched," he averred, declaring that experience in self-government was worth much more than mere "book-reading." He advocated gradual change, expounding the Lockean doctrine of tacit consent and believing "moderate imperfections had better be borne with; because, when once known, we accommodate ourselves to them, and find practical means of correcting their ill effects." On the other hand, Jefferson acknowledged, permanent adoption of such a passive outlook would result in a dangerous and unjust status quo, political inertia, and a calcification of existing social injustices: it would show contempt for the idea of human progress:

> I know also, that laws and institutions must go hand in hand with the progress of the human mind. As that becomes more developed, more enlightened, as new discoveries are made, new truths disclosed, and manners and opinions change with the change of circumstances, institutions must advance also, and keep pace with the times. We might as well require a man to wear still the coat which fitted him when a boy, as civilized society to remain ever under the regimen of their barbarous ancestors. It is this preposterous idea which has lately deluged Europe in blood.[12]

Jefferson blamed the kings of Europe for rejecting libertarian, "progressive" reforms, precipitating the French Revolution and the interminable wars that ensued. In this view, he agreed with Rousseau's concept in his essay "Universal Peace," that foreign nations remained in a "state of nature," tantamount to a state of war vis-à-vis one another.[13] The ancien regime's rulers had "obliged their

---

[12] Jefferson to Samuel Kercheval, July 12, 1816, in Peterson, ed., *Jefferson: Writings*, 1401.

[13] On Rousseau's ideas on international peace, see Howard, *War and the Liberal Conscience*, 22–29; Stanley Hoffmann, "Rousseau on War and Peace," in Hoffmann, *The State of War: Essays on the Theory and Practice of International Politics* (New York: Praeger, 1965), 54–87; Gay, *Enlightenment: An Interpretation*, 2:403–404; F. H. Hinsley, *Power and the Pursuit of Peace* (Cambridge: Cambridge University Press, 1963), 46–61.

subjects to seek through blood and violence rash and ruinous innovations, which, had they been referred to the peaceful deliberations and collected wisdom of the nation, would have been put into acceptable and salutary forms." Jefferson was alluding to the horrors of the Reign of Terror, which had aroused his disgust and suspicions of ersatz direct democracy.[14]

Disillusionment with France's inability to maintain a republic played a large role in Jefferson's conversion to cultural relativism, the belief that each country should adopt the form of government that was suited to its society and culture for the time being. Not all countries at all times were ready for the ideal form of government, direct democracy or its more easily adaptable, watered-down form, republicanism or "representative democracy," as it was often called. As Jefferson explained to the radical French republican Constantin de Volney in 1802, shortly after taking office as the third president, "I shall say nothing of your country, because I do not understand either its past or present state, nor foresee its future destiny. Those on the spot possess alone the facts on which a sound judgment can be formed." Implying that his countrymen's superior virtue and intelligence were demonstrated by their adherence to republican government, which they had reaffirmed in electing him president, Jefferson proceeded to dissect France's debacle. "Believing that forms of government have been attempted to which the national character is not adapted, I expect something will finally be settled as free as their habits of thinking & acting will admit. My only prayer is that it may cost no more human suffering," he concluded, reiterating his antipathy to Robespierre and the violent Reign of Terror.[15]

Nonetheless, Jefferson was enheartened by reports from John Hurford Stone, a radical Englishman residing in Paris, where he printed pro-Revolutionary pamphlets. Stone was Joseph Priestley's friend and a member of his Unitarian church. He observed that the French people maintained a desire to return to elective government and regain their civil liberties, which Napoleon had severely curtailed despite granting equality before the law. "It delights me to find that there are persons who still think that all is not lost in France;" Jefferson replied upon hearing the news, "that their retrogradation from a limited to an unlimited despotism, is but to give themselves a new impulse. But I see not how or when." Thus, Jefferson's optimism about all nationalities' seizing on the "rights of man" had given way to a gentle cynicism, even about the French people's attainment of that objective. "The press, the only tocsin of a nation, is completely silenced there," he pointed out, "and all means of a general effort taken away. However I

---

[14] Jefferson to Samuel Kercheval, July 12, 1816, in Peterson, ed., *Jefferson Writings*, 1401.

[15] Jefferson to Volney, April 20, 1802, in Oberg, ed., *Jefferson Papers*, 37:295. As he wrote later, "Robespierre met the fate, and his memory the execration, he so justly merited" (Jefferson to Madame de Staël, May 24, 1813, in Peterson, ed., *Jefferson: Writings*, 1271).

am willing to hope as long as any body will hope with me: and I am entirely persuaded that the agitations of the public mind advance it's [*sic*] powers." The friend of the Shays' and Whiskey rebellions still believed that popular revolt, no matter what the temporary cost, was worthwhile in the permanent gains made for posterity's freedom. He maintained his conviction "that at every vibration between the points of liberty and despotism something will be gained for the former. As men become better informed, their rulers must respect them the more." Writing to Thomas Cooper, who conveyed him Stone's reports on French conditions, Jefferson quixotically hoped that the French, by demanding a free press, would somehow obtain liberal concessions from Bonaparte and regain their republic.[16]

On a sober note, with the French debacle in mind, he returned to an almost Burkean concept of cultural relativism. Referring to (unfounded) rumors that Russia's Tsar Alexander I had instituted freedom of the press and abolished serfdom, he suspected that a country full of people without a history of liberty would find it difficult to cope with their newfound freedom (if indeed Alexander I had intended to offer it to them, of which he did not seem certain). "The apparition of such a man on a throne is one of the phaenomena which will distinguish the present epoch so remarkable in the history of man," he observed. "But he must have an Herculean task to devise and establish the means of securing freedom & happiness to those who are not capable of taking care of themselves." He wrote about Russian serfs and Virginian slaves in similar terms, of his expectations of their inability to take care of themselves because of centuries of oppression and depravation. It was not a racial thing with him. With undue optimism about the Russian tyrant, primarily the product of his appreciation for the Tsar's rhetorical praise of the United States, Jefferson wrote, "Some preparation seems necessary to qualify the body of a nation for self-government. Who could have thought the French nation incapable of it? Alexander will doubtless begin at the right end, by taking means for diffusing instruction & a sense of their natural rights through the mass of his people, and for relieving them in the mean time from actual oppression."[17]

Jefferson did not volunteer to write the synopsis of US laws and constitutions for Tsar Alexander I that Joseph Priestley informed him he was seeking. In keeping with his view that different cultures had different modes of perceiving political

[16] Thomas Cooper to Jefferson, October 25, 1802, in Oberg, ed., *Jefferson Papers*, 38:550–52, with "Enclosure: Extracts from a Letter of John Hurford Stone to Joseph Priestley," and notes, ibid., 38:554–64; Jefferson to Thomas Cooper, November 29, 1802, ibid., 39:83.

[17] Jefferson to Joseph Priestley, November 29, 1802, in Oberg, ed., *Jefferson Papers*, 39:85–86.

and social history, he considered a bilingual Russian author better qualified to perform the task than an Anglo-American. As he wrote Priestley at length,

> I should be puzzled to find a person capable of preparing for him the short analytical view of our constitution which you propose. It would be a short work, but a difficult one. Mr. [Thomas] Coopers Propositions respecting the foundations of civil government; your own piece on the First principles of government; [Nathaniel] Chipman's Sketches on the principles of government, and the *Federalist* would furnish the principles of our constitution and their practical development in the several parts of that instrument. I question whether such a work can be so well executed for his purpose by any other, as by a Russian, presenting exactly that view of it which that people would sieze [*sic*] with advantage. It would be easy to name some persons who could give a perfect abstract view, adapted to an English or American mind: but they would find it difficult perhaps to disengage themselves sufficiently from other pursuits.[18]

Thirteen years later, Jefferson was forced to admit that, by enthusiastically accepting Napoleon's imperial dictatorship for over a decade, the French people showed themselves unprepared for self-government, despite their superlative culture and educational structure. "A full measure of liberty is not now perhaps to be expected by your nation, nor am I confident they are prepared to preserve it," he wrote the Marquis de Lafayette, his friend from the American and French revolutions. "More than a generation will be requisite, under the administration of reasonable laws favoring the progress of knowledge in the general mass of the people, and their habituation to an independent security of person and property," he believed, "before they will be capable of estimating the value of freedom, and the necessity of a sacred adherence to the principles on which it rests for preservation." Adhering to his view that in a prehistoric state of nature, all societies had been democracies based on a social contract ensuring the liberty of all, Jefferson regretted that, unlike the Anglo-Americans, the French lacked the option to recur to historical traditions of representative government. In revolting against the king and rejecting moderate constitutional monarchy, a point at which he thought their progress should have temporarily ceased, and instead embarking on Robespierre's violent republicanism, revolutionary armies, and Paris communes, they courted disaster. "Instead of that liberty which takes root and growth in the progress of reason, if [liberty is] recovered by mere force or accident, it becomes, with an unprepared people, a tyranny still, of the many, the few, or the one," he

[18] Ibid., 86; Joseph Priestley to Jefferson, October 29, 1802, in Oberg, ed., *Jefferson Papers*, 38:598; Jefferson's undated "Extract from a Letter of John Hurford Stone to Joseph Priestley," ibid., 38:599–600.

said.[19] In this, he might have added, Western Europe's French had shown themselves hardly more successful than Louverture's Haitians. He did not recall the enthusiasm he expressed in 1793, when, safely ensconced in Philadelphia as secretary of state, he extolled France's proclamation of a republic although he considered the execution of Louis XVI unnecessary.[20]

Jefferson's prescription for evolutionary social and political change as peoples increased in education and scientific and cultural progress seemed to apply only to countries that were already "Westernized" or "European" to some extent. They had to possess a political culture of respect for the individual, some understanding of popular rule, a heritage of scientific curiosity, and a written language. Where such prerequisites left the tribes of Africa or Asia or even the fledgling, nearby Caribbean nations of Latin America and Haiti was a question that Jefferson did not directly address in his letter to Kercheval, insisting that, "laws and institutions must go hand in hand with the progress of the human mind." He was unimpressed with the progress of the South American "republics" toward democracy and greatly disappointed by the failure of France and other European countries to maintain popular government during the great wars of the French Revolution and Napoleon.

Jefferson's burgeoning cynicism manifested itself in an unlikely venue. Propagandizing for his new university in Virginia in 1818, he found it expedient to impugn the firmness of the "moral sense" of the Native Americans to whom he had originally ascribed that virtue in *Notes on Virginia* nearly forty years earlier. Despite his admiration for the Indians' anarchical democracy, he sardonically denounced them as intellectual throwbacks, similar to his aristocratic, atavistic Federalist political enemies who, he believed, rejected the idea of inevitable human progress. He was convinced that the Federalists sought to retard advancement in the arts and sciences, as proven by their Alien and Sedition Acts, which persecuted foreign scientists and opposition political writers. After his election as president in 1801, partly in reaction to Federalist repression, Jefferson buoyantly wrote his old colleague John Dickinson,

> What a satisfaction have we in the contemplation of the benevolent effects of our efforts, compared with those of the leaders on the other side [Federalists], who have discountenanced all advances in science as dangerous innovations, have endeavored to render philosophy and republicanism

---

[19] Jefferson to Lafayette, February 14, 1815, in Peterson, ed., *Jefferson: Writings*, 1360–61.

[20] Malone, *Jefferson and the Ordeal of Liberty*, chs. 3 and 4.

terms of reproach, to persuade us that man cannot be governed by the rod, etc. I shall have the happiness of living and dying in the contrary hope.[21]

Seventeen years later, praising his new university, he tacitly compared his Harvard- and Yale-educated Federalist opponents with illiterate American Indians. Insisting that education was indispensable to scientific discovery and increased comforts and inventions, he expostulated,

> What, but education, has advanced us beyond the condition of our indigenous neighbors? And what chains them to their present state of barbarism and wretchedness, but a bigoted veneration for the supposed superlative wisdom of their fathers, and the preposterous idea that they are to look backward for better things and not forward, longing, as it should seem, to return to the days of eating acorns and roots, rather than indulge in the degeneracies of civilization?[22]

For Jefferson and many others, American Indians' technological backwardness now seemed morally culpable. They believed that the Native Americans' possession of millions of acres of unused land hindered humankind from achieving the higher quality of life afforded by modern inventions and productive implements and conveniences. However, it is likely that Jefferson, in his own mind, was covertly attacking his Federalist and evangelical opponents, who opposed the

---

[21] Jefferson to John Dickinson, March 6, 1801, in Koch and Peden, eds., *Life and Selected Writings*, 561.

[22] [Jefferson] Report of the Commissioners for the University of Virginia, August 4, 1818, in Joyce Appleby and Terence Ball, eds., *Jefferson: Political Writings* (New York: Cambridge University Press, 1999), 301. Jefferson made a nearly-identical analogy between the views of the Indians, who "inculcate a sanctimonious reverence for the customs of their ancestors; that whatsoever they did, must be done through all time; that reason is a false guide," and his conception of the Federalists' ideology when they forced through the Alien and Sedition Acts, in his Second Inaugural Address (Peterson, ed., *Jefferson: Writings*, 520–21). For Jefferson's critique of the intellectual myopia and intolerance of his Federalist enemies in church and state, see also, e.g., Jefferson to Elbridge Gerry, January 26, 1799, in Boyd et al., eds., *Papers of Thomas Jefferson*, 30:646–47; Jefferson to Joseph Priestley, January 27, 1800, in Ford, ed., *Works of Thomas Jefferson*, 9:18–19; Jefferson to Priestley, March 21, 1801, in Koch and Peden, eds., *Life and Selected Writings*, 562–63. See also the excellent summary in Joseph Charles, *The Origins of the American Party System* (Chapel Hill: University of North Carolina Press, 1956), 76–80. On the popular and scientific obsession with inventions and discoveries that would contribute to the happiness and convenience of the individual during this period, see John E. Crowley's "The Sensibility of Comfort," *American Historical Review* 104/3 (June 1999): 749–82, and his *The Invention of Comfort: Sensibilities and Design in Early Modern Britain and Early America* (Baltimore: Johns Hopkins University Press, 2001). See also Cary Carson et al., eds., *Of Consuming Interests: The Style of Life in the Eighteenth Century* (Charlottesville: University of Virginia Press, 1994).

secularized, liberal curriculum he proposed for the University of Virginia. He used the Native Americans as a convenient metonym for the educated White "savages" who denounced his enlightened educational philosophy.[23]

Despite general fears in the slaveholding states that an educated Black population would foment slave insurrection, Jefferson favored educating slaves. He or his family members had taught several of his most favored and valuable slaves to read and write, among them his personal servant Burwell Colbert, his cooper (barrel-maker) Barnaby Gillette (surname), and Sally Heming's brothers, the furniture-maker John and the chef James. A slave at Poplar Forest, Hannah Hubbard, was also literate. In 1818, she wrote Jefferson a letter, regretting that his poor health prevented him from making his annual visit to Poplar Forest and urging him to accept Christ into his life before he died.[24]

Before the 1830s, most Southern states had no laws prohibiting slaves or free Blacks from learning or being taught how to read. In accordance with Protestant doctrine, slaveholders often taught their slaves to read so that they could peruse the Bible. Hoping to use Scripture as a benign weapon of social control, they would try to convince their slaves to accept the idea that bondage was God's will. During Jefferson's lifetime, Virginia law did not prohibit slaves from learning to read and write. Even during the 1850s, when fear of slave uprisings in Virginia was at its height, the state continued to permit masters to teach their slaves to read and write although outsiders were barred from instructing them. During the 1850s, only North and South Carolina, Georgia, and, to a limited extent, Virginia, prohibited slaves from achieving literacy. Sporadically during the 1830s and 1840s, Alabama denied slaves and free Blacks the right to learn to read and write; from 1830 to 1841, Louisiana laws imposed fines and imprisonment on any person who taught slaves literacy. Even these few laws, which violated the slaveholders' assumed right to treat their slaves as they pleased, were not strictly enforced.[25]

---

[23] This is Eugene R. Sheridan's argument in his introduction to Adams, ed., *Jefferson's Extracts from the Gospels.*

[24] For examples of the literacy of some of Jefferson's slaves, see McLaughlin, *Jefferson and Monticello*, 120–21, and ch. 4, "To Possess Living Souls," passim, and Stanton, *Free Some Day*, 98–100. For Hannah Hubbard to Jefferson, November 25, 1818, see McLaughlin, *Jefferson and Monticello*, 120–21. Cameron Addis, *Jefferson's Vision for Education, 1760–1845* (New York: Peter Lang, 2003), 12, claims that Jefferson unconditionally opposed Black literacy.

[25] Janet Cornelius, "'We Slipped and Learned to Read': Slave Accounts of the Literacy Process, 1830–1865," *Phylon* 44/3 (1983): 171–86, at 173–74n. Calculating based on ex-slaves' narratives conducted during the 1930s, Cornelius estimated that about 5 percent of Southern slaves knew how to read and write (172). On Virginia slaveholders' obsessive fear of slave revolt in the decade before the Civil War, see William A. Link, *Roots of Secession: Slavery and Politics in Antebellum Virginia* (Chapel Hill: University of North Carolina Press, 2005).

Jefferson probably felt misgivings that most slaves were illiterate. He was aware that, if kept uneducated and uninformed, they would be unsuited for liberty and less useful and efficient as enslaved workers on his estates. Contributions of funds by a few benevolent, religiously motivated Quaker and Methodist slave-holders would be insufficient to educate all Virginia's slaves for freedom, he pointed out. A public educational system financed by state taxes would be required. This was among the assumptions behind Jefferson's proposed law for the emancipation and deportation of all Virginia's slaves, which, published in *Notes*' Query XIV but never debated in the assembly, stipulated the state government's responsibility for educating the Blacks and teaching them a trade or profession to accommodate their disparate abilities. He intended his new law,

> To emancipate all slaves born after passing the act...and further directing, that they should continue with their parents to a certain age, then be brought up, at the public expence, to tillage, arts or sciences, according to their geniusses, till the females should be eighteen, and the males twenty-one years of age, when they should be colonized to such place as the circumstances of the times should render most proper, sending them out with arms, implements of household and of the handicraft arts, seeds, pairs of the useful domestic animals, &c. to declare them a free and independant [*sic*] people, and extend to them our alliance and protection, till they shall have acquired strength.[26]

As Jefferson's ill-fated statute suggests, as a young man in his thirties he may have regretted failing to instruct his slaves in literacy. G. K. Van Hogendorp, a young Dutch geographer who visited Monticello in 1784, recorded, "the gradual emancipation of the Negros [*sic*] is one of his favorite projects."[27] Hogendorp, who later became a conservative opponent of the French Revolution, much admired Jefferson. However, his notes of his visit, which he showed to Jefferson, to whom he had become devoted, decried the deep class divisions in Virginia between rich slaveholders and poor non-slaveholding farmers. He argued that the disparity between rich and poor was most evident in their educational attainments. Wealthy planters aspired to be great scientists and intellectuals like European philosophes while the poor Whites remained "brutes," as illiterate as Black slaves. Hogendorp charged that such vast differences in education did not exist among New England farmers. Perhaps suspecting that he was the covert target of this attack on the planters' intellectual elite, Jefferson indignantly wrote (privately) in English in the margin of his copy of Hogendorp's notes, which were in

---

[26] Query XIV, *Notes on Virginia*, in Peden, ed., *Notes on the State of Virginia*, 138.

[27] Jefferson's desire for abolition was mentioned in Hogendorp's "Notes" [1784], quoted in Boyd et al., eds., *Papers of Thomas Jefferson*, 7:82n. For details on Hogendorp's life, see Howard C. Rice, ed., *The College at Princeton* (Princeton: Princeton University Library, 1949).

French, "If this [commentary] be confined to the slave, the observation will be just but if it is meant to be extended to the poor among the Whites in Virginia, I believe it will be found that they possess the first elements of learning equally with the poor citizens of Massachusetts. By the first elements I mean reading, writing, and some arithmetic, which 9 out of 10 of our poor possess."[28]

Twelve years later, in 1796, a devout Quaker abolitionist who had earlier freed his eighty bondspersons, Robert Pleasants, a wealthy Henrico County merchant-planter who owned the estate at Curlis, asked Jefferson to join him in a program to educate plantation slaves. On the question of slaves acquiring a modicum of grammar school education, Jefferson combined pragmatism and cynicism. He advised Pleasants that, if the state emancipated all Virginia's slaves, they should receive public education to make them better citizens—a more thorough schooling than the "private liberalities" of individual planters would provide. Proposing to expand the defeated public education law he had proposed in the state assembly in 1776, his famous Bill for the More General Diffusion of Knowledge, which had ignored slaves, Jefferson advised that county governments would do a better job than private individuals in administering bondspersons' instruction. "I apprehend that private liberalities will never be equal but to local and partial effects," Jefferson wrote. "Permit me therefore to suggest to you the substitution of that [i.e., public education] as a more general and certain means of providing for the instruction of the slaves, and more desireable [*sic*] as they would in the course of it be mixed with those of free condition." (It seems probable that Jefferson intended free and enslaved Blacks to sit in the same classroom, rather than that free Whites and all Blacks learn together in integrated facilities, although this is not clear.) Considering, apparently facetiously, the possibility that an education might encourage slaves to develop schemes of violent emancipation, Jefferson pondered whether it was best that slaves whose masters did not intend to manumit them in the near future should remain illiterate. Apparently, he expected some masters would want to thwart their slaves' gaining ideas of their natural right to liberty and other incitements to revolt against the White man's "despotism" by reading such documents as the Declaration of Independence. In an unjust, slave-based society, he reasoned, the acquisition of knowledge of human beings' "natural right" to freedom, a legacy of the Enlightenment individualistic calculus that enslaved them, might contribute to the slaves' despair, anger, and likely violence instead of to their well-being ("happiness"). While expressing his

---

[28] Jefferson's comments are in "Hogendorp Notes" (1784), in Boyd et al., eds., *Papers of Thomas Jefferson*, 7:218n. For additional information on Hogendorp and Jefferson, see Thomas K. Murphy, *A Land without Castles: The Changing Image of America in Europe, 1780–1830* (Lanham, MD: Lexington Books, 2001), 61–63.

disgust for slaveholders' "despotism," he implied that in such cases ignorance might be bliss. As he pointed out, with some irony, "Whether, for their [the slaves'] happiness, it [schooling] should extend beyond those destined to be free, is questionable. *Ignorance and despotism seem made for each other.*"[29]

At bottom, this caustic remark stridently displayed Jefferson's contempt for the institution of slavery. He understood that, despite his efforts to be a kind master, African American bondage was even under the best of conditions naked tyranny ("despotism"). If he expected Pleasants to take him literally, Jefferson's words imply that in discussing slavery he could occasionally be coldly realistic and self-protective, rather than magnanimous. However, since Pleasants was a leading abolitionist, it is more likely that Jefferson knew he would take his statement as a sardonic expression of his antipathy to slavery, especially since he simultaneously expressed hope that the assembly would eventually proclaim mass emancipation. This accorded with his lifelong belief that all slaves should be liberated, and in adulthood exiled from the United States.

☙

During the 1820s, Jefferson compellingly stressed the indispensability of a system of public education in fostering morality, and by implication, successful Black citizenship. This was the period when his original preference for Haiti as the "receptacle" of emancipated slaves, quasi-officially expressed to Monroe in November 1801, revived. He agreed with the English Quaker communist Cornelius Camden Blatchly, whose works he owned and probably read, that the common ownership of property in small societies would promote the "equal rights of man" and enable people to "exist in habits of virtue, order, industry, and peace." Such a

---

[29] Jefferson to Robert Pleasants, August 27, 1796, in Catanzariti, ed., *Jefferson Papers*, 29:177–78 (my italics). Regarding Jefferson as "a real friend to the cause of liberty," Pleasants hoped he would join him in undertaking the "Instruction of Black children" to prepare them for freedom, which he considered their inevitable "right" (Pleasants to Jefferson, June 1, 1796, ibid., 29:120). Pleasants was disappointed at the education bill the Virginia assembly passed in December 1796, which ignored slaves. Although free Blacks were nominally included, Pleasants predicted that the "prevailing prejudices against that unfortunate race of people, will be an obstruction to an equal participation," and that the county courts would discriminate against them in enforcing the act (Pleasants to Jefferson, February 8, 1797, ibid., 29:287–88). For a detailed case study of Robert Pleasants's efforts in the Virginia courts during the 1790s to free his deceased father John's slaves in accordance with his father's wish, despite the opposition of the nominal heirs, see James H. Kettner, "Persons or Property? The Pleasants Slaves in the Virginia Courts, 1792–1799," in Ronald Hoffman and Peter J. Albert, eds., *Launching the Extended Republic: The Federalist Era* (Charlottesville: University of Virginia Press, 1996), 136–55. See also Kenneth L. Carroll, ed., "Robert Pleasants on Quakers," *Virginia Magazine of History and Biography* 86/1 (January 1978): 3–16.

community, Jefferson said, was "a state of as much happiness as heaven has been pleased to deal out to imperfect humanity." Probably with Native American tribes in mind, he said that he had personally observed such societies. Nevertheless, he believed that in large groups, including the Union's individual states, communism was not feasible. He added that he was aware that, despite the existence of an innate moral sense, there would always be immoral people in the world; therefore, he doubted that the principle of equal ownership of property was enforceable. Instead of the quixotic ideal of a uniform and universal moral sense, Jefferson confessed, "I look to the diffusion of light and education as the resource most to be relied on for ameliorating the condition, promoting the virtue, and advancing the happiness of man." Expounding his matured, relativist moral sense theory, he continued, "That every man shall be made virtuous, by any process whatever, is, indeed, no more to be expected, than that every tree shall be made to bear fruit, and every plant nourishment. The briar and bramble can never become the wine and olive; but their asperities may be softened by culture, and their properties improved to usefulness in the order and economy of the world."[30]

As he had written Law eight years earlier, though he now employed horticultural analogies, Jefferson believed that even evil-disposed individuals could be educated to contribute to society. "And I do hope, in the present spirit of extending to the great mass of mankind the blessings of instruction, I see a prospect of great advancement in the happiness of the human race; and that this may proceed to an indefinite, altho' not to an infinite degree." Despite the collectivist tendencies of Blatchly's project, he wished "every success to the views of your society which their hopes can promise."[31]

Thus, in his waning years Jefferson aptly summarized his cautiously optimistic philosophy of cultural relativism. Although he hoped for human progress, and considered its prerequisites present, he did not view it as inevitable.

☙

Just as he derided American Indians' alleged savagery and failure to contribute to their women's comfort, Jefferson denounced in similar terms those national avatars of science and education, Great Britain and France. Their savagery, selfishness, and violations of the laws of nations in conducting the Napoleonic Wars, the bloodiest conflict on record up to that time, and their accompanying violations of neutral rights on the seas, including seizures of American shipping and Britain's impressment (kidnapping) of American sailors into the British Navy,

---

[30] Jefferson to Cornelius Camden Blatchly, October 21, 1822, in Lipscomb and Bergh, eds., *Writings of Jefferson*, 15:399–400.

[31] Ibid.

inflamed him against their depraved moral sense. He felt ashamed of the recourse to barbarous, unstinting warfare in the nineteenth century by the most ostensibly civilized nations. As he said of Napoleon's deceitful diplomacy and its emulation by his British, Russian, and Prussian enemies:

> The total banishment of all moral principle from the code which governs the intercourse of nations, the melancholy reflection that after the mean, wicked and cowardly cunning of the cabinets of the age of Machiavelli had given place to the integrity and good faith which dignified the succeeding one of a Chatham and Turgot, that this is to be swept away again by the daring profligacy and avowed destitution of all moral principle of a Cartouche and a Blackbeard, sickens my soul unto death.[32]

Reflecting that the major powers' immoral wars and commercial restrictions made it imperative for the United States to become self-sufficient in manufactures and produce its own weaponry, Jefferson wrote,

> Who in 1785 could foresee the rapid depravity which was to render the close of that century the disgrace of the history of man? Who could have imagined that the two most distinguished in the rank of nations, for science and civilization, would have suddenly descended from that honourable eminence, and setting at defiance all those moral laws established by the Author of nature between nation and nation, as between man and man, would cover earth and sea with robberies and piracies, merely because strong enough to do it with temporal impunity.[33]

Between 1810 and 1820, Jefferson often reiterated his disillusionment with European violence and wars of aggression, believing they called into question his entire Enlightenment perspective of inevitable progress. In terms of higher education's beneficial effect on the moral sense, he contradicted himself: even highly educated European peoples and rulers behaved like savages in conducting their technologically superior wars of mass destruction, thereby demonstrating that advanced education and lofty cultural achievements did not necessarily guarantee a

---

[32] Jefferson to William Duane, April 4, 1813, in Lipscomb and Bergh, eds., *Writings of Jefferson*, 13:230, quoted in Charles M. Wiltse, *The Jeffersonian Tradition in American Democracy* (Chapel Hill: University of North Carolina Press, 1935), 180–81. Cartouche was a young eighteenth-century French robber, notorious for his reckless exploits.

[33] Jefferson to Benjamin Austin, January 9, 1816, in Appleby and Ball, eds., *Political Writings*, 567. For more on Jefferson's concept of international moral order and his disappointment at its wanton violation by the British and French (who thereby also harmed American interests) during the Wars of the French Revolution (1789–1815), see Wiltse, *Jeffersonian Tradition*, 178–200, and Peter S. Onuf and Nicholas G. Onuf, *Federal Union, Modern World* (Madison: Madison House, 1993).

greater degree of human decency and "moral sense." How could he blame Dessalines and Henry Christophe for emulating their intellectual "superiors" and mentors in carnage, Jefferson might have asked himself, thereby justifying his silence in the face of their destructive, dictatorial regimes.

The French Revolution's failure to install a stable republic, like the Haitian Revolution's triumph in overthrowing European rule—both cataclysms inspired by the paradigmatic American Revolution of 1776—only to grotesquely metamorphose into military dictatorships, caused Jefferson to modify his assumption that every people was as ready as his own for self-government once it eliminated oppressive rulers.[34] It also undermined his belief that a single, Enlightenment-rationalist "moral sense" was valid for every culture and nationality. Impelled by disgust at the failure of both illiterate Haitians and "enlightened" Frenchmen to achieve popular self-rule, he now glorified the "will of the majority" in his own country, recklessly ascribing to it an infallibility he would never have done earlier in life.

For instance, in a letter in 1823 to the young Philadelphia abolitionist Thomas Earle, the Liberty Party's candidate for vice-president in 1840, Jefferson revived his idea of thirty-four years earlier that all laws should automatically become void after twenty years unless specifically re-approved by a legislative majority. According to his interpretation, private property, as a creation of "civil society," only received its sanctity from positive, statutory law. "The laws of civil society indeed for the encouragement of industry, give the property of the parent to his family on his death; and in most civilized countries permit him even to give it, by testament, to whom he pleases," he observed. By failing to repeal an existing law, the legislature granted it an "implied assent," as Jefferson called it, emulating Locke, but it "does not lessen the right of that majority to repeal, whenever a change of circumstances, or of will calls for it." The legislature's mere "habit" of leaving most laws in force, in compliance with "civil practice," did not obviate its "natural right" of revocation.[35]

Alarmed by the disturbing political situation in Europe, South America, and Haiti, the aging Jefferson became skeptical of man's capacity for virtuous self-government. He turned resignedly from stressing the probity of the individual "moral sense" to the self-evident justice of the *lex majoris partis* (will of the majority) or, should that prove unfeasible, autochthonous self-determination—even by a minority—as a source of legitimate leadership. Disappointed that the Roman Catholic population of South America paid homage to priests and dictators

[34] Patrice Higonnet, *Sister Republics* (Cambridge: Harvard University Press, 1976); Gary B. Nash, *Death or Liberty* (Cambridge: Harvard University Press, 2005).

[35] Jefferson to Thomas Earle, September 24, 1823, microfilm reel 54, Jefferson Papers, LC (hdl.loc.gov/loc.mss/mtj.mtjbib024757).

instead of creating republican governments, Jefferson aptly warned, "History, I believe, furnishes no example of a priest-ridden people maintaining a free civil government. This marks the lowest grade of ignorance, of which their civil as well as religious leaders will always avail themselves for their own purposes.... These last, I fear, must end in military despotisms." Nevertheless, he acquiesced in such negative outcomes for republicanism, in South America as in Haiti, taking solace in the circumstance that independent colonies, like the United States after 1783, would at least be free of European domination, free to make their own mistakes without external coercion or forced involvement in foreign wars. As he eloquently put it in a letter in 1813 presaging the Monroe Doctrine ten years later, "But in whatever governments they end they will be *American* governments, no longer to be involved in the never-ceasing broils of Europe. The European nations constitute a separate division of the globe; their localities make them part of a distinct system; they have a set of interests of their own in which it is our business never to engage ourselves." Perhaps deliberately avoiding mention of the Haitian regime, a dictatorship that had bungled along for a decade as an ersatz empire, Jefferson put an optimistic gloss on the ongoing hemispheric revolution. "America has a hemisphere to itself," he said. "It must have its separate system of interests, which must not be subordinated to those of Europe." Jefferson thoughtfully reminisced about the political changes occurring in the fifty years after 1763, when he was only twenty, including the establishment of the United States, history's first successful republic. He hoped that, over the next fifty years, "the other parts of the American hemisphere" would adopt "the principles of our portion of it, concurring with us in the maintenance of the same system."[36]

Looking toward the future, Jefferson embraced the possibility that the illiterate, non-English peoples of the hemisphere might evolve toward popular self-government and liberal reform. Aware that this would probably not happen during his lifetime, he accepted the reality of violent, priest-ridden dictatorships as preferable to persisting colonialism under the aegis of European monarchies. He went so far as to envisage the United States acting as a republican policeman in the Americas, carrying a big stick to protect its neighbors' evolving national self-determination, whatever its political form, from the intervention of European autocracies. As he put it, "When our strength will permit us to give the law of our hemisphere, it should be that the meridian of the mid-Atlantic should be the line of demarcation between war and peace, on this side of which no act of hostility should be committed, and the lion and the lamb lie down in peace together."[37]

---

[36] Jefferson to Alexander Von Humboldt, December 6, 1813, in Lipscomb and Bergh, eds., *Writings of Jefferson*, 14:21–22.

[37] Jefferson to Dr. John Crawford, January 2, 1812, ibid., 13:118–19.

Jefferson tried to dispel his doubts about the future by substituting his newfound political relativism for his longtime adherence to traditional, uniform Enlightenment principles of virtue, democracy, and freedom of thought. Writing to the optimistic, world-renowned German geographer, explorer, and natural scientist Alexander von Humboldt, he acknowledged, "Whether the blinds of bigotry, the shackles of the priesthood, and the fascinating glare of rank and wealth, give fair play to the common sense of their people, so far as to qualify them for self-government, is what we do not know. Perhaps our wishes may be stronger than our hopes."[38] He resigned himself to the South American "republics'" likely failure, fettered by traditions of glowering aristocratic and religious intolerance, to adopt genuinely representative institutions in his lifetime.

[38] Jefferson to Alexander Von Humboldt, June 13, 1817, ibid., 15:127.

Chapter 20

Echoes of American Exceptionalism: Jefferson's Cultural Relativism, Haitian Independence, and the Latin American Revolutions

Despite adhering to the Enlightenment's universal values, Jefferson would have allowed races and peoples embarked on the road to political freedom time to adjust to self-government before labeling them politically "inferior" to America's democratic republic. Jefferson, ostensible paragon of the Enlightenment's struggle for the "rights of man," became a political relativist in his final years. This was partly in response to several contemporary occurrences: the relatively successful Haitian Revolution, the disappointing failure of the French Revolution, and the Spanish-American revolutions' degeneration into military dictatorship. As he aged, Jefferson applied forward-looking, progressive reasoning to his predictions for Haiti's freedom-seeking population. After retiring from the presidency, seeking some cause for optimism on the world scene, he speculated that the new Haitian state's accomplishments might eventually prove Blacks' intellectual equality with Whites, observing, "St. Domingo [Haiti] will, in time, throw light on the question."[1]

Aware of the Haitians' success in defeating the greatest European powers and abolishing slavery, Jefferson seemed permanently dejected over the French Revolution's termination in Napoleon's dictatorship. Out of desperation, perhaps, he became inclined to exonerate Haiti's autocratic regime. While simultaneously exploiting the island as a "receptacle" for American ex-slaves, despite its repressive rulers—monarchs Dessalines and Christophe in the north, and to a lesser extent, presidents Alexandre Pétion and Jean-Pierre Boyer in the south—his project would coincidentally aid the Black governments by supplying them with useful immigrants. Indeed, for a time, Haiti's rulers welcomed all "black"

---

[1] Jefferson to Joel Barlow, October 8, 1809, in Ford, ed., *Works of Thomas Jefferson*, 11:121.

emigrants (including American Indians) to their shores with incentives and subsidies.[2]

Jefferson was not alone among Democratic-Republicans in tolerating Haiti's dictatorship. Despite their belief in human freedom and self-government, Jefferson and his colleagues (contrary to historians' assumptions) generally failed to criticize the iron rule exercised by Haiti's dictator, Jean-Jacques Dessalines, a former slave who proclaimed himself emperor in late 1804. After declaring the colony's independence on January 1, 1804, Dessalines instituted a military dictatorship, denied his people a voice in politics, and killed off most of the country's remaining White French population, between 3000 and 5000 people. Despite Dessalines's actions, William Duane's *Philadelphia Aurora*, the foremost Jeffersonian newspaper, overlooked the Black regime's atrocities and accepted its dictatorship. Duane condoned Dessalines's brutality, asserting that, if US merchants wanted increased trade with the Blacks, they would have to tolerate his rule. Moreover, Duane argued, Dessalines was essentially only imitating France's path under Napoleon. If the French, who were more "enlightened" and better educated than the Haitians, could not maintain a republic, those who had recently emerged from slavery should not be expected to. "We cannot but regret, that all people have not so much wisdom or have not arrived at such a state of civilization as to know their actual rights and to determine to maintain them," he lamented. Regretting that Blacks were enslaved throughout much of the "western world," Duane advised the United States to maintain trade relations with the Haitians, whose goal in overthrowing their French overlords was only the "mutual happiness" that all deserved. Duane concluded by advising that, in seeking an advantageous commercial relationship with Haiti, the US government should treat Dessalines respectfully, but not so amiably as to provoke French hostility. Recommending cautious diplomacy, he wrote, "As respects the relative situations of the United States and St. Domingo [Haiti], the late occurrences [proclamation of independence and retaliation against Whites] in the latter will make it necessary to follow a delicate and circumspect line of conduct, for reasons too obvious

[2] Loring D. Dewey, *Correspondence Relative to the Emigration to Hayti, of the Free People of Colour, in the United States* (New York: Mahlon Day, 1824); Baur, "Mulatto Machiavelli," 324–27; Chris Dixon, *African America and Haiti: Emigration and Black Nationalism in the Nineteenth Century* (Westport: Greenwood Press, 2000), 18–21; Floyd J. Miller, *The Search for a Black Nationality: Black Emigration and Colonization, 1787–1863* (Urbana: University of Illinois Press, 1975), 74–81; Chris Dixon, "Nineteenth Century African American Emigrationism: The Failure of the Haitian Alternative," *Western Journal of Black Studies* 18/2 (Summer 1994): 77–88; Scherr, *Jefferson's Haitian Policy*, 377, 402n.

to need elucidation."[3] Like Jefferson during his presidency, Duane considered it prudent to conciliate Dessalines and simultaneously not antagonize Napoleon by adopting an offensively friendly policy toward his revolted Caribbean colony.[4]

Despite several historians' insistence that Jefferson wished to destroy Haiti or convert it into a puppet regime, from 1801 until his death he recommended Haiti as a desirable sanctuary for Southern Blacks emancipated en masse from bondage.[5] His willingness to conceive of the moral sense as a kind of muscle

---

[3] *Philadelphia Aurora*, March 28, 1804, p. 2. For a different interpretation of this editorial, claiming that it showed that Jefferson's partisans were horrified by the Haitian Revolution and the prospect of Black rule, see Dun, *Dangerous Neighbors*, 217. For an account of Dessalines's actions, see Girard, *The Slaves Who Defeated Napoleon*, 320–22.

[4] Duane's reasoning here, employing analogies between the course of the Haitian and French revolutions, was nearly identical to that which Toussaint Louverture, Haiti's ruler, used in refuting French émigré planters' charges in 1797 that he was guilty of arbitrary violence. See Dubois, *Avengers of the New World.* Writing to Jefferson in February 1806, Federalist senator Timothy Pickering of Massachusetts, the Democratic-Republicans' bitter enemy, employed similar reasoning. Denouncing the president's anticipated approval of an embargo on trade with Haiti, Pickering pointed out that critics who accused Haiti's government of barbaric, murderous actions in annihilating its White population should acknowledge that Dessalines's brutality paled by comparison with the crimes Robespierre and his followers perpetrated against innocent citizens during the Reign of Terror (Timothy Pickering to Jefferson, February 24, 1806, microfilm reel 35, Jefferson Papers, LC [hdl.loc.gov/loc.mss/mtj.mtjbib015910]. See also Donald R. Hickey, "Timothy Pickering and the Haitian Slave Revolt: A Letter to Thomas Jefferson in 1806," *Essex Institute Historical Collections* 120 [July 1984]: 149–63).

[5] See, for example, Jefferson to William Short, January 18, 1826, microfilm reel 55, Jefferson Papers, LC (hdl.loc.gov/loc.mss/mtj.mtjbib025635). Works taking for granted that, as president, Jefferson opposed Haitian independence and cooperated in suppressing the revolution include Tansill, *United States and Santo Domingo*, 78–81, 108–9; Simon P. Newman, "American Political Culture and the French and Haitian Revolutions: Nathaniel Cutting and the Jeffersonian Republicans," in David P. Geggus, ed., *The Impact of the Haitian Revolution in the Atlantic World* (Columbia: University of South Carolina Press, 2001), 83; Zuckerman, "Power of Blackness," 175–218; Egerton, *Gabriel's Rebellion*, 160–61, 168–72, and Egerton, "The Empire of Liberty Reconsidered," in James P. P. Horn, Jan Lewis, and Peter Onuf, ed., *The Revolution of 1800: Democracy, Race, and the New Republic* (Charlottesville: University Press of Virginia, 2002), 309–30. For a recent example of an historian's *a priori* assumption of Jefferson's hostility toward Haiti, see Maurizio Valsania, *Jefferson's Body* (Charlottesville: University of Virginia Press, 2017), 161–62, 235. Valsania follows Timothy M. Matthewson, "Jefferson and the Nonrecognition of Haiti," *Proceedings of the American Philosophical Society* 140 (1996): 22–48, a less compelling interpretation than Matthewson's previous "Jefferson and Haiti," *Journal of Southern History* 61 (May 1995): 209–48. Such detailed studies as Logan, *Diplomatic Relations of the United States with Haiti*; Gordon S. Brown, *Toussaint's Clause: The Founding Fathers and the Haitian Revolution* (Jackson: University Press of Mississippi, 2005), and Scherr, *Jefferson's Haitian Policy*, address the above works' assumptions. For an earlier, balanced brief treatment of Jefferson's views on the Haitian Revolution, see Ludwell Lee

(epitomized by "an honest heart") that grew stronger with exercise and time increased his confidence that in Haiti, a popularly elected government, which he considered synonymous with a moral political order, would eventually replace the rigid dictatorship.[6] A moral and democratic [r]evolution in the Black regime would ease his misgivings over utilizing the island to redeem the United States' experiment in White democracy, abolishing slavery and most of its Black population at the same time, employing Haiti as the "receptacle." Perhaps, assisted by the leadership of Southern former slaves who gained notions of popular rule after observing their masters' political conclaves, the Haitian people themselves would eventually experience the blessings of liberty and its frequent concomitant, prosperity.[7]

As a budding "natural philosopher," although *Notes* expressed his opinion that the Black poets Phillis Wheatley and Ignatius Sancho were essentially religious enthusiasts, not engaging poets (such evaluations are notoriously subjective, in any case), Jefferson did as much as anyone to ensure a hearing for Black claims to intellectual and moral equality. For instance, in 1791 he hired the African American Benjamin Banneker to work on surveying the national capital, making him the first free Black to work for the federal government. Jefferson even attempted to publicize abroad the mathematical talents evident in Banneker's almanac, in a letter to the Marquis de Condorcet.[8]

Likewise, in the political arena, Jefferson's efforts early in his presidency to save the lives of Black rebels in Virginia and find in Saint-Domingue and Africa (Sierra Leone), a refuge for free and enslaved Blacks in the future, established

---

Montague, *Haiti and the United States, 1714–1938* (Durham: Duke University Press, 1940), 35–40. For Jefferson's anticipations regarding Haiti, see Jefferson to Joel Barlow, October 8, 1809, in Ford, ed., *Works of Thomas Jefferson*, 11:121.

[6] As Jefferson wrote his nephew, Peter Carr, advising him on his future education, "An honest heart being the first blessing, a knowing head is the second" (Jefferson to Peter Carr, August 19, 1785, in Peterson, ed., *Jefferson: Writings*, 815). In general, see Holowchak, "The March of Morality: Making Sense of Jefferson's Moral Sense," in Holowchak, ed., *Jefferson and Philosophy*, 147–64. Unfortunately, Holowchak depicts Jefferson's philosophy in a contextual vacuum, ignoring his political activities and diplomacy in such matters as the Haitian Revolution.

[7] See also William G. Merkel, "To See Oneself as a Target of a Justified Revolution: Thomas Jefferson and Gabriel's Uprising," *American Nineteenth Century History* 4/2 (Summer 2003): 1–31, at 23.

[8] Jefferson to Condorcet, August 30, 1791, in Boyd et al., eds., *Papers of Thomas Jefferson*, 22:98–99. On Jefferson and Banneker, see Silvio A. Bedini, *Thomas Jefferson: Statesman of Science* (New York: Macmillan, 1990), 212, 222–25; and Bedini, *Life of Benjamin Banneker* (New York: Scribner, 1972), 108–109, 137–52.

him as a sort of godfather to experiments in Black liberty and self-rule in Haiti and Liberia. His disciple President James Monroe helped effect the latter.[9]

Jefferson's acceptance of Southern Blacks' capacity for self-government gradually evolved into an urge to incorporate their revolutionary potential within Haiti's existence as an independent state. The slave rebellion in Saint-Domingue and other slave revolts, including Gabriel's abortive uprising in Virginia in 1800, accelerated the progress of his thought. Contrary to most historians, whose sole "proof" is a remark that Jefferson allegedly made in July 1801 to Louis-André Pichon, France's chargé d'affaires at Philadelphia, Jefferson generally favored the Haitian revolt. Critics of Jefferson's Haitian policy, who insist that he was a racist who wanted to see Haiti returned to French rule, often cite Pichon's report to Napoleon's foreign minister, Talleyrand, of his July 20, 1801, conversation with President Jefferson. According to Pichon, Jefferson replied when asked whether the United States would consider cooperating with France in re-conquering Saint-Domingue: "Without difficulty; but in order that this concert may be complete and effective you must make peace with England; then nothing would be easier than to furnish your army and fleet with everything, and starve Toussaint."[10]

---

[9] Miller, *Wolf by the Ears*, 126–28, 132, 138; Egerton, *Gabriel's Rebellion*, 160–61, 168–72; Burin, *Slavery and the Peculiar Solution*, 14–15.

[10] Pichon to Talleyrand, July 22, 1801, *Archives, Ministère des Affaires Étrangères, États-Unis*, vol. 53, fols. 177–84. The letter was first quoted in Carl Ludwig Lokke, "Jefferson and the Leclerc Expedition," *American Historical Review* 33 (January 1928): 324, although he slightly mistranslated the French. In addition to the works already cited, studies emphasizing Jefferson's alleged hostility to Haitian independence and his (broken) promise of cooperation with France in suppressing the uprising include Douglas R. Egerton, "Race and Slavery in the Era of Jefferson," in Frank Shuffelton, ed., *The Cambridge Companion to Thomas Jefferson* (Cambridge: Cambridge University Press, 2009), 75–76; Forbes, "Cause of this Blackness," 90n.; Robert L. Paquette, "Revolutionary Saint-Domingue in the Making of Territorial Louisiana," in David B. Gaspar and David P. Geggus, eds., *A Turbulent Time: The French Revolution and the Greater Caribbean* (Bloomington: Indiana University Press, 1997), 209–12, 222n20; Robert W. Tucker and David C. Hendrickson, *Empire of Liberty: The Statecraft of Thomas Jefferson* (New York: Oxford University Press, 1990), 299–301n.; Gerald Horne, *Confronting Black Jacobins: The United States, the Haitian Revolution, and the Origins of the Dominican Republic* (New York: Monthly Review Press, 2015); Horne, "The Haitian Revolution and the Central Question of African American History," *Journal of African American History* 100/1 (Winter 2015): 26–58; Ronald Angelo Johnson, *Diplomacy in Black and White* (Athens: University of Georgia Press, 2015); and Dun, *Dangerous Neighbors*, 23–25, 34, 204, 207. In Dun's opinion, however, both Federalists and Republicans deserted the Haitian Revolution after the undeclared war with France ended around 1800. "As the French threat receded, all parties described this place [Haiti] as Black, and alien," he says. Federalists feared Haiti because they thought it embodied the disorders of Jacobinism and the excesses of the French Revolution, while Republicans dreaded it as a manifestation of Black power: "Where Federalists had posed

It is by no means certain that these were Jefferson's exact words. Moreover, as historian Rayford W. Logan observed long ago, he was not specifically promising to supply France with provisions but merely advising the French to make peace with the British. After that, French or even British ships could "furnish your army and fleet with everything," without risking confiscation by British ships' blockade. Several historians argue that this alleged conversation with Pichon revealed Jefferson's antipathy to the Haitian Revolution. They ignore the obvious: that, even if he uttered these words, they were insincere. During his presidency, Jefferson did nothing to thwart the revolution in Haiti. Years after the Haitians expelled the French and declared national independence, he acquiesced in congressional passage of a weak, poorly enforced prohibition of US trade with Haiti, from February 1806 to Februlary 1808; it was too little and too late. His objective was to make a show of accommodating and appeasing Napoleon, who objected to US merchants' arms shipments and indeed all trade with Haiti. Jefferson's acceptance of the 1806 embargo on Haiti (which he did not initially propose), years after Haiti had defeated Napoleon and secured independence, was not motivated by racist malice but by his hope to gain Napoleon's diplomatic support for US acquisition of Florida from Spain. Had he seriously wished to help France re-conquer Haiti, he would have imposed the embargo in 1802–1803, when fighting between Napoleon's troops and the Haitian revolutionaries was at fever pitch. Instead, he allowed US merchants to ship weapons and provisions to the Black government.[11]

After 1801, President Jefferson semi-officially recommended that Virginia and the United States utilize Haiti as a "receptacle" for the South's Black population, beginning with rebellious Virginia slaves scheduled for hanging (a course that his friend Governor Monroe found unacceptable). Initially, conspiratorial slaves, like the participants in Gabriel's uprising, who would otherwise suffer execution, and eventually all slaves, would be emancipated and "transported," whether they liked it or not, to Haiti, the only government in the Atlantic world ruled by Blacks. This was Jefferson's hope.[12]

---

the danger in terms of French ideals, Republicans described a Black menace" (Dun, *Dangerous Neighbors*, 207).

[11] Logan, *Diplomatic Relations of the United States with Haiti*, 120. On Jefferson's "interview" with Pichon, see also Scherr, *Jefferson's Haitian Policy*, ch. 4. For Jefferson's failure to prevent widespread violations of the Haiti embargo, see Gaffield, *Haitian Connections in the Atlantic World.*

[12] Jefferson to Monroe, November 24, 1801, in Peterson, ed., *Jefferson: Writings*, 1097. For Monroe's initial objection to Jefferson's suggestion, which would bestow freedom on rebels while keeping obedient slaves in bondage, see Monroe to Jefferson, June 11, 1802, microfilm reel 26, Jefferson Papers, LC (hdl.loc.gov/loc.mss/mtj.mtjbib011443).

Intent on facilitating his scheme for emancipating and deporting Virginia's rebellious slaves, and eventually all slaves, Jefferson downplayed the Haitian government's 1804 outlawry of Whites. He also ignored Louverture's, Dessalines's and Henry Christophe's oppression of Haiti's Black citizens, who either were forced to work on "government" lands as virtual serfs, receiving one-quarter of the crop or were conscripted into the army. Denying Haiti's Black population the right to elect their leaders, Louverture and his successors proclaimed themselves lifetime rulers and seized most of the country's land. Overlooking the disheartening outcome of Haiti's "republican" revolution—or perhaps ignorant of the details, as many in the United States were, judging from prominent Baltimore editor Hezekiah Niles's naïve articles in his *Weekly Register*—the aging Jefferson endorsed Haiti's regime.[13]

Consistent with Jefferson's support for Haiti as the final destination of liberated Southern slaves were the broadening and relativization of his moral sense theory to accommodate cultural diversity. He made allowances for other societies' slower political progress toward representative government, which in his perspective epitomized political morality. Since White Europeans, most notably the French, and non-White Haitians had failed in their efforts at representative government, Jefferson was willing to forgive them both and sacrifice his original theory that true "moral sense" and the republican government that went with it, were identical for all countries and cultures. He understood that foreign political leaders needed time both to develop their citizens' moral sense and to allow for all parties' voluntary acceptance of republican government, "self-evidently" designed for the happiness and prosperity of the greatest number. (Francis Hutcheson and Jeremy Bentham, founders of Utilitarianism, had rendered this judgment before Jefferson did.) Beginning with his letter to Thomas Law in 1814, he replaced a generalized, Enlightenment attitude of uniform standards for moral and political progress with a utilitarian view, arguing that what was moral and "virtuous" was whatever beliefs or actions helped maintain social stability and the greatest feasible approximation of justice and legal equality at the time. Ironically furnishing an ideological justification for the emancipation of US slaves and simultaneously condoning their deportation to a Black dictatorship whose "citizens" or "subjects" (in northern Haiti's monarchy) were not entirely free, Jefferson temporarily qualified his moral, democratic, universal Enlightenment values. He also validated

[13] "Hayti," September 27, 1823, in *Niles' Weekly Register* 25 [or vol. 1, 3rd ser.] (September 1823–March 1824): 50–53. Jefferson said he read no newspapers other than Ritchie's *Enquirer*, but he subscribed to *Niles' Weekly Register* until his death (Bear and Stanton, eds., *Jefferson's Memorandum Books*, 2:1307, 1417). *Niles' Weekly Register* is among the works listed in Nathaniel P. Poor's *Catalogue of President Jefferson's Library* auctioned off years after his death, in 1829 (accession no. 158, *Catalogue*, 7).

the hemisphere's first sovereign Black government, administered by ex-slaves who had overthrown White imperial rule.

Thus, Jefferson replaced his original idea of a universal, uniform moral sense with an amoral, environmentalist, relativist creed, which he considered "utilitarian," but which had potentially fascistic or totalitarian overtones. His elastic definition of values, albeit inadvertently, mocked the whole idea of "moral sense." At least potentially, he justified the introduction or reintroduction of slavery through the backdoor, the front door, or the side door, whenever those in charge determined it would be socially "useful" to the community. At the same time, he never fully abandoned his kinship to the Enlightenment, whose leading figures, Voltaire, Rousseau, and Lord Kames, as well as the Scottish common sense philosophers David Hume, Adam Smith, and Francis Hutcheson, preceded him in vaunting the human conscience's potential for virtue. As Jean-Jacques Rousseau put it in *Emile*, conscience was a more valuable moral guide than reason was: "Too often reason fools us, we have only too well acquired the right to accuse it, but the conscience never fools; it is the true guide of man; it is to the soul what the instinct is to the body."[14]

Rousseau's adversary Voltaire also believed there was a natural moral sense, based on natural law, valid for all peoples and common to all races. Although Voltaire viewed Blacks as mentally and physically inferior to Whites, like Jefferson he believed they were imbued with a similar innate sense of right and wrong. As historian Harvey Chisick writes, "His [Voltaire's] doubts about biological equality…were overcome by his conviction that there existed an objective, universally valid, natural morality."[15]

Further amplifying the concept, Jefferson attempted to substitute Americans' ample possession of the "moral sense" for their lack of major universities and their apparent remissness in contributing to scientific knowledge. He implied that his fellow citizens were "noble savages," in John Dryden's phrase. In a letter in 1803 to Marc Auguste Pictet, a renowned astronomer at the Genevan Academy of Science whom Jefferson hoped to convince to move to the United States, he depicted Americans as pragmatic doers interested in advancing material well-being rather than abstract thinkers and philosophers. He also stressed the divergence in politics and habits between the farming majority, whom he considered largely Republican, and the urban commercial minority, which tended to favor the Federalist Party. "In the line of science we have little new here," he wrote,

---

[14] *Emile*, quoted in Nicole Fermon, "Domesticating Women, Civilizing Men: Rousseau's Political Program," *Sociological Quarterly* 35/3 (August 1994): 434.

[15] Harvey Chisick, "Ethics and History in Voltaire's Attitudes toward the Jews," *Eighteenth-Century Studies* 35/4 (2002): 577–600, 590 (quotation).

> Our citizens almost all follow some industrious occupation, and therefore have little time to devote to abstract science. In the arts, & especially the mechanical arts many ingenious improvements are made in consequence of the patent-right giving an exclusive use of them for 14 years, but the great mass of our people are agricultural; and the commercial cities, tho' by the command of newspapers they make a great deal of noise, yet they have little effect in the direction of the government. They are as different in sentiment & character from the country people as any two distinct nations, and are clamorous against the order of things established by the agricultural interest.[16]

Identifying his presidency with the "agricultural interest," Jefferson depicted himself as leading a society in which the majority's devotion to a government that they trusted and which they believed treated them fairly transcended class and sectional conflicts. On an "exceptionalist" note, emphasizing public unity in defense of the commonwealth as he had in his first inaugural address, Jefferson proudly continued, "Under this order our citizens generally are enjoying a very great degree of liberty and security in the most temperate manner. Every man being at his ease, feels an interest in the preservation of order, and comes forth to preserve it at the first call of the magistrate."[17]

Jefferson's readiness to differentiate between urban and rural mentalities, albeit often attributing a purer moral sense to the farmer than to the merchant, signified his incorporation of cultural diversity into humankind's ongoing if stumbling political, social, and moral progress. Among his goals were to eliminate waste, bribery, and corruption from government; implement governmental frugality by reducing the size of the army and navy; and consequently reduce taxes and increase the people's freedom and happiness. As he explained to the foreigner Pictet, "We are endeavoring too to reduce the government to the practice of a rigorous economy, to avoid burthening the people, and arming the magistrates with a patronage of money and office which might be used to corrupt & undermine the principles of our government."[18]

---

[16] Jefferson to Marc Auguste Pictet, February 5, 1803, in Oberg, ed., *Jefferson Papers*, 39:456–57. In this letter I have modernized punctuation for clarity.

[17] Ibid., 457.

[18] Ibid. For Jefferson's retention of the Army in essentially the same strength as Adams left it, see Russell F. Weigley, *History of the United States Army* (New York: Macmillan, 1967), 104–6. The Adams Administration disbanded many troops in 1800, and Jefferson increased its numbers before his presidency ended. According to Weigley, under Jefferson and Madison the "regular army was destined to reach its highest authorized strength [under congressional legislation] before the Spanish War of 1898" (105). For an interpretation of Secretary of the Treasury Albert Gallatin's policies that stresses that tariff revenues rather than government

Jefferson was enraged by the calumny to which Federalist newspapers, reinvigorated by his former supporter James T. Callender, subjected him, and he warned Pictet of US newspapers' unreliability. "I state these general outlines to you, because I believe you take some interest in our fortune, and because our newspapers for the most part, present only the caricatures of disaffected minds," he explained. "Indeed the abuses of the freedom of the press here have been carried to a length never before known or borne by any civilized nation."[19] Jefferson's chagrin that the free press, an institution he relied on in his younger days to promote truth, knowledge, and education among the public, had betrayed him because the urban men of wealth who bought most of the newspapers were his political opponents, extended into old age.[20]

ꝏ

As the new consciousness of moral and cultural relativism pervaded his thought in his final years, Jefferson felt increasingly grateful when European writers examined his fellow citizens more objectively, counteracting those aristocratic observers who were prejudiced against the United States' bourgeois-democratic political economy. Despite its imperfections, Jefferson consistently upheld the US republic as superior to other governments because of its citizens' freedom, intelligence, morality, and prosperity. His hope increased that his country would stand as a role model for political, social, and moral progress. Perhaps reflecting Adam Ferguson's philosophy, described earlier, Jefferson praised one English traveler's attempts at impartiality, while admitting he did not agree with everything he wrote. "The candor with which you have viewed the manners and condition of our citizens, is so unlike the narrow prejudices of the French and English travellers preceding you," he said, "who, considering each the manners and habits of their own people as the only orthodox, have viewed everything differing from that test as boorish and barbarous, that your work will be read here extensively, and operate great good."[21] Regretting that many European aristocrats disdained self-

---

economy were the most important factors in balancing the budget and paying off the public debt, see Alexander Balinky, *Albert Gallatin: Fiscal Theories and Policies* (New Brunswick: Rutgers University Press, 1957).

[19] Jefferson to Marc Auguste Pictet, February 5, 1803, in Oberg, ed., *Jefferson Papers*, 39:457.

[20] See Dumas Malone, *Jefferson the President: Second Term*, vol. 5 of *Jefferson and His Time* (Boston: Little, Brown, 1974), 371–88; Frank L. Mott, *Jefferson and the Press* (Baton Rouge: Louisiana State University Press, 1943).

[21] Jefferson to John Melish, January 13, 1813, in Peterson, ed., *Jefferson: Writings*, 1268.

governing Americans' capitalist virtues and inherent moral quality, he extolled foreigners who appreciated the American character.

Jefferson was confident that Americans were sufficiently ethical and intelligent to handle representative government. In 1823, in a famous letter to Judge William Johnson analyzing the origins of political parties, Jefferson stressed Democratic-Republicans' respect for the average citizen. His party's success in preserving republicanism proved that "man was a rational animal, endowed by nature with rights, and with an innate sense of justice; and that he could be restrained from wrong and protected in right by moderate powers, confided to persons of his own choice, and held to their duties by dependence on his own will."[22]

During his lifetime, Jefferson learned that not all peoples and rulers readily applied reason to government. They needed time to merge instinct and emotion with rational republicanism. He was shocked to find this true even of the highly "civilized" French, whose revolution aborted in Napoleon's dictatorship and empire, followed by the restoration of the Bourbons' aristocratic constitutional monarchy. In the Western Hemisphere, South American revolutionaries' fervid fight for liberty, which he initially welcomed, crumbled in a welter of military dictatorships and clergy-dominated monarchies, severely disappointing to him. In the final decades of his life, he lamented his hemispheric neighbors' fate.[23]

He wrote David Bailie Warden, an Irish revolutionary he earlier befriended at Monticello, that many of the Latin American revolts had self-destructed. "I wished them success because they wished it themselves; but I fear they have much to suffer until a better educated generation comes on the stage, one formed to the habits of self-government," he observed. "They have already begun to disgrace our hemisphere with emperors, and kings, and will, I fear, fall under petty military despotisms."[24]

---

[22] Jefferson to Judge William Johnson, June 22, 1823, ibid., 1470.

[23] Although Jefferson supported the South American revolutions, he simultaneously feared their failure, because of the people's illiteracy and subservience to the Roman Catholic Church and nobility. In numerous letters written during his retirement, Jefferson complained that the Roman Catholic Church and militarism vitiated South America's revolutions (Jefferson to Alexander von Humboldt, April 14, 1811, and December 6, 1813; to Du Pont de Nemours, April 24, 1816; to Lafayette, May 14, 1817, in Peterson, ed., *Jefferson: Writings*, 1247–48, 1311–13, 1384–88, 1408–409; Jefferson to John Adams, January 22, 1821, in Cappon, ed., *Adams-Jefferson Letters* [1988], 570). For Jefferson's support of the Greek and Spanish-American revolutions against European and Turkish autocracies, see, e.g., Jefferson to David Bailie Warden, October 31, 1823, in Diamond, ed., "Some Jefferson Letters," 225–42, at 242, and Jefferson to A. Coray, October 31, 1823, in Lipscomb and Bergh, eds., *Writings of Jefferson*, 15:480–90.

[24] Jefferson to David Bailie Warden, October 30, 1822, in Saul K. Padover, ed., *A Jefferson Profile as Revealed in His Letters* (New York: J. Day Co., 1956), 323; Malone, *Sage of Monticello*, 83.

Retaining his residual optimism, Jefferson placed his trust in a future in which democracy and republicanism would inevitably triumph. Jefferson acclimated himself to the fact that the planet's diverse cultures, races, and nationalities were not all equally suited for self-government. Nonetheless, he thought they had the potential for it, and would eventually find their way on their own, utilizing the United States as a role model. Although he never recorded an opinion on Haiti's political fate, Jefferson was probably aware that absolute monarchy prevailed in northern Haiti under an "empire" ruled by Jean-Jacques Dessalines and, after his assassination in 1806, in a more modest "monarchy" led by King Henry Christophe. The advent of an oppressive, corrupt autocracy and ersatz aristocracy mocked the people of Saint-Domingue's struggles as colonists-in-revolution since 1791 and as citizens of independent "Hayti" after 1804. Haiti's southern part was a pseudo-"republic" governed by an oligarchy under the mixed-race General Alexandre Pétion and his cronies, who exercised unbridled rule. Dividing some of the land into small plots for subsistence farming among army veterans, Pétion instituted a more benevolent socioeconomic regime than Christophe permitted.[25]

In old age, echoing Montesquieu's *Spirit of the Laws*, Jefferson accepted the likelihood that certain governments, like those in Latin America, long dominated by the clergy and aristocracy, might become the norm for cultures or nationalities historically deprived of economic and political self-rule. These peoples and states might suffer indefinitely from a retarded collective "moral sense." On the other hand, Jefferson disagreed with Montesquieu's assertions that republicanism was impracticable in large landmasses like the United States, and that, overall, constitutional monarchy was the best government.[26]

Still, at least before the horrors of the Reign of Terror, Jefferson was optimistic that France would emerge from its internal strife with a constitutional monarchy like that of Great Britain, if not a democratic republic. Indeed, in 1790, when France seemed destined for a representative government under a king and a popularly elected unicameral Legislative Assembly, he sought to assuage the fears of his friends among the French aristocracy, whom he had left in 1789, ultimately assuming the position of US secretary of state. As he wrote the Duchesse d' Enville, "Heaven send that the glorious example of your country may be but the beginning of the history of European liberty, and that you may live many

[25] For an engaging general survey of the Haitian Revolution, see Dubois, *Avengers of the New World.* As a rule, US historians writing about Jefferson's era eschew mention of the Haitian Revolution's outcome.

[26] Carrithers, "Montesquieu, Jefferson, and the Fundamentals of Eighteenth-Century Republican Theory."

years in health & happiness to see at length that heaven did not make man in its wrath."[27]

Within a few years, he was more pessimistic. After learning of the legislative dictatorship and mass executions perpetrated in 1793–1794 by the French Revolution's Jacobin "Montagnard" Party, under the nominal leadership of Maximilien Robespierre, he became more appreciative of the United States' unique success as a republic. Without boasting of "American exceptionalism," as later generations, infused with ideas of Manifest Destiny and democracy's superiority would do, Jefferson regretted that the French lacked the historical political experience to make representative government work. Writing to the Republican political economist Tench Coxe in June 1795, he expected the French soon to resume their efforts at republicanism with greater success. "This ball of liberty, I believe most piously, is now so well in motion that it will roll round the globe," he asserted. "At least the enlightened part of it, for light and liberty go together. It is our glory that we first put it into motion, and our happiness that, being foremost, we had no bad example to follow. What a tremendous obstacle to future attempts at liberty will be the atrocities of Robespierre!"[28]

Jefferson learned hard lessons from experience, especially in the decline of the French Revolution's happy prospects in the excesses of the Reign of Terror's direct democracy, and then again five years later in the overthrow of the corrupt republican Directory by Bonaparte's coup d'état. In 1817, responding to a French gardening society's request that he write its constitution, Jefferson acknowledged the unique historic political past and cultural traditions of other peoples. Politely refusing the request, Jefferson said that, not being a Frenchman, he felt himself unqualified to prescribe a mode of government for their organization and insufficiently acquainted with their expectations of social and governmental associations. Conveying a mindset that accepted the Haitian dictatorship and hoped that emancipated slaves, with assistance from the state and/or federal government(s), would emigrate there, increasing the Black state's power and perhaps eventually advancing democratic views there, Jefferson blended erudition and common sense:

> Every people have their own particular habits, ways of thinking, manners, etc., which have grown up with them from their infancy and become a part of their nature, and to which the regulations which are to make them

---

[27] Jefferson to Madame d'Enville, April 2, 1790, in Peterson, ed., *Jefferson: Writings*, 965–66.

[28] Jefferson to Tench Coxe, June 1, 1795, microfilm reel 20, Jefferson Papers, LC (hdl.loc.gov/loc.mss/mtj.mtjbib008505). See also Jefferson to Lafayette, February 14, 1815, in Peterson, ed., *Jefferson: Writings*, 1360–61.

> happy must be accommodated....The institutions of Lycurgus, for example, would not have suited Athens, nor those of Solon, Lacedaemon. The organizations of Locke were impracticable for Carolina, and those of Rousseau and Mably for Poland.[29]

In the economic realm, Jefferson preferred a modified system of free enterprise that promoted social and economic justice and limited excessive accumulations of wealth.[30] In the political sphere, he remained convinced that the representative republican government practiced by the United States was superior to any other. He allowed the ancient Greeks credit for their aesthetic creativity, which, neglecting to mention that half the Greek population was enslaved, he considered an outgrowth of their respect for the citizen's freedom. "They had just ideas of the value of personal liberty, but none at all of the structure of government best calculated to preserve it," he contended. "They knew no medium between a democracy (the only pure republic, but impracticable beyond the limits of a town) and an abandonment of themselves to an aristocracy, or a tyranny independent of the people." After thus mocking the ancient Greeks notwithstanding their great cultural achievements, he extolled representative democracy, epitomized by Madison's *Federalist* no. 10. "It seems not to have occurred that where the citizens cannot meet to transact their business in person, they alone have the right to choose the agents who shall transact it," he observed, "and that in this way, a republican, or popular government of the second grade of purity [direct democracy was the purest], may be exercised over any extent of country." He implied that the ancient Greek and Roman republicans were dullards, ignorant of the benefits of representative democracy, who yielded their liberties to a dictator or an aristocracy rather than elect legislatures to decide public concerns.[31]

Without ascribing to Americans' superior abilities or intelligence, Jefferson emphasized their uniqueness in bringing Anglophone concepts of republicanism (representative government) nearest to perfection. "The full experiment of a government democratical, but representative, was and is still reserved for us," he said, optimistic that the United States would long remain a republic, rather than decline into anarchy and tyranny like the ancient Greek democracies and republican

---

[29] Jefferson to William Lee, January 16, 1817, in Lipscomb and Bergh, eds., *Writings of Jefferson*, 15:101.

[30] C. Katz, "Thomas Jefferson's Liberal Anti-Capitalism," 1–17; Stanley N. Katz, "Republicanism and the Law of Inheritance in the American Revolutionary Era," *Michigan Law Review* 76/1 (November 1977): 1–29; S. N. Katz, "Thomas Jefferson and the Right to Property in Revolutionary America," *Journal of Law and Economics* 19/3 (October 1976): 467–88.

[31] Jefferson to Isaac H. Tiffany, August 26, 1816, in Lipscomb and Bergh, eds., *Writings of Jefferson*, 15:65–66, and microfilm reel 49, Jefferson Papers, LC (hdl.loc.gov/loc.mss/mtj.mtjbib022558).

Rome. As was often the case, Jefferson gave at least some credit to his British forebears. The English "mixed monarchy" installed the representative process in the parliamentary system but became "corrupt" with the eighteenth-century rise of Robert Walpole, George III, and others, who used bribes, patronage, and other forms of "influence" to manipulate voting in the House of Commons. Jefferson regretted that some offices, such as the US judiciary, remained non-elective and virtually independent of popular control:

> The idea [of popular representation] (taken, indeed, from the little specimen formerly existing in the English constitution, but now lost), has been carried by us, more or less, into all our legislative and executive departments; but it has not yet, by any of us, been pushed into all the ramifications of the system, so far as to leave no authority existing not responsible to the people; whose rights, however, to the exercise and fruits of their own industry, can never be protected against the selfishness of rulers not subject to their control at short periods.[32]

Jefferson concluded, "My most earnest wish is to see the republican element of popular controul pushed to the maximum of it's [*sic*] practicable exercise. I shall then believe that our government may be pure & perpetual."[33] He continued to disparage the ancient Athenian and Spartan governments as pseudo-democracies inferior to the United States' representative republicanism. In 1823, he boasted to a Greek republican philosopher and historian who supported his people's quest for liberty from the Turks, "Possessing ourselves the combined blessings of liberty and order, we wish the same to other countries, and to none more than yours, which, the first of civilised nations, presented examples of what man should be. Not indeed that the forms of government, adapted to their age and country, are practicable, or to be imitated in our day."[34]

Persisting in praise of the ex-mother country's "small and imperfect mixture of representative government impeded, as it is, by other branches, aristocratical and hereditary," he believed Britain's constitutional monarchy "shews [*sic*] yet the power of the representative principle towards improving the condition of man," even in the benighted Old World. He died believing that republicanism was the governmental form closest to perfection and that the citizens of an agrarian

---

[32] Ibid.

[33] Ibid.

[34] Jefferson to Adamantios Coray, October 31, 1823, in Koch and Peden, eds., *Life and Selected Writings*, 711, and microfilm reel 54, Jefferson Papers, LC (hdl.loc.gov/loc.mss/mtj.mtjbib024782).

republic were the happiest and most virtuous.[35] If any government were capable of removing the blistering affront of Black slavery, the representative democracy existing in the United States could.

[35] Ibid.; Leo Marx, *The Machine in the Garden: Technology and the Pastoral Ideal in America* (New York: Oxford University Press, 1964); Jean M. Yarbrough, *American Virtues: Thomas Jefferson on the Character of a Free People* (Lawrence: University Press of Kansas, 1998); Adair, *Intellectual Origins of Jeffersonian Democracy*. See also Holowchak, "Individual Liberty and Political Unity," 41–60. Emphasizing Jefferson's credo that the citizens of a republic had the right to choose whatever outlets they desired for happiness, Holowchak, ignoring the question of slavery's morality, considers Jefferson the staunch advocate of human "flourishing" and "thriving." One reason Jefferson endorsed national territorial expansion and pushed through the precedent-setting, arguably unconstitutional Louisiana Purchase, was that it preserved the republic's agrarian makeup, which he considered indispensable for its future happiness. The Jeffersonian belief that expansion across space was essential to the republic's temporal duration is J. G. A. Pocock's theme in *Machiavellian Moment*, amplified in McCoy, *The Elusive Republic*.

Chapter 21

An End and a Beginning: Jefferson's Antislavery Legislation and His Relationship with Sally Hemings

In his last years, Jefferson accepted the Haitian Revolution and the essence of the Missouri Compromise: Congress's right, invoked during the Missouri crisis, to prohibit slavery in the territories. Undergoing a significant moral evolution from his younger days, he transcended even the idealistic period of the Declaration of Independence. In that heady era of "beginning the world again" (as Thomas Paine put it), he seemingly felt only revulsion at viewing what he interpreted as the oversexed and immoral life of enslaved African Americans implied in Query XIV of *Notes*.[1]

The great historian Winthrop Jordan viewed Query XIV's insulting remarks about Black slaves' sexuality as Jefferson's projections of unconscious, disavowed, prurient, perhaps perverse sexual desires. In *White over Black*, Jordan wrote, "His [Jefferson's] libidinal desires, unacceptable and inadmissible to his society and to his higher self, were effectively transferred to others and thereby drained of their intolerable immediacy. Having allowed these dynamic emotions perilously close to the surface in the form of the orang-outang, he had immediately…denied his exposure by caricaturing it."[2]

---

[1] Holowchak, in "The spirit of the master is abating," concludes that in *Notes*, Jefferson, despite his protestations of uncertainty, had already decided in his own mind that Blacks, though entitled to the same civil rights as Whites, were an inferior race. At the same time he acknowledged the suffering and abuse they endured. "Among the blacks is misery enough, God knows, but no poetry. Love is the peculiar oestrum of the poet. Their [enslaved Blacks] lofe is ardent, but it kindles the senses only." Query XIV, in Peterson, ed., *Writings*, 267.

[2] Jordan, *White over Black*, 459. [I have slightly changed the tense of the quotation.] In assessing the motives of Jefferson and Southern White males in general, Jordan makes some extreme psychoanalytic evaluations, claiming they projected their obsessive sexual and aggressive instincts toward Blacks in racist rhetoric depicting Blacks, especially free Blacks, as violent criminals. Jordan argues that Whites' repressed refusal to admit that they, rather than Blacks, were violent sexual predators, was the real motivation behind the 1806 legislation requiring manumitted slaves to leave the state within a year of emancipation (574–82). The evidence he provides, in the debate on bills prohibiting or restricting manumission in 1805–1806, reveals

However, as Jordan's own evidence amply demonstrated, Jefferson's assertions mimicked the latest "discoveries" of "natural science" in his time, as validated by the greatest thinkers, from Kant and Hume to Voltaire and Rousseau. A noted amateur scientist, elected to the American Philosophical Society in January 1780 (less prestigious than it sounds; even the traitor General James Wilkinson and secretary of the treasury Alexander Hamilton, men who lacked interest in natural science, were members), Jefferson was merely adopting the role of "natural philosopher" when he reiterated these ideas. Jefferson did not seem sexually repressed. His correspondence with women freely expressed his sexual urges. The best examples of Jefferson's eroticism are his romantic letters to Maria Cosway, for example that of April 24, 1788, with its phallic allusions. After describing some erotic paintings he viewed at Dusseldorf, Germany, while touring that region, he wrote her, "I am but a son of nature, loving what I see & feel, without being able to give a reason, nor caring much whether there be one. At Heidelberg I wished for you too. In fact I led you by the hand thro' the whole garden."[3]

In his conscious thoughts and political actions, Jefferson separated his legislative proposals concerning slavery from his erotic life. According to his memoirs, his first activities against slavery occurred as early as his first year in Virginia's colonial legislature in 1769 when he seconded a proposal by his cousin Richard Bland, a senior member of the House of Burgesses, to revive laws permitting manumission of slaves. He reminisced in his *Autobiography* that the bill was defeated because of pressure from George III and Virginia's royal government, in which British slave traders exerted great influence. Jefferson wrote,

> I made one effort in that body for the permission of the emancipation of slaves, which was rejected: and indeed, during the regal government, nothing liberal could expect success. Our minds were circumscribed within narrow limits by an habitual belief that it was our duty to be subordinate to the mother country in all matters of government, to direct all our labors in subservience to her interests, and even to observe a bigoted intolerance for all religions but hers. The difficulties with our representatives were of habit and despair, not of reflection & conviction.[4]

Meditating on his political life in old age, Jefferson stressed his activities against slavery. In his *Autobiography*, he took credit for legislation passed in October 1778 prohibiting the importation of slaves into Virginia. The British

---

that, though several White legislators feared that free Blacks' very presence encouraged slave revolts, these same men apologized for flouting Revolutionary era ideals and did not mention Black sexuality. Moreover, the 1806 law passed by the relatively close vote of 94 to 65 (575).

[3] Jefferson to Maria Cosway, April 24, 1788, in Peterson, ed., *Jefferson: Writings*, 921; Holowchak, "Spirit of the Master."

[4] For Jefferson's comments in his *Autobiography*, see ibid., 5.

blockade prevented their entry for most of the American Revolution, Jefferson noted, and "this subject was not acted on finally until the year 78, when I brought in a bill to prevent their further importation. This passed without opposition, and stopped the increase of the evil by importation, leaving to future efforts its final eradication." Prohibiting importation of slaves for sale "by sea or land, nor shall any slaves so imported be bought by any person," the law stipulated, "Every slave imported…contrary to the true intent and meaning of this act, shall, upon such importation, become free."[5]

In a memorandum he wrote in summer 1800, assessing his life's value to his country after false reports of his death circulated in Federalist newspapers, he again stressed his role, regarding "the act prohibiting the importation of slaves" as a major contribution to the "happiness of his country." (He mentioned the act in connection with being "the instrument of doing certain things.") Most of the contributions he listed (other than the Declaration of Independence and his actions as US minister to France in smuggling new varieties of rice and olives to Georgia and South Carolina) involved his liberal reform program in Virginia as a state legislator from 1776 to 1779.[6]

Jefferson's opposition to slavery was evident in the constitution he composed for Virginia in June 1776, which he never presented, being in Philadelphia composing the Declaration of Independence. The second and third drafts of the constitution he wrote declared that slaveholders were no longer welcome in Virginia, period. In words stronger than those in the state's final law, he asserted, "No person hereafter coming into this country [Virginia] shall be held in slavery under any pretext whatever," and, "No person hereafter coming into this country shall be held within the same in slavery."[7] Jefferson's categorical antislavery constitutional provisos prohibited even permanent settlers from legally bringing new slaves into the state. Hoping to slowly strangle slavery, Jefferson seemed relatively

---

[5] *Autobiography*, in Peterson, ed., *Jefferson: Writings*, 33–34. The act prohibiting the importation of slaves into Virginia, passed at the October 1778 legislative session, was titled "An act for preventing the further importation of Slaves." It prohibited all importation of slaves, even from other states of the Union, as well as from overseas (Hening, ed., *Statutes at Large*, 9:471–72). Jefferson was not present during the debates over the importation bill; he must have meant that he drafted the bill for introduction by others.

[6] For Jefferson's 1800 "Memorandum, Services to My Country," see Peterson, ed., *Jefferson: Writings*, 702–703; Malone, *Jefferson and the Ordeal of Liberty*, 477–78, 484–85.

[7] Jefferson's Second Draft Constitution for Virginia [before June 13, 1776], in Boyd et al., eds., *Papers of Thomas Jefferson*, 1:353, and third draft, 1:363.

unconcerned that this restriction might hinder Virginia's prosperity and population growth.[8]

Between 1776 and 1779, Jefferson's proposals as a member of the Virginia House of Delegates' committee to revise the colony/state's laws contained some features favorable to Blacks. Bill 51, as it was called, was the first measure in nearly a century to allow individual slaveholders to emancipate (manumit) their slaves. By a law passed in 1691, a master could only free his slave on condition that the slave leave the colony within six months, and the owner was required to pay for his transportation. Dreading the "inconvenience" of emancipated slaves remaining in the state, the assembly reasoned that freed Blacks would collude with slaves to fence goods stolen from masters and help them run away. Furthermore, they would burden the parish welfare system if they reached old age.[9]

As the province became more dependent on slavery, wealthy planters sought to discourage manumissions. In 1723, the 1691 law was superseded by an extremely restrictive statute, ordering that, "No negro, mulatto, or Indian slave, shall be set free, upon any pretence whatever, except for some meritorious services, to be adjudged and allowed by the governor and council." Few Blacks would be eligible for freedom under this statute, which in effect, prohibited a free Black community.[10]

From 1776 to 1778, Jefferson joined Edmund Pendleton, George Mason, Thomas Ludwell Lee, and George Wythe in compiling a "revision of the laws," finally presented to the House of Delegates on June 18, 1779. Jefferson's contribution was greatest. (Lee soon died and Mason resigned.) Although including the first manumission law in many years, "A Bill Concerning Slaves," which he apparently drafted, contained some harsh anti-Black provisions.[11]

---

[8] The 1778 law, which prohibited the interstate slave trade into Virginia as well as imports from abroad, did not apply to slaveholders who brought bondsmen into the state to settle; or to Virginia citizens who inherited slaves, or received them by marriage from someone from another state. It only stated that henceforth any slave imported into the commonwealth specifically for purposes of sale would be "free": "An act for preventing the farther [*sic*] importation of Slaves" (Hening, ed., *Statutes at Large*, 9:472; Merrill D. Peterson, *Thomas Jefferson and the New Nation* [New York: Oxford University Press, 1970], 152). In a scholarly article critical of Jefferson, William Cohen denied Jefferson's responsibility for the law prohibiting future slave importations. Like Robert McColley earlier, Cohen argued that the ban owed more to slaveholders' desire to increase the prices of bondsmen already in the state than to opposition to slavery (Cohen, "Jefferson and the Problem of Slavery," 508; Robert McColley, *Slavery and Jeffersonian Virginia* [Urbana: University of Illinois Press, 1964]).

[9] "Act XVI: An act for suppressing outlying Slaves," passed April 1691, in Hening, ed., *Statutes at Large*, 3:87–88.

[10] "An Act directing the trial of slaves," passed May 12, 1723 (ibid., 4:132); see also Jordan, *White over Black*, 124. The 1723 act was renewed in 1748.

[11] For Jefferson's brief account of the revisal of Virginia's laws, which mentions Lee's death and Mason's resignation, see "Autobiography," in Peterson, ed., *Jefferson: Writings*, 37–44.

Unlike his stillborn state constitution, Jefferson's Bill 51, written around 1778, intervened in slaves' personal lives. Because, as a "revision," it was required to incorporate to a degree the earlier 1691 legislation, it also regulated manumissions and interracial sexual relationships in ways that limited the growth of the free Black population. Jefferson's proposal, the first manumission law for the colony/state in nearly a century, required newly manumitted slaves to leave the state within a year of emancipation, allowing them six months more than the repealed portion of the 1691 law. However, the bill prohibited free Blacks from outside Virginia from entering the state. Jefferson wrote, "Those [Blacks] which shall come into the commonwealth of their own accord shall be out of the protection of the laws," except for Black seamen, who were allowed twenty-four hours to conduct their business. In addition, Jefferson's 1778 proposal stipulated that White women who bore children with "negroes or mulattoes"—like the 1691 law on which it was based, Jefferson did not specify whether the fathers were free or enslaved—would be exiled with their newborns, who would be free because their mothers were free. This provision resembled the harsher 1691 law, which banished the White partner to an interracial marriage from the colony. It was milder than a 1705 law, which imposed five years of slavery for the profit of the parish on White women who had "bastard children" with Black or mixed-race men. Under the 1705 law, after being taken from its mother, the illegitimate child was kept in bondage until the age of thirty-one.[12]

In many ways, as Jefferson tersely observed in his *Autobiography*, written in old age at Monticello, "The bill on the subject of slaves was a mere digest of the existing laws respecting them." To some extent, it merely codified existing statutes.[13] Jefferson may have only considered himself the state assembly's amanuensis in writing this bill, which did not affect already-resident free Blacks. He apparently did not defend the rights of Blacks to enter the state or to bear children with White women. (However, the legislature did not pass any law prohibiting the entry of free Blacks into the state until the 1790s). As is well known, Jefferson himself thought miscegenation caused "degradation" of the quality of the White race, while improving the Black.[14]

By substituting banishment for the White mother (and offspring) of a mixed-race child whose father was "negro or mulatto" instead of the five years of

---

[12] "51. A Bill Concerning Slaves," in Boyd et al., eds., *Papers of Thomas Jefferson*, 2:471. For the act of 1705, see Elizabeth Cobbs Hoffman, ed., *Major Problems of American History*, 2 vols. (Boston: Houghton Mifflin, 2007), 1:41.

[13] Jefferson's *Autobiography*, in Ford, ed., *Works of Thomas Jefferson*, 1:76, and Peterson, ed., *Jefferson: Writings*, 43–44.

[14] Jefferson to Edward Coles, August 25, 1814, microfilm reel 47, Jefferson Papers, LC (hdl.loc.gov/loc.mss/mtj.mtjbib021817); Peden, ed., *Notes on the State of Virginia*, Query XIV, 141, 143.

servitude she endured under earlier laws [passed in 1691, 1705, and 1753], Jefferson's revision had its moderate aspect. Still, Bill 51 would force her to "depart the commonwealth" with her children (but not necessarily with their father) "within one year," revealing Jefferson's determination to prevent an increased mulatto population. If the White woman sought to evade banishment, she would be "outlawed," a vague term, probably subjecting her to arrest and imprisonment. If her mixed-race children returned with her, they would be bound out as servants or apprentices by county aldermen as "poor orphans," "and within one year after their term of service expired [age twenty-one] shall depart the commonwealth," or be outlawed if they stayed. Although harsh, these provisions were less drastic than the thirty-one-year period of servitude existing laws imposed on "bastard" children.[15]

Many historians of Jefferson's views on slavery and race gloss over or completely ignore the proposals in Bill 51. For example, John C. Miller's standard work, *The Wolf by the Ears: Thomas Jefferson and Slavery*, the only monograph on this topic, omits it. Miller observed that from 1770 to 1772, as a young Williamsburg lawyer, Jefferson fought for mixed-race slaves' right to freedom. (Miller probably had especially in mind the case of *Howell v. Netherland* in 1770). Miller surmised that, during the Revolutionary War, fearing that free Blacks and mixed-races might form a "fifth column" allied with the British, Jefferson's racial opinions soured. Miller also conjectured that Jefferson developed another "reason for advocating their expatriation: since 1773 he had conceived an overmastering loathing for and fear of racial intermixture." Apart from such vague speculations, Miller provided no evidence of Jefferson's opinions at this time and never specifically noticed Bill 51.[16] Leading Jefferson scholar Merrill D. Peterson, in *Thomas Jefferson and the New Nation*, also ignored Jefferson's proposal. William Cohen's article, "Jefferson and Slavery," one of the few accounts to discuss Jefferson's Bill 51, argued that he wanted to banish manumitted Blacks because "he feared that a sizeable population of free Negroes would be an incitement to unrest among the slaves." Although this is plausible, Jefferson seldom if ever attributed incendiary motives to free Blacks. Moreover, Jefferson's bill did not banish free Blacks already in the state even if they impregnated White women; only the White women and their mulatto children had to leave. By reviving the slaveholder's power of manumission and modifying the 1691 banishment provision for slaves henceforth freed (giving Blacks six additional months to plan their future), thereby eliminating the alleged danger of a large free Black population, Jefferson's

[15] "Bill No. 51. A Bill concerning Slaves," in Boyd et al., eds., *Papers of Thomas Jefferson*, 2:471.

[16] Miller, *Wolf by the Ears*, 21.

bill might encourage chary slave-owners to free their slaves. Since the freedpersons were required to leave the state within a year of emancipation, the number of slaves would decline and the number of Virginia's free Blacks would remain small. The American Colonization Society later embraced similar logic in financing the transportation of free Blacks to Liberia.[17]

Especially during the last twenty years, historians have tended to merge Jefferson's sexual life with his views on race. They were inspired to a great degree by a research note in *Nature* magazine in 1998 revealing that DNA analysis of a male descendant of Jefferson's uncle, Field Jefferson, indicated that in 1808, Jefferson probably fathered Eston Hemings, Sally Heming's last child.[18] Despite a scholarly climate focusing on Jefferson's personal life, psychological paranoia, and sexual needs, Bill 51 remains overlooked.

While securing emancipation, which no existing Virginia laws permitted, Bill 51's banishment proposal would gradually reduce the rate of increase of Virginia's Black population. By prohibiting new slaveholders from entering the state, or slave dealers bringing in slaves for sale, Jefferson's proposal questioned slavery's legitimacy and simultaneously limited the number of Virginia's slaves. Following existing law, he specified that no persons would be slaves in Virginia except those who were already slaves and "descendants of the females of them." The inherited status of slavery had followed the condition of the mother in Virginia since 1662. In that year, the Virginia assembly declared that, to eliminate "doubts...whether children got by any Englishman upon a negro woman should be slave or ffree [*sic*]...all children borne in this country shalbe [*sic*] held bond or free only according to the condition of the mother."[19]

Jefferson's law not only prohibited new slaveholders from entering the state but also required that any slaves they brought with them, after residing in Virginia

[17] Peterson, *Jefferson and the New Nation*, 152–53; Cohen, "Jefferson and the Problem of Slavery," 508–509, 509 (quotation); Egerton, "Its Origin Is Not a Little Curious," 463–80.

[18] E. A. Foster et al., "Jefferson Fathered Slave's Last Child," *Nature* 396 (November 5, 1998): 27–28. See, e.g., Onuf, *Jefferson's Empire*; Onuf, "Every Generation is an 'Independant Nation,'" 153–70; Ellis, *American Sphinx*; Gordon-Reed, *Hemingses of Monticello*; Clarence Walker, *Mongrel Nation: The America Begotten by Thomas Jefferson and Sally Hemings* (Charlottesville: University of Virginia Press, 2009); David Sehat, *The Jefferson Rule: How the Founding Fathers Became Infallible and Our Politics Inflexible* (New York: Simon and Schuster, 2015); Henry Wiencek, *Master of the Mountain: Thomas Jefferson and His Slaves* (New York: Farrar, Straus and Giroux, 2012).

[19] "Bill No. 51. A Bill concerning Slaves," in Boyd et al., eds., *Papers of Thomas Jefferson*, 2:470. For the 1662 law, see Act XII, "Negro women's children to serve according to the condition of the mother," in Hening, ed., *Statutes at Large*, 2:170 (passed December 1662). Spelling is original.

for "one whole year, together, or so long at different times as shall amount to one year, shall be free." However, as in Jefferson's provisions for manumission, these liberated ex-slaves were required to leave the state in the course of the following year, or "they shall be out of the protection of the laws" (i.e., considered criminals who could be re-enslaved). In addition, under Jefferson's bill, currently resident slaveholders were barred from bringing into the state from other places slaves they inherited or received through marriage, even if they were not slave-traders but bona fide settlers.[20] The legislature did not adopt this strongly antislavery statute, which implemented Jefferson's hope for slavery's eventual disappearance from his state.

Perhaps thinking that the state needed additional inhabitants, the House of Delegates was less eager than Jefferson, who seemed confident that the reproduction of the existing population would be ample, to exclude slaveholders and even free Blacks. Jefferson's bill, as already mentioned, specified that any free Blacks or mulattoes who entered the state would not be welcome. The House of Delegates rejected this section as well as Jefferson's partial exemption of Black seamen.[21]

Jefferson's proposal of the first Virginia general manumission law in nearly a hundred years was of great significance, since Virginia became the home of more free Blacks than any other state. By allowing individual slaveholders to free their slaves by deed or last will and testament without obtaining the governor's permission, the law might be a first step toward a law providing for the gradual emancipation of all slaves. The assembly passed Bill 51 in altered form in 1782, omitting Jefferson's provisions exiling newly freed slaves and the White mothers of mixed-race children and prohibiting free Blacks' entry into the state. Jefferson's version of the manumission act showed perhaps greater perception of the slave's

---

[20] "Bill No. 51. A Bill concerning Slaves," in Boyd et al., eds., *Papers of Thomas Jefferson*, 2:470–71. On the legal term, individuals "out of the protection of the laws," which early Western TV series and motion pictures denoted "outlaws," see Anthony D'Amato and Stephen B. Presser, "Anglo-Saxon Law," in [West's] *Guide to American Law: Everyone's Legal Encyclopedia*, 12 vols. (St. Paul: West Pub. Co., 1983–1985), 2:251.

[21] For Jefferson's assertion that Virginia did not need to rely on (White) immigrants for robust population growth, see Query VIII, "On Population," in *Notes on the State of Virginia*, any edition. Jefferson's proposal concerning Black sailors partially exempted Black seamen from the ban on Black immigrants; they obtained the dubious privilege of leaving the state within twenty-four hours. This was eerily similar to harsher laws passed by every Southern state except Virginia from the 1820s to the Civil War. Beginning with South Carolina in 1822, the Southern states prohibited free Black seamen (including members of the British Navy) from entering the state and required their imprisonment until their ships departed (Michael Schoeppner, "Peculiar Societies: The Seamen Acts and Regulatory Authority in the Antebellum South," *Law and History Review* 31/3 [August 2013]: 559–86).

plight than the 1782 law did. Aware that elderly or disabled slaves might prefer remaining in slavery to an insecure liberty, he required manumission "with the free consent of such slave, expressed in presence of the court of the county wherein he resides." Less benignly, of course, he required the emancipated slave to leave the state within a year, or "be out of the protection of the laws." Though Jefferson's law would increase the number of free Blacks, they would be required to leave the state.[22]

Ignoring Bill 51's recommendations, the assembly failed to repeal the harsh existing law, passed in 1705, subjecting free White Christian mothers of "bastard" Black children to a fifteen-pound fine or five years of servitude and their children to thirty-one years of enslavement within the colony. Although the White mothers and their children remained in the colony/state, they remained as slaves, either for five and thirty-one years, respectively.[23]

Sadly, Jefferson's provisions exiling White mothers of mixed-race children revived in principle the harsh April 1691 law, which banished "forever" the White member of an interracial married couple. Like Bill 51, the 1691 law intended to reduce the number of mixed-race children, in its words the products of an "abominable mixture and spurious issue." At the same time, the 1691 law, containing the first manumission act, required emancipated slaves to leave the colony within six months.[24]

The 1691 law, primarily concerned with preventing an "increase" of the "abominable mixture and spurious issue" resulting from either marriage or sexual relations ("unlawfull [*sic*] accompanying") between Native Americans, mulattoes, Blacks, and Whites, banished only the White spouse, allowing the other partner to remain. Contrary to later governmental desires to increase the White population as a counterweight to the Black, and to later, racist social beliefs that took for granted that Black men found White women irresistibly desirable, the exiled Whites were apparently blamed for interracial copulation. Racial and social control, especially of nonconforming Whites, rather than fear of slave rebellion was

---

[22] "Bill No. 51. A Bill concerning Slaves," in Boyd et al., eds., *Papers of Thomas Jefferson*, 2:470–71.

[23] "An act concerning Servants and Slaves," Hening, ed., *Statutes at Large*, 3:447–62, passed October 1705, at p. 453. It repealed previous acts (Section 41); "Bill No. 51. A Bill concerning Slaves," in Boyd et al., eds., *Papers of Thomas Jefferson*, 2:470–71. The final act, covering fewer topics relating to slaves than Bill No. 51, was "An act to authorize the manumission of slaves," passed at May 1782 session of legislature (Hening, ed., *Statutes at Large*, 11:39–40).

[24] "Act XVI: An act for suppressing outlying Slaves," passed April 1691 (Hening, ed., *Statutes at Large*, 3:87). The 1705 law used the same phrase (3:449).

ostensibly the motive of the House of Burgesses in prohibiting interracial marriage in 1691.[25]

The same 1691 law ordered that a White woman, either indentured servant or free, who had a "bastard child" with a Black, Native American, or mulatto man would be sold into five years of slavery if she could not pay the huge fine of fifteen pounds sterling. Her child would be sold into servitude for thirty years, to the profit of the "church wardens." If the White mother were an indentured servant, after her indenture to her master expired, she would be re-sold for a five-year term.[26]

In this way and others, the original manumission law, passed in 1691, was especially harsh, casting doubt on several historians' view that, because Blacks and White indentured servants often worked under similar conditions, White legislators in the early days of bondage were friendlier to Blacks.[27] Jefferson's proposal did not discuss interracial marriage, nor did he desire to reinstate the provisions of the repealed 1691 law.[28]

Although both the 1691 and the 1705 laws placed the onus for interracial marriage on the White members of an interracial nuptial pair, the 1705 act, unlike the original 1691 law, permitted mixed-race married couples to remain in the colony. The act of 1705 forced illegitimate mixed-race children into servitude

---

[25] "Act XVI: An Act for suppressing outlying Slaves," passed April 1691, Hening, ed., *Statutes at Large*, 3:87 (quotation). See also Jordan, *White over Black*, 80.

[26] Hening, ed., *Statutes at Large*, 3:87. The law was renewed in 1705 and 1753, except that in 1753 the White women's fine was reduced from fifteen pounds sterling to fifteen pounds "current money." In the case of *Howell vs. Netherland* (1770), which he lost, attorney Jefferson argued that these laws were invalid under "natural law," because they implied the perpetual thirty-year servitude of all descendants of the original White female defendant.

[27] The argument that the late 1600s was a halcyon period when Blacks had nearly the same rights and opportunities as White servants to own property, and servitude was only a temporary condition for both races, is found in T. H. Breen and Stephen Innes, *'Myne Owne Ground': Race and Freedom on Virginia's Eastern Shore* (New York: Oxford University Press, 1980).

[28] Historian Philip D. Morgan, *Slave Counterpoint: Black Culture in the Eighteenth-Century Chesapeake and Lowcountry* (Chapel Hill: University of North Carolina Press, 1998), 402–403, emphasizes the liberalization of the 1691 law in 1705. As previously mentioned, the 1705 law stated, or at least implied, that Blacks and Whites could remain married if the White partner was willing to pay a ten-pound fine and go to jail for six months. In 1738, Morgan notes, a White woman, Tamar Smith, served the prison sentence and paid the fine so that she could marry a mulatto man. "1705, Chap. XLIX, Sections XIX-XX," Hening, ed., *Statutes at Large*, vol. 3, is excerpted in a college text, Hoffman, ed., *Major Problems of American History*, 1:41. Depicting eighteenth-century Chesapeake society as more sexually progressive than most scholars do, Morgan also argued that the death penalty for rape was seldom if ever imposed (*Slave Counterpoint*, 405).

until they were thirty-one years old.[29] The 1691 legislation was the first to bar free White men and women from marriage with a Black, Indian, or mulatto, "bond or free." Judging by the terms of the 1691 and 1705 laws, which were revised and tightened in 1753, ample White hostility toward Blacks existed from the beginning of slavery.[30]

Section XIX of the October 1705 act modified the terms of the 1691 law. Although the 1705 act denounced interracial marriage and "unlawful coition" between the races (Whites, Blacks, mulattoes) as equally "abominable," it was more lenient than previous legislation. It subjected free White men and women who "intermarried with a negro or mulatto man or woman, bond or free," to six months of imprisonment and a fine of 10 pounds Virginia "current money." After they served their sentences and paid their fines, the Whites could rejoin their Black partners and live happily ever after, apparently without banishment or further punishment, as long as they did not have children.[31] In its provisions respecting interracial marriage, the 1705 law allowed the married couples to reside in the colony/state. By contrast, the April 1691 law banished the White marriage partner, but allowed the Black one to remain.

Nearly a century after these laws passed, Judge St. George Tucker's famous treatise, *A Dissertation on Slavery* (1796), advocating the compulsory gradual abolition of slavery and the freedperson's deprivation of civil rights, alluded to various forms in which their anomalous provisions persisted. After listing statutes that subjected slaves and free Blacks and mulattoes to more brutal punishments than Whites received, Tucker noted that the 1705 marriage laws constituted an absurd exception:

> Negroes and mulattoes, whether slaves or not, are incapable of being witnesses, but against, or between Negroes and mulattoes; they are not permitted to intermarry with any white person, yet no punishment is annexed to the offence in the slave; nor is the marriage void; but the white person contracting the marriage, and the clergyman by whom it is celebrated are

---

29 "An act for suppressing outlying Slaves," passed April 1691, Hening, ed., *Statutes at Large*, 3:87; "An act concerning Servants and Slaves," (October 1705), *Statutes at Large*, 3:453. The law no longer mentioned American Indians.

30 Section 13 of the law passed in November 1753, "An act for the better government of servants and slaves," which may be found in Hening, ed., *Statutes at Large*, [6:361; entire law is from 356-369], and online (catalog.hathitrust.org/Record/009714930), reimposed thirty-one years of servitude on an illegitimate mulatto child. The relevant provision is on p. 361.

31 "An Act concerning servants and slaves" (October 1705), in Hening, ed., *Statutes at Large*, 3:453–54, Sections XIX and XX. Cf. "An act for suppressing outlying Slaves [1691]" in Hening, ed., *Statutes at Large*, 3:86–87. Unlike the 1691 law, the 1705 act omitted American Indians from stigma.

> liable to fine and imprisonment; and this is probably the only instance in which our laws will be found more favorable to a Negroe [*sic*] than a white person. These provisions, though introduced into our code at different periods, were all re-enacted in 1792.[32]

Like Jefferson's Bill 51 and the 1691 miscegenation law, the 1790s laws attributed agency only to the White partners to an interracial union; however, they did not discriminate between men and women, as Jefferson did by exiling only the White mothers.

In addition to adopting a more humane version of Jefferson's manumission measure, permitting freed slaves to remain in the state, Virginia's legislature approved several of his antislavery suggestions. In December 1785, it renewed its 1778 decree automatically freeing any slaves brought into the state for purposes of sale and residing in Virginia for a whole year.[33] The acts passed by the Virginia Assembly at that time included several provisions of Jefferson's Bill 51, many of them repetitions of previous English common law and Virginia's colonial-era legislation. For example, Bill 51 declared that no Black or mulatto could be a witness except in civil and criminal cases against other Blacks and mulattoes; no slave could leave their master's property without a pass from the master or overseer; no slave would be allowed to own or carry a gun without their owner's written permission. The House of Delegates passed versions of all these measures.[34]

Jefferson had few encouraging precedents if he hoped to codify the laws in order to improve Blacks' condition. Despite banishing White women who bore children with non-Whites, Jefferson's Bill 51 was a comparatively benevolent reform of the 1691 and 1705 laws, which imposed virtual term slavery on a White mother and her mixed-race offspring if she could not pay an exorbitant fine. In restoring the planter's prerogative of manumission and granting freed persons six additional months to leave the state, Jefferson again slightly liberalized the defunct 1691 manumission law.[35]

---

[32] St. George Tucker, *Dissertation on Slavery* (Philadelphia: Printed for Matthew Carey, 1796), 54–55.

[33] "51. A Bill Concerning Slaves," in Boyd et al., eds., *Papers of Thomas Jefferson*, 2:470; "An Act Concerning Slaves," passed at October Session [December] 1785, Hening, ed., *Statutes at Large*, 12:182–83. See also Arthur Scherr, "Governor James Monroe and the Souhtampton Slave Resistance of 1799," The Historian 61/3 (Spring 1999): 557–78 [note 560-561].

[34] "51. A Bill Concerning Slaves," in Boyd et al., eds., *Papers of Thomas Jefferson*, 2:471–72.

[35] Ibid. Unlike the 1691 act, the 1723 law granting the governor sole authority to manumit slaves he favored did not require their banishment. For the 1723 law, see Section XVII of "An Act directing the trial of slaves," passed May 12, 1723 (Hening, ed., *Statutes at Large*, 4:132). Jordan, *White over Black*, 124, mistakenly asserts that an act passed by the Virginia

Like its predecessors, Jefferson's Bill 51 maintained a double standard with respect to race and gender; it did not banish the Black or mulatto father of the White woman's infant or declare him "out of the protection of the laws" as it did the White woman. Indeed, Jefferson's bill did not restrict the Black father in any way, perhaps because it was statistically likely that the father was not a free Black but a slave, and his banishment would inconvenience his master. By the terms of Jefferson's Bill 51, the White woman's mixed-race child would suffer servitude if she did not leave the state with him/her within a year. This was similar to the laws of 1691 and 1705.[36]

As early as the mid-1770s, Jefferson, in desiring to prohibit African American immigration from other states, had decided that his ultimate objective, later clarified in Query XIV of *Notes* was to emancipate Blacks and banish them. Keeping out new Black settlers was auxiliary to eliminating most Blacks from the state. However, Jefferson's desire to remove simultaneously both slavery and future freed Blacks from Virginia would hinder budding White planters and urban artisans who required a cheap labor supply. Predictably, the legislature disregarded these sections of Jefferson's bill.[37]

Significantly, in contrast to the legislature's 1782 manumission act, Jefferson's bill lacked a clause making a slave security for the manumitting master's debts. Perhaps Jefferson had personal reasons for this omission. Motives of humanity and fiscal wisdom dictated that he free many of the dozens of slaves he had recently inherited from the Wayles estate, a lifetime financial burden that helped cause his bankruptcy. By prohibiting manumitters from freeing their slaves unless they were first free of debt, the 1782 law made it impossible for Jefferson and many other debtors to emancipate their slaves legally during their lifetimes. Instead, in beginning to pay off his inherited debt, and before he felt personally attached to them as he later did to Sally Hemings and her siblings, Jefferson soon sold many of the slaves his father-in-law left him.[38]

Evincing no particular pride in Bill 51 despite its manumission provisions, Jefferson merely listed his authorship in his notes. On a slip of paper, enumerating

---

assembly in 1705 repealed the six-month time limit for manumitted slaves to leave the colony. The law he cites contained no such provision (Hening, ed., *Statutes at Large*, 3:447–62).

[36] Jefferson's Bill No. 51, in Boyd et al., eds., *Papers of Thomas Jefferson*, 2:471.

[37] Ibid., 2:471–72.

[38] "Bill No. 51. A Bill concerning Slaves," in Boyd et al., eds., *Papers of Thomas Jefferson*, 2:470–71. The final legislation was, "An act to authorize the manumission of slaves," passed at May 1782 session of legislature, in Hening, ed., *Statutes at Large*, 11:39–40. On Jefferson's early slave sales and the ultimately crushing financial burden that slavery imposed on him, see, e.g., Lucia Stanton, "Thomas Jefferson: Planter and Farmer," in Cogliano, ed., *Wiley-Blackwell Companion to Thomas Jefferson*, 253–70.

the bills he had drafted, he jotted, "T.J. govmt of slaves."[39] Since Jefferson's assignment was to codify past and present laws of the colony, he may not have felt it mandatory to embody every old statutory provision in his proposed draft. At the least, Jefferson deserves applause for ignoring provisions of the 1691 and 1705 laws that subjected White mothers and their illegitimate mulatto children to term slavery.

ↀ

On the other hand, Bill 51's harsh provisions do not comport with the traditional, pre-1960s image of Jefferson as a kind-hearted humanitarian. This portrait has been drastically revised over the past twenty-five years, especially since Dr. Eugene A. Foster's DNA revelations in 1998, which indicated that Jefferson indulged in frequent sexual intercourse with his slave, Sally Hemings, youngest child of his father-in-law John Wayles and a mixed-race slave, Elizabeth Hemings. The consensus among historians is that Jefferson fathered six or more children with Sally, and their relationship may have lasted from 1788 until his death although she had no more children after he retired from the presidency in 1809.[40]

A few scholars, such as historian Andrew Burstein, condemn Jefferson's likely coitus with Sally Hemings as sexual exploitation of a helpless, attractive young woman to satisfy his own physical and "hygienic" needs in middle and old age.[41] However, in his mid-twenties, Jefferson committed what his society viewed as a more serious moral transgression than having children with an enslaved young woman: He attempted to seduce Elizabeth Walker, wife of John Walker, his close friend and a fellow member of the Virginia gentry.[42]

Most historians agree, based on the 1998 DNA findings, that Jefferson at the age of sixty-five fathered Sally Hemings's son Eston. For his part, Jefferson, though tacitly denying a sexual affair with Sally, admitted in 1805 to friends and Cabinet members the truth of James Callender's newspaper accusations that in 1768–1769 he attempted to seduce John Walker's wife, Betsy Moore, like him from a wealthy, established planter family. During his presidency, he told his

---

[39] "Memorandum by Jefferson on Bills to be Drafted," in Boyd et al., eds., *Papers of Thomas Jefferson*, 2:665.

[40] Foster, "Jefferson Fathered Slave's Last Child," 27–28.

[41] Burstein uniquely argues that Jefferson, inspired by the writings of the eighteenth-century Swiss physician Tissot, thought his life span would increase if he had frequent sex in his later years (*Jefferson's Secrets: Death and Desire at Monticello* [New York: Basic Books, 2005], and Burstein, "Jefferson in the Flesh," in Boles and Hall, eds., *Seeing Jefferson Anew*, 172–94).

[42] On Jefferson's notorious "Walker Affair," see Kukla, *Mr. Jefferson's Women.*

private secretary, William Armistead Burwell, who became a Democratic-Republican member of Congress, that he had sexually harassed Mrs. Walker on a sudden impulse: "It was without premeditation & produced by an accidental event." Jefferson was appalled that Mrs. Walker, whose husband John had become a Federalist opposed to his policies, was apparently complicit in publicizing the incident thirty-five years later. With unintended humor, Jefferson, Burwell recalled, "told me the affair had long been known & that [Alexander] Hamilton about the time he was attacked for his connection with Mrs. [Maria] Reynolds had threatened him with a public disclosure."[43] It is appropriate to briefly discuss what Hamilton's "Reynolds connection" was about.

In 1797, the radical newspaper writer and pamphleteer, James Callender, charged that as secretary of the treasury, around 1790 or 1791, Hamilton was involved with Maria's husband, James, in stealing money from the government. Appalled by these charges, Hamilton published a pamphlet in which he denied having joined Reynolds in defrauding Revolutionary War veterans of their pensions, but he admitted that Reynolds was blackmailing him for having an extramarital affair with his wife. Thus, Hamilton, in attempting to clear himself of charges that he had defrauded the government, publicly confessed to a yearlong sexual affair. In rebuttal, Callender blithely assured his readers that Hamilton was guilty of both adultery and embezzlement. Perhaps Hamilton perceived that it wouldn't help his own credibility if he simultaneously implicated Jefferson, who by 1797 was vice president and leader of the political opposition, for committing a puerile, unsuccessful sexual escapade in his youth.[44] Whatever the reason for

[43] Jefferson admitted the "incorrectness" of his youthful indiscretion in a letter to Secretary of the Navy Robert Smith, in which he said, "I plead guilty to one of their charges, that when young and single I offered love to a handsome lady.... It is the only one founded on truth among all their allegations" (Jefferson to Robert Smith, July 1, 1805, in W. C. Ford, ed., *Thomas Jefferson Correspondence. Printed from the Originals in the Collections of William Bixby* [Boston: Plimpton Press, 1916], 114–15); William Armistead Burwell, "'Strict Truth': The Narrative of William Armistead Burwell," edited by Gerard W. Gawalt, *Virginia Magazine of History and Biography* 101/1 (January 1993): 103–32. Gawalt surmises that Burwell composed this narrative in 1808.

[44] Jacob Katz Cogan, "The Reynolds Affair and the Politics of Character," *Journal of the Early Republic* 16/3 (Fall 1996): 389–418, at 415–16 (citing *New-York Evening Post*, September 29, 1802, on Hamilton's indifference to the Walker Affair). For Jefferson's respect for Hamilton's character and his belief that he was personally honest as a government official, see Jefferson to John Taylor of Caroline, October 8, 1797, in Oberg, ed., *Jefferson Papers*, 29:546; Jefferson to Joel Barlow, January 24, 1810, in Looney, ed., *Jefferson Papers: Retirement Series*, 2:177. Jefferson did not believe that Hamilton was stealing money from the government although he regarded his fiscal policies as granting carte blanche to urban Northern financiers and speculators to defraud Southern agrarian holders of the public debt and reap inordinate

Hamilton's silence, Jefferson's youthful antics probably constituted a more serious offense against Virginia planter "morality" in those days than having sexual intercourse and children with one's slave. Planters did not usually consider a sexual relationship with a slave egregious even if the philanderer were married.[45]

Fawn Brodie was the first historian to position the controversial relationship between Jefferson and Hemings into a formative event his life in her *Thomas Jefferson: An Intimate History* (1974), the first biography of Jefferson to become a bestseller. Using Brodie's interpretation as a point of departure, Annette Gordon-Reed, who for many years has been the preeminent student of the Hemings-Jefferson relationship, in her heavily detailed studies of Jefferson, the slaveholding planter, and his relationship with the Hemings family, surmises that Jefferson was a relatively gentle lover.[46] Unfortunately, no documentary evidence exists concerning his treatment of Sally, and the "Sage of Monticello" was not always kind to the slave members of his "family," as he sometimes mawkishly called his chattel.[47] Occasionally, Jefferson could be a cruel taskmaster but without emulating the ugliest traditions of Southern patriarchy.[48]

By 1825, as we have seen, Jefferson, in letters to Frances Wright, William Short, and others, expressed relatively friendly feelings toward African Americans, especially by comparison with those implicit in Bill 51 and some passages from *Notes on Virginia*. According to several scholars, Jefferson's senescent experience of the joys of interracial erotic love inspired his new benevolence. During the most critical days of his presidency and afterward, as he allegedly sired children with lovely Sally Hemings, the full tide of racial humanism perhaps overwhelmed the aging Sage of Monticello.[49]

---

profits as investors in the Bank of the United States and similar institutions. As he reminisced to Benjamin Rush in a famous letter of old age, "Mr. [John] Adams was honest as a politician as well as a man; Hamilton honest as a man, but as a politician, believing in the necessity of either force or corruption to govern men" (January 16, 1811, in Looney, ed., *Jefferson Papers: Retirement Series*, 3:305).

[45] For slaveholding planters' philandering without concern for their wives' opinion, see Catherine Clinton, *The Plantation Mistress* (New York: Norton, 1984); William R. Taylor, *Cavalier and Yankee* (New York: Knopf, 1962); and Joshua Rothman, *Notorious in the Neighborhood* (Chapel Hill: University of North Carolina Press, 2004).

[46] Brodie, *Thomas Jefferson: An Intimate History*; Gordon-Reed, *Hemingses of Monticello*.

[47] See Stanton, *"Those Who Labor,"* passim. This is a convenient collection of most of Stanton's previous indispensable writings on Jefferson as a planter and slaveholder.

[48] Kathleen M. Brown, *Good Wives, Nasty Wenches, and Anxious Patriarchs: Gender, Race, and Power in Colonial Virginia* (Chapel Hill: University of North Carolina Press, 1996).

[49] The interpretations in this paragraph are expounded in Brodie, *Thomas Jefferson: An Intimate History*; Gordon-Reed, *Hemingses of Monticello*; Kukla, *Mr. Jefferson's Women*; and Jan Lewis, "Jefferson and Women," in Boles and Hall, eds., *Seeing Jefferson Anew*, 152–71.

The radical Scottish pamphleteer and agitator James T. Callender's scurrilous 1802 newspaper articles furnish the primary historical, written documentation for Jefferson's sexual relationship with his wife's half-sister, Sally Hemings. For several years during the 1790s, Callender was Jefferson's ardent political supporter; the Virginian even paid him to write pamphlets against the Adams Administration during the presidential contest of 1800. However, Callender turned against Jefferson when he rejected him for a patronage job after his election to the presidency in 1801. In articles in a Richmond Federalist newspaper that he co-founded in 1802, Callender claimed that not only was Hemings Jefferson's mistress starting from the time she was a teenager living with him in Paris; she was the concubine of many men, Black and White, with whom she bore numerous children. Displaying shockingly little sympathy or respect for the young woman, Callender viewed her as "a slut as common as the pavement." Satisfying her passions with "fifteen, or thirty" different lovers "of *all colours*," he said, her depraved unions produced a "yellow litter."[50]

An aspect of Virginia's marriage laws during the 1790s, not directly concerning slavery, may have affected Jefferson's decision not to emancipate Sally Hemings and perhaps eventually marry her: A law passed in 1788, overlooked by Jefferson scholars, prohibited a man from marrying his wife's sister.[51] The law banning marriage to one's sister-in-law was first passed in 1788, when Jefferson was in Paris with Sally Hemings. Renewed in 1792, it prohibited a man's marriage to his brother's widow or to his deceased wife's sister. Titled "An act concerning incestuous marriages," it stipulated that, if "any man shall marry his wife's sister," the marriage would be annulled and the parties fined. However, if the couple produced offspring, the children would apparently be legitimate ("nothing herein contained shall be construed to render illegitimate the issue of any marriage so annulled"). The prohibition on marrying in-laws was not repealed until 1849.[52]

---

[50] *Richmond Recorder*, September 15 and 22, December 15, 1802, quoted in Joshua D. Rothman, "James Callender and Social Knowledge of Interracial Sex in Antebellum Virginia," in Jan Ellen Lewis and Peter S. Onuf, eds., *Sally Hemings and Thomas Jefferson: History, Memory, and Civic Culture* (Charlottesville: University Press of Virginia, 1999), 87–113, quotations at 95. For a sympathetic brief biography of Callender, see Michael Durey, *"With the Hammer of Truth": James Thomson Callender and America's Early National Heroes* (Charlottesville: University Press of Virginia, 1990).

[51] "An act concerning incestuous marriage," passed December 8, 1788, in Hening, ed., *Statutes at Large*, 12:688–89. I owe this insight to Dr. Marc A. Jolley.

[52] Ibid. See also Martin Ottenheimer, *Forbidden Relatives: The American Myth of Cousin Marriage* (Urbana: University of Illinois Press, 1998), 28. In any case, had Jefferson married Sally Hemings while he was actively involved in politics, his political career would probably have been ruined.

According to African American oral tradition, which Jefferson may have learned (from his wife, perhaps) to be fact, Sally Hemings's father was John Wayles, the father of Jefferson's wife, Martha. Therefore, Jefferson perhaps felt additional hesitation in daring to take Sally in matrimony. A major omnibus law on marriage passed at the December 1792 legislative session, when Jefferson was a national figure, continued the prohibition on marrying one's sister-in-law. Section 14 of the law punished bigamy by death and made it illegal for a man to marry his brother's wife, apparently even after the brother died. More importantly in Jefferson's case, a man was forbidden to marry his wife's sister. In addition, Sections 15, 16 and 17 of the law virtually duplicated the 1705 racial legislation, discussed earlier. That law punished Whites who married Blacks or mulattoes but did not banish them from the state. White men or women who married Blacks or mixed-race individuals, free or enslaved, would be "committed to prison, and there remain six months; without bail or mainprize; and shall forfeit and pay thirty dollars to the parish." It is unlikely that Jefferson looked forward to the possibility of jail time.[53]

Likewise, oral tradition among Hemings's descendants and those of other slaves insists that Jefferson, a more libidinous scholar than his supporters knew, fulfilled his sexual needs with other slaves at Monticello, including Sally's sisters and half-sisters. Without specifically mentioning Sally, Jefferson's contemporary, the famous English writer Frances Trollope, in her travel narrative, *Domestic Manners of the Americans*, written in 1832, acknowledged these reports of Jefferson's promiscuity. She pointed to Jefferson's sexual depravity as proof of the absurdity, hypocrisy, and stupidity of the democratic ideology he ostensibly championed. Although the "democratic party" idolized Jefferson and considered him "one of the greatest of men," he was in fact a perverted libertine, Trollope assured her readers. Public acceptance of the known "facts I allude to, [which] are spoken openly by all, not whispered privately by a few," and most people's indifference to Jefferson's debauchery, revealed the hollowness of Americans' alleged religious devoutness. Notorious for the "drunken orgies" he conducted at Monticello, in which his slaves unwillingly participated, she emphasized, "Mr. Jefferson is said to have been the father of children by almost all his numerous gang of female slaves."[54]

---

[53] Moreover, any minister who officiated at these interracial marriages would pay a $250 fine. "An Act to regulate the solemnization of marriage, and prohibiting such as are incestuous, and otherwise unlawful, to prevent forcible and stolen marriages, and for punishment of the crime of bigamy," passed December 22, 1792, in Shepherd, ed., *Statutes at Large of Virginia*, 1:130–36, at 133.

[54] Donald Smalley, ed. *Frances Trollope's Domestic Manners of the Americans* (1832; New York: Knopf, 1949), 71–72. For Jefferson's rumored sexual relations with other female slaves at Monticello, see Gordon-Reed, *Hemingses of Monticello*, 682–83n.

According to Trollope, who did not disclose her sources and never visited Monticello, Jefferson retained his "wretched offspring" in bondage, and they "worked in his house and plantations." Outraged guests witnessed "that it was his especial pleasure to be waited upon by them [his "children"] at table, and the hospitable orgies for which his Montecielo [*sic*] was so celebrated, were incomplete, unless the goblet he quaffed were tendered by the trembling hand of his own slavish offspring." Informed that two of Jefferson's alleged children, Harriet and Beverly Hemings, escaped from Monticello in young adulthood (probably in 1821 or 1822) and that he made no attempt to recapture them, Trollope disgustedly observed,

> I once heard it stated by a democratical adorer of this great man, that when, as it sometimes happened, his children by Quadroon slaves [a possible reference to Sally Hemings] were White enough to escape suspicion of their origin, he did not pursue them if they attempted to escape, saying laughingly, "Let the rogues get off, if they can; I will not hinder them." This was stated in a large party, as a proof of his kind and noble nature, and was received by all with approving smiles. If I know any thing of right or wrong, if virtue and vice be indeed something more than words, then was this great American an unprincipled, tyrant, and most heartless libertine.[55]

According to Trollope, Jefferson's prurient sexual relations with his slaves, his flouting of their free will and agency, continued into his seventies: "The great, the immortal Jefferson himself, when past the three score years and ten, still taught young females to obey his nod, and so became the father of unnumbered generations of groaning slaves."[56]

Without accepting the scandalous charges propagated by Callender, Trollope, and others, it is certainly possible that, despite his age, Jefferson was attracted to young Sally. His trusted slave Isaac Granger reminisced to Charles W. Campbell, a clergyman who interviewed him in 1847, that, "Sally [Hemings] was mighty near white.... Sally was very handsome, long straight hair down her back."[57] In a conversation with Henry S. Randall, Jefferson's first major biographer, many years after Jefferson's death, Jefferson's grandson, Thomas Jefferson Randolph, alluded to Sally's beauty. Informing Randall that a "sooty room among

---

[55] Smalley, ed., *Domestic Manners of the Americans*, 72–73.

[56] Ibid., 317.

[57] James A. Bear, ed., *Jefferson at Monticello* (Charlottesville: University of Virginia Press, 1967), 4 (quotation). The interview was reprinted as "Memoirs of a Monticello Slave," first by Professor Rayford W. Logan in 1951, and then as part of James A. Bear, ed., *Jefferson at Monticello*. For a recent commentary, see Annette Gordon-Reed, "'Take Care of Me when Dead': Jefferson Legacies," *Journal of the Early Republic* 40/1 (Spring 2020): 1–17.

the colonnades of Monticello" had been "Sally Henings' [*sic*] room," Randolph claimed that Jefferson's Carr nephews, not Jefferson himself, had fathered children with the Hemings sisters (assertions that Foster's DNA disclosures in 1998 disproved). Randall wrote to historian James Parton in 1868, "Col. Randolph informed me that Sally Henings [*sic*] was the mistress of Peter, and her sister Betsey the mistress of Samuel—and from these connections sprang the progeny which resembled Mr. Jefferson. Both the Henings girls were light colored and decidedly goodlooking."[58] Thus, sexual attraction, and a possible physical resemblance between Sally and Jefferson's dead wife, Martha, since Monticello tradition linked them as half-sisters (although some people might consider such basis for an attraction macabre), may have prompted Jefferson to begin a sexual relationship with his young slave, so pleasurable that it continued for over thirty years. Even Annette Gordon-Reed's lengthy account of Jefferson and the Hemings family has not found substantive information to back up the findings of the DNA study of 1998. Common sense probably furnishes the strongest proof of Jefferson's likely sexual exploitation of Sally Hemings: She was young, attractive, reminded him of his beautiful wife in her youth before illness and numerous pregnancies precipitated her premature death; most importantly, she was nearby and available. Such a combination of circumstances would have proven nearly irresistible to a sexually functioning, relatively healthy slaveholder, who legally enjoyed virtual impunity where the sexual exploitation of his women slaves was concerned, short of mutilating or murdering them.

Apart from a newspaper interview that Madison Hemings, Sally Hemings's son, gave in 1873 to a Republican Party (Lincoln's, not Jefferson's) newspaper reporter seeking to defame the Democratic Party by excavating its shameful, slaveholding past and one or two other third-hand memoirs, no written, historical material exists on the Hemings-Jefferson relationship besides Callender's hard-bitten account. Madison Hemings, who was born in 1805, long after the events he discussed in the interview transpired, said that his mother told him that he was Jefferson's son. She further informed him that she had become Jefferson's mistress or "concubine" when he was minister to France during the 1780s, and that he had impregnated her there when she was a teenager, fifteen or sixteen years old. According to Madison Hemings's account, young Sally told Jefferson that she would

[58] Henry S. Randall to James Parton, June 1, 1868, quoted in Milton Flower, *James Parton: The Father of Modern Biography* (Durham: Duke University Press, 1951), 236–39; Annette Gordon-Reed, *Thomas Jefferson and Sally Hemings: An American Controversy* (Charlottesville: University of Virginia Press, 1997), 254–57; and partially quoted in Malone, *Jefferson the President: First Term*, 497. The entire letter is available from the online *Encyclopedia Virginia* (encyclopediavirginia.org/Letter_from_Henry_S_Randall_to_James_Parton_June_1_1868).

remain in Paris and not accompany him back to the United States because in France she would be free. He convinced her to return with him by promising that if they had children together, he would emancipate them.[59]

Eugene Foster, the scientist who published the DNA discovery (another scientist, a British geneticist, Chris Tyler Smith, at the Sanger Institute in England, performed the actual testing) observed that at least twenty-five of Jefferson's contemporaries might have fathered Sally's youngest child, Eston. Although it seems probable that Jefferson, as the most frequent resident of Monticello among all the "suspects" (although during his later years, he spent some time in Philadelphia, Washington, DC, and his Poplar Forest estate), was Eston Hemings's father, this impregnation occurred when he was sixty-four years old, rather elderly for fatherhood in those days.[60]

Either because some of them were his sons, or because they possessed sufficient skills to survive in freedom, or both, Jefferson emancipated five men (including Madison Hemings) by a codicil to his will dated March 17, 1826, a day after composing the original document. These slaves were Burwell Colbert (a painter and glazier); John Hemings and Joe Fossett, carpenters whom he expected would be hired to do skilled work at the University of Virginia; and Madison and Eston Hemings, allegedly his and Sally's children, whom he ordered apprenticed to their uncle John, Sally's brother, until the age of twenty-one. At that date, they would gain their liberty. These individuals were all related in some way to the Hemings family.[61]

ʘ

Although defeated in 1779, the section of Jefferson's Bill 51, forcing all future emancipated slaves to leave the state within a year of manumission, passed in revised form in 1806. Ironically, the slaves Jefferson freed by his will would suffer exile from their home state by legislation similar to that which he had proposed nearly thirty years before. Under the law of 1806, newly freed slaves who did not leave Virginia within a year would be resold into slavery, with the revenue derived going to the fund for the benefit of the poor. However, various loopholes were

---

[59] "Reminiscences of Madison Hemings" [1873], reprinted in Brodie, *Thomas Jefferson: An Intimate History*, 471–76, at 473.

[60] See Foster's obituary, Thomas H. Maugh II, "Eugene Foster; arranged test of Jefferson DNA," *Los Angeles Times*, July 27, 2008 (archive.boston.com/bostonglobe/obituaries/articles/2008/07/27/eugene_foster_arranged_tests_of_jefferson_dna/).

[61] Codicil to Jefferson's Will, March 17, 1826, in Lipscomb and Bergh, eds., *Writings of Jefferson*, 17:469–70. Jefferson's will did not manumit Sally Hemings. She was unofficially freed by his daughter, Martha Jefferson Randolph, in 1829, and went to Ohio to live with her children, Madison and Eston.

created in the law after petitions arrived from benevolent masters. In 1816, the Virginia legislature amended the law to enable freed persons to petition local courts for exemption from exile based on their "acts of extraordinary merit" and their generally "good character," attested by their White neighbors. However, they were eligible to be "transported" out of the state if afterwards convicted of a crime, and their residency in freedom was legally valid only in the county or corporation where the court granted it. Deviating from the letter of the law, the dying Jefferson in his last will and testament directly petitioned the state legislature. In manumitting his five bondsmen, he begged the state assembly to show his ex-slaves the preference it denied so many others:

> I humbly and earnestly request of the legislature of Virginia a confirmation of the bequest of freedom to these servants, with permission to remain in this State, where their families and connections are, as an additional instance of the favor, of which I have received so many other manifestations in the course of my life, and for which I now give them my last, solemn, and dutiful thanks.[62]

It is possible that Jefferson's daughter Martha, to whom he had grown increasingly close in his final years, influenced his decision to free the five slaves. In childhood, slavery sickened her, a reaction that Jefferson, judging from his remarks in Query XVIII of *Notes*, considered appropriate for a moral person. As a teenager in Paris in 1787, she boldly expressed her views to her father, who at the time was on a junket through France and Italy (and later Germany).[63] Implying that Virginians treated their slaves harshly, she wrote, "Good god [*sic*] have we not enough? I wish with all my soul that the poor negroes were all freed. It grieves my heart when I think that these our fellow creatures should be treated so teribly [*sic*] as they are by many of our country men."[64]

---

[62] Ibid. The emancipation law of 1806 may be found in Shepherd, ed., *Statutes at Large of Virginia*, 3:252. Amendments to the 1806 law, passed January 24, 1816, are in "An Act to amend an Act, entitled, 'An Act concerning the emancipation of Slaves,'" in *Acts Passed at a General Assembly of the Commonwealth of Virginia, 1815–1816* (Richmond: Thomas Ritchie, 1816), 51–52; see also *The Revised Code of the Laws of Virginia* (Richmond: Thomas Ritchie, 1819), 433–34, 436, and *Acts of the General Assembly of Virginia, 1836–1837* (Richmond: Thomas Ritchie, 1837), 47–49. Schwarz, "Thomas Jefferson and the Law of Slavery," in Schwarz, *Slave Laws in Virginia*, 35–62, and 194n77, is a helpful, often-overlooked study.

[63] See Jefferson to Maria Cosway, April 24, 1788, in Peterson, ed., *Jefferson: Writings*, 921.

[64] Martha Jefferson to Thomas Jefferson, May 3, 1787, in Boyd et al., eds., *Papers of Thomas Jefferson*, 11:334.

Martha's humane feelings toward slaves perhaps weakened over time. When she became a wife and plantation mistress several years later, she had no qualms about disciplining the Monticello slaves and selling runaways and troublemakers. Martha eventually adopted the view that some slaves deserved punishment. In 1804, she sided with overseer Gabriel Lilly in the matter of selling a mischievous and possibly dangerous slave named John. She did not question Lilly's claims that John disrupted the peace of the quarters, told lies about other slaves, destroyed Lilly's farmland, and tried to poison him.[65]

Martha apparently was silent when her father, in an effort to treat his daughters fairly, distributed thirty-one of his slaves to her sister, Mary (also called "Polly" and "Maria"), when she married John Wayles Eppes in 1797, the same number he gave to Martha when she married Thomas Mann Randolph, Jr., in 1790. In the process of achieving this dubious equity, he separated four slave children from their parents, among them Betsy, daughter of Mary Hemings, Sally's sister.[66]

Nevertheless, there was a humanitarian component in Jefferson's seeming callousness in assaying an "equitable" division of slaves in the marriage portions between his daughters Martha and Mary/Maria. Although he separated four slave children from their parents, they would be physically near their families, less than ninety miles away. Maria lived with her husband at her childhood home,

---

[65] Martha Jefferson Randolph to Jefferson, November 30, 1804, in James A. Bear, Jr., ed., *Family Letters of Thomas Jefferson* (Columbia: University of Missouri Press, 1966), 264; Schwartz, *Ties That Bound*, 197; Cynthia A. Kierner, *Martha Jefferson Randolph, Daughter of Monticello: Her Life and Times* (Chapel Hill: University of North Carolina Press, 2012), 123.

[66] "TJ's Comparison of Marriage Settlements, 1797, MHI [Massachusetts Historical Society]," cited in Stanton, *"Those Who Labor,"* 77, and 321n29; Schwartz, *Ties That Bound*, 183, citing Stanton. The table that Stanton found is not among the documents published in Oberg, ed., *Jefferson Papers*, 29:547–50 ("Marriage Settlement for Mary Jefferson") and Jefferson to Francis Eppes, September 24, 1797, ibid., 29:531–33. Stanton described the list (which has since disappeared from the Massachusetts Historical Society manuscript division) as follows:

> In 1797, when his younger daughter Maria married, Jefferson wished to make her marriage settlement equal in value to her older sister's. A surviving document (obviously a fair copy made after long spells of computation) has two columns of names, 31 on each side, divided into males and females and listed according to their ages and thus value. Family integrity inevitably came second in the effort to calibrate human fates to make a perfect match. In this case, four children, from ten to fourteen, were separate from their families." (*"Those Who Labor,"* 77)

(Stanton's essay originally appeared as a chapter in John Milton Cooper and Thomas J. Knock, eds., *Jefferson, Lincoln, and Wilson: The American Dilemma of Race and Democracy* [Charlottesville: University of Virginia Press, 2010]).

Eppington, in Chesterfield County, only a few hours from Monticello. The slaves heard news of their siblings and could occasionally visit them. After 1794, instead of selling slaves, Jefferson, who by this means might have eased his financial burdens at a time when debts overwhelmed him, chose to distribute these individuals to family members.[67]

According to Lucia Stanton, the leading authority on Jefferson and his slaves, by the end of 1794, Jefferson, who after his father-in-law's death had far more slaves than he needed, sold ninety slaves and gave away seventy-six to his sister and daughter as marriage presents. In 1774, Stanton writes,

> Jefferson acquired 135 slaves who, added to the 52 slaves derived from his inheritance from his father, made him the second largest slaveholder in Albemarle County. Thereafter, the number of slaves he owned fluctuated above and below the figure of 200—with increases through births offset by periodic sales that were part of an attempt to pay off the almost £4,000 debt that accompanied the Wayles inheritance. Between 1784 and 1794, he disposed of 161 people by sale or gift. Unlike his father-in-law, Jefferson never engaged in the commercial buying and selling of slaves.

In the 1790s, after selling the Goochland and Cumberland County estates he had inherited, the ratio in landholding acreage between his Albemarle and Bedford County estates was 3:2. In 1796, he owned 167 slaves, in 1810, 199 slaves, and in 1815, 223 slaves, virtually all of them from natural increase rather than purchase. Even when selling slaves, usually to friends like James Monroe, he tried to keep families together. In 1794, he freed a valuable artisan, Robert Hemings, Sally Hemings's older brother, to enable him to move to Richmond to be with his wife and daughter. The same year, he sold another of Sally's siblings, her older sister Thenia with her children, to his close friend James Monroe, who resided on a neighboring plantation and probably owned her children's father. As the great Black statesman Frederick Douglass later observed, masters who kept slaves together were highly regarded in the slave community.[68] After 1794,

---

[67] "[Jefferson's] Negroes alienated from 1784 to 1794, inclusive," Sol Feinstone Collection, David Library of the American Revolution, on deposit at American Philosophical Society; available in facsimile online at Monticello Digital Classroom (classroom.monticello.org). From 1784 to 1794, Jefferson sold or gave to relatives 158 slaves. Another estimate is that Jefferson sold 94 slaves from 1784 to1794 (Schwarz, "Thomas Jefferson and the Law of Slavery," in Schwarz, *Slave Laws in Virginia*, 41).

[68] Stanton, *"Those Who Labor,"* 4–8, 305n6, 4 (quotation). In 1774, after his father-in-law's death, he added 135 slaves to the 52 slaves he had inherited from his father in Albemarle county, for a total of 187. In 1782, the total number of slaves on his Albemarle County plantations (Monticello, Shadwell, Tufton, and Lego) was 129, second to Edward Carter with 242

Jefferson did not disturb the slave community apart from deeding slaves to his children, where he could keep an eye on them and be reasonably certain they would receive decent treatment.[69]

From a historical perspective, many scholars have reminded us, despite the alleged proclivity of slaves to run away and seek freedom amid the disruptions of the American Revolution, during the last quarter of the eighteenth century the slave population of the Chesapeake states (Virginia, North Carolina, and Maryland) nearly doubled. The proportion of slaveholders in the population exploded between 1782 and 1790. By 1790, two-thirds of White householders in the Upper South owned slaves. The biggest slaveholding planters, whom the historian Ira Berlin labeled "grandees," were distressed to find that their native-born slaves' reproduction rates increased so fast that in order to avoid severe financial loss, they found it necessary to sell the "surplus" slaves. As Ira Berlin, among many other recent historians, noted, "On many estates, the number of slaves soon exceeded the number of workers needed. George Washington spoke for his class when he observed that it was 'demonstratively clear that…I have more working Negroes by a full moiety [50 percent], than can be employed to any advantage in the farming system.'"[70]

Although in old age Washington was reluctant to sell additional slaves or separate slave families, he concluded that his only alternative to poverty was to send troops of slaves to clear his lands in western Virginia, or evict his tenants from their leases (if the property was fertile) and produce wheat, corn, and tobacco for his own profit. He believed that he could be more financially successful with half the number of slaves (he owned over three hundred). "Something must be done, or I shall be ruined," he wrote his agent.[71]

Many planters sold their slaves, merely to avoid mounting losses resulting from taking care of them, as well as to reap a profit. Teenagers were especially popular sale "items." As Berlin pointed out, "The practice was adopted by many [slaveholders], as even the most conscientious masters found it necessary to reduce their holdings periodically."[72]

(ibid., 4). Douglass is quoted on p. 5. For Thenia and Robert Hemings, see Brodie, *Thomas Jefferson: An Intimate History*, 289–90.

[69] Stanton, *"Those Who Labor,"* ch. 1.

[70] Ira Berlin, *Many Thousands Gone: The First Two Centuries of Slavery in North America* (Cambridge: Harvard University Press, 1998), 264, citing Washington to Robert Lewis, August 17, 1799.

[71] Washington to Robert Lewis, August 18, 1799, available at Founders Online, National Archives (founders.archives.gov/documents/Washington/06-04-02-0211).

[72] Berlin, *Many Thousands Gone*, 264.

The aging Jefferson, mainly because of his father-in-law's debts and his own loans to friends, generosity to family members, failure to collect numerous debts owed to him, extravagant purchases of books and artwork in Europe, and excessive hospitality to visitors (including serving fine wines during his presidency), confronted a financial situation far worse than Washington's was. In his final years, Jefferson was unable to pay his creditors and was forced to rent out land and slaves at Poplar Forest to his son-in-law John Wayles Eppes (which he had promised to bestow on Eppes's son Francis) in exchange for $4000 to meet current expenses.[73] Despite his financial plight in his last years, he refused to sell any slaves. Strangely enough, at that time he ended up giving financial assistance to a free Black farmer he did not even know.

---

[73] Malone, *Jefferson and the Ordeal of Liberty*, ch. 10, esp. 178–79; Malone, *Sage of Monticello*, 311–14, 390, 478.

Chapter 22

Jefferson's Unknown Friendship with Patrick Henry, a Free Black Farmer

In addition to his purported love for Sally Hemings and his emancipation of several slaves in a codicil to his will, another act of Jefferson's old age demonstrated increasing good will toward oppressed African Americans. On July 5, 1774, young Jefferson, enchanted by its distinctiveness, purchased the Natural Bridge, uniquely composed of pure limestone, as part of a 157-acre plot of public land near Lexington in western Virginia. He paid a twenty-shilling registration fee. (Jefferson first visited the Natural Bridge seven years earlier, on August 23, 1767.) The acreage that Jefferson obtained so cheaply was not of the best quality. Most of it was not arable, and it was strangely shaped because several farmers had already bought up the best parts of the surrounding area.[1]

Jefferson was the first private owner of the Natural Bridge. In *Notes on Virginia* he proudly called it "the most sublime of Nature's works."[2] Although in *Notes* he did not mention owning the Bridge, he boasted of its beauty.[3]

Most Jefferson aficionados probably know that the Natural Bridge and its adjoining land in western Virginia were Jefferson's only deliberately made personal acquisitions of property outside his home county of Albemarle. It is virtually unknown that in 1817, Jefferson gave land on the Natural Bridge site, gratis, to a free Black farmer bearing the same name as the great Virginia patriot Patrick

---

[1] The acreage became part of Rockbridge County, named after its most distinguishing feature, the Natural Bridge, when that county was created in 1778 (David W. Coffey, "Thomas Jefferson, Patrick Henry, and the Natural Bridge of Virginia," *Proceedings of the Rockbridge Historical Society* 12 [1995–2002]: 135–45, 138; Malone, *Jefferson the Virginian*, 162, 377, 440).

[2] Query V, "Its Cascades and Caverns?" in Peterson, ed., *Jefferson: Writings*, 148; Coffey, "Jefferson, Henry, and the Natural Bridge," 139–40.

[3] For Jefferson's affection for the natural environment, see Miller, *Jefferson and Nature;* Engeman, ed., *Thomas Jefferson and the Politics of Nature*; Keith Stewart Thomson, *Passion for Nature: Thomas Jefferson and Natural History* (Chapel Hill: University of North Carolina Press, 2008); and Malcolm Kelsall, *Jefferson and the Iconography of Romanticism* (New York: St. Martin's Press, 1999). See also Jefferson to William Carmichael, December 26, 1786, in Boyd et al., eds., *Papers of Thomas Jefferson*, 10:633.

Henry. Historians have generally ignored this significant aspect of Jefferson's life, which starkly revealed the evolution of his views on race relations. At the age of thirty, in 1817, Henry, after working for several years as a farm tenant or laborer in Rockbridge County, near the Natural Bridge and Jefferson's Bedford County estate, Poplar Forest, found a permanent place to live and a permanent job: as caretaker of Jefferson's Natural Bridge. Among his duties was to prevent trespassers and ornery neighbors from stealing Jefferson's timber and encroaching on his land.[4]

Recruiting Jefferson's agent William Caruthers as an intermediary, Henry, who had recently married a slave woman whose freedom he had purchased, asked Jefferson to lease him the Natural Bridge lands. In June 1817, Caruthers wrote Jefferson,

> Patrick Henry a free Man of Coular [*sic*] requested me to write you that he will rent what land is cultivatable on the Bridge Tract—which is perhaps about 10 acres all of which [he] is to clear off and enclose and for which he is willing to pay a fair value. Patrick is a man of good behavior and as the neighbours are destroying your timber verry [*sic*] much it might not be amiss to authorize him to take care of it in order to which it might be well to have the lines run by the surveyor of the county.

Henry offered to farm the Natural Bridge acreage and serve as the custodian of the log cabin on the grounds.[5]

Having recently learned that there was a federal tax lien on the Natural Bridge, Jefferson worried that he might forget to pay future state and federal land taxes on the property. In June 1817, from Monticello, he wrote Caruthers,

> readily consent[ing] that Patrick Henry, the freeman of colour whom you recommend, should live on my land at the Natural bridge, and cultivate the cultivable lands on it, on the sole conditions of paying the taxes annually as they arise, and of preventing trespasses. I some time since saw the

---

[4] There are three overlooked articles on Jefferson's relationship with Patrick Henry and the Natural Bridge: Robert L. Scribner, "Mr. Jefferson's Rock Bridge," *Virginia Cavalcade* 4/4 (Spring 1955): 42–47, E. P. Tompkins, "Notes and Queries: The Will of Patrick Henry, the Negro Caretaker of the Natural Bridge," *Virginia Magazine of History and Biography* 58/1 (January 1950): 134–35, essentially a republished document; and Coffey, "Jefferson, Henry, and the Natural Bridge," 135–45.

[5] William Caruthers to Jefferson, June 2, 1817, Jefferson Papers, Coolidge Collection, Massachusetts Historical Society, Boston, MA. See also, Founders Online, National Archives (founders.archives.gov/documents/Jefferson/03-11-02-0330).

tract advertised for sale by the U.S. collector, and immediately sent him the taxes, but I do not know how it is with the state taxes.[6]

The oral agreement between Henry and Jefferson—or more likely, with Caruthers as his surrogate, although Jefferson spoke with Henry in person on several later visits to the Natural Bridge—was that Henry would live on and cultivate the Natural Bridge tract in exchange for keeping away trespassers and paying the taxes on it.[7] Jefferson promptly accommodated Henry's needs, both for his own convenience and out of eagerness to assist a well-recommended free Black man.

Some historians who incessantly denounce Jefferson's racism, would find it shocking that Jefferson trusted Henry, a free Black, member of a group he had recently disparaged (in his letter to Edward Coles in 1814), to administer one of his favorite properties. Perhaps Jefferson looked to Henry to belatedly fulfill his prediction to Edward Bancroft many years earlier that free Blacks would succeed as much as Whites did if they were given comparable incentives and opportunities.[8]

Patrick Henry and his wife, Louisa, moved to the Bridge, and Patrick built a cabin within 150 yards of the arch. Since Jefferson seldom visited Natural Bridge, Patrick was in effect the independent landowner of a natural wonder.[9] Jefferson was generally indulgent toward his unlikely new estate manager. Even though Jefferson leased Patrick Henry the arable land on the Natural Bridge (and allowed him to keep the produce) on the condition that he pay the annual taxes, Jefferson apparently ended up paying the taxes himself, along with giving Henry a gratuity. There is a notation in his account book for August 14, 1817: "Natural bridge pd. to PATRICK HENRY 5D to be pd. to the Sher. of Rockbridge for [state] taxes past & to come—gave him [Henry] 1.D."[10] A later note in Jefferson's *Memorandum Book* suggests that Jefferson reimbursed him for providing entertainment for tourists who viewed the Natural Bridge and for laborers' services:

---

[6] Jefferson to William Caruthers, June 11, 1817, microfilm reel 49, Jefferson Papers, LC (hdl.loc.gov/loc.mss/mtj.mtjbib022886). I have modernized the capitalization.

[7] Ibid.

[8] Finkelman, "Jefferson and Slavery: 'Treason Against the Hope of the World,'" in Onuf, ed., *Jeffersonian Legacies*; Wiencek, *Master of the Mountain*; Jefferson to Edward Bancroft, January 26, 1789, in Boyd et al., eds., *Papers of Thomas Jefferson*, 14:492; Jefferson to Edward Coles, August 25, 1814, in Peterson, ed., *Jefferson: Writings*, 1345 .

[9] Coffey, "Jefferson, Henry, and the Natural Bridge," 144.

[10] Bear and Stanton, eds., *Jefferson's Memorandum Books*, 2:1337.

"Nov. 14, 1821. Patrick Henry at Nat. br. Entertt. [entertainment], services & laborers 10D."[11]

Jefferson's confidence in Patrick Henry indicates that he was inclined to blame the deplorable state of free Blacks' condition on the unjust manner in which the dominant Whites treated them. He probably did not have many opportunities to deal with free Blacks since he seldom traveled to Norfolk, Richmond, or other towns where they often settled following manumission by their plantation-owning masters.[12]

Apparently, Jefferson met Patrick Henry for the first time in summer 1817. He visited Henry's farm at the Natural Bridge. He wanted to protect Patrick Henry's interests, give him control of more of the land by defending him against aggressive, racist neighbors, and make his life more comfortable by voiding the five-year leasehold of the gunshot manufacturer Dr. Philip Thornton at the Bridge site.[13] In January 1818, Henry conferred with Jefferson at his Poplar Forest estate, near the Bridge. Henry reported vandalism at the gunshot factory. Jefferson was grateful for Henry's attempts to protect his property.[14]

Despite Jefferson's status as an elder statesman and retired chief executive, he found his property victimized by incursions from vandals and unfriendly neighbors. In confronting his neighbors over the disputed boundaries between his land and theirs, Jefferson acted as agent for Henry's interests as well as his own. "I shall certainly be with you in autumn to get my lines settled," he assured him. A March 1818 letter from Jefferson to Henry reveals that he had met Henry personally and they had even schemed to expropriate Thornton. He regretted his inability to turn Thornton's share of the Bridge estate over to Henry, "in consequence of my conversation with you while I expected he would give up the lease." With cordiality and respect, Jefferson ended the letter, "I salute you with my best wishes."[15]

---

[11] Bear and Stanton, eds., *Jefferson's Memorandum Books*, 2:1380 (November 14, 1821); Coffey, "Jefferson, Henry, and the Natural Bridge," 144.

[12] See Michael L. Nicholls, "Strangers Setting among Us: The Sources and Challenge of the Urban Free Black Population of Early Virginia," *Virginia Magazine of History and Biography* 108/2 (2000): 157–58.

[13] Jefferson to Dr. Philip Thornton, March 10, 1818, microfilm roll 9, Jefferson Papers, Coolidge Collection, Massachusetts Historical Society, Boston, MA.

[14] Jefferson to John Adams, Monticello, May 17, 1818, Cappon, ed., *Adams-Jefferson Letters* (1988), 523; Jefferson to Dr. Philip Thornton, Monticello, March 10, 1818, microfilm roll 9, Jefferson Papers, Coolidge Collection; Jefferson to Mr. Patrick Henry, Monticello, March 10, 1818, microfilm roll 9, Jefferson Papers, Coolidge Collection, Massachusetts Historical Society.

[15] Jefferson to Mr. Patrick Henry, Monticello, March 10, 1818, microfilm roll 9, Jefferson Papers, Coolidge Collection. I am grateful to Dr. J. Jefferson Looney, editor of the *The*

Jefferson's White neighbors argued with Henry over the boundaries of the territory that Jefferson owned. Henry's White neighbors resented him, perhaps more because he prevented their poaching than because he was half Black. They seemingly did not care that the land's formal owner was a great ex-president.[16] They were probably aware that he and the freedman communicated as virtual equals. Edward Graham, surveyor of his lands at the Natural Bridge, knew of the quasi-friendship between Jefferson and Henry. In January 1818, requesting payment for surveying Jefferson's holdings at the Natural Bridge, Graham wrote him, "My fee for surveying your land is five dollars, which Patrick [Henry] has promised to pay. Should he not, you can do it next Summer when you are at the Bridge."[17] Despite calling him "Patrick," not "Mr. Henry," Graham apparently respected Henry.

If Patrick Henry wrote Jefferson, his letters have not survived. His literate brother John V. Henry wrote Jefferson from Lexington, Virginia, in April 1819, asking his help in resisting Patrick's unruly neighbors. John Henry informed Jefferson of Patrick's "Disagreeable Situation" with his neighbors, who threatened to confiscate the house it had taken him two years to build. Patrick wanted to see Jefferson "soon." He would have trekked to Poplar Forest, "but being so bisy [*sic*] plowing on the place Joining your land which he has rented prevents his comeing [*sic*]." Hardly awed by Jefferson's reputation, John Henry baldly stated that his hardworking brother was too busy to visit his patron. John's letter indicates that Jefferson met Patrick Henry several times before, treated him respectfully, and probably entertained him at Poplar Forest, about twenty-eight miles from the Bridge.[18] Henry's letter lacked obsequiousness, perhaps because the aging social democrat Jefferson, notorious for his personal informality and worn-out slippers and robes, did not require or expect any. Jefferson treated the Henrys as his equals, perhaps even as friends, just as he would have treated a White farmer or business

---

Papers of Thomas Jefferson: Retirement Series, for informing me of this letter and other correspondence between Jefferson and Patrick Henry. I am also grateful to Betsy Boyle, librarian at the Massachusetts Historical Society, for her help in providing letters relevant to Jefferson and Patrick Henry in the Coolidge Collection.

[16] Coffey, "Jefferson, Henry, and the Natural Bridge," 138.

[17] Jefferson to Edward Graham, March 10, 1818, microfilm roll 9, Jefferson Papers, Coolidge Collection; Edward Graham to Jefferson, January 24, 1818, in Looney, ed., *Jefferson Papers: Retirement Series*, 12:394.

[18] John V. Henry to Jefferson, April 25, 1819, microfilm roll 10, Jefferson Papers, Coolidge Collection. I have modernized some of the capitalization. For evidence that Jefferson was at Poplar Forest in April 1819, see Jefferson to Charles Clay, Poplar Forest, April 28, 1819, Peale-Sellers Papers, American Philosophical Society, Philadelphia, PA, and Founders Online, National Archives (founders.archives.gov/documents/Jefferson/03-14-02-0244).

acquaintance. His actions strikingly contrasted with his earlier insinuations in Query XIV of *Notes on the State of Virginia*.

Jefferson personally intervened to assist Patrick Henry and requested Graham's help in dealing with the neighbors' threats to seize his (and Henry's) property. Writing to Graham and Patrick Henry simultaneously from Poplar Forest, Jefferson told Graham that he had been unable to visit the Natural Bridge to supervise the surveying because of "ill health," but he expected to arrive there soon.[19] He attached notes concerning his property's exact bounds. He was aware that Henry would be vitally affected by the dispute's outcome. "I enclose a letter to Patrick Henry, open for your perusal," he wrote Graham, "after which I will pray you to forward it to him by such opportunity as occurs."[20]

Jefferson's letter of the same day to Henry, with its attention to detail and respectful tone, suggests he modified his racial prejudice in his final years. As unique testimony of his familiar relationship with a free Black to whom he had practically granted as a gift one of his most cherished properties, the letter deserves quotation in full:

> Poplar Forest, Oct. 22, 1821
> Sir,
>
> I should long ago have been at the Natural bridge to have my lines there ascertained, but that during the years [18]19 and 20 I was in a state of low health which rendered it impossible. I am now as well as usual, altho not absolutely well. But if no change occurs I shall try to go to the bridge. I shall set out for Albemarle in 3 days; where however I shall not stay more than a week and endeavor to be back here about the 6th or 7th of November, and on the 11th I will be at mr Greenlee's [tavern] perhaps in time to go on to the bridge and take measures for sending to ask mr Graham's attendance.... my stay will be short. These dates may be varied a little by bad weather.
>
> If the dam below the bridge has not been opened to let off the stagnant water and clear the bridge of it below, I shall ask your aid in procuring what laborers you think necessary to do it while I am there.[21]

---

[19] Between 1819 and 1821, as Jefferson wrote Henry and numerous others, he was ill with boils, severe rheumatism, a prostate infection, and diarrhea.

[20] Jefferson to Edward Graham, October 22, 1821, Jefferson Papers, Coolidge Collection, Massachusetts Historical Society.

[21] Jefferson to Patrick Henry, October 22, 1821, microfilm roll no. 11, Coolidge Collection. I have modernized the punctuation. Since historians have ignored Jefferson's acquaintance with Henry, quoting the letter at length seems justified.

Jefferson closed the letter as he did with friends, such as William Duane, the Democratic-Republican editor, and the famous naturalist John Bartram: "I salute you with my best wishes."[22]

No detailed information exists about Jefferson's activities once he arrived at the Natural Bridge in October or November 1821 to defend his and Henry's rights. He stayed at nearby Poplar Forest for some time but was at Monticello by late November.[23] Jefferson's efforts must have succeeded: Henry, his wife, Louisa, and their two children remained on the property for three years after Jefferson's death, until Patrick died in 1829.

Although Jefferson died insolvent in 1826, no legal action was immediately taken to liquidate his Rockbridge County holdings. Apparently, Jefferson had granted Patrick Henry de facto ownership of the land on the Natural Bridge site even though Henry lacked a duly executed deed from Jefferson. Rockbridge County tax lists for the period list Jefferson as the owner, but many tax assessments include the notation "Patrick Henry in possession."[24]

Dated January 10, 1829, and probated March 2, 1829, Patrick Henry's will stipulated his wish to be buried in the "back part of the garden attached to the house in which I now live." He hoped that the law would permit him to leave the acreage at the Natural Bridge to his heirs. The will stated his desire to divide equally between his wife and two children "the land now in my possession, conveyed to me by Thomas Jefferson, if it can be retained by said conveyance."[25] He would have liked to consider it the dead ex-president's gift to him.

Unique among the leading Founders, including Adams, Washington, Hamilton, and Madison, in old age Jefferson intervened to help a free African American achieve a better life and self-respect in a White-dominated society. At least in his relationship with Patrick Henry, he overrode the evil temptations and obstacles that slavery presented to White men's moral sense (including his own), about which he had so eloquently warned in Query XVIII of *Notes*. Trusting Patrick Henry's competence and honesty, he undertook a leap of faith in African

---

[22] Ibid. In 1801, for example, Jefferson used the salutation, "best wishes," in letters to Duane, Bartram, and others. See Oberg, ed., *Jefferson Papers*, vol. 34. To his closest friends, such as James Madison and James Monroe, Jefferson usually ended his letters with such phrases as "affectionately," or "with constant friendship and respect."

[23] Jefferson to Nathaniel Macon, November 22, 1821, microfilm reel 52, Jefferson Papers, LC (hdl.loc.gov/loc.mss/mtj.mtjbib024209).

[24] Tompkins, "Will of Patrick Henry," 135.

[25] Patrick Henry's Last Will and Testament, January 10, 1829, Rockbridge County Will Book, 6:340, ibid., 135. The brief introduction to Henry's will incorrectly identified him as "a Negro slave of President Thomas Jefferson" (135).

American decency (although even the notorious Query XIV affirmed that Blacks were at least as moral and sincere as Whites were).

As he neared death, Jefferson, perhaps unexpectedly, forged a character for humanity, candor, and civility in relating with African Americans. His moral sense instinctively trusted a recently freed slave, whom he had never met, to supervise and cultivate his most prized possession, the Natural Bridge. Pleased by Henry's fulfillment of his responsibilities, in their business relationship he treated him virtually as an equal.[26] He transposed his credo of social and moral progress from the world of public affairs to private undertakings on his landholdings. In his political and racial views, he had finally, at least in part, rejected prejudice, racism, and fear and, as in other aspects of his life and thought, embraced "common sense." On a personal as well as a political level, he showed himself to be a friend of liberty and of man.[27]

---

[26] For a recent, more detailed account of Jefferson's unique relationship with the free Black Patrick Henry, see Arthur Scherr, "'An Honest, Intelligent Man': Thomas Jefferson, the Free Black Patrick Henry, and the Founder's Racial Views in His Last Years," *Virginia Magazine of History and Biography* 127/4 (2019): 300–39.

[27] Edward P. Alexander, "Jefferson and Kosciuszko: Friends of Liberty and of Man," *Pennsylvania Magazine of History and Biography* 92/1 (January 1968): 87–103.

Conclusion

Jefferson, the State of Nature, and the Moral Sense over Time

In evaluating his political conduct and that of his contemporaries, Jefferson tended to view actions and reaction through a "moral sense" lens. For example, he assessed the likelihood of slavery's abolition, whether undertaken by government legislation or slower personal manumissions, based on what he believed was the "moral" or "immoral" mindset of Southern slaveholders at the time he wrote. The tentativeness and ever-changing nature of Jefferson's evaluation of the goodness or evil of those whose behavior he was gauging led Jefferson to embrace, in qualified form, a type of political and cultural relativism. This kaleidoscopic perspective enabled him to condone, at different junctures, such extreme actions as the Henrico County Court's hanging of thirty conspirators in Gabriel's plot in 1800 and Haitian army massacres of the White population after the country achieved independence in 1804. In the less sanguinary, more numerous instances of his accommodation to official decisions, Jefferson's passive reaction to Congress's temporary rejection of Missouri's constitution in 1821 reflects his moral relativism and neutrality in matters involving slavery and sectional relations.

From his early twenties, copying Montesquieu's writings into his Commonplace Book, Jefferson knew that slavery was wrong. He had no doubt that Missouri's enslaved, and those in bondage worldwide, were owed their natural right to liberty. Perhaps for this reason, and the value he placed on his own freedom, he seemed certain that if immediately emancipated and allowed to remain in the United States, the ex-slaves would seek violent revenge for their oppressed past. He voiced this notion as early as the mid-1780s in *Notes on Virginia*.

Jefferson's belief that liberty was a natural right of all human beings may explain his refusal to purchase slaves although during the 1780s and 1790s he sold many of those he inherited, ironically to pay some of the debts bequeathed with them. He apparently considered human liberty an aspect of the "state of nature," which he viewed as an historical reality. Although most historians automatically assume that Jefferson was a strong believer in inevitable "progress," there is little in his corpus of writing to confirm this. Especially toward the end of his life, he often pointed out that humanity's ostensible advances in civility, science, and philanthropy during the eighteenth-century Enlightenment were undone by the "barbarous," technological mass destruction produced by twenty-five years of war between revolutionary France and its monarchical opponents, leading him to seriously doubt the concept of inevitable progress. At least in terms of his ideas about humanity's moral advance, respect for freedom, and concern for members of the community, he viewed the current state of affairs as a serious decline from the pre-historic state of nature: a Golden Age in which all people were free. This was his position in some of his most famous addresses, including his first inaugural address. Referring to the French Revolution's effect on American politics and society, he asserted, "During the throes and convulsions of the ancient world [Europe, the Old World and its ancien régime], during the agonizing spasms of infuriated man, seeking through blood and slaughter his *long-lost liberty*, it was not wonderful that the agitation of the billows should reach even this distant and peaceful shore."[1] Jefferson's allusion to "long-lost liberty" could only refer to some distant, irretrievable past, the state of nature, unrecorded in historical annals.

Likewise, in his famous letter to Roger C. Weightman on the fiftieth anniversary of the Declaration of Independence, his final public pronouncement, he praised the ongoing efforts of European and South American revolutionaries to recover their lost liberty. Extolling the American Revolution, Jefferson hoped that all the world's peoples would follow its example, revolt against their oppressors, and seize "the rights of man." "May it be to the world, what I believe it will be (to some parts sooner, to others later, but finally to all), the signal of arousing men to burst the chains under which monkish ignorance and superstition had persuaded them to bind themselves, and to assume the blessings and security of self-government," he declared, reaffirming the Revolution's liberating purpose. "That form which we have substituted, *restores the free right* to the unbounded exercise of reason and freedom of opinion." The term "restores" had meaning only in the context of Jefferson's belief in a state of nature since, historically, these peoples had always suffered oppression under absolute or arbitrary regimes.[2]

Preferring an idealized state of nature, Jefferson, as we have seen, refused to look up to ancient Greece and Rome as proverbial, exemplary democracies. Unlike many of his contemporaries, who glorified the Roman Republic, Jefferson lamented that Rome's "unenlightened and vitiated" people had never experienced "one single day of free and rational government." In his opinion, their general pursuit of vice rendered them incapable of "Freedom and good government," even

[1] Jefferson's First Inaugural Address, March 4, 1801, in Peterson, ed., *Jefferson: Writings*, 493. My italics.

[2] Jefferson to Roger C. Weightman, June 24, 1826, in Peterson, ed., *Jefferson: Writings*, 1517. My italics.

had they been governed by such oppositionist paragons of virtue as Cicero, Cato, and Brutus.[3]

Adhering to his view that in the prehistoric state of nature, all societies had originally been democracies based on a social contract ensuring the liberty of all, Jefferson regretted that, in recent times, the French, unlike the Anglo-Americans, had no option to recur to traditions of representative government, which they had never experienced historically before the Revolution. He believed that this elision accounted for their revolution's fiasco, its inability to follow either the American or the British model.

In at least one instance, Jefferson applied the assumption of a primordial state of nature, in which races and peoples lived in social equality and apparently possessed equal abilities, to the question of African American intellectual equality. In his letter to Abbé Henri Grégoire in 1809, quoted earlier, he admitted that Blacks' conditions of enslavement and quasi-freedom in Virginia denied them opportunities for developing or "exercising their genius." Perceiving Haiti's victory over the European colonialist powers and its retention of self-government as evidence of Black equality, he claimed that Blacks had recently improved "in the opinion of nations, and hopeful advances are making towards their *re-establishment* on an equal footing with the other colors of the human family."[4] Unless it pertained to a semi-mythical "state of nature," the term "re-establishment" made little sense in light of the hegemony that White, "European" powers had always exercised over Blacks.

That Jefferson held a glorified view of the state of nature, one he seldom articulated, and similar to Rousseau's *First* (1750) and *Second* (1755) *Discourses*, is implicit in his ready acceptance of the moral equality or superiority of Blacks and Native Americans and of the average White American "ploughman" to more highly educated, "civilized" Whites. European nations' advances in science, he often insisted, led only to increasingly successful efforts at annihilating the human race by means of weapons of mass destruction and interminable wars. Indeed, Jefferson's letters to Bancroft, Coles, and Sparks on abolition, extending from the 1780s into the 1820s, asserted that government emancipation of Black slaves was only "restoring" and "recovering" that liberty to them which had been

[3] Jefferson to John Adams, December 10, 1819, in Cappon, ed., *Adams-Jefferson Letters* (1959), 2:549–50. See also Reinhold, *Classica Americana*, 108–109; Crowley, "Classical and Other Traditions for the Understanding of Change in Post-Revolutionary America," 213–53; and Richard, *Founders and the Classics*, ch. 4.

[4] Jefferson to Henri Gregoire, February 25, 1809, in Peterson, ed., *Jefferson: Writings*, 1202. My italics.

unquestionably theirs in the state of nature. It did not matter whether, in historical time, they had been free in sub-Saharan Africa, the West Indies or the US.[5]

An implicit feature of Jefferson's moral thought was that over time, human nature had declined from its original pristine quality, when freedom and equality for all were taken for granted, or perhaps it had correspondingly evolved in cycles of benevolence and enlightenment, counterpoised with "Gothic darkness" and arbitrary rule by church, state, feudal lords, or all combined.[6] Despite his perennial praise of education for all as a great democratic leveler, Jefferson was by no means certain that higher education, scientific progress, and modern "civilization" guaranteed a greater degree of human virtue than did the primordial societies of Native Americans and Black Africans; indeed, at times he placed greater reliance on the latter for humane and philanthropic acts.[7]

For his part, Jefferson considered it a matter of course ("self-evident") that a self-governing people would pursue democracy, freedom, equality, and happiness. He expected its leaders, a "natural aristocracy" who by definition deferred to the popular will, to promote liberty, equality, and the opportunity for individuals and societies to learn and achieve as much as their talents and potential permitted.[8] In following this principle, he remained hopeful that Haiti would eventually adopt a republican form of government.[9]

Complementing his altered theory of human nature and the "moral sense," Jefferson's concept of Black capacity for self-government gradually evolved. In his later life, the slave rebellion in Saint-Domingue (Haiti), and slave revolts in general, including Gabriel's abortive uprising in Virginia in 1800, played a pivotal role in the progressive direction of his thought toward large-scale emancipation.

---

[5] Jefferson to Peter Carr, August 10, 1787, in Boyd et al., eds., *Papers of Thomas Jefferson*, 12:15 ("ploughman").

[6] Jefferson to Joseph Priestley, January 27, 1800, and March 21, 1801, in Peterson, ed., *Jefferson: Writings*, 1073–74, 1084–87; Jefferson to A. Coray, October 31, 1823, Founders Online, National Archives (founders.archives.gov/documents/Jefferson/98-01-02-3837).

[7] During the debate over the Constitution, Jefferson implied that he favored a national system of common schooling. "Above all things," he said, "I hope the education of the common people will be attended to; convinced that on their good sense we may rely with the most security for the preservation of a due degree of liberty" (Jefferson to Madison, December 20, 1787, in Peterson, ed., *Jefferson: Writings*, 918).

[8] On this theme, see M. Andrew Holowchak, *Thomas Jefferson: Uncovering his Unique Philosophy and Vision* (New York: Prometheus Books, 2014); Edmund S. Morgan, *The Meaning of Independence: John Adams, George Washington, and Thomas Jefferson* (Charlottesville: University Press of Virginia, 1976); Bernard Bailyn, *To Begin the World Anew: The Genius and Ambiguities of the American Founders* (New York: Knopf, 2003).

[9] Jefferson to Joel Barlow, October 8, 1809, in Ford, ed., *Works of Thomas Jefferson*, 11:121.

Perhaps even more important was his perception, starkly manifested in the debate over Missouri's admission to the Union, that sectional antagonisms over slavery might lead to the American republic's demise.

Jefferson's relativist depiction of the moral sense in his letter to Thomas Law in June 1814 sharply contrasted with his earlier ascription of a universal quality (analogous to Enlightenment rationality and democratic republicanism) to that trait in letters to Peter Carr and others. This later ambivalence may have served as an unconscious means by which he impliedly condoned Haiti's dictatorship, whose rulers he hoped to recruit to save the United States' experiment in White democracy. Haiti was to become the "receptacle" for the emancipated slaves, simultaneously disposing of slavery and the South's Black population.[10]

Occasionally this ingenuous point of view led him to approach dangerous crossings, seeming to condone the liberation of oppressed peoples by externally induced violence (concluding, to put it in popular terms, that the end justifies the means). For example, during the late 1790s, when France's armies were conquering Europe, Jefferson looked forward to monarchical Great Britain's "republicanization" by the French. At the same time, he admitted, "I do not indeed wish to see any nation have a form of government forced on them; but if it is to be done, I should rejoice at it's [*sic*] being a freer one."[11]

Jefferson learned the hard way that it was dangerous to force people to adopt laws to advance freedom—such as trial by jury, freedom of religion, a free press, habeas corpus—and take steps toward abolishing chattel slavery when their previous history and traditions ran counter to these enlightened measures. For example, when he tried to accomplish some of these objectives, particularly attempting to curtail the slave trade, by exerting virtually dictatorial rule over the Orleans Territory, he aroused vigorous opposition from its Spanish and French citizens, the vast majority. He was forced to retreat. The Democratic-Republican Congress, which passed a law to abolish the internal and external slave trade in the Louisiana Purchase in 1804 with Jefferson's approval, backtracked a few years later, confronted by a virtual revolt of the territory's slaveholders, and restore the domestic slave trade. Jefferson's frustrating experience in Louisiana taught him that a leader could not force a community to adopt freedom, democracy, and enlightenment when its people were unacquainted with, even hostile toward them.[12]

---

[10] See also Merkel, "To See Oneself as a Target of a Justified Revolution," 23; Onuf, *Jefferson's Empire*, 175, 179.

[11] Jefferson to Peregrine Fitzhugh, February 23, 1798, in Ford, ed., *Works of Thomas Jefferson*, 8:378.

[12] James E. Scanlon, "'A Sudden Conceit': Jefferson and the Louisiana Government Bill of 1804," *Louisiana History* 9/2 (Spring 1968): 139–62.

Jefferson genuinely opposed coercing foreign peoples into adopting governments antithetical to their habits and traditions and not initiated by their own actions. He applied this maxim to the people of Haiti, who had spent most of their lives enslaved, as well as to the British, French, and other "White" European peoples. He remained confident, however, that the "American Way" of representative self-government was best. Unlike the ideas embodied in Jean-Jacques Rousseau's masterpiece, Jefferson's notion of the "social contract" never advocated "forcing people to be free."[13]

Jefferson's failed attempts to promote justice and bestow the blessings of liberty on the newly acquired territory of Louisiana probably convinced him to adopt a more tolerant attitude toward Haiti's dictatorship, which declared its independence at this time. His misgivings over France's failure as a republic despite his early optimism and his ultimate exoneration of Haiti's dictatorship, which he was willing to exploit as a "receptacle" for American Blacks (despite its legacy of repressive rulers, the most benevolent of which was Boyer), led him to embrace a proto-Hegelian Weltanschauung of, "What is real is rational, and what is rational is real."

Similarly, the elderly Jefferson stood by the Missouri Compromise. As important as he viewed the promise that the violent debate over slavery in Missouri held out for renewed discussion of abolition and an emancipationist Haitian alternative, Jefferson insisted on Missouri's admission to the Union on an equal basis with the original thirteen states. He considered acceding to Missourians' wish for slavery as necessary to maintaining state equality and the federal principle, rather than imposing a semi-colonial status upon the first state carved from the Louisiana Purchase—the first state not part of the original Union. Denying Missouri entry into the Union threatened the integrity of the entire Louisiana Purchase and the stipulation, concomitant with the Ordinance of 1784, of each territory's eventual admission as an equal state. In addition to abolishing slavery, among the major achievements of Jefferson's Ordinance of 1784 and the succeeding Northwest Ordinance of 1787 was their premise that the public lands within the continental United States would eventually become equal members of the Union, rather than remain subservient colonies. Jefferson considered this principle essential to establishing the United States as an expansive, egalitarian,

[13] Although Jefferson recommended forcing the emancipated slaves to depart the United States for Haiti after emancipation, these people were not free to begin with. We might criticize him for forcing *slaves* to accept freedom on conditions imposed by the government, but this is not equivalent to Rousseau's concept of forcing all citizens' adherence to the General Will.

powerful republic. At least temporarily, he accepted slavery as a component of this American republicanism.[14]

Jefferson regarded the American people, whom he considered naturally social and political, as being most human when they were most reasonable and rejected violent and passionate behavior for peaceful compromise. This was a component of his definition of individual and national morality. Because Americans had a greater degree of self-government than any other country, he believed, they had developed their sense of individual and social responsibility more than other peoples and were therefore potentially most moral. Considering the US unique for its time because its government was "founded on principles of honesty, not of mere force," he thought that most Americans' economic independence, moderate degree of education, and political knowledge made the republic's indefinite duration likely. "Never was a finer canvas presented to work on than our countrymen," he wrote John Adams in 1796. "All of them engaged in agriculture or the pursuits of honest industry, independant [*sic*] in their circumstances, enlightened as to their rights, and firm in their habits of order and obedience to the laws." "If ever the morals of a people could be made the basis of their own government, it is our case," he continued; "and he who could propose to govern such a people by the corruption of their legislature, before he could have one night of quiet sleep, must convince himself that the human soul as well as body is mortal." This allusion to Alexander Hamilton's fiscal program revealed Jefferson's continued vexation at his alleged scheme to "corrupt" Congress during the 1790s, plying its members with shares of Bank of United States stock and holdings of the public debt, thereby ensuring passage of his financial program. By thus emulating English prime minister Robert Walpole's conduct during the mid-eighteenth century, Jefferson contended, Hamilton sought to "copy" the "corruption of the English government."[15]

---

[14] Although most historians assume that the Northwest Ordinance of 1787 prohibited bondage, in many respects the law was a dead letter. Neither the national nor the state governments effectively enforced its provisions against citizens who chose to ignore it. For example, in Illinois, where the issue of slavery attracted most attention, including the admirable antislavery exertions of Edward Coles discussed earlier, various forms of slavery persisted until several state supreme court decisions during the 1840s declared it illegal and the Constitution of 1848 permanently abolished it (Newborn, "Judicial Decision Making and the End of Slavery in Illinois," 7–33).

[15] Jefferson to John Adams, February 28, 1796, in Cappon, ed., *Adams-Jefferson Letters* (1988), 260. For a full-length discussion of Jefferson's and the Republican Party's castigation of the Hamiltonian Federalists as striving to reproduce the English monarchy's "corruption," see Banning, *The Jeffersonian Persuasion*.

Jefferson continued to emphasize his conception of Americans' rationality and potential for moral government as outgrowths of self-government, a model for other nations' emulation. During the Missouri crisis, he reminded Richard Rush of Americans' "sacred duty to suppress passion among ourselves, and not to blast the confidence we have inspired of proof that a government of reason is better than one of force."[16]

Nonetheless, Jefferson was invariably cautious when he applied his conception of the collective, consensual, social ("superego") facets of the moral sense to the abolition of slavery. He considered it necessary that peoples and governments that had suffered for centuries under oppressive rule in Europe and the Americas be allowed time to adjust to the transition from arbitrary government to representative democracy. It was unfair to label them inferior or incapable of emulating Anglo-American models of constitutional government and republicanism before they seized the opportunity to experiment with these forms of self-government for themselves. He applied these standards to peoples and governments in Haiti, North and South America, and Europe as well as to the White French and their rebellious Black Haitian colonists, who had defeated empires and set up their own independent nation.

Applying his theoretical merger of culturally relativist environmentalism and universalist democratic idealism to real-life political crises, Jefferson ultimately considered the bitter sectional debate over the Missouri Compromise a springboard for national slave emancipation. In keeping with his axiom that human bondage must eventually end, as he aged in retirement at Monticello, Jefferson became increasingly convinced that the solution to the problem of Southern slavery was the gradual emancipation of the slaves and their "transportation" to Haiti. Coexistent with Jefferson's advocacy of Haiti as Southern slaves' final destination was his moral sense theory's expansion to accommodate cultural diversity and other peoples' slower political progress toward representative government, his paradigm of political morality. Conversely, he believed that the Union's preservation, as the embodiment of republicanism, the ultimate political ideal, was necessary at all costs, short of civil war. The abolition of slavery, a supremely moral goal in itself, was a small price to pay for the republic's survival. Jefferson's "moral sense" intuitions, buttressed by the state and federal governments' satisfaction of the material economic needs of the Union's sections, confirmed that representative democracy was the best existing form of government for all peoples. Far from resting his argument solely on sentiment, Jefferson concluded that Northern and Southern self-interest dictated that they remain a single republic. He was

[16] Jefferson to Richard Rush, October 20, 1820, in Lipscomb and Bergh, eds., *Writings of Jefferson*, 15:284.

confident that, "The experiment of separation would soon prove to both that they had mutually miscalculated their best interests."[17]

Jefferson applied to the slavery issue his moral sense ideology's ethos that decent national policy required that the government's "duties and interests" complement one another, and that both parties to an agreement experience reciprocal benefits. Hence, he asserted that the forced resettlement of legislatively liberated slaves to Haiti would benefit Blacks as well as Whites. To his friend, the millionaire Virginia expatriate and investor William Short, he extolled sending emancipated Blacks to the Haitian nation-state rather than unincorporated Africa, arguing that they would best realize their quest for happiness and equal opportunity in "a government of their colour": their own nation in effect. As mentioned earlier, before his death Jefferson seemed optimistic about Haiti's future. "The experiment now in progress in St. Domingo, those of Sierra Leone and Cape Mesurado [present-day Liberia] are but beginning," he advised English abolitionist Frances Wright when she visited Monticello in 1825. He suggested she commence her projected colony of freedmen by studying them.[18]

Jefferson's moral sense ideology evolved in an increasingly pragmatic direction. He was aware of human nature's imperfectability and selfishness as much as of its benign propensities, but he hoped that the exercise of the moral sense, combined with education in community responsibility, would yield positive results for social friendship, cooperation, and peace. In 1822, expounding his matured moral sense theories, he wrote, "That every man shall be made virtuous, by any process whatever, is, indeed, no more to be expected, than that every tree shall be made to bear fruit, and every plant nourishment."[19]

In his personal financial dealings, the aging Jefferson upheld an ethical credo, merging self-interest and idealism. He showed his continuing belief in universal principles of natural law, such as the dignity of all human beings. In 1815 he voluntarily sold his 6,000-volume library, his most prized possession, rather than sell a single slave, revealing the profundity of his moral sense's evolution as he entered his last decade. His kindness and sense of egalitarian fellowship (*fraternité*, the French revolutionaries might call it) in lending a helping hand to Patrick Henry, an ex-slave, showed that on the stage of day-to-day existence he had, to some extent, surmounted his earlier prejudices. He seemed prepared to acknowledge that Blacks and Whites might be able to live together although

---

[17] Ibid., 283.

[18] Jefferson to William Short, September 8, 1823, in Lipscomb and Bergh, eds., *Writings of Jefferson*, 15:469–70 (first quotation); Jefferson to Frances Wright, August 7, 1825, ibid., 16:120–21 (second quotation).

[19] Jefferson to Cornelius Camden Blatchly, October 21, 1822, microfilm reel 52, Jefferson Papers, LC (hdl.loc.gov/loc.mss/mtj.mtjbib024471).

probably only in a future, reformed, more "enlightened" (indeed utopian) state of American society, a culture in which Whites could overcome their prejudices and feeling of superiority toward former slaves, and Blacks could overcome their hate and fear of former masters. Judging from his displeasure with his neighbors' surly conduct toward Henry, who appeared to better moral advantage than did the Natural Bridge's White inhabitants, Jefferson inevitably perceived that Blacks were the moral and intellectual equals (or superiors) of most Whites. His most glaringly brutal moment, the only one that has come down to us, was in ordering Jamie Hubbard whipped, violating his own principles of natural rights. Although Hubbard's rebelliousness exasperated him, Jefferson's moral sense, which justified slave revolt in *Notes* and elsewhere, prohibited his disparaging a slave's desire for freedom as improper or a sign of criminality. In his last years, Jefferson adopted a persona of humanity and decency in his attitudes toward and relationships with African Americans. As his commentaries to Frances Wright, William Short, and others demonstrate, he questioned his earlier prejudice, racism, and fear and, as in most other aspects of his life and thought, attempted to merge his moral sense and common sense. On the other hand, he probably never thought Blacks capable of reaching the creative mental heights of a Franklin, a Newton, or a Jefferson: "natural aristocrats" who constructed the shaky edifice of human progress.

APPENDIX

ELDER V. ELDER'S RELEVANCE FOR JEFFERSON

Although the prominent legal historian Paul Finkelman has argued that Jefferson could have hired out his slaves before composing his will, using the money he received from renters of his enslaved laborers to enable his executors to pay his debts and consequently emancipate his slaves, this course was illegal at the time of Jefferson's death. The Virginia case Finkelman utilized as the model that Jefferson should have followed was *Elder v. Elder's Executor* (1833). In his will, the deceased testator, Herbert Elder, gave his eighteen slaves a choice: if they agreed to immigrate to the Black colony of Liberia, set up by the American Colonization Society (ACS), they would be emancipated after his death; otherwise, they would remain enslaved to his brother, John. Herbert Elder died in June 1826, a month before Jefferson. Elder owned far fewer slaves than Jefferson, and had no living family other than his brother. Jefferson, on the other hand, owned two hundred slaves and had numerous living family members, including over a dozen grandchildren, for whose future he felt responsible. However, that is beside the point. In fact, Elder's will included no codicil directing that his slaves be hired out to pay his debts as a condition for their liberation. He manumitted them without this qualification, but stipulated that the American Colonization Society pay for the transportation of his emancipated slaves to Liberia. When he died, he was unaware that his debts were great enough to prohibit him from emancipating his slaves. Perhaps he knew that, at this time, it was illegal for a planter to hire out his slaves for the purpose of paying his debts posthumously to secure their liberty. He would probably have been shocked that his greedy brother John attempted to claim all the slaves as his property, although only one had refused the offer to go to Liberia as the price of freedom.[1]

---

[1] Paul Finkelman, "Jefferson and Slavery: 'Treason Against the Hope of the World,'" in Onuf, ed., *Jeffersonian Legacies*, 195. The legal case in question, *Elder v. Elder's Executor* (1833) involved Elder's brother's attempt to gain ownership of all the slaves for himself. *Elder v. Elder's Executor* (1833), 4 Leigh 252-254 (1833), in [Benjamin Watkins Leigh] *Virginia Reports*, Feb. 1833. See also John H. Russell, *The Free Negro in Virginia, 1619-1865* (Baltimore: Johns Hopkins University Press, 1913), 87; and Catherine Wisnosky, "The Will of the Master: Testamentary Manumissions in Virginia, 1800-1858" (M.A. Thesis, University of Nevada, Las Vegas, 2015), 58-63.

Although Elder's will emancipated those slaves volunteering to go to Liberia, it *did not* require the slaves to hire themselves out to pay his debts as a condition of their emancipation, an option that Virginia law currently prohibited. Many authorities considered the idea of slaves hiring themselves out after their owner's death dangerous because it granted the enslaved too much agency in deciding their fate. Nevertheless, Minton Thrift, Elder's executor, was determined to fulfill his goal of manumitting these individuals. As he later explained to the Virginia supreme court, he felt he had a choice: to sell enough slaves to pay the estate's debts and free the rest; or, what he considered a more benevolent and fairer alternative, rent out the slaves' labor as temporary indentured servants, until the debts were paid off and they could claim their freedom unimpeded. Elder's brother John sued Thrift. He claimed that Thrift had violated the terms of the will by using the slaves in this manner, and charged that the executor was secretly profiting from leasing out the slaves rather than using them to pay his dead brother's debts. He demanded ownership of all the slaves.

When the case came before Virginia's Supreme Court of Appeals in 1833, Thrift explained that he had illegally rented out the slaves' labor to fulfill the terms of Elder's will. The court sympathized with this benign motive, especially since Elder had stipulated that only the slaves that chose to go to Liberia would be emancipated. In this manner, the deceased Elder showed respect for Virginia's laws, which prohibited manumitted slaves from remaining in the state for a longer period than a year, and simultaneously saved the state the expense of temporarily paying for the care of emancipated slaves. Ironically, Jefferson's nephew, Judge Dabney Carr, composed the court's opinion, ruling that the executor could "hire out" the estate's freed slaves to pay the manumitting owner's creditors. The court decided against John Elder, and decreed that the slaves were free.[2]

Several other southern state courts adopted the *Elder v. Elder* precedent, enabling a greater number of slaveholders to emancipate their slaves. Had a Virginia court rendered such a decision during Jefferson's lifetime, he would have been able to manumit a greater number of slaves legally in his will. In rendering this unconventional decision, Carr revealed his antislavery sentiments, which he perhaps learned from his uncle, Thomas Jefferson. In 1857, however, in the case of *Drane v. Beall*, Georgia's courts rejected the "hiring out" expedient, arguing that such self-hiring by slaves after their owner's death constituted illegal quasi-slavery. Most ACS testamentary emancipations (i.e., freeing slaves by means of the owner's last will and testament) granted slaves the option of freedom in Liberia

---

[2] *Elder v. Elder's Executor* 4 Leigh 252 (1833); Wisnosky, "Will of the Master," 62-63.

or continued bondage in America, and by the 1850s postmortem emancipations outnumbered those made while the masters were alive.[3]

That Thomas Jefferson was not legally entitled to free his slaves, although he did manumit five of them in his will, begging the legislature to make an exception in his case by excusing his heavy debts, revealed his determination to emancipate people who had developed useful handicraft skills and loyally served him.[4] Jefferson's debts, most of them inherited from his father-in-law and his deceased friend Wilson Cary Nicholas, were so large that within three years of his death, the state seized Monticello and sold his slaves at auction to reimburse his creditors.

---

[3] Burin, *Slavery and the Peculiar Solution*, 140. See also Thomas Johnson Michie, *Virginia Reports* (Richmond: The Michie Company, 1900), available online at hathitrust.

[4] Codicil to Jefferson's Will, March 17, 1826, in Lipscomb and Bergh, eds., *Writings of Jefferson*, 17: 469-70.

Index